THE ULTIMATE GUIDE TO VINYL AND MORE

CONTENTS

PART ONE:
COLLECTING AND COLLECTORS

PART TWO:
COLLECTIONS AND COLLECTIBLES

PART THREE:
THE EYE OF THE BEHOLDER—
CASE STUDIES FROM THE FRINGES OF OBSESSION

PART FOUR:
THIRTY COLLECTIBLE RECORD LABELS

ACKNOWLEDGMENTS

A lot of people threw something into this book but, most of all, thanks to Amy Thompson, for a wealth of suggestions, ideas and "just a thought, but . . ."s.

Everybody at Backbeat: John Cerullo, Bernadette Malavarca, Kristina Rolander; to Jo-Ann Greene; Mike Sharman, Boz, Danny, Karen and Todd; Linda and Larry; Betsy, Steve and family; Jen; Chrissie Bentley; Tim Smith; Gaye Black; Oliver and Trevor; the Manifold Denizens of the Tank (past and present); Barb East; Bateerz and family; the Gremlins who live in the heat pump; and to John the Superstar, the demon of the dry well.

And to all the record store staff, today and yesterday, who lent their enthusiasm, knowledge, and suggestions to these pages. Especially Jupiter Records in Wilmington, Rainbow Records in Newark, and Beautiful World Syndicate in Philadelphia, without whom I'd have a lot more space on the record racks.

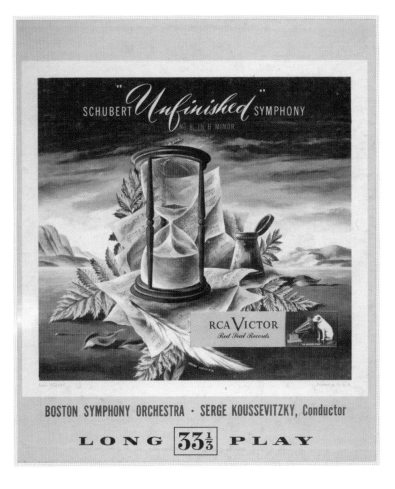

It (almost) starts here. From the dawn of vinyl Long Playing time, one of the earliest RCA Victor Red Seal 10-inch LPs, released in 1950.

INTRODUCTION

First things first. This book is not strictly, and merely, dedicated to collecting vinyl, as in the round, black, plastic discs that used to be our primary source of recorded music, and have regained that position again. A title that encapsulated its full scope, however, would be too unwieldy for words. Cylinders, 78s, 45s, LPs, picture discs, and flexidiscs are all included in here. So are cassettes, 4- and 8-Tracks, CDs, Pocket Rockers, and a host of other media. "Vinyl" just seems like a handy (if illogical) umbrella for all of them.

And so it should. Coin collecting has never been limited to collecting coins; medallions, tokens, and more are a vital part of the numismatic hobby. Stamp collecting incorporates envelopes, charity labels, and advertising stickers; and baseball card fairs rarely exclude vendors of football, basketball, and soccer images, simply because their subjects aren't wielding sticks. Record collecting (as it used to be called and, we hope, still is), by its very nature, concerns every medium in which music has been made available, a broad-mindedness that this book aims to embody.

It should also be noted that the book was written primarily with the rock and pop collector in mind. Although other publications may attempt to prove otherwise, it is impossible to do justice, in one slim volume, to every musical discipline that can fall under the record-collecting banner.

Jazz, classical, blues, reggae, soul and funk and R&B do all appear, of course. So do country, bluegrass, and gospel. There's even some spoken word, because records have been issued that encapsulate every sound a human has ever made. And that's before we even begin thinking about collections of whale song, birdcalls, and *The Authentic Sounds of the Savannah at Midnight*.

Sly Stone

"Buttermilk," Sly Stewart (AUTUMN 14, 7-INCH, 1964)

"Dance to the Music" (UK COLUMBIA DB 8369, 7-INCH, 1968)

Everything You Always Wanted to Hear By (EPIC AS 264, DJ LP, 1976)

Greatest Hits (EPIC EQ 30325, QUAD LP, 1970)

"Help Me with My Heart," Sylvester Stewart (G&P 901, 7-INCH, 1962)

"I Ain't Got Nobody" (LOADSTONE 3951, 7-INCH, 1967)

"I Just Learned How to Swim," Sly Stewart (AUTUMN 3, 7-INCH, 1964)

"A Long Time Alone," Danny Stewart (LUKE 1008, 7-INCH, 1961)

Sly and the Family Stone (EPIC 26397, JUKEBOX ALBUM, 1968)

"Temptation Walk," Sly Stewart (AUTUMN 26, 7-INCH, 1966)

Because that is what record collecting is really all about—gathering (as in acquiring), categorizing (as in deciding what you like and what you'd like more of), and listening (as in occasionally breaking open the airtight container, and finding out what the songs sound like). And it is for those reasons that this book does not address what are, for many would-be record collectors, the most important questions of all—"How do I start?" and "What should I collect?"

A first UK pressing of the Beatles' "Can't Buy Me Love." The initials ("KT") embossed around the spindle hole refer to the tax code applied to 45s at the time.

It does not address them because you already know the answers. How do you start? You buy some records, you keep them, and you have a collection. And what should you collect? Whatever you want. And that's that, whether you're lining your retirement fund with label varieties of the Beatles' first Vee-Jay 45, or simply filling a shoebox with old, ratty 8-tracks. Collect the music you like to listen to, and the songs you want to play. And don't ever, ever let anybody tell you that you're doing it wrong.

What Is Included in This Book? And What Isn't?

While it would be excellent to be able to answer that question with a confident "everything," clearly that is not the case. To attempt even a general discussion of the thousands of artists, bands, and performers who are considered "collectible" today, from Aardvark (one cool prog album on Deram's Nova subsidiary in 1970) to Zzebra (excellent jazz-rock from 1973), would require a volume many times the size of this one—and besides, that is what specialist publications such as *Goldmine* and *Record Collector* do in every issue, and a mountain of blogs in every posting.

Instead, the goal has been to offer a clear and concise summary of the many things that one could collect, and attempt to highlight at least some of the more interesting areas you might encounter: in an artist's career, a format's development, a label's history.

The book is divided into four sections. The first, "Collecting and Collectors," explores both the history of the hobby and some of its rules—how to grade a record, what to look for, and if you're lucky, where to find it.

Part two, "Collections and Collectibles," looks at the various different formats on which our music has been delivered over the years, from cylinders to Blu-ray; from acetate to UHCD.

Part three, "The Eye of the Beholder," ranges through a few (and we do mean, few) of the themes that a collector might choose to pursue, from annoying Christmas records to multiple versions of *Dark Side of the Moon*; from radio sessions to Stones-Beatles collaborations. You may or may not care for any of these artists or areas. But by example and anecdote, the lessons and observations contained within each will, hopefully, help you as you indulge your own fancies.

Finally, part four offers an alphabetical directory of thirty of the most collectible (and collected) American, British, and European record companies, each one emphasizing a label's history and pinpointing its most sought-after artists and releases.

Throughout the book, too, some 200 "Ten Top Collectibles" lists are scattered, some detailing the most significant era of an artist's career; others pinpointing the greatest rarities, variations, and oddities available to collectors of individual labels and musical genres. These lists include everything from the Holy Grails that collectors go to sleep dreaming about (but which only the fortunate few will ever discover) to the kind of relatively common, but increasingly desirable, one-offs and oddities with which every discography abounds. And others simply reference what we might regard as the very foundations of an individual artist or label's output. Each such list, however, is designed to illustrate the sheer variety of items available to the enterprising collector.

In each section, the emphasis frequently falls on the best-known and most collectible performers and records: the Beatles, the Rolling Stones, Elvis, the Beach Boys, Queen, David Bowie, Bruce

Banned in Australia for blasphemy, the Beatles' "The Ballad of John and Yoko."

Springsteen, and so on. But the spotlight also lights upon artists and aspects that may not immediately spring to mind as being "hot" topics—not out of any attempt at contrariness, but because it is often in record collecting's least-frequented corridors that one meets the most interesting people.

At the end of the day, the hope is that whatever your collecting interests are, you'll find something in this book that relates directly to them—and a lot of things that will simply make your collecting even more pleasurable and interesting.

What Is Collectible?

A term that appears again and again on these pages is "collectible."

It is a subjective term, and a somewhat loaded one. "Collectible," after all, is one of the buzzwords of the modern advertising age, usually applied to absolutely anything that is sufficiently useless that somebody has to work really hard to convince you that you need to buy it—"These precious heirloom possum-head egg-cups aren't simply whimsical, they are also very collectible."

In the context of this book, however, "collectible" means what it says. Whether you are shopping in person at a record fair, or in private on an Internet auction site, if a "collectible" item comes up for sale, you'll recognize it immediately. It's the thing that makes your heart skip a beat, as you look around to make sure that no one else is making a grab for it.

It doesn't have to be a particularly hard-to-find item, or an especially rare or valuable one. In fact, the words "collectible" and "valuable" share only a modicum of common ground. But it will attract the attention of more than a handful of casual browsers.

It may look unusual—a radically shaped picture disc is always going to draw more glances than a straightforward black-vinyl single; a barely-touched Deutsche Grammophon album with the old tulip label should always receive more admiring comments than a still-sealed copy of the Bee Gees' *Spirits Having Flown*; a U2 single with a foreign-language picture sleeve will have more people trying to read it than an 'N Sync record in its domestic cover.

It's not an inviolate rule . . . some of the hobby's most notable prizes, for example, can be identified only by the number, or the inscription, that is scratched into the dead wax that surrounds the label. But, however it may manifest itself, "collectible" means something that is sufficiently out of the ordinary that you should probably buy it now, while it's sitting in front of you, rather than risk losing it to the next person who passes by.

What Is a Rarity?

"Rare" is another word that gets thrown around a lot, and in many ways, it means quite the opposite to collectible, in that some of the rarest records in the world are actually among the dullest looking things you'll ever see.

Drab-labeled 45s from the dawn of the rock 'n' roll era have a shocking tendency to fetch four- or five-figure sums among collectors, yet to look at them you wouldn't think they had the bus fare home. Soul singles you've never heard of, on labels you never dreamed existed. Privately pressed progressive rock albums by bands that never landed a "real" record deal. Things like that.

Other rarities are marked out by such infinitesimally tiny details that you wonder how anybody noticed them to begin with. The dead wax inscriptions noted above. Maybe the catalog number on the label is printed half an inch to the left of center, rather than the quarter inch it normally lies. Maybe the composer credits have been listed back to front, an error that was corrected after just a few hundred pressings.

These records used to simply hang on dealers' walls with their weight-in-gold price tags. Today, you're more likely to find them lurking on the Internet, waiting while the bidding rockets into the stratosphere—and isn't it fascinating to watch these competitions, hitting your browser's refresh button as the auction timer ticks toward zero, imagining the last-minute high bidder poised at his computer, the national debt of a medium-sized European nation entered into the bid box, timing his actions to the very last moment . . . and then getting sniped with ten seconds to spare, because somebody wants the only known pale-green-label copy of an otherwise unremarkable doo-wop 45 $100 more than he does.

What all true rarities have in common is, there aren't many of them around. Or, at least, not as many as there are collectors who are hunting them.

Rarity is measured by supply and demand. There must be thousands of records whose total sales can be counted on the fingers of one hand, that exist now only in the crazed mind of the unknown hopeful who sank his savings into pressing them, and who was last seen digging a very deep hole in his back garden.

There are discs that were pressed in limited editions of just five copies, and you can't get much rarer than that. But if only two people ever want one, then the market is swamped. Copies might be painfully hard to find, they may be excruciatingly scarce, and anyone who finds a spare might price it in the high thousands of dollars. But they are not considered among the field's great rarities. And why? Because nobody cares.

On the other hand, there are records that may have sold several hundred thousand copies. But when twice that many collectors are chasing them, then you're in the big time.

Am I a Completist?

Completists are collectors for whom, as James Bond's family motto puts it, "the world is not enough." In extremis, they seek out every

REM

"Academy Fight Song" (UK BUCKETFUL OF BRAINS/LYNTONE BOB 32, FLEXIDISC, 1992)

Acoustic Songs (FRANCE WEA/LES INROCKUPTIBLES PRO 2002-2, CD SINGLE, 1991)

The Alternative Radio Staple (IRS CDREM 92, PROMO CD, 1992)

Chronic Town (IRS SP 70502, 12-INCH WITH CUSTOM LABEL, 1982)

"Ghost Reindeer in the Sky" (FAN CLUB 122589, 7-INCH, 1990)

"Good King Wenceslas" (FAN CLUB 122589, 7-INCH, PICTURE SLEEVE, 1989)

"Parade of the Wooden Soldiers" (FAN CLUB U23518, GREEN-VINYL 7-INCH, PICTURE SLEEVE, 1988)

"Radio Free Europe" (HIB-TONE HT 0001, 7-INCH, PICTURE SLEEVE, 1981)

The Source Concert 1984 (SOURCE CONCERT NBC 8428, 2-LP TRANSCRIPTION DISC, 1984)

"Wolves, Lower" (TROUSER PRESS FLEXI 12, FLEXIDISC, 1982)

variation of every version of every release in a band or artist's catalog, every bootlegged live show and studio outtake, every session appearance and semi-conscious guest spot—and then they deluge Internet chat rooms to ask if there's anything else out there.

In the UK, such fans are also known as "train-spotters," for their avid attention to detail, and "anoraks," after the traditional clothing of real train-spotters. In America, they're just a fact of life and most dealers welcome their attentions. Any knowledgeable fan might point out that your copy of the King Bees' 1964 Vocalion single "Liza Jane" was the first-ever record to feature the young David Bowie on lead vocals. But a completist is the only person who'll give you $5,000 for it, and then ask if you can find him or her a spare.

Most self-described completists set themselves less lofty aims, though their targets can still be high. Pursuing one copy of every record an artist has released in any given country is a form of completism; so is simply acquiring one copy of every released song, regardless of its original format.

This is the market that many box set compilers bear in mind. The powers behind Cat Stevens' 2001 box set *On the Road to Find Out*, for example, knew that collectors were unlikely ever to find an authentic acetate copy of the 1965 recording "Back to the Good Old Times," so they featured the performance at the start of disc one. Even if a collector has, somehow, acquired every other rarity and outtake included in the package, the presence of that one song will make the box a worthwhile purchase.

So, are you a completist? You tell me.

What Is a Record Actually Worth?

With just a handful (literally) of exceptions, actual values for records are not addressed in this book. Partly, this is because the market itself is constantly changing, rendering out of date any attempt to give a definitive price for an item, before the words have even hit the page. But it's also because the fact that a record is "worth" $200 does not mean that it cannot be found for $2 . . . or vice versa.

The late 1990s advent of Internet auctions, in particular, threw the accepted value of many records into utter confusion, sending the perceived value of some long-established rarities into free fall, while at the same time blasting other, hitherto unrecognized, gems into hyper-space.

Even more spectacularly, records and artists that had never previously been paid any heed by the hobby suddenly exploded into prominence, with more racing to join them all the time. Records that once seemed ten-a-penny in the bargain bins were

now being avidly sought out, and at a pace that neither brick-and-mortar dealers (that is, non-Internet dealers) nor price guide editors would ever be able to keep up with. Often because as soon as the market hit a certain level, it would then start dropping down again.

Early on in the career of eBay, for example, puzzled dealers suddenly noticed that an entire wave of '70s teenybop idols—the Osmonds, the early Jackson Five, and most notably David Cassidy and the Partridge Family—were suddenly "hot"; that albums and singles that had sat unsold for decades were flying out of the door.

But then, just as suddenly, they weren't. It was as if an entire flock of seagulls had suddenly descended upon a beach, eaten absolutely everything in sight, and then flown back out to sea. And the funny thing is, that's exactly what happened. Well, without the seagulls and the beach. And the eating. But yes, a generation of old-time fans had discovered their long-discarded past was up for sale, and they fell on it like locusts. Or seagulls. Then, when they were sated and they all had what they wanted, they moved on, leaving dealers scratching their heads in bemusement, with a lot of overpriced LPs on their hands.

Sometimes the market is easy to predict. REM collectors will always bid high for a picture-sleeve copy of that band's first single; Foreigner fans will do likewise for a clear-vinyl UK pressing of "Cold As Ice." Frank Zappa fans know the difference between an original release of *Weasels Ripped My Flesh* and its 2016 reissue.

On other occasions, however, a record will escalate in value for reasons that conform to none of the "rules" by which all hobbies are governed; it will become wildly popular for reasons that cannot be easily quantified.

We've already seen what happens when a generation "comes of age" and is suddenly, more or less simultaneously, stricken by nostalgia for its misspent youth. But it also happens when an artist unexpectedly

The Osmonds

"Be My Little Baby Bumble Bee" (MGM 13162, 7-INCH, 1963)

"I Can't Stop" (UNI 55015, 7-INCH, 1967)

"I've Got Loving on My Mind" (BARNABY 2004, 7-INCH, 1968)

"Mary Elizabeth" (BARNABY 2002, 7-INCH, 1968)

"Mr. Sandman" (MGM 13281, 7-INCH, 1964)

New Sound of the Osmond Brothers (Capitol Record Club ST 90403, LP, 1965)

Osmonds World (UK Lyntone, LYN 2705, flexidisc, 1972)

Songs We Sang on the Andy Williams Show (MGM SE 4146, stereo LP, 1963)

"Taking a Chance on Love" (Barnaby 2005, 7-inch, 1969)

The Travels of Jaimie McPheeters, Various artists (MGM PM 7, LP, 1963)

breaks out of a career-long journey through the recesses of underground cultdom, and a vast new audience needs to discover his past. Or when a TV show or commercial unearths some forgotten old record and the entire prime-time viewership cannot live without owning it.

Anniversaries can reignite interest—the fiftieth anniversaries of the Beach Boys' *Pet Sounds*, the Beatles' *Sgt. Pepper*, and the Doors' self-titled debut have all just passed through the calendar, and both hallowed old records and freshly-pressed new were quickly devoured.

The Monkees' comeback in 2016 saw that band's old records suddenly rejuvenated, and of course the death of a musical icon can often spark an incredible rush for his or her records. It is a matter of historical record, for example, that the day before Elvis Presley died, in August 1977, many record outlets no longer even stocked his back catalog, so low was the demand from customers. Twenty-four hours later, on the other hand, the greatest fleet of delivery trucks on earth would not have been enough to keep up with the demand for fresh stock.

More recently, in January 2016, the death of David Bowie prompted great swathes of his back catalog (the good parts of it, anyway) to race towards the top of the charts, while used dealers simply rubbed their hands with glee, and gave that scratchy old *Hunky Dory* another spin through the record cleaner.

Attempts to predict these shifts are almost unanimously doomed to failure. When Bowie died, the market went mad and it still hasn't

The Monkees

The Birds the Bees and the Monkees (COLGEMS COM 109, MONO LP, 1968)

"D.W. Washburn" (COLGEMS 66-1023, 7-INCH, PICTURE SLEEVE, 1968)

Head (UK RCA 8051, MONO LP, 1969)

Headquarters (COLGEMS 103, LP, "BEARD" PHOTO, 1967)

Instant Replay (UK RCA RD 8016, MONO LP, 1968)

"Last Train to Clarksville" (COLGEMS 66-1001, 7-INCH, PICTURE SLEEVE, 1966)

The Monkees (COLGEMS COM 101, LP WITH "PAPA JEAN'S BLUES" MISSPELLING, 1966)

The Monkees (UK ARISTA 112 157, 10-INCH EP, 1989)

"Oh My My" (COLGEMS 66-5011, 7-INCH, PICTURE SLEEVE, 1970)

That Was Then, This Is Now (ARISTA 1-4 673, LP, FOUR DIFFERENT PICTURE DISCS, 1986)

really recovered. When Prince passed away scant months later, there was a flurry of buying and selling, but overall, things remained calm.

So, no. You cannot predict what's going to happen in collecting, any more than pollsters seem able to predict the result of a general election, or weathermen get the next-day forecast right. Which means the safest rule of thumb when contemplating a record's true worth is: What is it worth to you?

Stay within those limits and you will never be ripped off.

One final point, though. If a record you own is going to go through the roof, it will only do so after you've sold it. Usually for a dollar.

1 | COLLECTING AND COLLECTORS

AN INFORMAL HISTORY OF RECORD COLLECTING

I was lucky. I got my start in record collecting in what was a golden age—probably the last one there ever was. Looking back today on the 45s and LPs for which I carelessly plonked down my pocket money, it seems incredible to believe that such fabulous treasures could be picked up so readily; that the store owner didn't go home every night and kick himself to death for allowing another priceless gem slip by for the cost of a can of soda.

You'll forgive me if I don't say exactly when this was, because it really doesn't matter. Or if I fail to name those "priceless gems," because most of them were probably as common as muck. They were priceless to me, which is why I was so astonished to find that I could afford them. Besides, everyone who picks up this book and can blissfully recall their own early days in the hobby will know those answers intuitively, because that's when they, too, got their start. A golden age, a time when there was magic in the air and glory in the grooves, and every record that hit the streets was another of the greatest ever made.

Of course it was, because why else would we have started collecting? There were, after all, so many more important things we could have been doing, like improving our grades or cleaning our rooms, or washing behind our ears every day. But no. Instead, selflessly, heroically, we sacrificed the pleasures of a normal, happy childhood to embed ourselves in the minutiae of music. And, just as we can now look back on our school days, convinced that the establishment was at its social, creative, and educational peak during the years in which we attended, so we reflect upon that other most formative moment in

childhood, the discovery of music, with the same sense of wide-eyed wonder. Could things ever be so great again?

It might have been the mid-'50s, when Elvis was on Sun, or the early '60s, when America found the Beatles. It could have been five years later, when every garage was a psychedelic shack, or a decade after that, when new wave ruled the roost. It may have been the early '90s, with the Sub Pop Singles Club blasting classics through the mailbox, or the mid-2000s, with Babyshambles on the march.

It might even have been just a couple of years back, with whatever nonsense it is that you kids listen to these days, but I'll tell you one thing, it isn't music . . . I'm sorry. I just turned into your parents.

Whenever it was, record collecting is possibly the only (legal) hobby around that offers a shortcut to your soul. Others—excellent schoolwork, tidy rooms, and clean ears among them—may be more aesthetically beautiful or educationally fulfilling. But records alone can make you laugh or cry without you ever knowing why; can make you get up and dance or run off to be sick; can force you to experience the entire range of human emotions; and—and this is the clincher—can do it all so quickly that almost before the moment's begun, and certainly before you can begin to analyze it, it's over. Until the next time you hear the same song.

Sometimes it isn't even the music with which we connect. Or rather, it isn't *only* the music. The record's very label might possess a resonance that mere words can never begin to explain. Perhaps this is why many collectors, desperately searching for a particular song, will nevertheless reject a copy on a foreign, or even domestic reissue label. For it isn't merely the *song* they are searching for. It is the artifact itself, the tangible embodiment, if you will, of whichever experience or emotion that dictated their need for the record in the first place.

It could be a classic RCA Victor release, with Nipper the dog and the gramophone horn. Maybe it's an old black British Parlophone, the giant silver 45 logo a trademark of quality that has never been matched. The checkerboard of Chess, the wholesome crunchy promise of Apple, the lascivious lips of the Rolling Stones, the bespectacled pig of Trademark of Quality. And, if a logo's worth a thousand words, then the slogans are worth many more: "Sounds great in stereo." "If it ain't Stiff, it ain't worth a fuck." "All rights of the producer and of the owner of the recorded work reserved."

Remember when, in the first flush of youth, a new record wasn't simply something you'd spin a few times and then file away, carefully alphabetically, in an archive-quality protective jacket? The days when the first thing you did was rip away the shrink-wrapping . . . onto the floor, then into the trash. Out with the record, all fingers and thumbs (you'll wipe away the fingerprints on the front of your

Apple

Celtic Requiem, John Tavener (UK APPLE SAPCOR 20, LP, 1971)

"F Is Not a Dirty Word," David Peel (PRO 6498/9, DJ 7-INCH, 1972)

"Hippie from New York City," David Peel (PRO 6545/6, DJ 7-INCH, 1972)

"How the Web Was Woven," Jackie Lomax (UK APPLE 23, 7-INCH, 1970)

In Concert, Ravi Shankar (UK APPLE SAPDO 1002, 2-LP, 1972)

"The King of Fuh," Brute Force (UK APPLE 8, 7-INCH, 1970)

"That's the Way God Planned It," Billy Preston (AMERICOM 433, FLEXIDISC, 1969)

"Those Were the Days," Mary Hopkin (AMERICOM 238, FLEXIDISC, 1969)

Walls Ice Cream, Various artists (UK APPLE CT 1, EP, 1969)

Columbia Records' March 1920 catalog included both records and sheet music.

sweater tomorrow), onto the turntable, drop down the needle, up with the volume.

Then you'd sit with the sleeve and consume every word. More than that, you'd absorb them. Every lyric, every credit, every last iota of information sucked in as if you were the kind of sponge your teachers had despaired of your ever becoming in the classroom—and they were right, because that kind of stuff didn't matter half as much. So what if Wellington won Waterloo? Benny Andersson, Björn Ulvaeus, and Stig Anderson wrote it, and they won the Eurovision Song Contest. In 1974, that was a lot more significant than some dusty old battle.

Old-timers deny it, but it's the same today. No matter that information now zips around the planet at the speed of thought, and that the average eight year old knows more about their pop idols' lives than his or her parents even cared to imagine. Album jackets are still a mine of arcane information and secret knowledge, the thrill of a new acquisition is still as physical as it is aural, and fingerprints can still be removed with a quick swipe down the front of a sweater.

The Vertigo swirl in all its glory.

Maybe some things have changed. No matter how garish and arty they may look, CD labels simply don't have the resonance of their vinyl counterparts, all the more so since they revolve so fast you can't even try to discover if you can read things in circles.

But mp3s *can* be listened to backwards, to check for Satanic messages; and, though a single piece of vinyl these days is heavier than an entire boxful of old-time RCA Dynaflex pressings, you can still soften them with boiling water and turn them into flowerpots when you get sick of listening. Back to labels, though. Remember the old Vertigo label? A Phonogram subsidiary, its US catalog included Jade Warrior, the Spencer Davis Group, Atlantis, and Aphrodite's Child, while its UK operation effectively swept up some of the most eclectic sounds in the entire local underground.

Daddy Longlegs, Dr Z, Gravy Train, Still Life . . . Catapilla, whose second album arrived in a die-cut sleeve that was indeed beautifully bug-shaped.

And then you took out the record.

True fact. If every record company had selected a wild spiral of black-and-white concentric circles for its logo, in the manner of the original Vertigo, the entire psychedelic movement might never have happened. Or, it might never have ended. Comedians Cheech and Chong, during one of their early-'70s routines, referred to playing

Black Sabbath at 78 rpm "and seeing God." To American listeners, accustomed to Sabbath releases appearing on staid old Warner Bros., the remark was little more than a throwaway that could have been applied with equal validity to any band in the world.

To British listeners, however, it wasn't a joke. Play one of Sabbath's Vertigo records at 78, keep your eyes firmly focused on the whirling spiral before you, and seeing God would be the least of the revelations in store. When Vertigo dropped the design in 1973, urban myth insisted that the government had forced it to, because someone went mad just watching the logo spin.

It probably wasn't true—the story was spread by the same sort of people who claimed the B-side of Napoleon XIV's "They're Coming to Take Me Away Ha-Haaa!," the catchily titled "!Aaah-Ah Yawa Em Ekat Ot Gnimoc Er'yeht," was banned by British radio because someone else went insane trying to decipher the lyrics.

The possibility that radio rarely plays records that are simply the A-side spun backward never crossed anybody's mind. It didn't need to. The legends are always more interesting than the truth. It is true, however, that record collecting isn't what it used to be. It's a lot more than it ever was.

Turn back the years, to as (comparatively) recently as the mid-seventies, and record collecting as a formal hobby barely even existed.

Yes, people did collect records; yes, there was a thriving network of specialist stores whose sole business was to buy and sell rare music. Even then, records had value; even then, dealers were well aware which would sit gathering dust on the shelves and which would fly out the door the moment they were put on display.

But they gained that information through experience. There were no publications on the subject, or if there were, they were obsessive little discographical creations run off in small-run private editions, barely available and prohibitively priced (by the standards of the day). *Goldmine,* today regarded as the foremost record-collecting publication in the US, was little more than a fanzine, sold at record fairs, swap meets, and via mail-order subscriptions; *Record Collector,* its UK counterpart, was barely a gleam in its creator's eye.

Price guides were nonexistent. The first, Jerry Osborne and Bruce Hamilton's self-published *33⅓ and 45 Extended Play Record Album Price Guide,* didn't appear until 1977. Grading was an unfathomable mystery (okay, so some things haven't changed), and a book like this would never even have been written, let alone mass-produced, by a major American publishing house.

Things began to change around the end of the 1970s, and the *Price Guide* had something to do with that. For the first time, a book was available that not only unlocked the mysteries of a rare record's worth, it also went some way toward explaining why such a record was valuable in the first place. But equally important was the music industry itself, and the sudden realization that it wasn't simply marketing music and musicians. It was also marketing a product, and the more eye-catching that product looked, the more likely it was to be sold.

The concept was road-tested in the UK. British 45s had traditionally been issued in generic paper sleeves since the dawn of recorded history. During 1976–77, however, an increasing number of limited-edition picture sleeves were the first manifestation of this new mood, and they proved an instant hit. Singles in picture sleeves sold. So more picture sleeves began appearing. Soon they stopped being limited editions. Soon they stopped even attracting attention. By the early 1980s, if you wanted to be noticed, you *didn't* have a picture sleeve. People started collecting those records as well.

The advent—again in the UK—of the first commercially available 12-inch singles raised the temperature even further. Embarking on another of their frequent raids on the Who's back catalog in fall 1976, but searching for a new way of persuading people to buy it (again), Polydor reissued the 1966 classic "Substitute" on LP-sized vinyl and found itself with the group's first Top Ten hit in five years. A few weeks later, Ariola-Hansa issued the first single by German disco band Boney M. in the same format. "Daddy Cool" shot to number six.

By the turn of the year, and certainly by the following spring, 12-inch singles were pouring out of every label in the land, and again they usually bore the magic words "limited edition." Some of them even were, but it didn't seem to matter either way. Bands that might never otherwise have had a shot at a UK chart single suddenly found themselves rubbing noses with the richest, most famous hit-makers in the land—New York new wave acts Television, Talking Heads, Blondie, and the Ramones were all promoted early on with the format, while new disco releases were scarcely given a second glance unless they appeared in the large format.

Gimmick followed gimmick. Colored vinyl was next, and this time it was a transatlantic conspiracy. The technology had been around since the days of the 78 and was especially rife in the US during the early fifties. But only a handful of labels had even tried to bring it into the rock age, most recently such enterprising UK independents as Stiff and The Label.

Now the majors got to work, utilizing the same limited-edition tactics that had worked so well with picture sleeves and the 12-inch, and reaping precisely the same rewards. It didn't even matter that, in many cases, the limited-edition colored vinyl seemed far more common than the regular, boring, black variety. By early 1979, a band without a strangely shaded single was a band without a prayer.

Suddenly record companies were falling over themselves trying to create the next marketing phenomenon. In the US, A&M became

Stiff

"Alison," Elvis Costello (UK STIFF BUY 14, 7-INCH, WHITE-VINYL MISPRESS, 1977)

Excerpts from Stiff's Greatest Hits (UK STIFF FREEB 2, EP, 1977)

"I Think We're Alone Now (Japanese Version)," Lene Lovich (UK STIFF BUYJ 32, 7-INCH, 1978)

"New Rose," The Damned (UK STIFF BUY 6, 7-INCH, PUSH-OUT CENTER, 1976)

"Sex and Drugs and Rock and Roll," Ian Dury (UK STIFF FREEB 1, 7-INCH, PICTURE SLEEVE, 1977)

"Stretcher Case Baby," The Damned (UK STIFF DAMNED 1, 7-INCH, 1977)

"Toe Knee Black Burn," Binky Baker and the Pit Orchestra (UK STIFF BUY 41, 7-INCH, PICTURE SLEEVE, 1978)

The Wonderful World Of, Wreckless Eric (UK STIFF SEEZ P9, PICTURE-DISC LP, 1978)

"You Caught Me Out," Kirsty MacColl (UK STIFF BUY 57, 7-INCH PROMO, 1979)

You're Either on the Train or off the Train, Various artists (UK STIFF DEAL 1, PROMO LP WITH BOOKLET, 1978)

one of the first labels to successfully create multicolored records that didn't resemble discarded slabs of chewing gum—the Stranglers' *Something Better Change* EP not only came in fetching pink-and-white marbled vinyl, it also featured liner notes warning that its very label design "may [cause] slight dizziness" if viewed while rotating. It could, indeed. Vertigo revisited! Now, of course, such things are routine, especially when Record Store Day rolls around.

Experiments were made with odd and awkward-sized vinyl. In America, A&M, again, was among the first to pioneer a rebirth of the 10-inch LP format, all but unseen since the 1950s; in Britain, Chiswick went the other way entirely and resurrected the miniaturized "hip-pocket editions" of the 1960s.

Picture discs were next. Again, an old 78-era technology found new life after years in the marketing dustbin. In spring 1979, Elektra's UK wing launched Boston bar band the Cars with a very fetching picture disc depicting, of course, a car. It sold like hotcakes, and "My Best Friend's Girl" had already stormed into the upper reaches of the chart when the first disquieting media reports suggested that, whereas other limited editions might have bent the walls of mathematical credulity, the Cars were driving a freight train through them. An acknowledged printing of 5,000 copies had, by some estimates, exceeded that figure ten times over, and the presses were still working.

The ensuing contretemps came close to demolishing the entire concept of limited-edition releases in the UK, all the more so since this scandal was very swiftly followed by even more serious allegations of chart hyping (illegally influencing a record's sales to ensure higher chart positions) at other labels.

By that time, however, America, Britain, Europe, Asia . . . the whole world, it seemed, was transfixed by an even greater obsession.

The problem with picture discs, colored vinyl, novelty-shaped discs, and all the so-called collectible gimmicks that launched so many sparkling careers was that they demanded a certain show of confidence on the record buyer's part—not only that the edition truly was limited, but that the record was worth buying in the first place. If every new release was issued with one collectible variant, regardless of whether the record was any good or not, how did you know what to buy? Easy answer—you didn't. So you stopped.

However, what if the same technologies were utilized retroactively, to pretty-up records that you already knew, already loved—and possibly, already owned?

The Beatles' *Sgt. Pepper's Lonely Hearts Club Band,* with a picture of the Lonely Hearts Club Band embedded in the grooves. *The Beatles,* also known as *The White Album,* in pure white wax. The possibilities

Record Store Day Rarities

Paul McCartney, "Sweet Thrash" (PROMO WHITE LABEL, RSD 2015)

Cake, *Vinyl Box Set* (RSD 2014)

Dave Matthews Band, *Live Trax* (RSD 2014)

Brand New, *Deja Entendu* (RSD 2015)

Haim, *Better Off* (100-COPY LIMITED EDITION, RSD 2013)

De La Soul & J Dilla, "Smell the Da.I.S.Y." (12-INCH, RSD 2014)

Mudhoney, *On Top* (TEST PRESSING, RSD 2014)

Elton John, "Bennie & the Jets" (100 COPIES, LIMITED EDITION 7-INCH, RSD 2013)

Pink Floyd, 1965: Their First Recordings (1,050 COPIES, LIMITED EDITION, RSD 2016)

Red House Painters, *4AD Numbered LP Box Set* (RSD 2015)

seemed endless, and so it proved. Every major David Bowie hit of the past ten years reissued with period artwork embedded into the playing surface. Entire classic album catalogs were remarketed in exciting new permutations, and if, as it very swiftly transpired, these new pressings did not have as high fidelity as they could have, then that simply proved what great investments they were. Unplayed or unplayable—either way, they remained in tip-top condition.

It is difficult to say at what precise point the army of gullible consumers that went into these booms metamorphosed into the army of serious collectors who emerged from the other side. But it happened, and it happened swiftly.

In the mid-'70s, the only people who knew what a rare record was worth were the people who actually **determined** such things . . . in other words, the people selling them. By the early '80s, the information wasteland of just a few years before had been neatly spruced up and completely paved over.

Rare record mega-marts were springing up where once only cultish swap meets had lurked. Price guides grew from obscure private publications—which are now, in some instances, changing hands for as much money as many of the records they list—to sprawling encyclopedias packed with microscopic print.

Little old ladies with antique stores on Main Street were adding rows of extra zeros to the price tags on their Beatles LPs, and casual browsers, stunned to discover that a long-forgotten component of their childhood was now worth its weight in gold, suddenly realized that they *had* to have it. And just when it seemed that record collecting had gone as far as it could, that every conceivable gimmick had been pulled out of the sack, and every conceivable notion for repackaging the past had been driven into the ground, some bright spark invented the CD, and the whole process began again.

More than three decades after the first five-inch aluminum discs began appearing in record stores, claiming to offer superior sound in half the space, and swearing that they were the future of music, it's difficult to remember precisely how much cynicism greeted them.

Indeed, even the most optimistic supporter of this exciting new format could never have imagined that, within a surprisingly brief period of time, not only would almost every prized album of the past have been revived, remastered, and remodeled with bonus tracks galore, but that many of the old bands themselves would be back, rejuvenated by the interest stirred up by the reissue of their catalog.

True, there were casualties. Record collections gathered painstakingly together over a course of so many years became . . . not obsolete, for no format (not even the 8-track) can ever truly be said to have died out completely . . . but certainly outmoded. New releases no longer appeared on vinyl; older issues were deleted and disappeared.

On the secondary market, in the world of used-record dealers, swap meets, and fairs, the very nature of the business changed overnight. Still a search for hits-you-missed and oldies-but-goodies, the business now needed to expand to assimilate the new format even as it struggled to absorb the vast flood of old material, as entire vinyl collections were discarded by owners upgrading to CDs.

Sheet music for one of the highlights of the first-ever Ziegfeld Follies, *in 1907. Murad was a popular brand of cigarettes.*

In the realm of the rarest records, of course, nothing changed. An Elvis 78 is an Elvis 78, no matter how far technology moves away from wind-up gramophone players. Vinyl that was collectible before CDs remained collectible after. But no matter how many thousands of records there may be with some kind of inherent value, there are millions more that are simply filler for the dollar bin, or that rot on the street in a box marked "Please take me away." Elvis 78s are the caviar of collecting. *Frampton Comes Alive* is the bread (without butter).

The thing was, a lot of people were now hungry for a few slices. CDs, so perfect for those occasions when you require uninterrupted music for more than twenty minutes at a time, nevertheless seemed cold and sterile in comparison to previous formats. Besides, no matter how much music was now being reissued in the CD format, there was many times more that remained stubbornly unavailable, as the most avid collectors were swift to point out.

RCA reissued Jefferson Airplane's *After Bathing at Baxter's* as a stereo CD, and suddenly it became imperative to pick it up as a mono LP. Polygram reissued Roxy Music's *Country Life* with its topless-Fräulein jacket restored, and suddenly, the old American cleaned-up version made a fascinating conversation piece. Old-record collecting skyrocketed in popularity for many different reasons, but new CD reissues had a lot to do with it.

In and of themselves, CDs at first appeared to offer little of interest to the traditional collector, beyond the obvious advantages of previously unissued or rare bonus material and, increasingly as the format aged, an attention to detail and to consumer and collector requirements that vinyl had never taken into consideration.

The medium itself was singularly unappealing; the words "cold" and "sterile" again come to mind. As it developed, however, and ironed out the kinks, a whole new discipline came into being—one that has possibly climaxed with the bank-account-crashing mega box sets of recent renown: every album Elvis (or Dylan or whoever) ever issued in a box that will fit on a bookshelf. Twenty-six hours of unreleased Pink Floyd across audio and video discs alike. Nineteen CDs of Dead or Alive; twenty-two of Steve Hillage. And so on.

By the early 1990s, CDs were firmly established, both in the marketplace and in the collecting community. Promotional releases, one-track CDs that replaced the DJ 45s of old, assumed at least some of the glamour of their predecessors, while record labels' increasing propensity for samplers heralding forthcoming box sets, hitherto restricted to cassette tapes, took on immeasurably higher value following the switch to CD.

Soon, advance (media) copies of almost every new album were being issued on CD (again, as opposed to the earlier cassette), a handful of which have since ascended to unimaginable heights of desirability and price. The advent later in the 1990s of officially produced promotional CD-Rs appears to have throttled this particular area somewhat, since the gold-colored discs and computer-generated white labels are simply too easy to counterfeit to allow their collectibility to survive. But collectors are adaptable. They'll find a way around that eventually.

It is true that some stalwarts of the old vinyl-collecting world will never be recaptured on CD. But many more have, ranging from inadvertent pressing errors that gift the first few lucky purchasers with alternate versions, mistaken masters, and so on, through to limited-edition "secret" tracks.

The increasing globalization of the world's record companies has done nothing to stem the flow of exclusive mixes, unavailable B-sides, and unusual sleeves issued all around the world.

And while the 7-inch single may be dead from a major corporate point of view, an entire generation grew up for whom the multisong CD single, the mini-album, was all they ever knew, and all they will ever care about.

The 1990s-era European fashion for issuing multiple versions of any given CD single, each bearing its own unique B-sides and mixes, will bedevil completist collectors of many individual artists for years to come, and that's as true for such then-contemporary stars such as Garbage, No Doubt, and Moby as it is for crusty old veterans like David Bowie, Paul McCartney, and Madonna. In 1994, the Rolling Stones issued five different versions of their "Out of Tears" single in Britain alone—proof, as if any was needed, that even traditional icons have found a comfortable place in the modern industry.

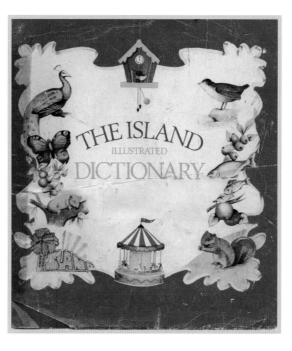

Record companies were still issuing colorful catalogs into the early 1970s. This one covers the UK Island label's available releases.

And then everything changed. The development and the introduction of mp3s, tiny globs of digital detail that were capable of capturing everything from the slightest pop song to the most dramatic symphony, and then playing it back through your computer; and, in tandem, a network of mp3 owners who were willing to "share" their possessions with strangers on the Internet was the first, and most potent game changer.

Piracy was born, and along came the second major development, the ease with which the general public accepted the concept of "free" music, regardless of whether it was provided by an authorized or unauthorized source. They then, it is said, embarked upon such an orgy of downloading that even some of rock 'n' roll's wealthiest proponents claimed that they were feeling the financial pinch. All of which led up to the music industry's throat-cutting response, with mergers and cost-cutting; by slashing investment, prosecuting offenders, and, most of all, boosting prices.

Fewer bands were being signed, and the majority of those that were came not from the clubs and bars of the nation, but the mass-exposure medium of television talent shows. Fewer discs were being sold, so prices soared for those that were. Pink Floyd could *never* have charged $500 for a box set in 1996. They happily did it in 2016, and people purchased it, too.

Sales were in decline, however. At the beginning of 2016, Nielsen Music tabulated the top-selling albums in America over the previous twelve months.

Billy Strange

The Best of Billy Strange (SURREY SS 1002, LP, 1965)

Billy Strange with the Challengers (GNP CRESCENDO GNPS 2030, STEREO LP, 1966)

English Hits of '65 (GNP CRESCENDO GNP 2009, MONO LP, 1965)

The Funky 12 String Guitar, The Transients (HORIZON SWP 1633, LP, 1963)

"I'll Remember April" (BUENA VISTA 406, 7-INCH, 1962)

"James Bond Theme" (GNP CRESCENDO 341, 7-INCH, 1965)

"Johnny Shiloh" (BUENA VISTA 417, 7-INCH, 1963)

Limbo Rock (COLISEUM CM 1001, LP, 1962)

"Long Steel Road" (LIBERTY 55362, 7-INCH, 1961)

"A Lotta Limbo" (COLISEUM 605, 7-INCH, 1963)

Number one was Adele's *25*, with a shade of eight million units shifted. In second place, Taylor Swift's *1989* had moved less than half that total, 3,105,000. Justin Bieber's *Purpose*, in third, had sold 2,225,000; with Ed Sheeran's *X* and the Weeknd's *Beauty Behind the Madness* the only others to have topped the two-million mark.

Altogether, the top ten bestselling albums of the year had sold a combined 25,717,000 copies, and this, thanks to Adele, was a good year. You need to travel back to 2000—not at all coincidentally, the year in which the industry first began taking downloads seriously—to find any album that outsold *25* over the course of just twelve months, and the fact that it was by 'N Sync reminds you of just how long ago that was.

Nevertheless, the remedy for such shortfalls and shortcomings does seem drastic. Writing in the *Guardian* newspaper in November 2016, journalist John Harris reflected upon the ease with which music had shaken off every orthodox business model that it had ever adhered to, from pocket money–priced records to cheap-night-out concerts, and "recast [itself] in the image of 21st-century capitalism, the culture of inequality, and the dread word 'bespoke'."

"It is suggestive of one of Pink Floyd's most renowned songs, 'Money,' which begins with the sound of a cash till and then archly celebrates the easy pleasures of wealth. 'Grab that cash with both hands and make a stash,' sings David Gilmour. 'New car, caviar, four star daydream/Think I'll buy me a football team.' Or, perhaps, another £375 album, or a gig ticket for £1,000."

Even vinyl, riding back to prominence on an utterly unexpected wave of A) nostalgia; B) novelty value; and C) the realization that, in the main, it sounds better than CDs, is no longer the cheap and cheerful medium it once was.

Not when the average price of a new release is more or less double the cost of a CD (a neat reversal from when the two formats last went head-to-head in the mid-1980s); nor when even the most barebones new album can then be split over four sides of vinyl when two would have held the music with room to spare, packaged with a "deluxe" box and a few pieces of ephemeral tat, and then put on the shelf with an even higher tag, in the knowledge that people would still want to buy it.

Which does pose a very interesting dilemma—how, with one breath, the industry bemoans the fact that people have grown so accustomed to getting their music for free, and with the next, it celebrates the fact that, with a few additional extras on board, no price seems so high that the audience is turned away.

Or perhaps it isn't a dilemma after all, and merely the consequence of the arrogance with which the majority of CDs had been marketed

Rolling Stones in the 1990s

"Almost Hear You Sigh" (UK CBS 656 065 5, TINNED CD SINGLE, 1990)
"Anybody Seen My Baby" (UK VIRGIN VS 1653, NUMBERED 7-INCH PICTURE DISC, 1997)
Bridges to Babylon (UK VIRGIN IVDG 2840, PROMO 2-CD WITH INTERVIEW DISC, 1997)
"Out of Control" (VIRGIN DPRO 13159, PROMO CD SINGLE, 1998)
"Out of Tears" (UK VIRGIN VSCDG 1524, WITHDRAWN CD, NUMBERED, DIGIPACK, 1994)
Pleasure and Pain (JAPAN VIRGIN XDDP 93082/3, PROMO 2-CD, 1990)
"Saint of Me" (UK VIRGIN VSTDT 1667, 2X12-INCH, 1998)
Stripped (UK VIRGIN IVDG 2801, PROMO 2-CD WITH INTERVIEW, 1995)
Too Great to Make You Wait (SONY CSK 4004, PROMO CD, 1991)
Voodoo Lounge, A Sampler (VIRGIN DPRO 14158, PROMO CD, 1994)

over the past thirty years, as no-frills discs in dull plastic cases, with minimal artwork and scant sense of occasion. It is very easy indeed to be shocked by the cost of certain records and box sets today. But at least their release feels like an event, and you get something more than a coaster-in-a-case to file on the shelf.

Besides, it's not as if vinyl is the only past relic moving back into commercial contention, and overthrowing what once felt like the inexorable dictatorship of digital. Simon Jenkins, in *The Guardian* in February 2017, noted not only had "sales of old-fashioned vinyl . . . soared to a twenty-five year high, requiring more factory reopenings," but also, "printed books are also recovering, with ebook readers disappearing from bookshop shelves. Knitting clubs are all the rage, along with gin cocktails and ballroom dancing. Even canals are running out of moorings."

Convenience and algorithms have lost their appeal for so many people; active experience is back in vogue. (And yes, listening to music on vinyl is an activity. Those discs don't turn over by themselves, you know.)

Either way, and however you choose to consume, today we have music coming out of our ears. It can be downloaded from the Internet, fed into our televisions, and programmed into the ringtones of our cell phones. It permeates every fiber of modern society, with every year seemingly promising further new audio formats that will deliver ever more perfect listening experiences, until that fateful day that science fiction has been predicting for so long, when we all have microchips embedded into our skulls, so that all we have to do is think of a song and we will hear it instantaneously.

And through it all, and whatever the cost, we still collect. People are, seemingly instinctively, acquisitive creatures, and music is what many of us enjoy acquiring. And no matter how it is packaged—on a small spiky cylinder or a flat metal disc, on a scratched-up 45 or a reel of tape, in a folder on the laptop or a tower of 12x12 inch shelves—for as long as people have ears to hear with and eyes to see with, they will continue to collect it.

It is the nature of the beast.

HOW TO GET STARTED

Well, you just start, don't you?

In fact, if you're reading this book, you probably have already. There's no magic formula, after all, or set of rigid rules and guidelines you need to follow. A collection is whatever you've collected, and whatever you decide to keep going with. Or not. Some people allow their collections to lie dormant for years. Others feed them on a regular basis. It's completely up to you.

That said, there are a few things that it might help for you to pick up, if you really are planning to take things "seriously." A rough guide to "what's out there," for example. If you collect Rush albums, it is useful to know their names; and, from there, to have an idea of their values. To enlarge upon an observation from the previous chapter, it is easy to walk into a Main Street antique mall, browse through the LPs in their cardboard boxes, and pay $20 for something that, with a little more research, you could have got for $5 including shipping on eBay.

You need to have something to play your music on, that works with the records you're buying—not in terms of technology, but . . . put it this way. If you decide only to purchase new reissues of classic albums, 180-gram vinyl, heavyweight sleeves, the whole nine yards, you don't want to then turn around and buy a $50 turntable, which will wind up grinding through the grooves and ripping the sound to shreds. Contrarily, if you go for quantity over quality and do most of your shopping in the dollar bin, there's no point in laying out the next few months' mortgage on a super-snazzy audiophile deck.

Shop around. Read the online reviews—and not just the one- and five-star ones. Pay attention to the ones that fall in between, because they are often the most accurate ones.

Think about what you actually want from the turntable. At the risk of over-simplifying matters, there are effectively two types of turntable—fully manual ones, in which everything from placing the needle on the record (and removing it at the end), to changing the speed at which the platter revolves, is done by hand; or automatic ones, which can do a lot of that for you.

For example, if you will be switching between playing singles and LPs, 45s and 33s, on a regular basis, you should probably choose an automatic deck, one that allows you to make that change at the flick of a switch (or the push of a button). The alternative is to be repositioning the belt that drives the platter in the first place, a procedure that often involves having to take the platter off. It's not difficult (or, at least, it shouldn't be), but it can be a pain. And it devours valuable listening time.

Do you want to press a button and watch the arm position itself exactly over the edge of the record, or, if you're sick of a song, raise itself and return to rest? You want an automatic player. Do you want a turntable that will sync with Bluetooth? One that will allow you to record direct to mp3? Those are both available options today.

In truth, there's a lot more that can go wrong with an automatic player than with a manual, simply because of all these extra bells and whistles. But in terms of convenience, there's a lot to be said for them, as well.

The other thing to consider is how much it costs to keep your turntable in optimum condition for playing your records. A good turntable can keep you spinning records for years, if not decades. But the stylus, or needle, which actually draws the music out of a record's grooves, and the cartridge into which it is inserted, are considerably less durable.

"Lost Albums" That Have Since Been Found

Bat Chain Puller, Captain Beefheart (RECORDED 1976, RELEASED 2012)

Blood on the Tracks (original version), Bob Dylan (RECORDED 1974, RELEASED PIECEMEAL OVER THE YEARS)

First Rays of the New Rising Sun, Jimi Hendrix (INCOMPLETE AT TIME OF DEATH, 1970; "OFFICIAL" COMPLETE RELEASE 1997)

Get Your Ya Yas Out, Rolling Stones (DOUBLE ALBUM SCHEDULED 1970, RELEASED 2009)

Kill City, Iggy Pop: Kill City (ABANDONED 1975, RELEASED 1978)

Let It Be (original "Naked" mix), The Beatles (RECORDED 1970, RELEASED 2003)

Live, 1962, Cliff Richard (RECORDED/SCHEDULED 1962, RELEASED 2002)

Live at the Hollywood Bowl, The Beatles (RECORDED/SCHEDULED 1965, RELEASED 1977)

Smile, The Beach Boys (RECORDED 1966, RELEASED 2003)

Untitled, the Velvet Underground (RECORDED 1969, ABANDONED WHEN BAND CHANGED LABELS, RELEASED IN VARIOUS PERMUTATIONS BEGINNING 1985)

A dozen different websites will offer you a dozen different suggestions as to how frequently a stylus should be changed, often conveying that information in terms of playing hours—as if anybody actually logs every record they play, totting up the total times until they hit the magic number. But you should invest in a new needle at least once a year, and sooner if you play a lot of records a lot of the time, or if you enjoy churning through scratchy and/or dirty discs.

One thing is certain. Do not wait until you notice the sound of your records deteriorating as you play them. Because it's not only your needle that is finished. The original fidelity of your record is on the way out as well.

What needle do you need? That can be tricky. Recent years have seen a lot of turntable manufacturers (particularly at the lower end of the price scale) neglect to offer this information on either their websites or in the literature that comes with the player—why, one can only guess.

Thankfully, a lot of stylus merchants will provide a checklist on their website, allowing you to match the make and model of your turntable to the appropriate needle.—so, again, before purchasing a particular turntable, do yourself a favor. Find out A) if replacement needles are readily available from any source beyond turntable's own manufacturer; and B), how much they're going to cost you. Because that can sometimes be a shock.

The cartridge that holds the needle will also require replacing at some point, although that is further on down the road—and it can often also be upgraded as well, to improve the turntable's sound even further. (Just remember, the stylus you require might also change, to fit the new cartridge's specifications.)

The final thing to watch, or rather listen, for is the condition of the turntable belt—the fat elastic band that makes the platter spin. These will, over time, begin to stretch, subtly altering the speed at which you are listening to a record. This will not harm your record, but it might damage your appreciation of what you're listening to. So pay attention!

There is one other area that you need to get a grounding, and that is how to look at a record and decide whether or not it's in good enough condition to actually listen to.

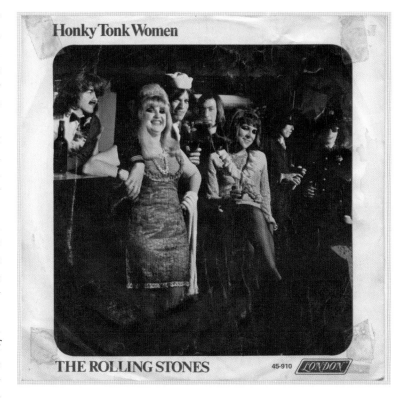

Split seams and sellotape stains establish this 1969 Rolling Stones picture sleeve as a solid G+.

HOW TO GRADE RECORDS (AND CDS AND TAPES)

Grading records is like eating spaghetti. Everybody has his or her own way of doing it, and sometimes it can be messy. It is, after all, an extraordinarily subjective topic, largely dependent upon whether one is buying ("That's one helluva gouge across the whole of side one") or selling ("It's only a surface mark; I played it and it's fine"). Attempts to formulate a universal standard founder on so many counts that it isn't even annoying any longer. Accurate grading is, in many ways, the most crucial element in the entire hobby. So why is it so difficult?

The finest grading systems currently in service apply to coin and baseball card collecting, hobbies in which visual appeal and visual perfection are (or, at least, should be) of paramount importance in evaluating an item's value—after all, what else can you do with coins and cards, than stare at them for hours on end? But hobbies in which the collected item actually does something—for example, transmitting music—are equally concerned with making sure that function remains as unimpaired as is possible.

The only way to truly grade a record, tape, or CD is to play it. Eyes can detect any obvious visual flaws; a magnifying glass (some collectors won't leave home without one) will pick up the tiniest ones. But until the music is actually booming out of the speakers, there is no way of detecting the myriad other little pings, dings, and clicks that can send an apparently brand-new disc hurtling down the scale to unlistenable oblivion . . . click . . . oblivion . . . click . . . oblivion.

But you, the listener alone, have the time and inclination to play every piece of music that you purchase, and you alone can tell whether the barely audible pop between tracks two and three is catastrophic enough to merit regrading a disc from Mint to miserable.

For the individual you purchased it from, it's often enough that the item fulfilled the visual criteria of whichever grading guide he or she applied to it. The best that you can realistically hope for is that the guide was published on this planet. It's surprising how many seem not to have been.

Remember, too, that grading a record's condition is not the last word in its description. A disc might fulfill every criteria for a particular grade, but still demand further attention: Is it a promotional, DJ, or cutout? Is it mono, stereo, or quadraphonic? Is it autographed? (And remember, there are autographs out there whose presence could turn the most trashed piece of vinyl detritus into a veritable nest egg, if they can be authenticated.)

There are dozens of variables that can seriously affect a potential purchaser's decision, and all the more so online, where the item is unavailable for hands-on inspection. When selling, provide as much extra information as you can. When buying, ask before you bid.

Records (45s, LPs, 78s, etc.)

American dealers tend to work from an eight-point scale developed for use in the monthly magazine *Goldmine* and in the myriad price guides that it publishes. In the UK, the seven-point scale formulated by the monthly *Record Collector* is now the accepted system. These scales are applicable to both vinyl and packaging; many sellers will now grade both separately, particularly if there is some disparity between the two—a clean disc and a torn sleeve, for example.

Family UK 45s

"Boom Bang" (RAFT RA 18501, 1973)
"Burlesque" (REPRISE K14196, 1972)
"In My Own Time" (REPRISE K14090, 1971)
"Me My Friend" (REPRISE RS 23270, 1968)
"My Friend the Sun" (REPRISE K14218, 1973)
"No Mule's Fool" (REPRISE RS 27001, 1969)
"Scene Through the Eyes of a Lens" (LIBERTY LBF 15031, 1967)
"Second Generation" (REPRISE RS 23315, 1968)
"Strange Band" (REPRISE RS 27009, 1970)
"Today" (REPRISE RS 27005, 1970)

Neither scale is right or wrong. Both function perfectly within those countries' borders. However, problems can arise when transactions cross international boundaries, especially when a record falls outside of the most self-evident of grades.

To begin at the bottom, Poor (P), or in the UK, Bad (B), should leave nobody in any doubt. In a nutshell, the record is wrecked. The sleeve is tattered, if it is even present. The vinyl might be cracked or broken, it might be scratched or warped. It certainly will not play very well, and unless the record represents one of the world's most fabulous rarities—say, a red-vinyl pressing of the Hornets' "I Can't Believe" (copies of which have sold for up to $20,000, if you care for such things), its value can only be measured in fractions of a cent.

Don't let the seller try to sweet-talk you, either. Every collector, finding a shot-to-hell Shangri-Las LP and asking why it's still $50, has been informed that, "if it weren't for the bullet holes, it'd be in Mint condition." And that's true, especially if the bullet holes are indeed the only imperfection.

Yes, it can be tempting to grab a bargain price for a medium-rare album with a scrappy jacket and some audible scratches, but think of what you might be able to find were you to be willing to invest a few dollars more. Indeed, as I write these words, I have just emerged from an e-mail exchange with a seller who justified charging $100 for an LP that did indeed suffer from such faults, by pointing out that the next-cheapest available copy on the Internet was priced at $150.

"Yes," I replied. "But that one's in near-mint condition."

Basically, if the record won't play, it's a Frisbee. And some don't even fulfill that function properly.

Mint (M), at the other end of the scale, means that one is purchasing a factory-fresh, unplayed, perhaps even unopened, disc. There will be no creases or ring wear on the cover (picture sleeve for 45s and EPs), no fingerprints on the vinyl, no spindle marks (light silvery lines) around the center hole. Any original extras, ranging from lyric sheets and posters to printed inner sleeves, will be present and pristine.

There will be no indication at all that human hands have ever touched the record. And one will notice that very few experienced American dealers or price guides ever advertise their wares in this state, no matter how perfect they appear. Instead, Near Mint is the preferred term, simply because even unplayed, unopened records may well have some undetected defect. Mint, in America, implies "perfect." Near Mint adds "as far as we can tell."

This latter is especially helpful when contending with what seems to be a growing problem among purchasers of newly released vinyl—an LP that, in every other way, can be described as factory fresh, mint condition, etcetera etcetera, but whose very weight and thickness has torn through the seams of the inner sleeve, and is maybe even worrying the outer sleeve too.

Of course, you can find plenty of battered old albums that have torn and split seams. The operative terms there, however, tend to be "battered" and "old." It is only in recent years that a brand-new album is as likely as not to reach you with these flaws at least beginning to show, and it is indeed a consequence of the weight of the vinyl, as it jostles around during shipping. Or so we are told.

It's an infuriating development, for sellers as well as purchasers, and one imagines the record company boffins are busily seeking a solution, even as we read these words. But don't bank on it.

Back to "Near Mint." British grading does not make this same distinction. Mint still means exactly the same as it does in the US, but there is no safety net a few points down the grading scale to catch any unforeseen problems. Perhaps the British trust the dealer to make good any serious shortfall in the quality of the disc. Perhaps British customers understand that once they break the seal and spin the record, it is no longer either unopened or unplayed. Or maybe they have simply come to terms with the fact that *Perfect* is just an old John Travolta movie. However they look at it, the system works for them. American buyers may not be so sure.

These are the extremes. On a numerical scale, a Mint record should score 100 (with Near Mint no less than 95); a Poor would barely scrape zero. What, however, of all the numbers in between—for it is there that the majority of used records one finds, whether on the Internet, in a thrift store, or at a record fair, will lie. And it is there that controversy is most likely to rear its head.

There are four basic flaws to which vinyl is commonly prone, most brought about through misuse of some sort—warping, dishing, scratching, and breaking.

The last of these is self-explanatory. If the record is broken, and that means anything from a minor crack on the edge to a huge chunk torn from the soul of the disc, then that's the end of the story. It's broken. Move along.

Warping, caused by exposure to excessive heat, is the term applied to records that, in the simplest terms, are no longer flat. Sometimes, the warp will gently bow the vinyl, so that when viewed edge-on, it takes on a pronounced wave. In more extreme cases, just one area of the record

will be buckled, while the remainder of the disc is unharmed. Playing and careful listening is the only way of deciding whether it materially affects the value's sound quality, but it should certainly affect the grade. Dishing is similar to warping, but this time, when viewed edge-on, the record takes on the appearance of, indeed, a dish. Again the effect can be minimal and may not affect the sound quality. But it may.

Scratches are more problematic. Every grade below Near Mint makes some allowance for wear and tear; the question is, how much wear and tear can one expect in any given grade? Some scratches are so light as to barely touch the vinyl—"surface marks," as they are commonly called, can be caused by the record itself coming into contact with absolutely anything, including the stylus that is playing it, or even its own packaging.

However, since surface marks lay across the surface of the record and do not cut into the grooves, where the music is stored, they will not affect the sound in the slightest. Scratches, on the other hand, cut deeper, and you can hear them. The American Very Good Plus (VG+) and British Excellent (Ex) indicate a record that, while showing some signs of use, was also clearly the property of a very careful owner. This is the province of the surface marks and similar light scuffs that do not interfere with the play, but that may be considered unsightly; a barely noticeable warp or dish might also creep into this grade if no other damage is in evidence. Spindle marks will be minimal and the spindle hole will still be tight.

As far as the packaging goes, all original inserts will be present, but will show some signs of handling. There may be some light creasing to the corners of the jacket or a little splitting around the spine. The only permissible "additions" to the original sleeve will be original autographs, items added at source to either point out bonus extras or notable tracks (stickers proclaiming "features the smash hit . . ." or similar), or devices designating the record as a promotional copy, produced for DJs, journalists, and other members of the media.

These can range from "property of" stickers and stamps to "timing sheets" spread across the lower front cover, listing the tracks and their duration—an invaluable service to DJs, of course. Many collectors regard these extras as a defect. However, specialists (and, of course, promo collectors) treat them as an integral part of the packaging and expect the grading to reflect that.

Otherwise pristine LP jackets might also have a punch-hole or indentation in one corner, or might have had about half an inch of corner physically chopped away, branding them as "cutouts"—factory-fresh records whose jackets were thus disfigured by the issuing record company, to indicate that they were made available at a discount price. Because of this damage, no cutout can reasonably be graded higher than VG+/Ex, even if it fulfills all the criteria of a higher grade.

So-called light scratches are those that have cut into the groove and are responsible for occasional, and very brief, sequences of light clicks as a record is playing. Clicking, however, is all that they will do. Medium scratches are those that actively interfere with the music, without actually causing the needle to skip or stick. They can be felt by running a fingertip over the surface of the record (make sure it's a clean tip, though, or you'll just add to the problem). On both sides of the ocean, the grade Very Good (VG) allows these scratches to intrude into the listening experience, together with further deterioration of the packaging, but without significant damage to it.

Another accepted VG ailment is surface noise that is evident during quiet passages. If the record belonged to somebody who regularly played certain cuts, there may be some minor clicking at the beginning and end of each favored cut, caused by the needle having been placed less than delicately down on the vinyl. In extreme cases, this can also affect (again, without skipping or sticking) the outro of the preceding cut and/or the intro of the next.

On a VG record, the spindle hole will probably be surrounded by a maze of silver lines; there may be some wear to the hole itself. The packaging may also be showing both its age and its history. Labels and sleeves alike may have writing, stickers, tape or the like either attached or showing signs of once having been adhered (tape residue will probably outlive cockroaches); tears and creases will be more apparent, and loose extras may well have disappeared.

It is important to note that while a VG record will suffer from some of these faults, it should not suffer from them all. Two or three is more than enough; a record with any more requires a serious reappraisal. Most US price guides regard VG as the lowest grade worth valuing.

On both sides of the Atlantic, the grade Good describes records that have been played a few times too often. Groove wear will be evident in the loss of the shiny black glow that a better-conditioned disc should retain. Label and sleeve alike will be tatty—stained, torn, or defaced. The corner areas of the sleeve, those portions that do not rest against the record itself, may feel soft and droopy, and will prove much more easily creased or folded than they ought.

Upon playing, the record will not sound as sharp as it once did; surface noise will be audible throughout, and the scratches will be louder, too. The record will still be playable without skipping or sticking, but it's a sorry sight to behold, regardless. The wholly unnecessary American grade of Good Plus (G+) is differentiated as not having quite as many defects as a mere Good.

The lowest grade in which a record is actually playable is the American Fair (F), which equates to the British Poor (P). In this state,

the deepest scratches come into play, those that not only cut through the grooves but also force the needle to follow them, leading to the dreaded skips and jumps. Or maybe they displace one of the groove walls, shifting it into the path of the needle, thus causing it to become stuck. (Dirt, hair, grease, and a million other foreign bodies can also cause this.) Or maybe they do both and really give you your waste-of-money's worth. The sleeve may still be intact, but it just as likely may not; and if there was a lyric sheet or similar included, it long ago went astray.

Basically, unless we are again discussing some fabulous rarity, records in this condition are worthless, and the only reason they are even offered up for sale is because modern society frowns so fiercely on simply giving rubbish away. One man's meat and all that. Likewise, there are few worthwhile reasons, and even fewer good excuses, for wanting to purchase a record in this state—unless, perhaps, you really hate the song and want to watch it suffer. In which case, are you sure you even need to know about grading?

Top-Dollar Acetates

Born to Run, Bruce Springsteen (THE MASTER CUTTING ROOM 12-INCH, 1975)

"Andrew's Blues," Rolling Stones (EMIDISC 7-INCH, 1964)

"Babooshka," Kate Bush (EMI 7-INCH, 1980)

"Don't Use Me," Dee Clark (UNIVERSAL RECORDING CO. 7-INCH, 1964)

"Give Me a Reason," Praying Mantis (PORTLAND RECORDING STUDIOS 7-INCH, 1983)

"I Feel Fine," the Beatles (CAPITOL 8-INCH, 1964)

"I Just Don't Know," Jackie Lomax (APPLE ONE-SIDED 7-INCH, 1969)

"Memory of Water," Marillion (WHITFIELD ST. STUDIO ACETATE 12-INCH, 1997)

"The Clown," Status Quo (ADVANCED PROMOTION ACETATE 7-INCH, 1969)

The Open Mind, The Open Mind (PHILIPS 12-INCH, 1969)

CDs/Tapes
(Reels, 4- and 8-Tracks, Cassettes, etc.)

In these fields, grading is basically a matter of whether or not the product plays perfectly. CDs, while not the indestructible heirlooms that early publicity insisted they were, are nevertheless very difficult to damage in normal use, despite their propensity to hastily accumulate the most unsightly collection of scratches, fingerprints, and dents.

Such eyesores have become especially prevalent as the industry turns more and more to "miniature LP sleeve"-style packaging, without also including a "miniature LP inner sleeve" to protect the

CD from the harsh card sleeve. A number of box set packages, too, seem custom-designed to scar and scratch the discs they are supposed to protect.

In all but the most drastic cases, however, not only will these problems not affect play, they can often be camouflaged with any one of the many CD cleaning products on the market. Certainly, unless factory freshness is a prerequisite of admission to your collection, a wanted CD should never be rejected simply because the disc looks a little battered.

Just make certain it's still the right color, though. A wave of CDs from the early years of the format are notorious for "bronzing," or CD rot—a very visible condition that ultimately renders them unplayable. So are the bootleg standbys of CD-R and DVD-R. So are laser discs, and so are computer games, should you collect those as well.

A simple rule of thumb when considering a purchase, then: Always check the playing surface for anything that shouldn't be there, be it tiny white flecks, odd-looking pin-pricks, or great blotches of brown. It means the protective surface has failed, the data is corrupting, and the disc will soon be unplayable.

At which point, it's also worth mentioning that it's not only the used CDs you are planning to buy that might well be suffering from this blight. The discs that you purchased brand new might, as well—online audiophile forums frequently address this issue, usually after one member or another went to play a favorite disc for the first time in years, and found it had fallen victim to the rot.

Neither is it only music fans and purchasers who suffer. Professional archivists, including the Library of Congress, have also acknowledged the problem; indeed, the latter has launched what it calls a "longevity research" project, in which it is stated: "Aging, storage environment, and handling can cause changes in the materials leading to deterioration and loss of data, sometimes referred to as 'CD-Rot' or 'Laser-Rot.' Oxidation, hydrolysis, and damage caused by mechanical stress can result in errors in signal playback, which can be assessed by measuring a disc's 'block error rate,' or BLER. When BLER exceeds 220/s, the maximum limit specified in the ISO 10149 standard for CD-ROM, the disc can begin to develop uncorrectable errors, indicating that information may have been lost, or the disc may become unplayable altogether."

In the UK, the problem was so pronounced that several manufacturers even instituted a return program for consumers to have affected discs replaced. This lapsed, however, over a decade ago and it now seems to be accepted that, just as cylinders, 78s, and the first (1930s) attempts at a long-playing record all possessed some kind of built-in self-destruct mechanism, so did/do CDs.

And so do cassettes, cartridges (4- and 8-tracks), and reels, with the most common problems—twisted, bunched, and/or broken

CD rot! Not as extreme here as some examples, but the white patches on the playing side as just as destructive as more colorful stains.

tape—often visible as soon as you look at them. But of course, there are other potential flaws to be aware of. In cassettes, defects can be seen either in the open playing area or through the transparent plastic window between the spools; in cartridges, the nature of the format can allow problems to be absorbed back into the case, but more often the tape itself jams, ensuring that the flaw is forever visible in the playing area. Or even hanging limply out of it. Always look at the tape itself to check that it has not twisted; the playing area, facing out, is light brown in color, while the backing, which should not be seen, is shiny black.

Another problem to which 8-tracks are heir are the large globules of an eternally adhesive black goo in the place where the roller once was. The problem is as common among sealed tapes as it is among those that have been well played, and is caused simply by age and decay. Unless extreme care is exercised upon opening the case and transferring the tape to a new cartridge case, this is a fatal condition; once that goo gets on the tape, you'll never get it off again.

These are the visual checks one should always make. However, tape formats are also prone to a number of flaws that remain undetectable until the tape is played. Magnetic tape also deteriorates with age, with the thin cassette tape especially vulnerable; even a factory-sealed cassette can prove unplayable if the circumstances are right. (Or, in this case, wrong.)

Tape is also irreversibly damaged by exposure to magnetic sources, and alarmingly, by the irradiation process introduced by the US Postal Service following the fall 2001 anthrax attacks. Paper products (LP sleeves, CD booklets, etc.), too, could also be adversely affected by the process, and had the irradiation system become universal, the ramifications for America's musical mail-order industry scarcely bore contemplating. Thankfully, the procedure was eventually scaled back and, apparently, is now a concern only if you are mailing that 8-track to a government office. Both 4- and 8-tracks can also suffer from the loss of the metallic strips that communicate the conclusion of each program to the playing head of the machine—without them, a player will just loop the same songs over and over, and the most varied album in the world will swiftly start sounding somewhat samey. Back in the heyday of cartridges, this problem was prevalent enough that several companies actually marketed replacement strips. For obvious reasons, these are less commonly available today.

Reel-to-reel tapes, produced as they generally were for the audiophile market, and uncluttered by rollers and the like, are less susceptible to hidden dangers. However, the very action of preparing to play a reel—looping the tape manually into the second spool—can cause terrible problems, ranging from grease on the playing surface to kinks, twists, and even breakage. When purchasing reels, always check for the presence of a short length of blank (and usually opaque) "run on" tape at the loose end of the reel.

The other key to tape collecting, no less than with LPs and 45s, is to ensure that the packaging is complete and clean.

As far as CDs and cassettes are concerned, this applies only to any appropriate artwork—booklets, liner cases, and so forth. It does not refer to the piece of mass-produced plastic that holds it all together, which is bad news for all those lost souls who complain loudly and bitterly because a mail-order CD arrived in a cracked or otherwise damaged jewel case, and good news for the sellers who know that the case was fine when it was dispatched.

Except in those cases where some kind of customizing incorporates the jewel case into the actual packaging (the personalized "Q" logo on the spine of Queen's *Made in Heaven* CD, for instance, or the gold symbol on front of Prince's *3121*), a jewel case (or cassette case) is a jewel case (or cassette case) is a . . . . Damage is regrettable, of course. But it is not the end of the world and it does not irreparably devalue your purchase. Just run down the road and buy a new one.

THE WORLD'S MOST VALUABLE RECORDS

No book on record collecting would be complete without a list of the world's most valuable records—and no two books on record collecting ever seem to agree on what should actually be included on such a list.

There are those supremely elusive nuggets from the dawn of rock 'n' roll—the first R&B LP of all time, a self-titled release by Billy Ward and the Dominoes; the Midnighters' *Greatest Hits*; *Johnny Burnette and the Rock 'n' Roll Trio*; Frank Ballard's *Rhythm-Blues Party*; UK pressings of Ron Harraves' "Latch On"; and Bobby Charles' "See You Later, Alligator."

There are acetates and demonstration discs that one can only dream about, such as a second copy of the Quarrymen's original 78 rpm acetate of "That'll Be the Day," or one of the fifty replicas that Paul McCartney had manufactured in 1981; Elvis's one-sided "How Do You Think I Feel" test pressing; Queen's five-song Trident Studios demo acetate; or the CD promo for Nirvana's unreleased UK single of "Pennyroyal Tea (Scott Litt Mix)." Dream on.

There are colored-vinyl albums that exist in quantities of just one copy, surreptitiously pressed by a factory worker to take home as a souvenir. There are hopelessly obscure private pressings by now-fashionable British prog and folk bands. There are demo tapes (or CDs) by every band that ever sought a record deal, and that includes the groups that got one—even U2, Radiohead, and the 1975 had to start somewhere.

There is so much that could be listed—and so little that anyone will ever actually find. The following, therefore, concentrates on releases that, theoretically, could turn up at any time, any place, mass-produced (more or less) items that might readily pass for just another everyday issue, and that, very occasionally, have done so.

All have accepted values in excess of $1,000 (well in excess, in most cases); all, to be honest, are as likely to turn up in your local thrift store, garage sale, or grandmother's loft as any of the fabled obscurities mentioned above. But the devil, as they say, is in the details, and if you don't know what the details are, then you'll never know when you're holding a little slice of record-collecting heaven in your hand.

The Beatles, *Introducing the Beatles*
(US VEE-JAY SR 1062, INCLUDES
"LOVE ME DO"/"PS I LOVE YOU"—1964)

The Beatles' first American LP was issued in January 1964, at a time when no sane American gave a fig for these longhaired lurkers from Liverpool . . . wherever that was. The album featured a dozen songs, including both sides of the band's first UK single, "Love Me Do"/"PS I Love You," plus ten others featured on the band's UK debut album, *Please Please Me.* Planning an issue in both mono and stereo, Vee-Jay ordered 6,000 cover slicks from its printers (Coburn and Co., Chicago), utilizing the same formal band shot that was used on the UK *Beatles Hits* EP (Parlophone GEP 8880); the reverse of the sleeve depicted tiny color photographs of twenty-five other Vee-Jay album releases, and no track listing.

A revised sleeve, with a full accounting of the record's contents, appeared soon after, leading some researchers to believe that both the ad back and what is now regarded as an intermediate issue, with its back cover absolutely blank, were either an oversight or a subtle subterfuge to postpone the inevitable wrath of Capitol Records, which was now taking a close look at Vee-Jay's right to release the Beatles' music. Ultimately, this led to the production of a revised edition of *Introducing the Beatles,* replacing "Love Me Do"/"PS I Love You" with the hitherto abandoned "Please Please Me"/"Ask Me Why" coupling.

Whatever their origins, the ad-back and blank-back editions of the album are extremely rare in any form, with stereo pressings even harder to find. And then there are stereo versions of the title back, a variation that was not even known to exist prior to 1995.

The Beatles, *Please Please Me*
(UK PARLOPHONE PCS 3042, GOLD-ON-BLACK LABEL, 1963)

If stereo releases were sporadic and limited in the US, they were even more so in Britain, where the market was limited exclusively to hi-fi freaks. The initial stereo issue of the Beatles' debut album, then, was always going to be tiny, but it was about to get even tinier. The first pressing utilized the gold-on-black label that had served Parlophone LPs for several years, but that was now being phased out in favor of a new yellow-on-black design. And the first pressings of *that* credit the publishing to "Dick James Mus[ic] Co."—later ones (and that's just days later) to the Beatles' own newly formed Northern Songs.

The Beatles, *The Beatles Deluxe Three Pack*
(CAPITOL 8X3T 358, 8-TRACK BOX SET, 1969)

Who says 8-tracks aren't worth anything? Released in September 1969, the fabled *Deluxe Three Pack* comprised three apparently randomly selected Beatles albums in a unique 12-inch box set. *Meet the Beatles, Yesterday and Today* (with the trunk cover, of course), and *Magical Mystery Tour* were the chosen ones, none of which have especial value in their own right. It is estimated, however, that no more than a dozen copies of the complete box set exist, establishing this as the rarest 8-track release of all time.

Kate Bush, "Eat the Music"
(UK EMI EM 280, 1993)

Most collectors believe that the greatest Kate Bush rarities relate either to her pre-fame days and the so-called Cathy demos, or to the 1978–87 period when she was at her most active. In fact, the acknowledged rarest Bush record of all was the projected first British single from her 1993 album, *The Red Shoes,* "Eat the Music"/"Big Stripey Lie"—projected, that is, until radio positively refused to bite.

Moving fast, EMI scrapped the entire first-print run, and slammed the decidedly jauntier "Rubberband Girl" into its place, while retaining the same catalog number and B-side. Picture-sleeve copies of the abandoned "Eat the Music" escaped regardless, to wreak havoc on the most complete Kate collections—and, doubtless, to raise the hopes of everyone who owns a copy. Good luck. "Eat the Music" was issued as planned in Europe, Australia, and the US, so it's only the British one that's worth a fortune.

Bob Dylan, "Mixed Up Confusion"
(COLUMBIA 42656, ORANGE LABEL, 1963)

Dylan's first-ever single was recorded in November 1962, and released on the heels of a less-than-world-beating debut album, before his second album finally broke Dylan out of the narrow confines of New York's Woody Guthrie–impersonation circuit. Hardly surprisingly, then, "Mixed Up Confusion" sold poorly, and while re-pressings would follow the singer's breakthrough, this original issue is extremely rare.

Bob Dylan, *The Freewheelin' Bob Dylan*
(US COLUMBIA CS 8786/CL 1986, INCLUDES FOUR MISSING TRACKS, 1963)

This is one of those rarities whose legend is now so well-known that it is probably more famous than the album that replaced it. When recording his second LP, Bob Dylan included four songs that—for reasons that are still somewhat obscure—were first placed on, and then removed from, the finished product: "Rocks and Gravel," "Let Me Die in My Footsteps," "Gamblin' Willie's Dead Man's Hand," and a pointed piece of anti–right wing politicizing, "Talkin' John Birch Blues." (Alternate titles "Talkin' John Birch Society Blues" and " . . . Paranoid Blues" have since appeared on bootleg and official anthologies alike.)

The removal of the latter track echoed a decision taken earlier in the year when Dylan appeared on CBS-TV's *The Ed Sullivan Show* and was pointedly refused permission to perform the song. The favorite theory is that Columbia, acknowledging the logic of its broadcasting department, prevailed upon Dylan to drop the song from the record, at which point Dylan decided to revise the entire disc to annoy the label as much as it was annoying him.

The album had already been manufactured at this point, with all four songs included. The entire run was withdrawn and prepared for destruction, while the revised edition went into production. Of course not all the original LPs were lost—a tiny number of stereo pressings are known, though all have (so far) appeared in the "corrected" sleeve. Neither would the re-pressing itself go as planned. An unknown quantity was produced mistakenly using the original mono master, featuring the four deleted tracks, though the correct new label and sleeve were employed. No sleeves listing the four deleted tracks have ever been located. (Interestingly, the precise opposite situation exists in Canada, where no "original" or "mispressed" versions of the LP have yet surfaced, but sleeves have.)

There are American promo editions with the deleted tracks listed on both the timing strip affixed to the front cover and on the label. But none found to date have yet played the banished quartet. No matter: unedited versions of *The Freewheelin' Bob Dylan* are already regarded as the rarest and most valuable record in America. What difference would another variation really make? Have you checked your copy yet?

Jefferson Airplane, *Takes Off*
(US RCA VICTOR LSP 3584, WITH MISSING/REVISED TRACKS, 1966)

The Airplane may have reveled in a world of chemical and sexual stimulation, but their record company certainly didn't. Original mono editions of the group's debut album hit the stores bearing three songs—"Runnin' 'Round This World," "Go to Her," and "Let Me In"—that should probably never have passed the label's internal censorship department. And when they did . . . the album was promptly sent back for a cleanup.

New versions of the latter two tracks were substituted for the original versions. The cleaned-up versions featured politely revised lyrics (the line "as you lay under me" in "Let Me In" was replaced by "as you stay here by me"). "Runnin' 'Round This World"—which referred to both sex and drugs, and was thus clearly unsalvageable—was dropped altogether, not to be heard again until 1971 brought the *Early Flight* compilation. The other two cuts are still in the vaults today, though alternate uncensored versions appeared on the *Jefferson Airplane Loves You* box set in 1991.

John's Children, "Midsummer Night's Scene"
(UK TRACK 604 005, 1967)

Alongside the edition of Queen's "Bohemian Rhapsody," listed below, this is the rarest British single of them all. Scheduled for release in June 1967, as the follow-up to the band's mini-hit "Desdemona" (604 003), the creepily psychedelic "Midsummer Night's Scene" was withdrawn from the schedules for reasons that still aren't clear. It was replaced, using the same catalog number and B-side, by "Sara Crazy Child."

Judged a rarity even at the time, the single's value began soaring after John's Children's guitarist, Marc Bolan, emerged at the front of T. Rex, the biggest British band of the early '70s, and still one of the UK's most fanatically collectible artists. Between twenty-five and fifty copies of this single are rumored to exist today—considerably fewer have actually been accredited.

Paul McCartney, *Ram*
(US APPLE MAS 3375, MONO PROMOTIONAL ISSUE, 1971)

By 1970, mono was dead. In just two years, the industry had risen up and squashed it like a bug beneath the shimmering brilliance of stereo sound. A number of radio stations still appreciated it, though, and new singles pressed for DJ use regularly featured a stereo mix of the song on one side, and a mono mix on the other. Mono promos of LPs, too, still appeared on occasion—1971 also saw a limited pressing of the Rolling Stones' *Sticky Fingers,* produced for the delight of DJs everywhere.

It was not, then, notable when Apple pressed up a small quantity of McCartney's second album in marvelous mono; what is eyebrow-raising is the value attached to copies. The mono catalog number and "MONAURAL" legend on the label are the only visibly distinguishing factors—there were no promo markings, nor was there a custom sleeve. Rather, most copies were delivered sharing a jacket with the regular stereo issue, and many were probably passed by without a second glance. Today, of course, it's a different story. Bootlegged through the '70s and beyond, the mono *Ram* has since been granted a full, official reissue, complete with a plain white, hand-notated sleeve.

Madonna, "Erotica" 12-inch picture disc
(MAVERICK W 0138 TP, 1992)

This is one of those stories that you simply couldn't make up. Barely had the pressing plants completed manufacturing this disc—complete with an image of Madonna sucking somebody's toe—than the British tabloid press went to town on real-life images of Sarah Ferguson, the Duchess of York, having the same thing done to her.

Why this should be considered news is anybody's guess. Nevertheless, the ensuing "scandal" engulfed the UK media, and over at Maverick, it was felt that Madonna's latest imagery could well be seen as heaping further insult upon the beleaguered Fergie. The manufactured discs were hastily collected from the pressing plant for destruction. Yet some survived, with rumors insisting that one copy was taken from each of the 138 boxes and sold on to a Liverpool record dealer. Or maybe more than one. Nobody knows for sure.

The Misfits, "Horror Business"
(PLAN 9 PL 1009, BLACK VINYL, 1979)

The New Jersey horror punk band has ascended into the upper realms of collectibility without most "traditional" (read "older") collectors even noticing. The majority of releases on the group's own Blank and Plan 9 labels are extremely rare, but this is the daddy of them all. Conventionally issued on yellow vinyl, twenty-five copies were produced in exciting black, and if you can find the unreleased picture sleeve too, featuring a group photograph on the reverse, you're really on to a winner.

Elvis Presley, "Can't Help Falling in Love"
(RCA VICTOR 37-7968 "COMPACT SINGLE 331/3,"
WITH/WITHOUT PICTURE SLEEVE, 1961)

RCA's Compact Single series was launched in 1961, primarily to offer fans an improved audio experience—like the 12-inch 45s of later years, 7-inch 331/3s allowed more information to be packed into the (wider) grooves, thus leading to better sound. Special picture sleeves were designed for each issue and some 150 releases were made over the course of the next year, none of which are especially common. But three of the five Elvis issues are much sought after—"His Latest Flame" (37-7908), "Good Luck Charm" (37-7992), and "Can't Help Falling in Love" are the rarest of the lot.

Elvis Presley, *Moody Blue*
(RCA AFL1-2428, 1976)

The world's most valuable picture disc was produced by RCA, apparently as an executive Christmas card, and it depicts, odd as it may sound, Elvis manager Colonel Tom Parker dressed as Santa Claus. That's on one side, anyway; on the other is a photo of an RCA staff Christmas party. Gripping stuff. But apparently no more than a dozen discs were pressed, and even fewer have surfaced on the open market.

Prince, *The Black Album*
(US WARNER BROS. 25677, 1987)

Scheduled for release for Christmas 1987, *The Black Album* was intended as the big pop secret of the year. It was listed on the Warner Bros. schedule as being, simply, by "somebody," and was to be launched into circulation beneath a cloak of impenetrable anonymity. A plain black sleeve (of course) included no artist information and no track details (even the CD long box was plain black), this Stygian vista broken by just two stickers, the requisite barcode and an "Explicit Lyrics—Parental Advisory" warning. Even the Warner Bros. promotions office was instructed to ignore the release altogether: no copies to reviewers, no information to the media, and no advertisements in the press.

Only the club circuit would be served with prerelease copies. Promos, dispatched shortly before the album's street date, were manufactured as two 45-rpm 12-inch discs; stock copies were prepared as conventional 12-inch 331/3 rpm LPs, and also as CDs. Then, with buyers apparently not gearing up for the release according to plan, Prince abruptly pulled it from the schedules. Suddenly, an album intended to be utterly anonymous was transformed into one of the most famous records of the decade.

Bootleg copies of *The Black Album* began appearing very swiftly; they are convincing, so beware. Authentic vinyl copies are practically nonexistent, while no more than twenty-five to fifty genuine examples of *The Black Album* CD are believed to have survived. The first to appear on the collectors market in 1991 sold for a then-record $13,500; in 2016, another went for $15,000. An official, albeit limited-edition, release finally arrived in 1994.

Queen, "Bohemian Rhapsody"
(UK EMI 2375, BLUE VINYL,
QUEEN'S AWARD FOR EXPORT PICTURE SLEEVE, 1978)

Currently ranked the rarest UK single ever issued, this blue-vinyl pressing dates from 1978, three years after the song's original release. It was housed in a maroon-and-gold custom sleeve, celebrating EMI's receipt of the prestigious Queen's (the other one) Award to Industry for Export Achievement.

Just 200 copies were pressed, the majority of which were distributed alongside a pair of etched goblets and a commemorative pen, to guests at a three-hour luncheon at London's Selfridges, celebrating the award on July 26, 1978. Check your diary—do you remember where you ate that afternoon?

Rolling Stones, "I Wanna Be Your Man"
(US LONDON 9641, 1964)

The Rolling Stones' debut US single was a proven UK smash, and should have been just as big in America. It was loud, it was brash, and it was custom written for the group by John Lennon and Paul McCartney. Even allowing for the band's unknown status in the US, it should have done something. Instead it sank like a stone, so hard and fast that many of the band's soon-acquired fans weren't even aware that it existed. And by the time they found out, it was too late. There are a lot of DJ copies around, mailed out to people who probably never even played them. But stock copies never seem to turn up.

Rolling Stones, *The Rolling Stones Promotional Album*
(US LONDON/UK DECCA RSM/RSD 1, 1969)

Or, how to turn the mundane into the magnificent. In 1969, the Stones' US and UK labels, London and Decca, respectively, compiled a catalog-spanning promotional album to help publicize the band's latest LP and tour. Just 200 copies were produced in one country, with the catalog number RSM 1; 200 sleeves were printed in the other, with the number RSD 1. The albums were then equally distributed between the two markets—never (or very rarely) to be seen again. It isn't only the album's rarity that attracts attention, either; the album is also the only source for an (admittedly minor) alternate mix of the song "Love in Vain."

Many collectors guides caution their readers not to confuse this issue with a similarly packaged Australian LP, *The Rolling Stones Limited Edition Collectors Item* (which features the "correct" "Love in Vain"). This is indeed sound advice if you're about to drop a couple of grand on a copy. However, since the Aussie release, too, is extraordinarily scarce, it probably wouldn't hurt to lay a copy or two by if you get the chance.

Sex Pistols, "God Save the Queen"
(UK A&M AMS 7284, 1977)

Signed and sacked in the space of one week, the Sex Pistols, and the group's A&M sojourn, is the stuff of which punk rock legends were made—all the more so since production of the group's "God Save the Queen"/"No Feelings" single was already underway.

With rumors swirling that outraged A&M superstars had deluged the office with complaints and disgust, unable to believe such a nice, sedate label had inked a pact with Satan's foulest demons, the company commenced destroying every manufactured copy of the

Not one of the world's greatest rarities, but this early CD promo for Marilyn Manson's fourth album certainly had its day in the highly-priced sun.

Pistols' record the moment the group was fired. And when "God Save the Queen" did finally appear two months later, it was on a different label (Virgin), with a different B-side ("Did You No Wrong").

The A&M single lived on, however. Up to 300 copies are now believed to have escaped the cull (earlier estimates were considerably more conservative), with the band members apparently owning several apiece. Another dozen were distributed among laid-off A&M executives, following the UK label's closure in 1999.

Tony Sheridan and the Beat Brothers, "My Bonnie"
(US DECCA 31382, 1962)

The Beatles by any other name, and this 45 has the honor of being the group's first-ever US release, almost a full year before Swan, Vee-Jay, Tollie, Capitol, and all the rest got in on the fun. It sold next to nothing at the time—even in their homeland, the "Beat Brothers" were an unknown quantity, though it was amazing the difference that a couple more years made. In 1964, not only was this single reissued (MGM K13213), an entire album's worth of similar tracks also made it out. In fact, they're still coming out today, so if you're looking for this particular issue, it's unlikely that you want it for its musical content. You probably don't want the bootleg copies, either.

Original pressings feature the then-standard black Decca label with colored bars; original DJ copies feature a pink label with a star beneath the word Decca. Black-label variations on this latter are generally regarded as counterfeits.

Frank Sinatra and Antonio Carlos Jobim, *Sinatra Jobim*
(REPRISE W7 1028, 8-TRACK, 1969)

Who says 8-tracks aren't worth anything (part two)? *Sinatra Jobim* was scheduled for release in 1969, with production of the 8-track carried out by the Ampex plant in Illinois. The production—and, indeed, shipping—in that format had already begun when the release was canceled.

Just one LP test pressing is known to have been made; on the other hand, some 3,500 8-tracks had been produced, and Warner Bros., Reprise's distributors, immediately circulated a memo requesting that all copies be returned for destruction. The company's efforts appear to have succeeded, as no more than half a dozen copies of the 8-track are known today.

Much of the album (seven of the ten songs) reappeared two years later on the *Sinatra and Company* (Reprise FS 1033) album.

Bruce Springsteen, "Spirit in the Night"
(US COLUMBIA 45864, 1973)

Many artists' rarest releases fall within the earliest days of their careers, and so it is with the Boss. "Spirit in the Night"/"For You" was his second 45, following "Blinded by the Light"/"Angel" (itself a considerable scarcity), issued at a time when Springsteen's future preeminence was already an open secret in the media, but had yet to communicate itself to the general public. DJ copies of this, with a mono/stereo coupling of "Spirit," are relatively common. Stock copies, however, have a nasty penchant for elusiveness.

Thin Lizzy, "The Farmer"
(EIRE PARLOPHONE DIP 513, 1970)

A lot of groups debuted under misspelled names. Jethro Tull became Jethro Toe for a now-scarce UK debut 45, and U2 played its first British show under the mistaken name of V2—posters for the show are worth an absolute mint. So Thin *Lizzie* probably got off fairly lightly—at least it still worked phonetically.

Still, even the band members could never have foreseen just how hard it would be for future collectors to get to hear what their first effort sounded like. Released in Ireland only in July 1970, just 500 copies of "The Farmer" are believed to have been pressed, of which 217 went unsold and were subsequently recycled. Absent from every Lizzy album and collection over the next 15 years, "The Farmer" finally resurfaced in 1986 on EMI's *Supernova* various-artists collection (GAS 101). But this, too, was available only in Ireland, and only for a very brief period.

The song was then exhumed for inclusion (as the opening track) on Universal's *Vagabonds, Kings, Warriors, Angels* four-CD box set in 2000—only for that entire project to be mired down in sufficient difficulties that, for a long time, it looked as though this release, too, was doomed to oblivion. It finally made it out in late 2001 in the UK, but precedent recommends picking up a copy quickly.

Ike and Tina Turner

Dynamite (SUE LP 2004, LP, 1963)
"A Fool in Love" (SUE 730, 7-INCH, 1960)
Get Yer Yah Yahs Out (by the Rolling Stones)
(UK DECCA, NO CATALOG NUMBER, 2-LP TEST PRESSING, 1970)
Ike and Tina Revue Live (KENT KST 514, STEREO LP, 1964)
"I'm Through with Love" (LOMA 2011, 7-INCH, 1965)
In Person (MINIT 24018, LP, 1969)
Live! The Ike and Tina Show (WARNER BROS. WS 1579, STEREO LP, 1965)
River Deep Mountain High (PHILLES 4011, LP, NO SLEEVE, 1966)
Soul of Ike and Tina (UK SUE IEP 706, EP, 1964)
"Two to Tango" (PHILLES 134, 7-INCH, 1966)

Ike and Tina Turner, *River Deep Mountain High*
(US PHILLES PHLPS 4011, 1966)

Phil Spector believed that his production of the Turners' "River Deep Mountain High" single was his greatest piece of work yet—though it was translated into his greatest rejection ever, when the 45 crashed and barely scraped the top ninety. An album cut to similar standards for release in the single's wake was promptly scrapped, even though the records had already been manufactured (though no sleeves had yet been printed). The vast majority were destroyed; a handful, however, drifted onto the marketplace over the years and should not be confused with either the UK issue, which did go ahead as planned (London HAU 8298/SHU 8298), or the eventual US issue released by A&M in 1969 (SP 4178).

The Velvet Underground, "All Tomorrow's Parties"
(US VERVE 10427, 1966)

No original Velvet Underground single can be accused of being common, but this, the group's debut, is by far the scarcest of them all. Featuring edited versions of both sides, lucky (and wealthy) collectors have a choice of two equally rare issues: stock copies, and promos in a custom picture sleeve, which is reproduced on the back cover of the Victor Bockris/Gerard Malanga biography *Up-Tight. The Story of the Velvet Underground.*

AND THE WORLD'S LEAST VALUABLE RECORDS

Let's make a list!

The ten best albums of all time. The ten bestselling albums of all time. The ten most influential albums . . . the ten most eagerly awaited . . . the ten most downloaded. The ten most disappointing . . . .

Or, the ten you are most likely to find in a thrift store, priced to sell at $1 or so, and all of them gazing out at you with great big puppydog eyes that ask, "What did we do to deserve this?"

There are lots to choose from. The history of the long-playing record is littered with releases that, today, we are forced to wade our way through with the tenacity of polar explorers, fighting an Arctic blizzard. Budget-priced Christmas collections. Awkward AOR recreations of contemporary pop hits. *Hooked On Classics.*

Can you even begin to imagine a time when sufficient numbers of people were so excited by the prospect of Louis Clark and the Royal Philharmonic Orchestra fiddling their way through a bevy of disco-fied classical music gems that they raced out to purchase so many copies that it remained on the chart for *sixty-eight* weeks? And who then so tired of tapping toes to it that they offloaded it to the local Goodwill at the first available opportunity?

It would be intriguing indeed to poll sundry donors to demand, "But why are you getting rid of this record? It's great!" Because, when we do look at the albums that most frequently turn up, it's shocking how many of them are as likely to turn up on a Certain Type of Person's "favorite LPs" list.

Some of the exceptions are understandable. Fallen teenybopper idols, purchased in a rush of devotion when you're twelve or thirteen, are often among the first things to go when you reach . . . ooh, fourteen or fifteen. All those Wham! and Duran, Andy Gibb and John Travoltas, the detritus of an adolescence spent gazing lovelorn at the bedroom wall and then discovering someone even better on the next installment of *Bandstand.*

Others . . . television tie-ins by oddly misguided actors (Bruce Willis is a favorite offender); budget-priced hit compilations; and those *Multitudinous Guitars of Turgidity Play The Best of the Beach Boys*-

style waxings… testify equally to precise moments in time when an entire nation, it seems, was so enamored by one thing (*Moonlighting*, the hustle, the Beatles) that it rushed out to buy others, simply to feel a part of the party.

Saturating a market that is ultimately uninterested can also lead to a plethora of Salvation Army shelf fillers. Prior to the release of the horribly miscalculated *Sergeant Pepper* movie in the late 1970s, the accompanying soundtrack album shipped an unheard of triple platinum. According to Fred Gershon at RSO Records, however, most of them came back as returns, together with maybe another million in bootleg copies. And the rest, the ones that weren't returned at the time . . . well, you know where they are.

Peter Frampton Albums

As Safe As Yesterday (with Humble Pie) (UK IMMEDIATE IMSP 025, 1969)

Frampton (A&M SP 4512, 1975)

Frampton Comes Alive (A&M SP 3703, 1976)

Frampton's Camel (with Frampton's Camel) (A&M SP 4389, 1973)

I'm in You (A&M SP 4704, 1977)

Performance: Rockin' the Fillmore (with Humble Pie) (A&M SP 3506, 1972)

Rock On (with Humble Pie) (A&M SP 4301, 1971)

Something's Happening (A&M SP 3619, 1974)

Town and Country (with Humble Pie) (UK IMMEDIATE IMSP 027, 1969)

Wind of Change (A&M SP 4348, 1972)

Sergeant Pepper is an interesting case study, too, because in many ways its doomed release marks the end of what we might call the Golden Age of Thrift Store Thunderbolts—those albums that thought they were in our lives for the long haul, when really, we got rid of them before you could sing a verse of "Mr. Blue Sky."

Between 1975 and 1979, a raft of albums was released that set new standards for record sales. Peter Frampton's epochal *Frampton Comes Alive*, as the man himself has said, "changed the music industry. Singlehandedly, that one record. I am responsible . . . not for better or worse, for worse alone . . . I am responsible for turning the record business into an industry.

"Up to that point we'd been learning. Everything was new with rock 'n' roll, every year was new, everyone was having fun and making some money, and people got screwed but it didn't matter because you were having fun. And then, all of a sudden, all these people saw that one record or one artist could sell that many records in one go, and they got interested in the corporate world. That's when all the big mergers started, that's when all of that started."

It's also when every new album by every putatively major star was heralded as the ultimate in musical virtuosity, and proceeded to sell accordingly. Between them, the albums on this list do indeed deserve a ranking on most reasonable "all time best sellers" lists.

But they also merit one on the "and all-time rather quickly disposed of" list too, for they were piling up in the bargain boxes even before compact discs arrived to coerce the entire record-buying community to trade in their treasured vinyl for a pile of tin coasters with extra-added "if we tell you they sound great, will you believe us? YES!!" deception.

The Electric Light Orchestra's *Out of the Blue* was released in fall 1977, a double album package that was regarded by snarky critics as the apex of Jeff Lynne and co.'s career-long struggle to sound exactly like the Beatles would have, if they'd sacrificed soulful songwriting for clever sounds played on smarty-pants instruments, then layered with pseudo-meaningful lyrics.

Not that it's a bad record. Indeed, *Out of the Blue* is positively littered with classic pop tones. "Turn to Stone" and "Sweet Talking Woman" deserve their berth of any Best of the Seventies collection; "Wild West Hero" has a yearning majesty that reaches as high as any of Lynne's sentimental sing-songs, and then there's that cover, a gargantuan gatefold so lavishly lifelike that if you ever rolled a joint on it, you will remember the first thought that ran through your head: "Wow, a few puffs on this, and I'm going to riding that spaceship. Man."

And then you donated your copy to charity.

Massive sales did not necessary guarantee a spot on the thriftstore countdown. Fleetwood Mac's *Rumours* sold so many bucketloads that you could probably build a stairway to heaven from them, but it has also remained such a consistent favorite that used copies readily find an after-market several rungs up from the thrift store.

Less so *Fleetwood Mac Live,* the double album package that followed *Tusk* as a space- (or contract-) filling reminder that the bigger Mac got, the less spontaneous their live show became. Surely ranking among the least live-sounding live albums ever, it wasn't simply a disappointment to fans who wanted to recapture the glories of the Buckingham-Nicks lineup's earlier shows (catch the 2018 deluxe edition of the 1975 *Fleetwood Mac* LP)), it was also a letdown for casual listeners who were looking for the perfect peaks of the earlier albums. Result? A swift donation to the charity store of your choice.

Abba's *The Album.* The Carpenters' *A Kind of Hush*—all have as many supporters today as they ever had, but you are not going to get rich from stockpiling copies. Further RSO Records leviathans, the soundtracks to *Grease* and *Saturday Night Fever.* And, from a slightly later era (1984), David Bowie's *Tonight.*

You rarely find any of his other records filed in among the budget country compilations, and the *No-Name Philharmonic Plays Debussy's Greatest Hits*, but poor old "Blue Jean" and co. just can't keep away from them, a still-bitter reminder of the day when David Bowie released a new album and more or less *everyone* hated it. But only after they'd purchased it in sufficient quantities that it topped charts all over the world in its first week of release.

Seasoned bargain hunters complain today that thrift stores are no longer the Aladdin's Caves they used to be; that many of them now employ staff whose sole function is to wade through the day's donations in search of items that will never see the business end of the shelves, and go straight up on eBay instead.

But some things will never change. Claudine Longet's early A&M albums can still be found selling for a buck apiece, despite ranking among the most enjoyable easy-listening LPs of the '60s. There will never be a paucity of Bee Gees records, or off-loaded copies of *Stars on 45*.

And the biggest landfill in the world could not hope to hide all those copies of the Eagles' *Hotel California.* The album that everyone seems to own; everyone says they like. And everyone can play air guitar to.

So why can nobody seem to hang onto a copy for more than a couple of weeks?

"Lost Albums" That Remain Lost

1984, David Bowie (RECORDED 1974, ABANDONED)

Berlin, Lou Reed (1973 PROPOSED DOUBLE ALBUM TRIMMED TO SINGLE FOR RELEASE)

Crush All Boxes, Frank Zappa (RECORDED 1980)

Household Objects, Pink Floyd (RECORDED 1972, SCRAPPED; EXCERPTS ONLY SINCE RELEASED)

Live at the Rainbow, Mick Ronson (RECORDED 1974, SCRAPPED)

Madman Across the Water, Elton John (RECORDED 1970, SCRAPPED AND RERECORDED)

Police Car, Larry Wallis (RECORDED 1977, SCRAPPED)

Touchdown, Ian McCulloch/Johnny Marr (RECORDED 1993, TAPES STOLEN)

Untitled, Bruce Springsteen (RECORDED 1976, SCRAPPED DUE TO INJUNCTION)

Untitled, Ringo Starr (RECORDED 1986, INJUNCTED BY STARR)

The World's Most Valuable Sleeves

It might come as a surprise to learn that not all of the world's rarest records are, in fact, records (or tapes, cassettes, CDs, or whatever). Sometimes it's the packaging that attracts the attention and brings in the biggest bucks.

It is important always to distinguish between genuinely rare sleeves, such as those below, and sleeves that have simply gained some form of notoriety—so-called censored jackets for Nirvana's *In Utero* (DGC 24607) album and Jane's Addiction's *Ritual de lo Habitual* (Warner Bros. 25993), for example, are certainly both very collectible, but as yet have attracted no more than modest premiums over their uncensored counterparts, for the simple reason that both versions were readily available in stores, in vast quantities.

Much the same can be said for Lynyrd Skynyrd's *Street Survivors* (MCA 3029), whose original artwork—depicting the group wreathed in flames—was replaced following the plane crash that claimed the lives of three band members, just three days after the album's October 1977 release. Copies can prove elusive, but are by no means rare.

The following, then, lists a selection of sleeves that are known to have made the journey from drawing board to printing press, and sometimes even beyond. But then, on very eve of release, their journey ended. Or did it?

The Beatles, *The Beatles*
(UK APPLE PMC/PCS 7067/8, EMBOSSED NUMBERING IN LOWER RIGHT OF FRONT COVER BETWEEN 00000001–00000020, 1968)

The Beatles' eponymous 1968 double album is popularly known as *The White Album,* because that's what it looks like. The sleeve is plain white, with even the band's name merely embossed on the front, and only an individually printed number in the bottom right-hand corner to break up the view.

It is unclear how high the individual numbering went before the printers stopped counting—one short of ten million was the highest figure allowed for by the sleeve. What is certain is that the lower the number, the more someone is likely to pay for a copy—with the first twenty (which essentially means the Beatles' own copies, plus those given away to family, friends, and other associates) fetching the greatest premium.

Several of these have appeared at auction, though the prices realized seem absurdly low today. The copy numbered 00000001 (owned by John, but autographed by Ringo) was sold by Sotheby's in New York, back in 1985, for the then-incredible sum of $715. Number 00000002 (John's landlord's copy) was auctioned by the Bristol, England, record store Plastic Wax in 1990 and fetched around $750. In 1999, a previously undocumented duplicate copy of 000000001

went under the hammer at Sotheby's for around $15,000; in April 2002, 000000005 was sold by Bonham's for almost $13,000. And in December 2015, Ringo Starr's personal copy of the Beatles' *The White Album,* numbered No. 0000001, sold for an absolutely staggering $790,000 at Julien's Live auction house, more than *ten times* its pre-sale estimate.

The Beatles, *Yesterday and Today*
(US CAPITOL ST 2553, "BUTCHER COVER," 1966)

Is this the most over-recited story in record collecting history? For the Beatles' tenth US album, Capitol selected a portrait of the band members clad in butchers' smocks, apparently reveling in the dismemberment of sundry dolls and other meaty items. After 750,000 sleeves were printed, the vinyl was inserted, and copies were distributed to media and radio, the complaints began pouring in.

No matter that the same shot had already decorated the UK press without any ill effect (Robert Whitaker's photograph was used in print ads for the British "Paperback Writer" 45); no matter that the album was scheduled for release just days later. The sleeve could not be allowed to stand.

A new design was hastily obtained—an utterly uncontroversial shot of the band posing around a traveling trunk (ah, but what was in the trunk?), and Capitol staff spent the entire weekend hurriedly gluing this new image over the offending one. And the great thing about glue is, it can sometimes be removed.

Three states of "butcher cover" are universally recognized: "First state" refers to copies that somehow missed the pasting-over process altogether. "Second state" refers to copies on which the "trunk cover" is intact, but the underlying butcher is apparent (look carefully—a black "V" on butcher Ringo's sweater can be discerned halfway up the right-hand side). "Third state" describes a cover from which the trunk has been removed. Different grading points thereafter note how well (or otherwise) the removal was accomplished.

In addition, sleeves intended for stereo pressings of the LP are considerably scarcer than those made for mono.

David Bowie, "Time"
(RCA APBO 0001, 1973)

Despite now being proclaimed for possessing the most valuable US picture sleeve of them all, "Time" was just another David Bowie single when it was released in 1973—and it remained so until 1998, when a photograph of its picture sleeve appeared in *Goldmine's 45 RPM Picture Sleeve Price Guide*, at a time when most people didn't know it had even been released with one.

Which, apparently, it wasn't. Despite being nothing more than a miniaturized reproduction of the parent *Aladdin Sane* album's cover, the "Time" sleeve was apparently planned and then scrapped with such haste that no more than two copies have been sighted so far, a less than perfect example which was bid up to $3,550 at auction in 2008, and a near mint copy that more than doubled that price in 2013.

David Bowie, *Diamond Dogs*
(US RCA APL1 0576, VISIBLE GENITALS ON DOG, 1974)

It was, as they say, "the dog's bollocks." Ordinarily, that's an astonishingly wonderful thing—just another of those quaint English expressions that seems quite incomprehensible, even after you know what it means. In the matter of David Bowie's latest album art, however, RCA was not so sure.

The artwork for *Diamond Dogs,* quite sensibly, featured the singer himself in the form of a dog, a vision hatched by the doyen of rock artists, Dutchman Guy Peellaert. But when Bowie told Peellaert to make the representation as realistic as possible, maybe he should have added, "but not *too* real." Flip the familiar album sleeve over, peer between the hound's rear legs . . . and if those generous genitals are jammed in there, then that's the dog's bollocks.

Almost every first-run edition had the offending bagatelles primly airbrushed into oblivion. But a handful—how does one put it?—slipped out. A word of warning, however. The search for the secret scrotum applies only to original RCA LP pressings of *Diamond Dogs.* Reissued in 1990 by Rykodisc, the original artwork was restored in all its original glory. And nobody batted an eyelid.

David Bowie, "Space Oddity"
(UK PHILIPS BF 1801, PICTURE SLEEVE, 1969)

Quite simple, this one. In 1969, David Bowie released a new UK single called "Space Oddity." It was not issued with a picture sleeve. However, when Philips's Dutch branch was called upon to press up stereo copies for the British market, it appears that somebody there decided to manufacture sleeves to go with them—presumably unaware that Britain, alone in the industrialized world, had yet to embrace that particular concept. Philips UK took one look at these alien artifacts and probably junked them; either way, no more than a handful are known to exist today. The first wasn't even discovered until 1996.

In terms of monetary value, this Heart picture sleeve is medium rare at best, but only a handful were issued to UK record dealers in February 1977, hence its uncanny resemblance to a Valentine card.

Bob Dylan, "Subterranean Homesick Blues"

(COLUMBIA 43242, DJ PROMO WITH PICTURE SLEEVE, 1965)

A picture sleeve was issued only with DJ promo copies. However, DJs are not a breed especially well-known for retaining such things . . . not when there are those nice stiff generic cardboard sleeves to tuck new records into. The sleeves were discarded, the stock copies arrived unadorned—hey, presto, an instant rarity.

Vince Everett, "Treat Me Nice"

(LAUREL 41623, 1956)

Vince who? Only confirmed Elvis fans, those who've watched *Jailhouse Rock* enough times to memorize the name of the character he plays, might detect something intriguing about this picture sleeve. It was printed for a record that was never made, by an artist who never existed. Rather, it was a prop used in the movie, and it haunts devoted collectors like no other piece of paper.

Elvis Presley, Elvis/Jaye P. Morgan

(RCA EPA 992/689, 1956)

Reputedly the rarest Elvis Presley release of all, this double-EP package featured Presley's recent *Elvis* offering, the first record in that format ever to sell a million-plus copies, together with an earlier release by Ms. Morgan, accompanied by Hugo Winternalter's orchestra. It was issued as a promotional device only, with the gatefold sleeve reproducing the original EP covers on the front, and an array of sales facts and figures within. The enclosed EPs themselves were no different from regular stock copies.

Elvis Presley, *The International Hotel Presents Elvis 1969/1970*

(RCA VICTOR COMPLEMENTARY BOX; 1969, 1970)

The King's live reinvention, at the International Hotel in Las Vegas, was a big deal—so big that RCA and the hotel got together to offer guests at the first two shows (July 31 and August 1, 1969) an extra-special souvenir of the event. The gift box included a press release, three photographs, a thank-you note from both Presley and manager Colonel Tom Parker, an RCA label catalog, and two LPs: regular stock copies of the soundtrack to the previous year's NBC-TV special (LPM 4088) and the recent *From Elvis in Memphis* (LSP 4155).

It was a popular gift, so when Elvis returned to the venue in January 1970, a similar package was presented at the show on January 28. This time, the box included a press release, a photograph, a booklet, a dinner menu, the latest RCA catalog, the LP *From Memphis to Vegas/From Vegas to Memphis* (LSP 6020), and the 45 "Kentucky Rain" (47-9791). Find the box, ignore the records. They make no difference whatsoever to the value.

Rolling Stones, "Street Fighting Man"

(US LONDON 909, PICTURE SLEEVE, 1969)

The Stones were no strangers to conceptual controversy. One UK album title, the delightful *Can You Walk on Water,* was outlawed by Decca for blasphemy, while the original sleeve design for the *Beggars Banquet* album, a graffiti-strewn bathroom, was blocked for indecency. (It was finally restored in 1984.)

Of course the Stones' American label, London, would have to get in on the act at some point, finally pouncing in 1969 when the Stones delivered their chosen image for the "Street Fighting Man" 45, a civil-disturbance scene in which the law, not the rioters, were the street-fighting men. But police brutality has always been a sensitive subject in America. Though the sleeve was printed, London then had second thoughts and the sleeve was hastily withdrawn. With the exception of Bowie's "Time" bag, it is now considered America's rarest picture sleeve, whether or not there's a record inside.

Neither was that the end to the band's shenanigans. Almost exactly a decade later, in 1978, the Stones' "Beast of Burden" (Rolling Stones 12309) arrived with a possibly saucy shot of a young lady and a lion. The lion is sitting on her, but she doesn't seem to mind. She doesn't seem to be dressed, either. It is all very strange, but the sleeve was withdrawn, just in case. For some reason, the world's loudest prudes always have far filthier minds than the rest of us.

COLLECTING ON THE INTERNET

The arrival of the Internet turned the collecting world on its head. From the online presence maintained by brick-and-mortar record stores, which brought a world of new and used releases into your home at the click of a mouse, to the "collection for sale" sites set up by so many individuals, the World Wide Web so revolutionized the way in which we sell, buy, and research music that it is now scarcely possible to remember life without it.

But there it was. Barely twenty years ago, and for decades prior to that, the hunt for a rare record involved traveling from store to store, from record fair to market place, and thumbing through racks of old vinyl. Or sitting patiently with the latest issue of *Goldmine* or *Record Collector,* plowing through the classified ads. Or subscribing to a mail-order dealer's catalog, studying the small print by the light of a guttering candle.

Today, you just type a title into the search engine, and the hardest choice is usually "Which copy do you want to buy?" Of all the options available today, however, no one area has had so profound an impression as the Internet auction sites.

Of these, the largest and best-known (and the only one that has actually survived intact since the early days) is eBay, a forum that started life as a marketplace for an informal circle of Pez collectors. It slowly gathered momentum and scope as the mid-'90s progressed, and in the first edition of this book (2002), we wrote "even three years ago, if you wanted to shop for rare or unusual records, you attended a record fair, those vast concourses stuffed with dealers and their wares, where Beatles' butcher covers rubbed shoulders with Electric Light Orchestra cutouts; where Presley promos hung alongside Sex Pistols picture discs; and the smell of old vinyl lingered so tantalizingly in the air that you knew that soon, very soon, you'd stumble upon that elusive stock copy of TV Smith's Explorers' *Last Words* debut album."

Now you just logged on.

Even there and then, of course, there were already mumblings of disquiet. The muttered grumbling of dealers bemoaning the poor attendance, the lack of sales, and the seemingly insatiable need of every customer to come across the greatest bargain in record-collecting history ("Great! *TV Guide Presents Elvis* and it's only 50 cents!"), because that is what eBay had led them to expect.

But slowly, around 1998, there were heard the first sounds of an answering grumble, one that—were one to be so gauche as to eavesdrop on other peoples' private conversations—seemed to offer an alternative to all the weary thumbing through endless LPs, the sight-searing scanning of countless CDs, the back-breaking stoop over the $1 singles: "I'm probably not going to be doing fairs anymore. I do much better on eBay."

And back at home, late that night, you'd type the appropriate URL into your browser window, half convinced that it probably wasn't any place you'd ever end up visiting again; half repressing the guilty belief that you were somehow betraying all the principles that had sustained your hobby for as long as you remembered. And dimly aware, through all of that, that your collecting life was never going to be the same again.

Ten Classical Vinyl Rarities

A Recital of Works . . ., Ida Haendel with Gerald Moore (HMV CLP 1021, 195?)

Carmen Fantaisie etc., Ruggiero Ricci (DECCA SXL 2197 ED1, 1960)

Deutsche Grammophon Avant Garde Vol. 1, various (104 988/93, 1968)

Deutsche Grammophon Avant Garde Vol. 4, various (2720 038, 1971)

Encores, David Oistrakh (COLUMBIA SAX 2253, 1954)

Les ouvres pour violon Volume I, II, and III, Jacques Dumont: Bach (BELVEDERE BWV 1001-1006, 196?)

Mosaics, Michael Rabin (CAPITOL SP-8506, 1959)

Mozart a Paris, various (PATHÉ DTX 191/7, 1955)

Music of Old Russia, Nathan Milstein (COLUMBIA SAX 2563, 1963)

Ravel Complete Orchestral Works, André Cluytens (COLUMBIA SAX 2476-9, 1963)

Let us make one thing clear. Neither eBay nor any other Internet auction site is any alternative whatsoever to attending a fair or entering a store; there is no substitute for interacting with a dealer, and his or her customers and stock. No matter how accurate a cyber-description appears to be, no matter how generous an online seller's return policy is, and no matter how pristine the record looks in the scanned photographs, there are still a hundred other issues that you won't have answered until the system finally spits your purchase into your mailbox. Including whatever vicissitudes the mail itself might involve.

But, for every brick-and-mortar dealer you visit, and for every amazing find (or even passing fancy) you return home with, there are a dozen more occasions when an entire day of sore thumbs, blurred vision, and aching spine turns up nothing more than a couple of 8-tracks you grabbed on the way out, simply so you wouldn't leave empty-handed, and the nagging certainty that the day could have been somewhat more profitably spent watching paint dry. Or, seated at the computer with a harry in your hand (seasoned Ray Davies fans will understand), scrolling through an online marketplace in search of a clean mono copy of the Kinks' *Something Else.* Because you've never managed to find one at any conventional fair you've ever been to.

The early years of the Internet auction have been described as a wild west, a free-for-all during which the most unlikely items were bought and sold for the most equally unlikely sums. In 1999, was the astonishing $200 bid for a mid-'70s Moody Blues vinyl bootleg a one-off aberration or indicative of a major market surge? Did the paltry $20 received for an unknown Venezuelan pressing of the almost equally unknown second Hotlegs LP bring further copies to light, or drive them deeper underground?

At the time, the majority of traditional collectors and dealers chose to regard unusually high auction results as one-offs, with prices driven to extremes either by two equally determined fanatics (or hoaxers), or by the simple thrill of the auction. Poor results, on the other hand, were evidence that the majority of Internet users were mere hoarders who knew nothing about the "true worth" of rare records, or even as proof that computers had not penetrated our world as deeply as the cheerleaders reckoned.

The emergence of such sites as popsike.com, and various magazines' now-engrained habit of tracking the biggest sales and surprises, has taken a lot of the guesswork out of that, to prove that the truth is somewhere in between each of these views: that a successful Internet auction, for buyers and sellers alike, is dependent on a number of criteria.

Demand

From a seller's point of view, the most crucial point in any sale, whether conducted online or on Main Street is—does anybody actually want the thing? In the early days of Internet auctions, many people regarded them as a forum in which any piece of household junk could find a willing buyer, and they were often proved correct. Balls of string, bags of dirt, pizza slices with the face of a saint burned into the onions—anything could be listed and, amazingly, anything could be sold. As more people became sellers, with the corresponding influx of increasingly interesting material, that mentality began to fade. (Although the junk is still up there, and it still attracts bids). Slowly, Internet auctions began to uncover some fascinating items, hitherto unknown or ultra-rare oddities, as attics were cleaned, storerooms wee emptied, and thrift stores, once the number one repository for untapped treasures of all descriptions, were swept bare of anything that looked even remotely saleable.

With this flood, of course, came trouble. Not *all* of the items considered one-of-a-kind finds by their owners were suddenly revealed as mass-produced trinkets in the cold light of cyber-day. But one of the most frequently heard gripes among professional record dealers involved the hours they spent listing their rarest records at "reasonable," "heavily researched" prices, only to discover that a couple of dozen know-nothing amateurs had listed the same discs at a fraction of the price. A sale was lost, the market was flooded, and an LP once cataloged at $100 was frustratingly revealed to be as common as muck.

Or, the opposite occurred; a would-be seller comes across a heap of, for example, vintage Who memorabilia—an outtake from the band's *My Generation* photoshoot, and the typewritten lyrics to that album's title track; handwritten lyrics to a *Tommy* highlight; a receipt for an order of smoke bombs; a rejection letter from EMI, and so on.

Quite the treasure trove, you will agree. Unless, of course, you already know that it was all given away free with original copies of the band's *Live at Leeds* album and that, unless the stash also includes a copy of the band's contract for the Woodstock Festival (of which just 500 were printed), it'll fetch a far higher price if it's tucked back into the album cover. Exit one disgruntled seller; enter a horde of laughing browsers.

Another example: the seller who, in 2016, listed what was described as a rare David Bowie picture disc, printed with the image inverted. Presumably it never crossed his mind that the disc had simply been placed into its plastic sleeve upside down. Before listing any seemingly unusual item, then—or, if you're buying, placing a bid on one—it isn't a bad idea first to research it, and then to run a search on the site to see how many (if any) similar items are already on display, and how they are faring. That way, one can also get a good idea of the demand for the item, and figure out if it's even worthwhile trying to compete with other similar listings. Sometimes it can pay to wait until the crowd has dispersed.

Price

This is the area in which most sellers come unglued, be they experienced dealers with a lifetime of buying and selling old records behind them, or impoverished students looking to raise some spare cash for a pizza party.

There are no laws whatsoever. A record can have a catalog value in excess of $100. But if only one person wants to buy it, and that person thinks that $10 is more than a fair offer, then the catalog

Del Shannon

Best of Del Shannon (DOT DLP 3824, MONO LP, 1967)

"From Me to You" (BIG TOP 3152, 7-INCH, 1963)

The Further Adventures of Charles Westover (LIBERTY LST 7539, STEREO LP, 1968)

Handy Man (AMY S8003, STEREO LP, 1964)

"I Can't Believe My Ears" (AMY 947, 7-INCH, 1966)

Little Town Flirt (BIG TOP 12-1308, STEREO LP, 1963)

1661 Seconds with Del Shannon (AMY S8006, STEREO LP, 1965)

Runaway (BIG TOP 12-1303, STEREO LP, 1961)

"Runnin' On Back" (LIBERTY 56018, 7-INCH, PICTURE SLEEVE, 1968)

Sings Hank Williams (AMY S8004, STEREO LP, 1964)

counts for nothing. Price guides are, as their name should make plain, merely guides to the recommended worth of an item. But they themselves are worthless in a market in which the vast majority of buyers (and many sellers too) have never even heard of such volumes, and probably wouldn't read them if they had. The cold reality is, for sellers, a record is worth the most that they can get for it; for buyers, it's the minimum they have to pay for it.

The stated opening bid sets the scene. The seller needs to have established a reasonable amount, with the knowledge that, in this forum, "reasonable" does not mean settling for a sum similar to, or in excess of, any catalog or retail value the item might have.

It is an immutable fact of life that the majority of potential purchasers are in search of a bargain, which is why a CD available elsewhere around the country for $15 has more chance of selling in auction for $5, than for $10 plus postage, plus insurance, plus all the other extras that a seller can apply. Indeed, a seller does need to look at these extras too, and either establish a set rate for shipping and handling, or allow the bidder to choose a preferred method. It is surprising how many will opt for a more expensive, but faster, method of delivery when given an option, yet balk at bidding if confronted with a *fait accompli*.

If establishing a fair price for an item is a minefield for sellers, it can be just as traumatic for buyers. Again, there are no rules—value is set by demand alone, and if you're going head-to-head with a rival bidder for whom money is no object, there are just two possible outcomes: One of you will win the item for a stratospheric price, and the other will get the (admittedly reprehensible and utterly unsporting) satisfaction of having pushed the winner to those heights. And then sit back and wait for another copy to come along. It's surprising how many things do.

The vast majority of Internet auction sales are completed with just one bidder, a statistic further buoyed on eBay by the proliferation of "Buy It Now" offers, in which an item is listed with both an opening bid price and a firm selling price.

With this provision, however, there are several points worth bearing in mind. First, the temptation can be great to simply purchase an item on the spot, without either the delay of waiting till the auction's end or the fear of losing out to another bidder. Against that, however, one must balance the possibility that there will be no other bidder and that an item one could have purchased for $5 is now going to cost $25.

Nobody can counsel you on this area. Many items do not even receive an opening bid until minutes before the auction is due to an end, as potential purchasers hold fire for fear of igniting some kind of bidding war; many more items that hold a single bid for days

Free

Barbed Wire Sandwich, Black Cat Bones (UK NOVA SDN 15, LP, 1970)
BBC Classic Tracks (WESTWOOD ONE, CD, 1993)
"Broad Daylight" (UK ISLAND WIP 6054, 7-INCH, 1969)
The Free EP (UK ISLAND PIEP 6, 12-INCH EP, 1982)
The Free Story (ISLAND OLSD 4, 2-LP, 1975)
Heartbreaker (ISLAND ILPS SW 9324, LP, 1973)
"I'll Be Creepin'" (UK ISLAND WIP 6062, 7-INCH, 1969)
"King Fu," Sharks (MCA 40246, 7-INCH, 1974)
Mr. Big/Blue Soul, Paul Kossoff (UK ST. TUNES 0012PD, PICTURE-DISC LP, 1982)
Tons of Sobs (UK ISLAND ILPS 9089, FIRST-LABEL LP, 1969)

will then skyrocket at the end as the "snipers"—last-minute bidders with hair-trigger mousing-fingers—move in on their prey. The safest rule of thumb, if you want an item badly enough and feel the stated asking price is reasonable, is to just go for it. You may see other copies at cheaper prices in the future, but by then you'll be looking for something else. A bird in the hand is not a bad thing to have.

The final point to be aware of involves international buying. The Internet is a global marketplace, with prices quoted in what may seem a bewildering variety of currencies. Most sites do utilize software that translates these into local currency, so one always knows precisely how much one is bidding for an item.

Remember, however, to factor in delivery and any applicable customs charges. When purchasing CDs from abroad, it should be no problem for the seller, if requested, to remove the discs and their artwork from the jewel cases (which account for some two-thirds of a CD's total weight, and therefore, its mailing cost). Just ask an international seller to wrap your CD in tissue or bubble-wrap before mailing. (But do keep such requests to a minimum. Not every seller can afford to devote half an hour to wrapping every package, and is just as likely to cancel the sale as fulfill every demand.) Vinyl discs, particularly LPs, do not offer this same luxury, however, and can prove extremely expensive to mail. Especially when bidding on bulk lots, always take a moment to visualize how big and how heavy the stack will be. You can e-mail the seller to request a postage estimate before the auction's end; alternately, many foreign postal administrations now offer international rate tables on their websites. Either way, make sure you know what you're letting yourself in for.

Customs fees, assessed when a package crosses an international border, are another matter entirely. One person may go an entire lifetime without ever being hit with duty charges; another may be billed every time he or she receives a package from abroad. Like death and taxes, customs charges are a fact of life. Expect the worst and you'll never be disappointed.

Description

For both seller and buyer, an item's description is crucial, especially if an illustration is either not present or leaves room for doubt on the viewer's part. "Rare Genesis 45" might make for an eye-catching headline, but that is all it is.

Titles and catalog numbers are vital; concise, but detailed grading is essential. Are there any visible faults, either to the record or, if applicable, to its packaging? Are there any all-but-invisible ones? Has the record been played? If so, how did it sound the last time it was listened to? "Slightly warped with some scratches but plays great" might satisfy some bidders, but what if the seller's definition of "great" or "slightly" is more lenient than yours? And, finally, is it genuinely rare, or is the seller simply assuming that every other single copy of this mid-1980s chart-topper has been mysteriously lost or destroyed? Nobody is suggesting (although some buyers might expect) that a seller sit down and patiently play through every record, tape, and CD that he or she is listing, noting every audible pop, click, and crackle. However, outside of manufacturing and mastering errors, few audible faults are utterly invisible to the naked eye, and careful grading will identify almost all of them.

Most sellers will happily answer questions about the items they are selling; they will be happier still if both the questions and the subject are clearly delineated in the e-mail. Simply typing "What are the songs?" is *not* acceptable. Many sellers list more than one item at a time; always make sure you name the item you are inquiring about. Similarly, many sellers do conduct personal lives in between waiting expectantly for your life-and-death queries so, again, always try to keep your requests reasonable. Oh, and please don't get pissy if they don't reply immediately.

Also, going back to track listings: Yes, it's a straightforward enough request, and should not inconvenience anybody. But a faster way of procuring that information would be to get the details yourself by visiting one of the multitude of online sites that list that same information.

If requesting more specialized information, tailor your question so that it involves the least amount of work and/or time on the seller's part. If there are two pressings of a certain album and you want to ensure you are bidding on the right one, better to ask "Does it contain this song/credit/variation?" than to demand a full accounting of every feature of the disc. And if you have specific concerns about the state of the item, voice them.

Condition

Many sellers will impose conditions upon their auctions, lengthy lists of dos and don'ts that might weed out any possible time-wasters but can also have the effect of discouraging honest bidders.

A refusal to sell to bidders with fewer than a specified number of "feedbacks" (successfully completed auctions, as detailed on the site by other buyers and sellers) might seem a sound way of protecting oneself from newly enrolled idiots who have no intention whatsoever of paying. But don't forget that every single person on the site was, at one point, a beginner without a feedback to his or her name. Yourself included.

Also frowned upon are those sellers who threaten dire retribution if what might otherwise be construed as reasonable terms are not met. Remember, most bidders are as anxious to receive their item as you are to receive their payment. Treat them with the same respect you would expect them to extend to you. (For an outline of reasonable terms, see "Concluding the Auction" below.)

Locating Items

The next factor to consider is visibility. Although most auction sites do offer subcategories within each subject, into which items can be placed, potential buyers may find it easiest to simply do a general search within the overall category for an artist's name or for the title of a desired song or album, since not every seller will be aware of the precise place in which any given record belongs.

Successfully narrowing searches down within given fields is, unfortunately, an effort in which trial and error alone can assist you. Searching, say, for "the Beatles" will bring up thousands upon thousands of items; you need to specify the kind of Beatles items you require. Searching for "Scott Walker" will present you with far more baseball memorabilia than musical items. Seeking out "10cc" will bring up an awful lot of syringes. Again, you need to specify, either by item or category. And woe betide fans of the bands Free, If, Yes, and the Killers.

Concluding the Auction

Death, dismemberment, or similar crisis excepted, there is no defense for a high bidder failing to complete an auction. You bid, you win, you pay. It's as simple as that.

Similarly, sellers should always dispatch items as soon as possible after receipt of payment. This may (and, indeed, should) include a waiting period while checks clear (at least on those increasingly rare occasions when the buyer doesn't simply use PayPal), but the seller who takes a month to mail out items that have been paid for is as reprehensible as the buyer who takes as long to send in payment—more so, in fact, because the sloppiest sellers are often the ones whose auctions are governed by the most stringent and unfriendly regulations.

All of which, looking back at these pages, seems to involve an awful lot of fuss for what should be a simple and enjoyable transaction between two individuals. And probably, some of the fuss results from being overly cautious. Seasoned Internet auctioneers, bidders, and sellers will develop a set of practices that work for them, and when all is said and done, that's all that really matters. Internet auctions are unique to our age. Enjoy them.

2 | COLLECTIONS AND COLLECTIBLES

INTRODUCTION

There are as many ways to collect as there are collectors to find new ways. And just as nobody can tell you what you *should* be collecting, nobody can tell you what you shouldn't. This section is devoted to that freedom.

Arranged alphabetically, the bulk of the entries center on the myriad different formats in which we, the consumers, have been offered our music over the years. From cylinders and 78s to CDs and mp3s; from uncluttered mono to full surround sound, the music industry has never ceased offering up new and improved ways of hearing and storing the songs we love—and each of those ways has its die-hard adherents.

The stories told, however, are not simply dry dissertations on the history, development, and where appropriate, the quiet discontinuation of these formats. Each entry digs deeply into the collecting lore that surrounds its subject, to unearth the releases that collectors are most commonly searching for, and to find out what makes them so special.

Why is Pink Floyd's *Animals* such an in-demand 8-track? What is so special about the mono version of *Trini Lopez at PJ's*—or the quadraphonic pressing of Black Sabbath's *Paranoid*? Why is a UK export pressing of the Beatles' *Something New* album worth a hundred times more than an American edition? And what on earth is a Pocket Rocker?

Even if you don't collect, say, Mini-8s, the information within will, hopefully, help you with the formats you do collect.

A BRIEF HISTORY OF RECORDED SOUND

As explained earlier in this book, record collecting has never been restricted to simply collecting records. Cassettes, cartridges, cylinders, reels, CDs, and more are all embraced under that single heading, to become legitimate and popular pursuits in their own right, and to spawn ever more exclusive fields of specialization.

Because this book is primarily concerned with the modern collecting industry—that is, the so-called rock 'n' roll era that commenced in the mid-'50s, little consideration is given to those formats that were

already en route to the Ark when Bill Haley first rocked around the clock. However, interest in these earlier formats has never stopped rising, with prices escalating likewise. Plus, a quick glimpse at where we came from might help us understand where we're going.

Refinements and improvements in records, players, and markets continued to be made throughout the 1890s, the most important innovation being Emile Berliner's invention of the flat gramophone disc. Originally pressing his discs on celluloid and rubber-based compounds, Berliner finally switched to shellac in 1894, after noting how the same material had revolutionized telephone manufacturing (phones too were once made from hard rubber).

Revolving at 78 revolutions per minute (rpm), Berliner's earliest discs were seven inches across; by the turn of the century, this had increased to ten and even twelve inches. With very few subsequent improvements, this would become the principal format for recorded sound for the next half-century. It would also, even in its infancy, prove astonishingly versatile.

Despite the vast strides being made in developing and perfecting the medium, however, the very notion of the gramophone recording spent much of the early twentieth century battling to prove its viability. Broadcasting, in particular, regarded prerecorded music as an absolutely unnecessary addition to an already oversubscribed market; radio, at that time, relied largely on live entertainers for its content and did much to convince its audience that it was simply a waste of money to purchase prerecorded, or "canned," music.

In Britain, the hostility went even further, as the all-powerful Musicians Union introduced the policy of "needle time," by which broadcasters were forced to compensate union members for lost income for every minute devoted to prerecorded music. It was an unpopular regulation, but one that persisted for almost another century, until it was finally abandoned in the late 1980s.

No, it's not a song about a canine litter box—the dog's name is actually Tray. A 1915 Edison Records hit.

An Edison disc and vintage 1926 player at work. (Photo by Amy Hanson)

Broadcasters were not the gramophone industry's only foe. The medium itself was still primitive, with the quality of most sound recordings little better than tinny echoes. Attempts to improve the fidelity preoccupied the backroom boys, but even the genius Thomas Edison, and the eponymous discs he marketed between 1912–1929, was unable to break through the quality barrier.

Neither was Edison the gramophone's only foe. In 1929, the same year as the old inventor finally withdrew from the competition, the recording industry received another major blow, this one from the conductor Arturo Toscanini. Disappointed by his first recordings, he insisted he would never make another record again, because the technology was simply incapable of doing justice to his art. (He finally relented in 1936.)

Further setbacks followed. Early in the 1930s, technicians at both RCA and Columbia perfected what we would now recognize as the long-playing record—discs that were capable of carrying more than one or two songs per side. They did not, however, perfect the material from which they could be made, leading to those early LPs all but disintegrating whenever someone attempted to play them. Nor, at the height of the Great Depression, were their paymasters interested in spending more money in an attempt to remedy the problem.

The new format was all but stillborn, then. But the demand for recorded music continued even through these most straitened years, with the so-called jukebox sensation of the immediate post-Depression era providing the most powerful tonic. In 1938, more than thirteen million records were sold to US jukebox stockists alone and, buoyed by these successes, the music industry finally learned to market itself. The big-band craze of the late 1930s, and the bobby-soxer explosion of the early 1940s, might have been fired by musicians and live performances, but behind them the record companies were stoking the boilers furiously.

August 1942 brought all activity to a shuddering halt. In that month, with the US now at war, the American Federation of Musicians passed a resolution agreeing to stop recording any music that did not contribute directly to the war effort. In addition, there was a shortage of the very lifeblood of the industry: shellac. For two years, scarcely any new records were manufactured and released in the US.

Normalcy began returning in 1944, and by war's end the following year, it was as though the hiatus had never happened. However, hardly had the dust settled on an international conflagration than the music industry itself was riven by its own bloody battle, as Columbia and RCA Victor, the two mightiest powers in the business, went head to head in what has become known as the War of the Speeds.

No matter how bad the memories may have been, neither company had forgotten its long-ago attempts to increase the amount of playing time available on a record. The standard speed of 78 rpm was clearly impractical; for decades, musicians and performers had been tied to a maximum playing time of just five minutes per side. Which, in truth, was not so terrible for popular songs and dance music. But an hour-long symphony needed to be broken across twelve sides of six separate discs (packaged in bound "albums"), and a three-hour opera required a wheelbarrow simply to transport it.

In 1948, Columbia Records finally perfected long-playing (LP) 33⅓ rpm 10-inch "microgroove" records, capable of playing up to *twenty* minutes a side; they were accompanied by a new style of record player designed to play the new speed.

It was a staggering innovation that the company knew could change the face of the recording industry forever. Yet when Columbia offered the technology to RCA Victor, with the suggestion that the two giants join forces to market it, RCA chief David Sarnoff instead flew into a fury, demanding that his technicians come up with a format that was even better.

The result, unveiled the following spring, was the 45 rpm disc (and its own, correspondingly calibrated, automatic record player). Little better in terms of playing time than the 78, these 45s were superior in that their "unbreakable" vinyl construction allowed them to be stacked on top of one another on the record player, each disc falling into place as the previous one finished. To add further fuel to the coming conflict, neither the Columbia nor the RCA record players were compatible with one another. Anybody purchasing both LPs and 45s required two separate players to listen to them on—and a third, of course, for 78s.

The formats did battle head to head, Columbia marketing full-length LPs that allowed the listener uninterrupted listening, and RCA sticking with the old style "album" presentation, trusting automation to keep the listener happy.

Of course the LP won, but by that time, RCA had already figured out that 45s were best targeted toward the hit parade. In 1951, RCA and Columbia agreed to accept that each invention had its own unimpeachable place in the market and began manufacturing and marketing both kinds of records. Multispeed record players followed and, with the rest of the industry falling in line behind the two new speeds, the day of the 78 was nearing its end.

The last commercially available 78s were produced in the US during the late '50s, with Britain following suit shortly after; 1958 was the last year in which 78s outsold other formats in the US. By 1963, 78s were no longer in production anywhere in the Western world, though they hung on elsewhere, and the last days of the format did give the modern record-collecting hobby some of its most magnificent—and deliciously anachronistic—collectibles, from

EMI's India subsidiary. Beatles singles were still appearing as 78s as late as 1965.

The late 1940s also saw magnetic tape recording emerge from the shadows of various laboratories, where its potential had been gathering pace since the late '20s. Germany was in the forefront of the research, with the BASF corporation perfecting tape capable of reproducing the frequency range of gramophone records, as early as 1938. (Hitherto, recordings had been made direct to disc.)

World War II saw the research come to an end. The technology survived, however, and peacetime saw it accompany so many other pioneering German inventions (rocket science included) to the US, where the Ampex and 3M (Minnesota Mining and Manufacturing) companies continued its development.

Much as Toscanini had given the traditional recording industry a major shot in the arm when he embraced its technologies in 1936, so Bing Crosby brought magnetic tape to prominence in 1948, when he declared the 3M-Ampex products to be infinitely superior to any of the direct-to-disc methods employed elsewhere. He began recording all his music onto magnetic tape—of course, others followed and, by the early 1950s, tape was not only the primary medium for recording, it was also being marketed for reproduction too, in the form of reel-to-reel tapes.

It is impossible to document all the advantages that magnetic tape brought to the recording process, but paramount among them is surely the development of stereophonic sound, hitherto an impossible dream. Overnight, tape revolutionized the capabilities of the recording studio, although stereo itself would initially prove a hard sell to the general public. While it found a ready market among audio enthusiasts, the overall public response was initially so lukewarm that even record companies who did invest in the required equipment continued to release the majority of their records in mono only (stereo mixes from the format's infancy are still being discovered today).

It was only as the 1960s rolled on that stereo began to increase its appeal, aided not only by the sometimes miraculous strides being taken elsewhere in the recording industry—many of the sonic effects we take for granted today were startlingly novel when first heard in the mid-'60s—but also by the development of a new rival to records, the all-American 4-track and 8-track cartridge tapes, and—from the European labs of Philips—the cassette.

Introduced just a couple of years apart, the cartridges immediately fell into competition for the lucrative in-car entertainment market, while the cassette ambitiously targeted everything in sight. All three, of course, were designed with stereo reproduction firmly in mind. (Half a decade later, when quadraphonic sound first became a reality, it, too, was pioneered by the 8-track, with the first commercially available Quad-8 cartridges appearing a full year before equivalent LP pressings.)

The cartridge formats offered little in the way of improved audio reproduction. It was their portability that sold them, with the first in-car sound systems appearing as early as 1964. And no matter what faults the formats were heir to, their ready absorption into the American art of motorvating ensured their immediate success.

Cassettes took off more slowly, suffering initially from poor sound and spasmodic performance. But with the arrival of the Dolby Noise Reduction System in 1969, they, too, moved into prominence, not only consigning cartridges to the junk heap, but moving in on vinyl as well. By the late '70s, the two formats were neck and neck in the marketplace.

Their joint reign was to be short. In 1982, the first digital compact discs (CDs) made their debut; by 1987, both LPs and 45s were well en route to being phased out by every major record company in the US and Europe, to be replaced by the CD. Cassettes lingered on in the marketplace, but the advent of DAT (Digital Audio Tape) in 1987 spelled a similar end to magnetic recording tape in the professional

Automobiles

Bonneville 1960 (RIVERSIDE RS 95506, STEREO LP, 1960)

Carroll Shelby: The Career of a Great American Racing Driver (RIVERSIDE RLP 5006, LP, 1957)

Cement Roadsters (BATTLE 96132, STEREO LP, 1964)

Dan Gurney: His World of Racing (MOBILE FIDELITY MF 101, LP, 1965)

Golden Age of Sebring (RIVERSIDE SDP 33, LP, 1959)

History of Drag Racing (CAPITOL STAO 2145, STEREO LP, 1964)

Mercedes Benz: 75th Anniversary (RIVERSIDE RS 95025, STEREO LP, 1962)

Racing Cars (FORTISSIMO XK 8003, LP, PLAYS FROM THE LABEL OUT, 1959)

1320 Special (FLEETWOOD FLP 4005S, STEREO LP, 1963)

Wonderful World of Sports Cars (RIVERSIDE SDP 44, LP, 1959)

John Mayall in the Sixties

A Hard Road (LONDON PS 502, 1967)

Bare Wires (LONDON PS 537, 1968)

Blues from Laurel Canyon (LONDON PS 545, 1969)

Bluesbreakers with Eric Clapton (LONDON PS 492, 1966)

Crusade (LONDON PS 529, 1967)

Diary of a Band (LONDON PS 570, 1970)

John Mayall Plays John Mayall (UK DECCA LK 4680, 1965)

Looking Back (LONDON PS 562, 1970)

Raw Blues (LONDON PS 543, 1968)

The Blues Alone (LONDON PS 534, 1967)

sphere. By 1992, some eighty percent of recording studios in the US had converted to DAT recording, and the race was on to draw the public to the format as well.

A decade later, and that battle, at least, seems to have been lost. Sony's MiniDisc (MD) and Philips's Digital Compact Cassettes (DCC) were introduced during 1993–94, both offering digital playback and recording possibilities—DCC even had the advantage of being compatible with cassettes, at least in playback mode. Within a year, however, DCC had fallen by the wayside, to be joined by MD, around the same time as computer technology introduced the first recordable compact discs (CD-Rs), offering all the advantages of MD but without the need for another total upgrade of one's hi-fi system.

If at first you don't succeed . . . further sonic advances were offered: Panasonic's DVD-Audio (DVD-A), Sony/Philips's Super Audio Compact Disc, and Sony's Blu-ray formats all repeat the old CD mantra of "best possible sound" in yet another attempt to persuade us to rebuild our collections once again. Yet if any one format has dominated the marketplace of the twenty-first century, it was one that contrarily offered the least sonic fidelity of all: the mp3. Quite frankly, in terms of the listening experience, listening to the average mp3 of a favorite CD is akin to playing a Quad 8-track through a mono earplug. Yes, you get the song. But there's more to music than a tune and some words.

The first edition of this book, back in 2002, outlined the average "serious" music collector's first impressions of this new format.

"They're Music, but Are They Collectible?" ("Probably Not," Says Little Nicola)

There is, as yet, no way to assess the impact that Internet music will have on record collecting. At present, it is largely overlooked—as with homemade cassettes and, more recently, CD-Rs, the mp3 and similarly downloadable music revolution is confined to collectors who simply require the music.

Record collecting, however, is concerned with the format as well—the tangibility of vinyl, tape, aluminum, whatever. Downloadable music does not intrinsically require any of these things; it is as comfortable being burned onto a CD as it is simply playing through a computer's software applications. There is no physical substance to the medium; therefore, in the commercial sense of collecting, there is no product.

Velvet Underground

"All Tomorrow's Parties" (VERVE 10427, 7-INCH, PICTURE SLEEVE, 1966)
Aspen **magazine,** Various artists (FLEXIDISC, DECEMBER 1966 ISSUE)
East Village Other **newspaper,** Various artists (ESP 1034, LP, 1966)
"Femme Fatale" (VERVE 10466, 7-INCH, 1966)
Live at Max's Kansas City (COTILLION SD 9500, PROMO LP, 1972)
Loaded (COTILLION SD 9034, PROMO LP, 1970)
Velvet Underground and Nico (VERVE V5008, MONO LP, WITH PEELABLE BANANA AND "MALE TORSO" BACK SLEEVE, 1967)
"What Goes On" (MGM 14057, 7-INCH, 1969)
"White Light/White Heat" (VERVE 10560, 7-INCH, 1967)
"Who Loves the Sun" (COTILLION 44107, 7-INCH, 1970)

The mp3 did have its supporters, of course, with *Ice* magazine pointing out, in October 2001, that "it's quite possible . . . because of the Internet . . . that there will never again be such a thing as a 'lost' album."

Once, bootlegs alone brought such unreleased masterpieces as the Beach Boys' *Smile* to the world. In 2000 and 2001 alone, scrapped, rejected, or otherwise abandoned albums by acts as far apart as the Dave Matthews Band, Juliana Hatfield, Whiskeytown, and Wilco were all circulating freely as mp3s on the Internet. Many, many more have since followed.

Neither was the perceived ephemeral nature of the mp3 viewed as a stumbling block to a certain breed of collectors. The pleasure was in the accumulation of music, not in the hoarding of multitudinous formats, sleeve designs, and varieties.

Without doubt, the mp3 remains the most influential and powerful single format in the modern music industry, most notoriously as the scapegoat for innumerable economic ills, but a power for great good, too. Artists who might once never have come within touching distance of a record deal are now enjoying vibrant careers with downloadable product, while downloads themselves have become as much a part of the mainstream retail landscape as physical product ever was.

Streaming, too, has utterly altered the way in which music is consumed, and while the financial model remains a cause for bitter concern from the artist's point of view (they receive approximately $0.0015593 per play), somebody is clearly doing very well out of it.

It's ironic, then, that with "free" (or the next best thing) music proliferating across the Internet, the two most significant changes in the way we consume music *today* are both what might be considered luxury items—sprawling box sets, in which great swathes of an artist's catalog are splayed across as many CDs as they can possibly be, and often priced at the stratospheric end of eye-watering; and a vinyl revival that habitually mocks the prices that collectors are willing to pay for a mint-condition original pressing by charging just as much (or more) for a reissue.

But people buy them, people collect them, and, one assumes, people cherish them. Just as they always have. Long may they continue to do so.

FOCUSING ON FORMATS: A QUICK CASE STUDY

How many copies of a single album does any collector require?

Of course, that depends on the collector . . . and the album. Tamsin Darke, author of *David Bowie: Rare Records Price Guide*, offers up a discography so exhaustive that it transforms what could have been a simple list of thirty or so LPs into almost seventy pages of label variations, matrix numbers, reissues, remasters, repackagings, and more. She notes almost forty different vinyl permutations of *Hunky Dory* alone, with values that range from a matter of dollars to $10,000 plus.

And that is perfect for some collectors.

Black Sabbath's Paranoid *in its US cassette incarnation.*

For others, it might be sufficient simply to pick up whichever version it is of the album that offers the most bang for the buck, via bonus tracks or whatever—and Pink Floyd's *The Dark Side of the Moon*, which we will be looking at later in this book, is a case in point.

For some, it could be a collection of every known pressing of a favorite Beatles LP; one particular variation of their UK debut, *Please Please Me*, sold for almost $20,000 in 2014, which is as good a reason as any to get involved. For others, any and every copy of an individual LP—in early 2017, collector Mark Satlof estimated he now owned 800 copies of *The Velvet Underground and Nico*.

And others still will seize upon a favorite disc and pursue every format variation they can find. Taking, as a case in point, Black Sabbath's second LP, *Paranoid*.

It is, after all, a significant album, and not simply in terms of its musical content, or even its subsequent influence. In the world of great rock "What Ifs," few resound more tantalizingly than . . . what if Black Sabbath had actually followed up their 1970 hit single "Paranoid"? If, instead of waiting eighteen months before releasing a new one (spring '72's "Tomorrow's Dream"), they had slammed "Iron Man" into action, or "War Pigs," or even "Fairies Wear Boots"?

Listened to today, the Birmingham band's international breakthrough LP is as close to a greatest hits collection as you could get without selling your soul (for rock 'n' roll); recalled from 1970, it was the *Thriller* of its generation, an album so jam-packed with potential 45s that the whole thing could have spun on two speeds forever.

Except . . . "serious" bands didn't chase hits in those days. Rather, they occasionally endured them as incidental adjuncts to the main affair. That's why a flick through the annals of British chartdom at the dawn of the 1970s will see all manner of unrepentant hairies scoring a hit (or maybe two) with records which, they fervently assured their following, were never intended as anything more than a taster for the album. Argent, Atomic Rooster, Curved Air, Deep Purple . . . and Sabbath, who hit number four in late 1970, and even appeared on British television's premier prime time pop program, *Top of the Pops*.

They could have changed the world.

Paranoid is no stranger to the reissue racks. Even if one concentrates simply on major variations, US pressings can be picked up on a variety of changing Warner Brothers labels, up to and including its most recent incarnations on Rhino; in the UK and Europe, early pressings on Vertigo's insanely collectible "spiral" label (the one that makes you dizzy just to look at) have been succeeded not only by that company's later designs, but also by releases through NEMS, WWA, Sanctuary and more.

But where's the fun in pursuing those? You know what you're going to get each time—eight songs (that were magically stretched to ten to adhere to American copyright laws, although you probably still can't whistle either "Jack The Stripper" or "Luke's Wall," tracks within tracks on the earliest pressings), and which remain the sound of Sabbath in ear-bleeding, soul stirring *excelsis*.

Paranoid is not simply an LP, after all. It is the blueprint for every so-called heavy metal record made in the almost half-century since then . . . and we say "so-called" because it was never intended to be metal to begin with. It was simply the blues, slowed down to quaalude drip-feed proportions, and then fed back through amplifiers whose knobs began at ten. It might be the most perfect record ever made.

And it's yours to collect in any format you like.

Start, if you can, with an acetate—a couple of which have been sold in recent years. Fetching almost $900 on eBay in 2013, the first was a one-sided 10" metal disc labeled "Guitar Solos," and featuring two versions of "Paranoid" itself, one with the solo included (clocking in at 2:20), the other, thirty-five seconds shorter, without.

The second, which collected almost $500 that same year, was a two-sided 10-inch, spinning at 45 and packing three tracks in glorious mono: "Paranoid" (3:45), "Planet Caravan" (4:20), and "Fairies Wear Boots" (6:09).

Next comes the test pressing, a number of which have appeared on the market over the last decade, and realized sums ranging from $155 (on eBay in 2008) for a US copy produced by Record Productions, down to $30 (eBay, 2016) for a 2015 example.

Onto the release racks, *Paranoid* made its debut on vinyl, cassette, and 8-track; and it's strange, but the latter—juggling the running order so as to balance the timings—is more or less an entirely new listening experience. It opens with "Iron Man," closes with "Paranoid" (tracks two and four on the vinyl and cassette), and leaves the traditional opener "War Pigs" until program three. Give it a listen; you might even prefer it.

There was a reel-to-reel, manufactured by Bell & Howell—one of five Sabbath albums to be released in that format, but strangely, the hardest to find. There's the quadraphonic vinyl pressing, famed for *not* speeding up the end of "War Pigs," but packing lots of other little sonic treats as well. And there's the UK double album version that

A well-loved copy of Paranoid's reel-to-reel release.

was released in 2009, and featured two extra sides of session alternates and instrumentals.

Then there are the compact discs, which you can pursue or eschew according to whim, but don't miss out on the three-CD deluxe edition that repeats those same bonus goodies, and then serves up a full surround-sound rendering of the original quadraphonic mix. Or the four-CD Super Deluxe box, which mixes the quad down to stereo (but still sounds impressive), and then adds a couple of period live shows to the brew.

And still there's more. A picture-disc pressing of the album; and the single of "Paranoid," with a worldwide wealth of picture sleeves and its own picture disc. Bootlegs of the April 1970 BBC session at which the band premiered "Fairies Wear Boots" and "War Pigs" (under its original title of "Walpurgis"), and an *In Concert* live show for the same broadcaster. Period TV appearances, including a 1970 *Beat Club* performance that added "Blue Suede Shoes" to the witches' brew.

The songs remain the same, of course, but if you already know *Paranoid*, you know that no other Sabbath album came close to its perfection (although yes, *Masters of Reality* tried, and the rest of the first five had their moments); and if you don't, then where have you been all your life?

"War Pigs" and "Iron Man" still crush the furniture; "Planet Caravan" and "Hand of Doom" could chill global warming. "Rat Salad" inching into "Fairies Wear Boots" are both so much fun it hurts, and if you've listened to "Electric Funeral," then you can skip watching more-or-less every futuristic "the robots are coming to kill us" movie ever made.

And then there's "Paranoid." The hit that could have set off an avalanche.

ACETATES: THE ROCK STAR'S ROUGH DRAFT

Acetates are a relic of the days before cassettes, DAT, and recordable CDs came into widespread use in recording studios. Otherwise identical to regular singles and LPs, but manufactured from aluminum coated in a thin veneer of vinyl, they were produced to allow the concerned parties to hear how a particular version of a recording would sound outside the studio, on their home hi-fi, for example.

Manufactured on very basic disc-cutting machines, most acetates exist in extremely limited quantities—sometimes no more than one or two copies would be produced, and when they are found on the open market, they often bear no identifying marks whatsoever. Most studios utilized a blank label, adorned with the studio's name and address at most; it was up to the disc's recipient whether the artist or song title was then scribbled on by hand.

Neither were acetates "built to last." The vinyl coating is so thin that even three or four plays will cut through it, while the aluminum is susceptible to problems of its own. A pale greenish mold can grow on the playing surface with surprising rapidity.

For these reasons, many of the acetates on the market today are irreparably damaged. That does not, however, mean that collectors ignore them. In fact, the field represents one of the most fruitful hunting grounds around, the source of some unimaginable treasures—financial and musical.

Many acetates contain music that is otherwise unavailable in any form. For every band that actually gets a record out, there are many, many more who book a studio under their own steam, record their

music, collect the acetates, and are never heard of again. Even among those who do go on to great things, their closets might still overflow with the acetate reminders of long-forgotten sessions, undertaken in their distant youth.

In July 1953, a young truck driver named Elvis Presley stopped by Sam Phillips' Memphis Recording Service to record a couple of songs, "My Happiness" and "That's When Your Heartaches Begin," as a gift for his friend Ed Leek. It cost him $4. In January 2015, Jack White paid Leek's daughter $300,000 for the only existing copy of the resultant 10-inch acetate.

White then permitted everyone else the opportunity to own a copy by reissuing it for Record Store Day that same April, a limited-run vinyl rerelease that, according to White's Third Man label, not only "reproduc[ed] the typewritten labels (printed on the reverse of extra Prisonaires labels that happened to be laying around Sun Records in July 1953)," but was also "packaged in a plain, nondescript, of-the-era sleeve." The intention was to produce a disc "so close to the historic original as to almost be indistinguishable from one other." In 1958, a young band from Liverpool, England, named the Quarrymen recorded two songs, "That'll Be the Day" and "In Spite of All the Danger," at a small studio operated by one Percy "P.F." Philips, from his living room at 38 Kensington, Liverpool, L7. Just one 10-inch 78 rpm acetate was produced—it was all the band members could afford—and, for more than twenty years, it lay all but forgotten in piano player Duff Lowe's personal collection.

In 1981, he rediscovered it and offered it for auction at Sotheby's. Three of his fellow Quarrymen, after all, had indeed gone on to greater things—John Lennon, Paul McCartney, and George Harrison later became three of the Beatles. If nothing else, this scratchy

A typical late-'60s acetate, this one for Gary Puckett and the Union Gap.

representation of their earliest strivings was a unique conversation piece. The auction never occurred. Shortly before the sale was scheduled, McCartney himself stepped in with a private bid that Lowe accepted. Since that time, both songs the group recorded have been released to the public, on the Beatles' own *Anthology* box set. The acetate itself, however, remains under McCartney's lock and key.

The Quarrymen 78 is certainly the best known acetate in the world today. The question that haunts many acetate collectors, however, is: How many similar items are out there that no one knows about?

In 1988, a three-track EMI studios acetate—bearing a standard Emidisc label, with its contents handwritten below the center hole—went on the block at Phillips auction house in London. Who would have known, without the catalog's guidance, that "Soon Forgotten," "Close Together," and "You Can't Judge a Book" represented the first-ever recordings by the embryonic Rolling Stones? So embryonic was the group that it had not even obtained drummer Charlie Watts and bassist Bill Wyman.

Acetates are not confined, however, to a group's first strivings. The Beatles, for example, produced acetates for almost every stage of their album *Sgt. Pepper's Lonely Hearts Club Band,* meaning discs were pressed for every mixdown of every song. The Beatles were not alone in their practice; many artists, at the end of a recording session, would have an acetate or two pressed up to listen to at home. Some would then return to the studio to try the song again; others would agree that they'd finally got it right.

Either way, acetates represent a key moment in the recording process and are both treasured and valued accordingly. The Beatles and the Stones, of course, are paramount among those acts whose acetates fetch high prices, no matter what the contents—even discs that offer no variation whatsoever from the released version of a song may fetch multi-figure sums. (Inevitably, a lot of these efforts have now made it into the public arena courtesy of modern CD box sets and compilations.) However, acetates by lesser-name acts can bring a decent price, and even unknown, or unidentified, acetates should not be passed over if the price is right.

Acetates were not only produced for individual songs. Entire albums would be pressed in this form, to allow listeners to contemplate such issues as running order, and again, these can be highly prized—especially

if the album itself was then never released, or more commonly, was released with songs rearranged and/or replaced. (Acetate pressings should not, incidentally, be confused with factory samples, known as test pressings. These are very different items, manufactured under very different circumstances.)

Legendary indeed is the acetate pressing for what became the Rolling Stones' *Get Yer Ya-Ya's Out!* album, in 1970. In its original form, it was envisioned as a double album, with one disc—rejected by the Stones' label of the time, Decca—given over to the support acts, B.B. King and the Ike and Tina Turner Revue; the other disc, while generally adhering to the familiar released version of the LP, offered raw and unedited performances that would be markedly cleaned up for release. Manufactured at the Apple studios, and bearing that company's familiar label (notated "*Get Your Yah Yah's Out*"), this fabulous item was auctioned in late 1985 at Christie's in London, where it sold for around $900.

Recording studios are not alone in cutting acetates. One of the most highly prized of all Beatles artifacts is a two-song acetate of "Kansas City" and "Some Other Guy," cut by the Granada TV company from the audio track for the *Look Now* TV special on the Cavern Club in Liverpool, shot in August 1962, before the Beatles even had a record deal.

Another unique acetate, in historical as well as numerical terms, is that cut by the BBC in 1951, preserving three of the first melodies ever performed by a computer (logician Alan Turing's Mark II): "God Save the King," "Baa Baa Black Sheep," and Glen Miller's "In The Mood". Just one copy of the acetate was produced, for engineer Frank Cooper, and it is now in private hands. But its status as the first ever recording of what we would now call "digital music" is surely even more precious.

It was even possible for the general public to cut acetates of their own, at the "Record Your Own Voice" machines that used to lurk

The Ventures

Another Smash (DOLTON BST 8006, STEREO LP, PALE-BLUE LABEL, 1961)

"Hold Me Thrill Me Kiss Me," Scott Douglas and the Venture Quintet (BLUE HORIZON 102, 7-INCH, 1960)

"Perfidia" (DOLTON 28, 7-INCH, PICTURE SLEEVE, 1960)

"The Real McCoy," Scott Douglas and the Venture Quintet (BLUE HORIZON 100, 7-INCH, 1960)

"Surfin' and Spyin'" (TRIDEX 1245, 12-INCH SINGLE, 1981)

The Ventures (DOLTON BST 2004, LP, PALE-BLUE LABEL, 1961)

Walk Don't Run (DOLTON BLP 2003, LP, PALE-BLUE LABEL, 1960)

Walk Don't Run (DOLTON 503, EP, 1960)

"Walk Don't Run," Scott Douglas and the Venture Quintet (BLUE HORIZON 101, 7-INCH, 1960)

"Walk Don't Run '64" (DOLTON 96, 7-INCH, PICTURE SLEEVE, 1964)

around railroad stations, department stores, and record shops across the US and Europe. Both Elvis Presley (at Sun Studios in Memphis) and Cliff Richard (at the HMV Records store in London) made their recorded debuts in this fashion, while Neil Young and Jack White combined to record an entire album in one such booth, Young's 2014 opus *A Letter Home*. So, do you want to devote your life to collecting acetates? Only if you own an endless supply of needles for your record player, and infinite patience for a lot of dreadful music. On more casual hunts, you have little to lose. The chances of stumbling upon a hitherto unrecognized gem are probably good enough; the chances of finding at least a recognizable song or artist aren't too remote either. And someone has to locate the rarities we read about.

A word of warning, however. When purchasing acetates, do not make any attempt to clean the disc, beyond a light swipe with a moist cloth, being careful not to allow moisture to gather on the playing surface.

It is also advisable to play an acetate just once, making a digital reference copy as you do so. No matter how clean and well cared for an acetate may look, every listen takes a huge bite out of its playable life, and no matter what a disc's worth may have been the day you found it, it's going to be an awful lot less after a couple more listens.

AUTOGRAPHS

Oh, don't even go there. The days when you could wander up to a celebrity, pen and piece of paper in hand; get their autograph; and go home happy are so far distant today that it scarcely seems possible that they even existed.

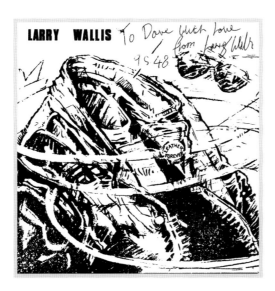

Former Motörhead/ Pink Fairies guitarist Larry Wallis autographed this copy of his "Leather Forever" 45 in 1986.

The final single by punk heroes the Adverts, in 1979, autographed by all but guitarist Howard Pickup—the band had actually disintegrated by the time this was released.

From those veteran celebrities who seem to spend their entire lives drifting from conference center to convention hall, charging a bundle of bucks to sign their name on a piece of official merchandise (that costs another bundle of bucks to purchase); to those who won't even sign a birthday card in case it somehow winds up on eBay; and onto those unscrupulous sellers who will fake a name on any old album in the hope of suckering someone into buying it . . . autographs are a minefield today, and one that is unlikely ever to be cleared.

There is no simple way of entering the field. In the lower echelons of the show-business pantheon, where there is little financial incentive to forge an artist's signature, the chances are that the autographed album you saw online is the real thing. Unless, of course, a previous owner was messing around one day.

In more rarified strata, however, "buyer beware" is an understatement. In early 2017, for example, the collecting community was convulsed by the appearance on an online auction site of an autographed copy of John Lennon's *Milk and Honey* album, supposedly the property of the seller's Beatles-loving grandfather.

It did not take long for the first Lennon fans to point out that John had been dead for almost four years before that album was released, and was thus exceedingly unlikely to have signed a copy for anyone. And it was not much longer before the auction was closed.

In the meantime, though, a few trusting souls had already placed bids on a not-inexpensive item, and many more might have followed them. Proof that even an authentic-sounding background story is only as honest as the seller who spins it.

For many general record collectors, and for these reasons, an autographed album is worth no more or less than an un-autographed one. It makes an interesting conversation piece, perhaps. But, unless you were the one who got the autograph in the first place, there's no way of knowing for sure what you've got . . . forgeries can always beat experts if they're good enough, and even that most familiar piece of proffered proof, a photograph of the artist actually signing the record, does not guarantee that someone else didn't then sit down and sign a bunch more.

So, collect autographs as much as you like. Fill a shelf with old records that have been lovingly inscribed to "Brenda" and "Barry," "my number-one fan" and "to Pooky, with love." Just don't pay over the odds for them.

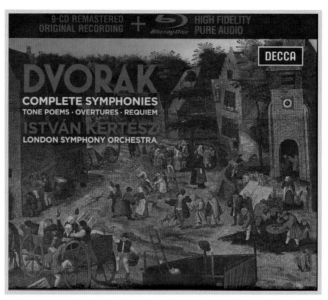

The CD/ Blu-ray box set for Czech composer Dvorak's complete symphonies.

BLU-RAY: CAN IT EVER GET BETTER THAN THIS?

Blu-ray has been described, with some accuracy, as the Rolls Royce of available sound formats. Mastered correctly, a Blu-ray audio disc sounds better than anything else . . . better than pristine original pressing vinyl, better than a mint condition reel-to-reel, better than anything you can name.

A case in point: In 2016, Decca released a box set comprising conductor István Kertész's re-envisioning of the complete works of Antonin Dvorak, as recorded in London between 1963 and 1966, and still regarded as the finest ever performances of the Czech composer's symphonies, tone poems, and requiem. Indeed, it was Kertész's attention to detail that raised Dvorak himself into the first tier of the world's greatest classical composers, after decades of languishing in comparative obscurity.

The box set itself was beautifully realized, with the CDs housed in an appropriately-sized recreation of an old-time (78s era) "record album," each one decorated with the distinctive Pieter Bruegel paintings that distinguished the original vinyl releases; a second book hosted liner notes and track information. And the sound quality, newly remastered from the original analogue tapes, was unimpeachable.

Nestled at the back of the second book, however, was a Blu-ray disc that not only crammed all of that music onto a single disc, it also improved on the already stellar sound of the CDs. Even without resorting to surround sound (the traditional default setting of Blu-ray, of course), every last aspect of the performances rings out with room-filling clarity, the highest fidelity that either Dvorak or Kertész have ever enjoyed.

And that is why Blu-ray is, at the time of writing, the best.

But Blu-ray is not only the most exquisite music delivery system yet developed. It is also among the most particular. Developed by Sony and Philips, what was originally called DVD-Blue (predicated on the format's use of blue laser diodes) officially launched in 2002, with the first players reaching the market in Japan in April, 2003, despite there not yet being any discs to play them on.

Its fidelity aside, the Blu-ray is also regarded as being effectively piracy proof, with the overseeing Blu-ray Disc Association (whose members include some of the world's largest and most influential movie houses) insisting on a plethora of safeguards being built into the format. These included a new, superior digital rights management system to that carried by CDs, and the removal from the Blu-ray player of any outlet ports that might tempt owners to try and make a copy of their discs.

Movies and television were the Blu-ray's initial preserve, and the format continues to favor them. However, a growing library of music-related discs (documentaries and concert footage, for the most part) has seen a number of albums released in what developers Universal Music called High Fidelity Pure Audio—that is, Blu-rays delivered without any accompanying visuals beyond the menu and track listings.

Launched in 2013 with the Rolling Stones's *Grrr!* compilation, the format received its earliest plaudits not simply for the quality of the sound, but also for its quite remarkable storage capacity—three hours of completely uncompressed music on a single disc.

Others followed and, of course, so did a variety of rival formats— msm-Studios' Pure Audio Blu-ray and AIX Records' Blu-ray 3D Music. All have their adherents among both purchasers and labels, but unlike past format wars, the public is not being forced to choose between competing players as well. Learning, one hopes, from previous mistakes, there is no specialized equipment demanded by any of them beyond a basic Blu-ray player.

Which is not to say, however, that Blu-ray is completely problem-free. As a still developing technology, certain firmware upgrades appear to have rendered a number of discs, movies and music alike, unplayable, in the same way as regular operating system upgrades can make redundant hitherto functioning computer programs. At the time of writing, we still wait and see how this particular drama will play out. But the technology itself remains unbeatable.

BOOTLEGS: BEAUTIES OR THE BEAST?

Half a block off Carnaby Street, the soul of swinging London, a dusty record store nestled between a souvenir shop on one side, a shoemakers' on the other. It was nothing special from the outside, and not that much better within; just an owner who looked like Neil from the Young Ones, and a shifting stock of Japanese imports, and French Stooges records.

But root through the racks often enough, and sooner or later you'd make a rare find. Or overhear a conversation which would lead you to an even rarer one, like this:

[Customer]: "Anything interesting come in lately?"

[Neil]: "Yeah, a couple of Bowie things, and—oh, are you interested in this?" And he'd reach for a shelf high over the cash register, and pull down . . . well, that's the point. You never knew what he'd pull down, but they certainly weren't records that you'd seen before. Pink Floyd's *The Coming of Kahoutek*; David Bowie's *Baby Doll*; Roxy Music's *Champagne and Novocaine*; and, within weeks, it seemed, of the first

The Avons

The Avons (HULL HLP 1000, LP, 1960)
"Baby" (HULL 722, 7-INCH, 1957)
"A Girl to Call My Own" (HULL 754, 7-INCH, 1962)
"Oh Gee Baby" (GROOVE 58-0022, 7-INCH, PICTURE SLEEVE, 1963)
"Our Love Will Never End" (HULL 717, BLACK-LABEL 7-INCH, 1956)
"We Fell in Love" (MERCURY 71618, 7-INCH, 1960)
"What Love Can Do" (HULL 731, 7-INCH, 1958)
"What Will I Do" (HULL 728, 7-INCH, 1958)
"Whisper" (HULL 744, 7-INCH, 1961)
"You Are So Close to Me" (HULL 726, 7-INCH, 1958)

time you heard of her, Patti Smith's *Teenage Perversity and Ships in the Night*. With a guest appearance from Iggy Pop!

You'd turn and look, and Neil would smile, and in that magic moment you were hooked. Welcome to the world of bootlegs. Take a poll of any sizeable grouping of serious music fans, and few issues raise so many emotions as bootlegging, the art of acquiring unreleased live or studio material by whichever band takes your fancy, and making it available to a fanatical underground of collectors, fans, and anal-retentives.

Legally, morally, and ethically, the subject is unquestionably among the most inflammatory issue in the hobby, particularly once mp3s emerged to relieve the bootlegger of the need to press up vinyl or CD copies of the offending stash. Indeed, even supporters of bootlegging are divided over where the advantages end and the problems begin.

No less an authority than the *New York Times* once described bootleggers as "cultural heroes," for liberating music that, under normal circumstances, might never have been heard. Today, it is more

Released in 1972, The Who's Closer to Queen Mary *remains one of those bootlegs that epitomize the allure of the format.*

10cc's Before They Were Four *rounded up two CD-Rs' worth of rare material recorded by the band members in the years before the band was formed.*

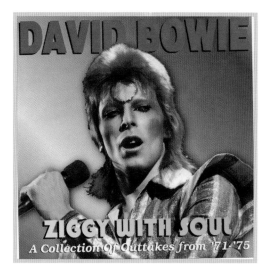

One of a multitude of bootleg CD collections compiling rare and unreleased David Bowie material.

From 1977, Genesis' Awed Man Out captured highlights from the band's 1976 UK tour, their last with Peter Gabriel.

likely to report on their being sent to prison for the unpardonable crime of copyright infringement.

The fact is, however, that bootlegs exist and they are collected. Whether a person cares to indulge in this forbidden fruit is entirely his or her own decision.

The popular history of bootlegs dates back to the mid-'50s and the advent of the first generally available reel-to-reel tape recorders. Live recordings of blues, jazz, and opera performances were the staples of the field, with both tapes and limited-edition vinyl pressings (often 7-inch 45s) circulating in an underground that was small, but astonishingly fertile.

Even before that, however, privileged enthusiasts were able to make recordings of live events. As far back as 1901, a Mr. Mapleson, the librarian at the Metropolitan Opera in New York, was using a cylinder recorder provided by inventor Thomas Edison to capture snatches of performances on the opera stage. None of the recordings were more than a few minutes in length, but still they offer a unique documentary of their subjects, one that a regular record company would never have deemed worthy of preserving. It is this historical record-keeping that, in many collectors' eyes, justifies the existence of bootlegs.

Bootlegging entered rock and pop music in 1969, with the release of Bob Dylan's *The Great White Wonder*. A two-LP set, it compiled hitherto unreleased material from three basic sources—a tape of home recordings that Dylan made in Minneapolis in 1961; a smattering of

studio outtakes which had themselves leaked into the collectors market over the years; and an acetate circulated in 1967 by Dylan's music publishers, soliciting cover versions of material that Dylan himself had apparently abandoned. (Hit versions of "This Wheel's on Fire," "The Mighty Quinn," and so on were developed from this tape.)

Popularly known as *The Basement Tapes* (because they were recorded in one), these recordings were frequently aired on radio and were inevitably recorded by fans and collectors. Less inevitably— simply because, to reiterate the fact, it had never happened before— somebody pressed these recordings on vinyl and marketed the result.

Response was immediate. Private tape (primarily reel-to-reel) collectors had long existed in rock circles, trading among themselves as new material somehow slipped out of record company vaults or concert halls, but rarely making waves beyond their own immediate circle. *The Great White Wonder*, on the other hand, seemed miraculously

George Martin Comedy Productions

Beyond the Fringe, Original cast (PARLOPHONE PMC 1145, LP, 1961)

"**A Gnu,**" Flanders and Swann (PARLOPHONE R4354, 7-INCH, 1957)

"**The Highway Code,**" The Master Singers (PARLOPHONE R5428, 7-INCH, 1966)

"**The Hole in the Ground,**" Bernard Cribbens (PARLOPHONE R4869, 7-INCH, 1962)

"**Little Red Monkey,**" Joy Nichols, Jimmy Edwards, and Dick Bentley (PARLOPHONE R3684, 78, 1953)

"**Morse Code Melody,**" The Alberts (PARLOPHONE R4905, 7-INCH, 1962)

"**My Boomerang Won't Come Back,**" Charlie Drake (PARLOPHONE R4824, 7-INCH, 1961)

"**Nellie the Elephant,**" Mandy Miller (PARLOPHONE R4219, 7-INCH, 78, 1956)

"**She Loves You (German Version),**" Peter Sellers (PARLOPHONE R6043, 7-INCH, 1981)

"**You Gotta Go Oww!**" Spike Milligan (PARLOPHONE R4251, 7-INCH, 78, 1956)

From the mid-1990s, the Goldtone label pioneered "gold" CD bootlegs. A bonus track-stacked version of The Great Lost Kinks Album *was one of their most popular offerings.*

by rush-releasing a double album called, prosaically, *Before the Flood.* He should have thought of that title five years before.

Radio, meanwhile, had moved on to another exclusive clutch of songs. In 1969, while the Beatles argued amongst themselves regarding the final form of their next (and final) LP, *Let It Be,* test-pressing copies of its provisional contents were made by producer George Martin for circulation among sundry interested parties. At least one of these somehow made its way onto American radio, where it was played in its entirety—and appeared on the streets just weeks later as the bootleg *Get Back and 12 Other Songs.*

Produced and sequenced by George Martin in the period before Phil Spector was invited in to sprinkle his magic over the proceedings, *Get Back and 12 Other Songs* would subsequently become one of the highest-selling bootlegs of all time, and is certainly one of the best known. Neither did the arrival of the next "real" Beatles album a few months after *Get Back and 12 Other Songs* damage its standing in the slightest. Indeed, if anything, the substantially remixed and rejigged *Let It Be* only increased demand for the original, unbeautified, recordings.

By the end of 1969, bootlegs were firmly established as a serious irritant to the music industry. Bootleggers sometimes used conventional pressing plants that either didn't know or didn't care what they were producing. Sometimes bootleggers reconfigured discarded 78 rpm presses and did the pressing themselves, producing easily identifiable discs, up to twice the thickness of a regular LP.

available to anybody who wanted it. Reviews and features discussing the album appeared as far afield as *Rolling Stone* and the *Wall Street Journal;* radio aired its contents with impunity. The legality of the issue was of no apparent concern—it was the music that mattered.

By the standards of many subsequent bootlegs, *Great White Wonder* was a primitive offering. The discs bore blank labels, the sleeve itself was a plain white gatefold with the title *GWW* hand-stamped on it. No more than 2,000 copies of this original issue made it out; within weeks, however, other enterprising entrepreneurs had stepped in to duplicate it—bootlegging a bootleg— and, though Dylan's record label, Columbia, did make litigious noises, the only positive response was another new Dylan album, *Self Portrait.*

Drawn from a variety of live and abandoned studio sources, *Self Portrait* was presumably Dylan's own idea of what a bootleg should be. But if that was the case, it just proved how out of touch Dylan had suddenly become. His fans wanted outtakes, but they wanted outtakes from his good albums. Not from *Nashville Skyline.* A second Dylan bootleg, *Flower* (so named for the hand-drawn picture on each sleeve), brought further *Basement Tapes* into circulation. A third, *Troubled Troubadour,* unveiled even more. It would be as late as 1971 before the entire original *The Basement Tapes* acetate was compiled onto one disc, *Waters of Oblivion;* in the meantime, however, the songs just kept trickling out. In 1974, on his first tour since the mid-1960s, Dylan would try and preempt the inevitable flood of in-concert bootlegs

An early bootleg souvenir of Mac's Buckingham-Nicks lineup in concert.

In late 1969, John Lennon was moved to rush-release a live recording of the first-ever Plastic Ono Band concert, at the Toronto Peace Festival, to quash a bootleg of the same performance. In the new year, both the Rolling Stones *(Get Yer Ya-Ya's Out!)* and the Who *(Live at Leeds)* acted against bootlegs of their own recent tours, the Stones' *LiveR Than You'll Ever Be* and the Who's *Closer to Queen Mary.* Both groups hoped that fans who might otherwise have purchased the bootleg would instead buy the "real thing"—in fact, they probably purchased both. But neither would deny the bootleggers' impact. The Stones sold a million albums and the Who went double platinum with recordings they might never have released without bootlegs to force their hand.

Even up and coming acts were being booted. When DJM released the still-rising Elton John's *11-17-70* live album, they did so fully aware that a bootleg version of the same radio broadcast was already in circulation. And they *still* cropped twenty minutes off the show, twenty minutes that the bootleggers, of course, had left intact. There was a certain pride in being bootlegged, too; admittance into what was—at least in the early days—an exclusive club of superstars whose appeal and audience extended beyond even the most generous record company's boundaries. Bootlegs themselves became legends—when Columbia, in 1974, chose to give an official release to Dylan's *The Basement Tapes,* what better title for the ensuing double album than that which the bootleggers had long since passed into common circulation? And, twenty-five years later, another fabled Dylan bootleg was not only released under its most commonly employed title, it appeared thus despite the fact that the bootleg's stated source, the Royal Albert Hall concert, was incorrect.

The tape that comprised Dylan's *Live 1966* album had been circulating on bootleg since the early '70s, and immortalized a concert taped in Manchester, England. The original bootleg, however, relocated the show to London's Royal Albert Hall and the error proved so adhesive that not only did every subsequent bootleg perpetuate it, but Sony, too, felt obliged to subtitle the official release, *Bootleg Series, Vol. 4: Live 1966,* as The *"Royal Albert Hall Concert"*—not to mislead purchasers, but to assure them that they were indeed receiving the same performance they knew and loved from years of bootleg listening. A stronger endorsement of bootlegs and the role they serve in the musical community could scarcely be imagined.

The "correct" Royal Albert Hall tapes were finally released in 2016, within a thirty-six CD box set that rounded up every other live show from that same tour,

many of which existed only through the efforts of the bootleggers, and this is where things become interesting.

Going back to the Stones and Who live albums, it could be (and has been) argued that, in many ways, bootlegs blackmailed artists and labels into releasing material they might otherwise never have deemed fit for public consumption. Indeed, along with the undeniable infringements of copyright and flouting of artistic freedom, this is the most frequently voiced of all cases against bootlegs.

However, frequently overlooked in the scramble for ethical sanctuary is the fact that the traffic is not totally one way. Bootleggers profit from bands, but bands profit from bootlegs, and in more important ways than merely financially.

Bootlegs—or, at least, that community of illicit tapers and hoarders who might be described as bootleggers—have unquestionably provided the modern, collector-oriented music industry with any number of now-much-valued recordings, each one effortlessly puncturing the popular record company insistence that bootlegs are low-fidelity, poor quality castoffs that rip off even the most aurally insensitive consumer.

Much of what is now regarded as jazzman Charlie Parker's most important work was only preserved because someone bothered to tape it. Someone who wasn't affiliated with the record company, someone who didn't then blank the tape the moment the next star came along to record.

Many of Hank Williams' classic radio broadcasts were recorded, some might say illegally, and circulated on bootleg long after the original performances were forgotten, and long before anybody decided to seek them out for an official release. By that time, of course, many of the original source tapes had themselves been lost. But bootleg tape and vinyl allowed musical history to be experienced once again.

Elvis Presley's 1961 USS *Missouri* performance is another example of bootlegs having saved the day. Not including television, this was

Emerson Lake and Palmer

Brain Salad Surgery (CASTLE CMRCD 201, 2001)

Emerson Lake and Palmer (ISLAND ILPS 9132, PINK LABEL, 1970)

Excerpts from Brain Salad Surgery (UK MANTICORE/LYNTONE LYN 2762, FLEXIDISC, 1973)

"Jerusalem" (UK MANTICORE K13503, 1973)

"Nutrocker" (JAPANESE ATLANTIC P-1128A, 1971)

Pictures at an Exhibition (UK VHS CHANNEL 5 CFV 00502, 1971)

Selections from Return of the Manticore (VICTORY SACD 757, PROMO, 1993)

Tarkus (MOBILE FIDELITY 203, 1994)

Trilogy (CAPITOL RECORD CLUB SMAS 94773, 1973)

Works Volume One (ATLANTIC PR 277, PROMO, 1977)

Grateful Dead

American Beauty (MOBILE FIDELITY 1-014, AUDIOPHILE PRESSING, 1980)

"Dark Star" (WB 7186, 7-INCH, PICTURE SLEEVE, 1968)

"Don't Ease Me In" (SCORPIO 201, 7-INCH PROMO, 1966)

Grateful Dead (WB W1689, MONO LP, 1967)

Grateful Dead Hour (MJI, WEEKLY TRANSCRIPTION DISCS, 1988–DATE)

King Biscuit Flower Hour 6/80 (KBFH, 2-LP TRANSCRIPTION DISC, 1980)

Sampler for Deadheads (ROUND 02/03, PROMO EP, 1976)

Terrapin Station (DIRECT DISC 16619, AUDIOPHILE PRESSING, 1980)

27 Years Playing in the Same Band (4-LP TRANSCRIPTION DISC, 1992)

Wake of the Flood (GRATEFUL DEAD GD 01, GREEN-VINYL LP, 1975)

the only live performance Presley gave between 1957 and 1969, and it exists purely because an onlooker had the presence of mind to record it, illegally, on a reel-to-reel player he brought into the performance.

The recording circulated on bootleg for close to two decades before RCA finally released it officially in 1980, giving Presley buffs a spectacular performance and a milestone event. There is not even room for doubt here; without bootlegs, or at least, bootleggers, this performance would have been lost forever. While RCA could argue that it had no reason whatsoever to record the show (who, after all, could have predicted that Presley would wait so long, and change so dramatically, before his next gig?), that very argument is a justification for the illicit recording of live performances. History is not a matter of hearsay. It needs evidence to back it up. Bootlegs provide that evidence.

There are countless more instances. Jon Astley and Chris Charlesworth, compilers of MCA's universally applauded series of 1990s Who remasters, turned on several occasions to the bootleg industry in search of certain rarities, having completely exhausted both official archives and the band members' own collections; and they are not alone.

Purchasers of Van Der Graaf Generator's much-applauded *Boxed* box set in 2000 were treated to early BBC sessions taken from exactly the same less-than-perfect tape source as the *Necromancer* bootleg; while live material from a 1975 show in Rimini, Italy, was lifted directly from a bootleg disc. Led Zeppelin did the same in 2016, when updating their own BBC sessions collection. Again, this is material that, in the first instance, had not survived the passing years in any official archive, and in the second, would never even have existed without somebody undertaking the task illegally.

Frank Zappa, Emerson Lake and Palmer, and Tangerine Dream are just three of the acts who have given official releases to original bootlegs, often replicating the boots' own covers—bootlegging the bootleggers, indeed. When David Bowie first delved into his archive in search of vintage live concerts to release, he chose two of his most legendary bootlegs, from Santa Monica in 1972 and Nassau Coliseum in 1976. And, perhaps most famously of all, there is the example of the Grateful Dead, who—as documented in the first-ever issue of *Relix* magazine—were once adamantly opposed to people taping their concerts. Today, however, those tapes provide fans with one of the most spectacular (and, via multiple releases overseen by the band itself, profitable) archives in rock history.

Yes, bootleggers do make an unauthorized profit from selling other people's work. But the trade-off is, if they had not recorded that work in the first place (this applies principally to live and occasional on-air performances), or arranged for it to be illicitly borrowed from a record label or radio station vault, it might no longer even exist today.

The 1970s were the golden age of the bootleg. Many of the best-loved boots of all time were produced during this period, together with some of the most successful. The labels Rubber Dubber, Kustom, Phonygraf—and most prominent of all, Trademark of Quality (TMQ or TMOQ) and The Amazing Kornyfone Record Label (TAKRL)—were especially prolific issuers, their wares not only incorporating all the superstars of the era—the Beatles, the Stones, the Doors, Led Zeppelin, Yes, and so forth, but digging deep into the ranks of newcomers, too. And once again, the quality of these releases is borne out by the eventual fate of much of the music contained within.

The Beatles' 1964 and 1965 Los Angeles shows both circulated on illicit vinyl for several years before Capitol finally released them as *At the Hollywood Bowl* in 1977. Deep Purple's *On the Wings of a Russian Foxbat*, featuring the tragically short-lived Tommy Bolin, was

Genesis

"Carpet Crawlers" (CHARISMA CB 251, 7-INCH, 1975)

"Firth of Fifth" (CHARISMA/LYNTONE 13143, FLEXIDISC, PICTURE SLEEVE, 1983)

"Happy the Man" (UK CHARISMA CB 181, 7-INCH, PICTURE SLEEVE, 1972)

"I Know What I Like" (CHARISMA CB 26002, 7-INCH, 1973)

"The Knife" (UK CHARISMA CB 152, 7-INCH, PICTURE SLEEVE, 1970)

"Looking for Someone" (UK CHARISMA GS 1-2, 7-INCH PROMO, 1970)

"Man on the Corner" (CHARISMA CB 393, BLUE-LABEL 7-INCH, PICTURE SLEEVE, 1982)

"That's All" (CHARISMA TATA Y-1, 7-INCH PICTURE DISC, 1983)

"Twilight Alehouse" (CHARISMA/ZIGZAG, NO CATALOG NUMBER, FLEXIDISC, 1973)

"Watcher of the Skies" (CHARISMA 103, 7-INCH, 1973)

reissued wholesale on an authorized disc by the same name. In fact, almost every single release in the official *King Biscuit Flower Hour Live* and *Live at the BBC* series—from the Beatles to Bowie, Nirvana to Julian Cope—existed on bootleg long before the vault was opened to "real" record companies.

Bootlegs also, on occasion, offer a far more authentic view of certain proceedings than official releases ever allow. David Bowie's *His Master's Voice* featured a recording of a 1974 ABC-TV broadcast of Bowie's final Ziggy Stardust show (recorded the previous year), prior to its remixing for the movie *Ziggy Stardust: The Motion Picture.* What is especially fascinating about the bootleg is that it includes Bowie's closing "retirement" speech in its entirety, plus an eight-minute "Jean Genie"/"Love Me Do" medley featuring guest guitarist Jeff Beck. Both were absent from the authorized issue.

Genesis's *As Though Emerald City,* excerpted from the 1975 Los Angeles Shrine concert, was released two decades later within the official *Archive 1* box set. Here, again, the bootleg fan receives a more lifelike version of show, via a full and perfectly listenable version of the closing track "It," which the box set claimed was so damaged that Peter Gabriel's vocal track needed to be rerecorded.

Meanwhile, 10cc's *Going Pink on Purpose* offered up five live songs taken from a King Biscuit broadcast recorded shortly after the group left the UK label for Mercury. What is interesting is that when this same concert was given an official release (by KBFH) two decades later, the entire disc was given over to the UK-era material performed that night. Tracks from the band's Mercury debut, including two of the cuts on the bootleg, were nowhere in sight.

Other classic recordings remain locked in the official archive, but thrive underground regardless. Linda Ronstadt's *Take Two Before Bedtime* recalls a sensational live act whose formidable powers have, perhaps, been overlooked by modern historians; Wings' *Live in Hanover, Germany 1972* not only offers an opportunity to experience the deeply underrated early live prowess of Paul McCartney's post-Beatles band, it also serves up a crop of rarely heard and never officially released songs. And Little Feat's Lowell George is widely believed to have mixed the concert tapes that comprised that band's *Electrif Lycanthrope*. Not every bootleg, even from this halcyon age, is actually worth its weight in vinyl. But an awful lot of them are.

During the mid-to-late '70s, when Bruce Springsteen's recording career was tied up by litigation, the singer went out on the road, honing a live show that still draws comparisons with the best on the block, and making sure

(tacitly if not overtly) that as many people got to hear what he was doing as possible.

Alongside Dylan, Springsteen is the most frequently bootlegged American artist in history (the Beatles and Led Zeppelin take that title among British bands), with the dynamic performance captured on the 1975 *Live at the Bottom Line* never far from any discussion of the greatest boots of all time. It was also one of the most influential, turning more potential listeners on to his music than any amount of hyperbolic press.

Appreciating this, Springsteen's 1978 American tour saw five entire shows, with over fifteen hours of live music, broadcast on American radio with one show famously including the exhortation "Bootleggers, roll your tapes." Another show found the Boss hoping that some distant friends would hear a dedication "through the magic of bootlegging." And when the British *New Musical Express* pinned him down on the subject in October 1978, Springsteen's support for bootlegs seemed unequivocal.

"Most of the time, they're fans. I've had bootleggers write me saying, 'Listen, we're just fans.' And the kids who buy the bootlegs buy the real records too, so it doesn't really bother me. I think the amount of money made on [bootlegging] isn't very substantial. It's more like a labor of love."

By the end of the decade, he had changed his mind and co-filed a civil suit in a California Federal District Court against two of these "fans," for "infringement of copyrights, unfair competition, unjust enrichment, unauthorized use of name and likeness, and interference with economic advantage." But at least he once understood what drove the bootleg industry on.

Pink Floyd is another band that has at least taken heed of the bootleggers' art. Again, the group's underground catalog features some essential titles: *In Celebration of the Comet: The Coming of Kahoutek* preserved the band's 1972 London premiere of the then-

---

Pink Floyd

Animals (COLUMBIA AP-1, PROMO LP WITH EDITED "PIGS," 1977)

"Apples and Oranges" (UK COLUMBIA DB 8310, 7-INCH PROMO, 1967)

"Arnold Layne" (TOWER 333, 7-INCH, PICTURE SLEEVE, 1967)

Dark Side of the Moon (MOBILE FIDELITY MFQR 017, BOXED LP
    "ULTRA HIGH-QUALITY RECORDING," 1982)

"It Would Be So Nice" (TOWER 426, 7-INCH, PICTURE SLEEVE, 1968)

"Octopus," Syd Barrett (UK HARVEST 5009, 7-INCH, 1969)

The Piper at the Gates of Dawn (TOWER T5093, MONO LP, 1967)

Saucerful of Secrets (UK COLUMBIA SX 6258, MONO LP, 1968)

Selected Tracks from Shine On (EMI SHINE 1, PROMO CD, 1992)

Ummagumma (HARVEST STBB 388, 2-LP WITH GIGI SOUNDTRACK VISIBLE ON SLEEVE, 1969)

Nirvana

Bleach (UK TUPELO LP 6, WHITE-VINYL LP, 1989)

"Blew" (UK TUPELO TUPCD 8, CD SINGLE, 1989)

"Here She Comes Now" (COMMUNION 25, COLORED-VINYL 7-INCH, 1991)

Hormoaning (AUSTRALIA GEFFEN GEF 21711, BURGUNDY-VINYL 12-INCH, 1993)

Incesticide (GEFFEN DGC 24504, BLUE-VINYL LP, 1992)

"Love Buzz" (SUB POP SP 23, 7-INCH, HAND-NUMBERED PICTURE SLEEVE, 1988)

"Molly's Lips" (SUB POP SP 97, GREEN-VINYL 7-INCH, 1991)

"Pennyroyal Tea" (UK GEFFEN NIRPRO, PROMO CD SINGLE, 1994)

"Sliver" (SUB POP SP 72, BLUE-VINYL 7-INCH, 1990)

"Smells Like Teen Spirit" (UK GEFFEN DGCTP 5, 12-INCH PICTURE DISC, 1991)

unreleased *Dark Side of the Moon*. *Embryo* featured a stunning 1971 show in San Diego, and most infamous of all, *British Winter Tour 74* (released in the US as *Raving and Drooling*), arrived so well-packaged and -recorded that many people thought it really was a new official album from the band.

It featured just three tracks: "Raving and Drooling," "Gotta Be Crazy," and "Shine On You Crazy Diamond," all of which were unavailable in any other form—and it sold, according to legend, like the proverbial hotcakes. Indeed, it continued selling even after the third of those tracks turned up a few months later on the Floyd's next studio album, *Wish You Were Here.*

The other two songs, however, were nowhere in sight, and six months later, in an interview with the French *Rock et folk* magazine, Floyd frontman Roger Waters finally bowed to the inevitable. Floyd's bootleg repertoire abounds with the unfulfilled promise of songs in the making, and it would have been very easy for this pair to go the same sad way as "Fingal's Cave," "Oenone," "Baby Blue Shuffle," and "Reaction in G."

Instead, when asked what he was going to do next, Waters admitted that public demand left him with little choice. "Record 'Gotta Be Crazy' and 'Raving and Drooling,'" he replied. Reworked as "Dogs" and "Sheep," the two songs appeared on the next Floyd album, 1977's *Animals.* And a little over three decades later, Floyd commenced the series of archive-sweeping box set projects that would give everyone a chance to hear what bootleg collectors had been enjoying for so long.

The record companies' take on bootlegs throughout this period was curious. On the one hand, they abhorred the things and worked feverishly to cut the cancer from their midst. The decline in the quantity of bootlegs and operating bootleg manufacturers during the late '70s was, at least partly, the result of increased law enforcement

crackdowns. On the other hand, labels were quick to recognize the cachet of outlaw chic that bootlegging could confer upon an artist.

Sony's release of Bob Dylan's *The Basement Tapes* in 1974 is the best-known early example of a bootleg being, effectively, bootlegged by its legal owners. The mid-'70s, however, saw this process reach magnificent heights, as labels began bootlegging their own artists as well.

Nils Lofgren, Tom Petty, and Graham Parker were all recipients of oxymoronically titled *Official Bootleg* promo releases at the dawn of their careers, as their labels hit upon the admittedly ironic notion of legitimizing an artist by making him appear palatable from an illegitimate angle.

If Nils Lofgren was worth bootlegging, the theory went, he must be worth listening to, and the fact that the limited-edition *Back It Up!! An Authorized Bootleg* would itself shortly be bootlegged only proves what an effective idea that was. (The album, one of Lofgren's finest, has since returned to official release schedules as the CD *Bootleg*.) Parker's *Live at Marble Arch* has likewise since reappeared on several official anthologies, while Petty's one-sided, five-track *Official Live Bootleg* has at least leaked out on B-sides and within the *Playback* box set.

History records that the ploy worked from the record companies' point of view—all three artists did indeed succeed. Interestingly, however, none became a star of the bootleg world itself; indeed, with the exceptions of the Sex Pistols, the Cure, Elvis Costello, and Patti Smith, none of the bands thrown up by, or in the chronological vicinity of, the punk and new wave movements ever became stalwarts of the underground industry.

Indeed, by the end of the 1990s, the entire alternative rock era, the history of which dates back to around 1975, had thrown up a mere handful of acts who could claim entry to the bootlegging hall of fame—Kate Bush, U2, Prince, Stevie Ray Vaughan, Nirvana, Pearl Jam, and Phish, with maybe Radiohead sneaking in under the wire. All of which means that the biggest names in the bootleg world today have remained essentially unchanged since the late 1970s.

That this was so became manifest during the early '90s, when bootleg CDs first began appearing on American streets in serious numbers. This in itself was an unexpected development—as late as 1987, it was a common industry belief that the new format was immune from the scourge of bootlegging, because the manufacturing plants were so tightly controlled. Instead, bootleg CDs were rapidly revealed as even easier to manufacture than vinyl.

Bruce Springsteen was the recipient of the first-ever bootleg CD, the *Castaway* collection of *Born in the USA* outtakes and live cuts, also in 1987. More followed, but the boom really began courtesy of a fascinating loophole in international copyright law. Releases that were deemed strictly illegal in the US suddenly turned out to be perfectly legitimate in a number of leading European and Far Eastern nations, and an industry that had lain moribund for close to a decade suddenly reemerged with renewed vigor.

The Italian Bulldog label was first out of these newly opened blocks, and by 1993, live CDs featuring virtually every major artist were selling freely across Europe and Asia, and making inroads into the American market as well. Indeed, so confident were these operators of their legal position that the San Marino–based Kiss the Stone label even began taking full-page advertisements in the mainstream American music press, promoting new releases ranging from a broadcast-quality copy of Nirvana's last-ever show in Rome to a string of top-selling Phish titles.

Some fabulous items came to the surface. Long out-of-print vinyl boots were revisited, often via a straightforward transfer from the LP, but sometimes from original source tapes (or from as near the original source as possible). Other discs delved into hitherto uncharted waters, unearthing from who knows where recordings whose existence had never even been suggested. Others still proved that no matter where one stands regarding the commercial and moral rights or wrongs of bootlegging, at the end of the line there sat collectors and enthusiasts who genuinely cared about the music.

Multiple volumes of the Beatles *Ultra Rare Tracks* (Swinging Pig) series cut through all the red tape that, even in the aftermath of the official *Anthology* collection, continues to snarl the Fabs' catalog. The series presents an unsurpassed collection of studio, broadcast, and live recordings. Even more specialized studies have, of course, followed, including all but full renderings of every note of music produced during the Beatles' *Get Back/Let It Be* sessions.

Vast sprawling anthologies became commonplace. The Rolling Stones were subject to an eight-CD examination of the sessions for 1967's *Their Satanic Majesties' Request* (Midnight Beat); other classic/legendary albums to be similarly documented (albeit within much smaller packages) include the Beach Boys' unissued *Smile,* Led Zeppelin's *Physical Graffiti,* and Bob Dylan's *Blood on the Tracks.*

The advent of digital recording technology (DAT) allowed for concert recordings to be rendered with unprecedented fidelity—all the more so on those occasions when concerts were simultaneously broadcast either on radio, pay-per-view TV specials, or via an enhanced audio system developed to aid the hard of hearing. The ease with which CDs could be manufactured frequently saw discs of recorded concerts hit the streets within days of the concert. And the most astonishing thing was, it was all completely legal.

Disparate copyright laws have always been with us. Throughout the nineteenth century and into the first years of the twentieth,

for instance, American book publishers were under no obligation whatsoever to pay, or even consult, those European authors whose novels were appearing stateside in such prodigious quantities. So, in the vast majority of cases, they didn't, reducing an entire industry to the level of pirates, and their product—those Victorian- and Edwardian-era US editions of Charles Dickens, William Thackeray, and Sir Walter Scott that collectors prize so highly today—to precisely the same status as the Italian CDs of the 1990s.

The same selfish and protectionist policies that ignited that controversy were still at work in the 1980s and 1990s. The difference was, whereas America's refusal to initiate reciprocal copyright agreements with other countries once worked to the Americans' advantage, the boot was now on the other leg. And you could cut the outrage with a tuning fork—or, in this case, a legal brief.

Beginning in 1996, the European and Asian loopholes were plugged as tightly as was humanly possible, while a succession of well-publicized busts targeted importers, distributors, and retailers across the US.

Even small-time operators are not exempt. Many record companies today employ staff whose sole purpose, it seems, is to trawl the Internet searching for potentially infringing items, be they physical discs or mp3 downloads, and attempt to close them down.

No sooner, after all, had the imported menace been beaten back, than a new domestic crisis emerged, with the arrival on the marketplace of recordable CDs (CD-Rs). The Head label set the pace for this new explosion, debuting with a staggering launch of forty titles, in individually numbered editions of 1,000 apiece, and rubbing salt into the industry's chagrin by timing its launch to within a week of a series of March 1997 busts that had the American industry trumpeting the worldwide elimination of bootlegging forever.

The Gold Standard label followed, joining Head in spinning out a dizzying array of what were, at that time, distinctive-looking golden-colored discs. It was, of course, a brief phase; within a couple of years, so many other CD-R labels had emerged to offer both original recordings and straight copies of other labels' bootlegs, that by the end of the century, the market for CD bootlegs was in a state somewhat approaching crisis.

Collectors, and even casual purchasers, wary of the ease with which any potential bootlegger could now spring into action, began differentiating loudly between gold (CD-R) and silver (factory-manufactured) discs—not because there was any discernible difference in quality, but because silver discs were somehow more "real." It is a backlash that reduced many CD-Rs to the status of the homemade and handwritten cassette bootlegs, which, while once the backbone of many a street market and classified advertisement, are nevertheless of no collectible value whatsoever.

Some fascinating dilemmas would arise, however, including the strange case of the Who's *The Blues to the Bush* Internet-only live album. The official release, in 2000, was issued on CD-R; the *Bridge to the Blues* bootleg, documenting the same show, was issued on a conventional silver disc. Which is the *real* real deal?

It is within this climate of self-imposed hostility that bootlegs have again dipped below the radar somewhat. New issues are still appearing, of course, with at least a few of them readily comparable to the best that official record labels can muster, even at a time when the labels themselves are digging deeper into the vault and expending more time and effort on packaging and presentation than at any time in the past. But many more simply rip an already existing mp3 to disc, with the resultant dip in sound quality; and others still are nothing more than copies of those.

The result has seen both the market for, and the visibility of physical CD bootlegs plummet, while attempts to relaunch the medium on vinyl are likewise being thwarted by the world of digital files.

Meanwhile, it is becoming increasingly apparent that artists and record companies alike have not only got a handle on why bootlegs are so popular with collectors, they have also learned to fight fire with fire. Throughout the 1980s, Fairport Convention, Richard Thompson, and Peter Hammill were among the first acts to recognize that the true fan's demand for music could never be sated by one new album issued every couple of years, so they began plugging the gaps with limited-edition, fan-club (or similar) albums containing live shows, outtakes, and the like.

Enter the 1990s, and Prince—whose public conflict with Warner Bros. hinged on similar notions of commercial freedom and artistic expression—likewise used the Internet to pioneer new means of making his music available to his audience, openly acknowledging a conflict that previous generations had only tacitly spoken of—that is, a record company's prime concern is to market music that is considered commercially viable; an artist's is simply to make music. Rightly or wrongly, bootlegs at least offered the consumer a middle ground between two so diametrically opposed viewpoints. Prince instinctively understood that the Internet could serve a similar purpose.

By the turn of the century, the Cure, the Beastie Boys, King Crimson, Jimmy Page/Black Crowes, Pete Townshend, and Brian Wilson were among the leading artists to utilize either their own Web sites, or suitable online retailers, to make available CDs that might never reach conventional retail outlets. Others, most notably David Bowie and They Might Be Giants, also started making rare music available for download.

Pearl Jam, meanwhile, pioneered an even more audacious step—one that fans of every act must surely was be wishing was common practice among artists. Well aware of the allure of bootlegs, but well aware, too, that words and threats could never stop people from buying (or manufacturing) them, the Seattle band regularly permitted radio stations to issue limited-edition two-CD albums of select live performances during the 1990s.

In 2000, however, the band itself recorded every night of its summer European tour, then made each show available as an individually (and suitably minimally) packaged, budget-priced two-CD set under the umbrella title *The Bootleg Series.*

A total of twenty-five discs were issued in 2000; the following spring, forty-seven more appeared, documenting every stop on the band's fall 2000 North American tour. Result? No more Pearl Jam bootlegs (at least from those tours), plus a record-breaking five simultaneous entries onto *Billboard*'s Top 200 LP chart.

Again, a myriad others (the Who and Peter Gabriel among them) have followed suit. Other artists, including the owners of the Marc Bolan, Jimi Hendrix, Doors, and Elvis Presley catalogs, have seen fit to cull the best of their own bootlegged archives for official releases, with rewards that far surpassed any profits made by the bootleggers. Once, collectors were starved for authorized issues of legendary releases. Now, some fans are literally groaning beneath the weight of them all.

Bill Levenson, former VP of Artists and Repertory at Universal Music Group, and the man responsible for many of the finest collector-oriented CD box sets of the past decades, acknowledged, "I am always mindful of what bootlegs are floating around on an artist, and I try to assess whether the presence of bootlegs implies that there is a market/music consumer for me to reach."

More specifically, "While working on the Velvet Underground *Bootleg Series Volume One: The Quine Tapes* (a three-CD box of previously unheard live recordings from 1968–69), we collected and reviewed many bootlegs to see: A) what was out there; B) how did they sound; and C) how were they packaged, so that when we moved forward with our ideas, we had an idea on how to improve on what was previously done by 'professional' bootleggers only."

The critical success that met the package indicates that the efforts were successful, all the more so since the greatest plaudits were drawn from a community notorious for its ambivalence toward "official" attempts to anthologize this most sainted of sixties rock legends.

For many collectors, the increasingly common phenomenon of hitherto bootleg-only material making it onto authorized releases is another reason why the market for illicit releases has declined.

Bootlegs of earlier periods, however, remain fiercely collectible, with many enthusiasts utilizing what might be perceived as a lull in the present climate to renew their acquaintance with the classics of the vinyl age.

Prices for 1970s-era issues by even relatively obscure artists have soared in recent years, particularly those that, making no pretense whatsoever toward professionalism (printed jackets, colored vinyl, etc.), arrive with the simplest of packaging: a plain white-card sleeve, shrink-wrapped around a single-sheet, one-color photocopied "cover," a blank (or occasionally, preprinted but wholly deceptive) label, a quirky message in the run-off groove.

The sound quality might be bog-awful, the contents mislabeled and misrepresented. The music might be rubbish—the artist might be of no conceivable interest to anyone but the most die-hard fan. But the bootlegs are irresistible for all that, a labor of love in every sense of the word. And isn't that what music should really be all about?

BOX SETS:
ALL YOU EVER NEEDED
TO KNOW (PLUS A BOOKLET)

Box sets have traveled a long way from the days when they were, simply, boxes with a handful of LPs in them. Today, even the most unambitious set will pack multiple discs with multiple rarities, while the package itself will hold as many extras as the budget will allow.

Box sets regularly contain booklets the size and thickness of small books (or even big ones: Germany's Bear Family label prides itself on its extravagant publications); most box sets boast discographical exhumations that the artists themselves might sometimes have forgotten about. Even those packages whose main goal is simply to recycle the catalog one more time will usually throw in an extra disc of rarely heard oddities, or a few bonus tracks, at the end of each album. Today, a box

set is a one-stop summary of everything you needed to know—and were probably not quite rich enough to have found out already.

For a number of reasons—size and cost among them—it is only in relatively recent years that box sets have come to be accepted as true collectibles in their own right, as opposed to budget-priced roundups of old hits and album tracks.

Of course, there have always been exceptions—'80s-era boxed collections of reissued albums by the likes of the Beatles, Queen, and Pink Floyd have remained in demand since their release.

However, even the then-extravagant offerings that date from the first years of the CD age, four-or-more disc examinations of Bob Dylan, Elton John, Rod Stewart, Led Zeppelin, David Bowie, and so on, swiftly declined in value when compared to their original (not inconsiderable) selling price.

Most collectors own a few releases that offer a comparatively inexpensive or uncomplicated way of obtaining music that might never come their way in its original format; but that, for many serious enthusiasts, is all that box sets are—substitutes for the "real thing," be it a long deleted B-side, a unique and precious acetate, a lost and forgotten radio broadcast—whatever.

One of several attempts to round up the best of Marc Bolan's oft-reissued back catalog into one little box.

Exactly what it says on the sleeve: a box set rounding up all that Peter Green's Fleetwood Mac recorded for Mike Vernon's legendary Blue Horizon label.

Recent years, however, have seen a number of once ubiquitous box sets become appallingly hard to find; make the jump from CD to vinyl and the hunt becomes even more expensive.

Like so many innovations in musical packaging and formatting, box sets owe their genesis to the classical market and, while it tends to be rock releases that get all the headlines, the classics still dominate the field in terms of girth and value. As far back as 2013, the *New York Times* was marveling at "the burst of special boxed-set collections of [classical] CDs that keep getting produced," in apparent defiance of all predictions of a major industry meltdown.

"This June, in honor of the centennial of the birth of Benjamin Britten, Decca issued *Britten: The Complete Works*, a comprehensive sixty five–disc set offering essentially every work he wrote, including some juvenilia . . . ." (The previous year had seen twenty-three discs' worth of Leon Fleisher's *The Complete Album Collection*; twenty-four of Gary Graffman's *Complete RCA and Columbia Album Collection;* a twenty-eight disc *Legendary Van Cliburn: The Complete Album Collection;* and the forty-two disc *Vladimir Horowitz: Live at Carnegie Hall.)* "The suggested retail price," the *Times* piece added, "is $149.98."

The market has only continued expanding since then. Fifty plus–disc boxes rounding up the cream of Deutsch Grammophon's mono output, Mercury's Living Stereo series, Decca's "analog years," and many others now feel commonplace.

The complete works of individual composers or conductors can stretch to just as many CDs . . . or more! One box set spreads one

Donovan

"Catch the Wind" (HICKORY 1309, 7-INCH, 1965)
Children of Lir (IRELAND FIONA, NO CATALOG NUMBER, CD, 1995)
Donovan Rising (UK PERMANENT PRESS PERMLP 2, LP, 1990)
A Gift from a Flower to a Garden (EPIC N2N 171, MONO 2-LP BOX SET WITH PORTFOLIO, 1967)
HMS Donovan (UK DAWN DNLD 4001, 2-LP WITH GATEFOLD SLEEVE, 1971)
"Remember the Alamo" (UK PYE 7N 17088, 7-INCH, 1966)
"Rock 'n' Roll with Me" (UK EPIC EPC 2661, QUAD 7-INCH WITH PICTURE SLEEVE, 1975)
Sunshine Superman (EPIC LN 24217, MONO LP, 1966)
"Sunshine Superman" (EPIC 10045, RED-VINYL 7-INCH PROMO, 1966)
Universal Soldier (UK PYE NEP 24219, EP WITH "SUMMER 1955" MISPRINT, 1965)

hundred Leonard Bernstein symphonies across sixty discs; another devotes eighty-four CDs and a DVD to Arturo Toscanini's *Complete RCA Recordings*; while Arthur Rubinstein's *The Complete Album Collection* weighs in at a staggering 144 CDs plus 2 DVDs.

And then there's 2016 *Mozart 225: The New Complete Edition,* a 200-disc collection of every work Mozart produced, featuring sixty different orchestras, 600 soloists, and a staggering 240 hours' worth of music. Which, according to reports, wound up the biggest selling album of the entire year, thanks to *Billboard* magazine's album sales chart counting each individual disc as a separate sale. Around 6,250 box sets shifted equated to total sales of 1.25 million copies, streets ahead of any of the year's more headline-worthy names.

Compared to heavyweights like this, even the most exquisitely anthologized rock legends (Elvis and Dylan lead that pack) have a lot of catching up to do.

There again, that's the story of rock box sets through and though. In 1967, Donovan became the first mainstream rock artist to at least

From France, the collected works of Jacques Brel were spread across ten CDs.

Ozric Tentacles' early career, documented on cassette and occasionally vinyl only, was given a CD release in a box set brilliantly designed to resemble a pack of breakfast cereal.

appropriate the notion of the box set for his *A Gift from a Flower to a Garden*, although it still contained just two LPs, plus a portfolio of lyrics and drawings.

Two years later, the boxed edition of John and Yoko Lennon's *Wedding Album* featured just one LP, but was weighed down regardless by a photo strip, a postcard, a poster of wedding photographs, a second poster of lithographs, a booklet, a sleeve, and a photograph of a slice of wedding cake. The following year, early British pressings of the Beatles' *Let It Be* swan song were boxed, a single LP accompanied by a booklet. And, in 1970, Beatle George Harrison's three-LP solo debut, *All Things Must Pass*, was luxuriously packaged in a custom box, with his *Concert for Bangladesh* all-star live album making a similar appearance in 1972. Capitol Records, constantly on the lookout for new and inventive ways of selling its back catalog, moved into the box-set market with a little more conviction in late 1967, releasing a series of *Deluxe Edition* packages, each featuring three albums by a host of popular stars, Dean Martin, Frank Sinatra, and the Beach Boys among them. The series employed both vinyl and 8-track, with the latter format not only seeing many more releases, but also turning up one of the scarcest Beatles items of all time, a *Deluxe Edition* 8-track collection.

Capitol also ventured into various-artists boxes by way of a short series of 1969 releases combining individual LPs by different bands into one package. One popular volume combines the Band, the Steve Miller Band, and the Quicksilver Messenger Service.

Crucially, many early box sets were limited editions, either as entities in their own right (none of the Capitol issues remained on sale for long) or, at least, in terms of packaging, with the boxes replaced by more traditional sleeves for later issues.

Equally important, from the modern viewpoint, is that the boxes themselves tended to be rather flimsily constructed, easily splitting and tearing unless treated with absolute care. The Donovan and George Harrison LPs are extremely common in poor condition, while the John and Yoko set itself is considered rare only if all the inserts are present. Like many other LPs that were originally issued stuffed with ephemera (the Who's *Live at Leeds* is the best-known example), it is the entire package that attracts attention, not the individual elements.

While one segment of the music industry was marketing box sets as a luxurious cut above the norm, another employed them as a cost-cutting exercise. The early-to-mid-'70s saw a number of budget labels (the TV-advertised Adam VIII label among them) produce a bewildering array of various-artists collections packaged as box sets, to obviate the need for printing individual sleeves for the discs themselves.

Such budget boxes have little value today, either as collectibles or as listening experiences. While rare or unusual stereo mixes may occasionally make their way on board, most discs packed so many songs onto the vinyl that not only did the sound quality plunge to new lows, the songs themselves were frequently presented in rerecorded, edited, and/or prematurely faded form. Much like the budget-CD collections of later years, these sets were targeted solely at an audience that wanted the biggest bang for its buck.

Another factor holding box sets back was the sheer paucity of artists whose careers actually merited anything more than a one- or two-disc *Greatest Hits* package. It was as late as 1970 before even Elvis Presley was deemed worthy of a boxed hits collection, the four-LP *Worldwide Gold Award Hits Volume One* compilation. A second volume serving up *The Other Sides* followed in 1971.

Mike Oldfield US Singles

"Family Man" (VIRGIN 1402877, 1982)

"Five Miles Out" (12-INCH, VIRGIN AS-1424, 1982)

"Hergest Ridge" (VIRGIN PR223 PROMO, 1974)

"Magic Touch" (LONG VERSION, 12-INCH, VIRGIN PR2113 PROMO, 1987)

"Magic Touch" (VIRGIN 7-99402, 1987)

"Portsmouth" (VIRGIN ZS8 9510 PROMO, 1976)

"The Wind Chimes Pt. 2" (12-INCH, VIRGIN PR2181 PROMO, 1987)

"Theme from Ommadawn" (VIRGIN ZS89505, 1975)

"Tubular Bells" (VIRGIN VR55100, 1973)

***"Tubular Bells* Extracts"** (VIRGIN PR196 PROMO, 1973)

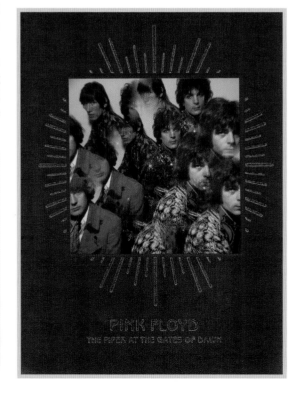

The fortieth anniversary edition of Pink Floyd's 1967 debut album The Piper at the Gates of Dawn, *boxed with both the mono and stereo versions of the album, plus a third disc of rarities.*

In Europe, Cliff Richard and the Shadows were anthologized across a World Record Club six-LP package, *The Cliff Richard Story*, in 1972, an exquisite issue that placed each individual LP into its own custom sleeve, with liner notes and exclusive photographs.

However, the most legendary of early boxes is surely the Beatles' *Alpha-Omega*, a four-LP compilation that tracked the group's entire 1962–70 career (plus a handful of solo recordings), via what its manufacturer, Audio Tape, perceived as a loophole in a newly instituted copyright law, which permitted them to release the music without being its legal owner.

The first full Beatles compilation ever issued in the US, in 1972, *Alpha-Omega* was released on both vinyl and 8-track and was made available via TV advertised mail-order. Unfortunately, the loophole that it exploited turned out to be a dead end.

Capitol, the rightful copyright owners of the material, swooped in and both *Alpha-Omega* and a projected *Volume Two* follow-up vanished overnight. Today, the common perception of the set is that it is a bootleg; in fact, it not only deserves the same place in the Beatles' catalog as any of the myriad Star Club–era collections issued elsewhere in the group's history, it can also be thanked for inciting the Beatles to finally issue their own compilations, the *1962–66* ("red") and *1967–70* ("blue") anthologies.

Another forerunner of the modern box set was Mike Oldfield's *Boxed*, comprising quadraphonic mixes of the albums *Tubular Bells, Hergest Ridge,* and *Ommadawn,* plus an exclusive fourth disc, *Collaborations,* featuring Oldfield's work with other artists. A far cry from other limited-edition, and now extremely scarce, packages of the age, *Boxed* became one of the most successful box sets of all time, reaching No. 22 on the UK LP chart in late 1976. From the same country and era comes *The Electric Muse*, the Transatlantic label's four-LP box set summarizing the story of English folk music as it transformed into folk-rock.

Similar collections had a long pedigree in budget circles, with the Vanguard label curating several budget-priced folk boxes during the early 1960s. Few of these are paid much heed today. *The Electric Muse*, on the other hand, remains regarded among the crucial compilations of the genre, and that despite the box suffering from poor distribution and low sales, and vanishing within a year or so of its 1975 release. (A book published to coincide with the album is even rarer.) Neither has a CD reissue taken the edge off the collectors' demand—licensing problems saw several key tracks deleted or replaced from the digital release.

Another Elvis Presley collection, 1980's eight-LP *Elvis Aaron Presley 25th Anniversary Limited Edition*, was the next boxed milestone, an exquisitely curated portrayal

littered with unusual material and surrounded by some extraordinary ephemera. A booklet and a set of calendars dated 1963–1980 accompanied original vinyl pressings; the cassette versions of the set featured four tapes, and additionally packed in eight color reproductions of the individual LP sleeves.

The complete works of Cream in a 1997 box.

Queen

At the BBC (HOLLYWOOD ED 62005, PROMO PICTURE-DISC LP, 1995)

"Bicycle Race" (UK EMI 2870, 7-INCH EXPORT, PICTURE SLEEVE, 1978)

"Bohemian Rhapsody" (EMI 2375, BLUE-VINYL 7-INCH, QUEEN'S AWARD, PICTURE SLEEVE, 1978)

"Hammer to Fall" (UK EMI QUEEN 4, 7-INCH, LIVE RECORDING, PICTURE SLEEVE, 1984)

The Highlander Selection (UK PARLOPHONE EMCDV 2, VIDEO CD, 1986)

"Man on the Prowl" (UK EMI QUEEN 5, 7-INCH TEST PRESSING, 1984)

News of the World (UK EMI; NO CATALOG NUMBER; BOX SET WITH LP, CASSETTE, AND EPHEMERA; 1977)

A Night at the Opera (MOBILE FIDELITY 1067, AUDIOPHILE-PRESSING LP, 1980)

Queen (UK EMI, NO CATALOG NUMBER, WHITE-LABEL DIE-CUT SLEEVE, 1973)

"Radio Ga Ga" (UK EMI QUEEN 1, 7-INCH, VIDEO-SHOOT PICTURE SLEEVE, 1984)

Igniting another modern tradition, single-disc samplers for this package also exist—one issued for retail, offering excerpts from thirty-seven songs, and one for radio, featuring twelve complete tracks. Both samplers are considerably rarer than the actual box.

Other noteworthy vinyl boxes abound. Frank Zappa masterminded several very collectible vinyl box sets. In 1987, three volumes of *Old Masters* between them reissued twenty classic Zappa/Mothers of Invention albums, with the first two bolstered by the inclusion of *Mystery Disc* bonus albums featuring outtakes, live recordings, and oddities from Zappa's earliest years as a recording artist. And, beginning in 1991, two volumes of *Beat the Boots* set about reissuing twenty classic bootlegs dating between 1968–'81, with original artwork, and in a wry twist, the original sound quality intact.

Working Backwards 1983–1973 was a nine-LP box set of Brian Eno's work, bolstered by the inclusion of one previously unreleased album, *Music for Airports Volume Two,* and a 12-inch EP, *Rarities.*

In Germany, the Rolling Stones were boxed first with a twelve-LP recounting of their entire LP catalog, *The Rolling Stones Story*, and then by a four-disc roundup of non-album material, *The Rest of the Best of the Rolling Stones,* which was the only official source for the Chess Studios outtake "Tell Me Baby How Many Times," and, via a bonus one-sided 7-inch disc, the legendary "Cocksucker Blues."

Bruce Springsteen answered a decade's worth of fan mail with the release of his five-LP *Live 1977–85* package; and Queen's *The Complete Works* box served up thirteen past albums and a unique fourteenth featuring non-album singles and B-sides, plus two album-sized booklets. Issued, of course, in a gold embossed, leather-bound box, this was one of the last genuinely significant vinyl box sets, before the advent of CDs.

That watershed, of course, introduced a whole new realm to box sets, with Bob Dylan's *Biograph* among the first to take full advantage of the new format, cherry-picking rarities and released highlights

Mono versions of Bob Dylan's 1962–1967 catalog were growing increasingly hard to find by the time they were repackaged together in a CD box set. This, however, is the original vinyl of the last in the sequence.

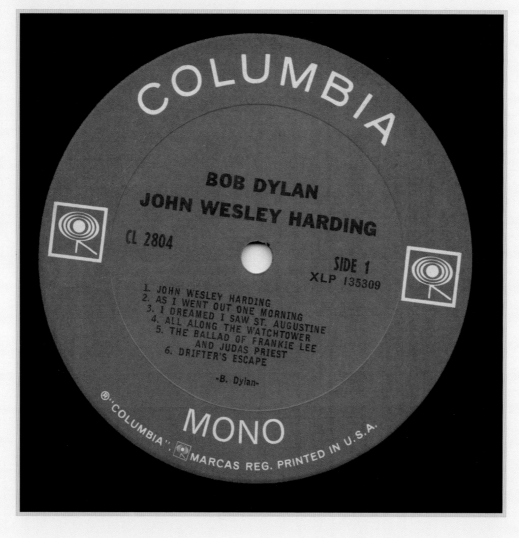

alike to show the world how box sets should really feel. Originally issued in a twelve-inch box, with your choice of five LPs or three CDs, the latter was subsequently repackaged in a far smaller format, a fate that has befallen a number of other early CD boxes.

Led Zeppelin's four-CD *Led Zeppelin* was another trailblazer, while David Bowie's three-CD *Sound and Vision* was further distinguished by the inclusion of a bonus fourth disc propagating the then-fashionable (but ultimately doomed) video disc format. These sets, too, were originally accompanied by vinyl versions, comprising six LPs apiece. In the realm of modern box sets, both are highly prized.

Many other early CD box sets have since disappeared, either because they've been deleted altogether, or because they've been completely reconfigured. Thrilling though they were at the time, the likes of Rod Stewart's *Storyteller,* Sandy Denny's *Who Knows Where the Time Goes?,* the Monkees' *Listen to the Band,* and the Carpenters' *From the Top* all look decidedly low-budget and unambitious today. All appeared in album-sized twelve-inch boxes; all featured a single, flimsy, glossy booklet; and all boasted just four discs, onto which an equal helping of hits, album tracks, and rarities had been spread.

That latter point set the pace for the majority of single artist box sets that followed. While packaging certainly improved, and booklets often became books in their own right, there was something about four-CD anthologies that, like the double album "best ofs" of the vinyl era, felt "right"—the perfect snapshot of a career, designed to appeal to both die-hard fans and casual purchasers alike.

More ambitious projects were soon to arrive, however, among them what became just the first in a long line of Pink Floyd's catalog repackagings.

Shine On offered remastered editions of seven Floyd albums, each uniquely packaged in an all-black jewel case, with the spines lining up to re-create the famous *Dark Side of the Moon* prism logo. A fold-out slipcase was included to hold the discs, alongside a packet of postcards, a lavish hardbound book, and an additional disc of early rarities. An expensive item at the time of its release, it is now one of those collections that can be picked up for considerably less than it originally sold for. Somewhat more highly prized is the limited-edition metal box within which Rykodisc packaged reissues of Bowie's *Low, Heroes,* and *Stage* albums. Although it contained just those discs, the box was designed to hold the entire sequence of rereleased CDs and was apparently available for just a few weeks at most. The box's value today exceeds that of all its intended contents combined. Since that time, a similarly imaginative multitude of extras have enticed would-be purchasers towards new box sets, ranging from the now near–*de rigueur* posters and booklets, on through the stickers and condom that were included with the twentieth anniversary remaster of Garbage's *2.0,* and onto marbles and coasters with which Floyd's *Immersion* boxes were bolstered.

The late eighties also saw a number of similarly limited boxes produced around the release of the first Beatles-catalog CDs. These have also escalated in value, but their worth should not be confused with the 1990s phenomenon of speculative limited editions produced not by record companies, but by wholesalers.

Custom boxes featuring one (or sometimes more) albums, packaged with T-shirts, key fobs, buttons, and the like, and offered for sale only through collector magazines and mail-order houses, may look attractive—and of course, they are described as being *desperately* collectible. But as legitimate entries into an artist's discography, they have little more than quasi-official status and minimal value to collectors.

Some box sets were never intended as rarities, but have ascended to that status regardless. Bob Marley's four-CD *Songs of Freedom* box astonished all observers when what was described as a hopelessly optimistic limited edition of one million copies worldwide not only sold out, but also created a ferocious secondary market. Originally issued in "bookshelf" form (a hardbound booklet the width of one CD and the height of two), this set, too, was subsequently reissued in a smaller single-CD-sized box, but its renewed availability would never dent the demand for the earlier format.

Other significant releases that have faded from view despite appearing set for long runs as catalog staples include the four-CD *Lennon* box set, originally issued in 1990 as a career-spanning roundup of the late Beatle John's solo career; and Elton John's . . . *To Be Continued* retrospective, which fell out of print around 1994, and was still picking up speed on the collectors market when Universal finally reissued it in 2000.

The reissue immediately saw the original's value plunge—but promptly engendered a new collectible, when it was revealed that the new set was itself a numbered, limited-edition release of just 55,000 copies, with a stated availability of a mere six months.

With these examples in mind, it is clear that even modern releases of vintage obscurities cannot be guaranteed to remain available for much longer than the discs they have reissued, with their future desirability only exacerbated by the obvious laws of supply and demand.

This is true even of such relatively recent releases as King Crimson's series of multi-disc live anthologies, seven (at the time of writing) boxes tracking every known live recording made during different periods of the band's lifespan; "complete catalog" roundups for Family, Jess Roden, Elvis Presley, and Wishbone Ash; and expanded "super deluxe" editions of sundry classic LPs (Mike Oldfield's *Tubular Bells*, Fleetwood Mac's post-1976 output, and the Who's *Quadrophenia* among them).

All, it seems, have fallen prey to the hoary old adage of "here today, gone tomorrow"; meaning even such 2016 releases as Pink Floyd's *The Early Years*, Steve Hillage's *Searching for the Spark*, Ian Hunter's *Stranded in Reality,* and Lou Reed's *The RCA and Arista*

Albums Collection might well have disappeared by the time this book is published. And, having done so, they might all seriously enrich anyone who was smart enough to buy them at the time (and, perhaps, careless enough to offload them again too swiftly).

Indeed, visit the online forums where fans congregate to discuss the latest releases, and you will quickly come across those buyers who admit they have purchased the latest "limited edition" box set specifically for the purpose of reselling it once the value has increased sufficiently. It is up to the individual reader to determine whether that makes them a smart investor, or the box set equivalent of the touts who snatch up tickets for an upcoming concert or sports event, purely to resell them at a monster profit.

Of course, their guile invariably pays off. A rare 45, after all, will appeal to only a handful of fans who are prepared to pay significant sums for a copy. A rare box set might be pursued by everyone who ever cared about the artist—and might well end up costing even more.

CASSETTES: AGAINST ALL ODDS

The cassette, without doubt, is the poor relation of the collecting world. Whereas every other format, even such utter obscurities as Pocket Rockers and 4-track cartridges, has its die-hard adherents, the cassette remains despised and derided by the majority of buyers.

Part of this is undoubtedly due to the poor quality with which cassettes were traditionally manufactured. Even in the early '70s, when standards were beefed up to compete with (and eventually overthrow) the 8-track cartridge, cassettes were markedly inferior to their counterparts in terms of packaging, durability, and sound quality.

They triumphed because they were cheaper (both to produce and to purchase), and because most listeners were simply looking for a format that could be easily transported, readily accessed, and that devoured little space. Four cassettes can fit into the storage space required by an 8-track, and that's a major consideration in such confined quarters as an automobile or a student dorm room.

In addition, cassettes possessed a versatility that the 8-track would not embrace for several years to come: Cassettes could be utilized for both playing and recording, the first genuinely affordable recording medium in the history of consumer electronics—and they could store more music.

The first blank, recordable, tapes could hold up to ninety minutes; by the early '70s, capacity had increased to two hours. Weighed

against the fact that few potential cassette buyers were numbered among the high-end audio buffs to whom fidelity is of paramount importance, such advantages ensured that the format could not lose.

Cassettes were developed by the Philips and Norelco companies during the early '60s, originally for use in Dictaphones and other business machines. Japan was the first nation to adapt the technology as an alternative to vinyl, with Europe following suit around 1966.

There, cassettes were marketed alongside small, portable, battery-operated players in much the same way that PlayTapes were in the US. The following year, when the first auto manufacturers began offering cassette players as in-dash accessories, the format moved onto the American market as well.

By the end of the 1960s, prerecorded cassette sales were running neck and neck with 8-tracks (PlayTapes and 4-tracks had both already given up the ghost); by the mid-'70s, it was a one-horse race. Adjustments to both the quality and reliability of cassettes vastly improved their performance, ridding the format of its early penchant for jamming, twisting, and fluttering. The Dolby Noise Reduction system was perfected to erase the hiss that plagued early tapes, and as the 1970s progressed, further innovations in the composition of the magnetic tape at least gave the format the aura of quality sound reproduction. Reel-to-reels marched on in their own tiny corner of the market, of course, their share of the listening public as unaffected by cassettes as by any earlier tape format. But from here on in, the cassette was unstoppable.

Home bootleggers grasped the format, both to record live shows in the first place, and then as a quick and easy means of distributing the

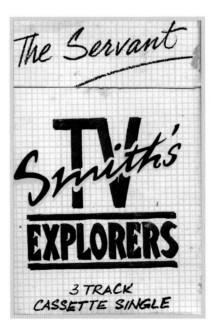

*TV Smith's Explorers'
first single for the UK
Kaleidoscope label was
originally intended to be
released on both vinyl
and cassette. The latter
plans were dropped,
however, with just
twenty-five or so copies
produced.*

The first ever cassette single? In 1974, more than five years before the majors caught on, Judy Dyble released "Satisfied Mind" in the format.

results. Simply hook one player up to another (or, later, pick up a high-speed dual cassette deck) and one could run off copies until the cows came home. Add a simple photocopied sleeve, and tapes of a concert could be available for sale within hours of the show actually ending. By the end of the 1970s, a flea market wouldn't feel complete without at least a couple of dealers selling unimaginable delights from a box of C-60s.

Musicians and disc jockeys took the cassette to heart as an easy way of distributing their all-important demo tapes—a few of which still turn up today, to delight their most completist collectors. A huge number of artists even opened their recording careers with cassette-only releases, sold at gigs or by mail-order—CD-Rs and downloads now fulfill this same function, but during the very late '80s and into the 1990s, Beck, the Smashing Pumpkins, and Marilyn Manson all went this route.

Friends and lovers *adored* cassettes, creating private mix tapes of favorite songs to pass amongst themselves. Indeed, novelist Rob Sheffield wrote a book on the subject, suitably titled *Love Is a Mix Tape: Life and Loss, One Song at a Time*, reliving seven particularly poignant years through the music on the mix tapes he was making at the time. Sonic Youth's Thurston Moore went even further, and convinced a bunch of friends to send him both details and the artwork from their favorite mix tapes for a book that he very sensibly titled *Mix Tape: The Art of Cassette Culture*. (And which he then spoiled by allowing them to include CD-Rs as well.)

And, once CDs took off in the eighties, record companies frequently deployed cassettes for promotional purposes, mailing them out to prospective reviewers as a (presumably) cost-effective substitute for the compact disc version.

So far as the cassette's public face was concerned, too, attempts were continually being made to broaden its appeal even further. In the past, cassettes had simply echoed the contents of their vinyl counterparts. Beginning around 1979, cassette-only bonus tracks came into vogue—one of the best-known early examples is the Kinks' 1980 double live album, *One for the Road*, issued on tape with the extra song "20th Century Man."

Cassettes also began to offer full-length versions of songs that had been edited down for vinyl releases. Cassette copies of Grace Jones' *Warm Leatherette* are prized for their unique inclusion of virtually a second LP's worth of music.

Jones' label, Island, also introduced a range of releases that featured an entire album on one side of the tape, but left the other side blank, allowing consumers to record their own choice of music onto the back of the album. Yet another innovation, frequently applied to the growing market in cassette singles, duplicated the entire playing program on each side of the tape, thus removing the need to turn the tape over midway through the listening experience.

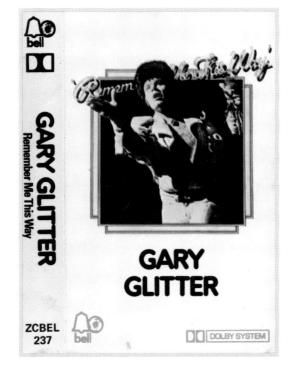

Gary Glitter's Remember Me This Way *live album was also the soundtrack to the movie of the same name.*

A promo cassette collection of Ozrics remixes.

The advent of the cassette single itself created a boom in the cassette's popularity. The first appeared in 1974, the brainchild of Simon de la Bedoyere, and featuring the first new recording in four years by former Fairport Convention vocalist Judy Dyble (Bedoyere's wife). Sadly, the "Cassertate," as he dubbed it, was too far ahead of its time; according to Dyble, "we gave away about four copies to friends, but we didn't sell a single one."

Six years later, Malcolm McLaren, former manager of the Sex Pistols and now overseeing a new band, Bow Wow Wow, tried again when that latter band issued the *Cassette Pet* single in 1980. The song was a hit, the format was a success. Within a year or two, virtually every new single released in the UK and the US was made available on cassette; some appeared *only* on cassette.

Today, there are numerous cassette singles that command high prices among fans of individual artists, often as a result of some extremely well-designed, limited-edition packaging or the use of exclusive material.

Promotional copies of the aforementioned Bow Wow Wow *Cassette Pet* were issued in a mock can of dog food, for example, while several of Frankie Goes to Hollywood's early cassette singles offered otherwise unavailable mixes. Other releases are sought after because the cassette was issued for promotional purposes only, or even abandoned for one reason or another—a 1981 cassingle of "The Servant," by ex-Adverts singer TV Smith's new band, the Explorers, falls into that latter category. The gradual elimination of vinyl during the mid-'80s only furthered the cassette's domination. Figures published in 1989 claim cassettes outsold both LPs and CDs in the US, and while those figures are necessarily warped by the fact that LPs and CDs were then engaged in their own, private battle for supremacy, splitting sales as they did so, still it was a remarkable achievement.

Available within days of the gig itself, a bootleg cassette captures John Cale's December 1985 London performance. The sleeve was a photocopy; the tape itself was a commercially produced C90.

Move outside of the rock market and the cassette's penetration is even more impressive. Long after CDs took off elsewhere, the cassette dominated the music industry in the Third World, both in official, record company–sponsored form, and under the auspices of pirates and bootleggers. In 2002, it was estimated that pirate cassettes, primarily emanating from Hong Kong, Singapore, Taiwan, and South Korea, had devoured as much as eighty percent of the African market, even forcing the closure of several official record companies.

This specter has long haunted the Western world, hence the periodic vociferous attacks launched by the industry on blank cassettes (subsequently, of course, supplanted as Public Bogeyman No. 1 first by recordable CDs, and then mp3s). Many an album from the early 1980s arrives with the printed message on its back cover, "Home Taping is Killing Music," with a cassette tape supplanting the skull in a piratical skull and crossbones logo.

Such misgivings aside, the prerecorded cassette was to remain the only mass-market alternative to the CD until the early 2000s at least, continuing to thrive because, first and foremost, it was cheap and cheerful.

Attempts to dislodge it as the world's No. 1 tape product with such high-end formats as DAT (digital audio tape) and DCC (digital compact cassettes) have consistently failed for those very reasons—these formats demanded new equipment, they required more outlay, and they insisted upon more care.

But all the consumer wants is something that will play music any time, any place, and can then be thrown into the glove compartment or dropped onto the floor until the next time it is needed. The actual quality of that sound is, understandably, secondary to those most pertinent capabilities.

The cassette version of the Adverts' debut album rearranged the vinyl running order. Perhaps it thought it was an 8-track?

While cassettes have never engaged the general collecting sensibilities, that is not to say they do not have the potential to do so.

Many conventionally released albums that are scarce, and thus, very high priced on vinyl, can be picked up for a fraction of the price on cassette, and that's a worthwhile consideration for fans who simply want to hear the music in its original (non-digitally remastered) form, and don't care for other considerations.

In some—indeed, many—instances, the cassettes might even be scarcer than the LPs. But while all the "serious" collectors are flipping through the vinyl racks, you're cleaning up in the corner with the tapes. Then watch how many of them ask you to make them a copy.

Outside of collecting circles, there is still a love for cassettes today . . . a revival, said *Rolling Stone*, "that almost no one . . . saw coming." It is being led, once again, by independent labels and unsigned bands, and seems utterly unhindered by the fact that neither cassette manufacturers nor, for that matter, working cassette *players* are exactly commonplace these days.

Indeed, the very obscurity of cassettes (remember, anyone under the age of twenty-one could be excused for never having seen one) seems to play into their appeal. But it is a real phenomenon, all the same.

"Cassette Store Day" has been established on the early-October calendar since 2013, bringing with it a host of new releases and reissues by the cream of the independent scene; headlining the 2016 celebration were albums by Laraaji, DJ Shadow, and Xiu Xiu, and a special triple-tape reissue of the first three Big Star albums.

The revival has also produced its first mainstream collectibles— including a limited edition (25,000 copies) cassette reissue of Metallica's seven-song *No Life 'Til Leather* demo, originally recorded in 1982, and a reproduction of the Flaming Lips' "Fuck You Frog" 1983 demo (twenty copies).

Of course, it is only a matter of time before all the old arguments against cassettes resurface among the collecting fraternity (sound quality, fragility, and so on and so forth). For now, with an entire new generation of performers choosing the cassette as their medium of choice, home taping is *revitalizing* music.

The ROIR label's mid-1980s cassette-only release of Judy Nylon's super-scarce On-U LP debut.

CDS: THE ULTIMATE HOSTILE TAKEOVER

Musical formats seem to roll in thirty or so–year cycles. The 78, though it was originally developed around 1900, did not truly take off until the early 1910s, but was facing extinction by the late 1940s.

The vinyl LP was born in 1949, only for compact discs to sound its death knell in the mid-1980s. And today, a little over those so-pertinent three decades . . . CDs are still the dominant force in the marketplace. But it is hard to open any music magazine and not read the latest predictions of their imminent demise, crushed on one hand by the inexorable rise of downloads and streaming, and on the other by the "rebirth" of vinyl.

Of course the true picture is a lot more complicated than that, and the fact remains: More people continue to buy their music on CD (whether new or used) than in any other physical format. Indeed, there can be little denying that the format has become *the* single most popular medium for retailing and collecting music ever developed.

Convenient to use, easy to store, and offering sound quality that (though some folks will disagree) generally outperforms any other media in sight, CDs revitalized the music industry at a time when everybody was predicting its imminent demise, and revolutionized collecting at a time when it, too, was beginning to flag.

There is no doubt that times are hard for the little silver discs. At the height of CDs' dominance, in the late 1990s, an estimated 750 million CDs were sold every year in the US alone. A decade and a half later, in a July 2016 report headlined "U.S. Record Industry Sees Album Sales Sink to Historic Lows (Again)," *Billboard* reported "the compact disc continued to crumble, losing 11.6 percent and moving 50 million [copies]." By comparison, "listeners streamed 208.9 billion songs (which translates to 139.2 million album units)."

Of course those figures only reflect sales of new CDs; add thrift stores and bargain bins, record fairs and the Internet to the tally, and the number of discs being purchased soars—particularly as dealers themselves respond to all the gloomy predictions, and begin consigning their own back stock to the dollar bins. None of which helps the mainstream industry's bottom line in the slightest, but it proves that the CD is likely to be around for a very long time to come.

Or at least until somebody comes up with a new format that cannot be deleted with a simple click of the mouse; devoured by a malevolent virus; or replaced by a software feature designed to "enhance" your online library of songs, but which also replaces your carefully curated library of irreplaceable songs with identically titled hits by the stars in its online database. (Yes, it happens.)

Meanwhile, the CD industry fights back with breathtaking élan, via the vast and sprawling box sets that are now such a dominant force on the collecting landscape. Indeed, the cry that once went up from "traditional" collectors, that CDs were not and never could be considered "collectible," today sounds too simpleminded for words. Not only are CDs extraordinarily collectible, they are probably favored by more collectors than any other format on earth—if we assume collectors aren't all running around dropping a month or two's mortgage payment on obscure singles with an alternate take on the B-side, and will sometimes seek out a more affordable alternative should one become available.

And we can journey beyond that example, too. Why bother hunting through rack after rack of dusty 45s in search of that one missing Saint Etienne B-side, when you can simply pick it up on CD? Why blunt your eyesight on the Internet all night, hoping to find the *1963 Newport Folk Festival* album, when the Bob Dylan track you're looking for is already on a Joan Baez CD? And why break the bank for fifty scratchy freakbeat 45s, when Rhino's *Nuggets II* box set has twice that many, and in pristine condition?

A shaped mini-CD ticket for Genesis' 1998 German shows. The CDs were issued as tickets, and the clip on the side would be broken off at the venue. The disc contains a spoken intro by the band and an edited version of the "Calling All Stations," their latest album's title track.

Once upon a time, the answer to those questions would have been obvious. Because the music is only part of the equation; because the artifact itself is what matters: the vinyl, the sleeve, the physical presence of an original recording.

CDs did not have that same presence.

Slowly, however, that mentality changed. CDs have become accepted as artifacts in their own right, as prone to change and variation as vinyl ever was, and just as valued an item. Particularly once the archives started dispensing treasures that had *never* even appeared on vinyl in the first place. True, no CD has yet climbed to the same peaks of scarcity as did the classic giants of the vinyl era. There is no CD equivalent of Bob Dylan's *Freewheelin'* with the four unissued songs, or the Beatles' Vee-Jay album in original stereo, with "Love Me Do" and "PS I Love You," and ads for the label's other releases spread across the back cover.

But for most collectors, the very existence of those records was more or less academic. We all hoped that one day we'd find one, but we never did, and what was worse, a lot of the time we never got to hear them either. CDs have made some staggeringly rare music available, so not only can we find out what the fuss is all about, we can also play them to death. A withdrawn pressing of *Freewheelin'* is so valuable you'd be afraid to even look at it.

Neither is it true that no CDs are actually "valuable." Again, there is nothing yet capable of competing with the storied legends of vinyl, but there are probably 50,000 CDs out there that habitually trade for over $100 apiece, and many times that number which, through deletion, withdrawal, or simply limited availability, are worth far more than they ever retailed at. And that is before one even considers promos, radio shows, and other specialist formats.

Fans of the Eurovision Song Contest will remember Turkey's MFÖ for their 1985 and 1988 assaults on the trophy. This is a Turkish cassette pressing of their second album, from 1985.

There are certainly some high-ticket items out there, too: the Rolling Stones' 2CD 1990 Japanese tour promo; Coldplay's 1998 *Safety* EP, of which just 500 were ever produced; a miniature flight case containing seventeen Johnny Halliday live discs; Mobile Fidelity's audiophile Woodstock album. These and more touch four figure values.

Even better, anybody who has been actively buying CDs since their inception probably already owns a few of the field's medium-rarities—that fold-out digipack version of the Foo Fighters' *There Is Nothing Left to Lose;* Capitol Records' slipcased *Essentials* rarities series; the first release of the Idle Race's complete works, and so on. CDs float in and out of print as regularly as vinyl ever did, and deletion from the catalog still awaits those whose useful lifespan is nearing its end. Just because CDs themselves are meant to last forever, that doesn't mean they will be available forever as well.

The commercial history of the CD dates back to the early '80s. The story of the format, however, stretches back two decades before that. Dutch electronics giant Philips began working on the concept in the late '60s, when physicist Klass Compan first conceived of utilizing digital technology as a means of recording and storing sound.

Neither was the company alone in its researches—as early as 1967, Japan's NHK Technical Research Unit was demonstrating a 12-bit digital audio recorder, with Sony perfecting a 13-bit recorder in 1969. ("Bits" refer to individual pieces of information stored within the disc. The first commercially available CDs were 16-bit; today, 22- and 24-bit discs are the norm, with every increase improving the sound just a little more.)

These earliest experiments utilized videotape as the host for the digital recordings. In 1970, however, Philips perfected a prototype glass disc that required a laser to read it. It would be another seven years, however, before the first digital audio disc prototypes were unveiled, at the 1977 Tokyo Audio Fair, by Hitachi, Sony, and Mitsubishi. The following year, thirty-five different manufacturers demonstrated their

own prototypes at a specially convened Digital Audio Disc Convention in Tokyo, at which point Philips proposed that a universal standard be set prior to any attempt to launch the system.

By the end of 1978, agreement had been reached regarding such essential topics as diameter, the type of laser required to read the disc, and the direction in which the data would be decoded: from the inside out, although even these essentials were subject to revision, which is what happened when Philips invited Sony, as the leading Japanese researcher, to collaborate in perfecting the system.

Hitherto, CDs were intended to be 11.5 cm in diameter. But Sony VP Norio Ohga held out for twelve, to ensure that a full seventy-four minute recording of Beethoven's *Ninth Symphony,* could be fit onto a disc.

The first commercial CDs were produced, by Philips, in August 1982, in the form of Claude Arrau's 1979 recording of the Chopin waltzes. (Arrau himself pushed the button that set the presses running.) The following year, David Bowie's *Let's Dance* became the first album to be released simultaneously on vinyl and CD, around the same time as the first discs and players were introduced into the US market.

They made an immediate impression. Some 800,000 discs were sold during the first year, together with 30,000 players. Within three years, those figures had exploded beyond anyone's wildest imaginings—three million players, fifty-three million CDs. America's first CD manufacturing plant went online in 1984, with Bruce Springsteen's *Born in the USA* becoming the country's first release in the new format; and, by 1988, there were more than fifty manufacturers operating worldwide. And suddenly, a bogeyman who had been hanging around the fringes of the record-buyer's imagination for a couple of years began taking his first giant steps forward. The possibility that the industry would begin phasing out vinyl in favor of CDs had been hanging in the air again since the introduction of the first discs. Now it was official.

The fact that rock music was so (comparatively) slow in embracing the CD should not be a surprise. Although it is by far the best selling genre in western music, it is . . . or at least *was* . . . viewed by record labels as the one least concerned with sound quality. Which, of course, was being peddled as the compact disc's greatest advantage over vinyl.

It was classical music that led the revolution, as it had so often in the past; it was the classical listener whose demand for the closest thing to sonic perfection had always rung loudest, and it was towards the classical listener that the record companies targeted their most exquisite developments.

Digital recording was common within the Deutsch Grammophon catalog, for example, long before the first rock artists invested in the necessary equipment, and anybody purchasing a CD player in the months after they first appeared in the stores would only have found classical CDs to play on it.

But, much to the labels' delight, it swiftly transpired that rock and pop fans were as partial to the promised superior sound quality as their classical brethren, and so the industry embarked upon what, looking back from a distance of thirty years, rates among the most impressive restoration programs of all time.

Even today, one cannot say that *every* record ever made is now available on official CD (as opposed to bootleg or "grey area"); nor even every one for which there would seem to be a ready market. But very many have been reissued and, if one considers both official and unofficial digitization, and its widespread availability on the internet, the ratio becomes even higher.

Was there ever a time in the past eighty years, for example, that one even imagined owning a complete collection of every 78 released by the legendary Paramount label? Two vast box sets issued by Jack White's Third Man label have made that possible, courtesy of a pair of mp3 stick drives. The contents of which can then, should you so desire, be burned to CD. A lot of CDs, it is true, but it can be done.

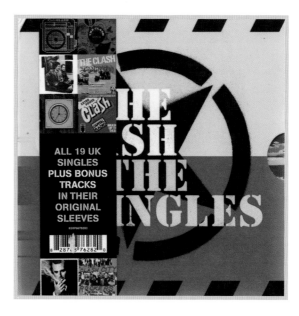

A CD box set rounding up the Clash's entire 45 rpm output.

Outside of the world of bootlegs, with their often questionable sound, how could you ever have heard Woody Guthrie's complete Library of Congress interview with Alan Lomax? It's now available to all on the *American Patriot* box set.

Without a lot of patience, and a lot of money too, how could you ever have heard every LP cut by the giants of fifties rock 'n' roll, with not a single scratch or click to mar the experience? All are now available, some within budget-priced box sets that cost less in their entirety than even one well-worn and possibly scratched-to-hell '60s repress.

Indeed, as yet another hitherto lost so-called masterpiece is scraped from the bottom of another veteran's barrel, some collectors are wondering whether they even want to keep buying the things. Frank Zappa issued sixty-two "new" albums throughout his lifetime. That total has almost doubled in the years since his death in 1993.

The advent of CDs aroused other fears, too. Doomsday predictions that, far from being indestructible, the discs were likely to self-destruct within a few years were raised, then dismissed when it became apparent that the vast majority were not going to do anything of the sort. Production problems apparently confined to the Philips-Dupont-Optical manufacturing plant did see a number of late-'80s discs issued by the UK Phonogram label turn brown and eventually deteriorate to become unplayable. But other CDs, even those dating from the first days of the format, play as perfectly today as they did in 1983.

Another supposedly significant drawback to the format was its seventy four–minute time limit—not a concern when reissuing a conventional single LP, but very problematic on those occasions

Love and Rockets Singles

"Ball of Confusion" (12-INCH, BIG TIME/RCA 6038, 1986)

"Body and Soul" (12-INCH, AMERICAN 014000, 1994)

"Kundalini Express" (12-INCH, BIG TIME/RCA 6018, 1986)

"Mirror People" (1988 RECORDING, 12-INCH, BIG TIME/RCA 6070, 1988)

"No Big Deal" (EXTENDED, 12-INCH, RCA 9097, 1989)

"No Big Deal" 7" (BIG TIME/RCA 9045, 1989)

"So Alive" 7" (BIG TIME/RCA 8956, 1989)

"Sweet FA" CD (UK BEGGARS BANQUET BBQ 67, 1996)

"The Bubblemen Are Coming" (as the Bubblemen) (BIG TIME/RCA 8335, 1988)

"This Heaven" CD (UK BEGGARS BANQUET BBQ 36, 1994)

when a two-LP set exceeded the time limit by so small a margin that a two-CD set simply didn't seem practical.

Early CDs of Joni Mitchell's *Miles of Aisles* and Bob Dylan's *Blonde on Blonde* were among the albums that would make their digital debut edited in some form . . . a few minutes of music in some cases, entire songs in another. The outcry was immediate, and grew even louder after Fleetwood Mac's *Tusk* was released, shorn of what many people considered its standout track, "Sara." The gradual pushing forward of the CD's storage capacity would eventually remedy this; so, ultimately, would the discovery that the public was happy to pay extra for the entire experience. But it is ironic to discover today, with the full versions of each album readily available, that a sizable market has developed for these earlier "edited" issues.

Even more ridiculous, in hindsight, were fears that record companies would confine the new format to new releases and past bestsellers only. Through the late 1980s and beyond, several magazines actually encouraged their readers to delve deep into their record cabinets and pull out LPs even they had forgotten about, to hold up, and then bemoan, "This'll never be reissued on CD." And fellow collectors would shake their heads in dismay, quite forgetting that it would never be *re*issued on vinyl either.

In fact, CDs rapidly came to embrace the most unlikely antiquities, and by the early '90s, it was getting difficult to predict what would be coming out next, as the major labels laid bare their archives, and enterprising indies pounced on any crumbs the majors had missed. And some of them even sold more copies this time than they ever did the first time around. Bad luck for anyone hoping to corner the market in original vinyl pressings of the one and only album by Tickawinda. Good luck for everyone who has finally got to hear one of the best British folk-rock albums of the late '70s in superb digital sound.

Even more excitingly, the bitter taste of needing to replace a lifetime's vinyl collection on CD was expunged first by the realization that many (not all) CDs *did* sound better than their predecessors, but also by the growing trend of appending old records with new bonus tracks.

Soon, it was difficult to even remember a day when a listening session necessitated getting up every twenty or so minutes to turn the record over, and (at least until the vinyl revival took hold) the result was an entire generation of listeners for whom such a chore was as unimaginable as using a mangle to do the laundry, or going to math class without a pocket calculator.

The arrival of the Beatles' back catalog on CD, beginning in early 1987, gave further impetus to a format that had, thus far, taken considerable flak for its claim to be the wave of the future, while the biggest stars of the past had still to endorse the product.

Both Capitol (US) and EMI (UK) were initially criticized for their approach to the subject. Unilaterally, they utilized the original British mixes and sequencing for LPs that appeared in very different form in the US, and they charged the full CD price for discs that barely topped half an hour of playing time (similarly brief Beach Boys albums were issued as "two-fers"—two CDs on one disc).

They were criticized, too, for issuing the first four albums in band-approved mono, rather than providing the subsequent stereo mixes—and for so much more. But time—and, of course, subsequent releases that have now mined almost every imaginable permutation of each record—has softened most collectors' views considerably. Today, the idea that a classic album could be reissued in anything *but* its intended form should be anathema, even to record company executives.

The Beatles, perhaps inevitably, are responsible for one of the earliest CD collectibles, when the *Abbey Road* album was issued in that format by Japan's EMI-Toshiba, some months before the official go-ahead was given, with sound quality several notches below what it was intended to be. Copies were hastily withdrawn, with the estimated 1,500 survivors fetching extraordinarily high prices in the period before an official issue made it out, and still attracting considerable attention today.

A number of other early Beatles discs also merit a second glance. As early as 1985, German Polydor issued the Tony Sheridan–era *Beatles: First* on disc, though a swift withdrawal saw this set, too, soar in value.

Discs translating the Star Club live recordings and the Decca audition tapes to the new format were also quick off the mark, and while all have been superseded (many times over), all predate the release of EMI's own catalog.

Among the other early signs that CDs were going to develop into a powerful force on the collectors market was the launch, in April 1987, of the CD newsletter *Ice (International CD Exchange)*. Destined to remain the leading source for new-release information and gossip for close to twenty years to come, *Ice* began life as an eight-page, photocopied publication, acting as both a watchdog for the infant industry and an invaluable lexicon of collector-oriented information.

"Bruce fans with CD players now have their first *bona fide* collectors item to chase down," reported that debut issue, revealing that the first Japanese CD pressings of Springsteen's *Nebraska* utilized a master tape prepared before the original album underwent its final mix.

It was a neat exclusive, but it was a significant story for other reasons, too, in that it demonstrated that a medium hitherto touted for its perfection was, after all, as prone to error and mistake as any of its predecessors. Indeed, many of the CD age's most treasured rarities are, similarly, errors that somehow passed unnoticed into production.

Some of these are, in themselves, little more than minor snafus, affecting the purchaser's recollections of the original song or LP more than the integrity of the release itself—an unissued stereo mix replacing the expected mono, for example. Occasionally, however, errors creep out that offer something far more precious.

Those original CD pressings of Bruce Springsteen's *Nebraska* are hotly pursued for the sake of four extra minutes of the song "My Father's House"; collectors identify the disc by its white spine with red lettering, and the absence of the "Now Made in America" notation, which appeared on discs after the opening of the Digital Audio Disc Corporation manufacturing plant in Terre Haute, Indiana.

The 1997 reissue of Bob Dylan's 1985 *Biograph* box set initially entered the market laden with four unexpected bonuses, in the form of two previously unissued live performances, one hitherto unavailable outtake, and one super-rare single. Even more bizarrely, two of these boo-boos actually corrected mistakes committed on the original 1985 package. Just 5,000 copies of the box had been distributed when the errors were discovered and the package was recalled. In the meantime, just days after the withdrawal, copies were spotted trading for up to $150.

The errors still occur. Preparing the release of 2016's *The Early Years* box set, Pink Floyd initially intended including a recording of their legendary live show among the ruins of Pompeii. Later, however, the decision was taken to replace it with a new mix of 1972's *Obscured By Clouds* soundtrack, and when the box's track listing was released to the media, that is how it lined up.

Only at the very last moment, with the boxes manufactured and awaiting release, did anyone notice that the change had not actually been made—that *Live at Pompeii* still lurked within, and *Obscured By Clouds* was nowhere in sight.

Hastily, stand-alone discs of the missing album were manufactured, to be packaged in simple paper sleeves, and laid alongside the *already factory sealed* boxes.

Pink Floyd caught their mistake. Other artists have not been so fortunate. In 2017, David Bowie's *A New Career in a New Town* box set made headlines when fans swarmed to bemoan a sound dropout on the newly commissioned remaster of the *Heroes* album. Though the record company (Rhino) insisted it was intentional, and present on the master tape, still the opprobium raged until finally the label conceded defeat and produced a replacement disc.

Dead or Alive fared even worse; errors forced the replacement of no less than ten of the nineteen discs in their 2016 *Sophisticated Boom Box* package. It is too early to tell whether such errors will themselves one day become collectors' items. Past precedent suggests that they may, if only as curios; a mono version of Dead or Alive's *Youthquake* CD probably doesn't excite too many people, regardless of how much they love the band. In many ways, however, future value is only a part of the appeal of items like this. A more important consideration might be: How complete do you want your collection to be?

The first widespread collectibles of the CD age were the so-called long box (six-inch by twelve-inch) packages within which the earliest CDs were issued, as an anti-theft measure. It was assumed that the size of this external packaging, which often attractively reproduced the cover art, would deter shoplifters who might be tempted by the otherwise pocket-sized format.

The boxes were never particularly popular and few people ever saved them. So when a phase-out initiative launched by the Rykodisc label promised, among other things, to reduce the cost of a CD by up to $1, few people were sorry to see the long box leave. Label after label followed Rykodisc's lead; store after store turned instead to similarly sized reusable clear plastic cases for their security concerns. And in April 1993, the Recording Industry Association of America, representing most of America's leading record companies, confirmed the permanent withdrawal of the long box.

By which time, of course, everybody who'd ever thrown them away were already wishing they hadn't. The fact that long boxes were beasts to open without tearing them up was, of course, conveniently forgotten.)

If the CD's first collectible gimmick was wholly inadvertent, it would soon be followed by some very deliberate ones.

Attempts to market some CDs as "picture discs" were, perhaps understandably, doomed to failure —with the label covering the entire non-playing side, every disc was effectively a picture disc and besides, once it was shut inside the player, it didn't matter what was printed on it.

(One is reminded here of the similarly asinine "selling point" to which early DVD manufacturers were prone, the interactive menus that effectively meant you still had one more step to go through before you could actually watch the movie. Seriously, it's not a special feature if it's an integral part of the process.)

But genuine (and genuinely collectible) gimmicks were on the horizon, in the form of "hidden" tracks that were included either as deliberate, or in some cases, accidental, bonuses. Usually secreted at the end of a disc, often following untold acres of silence, these unannounced bonuses created an awful lot of excitement when originally discovered. Nirvana's *Nevermind* breakthrough album was not the first to employ the device, but it certainly became the first CD to truly ignite the craze, all the more so after it was revealed that the bonus cut, "Endless Nameless," appeared only on the first 15,000 copies pressed—by which time sales of the album had topped 600,000.

The list of CDs featuring hidden material is, today, enormous. It includes such stellar names as U2 (1998's *The Best of 1980–90* collection), the Clash (the *Clash on Broadway* box set), and Cracker (whose *Kerosene Hat* album actually indexed ninety-nine tracks, though music and sound appeared on only a handful of them).

The Champs

All American Music from the Champs (CHALLENGE 2514, STEREO LP, 1962)

"Anna" (CHALLENGE 59322, 7-INCH, 1965)

Everybody's Rockin' with the Champs (CHALLENGE CHL 605, LP, 1959)

Go Champs Go (CHALLENGE CHL 601, BLUE-VINYL LP, 1958)

Great Dance Hits (CHALLENGE 613, LP, 1962)

"Hokey Pokey" (CHALLENGE 59103, 7-INCH, 1961)

"Tequila" (CHALLENGE 1016, BLUE-VINYL 7-INCH, 1958)

"Tequila 76" (REPUBLIC 246, 7-INCH, PICTURE SLEEVE, 1976)

"Tequila 77" (WE'RE BACK 1, 7-INCH, 1977)

"Turnpike" (CHALLENGE 59026, 7-INCH, 1958)

An even more unconventional hiding place was developed for such releases as the Essential label's reissue of the Adverts's *Crossing the Red Sea with the Adverts* and the Astronettes's *People from Bad Homes* archive release. In these instances, the bonus material was secreted at the *beginning* of the disc and could be accessed only by starting the disc playing, and then holding down the rewind button. Neither of these discs was intended as a limited edition or a rarity (although the short shelf-life of the latter, a David Bowie production from 1973, has certainly established it as one); the collectibility stems from technology.

As far as other CD innovations are concerned, the miniature CD-3 format was all but stillborn during the late '80s and early '90s, but has nevertheless spun off a number of now-popular collectibles. Video CDs were also short-lived, while enhanced CDs never took off as triumphantly as they deserved to.

However, one new trick did take off, in the form of the special editions created for, and/or by, major retail chains such as Best Buy and Blockbuster; many rapidly become highly sought after.

Bonus discs for the Who's *BBC Sessions,* Ringo Starr's *Third All-Starr Band,* and several of Paul McCartney's catalog revamps were hot commodities, even before the stores' own copies sold out; while the Pearl Jam live album *Give Way,* featuring seventeen songs from a concert in Melbourne, Australia, in 1998, simply went through the roof after the band's label, Epic, objected to its release. Another one to look for is Best Buy's Roy Orbison set, *Live at the BBC,* featuring fifteen otherwise unavailable recordings dating back to 1968.

Not all such supplementary releases feature exclusive music—the Best Buy bonus accompanying Paul McCartney's *Run Devil Run,* for example, merely duplicated a forty-minute interview disc available with all first pressings of the UK edition. The rival Musicland chain, meanwhile, offered a CD single featuring original versions of four

of the songs covered on the McCartney album—by Wanda Jackson, Gene Vincent, Fats Domino, and Ricky Nelson.

Moving on from the contents of various discs, there have also been several attempts to upgrade CD sound even further, pioneered by (among others) Sony's Mastersound series of SBM (Super-Bit Mapping) editions, Mobile Fidelity's Ultradiscs, and Atlantic's Gold Standard collectors editions, and still going strong today, in the shape of SACDs, DVD-Audio and Blu-ray audio. Most of these round up a hardcore coterie of believers, in much the same way as the various quadraphonic formats did in the '70s, and invariably are produced in such limited quantities that the aftermarket sometimes resembles a bull ring.

Furthermore, many of them *do* perform as the admen would like you to believe. Not every stated improvement, however, is so reliable. The late 1990s saw the industry afflicted by the belief that gold-colored CDs offered a far better listening experience than silver, and that despite the fact that it was the more painstaking mastering process that certain manufacturers employed, as opposed to the fabric itself, that differentiated the two.

Either way, the craze died out first when sundry budget labels took to manufacturing their own gold discs (without the additional care and attention); then when various cunning CD bootleggers got in on the game; and finally, when gold-colored CD-Rs became generally available. Today, with the exception of a handful of renowned and trusted label names, gold CDs are scarcely worth their weight in aluminum-colored polycarbonate. The heart of CD collecting, then, lies in the same place as LPs and 45s before it, in regular issues and rarities, in surprising deletions and unexpected famines. One of the earliest discoveries in this direction was, indeed, the fact that discs that appeared during the first few years of the CD were suddenly disappearing again, with David Bowie among the first major casualties. RCA issued his first CDs as early as 1984. By 1988, however, they had all but disappeared, prior to being reissued in expanded form by Rykodisc, two long, cold-turkey years later.

Overnight, and despite the promised superior packaging and content of the reissues, the RCA discs became highly collectible, reaching a plateau from which they have yet to descend. Ironically, Rykodisc itself did much to further this situation, at least in one instance—the promotion of Bowie's epochal *Rise and Fall of Ziggy Stardust* included the offer to exchange copies of the original RCA disc for a new Rykodisc pressing.

Whether as a consequence of this generosity or not, *Ziggy Stardust* (RCA PCD1 4702) is now among the scarcest of all Bowie's primary RCA CDs, with only such late-in-the-day compilations as *Golden Years* and *Fame and Fashion* proving harder to locate.

First CD issues of discs are also a popular hunting ground, particularly in the realm of the first-ever CDs. They were, after all, manufactured at a time when the format's future was still uncertain—nobody knew whether the CD was going to take off or simply vanish into obscurity, as the 8-track had done.

At the dawn of the CD age, even major artists' releases were limited by the fact that there were very few manufacturing plants operating anywhere in the world, with none at all in the United States. American CDs issued prior to 1984 were actually manufactured either in Japan or in Hanover, Germany, while the booklet was printed in America.

Spotting these details is the easiest way to identify a first issue; another detail to watch for is the label design—regardless of the issuing record company, the earliest CDs manufactured in Hanover all employed a distinctive row of colored squares across the center of the disc. Even the jewel case can clue in collectors: prior to 1985, the spindle that holds a disc in its tray had eight teeth; later cases had 12.

Other modern rarities include those acts whose careers were flourishing at the dawn of the CD age—and were, therefore, among the first to have their catalogs released—but whose subsequent fall from fame has seen those albums long since either deleted, or reissued in somehow revised form. Anybody wanting the original albums must turn instead to the collectors market—and the values there might surprise them.

Maybe the day when a shelf of old CDs could help put your kids through college is still a long way away. But it might well be worth more than you ever imagined it might be.

CD-3S: GOOD THINGS DON'T ALWAYS COME IN SMALL PACKAGES

The first collectibles—and the first major casualty—of the CD age were the 3-inch discs that the industry intended to represent the next wave in the revolution, as the replacement for the 7-inch single.

Capable of holding up to twenty minutes of music, 3-inch CDs were launched amid considerable fanfare during the summer of 1987, when the first promotional issues were dispatched to radio, with Fleetwood Mac's "Little Lies," Squeeze's "Three from Babylon," and Stevie Wonder's "Skeletons" among the earliest promo issues.

There was just one problem. While the discs' manufacturer, Digital Audio Disc Corporation, of Terre Haute, Indiana, launched the discs on schedule, the snap-on plastic adapters necessary to center the discs within the CD player didn't arrive quite so punctually.

The oversight was rectified within weeks, but the damage was already done. Nice format—a shame it can't be played.

From the start, the industry was hopelessly divided over the CD-3. Rykodisc, the newly established CD-only label, was first into the commercial marketplace with Frank Zappa's "Peaches en Regalia" remix.

But Philips, pioneer of the CD in the first place, announced that it wanted no part of this latest innovation. For every label that did seem set to jump on board, another seemed equally determined to sabotage the format by continuing to issue all its discs as 5-inchers. And the public, tired of waiting for the businesspeople to make up their minds, did it for them. They rejected the CD-3 outright.

Before that, of course, there was a flurry of releases, and some surprisingly spectacular ones, at that. The jazz and classical specialists at the Delos label issued a number of CD-3s in late 1987. The following year, Rhino launched a series of four-song packages under the overall title *Big Hits Come in Small Packages,* and featuring the Turtles, the Everly Brothers, the Beach Boys, and more. The first Beatles CD-3, Romance Records' repackaging of the pre-fame 1961 Tony Sheridan material, followed.

Atlantic, Dunhill Compact Classics, MCA, Polygram, Virgin (UK), and even Deutsche Grammophon were among the other labels to move into the CD-3 field during 1988–89, while EMI plowed ahead with a CD-3 box set of twelve Queen singles issued in the UK, Germany, and Japan.

Criticized at the time for a remarkably eccentric selection of material—the twelve seemed to have been plucked at utter random from throughout the band's entire catalog—*The 3" CD Singles* box is now one of the most in-demand CD-3 releases of all time . . . with or without an adapter to play it with.

Public resistance to the CD-3 was not unreasonable. The CD-3 offered not the slightest advantage over the CD, particularly when

The Chiffons

"After Last Night" (REPRISE 20103, 7-INCH, 1962)

Everything You Always Wanted to Hear . . . (LAURIE 4001, LP, 1975)

He's So Fine (CAPITOL RECORD CLUB DT 90075, LP, 1965)

"Lucky Me" (LAURIE 3166, 7-INCH, 1963)

"Never Never" (WILDCAT 601, 7-INCH, 1961)

One Fine Day (LAURIE LLP 2020, LP, 1963)

"Secret Love" (BT PUPPY 558, 7-INCH, 1970)

"So Much in Love" (BUDDAH 171, 7-INCH, 1970)

Sweet Talkin' Guy (LAURIE SLP 2036, STEREO LP, 1966)

"Tonight's the Night" (BIG DEAL 6003, 7-INCH, 1960)

COLLECTING AND COLLECTIBLES **71**

balanced against the tangible inconvenience of needing to attach an adapter to every disc (very few discs were packaged with one of their own) before playing.

Soon, only Sony remained unequivocal in its support for the 3-inch CD, even forging ahead with plans to launch a dedicated 3-inch player on the Japanese market in 1988. However, they, too, would run headlong into another of the format's drawbacks that same year, with the long-awaited release of Bruce Springsteen's *Chimes of Freedom* EP.

The original EP ran to twenty-five minutes, but the format could hold just twenty. Cuts were made, fans were outraged, the release vanished from view. How ironic, then, that when the EP was reissued on a 5-inch disc in 1999, the edited CD-3 master was inadvertently utilized for the first run of pressings! The oversight was corrected for subsequent issues.

Despite the format's unpopularity, however, it would survive a little longer. Several publishers adopted the CD-3 as an inexpensive way of presenting bonus musical material with books (the digital equivalent to the flexidisc, perhaps), while occasional new releases across the first years of the twenty-first century at least allowed the format an aura of dogged determination. It is not, after all, the disc itself that is outdated, simply its size. With an adapter attached, a CD-3 remains as viable a medium as its 5-inch brethren.

The CD3 promo for Nigo's "Kung Fu Fighting" (2000). Lined up alongside this one, the sleeves for the band's next two singles spelled out their name.

Nevertheless, there are just two primary areas upon which CD-3 collectors concentrate: the optimistic glut of early American issues (with many more existing as promos than as commercial releases), and the often grandiosely packaged Japanese issues that survived into the mid-'90s.

These include enduringly popular collections by the Beatles, Madonna, Depeche Mode, Pink Floyd, and Bruce Springsteen (again). Even with the greatest collectibles, however, CD-3 prices have remained comparatively low—testament, perhaps, to the uncertainty that haunted the format almost from the outset.

CYLINDERS: TUBULAR BLUES

The earliest records, as we would now term them, were metal cylinders, developed from earlier experiments with tin foil and other media, and pioneered not only by their inventor, Thomas Edison, but by a host of other sound pioneers as well—Emile Berliner; Chichester Bell and his cousin Alexander Graham Bell; Charles Sumner Tainter; the Frenchmen Charles Cros, Leon Scott, and Édouard-Léon Scott de Martinville; and others.

In fact, it was Chichester Bell and Tainter whose patents were sold in 1887 to what became the world's first commercial record manufacturer, the American Graphophone Company, who in turn launched the Columbia Phonograph Company in 1889. Merchandising rights were then leased to the North American Phonograph Company, under whose aegis the first commercial records were produced sometime before 1893 (the year in which the company folded).

P.F. Sloan

"All I Want Is Lovin'," Flip Sloan (ALADDIN 3461, 7-INCH, 1959)

"Halloween Mary" (DUNHILL 4016, 7-INCH PROMO, PICTURE SLEEVE, 1965)

"Karma," Philip Sloan (DUNHILL 4106, 7-INCH, 1967)

"Let Me Be" (MUMS 6010, 7-INCH, 1972)

"She's My Girl" (MART 802, 7-INCH, 1960)

"The Sins of a Family" (DUNHILL 4007, 7-INCH, 1965)

"Skateboard Craze," as Willie and the Wheels (DUNHILL 4002, 1965)

"Star Gazin' " (ATCO 6663, 7-INCH, 1969)

"Sunflower Sunflower" (DUNHILL 4064, 7-INCH, PICTURE SLEEVE, 1967)

Surfing Songbook, as Rincon Surfside Band (DUNHILL D/DS 5001, LP, 1965)

The market for these contraptions was understandably limited. A handful of coin-in-the-slot machines, the forerunners of the jukebox, were installed in various public gathering places; most would-be listeners, however, received their first exposure to the medium through the auspices of sundry traveling showmen, who would charge people five cents to listen to a cylinder via a nest of listening tubes connected to the player. The success of these showmen is an indication of precisely how exciting and novel this newfangled device was.

The arrival of the 78 saw cylinders consigned to the ash heap almost overnight—although, surprisingly, they are still being manufactured today, by the Vulcan Cylinder Record Company of Sheffield, England, among others.

Jed Davis of the decidedly twenty-first century Eschatone label explains, "Odd formats are fun, and even if you don't have the means to play them, they can still deepen the meaning of a release.

"We put out my track 'Yuppie Exodus from Dumbo' on cylinder because the song is in part about antiquarian fetishes. The format becomes part of the story."

He turned to Vulcan because "they're enthusiasts who take the format very seriously and do wonderful work," and Davis is not being immodest when he enthuses, "it happens to be a gorgeous package. Michael Doret did the design, and signed and numbered the lot." (For folks without access to a cylinder player, incidentally, the package came with an accompanying download of both mono and stereo mixes of the track, as well as a recording of the cylinder being played on a vintage Edison machine, so it's not like they just bought a pretty round brick.) History recalls the first "true" recording to be Edison's experimental reciting of "Mary Had a Little Lamb," then draws a long, thick curtain over the next few decades' proceedings. In fact, one might be surprised at the wide range of recordings that were available as early as 1895—a catalog published by Berliner's United States Gramophone Company that January advertised close to 100 "plates" (as the medium was then called), "with between 25 and 50 New Pieces [expected to] be added every month."

Included were selections of band music ("Dude's March," "The Star-Spangled Banner," Mendelssohn's "Wedding March"); vocal pieces ("When Summer Comes Again," "Old Kentucky Home," "The Maiden and the Lamb," "The Coon That Got the Shake"); opera; light classical pieces; solo instrumentals (cornet, drum and fife, trombone); pieces dubbed "Indian Songs"; Hebrew melodies; and even animal sounds.

Although one is more likely to find empty cases than the cylinders themselves, a number of cylinders have survived into the modern age, and are thankfully being both preserved and made available in a digital format. Especially noteworthy among these is the cache of intriguing spoken-word recordings released on a 2007 CD by Archeophone Recordings under the title *Actionable Offenses*—intriguing because, as the collection's subtitle, "Indecent Phonograph Recordings from the 1890s" makes clear, almost every one of them would still be considered risqué, or even X-rated, today.

Their survival is especially remarkable given that these particular cylinders were not only prey to the traditional deterioration of the cylinder; they were also targeted for destruction by the authorities!

DIGITAL COMPACT CASSETTES: OOPS. WELL, THAT DIDN'T WORK TOO WELL

The Philips company's Digital Compact Cassette, or DCC, was launched in 1992, amid the same flurry of excitement that saw rivals Sony produce the MiniDisc. Both formats offered consumers the opportunity to make home digital recordings without having to invest in a costly (or, more accurately, *even more* costly) DAT system; and both, after a few years spent tussling for the market, were effectively sidelined by the arrival first of recordable CDs, and then the portable mp3 player.

While they were in action, the DCC was probably the superior product, in as much as the new players were compatible (in play mode) with existing cassette tapes, although they required their own (not inexpensive) tapes for recording. Despite this, the DCC remained on the market for less than four years, during which time a number of albums had been produced in the new format—among them David Bowie's *Ziggy Stardust* and *Black Tie White Noise*, Kiss's *Revenge*, and

Flip

"A Casual Look," The Six Teens (FLIP 315, 7-INCH, 1956)

"Louie Louie"/"You Are My Sunshine," Richard Berry (FLIP 321, 7-INCH, 1957)

"Movie Magg," Carl Perkins (FLIP 501, 7-INCH, 1955)

"Sugar Sugar You," Richard Berry (FLIP 327, 7-INCH, 1957)

"Take the Key," Richard Berry (FLIP 318, 7-INCH, 1956)

"This Paradise," The Bel-Aires (FLIP 303, MAROON-LABEL 7-INCH, 1954)

"Uncle Sam's Man," The Elgins (FLIP 353, 7-INCH, 1961)

"White Port and Lemon Juice," The Bel-Aires (FLIP 304, 7-INCH, 1954)

"Why Do I Go to School?" The Six Teens (FLIP 346, 7-INCH, 1959)

"You're the Girl," Richard Berry (FLIP 331, 7-INCH, 1958)

Jimi Hendrix's *The Ultimate Experience*. However, as with the various MiniDisc releases, devoted collectors are in a tiny minority, and interest in most of these is restricted to the curious alone.

DVD-AUDIO: SOUND AND SOMETIMES, VISION

DVD-Audio, or DVD-A, was launched in 2000, around the same time as Sony/Philips introduced the SACD, and swiftly proved the most advantageous of the formats in that it did not require a stand-alone player. Rather, it was compatible with already-existing DVD players, and thus proved the format of choice not only for purchasers, but also manufacturers.

A number of albums have thus been released on DVD-A, usually remixed into surround sound, ranging from individual albums through to entire catalogs. As expected, many of the earliest issues are now very much in demand.

EDISON DISCS: THE FIRST FORMAT WAR

In 1912, horrified by the lack of fidelity common to the emergent flat records, Edison launched a new form of gramophone recording, the Edison disc, which claimed to offer "true representations of vocal and instrumental music as produced by living artists. They are not mere shadows. They are the very substance of the living music, alive with all the emotions of the living artist."

Compared to other discs of the day, Edison records did sound good. But improvement came at a price. Pressed on quarter-inch-thick discs, they were both recorded and manufactured to wholly different specifications than were the shellac 78s—Edison employed a substance called condensate, which was then sprayed onto a celluloid base that was bonded to a wood-flour core. His discs also required the use of a special Edison phonograph—attempts to play Edison discs on regular players not only damaged the discs, but could also harm the player.

Few of the artists who recorded for Edison are especially collectible today—Vernon Dalmart, a pioneer of what became country music, might well be the most highly regarded. Elsewhere, the catalog (which eventually amounted to over 25,000 different releases) was littered with vaudeville singers, Hawaiian guitarists, pianists, polka dances, comedians, and novelty acts.

True, there are some very early examples of the nascent jazz and blues to be unearthed, including releases by Genevieve Gordon, Wilbur Sweatman's Brownies, Nobble Sissle, and Eubie Blake and the Frisco Jass [sic] Band. Furthermore, the first known recorded reference to jazz itself was delivered by an Edison disc: Arthur F. Collins and Byron G. Harlan's 1916 "That Funny Jas [sic] Band From Dixieland."

There are also some stellar Rachmaninov recordings to be found, the composer and the inventor being close friends and supporters. For the most part, however, Edison's discs fall into that vast corpus of early twentieth century "light entertainment" that few collectors pursue. (Although, if you're really interested, the American Sound Archives maintain a vast database of digitized recordings, while Document Records have produced a magnificent series of compilation CDs.)

Attempts to harmonize the two rival formats were destined to failure, largely because of Edison's own, very jealous, sense of proprietorship. It has also been suggested that Edison discs were unpopular because they revolved at 80 rpm, although this was *not* actually a part of the problem. In fact, 78 only became the universal standard in 1934, five years after the last Edison came off the presses.

Record players capable of adapting to both a regular disc and an Edison disc's special characteristics were eventually manufactured, but—like the records themselves—they were expensive, and they never took off. The last Edison records were manufactured in 1929.

8-TRACKS: CLUNK, CLICK, EVERY TRIP

Has any format ever been so cruelly derided as the 8-track? It was not the first innovation to be superseded by better technology, nor will it be the last. But it is the only one that is continually held up as the butt of even non-collectors' jokes.

Some, including such close relations as 2-track and 4-track tapes, have been quietly forgotten. Others—78s and 45s, most notably—are either utterly sanctified, or are constantly on the brink of a major comeback.

But 8-tracks aren't simply remembered, they are remembered with such loathing that the growing band of enthusiasts who do actively collect them spend as much time trying to justify their dementia as they do actually buying and playing the things.

The disadvantages of the format are manifold, of course. But so are the advantages, and the 8-track can also claim to have one of the most fascinating histories in modern recording industry. With the emphasis on the word *modern.*

Several designers can be considered among the fathers of the format, though in reality, each was working toward decidedly different destinations. The basis of the format is the "endless loop," a single band of tape that moves through a hollow-body cartridge (affectionately abbreviated to "cart" by modern enthusiasts), and which, when it reaches the end of the recorded program, simply begins again. The advantage of this system is that (barring malfunction, of course) one would never need to touch the tape itself.

A Toledo, Ohio, inventor, Bernard Cousino, was the first off the mark, perfecting a loop tape that he intended to be marketed toward the retail community for point-of-sale advertising. He visualized, of course, the endless repetition of a slogan or jingle that makes the modern shopping experience such a joyful one. (The in-flight or "black box" recorders utilized by the airline industry also used the endless-loop technology.)

Another pioneer was George Eash, creator of the Fidelipac cartridge favored by radio stations to carry advertisements, spot announcements, and station IDs. A third was Earl Muntz, a former used-car and TV salesman who was now working to create a personal music system for use in automobiles. The fourth innovator was Chicago-based William Powell Lear, Sr., inventor, of course, of the Lear Jet, and a renowned pioneer in the field of instruments and communications devices for use in aircraft; back in the 1930s, he was a leading figure at Motorola, the car radio manufacturer.

What distinguished the formats of each of these men was the number of tracks the tape carried; that is, how the music was stored on the tape and how the player read it. The simplest devices, Cousino and Eash's territory, utilized 2-track technology, and are best visualized as a length of tape that has been divided into two bands, lengthwise, each containing one musical program. When inserted into the player, the machine first reads one band, then when reaching a (usually metallic) marker at the end, switches over to read the other band, and so on, until the tape is removed from the unit.

Muntz's tapes, utilizing the same technology, also contained two tracks, but because they were in stereo, each of those tracks was then divided again—hence the format was called "4-track." Lear's design, with four stereo tracks, requiring the tape to "turn over" after each one, therefore became the 8-track.

Although he had been experimenting with endless loops since the 1940s, Lear was inspired to action by Muntz's 4-tracks, which he began installing in his Lear Jets in 1963.

Unfortunately, both the quality of the 4-track tapes and their restricted length left him somewhat dissatisfied. The optimum length for the tape in any of these formats was no more than twenty minutes. The stereo 4-track tape was thus limited to a maximum of forty minutes' playing time; by doubling the number of tracks, the 8-track doubled the playing time too, with a loss of fidelity that was barely noticeable.

Working in partnership with one of the leading suppliers of tape heads, Nortronics, Lear also succeeded in vanquishing another of the Muntz tape's drawbacks, the need for the tape roller to enter the cartridge from the player's mechanism.

The Lear 8-track's roller was contained within, and while this would cause its own rash of problems should the tape tangle, or should the roller decompose (unforeseen at the time), it was still an improvement. Within a year, Lear was unveiling his prototype to widespread admiration.

With RCA having leaped aboard the format with a pledge to adapt its entire current catalog to the 8-track, Lear contracted with the Ford Motor Company to supply the Lear Jet 8-track as an optional extra in its 1966 models. Chrysler and GM followed suit in 1967. And, while the 8-track is remembered primarily as an in-car format, as its popularity increased, there was also vast demand for household players.

The 8-track was not a worldwide success. In the UK and Europe, where an American-style automotive culture has never been more

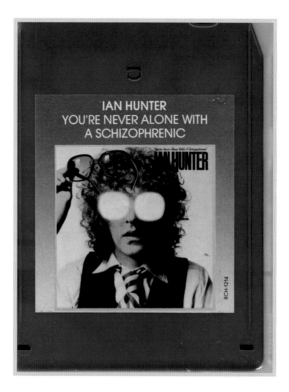

The 8-track for Ian Hunter's 1979 You're Never Alone with a Schizophrenic.

than a minority interest, the format struggled for acceptance and, by the mid-'70s, British manufacture of 8-tracks had ceased.

Back in the US, meanwhile, even the higher cost of 8-tracks when compared to LPs could not prevent the cartridge's forward march. All of the advantages that were trotted out to sell CDs in the mid-'80s—from portability and durability to non-deteriorating sound quality—were touted for 8-tracks, while fears that one's favorite records might not become available in the format (a hurdle that the competing 4-track was never able to overcome) were allayed by a virtual industry-wide leap onto the bandwagon.

The 8-track format was not perfect, of course. Among the features that modern-day comedians most enjoy abusing is the metallic "clunk" sound that the player makes as it reaches the end of one program and switches over to the next.

If this falls in a logical place—at the end of a song, for example, one swiftly becomes inured to it. However, particularly in the early days of 8-tracks, logic sadly appears to have been strangely lacking as record companies simply dubbed an entire album onto the tape, irrespective of where the program ended (and, therefore, where the clunks fell).

The only concession made was to fade the song out a few seconds before the end of the program, then fade it back in once the next was under way, and it is by no means unusual for a song to begin literally seconds before it needs to be faded, then to pick up again one resounding clunk later.

Further problems arise with especially lengthy tracks—"Southern Man" on Crosby, Stills, Nash and Young's *4 Way Street* 8-track begins on one program, continues across the next, and finally concludes on a third!

Not until the early '70s did record companies make a concerted effort to address this problem, at least where possible ("Southern Man" was never sorted out). Simply rearranging songs so that each program contained complete performances was a popular and sensible method, although this could create problems of its own. Concept and thematic albums, for example, would emerge utterly jumbled, with Genesis's *The Lamb Lies Down on Broadway* just one of those that sheds all semblance to its intended nature via the transference of much of the vinyl's third side to the 8-track's second program.

Another difficulty lay in trying to even-out the playing time of each of the four programs—an expanse of blank tape at the end of one of them, after all, completely obviated the benefits of the continuous loop, and while some labels did simply shrug their shoulders and let purchasers figure out what to do next, others found an ingenious solution that has resulted in what are now some very popular variations. Bonus tracks would be added, either repeated from elsewhere on the album, or imported from another release entirely.

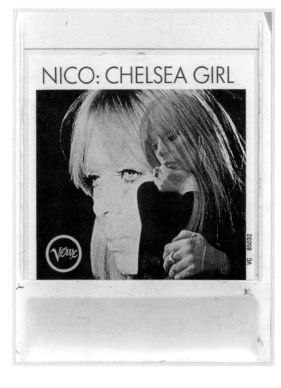

Until the reissues started rolling in, Nico's Chelsea Girls *was hard enough to find on vinyl. The 8-track was even tougher.*

This wasn't always a grandiose gesture. Elton John's *Greatest Hits Volume One,* for example, boasts a final track comprising a little less than half of a repeated "Bennie and the Jets." But several of Capitol's Beatles 8-tracks are prized for their additional inclusions—*Early Beatles* adds "Roll Over Beethoven" to the program, *The Beatles' Second Album* gains "And I Love Her," and *Something New* is bolstered by "Thank You Girl."

Even more exciting, from the collector's point of view, were those occasions when a well-intentioned engineer would return to the original master tape and extract a performance deleted from the album itself, using that to plug the gap. A mere handful of these have been documented, but all are extremely sought after by collectors, and of course, they fetch prices to match.

The Beatles' *Sgt. Pepper's Lonely Hearts Club Band* offers a slightly extended version of the title track reprise, while Lou Reed's *Berlin* includes approximately thirty seconds of lazy piano appended to the opening title track that is unavailable in any other format (Reed himself even blocked its inclusion on the 1998 CD remaster). Even more desirable is Pink Floyd's *Animals*, which features an unabridged version of "Pigs on the Wing," a piece presented in two abbreviated parts on vinyl, cassette, and CD.

A number of 8-tracks also offered up exclusive, alternate mixes, either on individual songs or throughout the entire album. According to several enthusiasts, King Crimson's *Court of the Crimson King* and

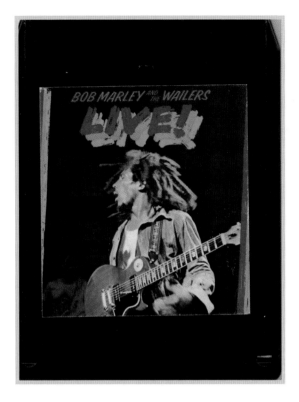

Bob Marley and the Wailers' Live! 8-track, from 1975.

Steeleye Span's *Commoners Crown* are both numbered among this select band of collectibles.

Another area of the 8-track collectors market is the format's packaging. The nature of the cartridge denied consumers many of the extras that LPs were beginning to incorporate—free posters, inserts, and so on. Proof-of-purchase slips were thus inserted, to allow the buyer to receive such goodies free of charge from the record company. Other issues, notably double album/tape packages, boasted custom boxes that are a thrill to find today.

Few, if any, record companies maintained their own 8-track manufacturing facilities. Rather, the majority entrusted both production and distribution to outside companies, with the majority opting for the market leader, Ampex. (Orrtronics, pioneers of its own superior, but ultimately doomed, 8-track format also did some manufacturing.)

This was obviously an ideal situation in the normal course of events. However, two of the 8-track hobby's most enduring rarities testify to what could happen when that course became disrupted.

In 1969, Reprise cancelled plans to release a new album by Frank Sinatra and Antonio Carlos Jobim, the follow-up to their 1967 collaboration *Francis Albert Sinatra and Antonio Carlos Jobim*. However, production and shipping of the *Sinatra-Jobim* 8-track was already well under way at Ampex's Illinois plant, when the Reprise label, in Los Angeles, made the decision to cancel the release. Though just a handful of copies are known to have survived the ensuing recall, still the 8-track stands as the only format in which this album was made available.

Five years later, Ampex's production schedule and Reprise's new release policy came into conflict once again, this time over Alan Price's *Savaloy Dip: Words and Music by Alan Price*. The follow-up to the Englishman's hit soundtrack *O Lucky Man!* was similarly already in production when Reprise decided not to issue it after all. Again, a handful of 8-tracks are all that remain of this rather enjoyable LP.

The golden age of the 8-track, at least in terms of sales, arrived during the early '70s, peaking around 1974. Only then did progressive advancements in the fidelity and quality of cassette tapes (hitherto a despicably poor relation to the mighty cart) begin nibbling away at the 8-track's market share, a meal that was garnished by record company economics, since the industry was reeling from the effects of the oil embargo of 1973–'74. Cassettes were considerably cheaper and easier to manufacture than 8-tracks, required fewer manufacturing materials, and demanded less storage space as well.

It wasn't cassette tapes alone that were cheaper to manufacture. Cassette players, too, required less effort, and by 1976, none of the leading American cartridge deck manufacturers were doing more than treading water with existing models, while putting their research-and-development efforts into cassette players and recorders. The cassette industry adopted the Dolby noise reduction system, for example. For the most part, 8-tracks ignored it.

Too late, the 8-track began to fight back. Recordable tapes (and, of course, machines) were introduced to compete with the cassette's

The Residents

"The Beatles Play the Residents and the Residents Play the Beatles"
(RALPH RR 0577, 7-INCH, 1977)

Blorp Esette (LAFMS 005, LP, 1975)

Freak Show (EAST SIDE DIGITAL OP 011, BLACK-VINYL PROMO LP, 1991)

"It's a Man's Man's Man's World" (UK KOROVA KOW 36, 7-INCH, PICTURE SLEEVE, 1984)

Meet the Residents (RALPH RR 0274, ORIGINAL MIX, LP, 1974)

The Pal TV LP (UK DOUBLEVISION DVR 17, RED-VINYL LP, 1985)

Please Do Not Steal It, Various artists (RALPH DJ 7901, PROMO LP, 1979)

"Santa Dog" (RALPH RR 1272, 7-INCH, 1972)

"Satisfaction" (RALPH 0776, BLACK-VINYL 7-INCH, PICTURE SLEEVE, 1976)

Uncle Willie's Highly Opinionated Guide to the Residents
(RALPH RZ 9302, PROMO CD, 1993)

most obvious advantage, while the storage issue was challenged by two distinct design changes: the folding Mini-8, which enjoyed a brief flicker of popularity during the mid-'70s, and a revolutionary effort from the Motorola company that was little more than half the size of traditional cartridges.

Neither truly took off, however, and even if they had, the cassette had one more trick up its sleeve, as the tape makers teamed up with car manufacturers. The day when more cassette players than 8-track players were installed in automobile dashboards was the day we kissed the cartridge goodbye.

Sensing the direction the wind was blowing, 8-track manufacturers themselves began to cut back on the quality of cartridges, with inevitable results.

If 8-tracks had one major flaw (one that was readily exploited by supporters of the cassette format), it concerned reliability. Tape jammed, twisted, or snapped, rollers slipped out of alignment, and so on. Of course, as quality control and design standards stagnated and slipped, these problems became more pronounced. Soon, it seemed, more new 8-tracks were turning up faulty than not, and the cassette took another mighty stride toward supremacy.

Many of the 8-track collecting hobby's most prized releases date from these last, desperate years, with particular emphasis on punk rock and new wave issues. A mint, sealed copy of the Sex Pistols' 1977 album *Never Mind the Bollocks, Here's the Sex Pistols* (Warner Bros. M8 3147) caused waves of disbelief and controversy to sweep through the 8-track community when one sold for $100 during the mid-'90s.

The tape itself is not especially rare, certainly not when compared with the Beatles' *Deluxe Three Pack*, valued at over $2,000, or the aforementioned *Sinatra Jobim*. However, like Lou Reed's legendary *Metal Machine Music*, there is an aura surrounding *Bollocks* that simply does not fit in with the popular image of the 8-track collection—that is, a teetering pile of Peter Frampton, Jethro Tull, Elton John, and country-and-western carts.

In fact, a surprising number of prized and primal punk albums did make it onto 8-track in the US, including issues by Patti Smith, the Jam, Television, the Ramones, Blondie, and Elvis Costello. Track back into the genre's prehistory, meanwhile, and early albums by the Stooges, the MC5, and the Velvet Underground can also be found on 8-track.

Prices for many of these items tend to be high. But only in the latter instances, where manufacturing figures were significantly lower than even the famously minuscule vinyl pressing runs, do the tapes truly merit the attention. In the other instances, it is the collectors' own perceptions of an item's collectibility, as opposed to its actual physical rarity, that buoys the market.

A budget-priced T Rex compilation, drawing tracks from 1967–1971.

As a general rule of thumb, a rare LP is always going to be rarer on 8-track. However, the relatively minor corner of the collectors market that 8-tracks occupy ensures that, with but a handful of exceptions, prices for carts are never going to begin attaining the same heights as vinyl.

It is well-known, for example, that the Yardbirds' *Live with Jimmy Page* LP was on sale for less than a week in 1971 before an injunction from Page saw it pulled from stores. Less well-publicized is the 8-track version that, due to a slightly later shipping date, saw the light of day for just twenty-four hours before the ax fell. The LP is today worth close to three figures; a 2000 CD reissue on the Mooreland St. label, similarly quashed at Page's insistence, looks set to join it there. But the 8-track is scarcely even noticed by collectors, despite its being many times rarer than either of them.

That collectors are so dismissive of even the 8-track's greatest rarities simply echoes the public response to the format's demise. As the 1970s ended and the 1980s began, fewer and fewer new releases made the stores, and by 1983, the battle was over. Only a handful of major labels were even producing the old format any longer, and of those that were, all had withdrawn them from stores by the end of the year.

The 8-track format continued to be sold through the RCA (now BMG) and Columbia House record and tape clubs for a few years longer, but even there, interest was fading. Among the very last releases

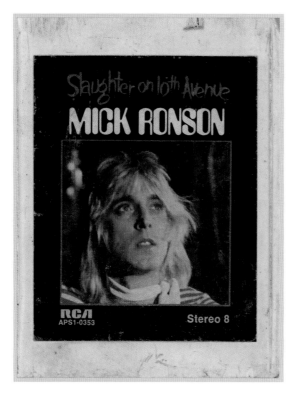

Mick Ronson's masterful Slaughter on 10th Avenue *solo debut.*

offered were John Lennon's *Live in NYC* (1986), George Harrison's *Cloud 9* (1987), Michael Jackson's *Bad* (1987), and Chicago's *XIX* (1988). It is an indication of how poorly even these mega-smashes sold, however, that many people—collectors of those particular artists included—are completely unaware that the 8-tracks exist. The digital era had, after all, already dawned. Today, it seems impossible that such a dinosaur as the 8-track could ever have walked the earth in tandem with the CD.

Even at the end, the format still had life in it, if only to keep people company as they joined the national exodus to Seattle at the end of the 1980s—for whatever reason, the "most live-in-able city in America" was, for a time, also the repository for some of the best used 8-track collections around.

It was already too late, though. The assassination of 8-track, like the vanquishing of vinyl, was as underhand an undertaking as you'll find this side of Agatha Christie. One day, the industry simply decided that enough was enough, that vinyl and cassettes had taken over the market, that CDs were coming, and there no room for anything more.

From being a vital component of every release, the schedule grew increasingly selective. Then, when sales plummeted, the Moguls sat back and said, "See, we told you. Nobody buys the things anymore."

But vinyl wasn't really dead, and maybe 8-track isn't either.

They Must Be Giants and Spinal Tap both released albums with cartridge-shaped promos; Mudhoney toyed with the format as well; and fellow Seattleites Sick and Wrong went the whole hog and released their debut EP on 8-track and cassette only.

Sonic Youth collected 8-tracks, as did members of Gumball. The Cramps' Lux Interior once declared that he'd like to have seen the band's entire catalog reissued on 8-track, and there was even a fanzine devoted to the things, brilliantly titled *8-Track Mind*.

And then, of course, there's the collector mentality, which simply *must* have every record, in every format, by their favorites.

When 8-track collecting first began to organize itself during the early '90s, it was initially viewed as little more than an offshoot of the then-burgeoning market in nostalgia-kitsch. Either that, or as a peculiarly damaged cult.

However, there was some support. A 1993 article in *Alternative Press* magazine extolling the sonic virtues of 8-tracks in preference to some of the shoddily mastered CDs then on the market, raised some eyebrows, and even prompted a wry commentary in a subsequent issue of *Billboard*.

The nationwide launch of the now-legendary (but sadly, after one hundred issues, defunct) *8-Track Mind* fanzine focused further attention on the hobby. The advent of eBay and other Internet auction sites had an immeasurable effect, as whole new supplies of vintage tapes were suddenly launched onto the market.

Cart collecting remains a backwater today, but it is probably better off for it. Few dealers price their 8-tracks higher than a couple of bucks;

According to legend, David Bowie's record label of the time, RCA, hated Low *so much that they didn't even want to release it. Once they agreed, of course, an 8-track was inevitable.*

few collectors (the aforementioned Sex Pistols fan notwithstanding) would pay any more than that.

In addition, the field remains wide open to both research and finds, all conducted in the knowledge that their discovery may not make the finder rich or famous. But they will leave him or her with a collectible rarity that nobody else had probably even dreamed existed.

ENHANCED CDS: ALL THIS AND MOVING PICTURES, TOO

Widely regarded as the future of CDs when the format was first ignited in 1995, "enhanced" CDs—also known as CD+ and CD-Extra—offered conventional CD releases with additional multimedia material accessible via a computer equipped with the necessary (and readily obtainable) software.

It was a remarkable invention. Video footage could now be added to discs, together with displays of discographical and biographical information, extra illustrative material, and so much more. In many ways enhanced CDs were comparable to the simultaneously emergent CD-ROM, the difference being that enhanced CDs also allowed one to enjoy the music without access to a computer. Moreover, enhanced CDs usually retailed at the same cost as a regular issue, providing the enhancements as a free bonus.

A number of acts, across the musical spectrum, latched on to the enhanced CD format very early on, with mid-1995 releases by Sarah McLachlan, Moby, 2 Minutes Hate, Bush, and the picturesquely named Techno Squid Eats Parliament. Other early entrants included Tom Robinson, London Suede, Marc Almond, and even Bob Dylan, whose 1995 *Greatest Hits Volume 3* collection included a wealth of additional material.

Unfortunately, conflict over the required operating systems ensured that buying enhanced CDs swiftly degenerated into a crapshoot. The industry's attempts to standardize the format were hampered both by the non-availability of appropriate software for some operating systems, and by the software makers' own updating of their product. Somehow it doesn't seem like a lot of fun to cram your hard drive with downloads, upgrades, and patches every time you want to watch a video flickering in a one-inch square.

Enhanced CDs are still appearing today, some with fascinating bonus material, and others offering an accompanying video or live footage, additional liner notes, and sundry other items. As collectibles, however, they have yet to take off as anything more than curios.

EPS: ALBUMS ON INSTALLMENT PLANS

EPs, short for Extended Play, are the most evocative of all "classic" vinyl stars. Neither single nor album, neither a quick burst of glorious noise (surely the hallmark of a truly great 45) or an overlong succession of songs you could live without (sadly, the hallmark of too many LPs), EPs offered four songs tailored for shocking, rocking fun, and through the 1950s in America and the 1960s in Britain, they served up some of the greatest music of the age.

The EP grew, naturally, out of the developing popularity of the 45, when the Columbia label—at the height of the so-called War of the Speeds with RCA—decided to counter that company's newfangled single with the mini-album. That format did not take off, but the principle was sound, and EPs began to move into the limelight.

The vast majority were pressed in considerably smaller runs than most 45s (or LPs), ensuring that even relatively unknown issues today can fetch high sums. Move into the realm of the accepted superstars of the rock 'n' roll era, and prices can balloon—it has been estimated that, in terms of percentages, there are more rare and high-priced EPs in the American rock 'n' roll catalog than either 45s, 78s, or LPs. Anybody who has devoted time to seeking out the things will doubtless agree.

Elvis, of course, was at the forefront of the EP release schedules. Between 1956–'59, RCA issued some two dozen Presley EPs, excerpting his albums and movie soundtracks, rounding up recent hits, or even offering all-new material. Many received custom picture sleeves, which of course only increases their modern worth even further.

The Cramps

"Bikini Girls with Machine Guns" (ENIGMA EPRO 253, 12-INCH PROMO, 1989)

"Fever" (UK ILLEGAL 017, 7-INCH, FULL-BAND PICTURE SLEEVE, 1980)

"Goo Goo Muck" (IRS 9021, COLORED-VINYL 7-INCH PROMO, 1981)

Gravest Hits (ILLEGAL SP 501, 12-INCH, COLORED SLEEVES, 1979)

"Human Fly" (VENGEANCE 668, 7-INCH, 1978)

Lux (UK WINDSONG 4; NUMBERED 3X12-INCH BOX SET, WITH T-SHIRT AND BOOK; 1991)

Off the Bone (UK ILLEGAL ILP 012, WHITE-LABEL LP WITH DIFFERENT MIX OF "DRUG TRAIN," 1983)

Songs the Lord Taught Us (ILLEGAL SP 007, LP, SLEEVE DATED, 1979)

Stay Sick! (ENIGMA 268, PROMO LP, 1990)

The Way I Walk (VENGEANCE 666, 7-INCH, 1978)

Some excellent collections are included in this canon. In 1956, two volumes of *Elvis* highlighted the King's first album in pocket-money pieces; that same year, *Elvis Presley* offered up his dramatic versions of "Blue Suede Shoes," "Tutti Frutti," "I Got a Woman," and "Just Because," together with a minefield of sleeve variations that have fascinated collectors for forty-five years.

To even begin to dwell on the Presley catalog, however, is to overlook a vast corpus of equally exciting issues by other artists. Gene Vincent's *Bluejean Bop, Gene Vincent and the Blue Caps,* and *Record Date* albums were each split across three EPs apiece during 1957–'58; Decca made a similar gesture with great swathes of the Bill Haley catalog. Sun released four fine Jerry Lee Lewis EPs; Del-Fi produced two Ritchie Valens EPs; and the first five EPs issued by Specialty were all by Little Richard and include some of his most incendiary performances. And this is merely to scratch the surface. Many collectors believe rock 'n' roll is best experienced on 45. But it is best collected on EP.

The late '50s saw the EP's popularity decline considerably. LPs were becoming more affordable, and perhaps appeared more attractive to younger customers. Suddenly it no longer seemed necessary to release LPs on "installment plans," and by 1962, only a handful of US labels were still issuing EPs in any great numbers, RCA (more Elvis) and Vee-Jay paramount among them.

The latter's Four Seasons EP catalog, two volumes of *The Four Seasons Sing*, is a wonder to behold, while Dee Clark's *Keep It Up*, originally released on the Abner subsidiary before being reissued on Vee-Jay, is also a fine find if your tastes drift towards classic Northern Soul.

For many collectors, however, mention of the Vee-Jay EP catalog brings just one title to mind: the Beatles' *Souvenir of Their Visit to America*, featuring four songs from the already oft-recycled *Introducing* LP. Advertising for the issue, incidentally, found a new meaning for the initials EP—"economy package."

Souvenir . . . sold close to 80,000 copies, a respectable quantity, but strangely, not enough to push it into the chart. Two subsequent Beatles EPs released by Capitol sold less but climbed higher: *Four By the Beatles* reached No. 92; *4-by the Beatles* hit No. 68. In defense of those lowly positions (this is the biggest band in the world, after all), it should be pointed out that EPs were costlier than 45s, were less well promoted, and offered no new material.

The *4-by* concept was not unique to the Beatles issues. Prompted by the success of EPs in the UK, Capitol contemplated launching an entire series of so-called super singles, featuring four tracks apiece. The Beatles issue was preceded by a Beach

Manfred Mann's extended play catalog was among the best produced by any of the British Invasion bands. This was their 1965 entry.

Boys EP, *4-by the Beach Boys*, featuring "Wendy," "Little Honda" (both of which charted, at No. 44 and No. 65, respectively), "Don't Back Down," and "Hushabye." Unfortunately, the super-single concept did not travel much further, and in December 1965, the releases were deleted from the catalog, and the EP as a flourishing American format was at an end.

In Britain, however, the EP survived until around 1967; was reborn as the three- or four-song maxi-single in the early '70s; and has never truly gone away. A strong revival during the punk era at the end of the 1970s was followed by the adaptation of the EP format first for 12-inch singles, and more recently, for CD singles. Many modern artists, particularly those with a strong feel for pop traditions, claim even now that they think of the three- or four-track CDs that for a long time were practically *de rigueur* in the UK marketplace, as EPs. In the meantime, of course, the 7-inch vinyl forebears just keep on rising in value.

Little Richard

"Baby Don't You Want a Man Like Me" (MODERN 1018, 7-INCH, PICTURE SLEEVE, 1966)

"Get Rich Quick" (RCA VICTOR 47-4582, 7-INCH, 1952)

"Good Golly Miss Molly" (SPECIALTY 624, 7-INCH, PICTURE SLEEVE, 1958)

Here's Little Richard (SPECIALTY 100, LP, 1957)

Little Richard (RCA VICTOR CAL 416, EP, 1956)

Little Richard (SPECIALTY SP 2103, LP, NO TRIANGLE ON FRONT PHOTO, 1958)

"Little Richard's Boogie" (PEACOCK 1658, 7-INCH, 1956)

"Please Have Mercy on Me" (RCA VICTOR 47-5025, 7-INCH, 1952)

"Taxi Blues" (RCA VICTOR 47-4392, 7-INCH, 1951)

"Why Did You Leave Me?" (RCA VICTOR 47-4772, 7-INCH, 1952)

Four hit singles on one disc!

Jacques Brel

American Debut (COLUMBIA AWS 324, LP, 1959)

Babar/Pierre et le loup (FRANCE BARCLAY 80 406, LP, 1972)

En public olympia 1961 (FRANCE PHILIPS 6332 077, LP, 1961)

Jacques Brel 3 (FRANCE PHILIPS 70-473, 10-INCH LP, 1958)

Le plat pays (FRANCE BARCLAY 70 475, EP, PICTURE SLEEVE, 1962)

L'homme de la mancha (FRANCE BARCLAY 80 381, LP, 1968)

Les bon bons 67 (FRANCE BARCLAY 71 18, EP, PICTURE SLEEVE, 1967)

Les bourgeois (FRANCE BARCLAY 70 493, EP, PICTURE SLEEVE, 1962)

Les paumes du petit matin (FRANCE BARCLAY 70 452, EP, PICTURE SLEEVE, 1962)

Vesoul (FRANCE BARCLAY 80 373, 10-INCH LP, 1968)

EPs were launched in Britain in 1954, in emulation of the format's success in mainland Europe. Many of France's top performers, in particular, apparently preferred the brightly sleeved EPs even to LPs, and collectors of such artists as Jacques Brel, Serge Gainsbourg, and Françoise Hardy, seeking first releases of their best-known songs, are known to pay high sums for required EPs.

Although the earliest British EPs were issued in generic record company sleeves, they swiftly began aping the Continental predilection for colorful jackets, often featuring unique photographs and artwork. It is crucial to remember, when collecting EPs, that the sleeve is as important as the music.

In Britain, the format was initially the preserve of middle-of-the-road and jazz artists, many of whom utilized the format not only for their more popular releases, but also to highlight successful aspects of their live shows. Jazzman Chris Barber, for example, turned tracks on several of his EPs over to Lonnie Donegan, a band member whose "skiffle" music style was showcased with a few numbers during the Chris Barber Jazz band's own performance. Donegan quit Barber's band soon after; *The Lonnie Donegan Skiffle Group* and *Backstairs Session*, the young iconoclast's first solo EPs, still stand as prime examples of the music's early years.

The Vipers skiffle group, led by future children's TV host Wally Whyton, also cut three extraordinary EPs: two volumes of *Skiffle Music* and *Skiffling Along with the Vipers*. Other skiffle acts to look for on EP include the Avon Cities Skiffle Group, Ken Colyer, Bob Cort, Chas McDevitt, and even blues legend Alexis Korner. Be warned, however. They won't be cheap.

Into the early '60s, jazz and light pop continued to dominate the EP release schedules. From 1959, Acker Bilk's *Mr. Acker Bilk Sings* is a popular issue, not only as, indeed, a rare opportunity to hear Bilk put down his trademark clarinet for a time, but also for a tiny credit published on the back of the picture sleeve: "Recording balance—Joe Meek."

Meek would soon spring to prominence as perhaps the most visionary independent British producer of all time, with a sprawling discography of considerable value. Less well-documented, his early years twiddling knobs for other producers (in this instance, Denis Preston) have caused some extraordinarily unexpected records to spring to collecting prominence.

Also popular in Britain at this time were EPs by comedians (a prime example is Tony Hancock's *Little Pieces of Hancock*), such children's entertainers as Uncle Mac, and pianists Russ Conway and Mrs. Mills. The pianists' releases, on Columbia

Vee-Jay

"Ask Me Why," The Beatles (VEE-JAY SPEC DJ 8, 7-INCH PROMO, 1964)

"Baby It's You," The Spaniels (VEE-JAY 101, RED-VINYL 7-INCH, 1953)

"Bobby Sox Baby," The Hi LiterS (VEE-JAY 184, 7-INCH, 1955)

"Fool's Prayer," The Five Echoes (VEE-JAY 156, 7-INCH, 1955)

"For Your Precious Love," Jerry Butler and the Impressions (VEE-JAY 280, 7-INCH, 1958)

"High and Lonesome," Jimmy Reed (VEE-JAY 100, RED-VINYL 7-INCH, 1953)

"Please Please Me," The Beatles (VEE-JAY 498, 7-INCH, BRACKETS LABEL, 1963)

"Please Please Me," The Beattles (VEE-JAY 498, 7-INCH, MISSPELLED LABEL, 1963)

Souvenir of Their Visit to America, The Beatles (VEE-JAY 1-903DJ, PROMO EP, 1964)

"Tell the World," The Dells (VEE-JAY 134, RED-VINYL 7-INCH, 1955)

Joe Meek Productions

Away from It All, The Tornadoes (DECCA LK 4552, LP, 1963)

"Diggin' for Gold," David John and the Mood (UK PARLOPHONE R5301, 7-INCH, 1965)

Dream of the West, The Outlaws (UK HMV CLP 1489, LP, 1961)

"I Take It That We're Through," The Riot Squad (UK PYE 7N 17092, 7-INCH, 1966)

"Jack the Ripper," Screaming Lord Sutch (UK DECCA F11598, 7-INCH, 1964)

"The Kennedy March," Joe Meek (UK DECCA F11796, 7-INCH, 1963)

"Magic Star," Kenny Hollywood (DECCA F11546, 7-INCH, 1962)

"March of the Spacemen," The Thunderbolts (DOT 16496, 7-INCH, 1963)

Tom Jones, Tom Jones (UK COLUMBIA SEG 8464, EP, 1965)

"Whatcha Gonna Do Baby?" Jason Eddy and the Centremen (UK PARLOPHONE R5388, 7-INCH, 1965)

and Parlophone respectively, are among the most common of all EPs of the pre-Beatles era. But, as domestic rock 'n' rollers began their ascent, the EP began to shake off its somewhat dusty image.

Tommy Steele, often described as Britain's first rock 'n' roller, issued nine EPs for Decca between 1956–60, though it must be confessed that long before that sequence reached its end, Steele's transformation into an all-round family entertainer was well under way. Certainly by 1958, his most innovative years were behind him, which left the field wide open for a new King of rock 'n' roll. And this one would not be abdicating.

Cliff Richard and the Shadows, both individually and collectively, were responsible for a wealth of fabulous EPs during the 1950s and 1960s. *Serious Charge*, Richard's first EP, and *Expresso Bongo*, his fourth, both took their titles and contents from Richard's first two movies, in 1959. Following each of the soundtrack EPs, two volumes of *Cliff* and four of *Cliff Sings* excerpted his first two albums. Beginning with *Expresso Bongo,* meanwhile, Richard was also among the first British pop stars to record and release in stereo. In total, Richard issued forty-six British EPs between 1959–'68, many of which featured music that had yet to make its way onto long-playing formats.

Richard was accompanied on many of his greatest hits by the Shadows, a band that ignited their own massively successful career with the guitar instrumental "Apache," in 1960; the Shadows issued a further twenty-five EPs. Again, the contents were drawn from both fresh and previously issued sources; again, a worldwide network of collectors is hot in pursuit of both British issues and the wealth of additional titles issued elsewhere. Australia,

New Zealand, Scandinavia, Germany, and France were all hotbeds of EP activity throughout the 1960s.

The popularity of these mini-LPs was economic and technological. Although multispeed record players were coming into use, they were still very expensive. British and European EPs, revolving at 45 rpm (many American issuers preferred 33⅓), allowed the public to accumulate LPs without having to invest in new equipment—a consideration that the fans repaid by sending many EPs into the chart. Indeed, between March 1960 and December 1967, Britain actually boasted a separate EPs chart; predictably, it was dominated by Richard and the Shadows, at least until 1963. Then the Beatles issued their first EP, *Twist and Shout*, and the world turned upside down.

The Beatles became the single most successful EP act in British chart history, and that despite releasing just a dozen conventional EPs between 1963–'66. Even the abandonment of the EP chart could not halt the group—their thirteenth and final EP simply took over the singles chart instead. Issued as an LP in America, December 1967's *Magical Mystery Tour* was a unique double EP in Britain, where it climbed to No. 2, held off the top spot by "Hello Goodbye," a regular 45 excerpted from the same EP.

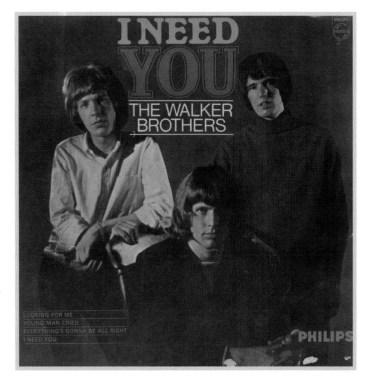

They weren't brothers, but the Walkers were huge in mid-'60s Britain. This was their first UK EP.

Richard, the Shadows, and the Beatles were by far the most prolific issuers of EPs during the 1960s, with the majority of their releases remaining in print for several years. (The Beatles issues have even been reissued on CD, with individual sleeves recreating the original EP jackets.)

Other bands considered among the era's most collectible, however, were less prolific. Throughout the heyday of the EP, Manfred Mann released eight EPs, the Kinks just five (both have also been reissued as CD box sets); the Rolling Stones no more than three (all comprising non-UK album/single material); and the Who a mere one, the legendary *Ready Steady Who* (Reaction 592 001), in 1966.

However, diligent searching can uncover EPs from as far across the pop spectrum as the Bachelors, Lulu, the Walker Brothers, the Barron Knights, and all of the important Merseybeat and Motown acts. Some fascinating statistics, too, come to light as one delves deeper into the subject: The Shadows' *To the Fore* shares the title of most successful British EP of all time with Nina & Frederick's eponymous EP, with a whopping 115-week chart life. And the Beach Boys' *Hits* spent more weeks at No. 1 (thirty-four) than any other release.

Most EP collectors pull down the curtains on the era with *Magical Mystery Tour;* some even fold before that, with the cessation of the EP chart and the corresponding abandonment of the format elsewhere around the UK industry.

However, the maxi-single boom of the early '70s does have its adherents, with the Dawn progressive label releasing a string of very collectible issues, including two UK chart-toppers, Mungo Jerry's "In the Summertime" and "Baby Jump." Other successful maxi-singles included the Who's 1970 opus *Excerpts from Tommy,* the Rolling Stones' "Street Fighting Man," and several releases within the Fly label's *Magnifly,* and from RAK's *Replay* series.

Finally, for collectors unable to spend the increasingly high sums that classic EPs now demand, the UK See for Miles label has done an admirable job compiling many of these onto CD in the *EP Collection* series, with the packaging including illustrations of the original artwork. Beware, however—several of these issues have themselves now gone out of print, and the series as a whole is rapidly becoming a collectible in its own right.

EXPLICIT CHAPTER: I CAN'T BELIEVE YOU JUST SAID THAT

Music censorship might not be as old as music, but it is certainly as old as recorded music. Did 1928 America really believe that Duke Ellington's "The Mooche" (Brunswick 4122) was an incitement to rape? Did *Variety* truly announce, in 1931, that songs with suggestive or otherwise objectionable titles would no longer be included in the trade publication's pop chart? And was "(I'm Your) Hoochie Coochie Man" genuinely one of the titles singled out for blacklisting?

Everybody knows that Elvis Presley was requested not to swivel his hips on the *Ed Sullivan Show* in 1957. It isn't so widely recalled that, two years earlier, Alan Freed's *Rock 'n' Roll Dance Party* was yanked from the network schedules after viewers saw Frankie Lymon dancing with a white girl.

The strange tale of "Louie Louie," investigated by FBI agents convinced that its lyrics contained some deeply, darkly disturbing obscenity, has become the subject of learned books and articles. But what of the equally bizarre saga of Van Morrison's "Gloria," so widely considered obscene that even a custom-built clean version by the Shadows of Knight was initially viewed with some suspicion?

The tale of censorship in music is as wry as it is, on occasion, weird. In Britain, where the BBC monopolized the airwaves, it was once an unwritten law of commerce that a record that landed a broadcast ban stood a greater chance of becoming a chart success than one that hadn't—a rule that was tested (and found to be absolutely correct) by artists as far afield as Twinkle, Judge Dread, and Frankie Goes to Hollywood.

Elsewhere, the varied applications of Chuck Berry's "Ding-a-Ling" (banned not from radio, but from television, after Berry's wrist movements were seen to be suggestive) seem childishly tame when compared to the dirty deeds perpetrated in the name of pop today. But the powers that be have long since learned their lesson. Even the most explicit record is no longer publicly banned. Instead, it simply doesn't get played.

In America, the issue of banishing records from the airwaves is confused somewhat by the absence of a central broadcasting authority such as Britain's BBC or IBA (Independent Broadcasting Authority), both of whose duties include a spot of moral watchdogging.

Recent years, however, have seen censors of another sort move into that void, in the form of the giant corporate retailers whose family-oriented policies have seen the retailers grow increasingly resistant to new releases that fail to meet certain moral criteria.

It is within this field that many collectors are finding variations on commonly available CDs that, while never likely to be declared true rarities, are certain to elude completists in years to come. The fact that many of them offer a wholly distorted view of what the original album was trying to say only adds to the fascination.

Slicing up albums to make them palatable to the masses is not, of course, a new practice. In 1962, Columbia bade Bob Dylan revise his forthcoming *The Freewheelin' Bob Dylan* (Columbia CL 1986) LP lest one track, "Talking John Birch Blues," inflame the then-influential society of the same name. In 1966, early pressings of Jefferson Airplane's *Takes Off* debut (RCA LPM 3584) were remastered to excise three songs seen as overtly promoting sex and drugs.

Deleting odd references from songs, too, has a long and proud history. Also in 1966, Lou Christie was forced to rerecord a lyric in his single "Rhapsody in the Rain" (MGM 13473) after radio found it sexually explicit—the single was then re-pressed and reissued with the letters "DJ" added to the matrix number in the run-off groove.

In the UK in 1970, the change of one simple word made the difference between the latest Kinks single, "Lola" (Pye 7N 17961), fading into oblivion or becoming a major hit. Singer Ray Davies actually flew home from the band's latest US tour to replace the word "Coca" (as in "Cola) with "cherry," to avoid contravening the BBC's strict policy on not advertising commercial products. Weeks later, "Lola" was No. 1 and British Kinks collectors have spent the last forty-plus years seeking the few thousand copies of the unaltered version that made it onto the streets.

The notion of providing "cleaned-up" versions of potentially offensive songs to radio also goes back at least to the late '60s. In 1967, psychedelic band John's Children recorded a new version of their "Desdemona" mini-hit after British radio objected to the line "Lift up your skirt and fly" (it was replaced with "Why do you have to lie?"). Unfortunately, radio then lost interest in playing the song altogether, and the rerecording exists only on a handful of rare test pressings.

Other examples abound. The first promo singles of Pink Floyd's "Money" were lifted directly from the group's *Dark Side of the Moon* album, with the word "bullshit" clearly audible. The disc was hastily withdrawn and replaced with an expletive-deleted edition. Two years later, Bob Dylan's "Hurricane" was similarly treated; "shit" was removed and the edited version was released with the legend "Special Rush Reservice" printed on the label.

Since that time, bleeps and edits have become a part of the furniture—so much so that, when an old song is heard on the radio today, even listeners familiar with the original might not notice the excision of sundry choice lines and rhymes. However, it was not until the late-'80s industry-wide adoption of Parental Guidance–type labels that these "cleaned-up" recordings also became available to the general public.

Van Morrison

BBC Classic Tracks (WESTWOOD ONE, TRANSCRIPTION DISC, 1991)

Blowin' Your Mind (BANG 218, STEREO LP WITH UNCENSORED "BROWN EYED GIRL," 1967)

"Brown Eyed Girl" (PHILCO HP 16, HIP-POCKET RECORD, 1968)

An Evening with Van Morrison (WB, 2-LP PROMO, 1989)

Live at the Roxy (WARNER BROS WBMS 102, PROMO, 1979)

Moondance (DIRECT DISC SD 16604, AUDIOPHILE PRESSING, 1981)

A Sense of Wonder (UK MERCURY MERH 54, LP WITH "CRAZY JANE ON GOD," 1985)

"Summertime in England" (WB PRO A 911, 12-INCH PROMO, 1980)

Them, Them (UK DECCA DFE 8612, EXPORT EP WITH LADDER PICTURE SLEEVE, 1965)

"Wavelength" (WB PRO A 755, 12-INCH PROMO, 1978)

These labels represent a major challenge to collectors and have become a very popular specialty. They range from what has become the generic, industry-standard wording, "Parental Advisory—Explicit Lyrics," to custom issues designed by individual bands, and on to private stickers applied by retailers themselves.

In both the former and latter categories, collectibility is subjective, often centering around inappropriate usage. Copies of Frank Zappa's *Jazz from Hell*, purchased from the Pacific Northwest chain of Fred Meyer department stores, for example, bore the retailer's own "Explicit Lyrics" warning, despite the fact that the album was wholly

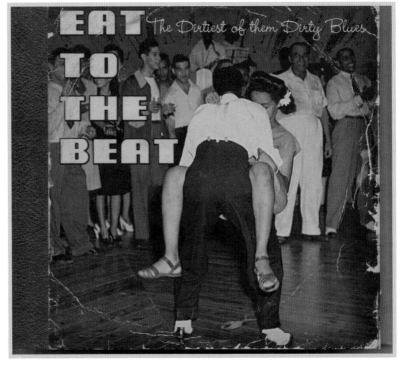

From the ever-enterprising Bear Family label, a glorious 2006 compendium of distinctly dirty blues.

Frankie Goes to Hollywood

Panic at the Whitehouse (ISLAND PR 665, EP TEST PRESSING, 1984)

Pleasurepak (ISLAND ISLP 1021; PROMO BOX INCLUDING LP; 2 X 12-INCH, 1985)

"Rage Hard" (UK ZTT ZCID 22, CD SINGLE, 1986)

Rage Hard Boxed Set (UK ZTAB 22; BOX SET, INCLUDING 7-INCH, 12-INCH, CDS; 1986)

"Relax (Original Mix)" (UK ZTT 12ZTAS 1 (1A1U), 33⅓ 12-INCH, 1983)

"Relax (Sex Mix)" (UK ZTT 12P ZTAS 1, 12-INCH PICTURE DISC, 1983)

Relax's Greatest Bits (UK ZTT CTIS 102, CASSETTE, 1984)

"Two Tribes (Hibakushu)" (UK ZTT XZIP 1, 12-INCH, 1984)

"Welcome to the Pleasuredome" (UK ZTT ZTAS 7 (7A7U), BLUE-LABEL 12-INCH, 1984)

Welcome to the Pleasuredome (UK ZTT ZTIQ 1, VINYL WITH TRACK LISTING AS CASSETTE, 1984)

instrumental. Shrink-wrapped copies still bearing this sticker may not be much more than humorous curios to many people, but censorship collectors regard them as something of a Holy Grail.

Other favorites include John Moran's *The Manson Family*, the first classical album ever to be stickered, and Serge Gainsbourg's 1986 *Love on the Beat*, which history records as the first album ever to receive a parental advisory. It warned that the album contained "explicit *French* lyrics."

Stickers produced of a band's own volition are also at a premium, again, if the shrink-wrap to which they were applied is still in place around the album (sealed or unsealed). These include the Cure's reminder, attached to its *Standing on the Beach* compilation (Elektra 60477), that the song "Killing an Arab" "has absolutely no racist overtones whatsoever . . . the Cure condemns its use in furthering anti-Arab feeling" (in recent years, the band have taken to performing the song as "Killing Another").

Also highly collectible is Ice-T's warning, applied to the ironically titled *Freedom of Speech*, that "some material may be X-tra hype and inappropriate for squares and suckers." It's worth watching out, too, for the lengthy anti-censorship diatribe accompanying another Zappa album, *Frank Zappa Meets the Mothers of Prevention*.

For several years, the use of Parental Advisory stickers appeared to be holding the forces of further censorship at bay, and any battles were fought out over album artwork (see below). Slowly, however, the climate began to change. Several stores greeted the proliferation of stickers by instituting their own policies of who such an album could or could not be sold to, in line with their policies regarding rated videos and magazines. Then, in 1991, Wal-Mart—the nation's largest retail outlet—announced it would no longer be stocking any stickered discs whatsoever, regardless of their content. With other family-oriented chain stores seemingly set to follow suit, the record

labels had just two choices: lose a massive chunk of the market, or lose the lewd lyrics. The lyrics lost.

"Clean" versions of albums involve removing—either with bleeps, gaps, or (less commonly) lyrics transplanted from elsewhere in the song—any word or phrase that can be considered objectionable. These tend to be the traditional vulgarities of "fuck," "shit," "asshole," and so on, yet during the decades through which these "PG" discs have now flourished, little attention has been granted them by discographers and researchers.

It is a void that future collectors and historians are certain to regret. Across the entire musical spectrum, the number of albums available in both "clean" and, for want of a better word, "unclean" versions certainly runs into the thousands. It will be interesting, in a few years, to discover which versions are the most common, though at present, the "clean" editions are lagging far, far behind in terms of both sales and visibility.

"PG" versions of Prince's *Emancipation* three-CD set swiftly became hard to find; so did Metallica's *Garage Inc.* (the Elektra label's first-ever censored rock record), Oasis's *Standing on the Shoulder of Giants,* and Lo-Fidelity All-Stars' *How to Operate with a Blown Mind* (Skint/Columbia 63614).

Perhaps oddly, no "classic" or even original punk rock records have yet been similarly treated, including such notoriously scatological jewels as John Lennon's *Plastic Ono Band,* the Sex Pistols' *Never Mind the Bollocks*, Marianne Faithfull's *Broken English* and the Pretenders' debut, all of which have seen high-profile rereleases since the dawn of this new age.

Readily audible in the above-mentioned records are such traditionally censured words as "fuck off" (the Pretenders), "fucking" (the Pistols and Lennon), and "cunt" (Faithfull); yet all four are

Marianne Faithfull in the Sixties

"As Tears Go By" (LONDON 9697, 1964)

"Come and Stay With Me" (LONDON 9731, 1965)

"Counting" (LONDON 20012, 1966)

"Go Away from My World" (LONDON 9802, 1965)

Go Away from My World (LONDON PS 452, 1965)

"Is This What I Get For Loving You" (LONDON 20020, 1967)

Marianne Faithfull (LONDON PS 423, 1965)

"Something Better"/"Sister Morphine" (LONDON 1022, 1969)

"Summer Nights" (LONDON 9780, 1965)

"This Little Bird" (LONDON 9759, 1965)

sold without any form of printed warning as to the nature of their contents, leading one to assume that foul language and contentious subject matter are not the only issues at stake.

Modern standards of political correctness and cultural bias would also seem to play a part in the cautionary labeling of music. Either that or, as Patti Smith remarks on her *Easter* album, "don't fuck with the past."

YOU CAN'T SHOW THAT HERE: COLLECTING "BANNED" RECORD SLEEVES

The field of banned record sleeves is, of course, a long-established favorite among record collectors. From 1966, the Beatles' "butcher cover," depicting the Fab Four draped in dismembered dolls and slabs of raw meat, is undoubtedly the best known—withdrawn on the very eve of release, the band's US label had time simply to paste a new photo over the offending one, and collectors have been painstakingly peeling them off ever since. There are, however, many more similar, if considerably less high-profile, examples of jackets that, having caused some offense to some sensitive soul, are then packed off to the darkest corners of oblivion.

The Mamas and the Papas' 1966 debut LP, *If You Can Believe Your Eyes and Ears*, exists with three different sleeves. The original depicted the four band members in a bathtub, with a toilet visible in the lower right corner of the picture.

Fearing that this oblique reference to bodily functions (even pop stars have to poo) could offend people, Dunhill revised the cover, placing a scroll over the contentious commode, emblazoned with the words "includes California Dreaming," before finally removing the toilet altogether.

The following year, the front jacket photo of Moby Grape's self-titled debut album was withdrawn in America (but not in Europe) after it was noticed that band member Don Stevenson's middle finger, as laid across his washboard, could be construed as making an offensive gesture.

In 1969, two sleeves were censored for promoting nudity; first, the original sleeve for Blind Faith's eponymous album, depicting a young, topless girl, was replaced by a band portrait; then a full-frontal-nude sleeve for John and Yoko Lennon's *Wedding Album* caused such a stir that it was repackaged in a brown paper sleeve, cut to reveal only the duo's faces.

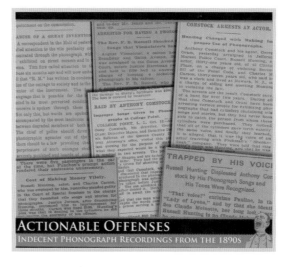

A CD compilation of risqué, rude, and occasionally downright disgusting cylinders, dating from the dawn of the recording age.

The climate was equally unyielding five years later, when the original European artwork for Roxy Music's *Country Life,* depicting two scantily clad females, one concealing her bare breasts behind her hands, was withdrawn from sale in the US and replaced with a close-up of the foliage that stands in the background of the scene.

Airbrushing came to the rescue with another banned artwork that same year—the original cover of David Bowie's *Diamond Dogs* depicted the singer sprawled out across the album's front and back, his head atop a large dog's body, and the hound's naughty parts clearly visible.

The bits were obliterated and the album went on sale—but not before a few copies of the untouched cover also made it out to send collectors frantically scouring their local emporia in search of what the English would call "the dog's bollocks" (a common phrase denoting something that is highly prized). Since those now-so-seemingly naïve days, withdrawn album art barely even makes minor headlines anymore, and rarely require radical surgery, either. When sundry retailers objected to Sky Ferreira appearing topless on the cover of her 2013 debut album, a simple sticker spared America its blushes. Likewise the buttocks that adorn St. Vincent's *MASSEDUCTION*. It's all a far cry from the absolute indifference that greeted Supertramp's pre-fame 1972 album *Indelibly Stamped*, with its own frontal image of two naked (but heavily tattooed) breasts. The collectors market, too, treats such events as all but routine—the Beatles and Bowie notwithstanding, nobody is ever going to get rich from stockpiling "banned" record sleeves. They are interesting conversation items, nothing more. Nevertheless, occasional pieces do rise above the average apathy to create a stir in wider circles.

Retail complaints over Jane's Addiction's *Ritual de lo Habitual* and Nirvana's *In Utero* both made headlines, with Jane's Addiction frontman Perry Farrell proving a formidable foe, even for the megacorporations ranged against him. His original sleeve design depicted Farrell in bed with two women, the covers drawn back to reveal a modicum of genitalia.

Having delightedly ascertained that it was his penis, as opposed to any other organ, that was creating the fuss, Farrell finally agreed to replace the art with a plain white sleeve emblazoned with the First Amendment. He then took similarly great pleasure from revealing that the original cover far outsold the "clean" one.

Nirvana's *In Utero* drew opprobrium on several levels. Included in the artwork, by vocalist Kurt Cobain, were several fetuses—an odd object to be deemed offensive, but no matter. The song title "Rape Me" also upset some people. A revised version removing the fetuses and retitling the offending song "Waif Me" was issued for sale in stores that required such alterations, though the song itself went untouched.

Like the Jane's Addiction release, copies of the doctored sleeve are far scarcer than the regular edition, perhaps indicating that the marketing departments who demand the changes are somewhat less open-minded than the consumers they seek to protect—as, perhaps, they always have been.

Possibly the most purposefully "naughty" sleeves of all time, Mom's Apple Pie's 1972 debut, is far more common in its original form—on which a beaming woman proffers the viewer a steaming pastry, sliced

to reveal a vagina within—than the hastily arranged replacement sleeve that shows the crevice plugged with a wall of barbed wire.

Another much-debated withdrawal surrounded the sleeve scheduled to accompany hip-hop act the Coup's *Party Time* album, in November 2001. As posted on the 75 Ark label's Web site that August, the sleeve depicted a massive explosion ripping through the twin towers of the World Trade Center, with band member "Boots" Riley in the foreground, holding a detonator.

The real life destruction of the building on September 11 led to the design's immediate withdrawal, with the Web site image being removed within two hours of the attack. No finished sleeves had been printed (production was due to begin that week), but printer's proofs and other preliminaries had long since been completed and circulated.

By macabre coincidence, Dream Theater's *Live Scenes from New York* (East West), issued just days before the attack, depicted both the World Trade Center towers and the Statue of Liberty engulfed in flames. This release, too, was promptly withdrawn, with stores and eBay both halting sales of the set. It remains to be seen whether these sleeves will become cherished collectors items in the future. (But spare a thought for Def Leppard, whose sleeve for 1983's *Pyromania* album—depicting the top of a skyscraper in flames—was likewise caught up in post-9/11 controversy. Several chains removed it from sale out of respect for the victims and their families.)

David Bowie's Diamond Dogs, *before RCA took the airbrush to it.*

EXPORT ISSUES: FOREIGNERS HAVE ALL THE FUN

A very specialized corner of the European 45 and LP collecting market revolves around so-called "export issues"—releases pressed in the UK during the 1960s by such major labels as the EMI and Decca groups, intended for release and distribution to countries whose own manufacturing capabilities were minimal or even nonexistent.

Readily detectable by their unique catalog numbers, many of these simply replicate standard UK releases, but are considerably more collectible than their domestic counterparts. Even more popular, however, are export issues that never received a full British release in any form.

The most attention in this area is, predictably, focused on the Beatles, the Rolling Stones, and Cliff Richard. Five different Beatles export-only singles exist, including three that have no UK counterpart

("If I Fell," "Yesterday," and "Michelle") and two more ("Hey Jude" and "Let It Be") that were issued by Apple in Britain, but as exports, bear the domestic Parlophone label.

Among the rarest export albums, meanwhile, are British Parlophone pressings of releases normally considered part of the Beatles' American catalog, and again, not conforming to any regular UK issue: *Something New*, *The Beatles' Second Album*, *Beatles VI*, and *Hey Jude*.

The Rolling Stones' export catalog is even more vast, comprising some twenty 45s and four EPs, and again including several unique issues. "Empty Heart," "Time Is on My Side," "Heart of Stone," and the live "Little Queenie" are all hotly pursued. US-only albums similarly manufactured include the radically different stateside configurations of *Out of Our Heads*, *Have You Seen Your Mother Live* (aka *Got Live If You Want It!*), and *Flowers*.

Not all export issues were lost to UK record buyers. In 1961, Cliff Richard's "Gee Whiz It's You" was produced for European use, yet the

German models Constanze Karoli and Eveline Grunwald don't quite bare all on the sleeve of Roxy Music's fourth album, but American censors were taking no chances. The ladies were airbrushed out altogether. The pair also helped Bryan Ferry translate the lyrics of his song "Bitter Sweet" into German.

Monty Python satirize the then-incumbent British Prime Minister with a lesson in how to talk just like him.

song proved so popular that copies were imported back into Britain in such numbers that the record wound up at No. 4 on the chart! In a field normally priced in the three-figure range, "Gee Whiz It's You" allows even the most impecunious collector to own at least one export 45. (Other Richard export issues are less accessible—neither "What'd I Say" nor "Angel" are at all easily found.)

The phenomenon was not restricted to these acts alone, of course— nor was it restricted to vinyl. In the early '60s, Britain was unusual in its failure to have adopted picture sleeves for singles. A number of labels, therefore, manufactured export-only sleeves that would be wrapped around both specially pressed and regular-issue singles. The Kinks' "All Day and All of the Night" and "Till the End of the Day" (7N 15981) are among the wealth of releases that exist in this form.

Export-single collecting is not an easy hobby to pursue. Releases were typically distributed throughout Europe and the British Commonwealth in quantities appropriate to the size of the host market—a few thousand here, a few thousand there. Of course a number of issues have come to light via the Internet, with many being offered by seemingly original purchasers who themselves had no idea of the records' significance to British collectors. Presumably the nature of the bidding swiftly alerted them to the true value of their holdings.

Along similar lines, several US record companies leased equipment at pressing plants in Germany and elsewhere in western Europe, to produce custom LPs for sale at American military PXs, largely in Germany. Using standard American artwork, these albums often used local labels (but printed in English), with "Manufactured in Germany" in the run-off groove. Few examples are known, though Elvis Presley's *Elvis* is a well-attested rarity.

FLEXIDISCS: BEND ME, SHAPE ME

Since its arrival on the scene during the 1930s, the flexidisc has proven itself to be *the* most . . . uh . . . flexible promotional medium available.

The advantages are manifold. Extraordinarily cheap to produce, flexidisc technology can be applied to any host material sturdy enough to withstand the light embossing required to impress the grooves. Thus, flexidiscs have appeared in the form of postage stamps (issued by the Asian nation of Bhutan), postcards, and greetings cards; they have been embedded into cereal packets and record sleeves; they appear on pieces of wood and sheets of metal.

Among the first flexidiscs to truly capture the public imagination was a series of "Hit of the Week" discs produced during the early 1930s. Manufactured from paper (sometimes adorned with a picture of the artist), with a shellac layer containing the music, these discs were produced in both 4-inch and 10-inch formats and sold at newsstands for between fifteen and twenty-five cents apiece. They were very fragile, and despite their popularity, few have survived to this day.

Since that time, flexis have filled every need. Manufacturers of almost every conceivable product have used them as promotional items. Thrift-store record bins once overflowed with instructional and advertising discs (much as they now teeter beneath similarly intentioned videocassettes).

They have been given away free with books and magazines, they have been affixed to food packages and dispatched through the mail. No matter what use a manufacturer could require, the flexi was capable of fulfilling it.

For the majority of rock and pop record collectors, the most familiar flexis are those that were distributed mounted on the covers of magazines and books; the most famous are those that the Beatles recorded as a Christmas gift to its fan-club members every year between 1963 and 1969.

Free with Britain's Record Mirror *newspaper, a 1974 flexi served up excerpts from seven past Bowie 45s, alongside the newly released "Knock on Wood."*

Containing greetings, comic routines, and snatches of music, these wholly ad-libbed performances are among the most popular of Beatles collectibles, all the more so since they rank among the only officially recorded and released Beatles performances never to have been fully reissued since the band's demise.

Only once was an authorized LP of the Christmas messages issued, 1970's *From Then to You: The Beatles' Christmas Album*—and it was again distributed only to members of the fan club. However, though these are the best-known issues, they are not the Beatles' only excursion into flexiland.

The greatest source of Beatles (and solo Beatle) flexis is, perhaps oddly, the former Soviet Union. The magazines *Club and Amateur Art Activities* and *Krugozor* both dispensed Beatles records with occasional issues during the 1970s and 1980s, including such extravagant four-song issues as "Can't Buy Me Love"/"Maxwell's Silver Hammer"/"Lady Madonna"/ "I Should Have Known Better." Many of the *Krugozor* issues, incidentally, echoed regular vinyl releases through the state-run Melodisc label.

Numerous other artists were featured on Soviet flexis; more still can be found on the so-called Polish Postcard singles issued in that country during the 1960s–'70s, and certainly a close relation of the flexi that we in the West know and love.

Flexidiscs were a popular vehicle for "special" and fan-club editions; they were also frequently distributed with fanzines and magazines: An Allman Brothers/Marshall Tucker disc that was cover-mounted to a 1975 issue of *Rolling Stone* is popular among Southern-rock aficionados. Genesis gifted the non-LP masterpiece "Twilight Alehouse" to a 1973 issue of Britain's *ZigZag*.

Robyn Hitchcock's reinvention of the Beatles' "A Day in the Life" has been a hot commodity since it appeared with a 1991 issue of *The Bob*. Mark Eitzel of American Music Club performed "Crystal Never Knows" on a disc issued with the satirical magazine *Breakfast*

The Freshest Fruits from Fruits de Mer

Various artists, *A Phase We're Going Through* (PINK MARBLE VINYL)

The Chemistry Set, *The Endless More And More* (LP/CD BOX SET WITH TEST TUBE, STAMPS, ETC.)

Various artists, "Friends of the Fish" (LATHE-CUT 7-INCH SINGLE)

Schizo Fun Addict, "Theme One" (7-INCH, PICTURE SLEEVE)

Vibravoid, *Krautrock Sensation* EP (PURPLE VINYL)

Sendelica, *Live at Crabstock* (BOX SET, ORANGE VINYL)

Various artists, *Postcards From The Deep* (7-INCH FLEXIDISC BOX SET PLUS USB)

The Pretty Things, *Live at the 100 Club* (TEST PRESSING)

Us and Them, *Julia Dreams of All the Pretty Little Horses* EP (CHARCOAL VINYL)

Stay, *Rainy Day Mushroom Pillow* EP (GOLD VINYL)

without Meat in 1990. And Michael Stipe, REM's lead singer, treated readers of *Sassy* to a solo interpretation of Syd Barrett's "Dark Globe" in 1989.

However, American collectors can pursue flexidiscs down even more esoteric paths. TOPPS, the gum manufacturers, issued a series of playable gum cards during the late '60s, featuring Motown artists. The Archies and the Monkees rank high among several pop acts featured on cereal packets, with cutaway discs actually printed into the packaging itself. The Shadows of Knight can be heard performing a song called "Potato Chip," distributed with a brand of potato chips. The Dave Clarke Five, in support of Pond's facial cream, delivered another very collectible piece of product endorsement in the mid-'60s.

Although US consumers have received by far the greatest number of now-collectible flexidiscs, the UK has served up some of the hobby's most in-demand individual issues.

One of the pioneers of the cover-mounted flexi in that country was the satirical magazine *Private Eye,* which produced a series of now-

A promotional flexi for Mick Ronson's debut LP.

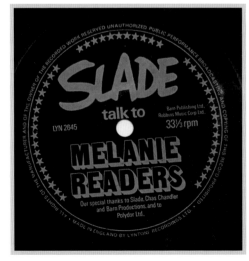

Glam superstars Slade deliver a message to readers of the UK girls' comic Melanie.

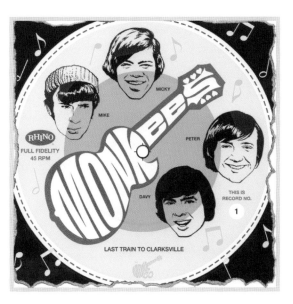

A twenty-first century rerelease for the Monkees' breakfast cereal flexi discs.

rare discs during the 1960s, featuring performances from, among others, Peter Cook and Dudley Moore, and the magazine's own takeoff on the Beatles, the Turds. These were subsequently compiled onto LP, *Private Eye's Golden Years of Sound 1964–70*, which itself was available to magazine subscribers only, and is now almost as scarce as the original discs.

The *New Musical Express* weekly produced a string of flexis during the early-to-mid-'70s, featuring, among others, Curved Air, the Faces, Monty Python, Emerson Lake and Palmer, and Alice Cooper. The latter two flexis are especially sought after today, since both contained what was then otherwise unavailable material.

Both discs were two-sided, one dedicated to medleyed excerpts from the group's latest album (ELP's *Brain Salad Surgery*, Cooper's *Billion Dollar Babies*), and the other given over to, respectively, a US-only B-side, "Brain Salad Surgery," which would not be given a full

UK release until its inclusion on the *Works Vol. 2* album five years later, and the session outtake "Slick Black Limousine," since reissued on several Cooper anthologies, but never included on a regular LP.

Missing from any other Cooper release, however, is a brief moment of speech appended to the excerpt of "Unfinished Suite" on side A— before the dentist drill starts up, and the pliers begin removing teeth, a sinisterly ethereal disembodied voice asks simply, "Have you ever had gas before?" Priceless.

High values also attach themselves to complete issues of a British music magazine called *Flexipop*, active through the early-to-mid-'80s, and offering, cover-mounted to every issue, colored vinyl flexidiscs by some of the biggest stars of the day.

These are especially valued, since again, the emphasis was on rare and unreleased material. Paul Weller of the Jam donated "Pop Art Poem" and a demo of "Boy About Town" (issue 2). Adam and the Ants recorded a version of the Village People's "YMCA," realigned as "ANTS" (issue 4). Soft Cell delivered up one track from their very first, privately produced EP *Mutant Moments* (issue 12). The Cure provided "Lament" (issue 22), and these are just a few of the many goodies presented by this enterprising publication. A mere handful of tracks from this impressive archive have since appeared on CD, via the individual bands' own anthologies and collections. Many more, however, await their rediscovery.

By their very nature, flexidiscs are difficult to find in Mint condition. They are easily bent, torn, and otherwise damaged, becoming utterly unplayable through everyday wear and tear that would not affect a vinyl disc.

However, as a repository for some genuine curios and rarities within so many bands' catalogs, they cannot be overlooked for a second. Whether it's David Cassidy sending greetings to readers of an early '70s teenybop magazine or Dick Clark imparting "inside stories" via a giveaway with 1973's *20 Years of Rock and Roll* compilation LP . . . whether it's EMI heralding a Cliff Richard box set with a flexi excerpting the best of its contents or a 1987 Guns n' Roses tour

Fruits de Mer's acclaimed ten-disc Postcards from the Deep *flexi-box set.*

One of several flexis released during the '60s by the British satirical magazine Private Eye.

promo, flexidiscs offer a world of apparently untapped possibilities, frequently at minimal cost.

Monty Python's Eric Idle teaching listeners how to impersonate the then-incumbent British Prime Minister, *Teach Yourself Heath*. The late English erotica superstar Mary Millington discussing all manner of naughtiness, while the needle went *ssshhhhh* in embarrassment behind her. Glam rock superstars Slade talking to readers of the *Melanie* comic.

Neither have flexidiscs fallen from grace. In 2014, the UK-based Fruits de Mer label released what surely ranks among the most audacious box sets ever issued, a collection of ten one-sided, see-through flexis, accompanied by a package of postcards upon which the music was very nearly pressed in the first place. Only problems in locating the necessary Communist-era Polish postcard pressing equipment derailed the initial dream, but once hatched, the notion would not fade away. And so it became reality instead. Just make sure you have a small coin handy, to weight the record down on the turntable.

One of the rarest singles in both the glam rock and Bell Records catalogs—a demonstration copy of Hello's "Teenage Revolution" 45, scheduled for release in 1976, but withdrawn after just a handful of these promos were produced.

45S: THE GREATEST SOUND ON EARTH

The 45 rpm single, the backbone of record collecting in the US (and around the world), arrived on the scene in 1949, as the result of a peculiar—and peculiarly vicious—battle between the giant record labels Columbia and RCA.

The previous year, Columbia introduced the 33⅓ rpm 10-inch "microgroove" long player and approached RCA—at that time its biggest rival—with an invitation to join in pioneering this new innovation, thus paving the way for its universal introduction. Instead, RCA head David Sarnoff was outraged at having been left so far behind in the technology stakes and, having raged at his own staff, he demanded they make amends by creating a new, competing format. They gave him the 7-inch 45.

The first advertisements for the 45, in March 1949, declared it to be a "50-year marketing achievement." In fact, it took RCA's engineers somewhat less than a year to develop the system, with perhaps the least thought of all going to the speed at which the disc would rotate. The 78 was the norm at the time; 33⅓s the alleged wave of the future. RCA simply subtracted the latter from the former, and let that be the guide.

Of course, it was not the speed of the Columbia innovation that mattered to the consumer. It was the fact that, for the first time ever, the listener would not have to get up every three or four minutes to change the record. Long players, as their name implied, played for a long time, up to twenty minutes in some cases.

RCA's 45 could not compete with this. At best, the format allowed for two songs to be placed on each side. At the same time as the 45 rpm record was being developed, however, another team was designing an automatic record changer that would permit the listener to stack up to half a dozen unbreakable vinyl 45s atop one another, with each falling to the turntable as the arm left the disc below.

The immediate advantage to this, of course, was that consumers could mix and match music to their liking, as opposed to the Columbia discs, which programmed the songs according to a will of their own. Even better, from a marketing point of view, were the dimensions of these new discs. The 7-inch disc offered a size that anybody could handle one-handedly, and devoured a lot less storage space as well. An ad in *Billboard* that April trumpeted that the "Convenient 7-inch size [means] more than 150 single

John's Children's 1967 single "Come and Play with Me in the Garden."

records fit in one foot of bookshelf space. No storage problems for your customers." Intriguingly (but possibly unknowingly), this latter innovation essentially returned records to square one—Emile Berliner's first gramophone records, fifty-four years earlier, also measured seven inches.

RCA simultaneously introduced a color-coding system that was itself unique. No more unbroken rows of boring black plastic. From now on, pop records alone would be pressed in that color. Classical recordings would use red vinyl, "light classics" were midnight blue, international (modern world music) appeared on light blue, R&B was cerise, country was green, and children's music was yellow. It was a short-lived innovation; by 1952, black vinyl was again the rule. But for the three years in between, during which the 45 rose from novelty status to something approaching its eventual preeminence, a collection of "singles" (so called because the majority featured a single song on each side) was a kaleidoscope of color.

RCA's initial launch comprised 104 singles (primarily reissues of popular 78s), plus seventy-six "album" collections, themselves comprising boxed packages of multiple 45s to be stacked onto the player in whatever sequence the listener chose.

Numbered sides, of course, indicated the company's own suggested listening order, with the first track on the album being backed by the last, the second by the penultimate, and so forth—again allowing for uninterrupted listening of the entire program. The practice of double albums being pressed with sides one and four on one disc, sides two and three on another, a scheme that continued into the early '80s, is a holdover from this early innovation.

Numerically speaking, the first RCA 45 was Eddy Arnold's "Texarkana Baby"/"A Bouquet of Roses," although any of the 104 records released that momentous day (including ten further Arnold singles) can share the honor of being the first 45s ever. Soon, RCA was releasing almost every new release on both 78 and 45, and by May 1949, the new format had scored its first American chart-topper, Perry Como's "'A'—You're Adorable."

Other labels watched RCA's activities with intense interest; Columbia even tentatively tried to take the conflict to a new level by introducing its own 33⅓ rpm 7-inch in April 1949—the forerunner of the later EP. However, low sales prompted the company to lose interest fairly quickly and, as the year wore on, there were signs that RCA's faith in

the 7-inch, too, was beginning to falter. Sales of 78s remained far higher than sales of 45s; Columbia's LPs, for all RCA's efforts, were taking off as well.

There was only one small crumb of comfort to be taken from the entire debacle, and that lay amid reports from around the country that kids, a hitherto untapped market for record companies, were the ones who most supported the 45. If RCA's marketing department could find a way to target this audience, the 45 might be saved.

An RCA retail bulletin from November 1949 fills in the gaps. "Coast to coast, teenagers are lining up for . . . neat little records they can slip in their pockets, with first-class bands playing their favorite hits for 49 cents." It was, the bulletin continued, the lowest price at the newest speed. The cavalry had arrived.

The sudden turnaround in the 45's fortune lost no time in communicating itself across the industry. Capitol, MGM, and Mercury were all early entrants to the fray, with the latter notching up the first non-RCA 45 chart-topper in 1950, with Frankie Laine's "The Cry of the Wild Goose."

National, London, Decca, Savoy, and Aladdin followed; and in late 1950, Columbia swallowed its pride and threw its first 45s into the market. By 1952, there was barely a record label in the land that was not issuing 45s; by 1955, the 45 was *the* most important musical medium in the Western world. In commercial terms, it remained so until the mid-'80s; in collecting terms, its supremacy remains inviolate.

As the late '70s progressed, picture sleeves became increasingly complex. Snatch's "All I Want" was released in a striking matte-laminated picture sleeve with gold print— which, unfortunately, started to peel as time passed.

There are as many ways of collecting 45s as there are collectors of 45s, and it would be impossible to even begin taking note of every one. There is no innovation in record-production history that has not, even in a tiny way, become integral to the format—colored vinyl, as already mentioned, was its birthright; picture sleeves its inheritance; picture discs an inevitable destiny.

Each and every one of these represents a fertile collecting area, and so do their corollaries. If a single was issued on colored vinyl, there are collectors who seek only black-vinyl pressings. If one was issued in a custom picture sleeve, there are collectors who collect only generic-label sleeves. There are even collectors for whom the record itself is not the point—they are after the metal and plastic adapters that were marketed to plug the hole in the record's center, and have elevated the search for even these ephemeral scraps to high science.

The introduction of stereo in the late 1950s saw several labels experiment with the format at 45 rpm—these issues are eminently collectible. At the other end of the spectrum, mono singles drawn from albums ordinarily available only in stereo have their own army of devotees. And, representing the best of both worlds, promo issues manufactured for radio play offer the hit song in stereo on one side, mono on the other.

Some of the rarest records in the world are 45s, and many of the most expensive. The history of the format is littered with records that are valued not because they are great, not because the band is famous, but because the label in question pressed just a handful of copies, and no one has ever seen more than one or two—and that is the *entire* history. Even today, major and minor record labels continue to produce 45s, albeit in such limited quantities that it seems impossible that their values have not already soared skyward.

Some of these are issued for the handful of jukeboxes nationwide that still play 45s; the 1990s even saw the Capitol-EMI group issue 45s specifically designated "For Jukeboxes Only." Others, however,

are marketed directly to the collectors market (Record Store Day routinely sees a plethora of such things), arousing some fascinating parallels in the process.

In 1963, the UK Decca label scheduled, then withdrew, a new Rolling Stones single, "Fortune Teller." No more than a handful of regular UK issues made it out; more were pressed for record club and export releases—they are identifiable by a solid center, rather than the standard push-out one. How many exist? A couple of thousand at most, and they are valued in the $1,000 range.

Fast-forward thirty years to 1994, and another new Stones single, "Out of Tears." It wasn't withdrawn; indeed, it reached No. 36 on the UK chart. But it did so on the strength of cassette and the two-part CD-single sales. The actual 45 was a numbered, limited edition of just 7,000 copies—more than exist of "Fortune Teller," of course, but still an insignificant number compared to how many Stones collectors there are. Value? Not so much right now, but you should keep an eye out for a scheduled third CD of the song: 4,000 were pressed and then withdrawn, and have already reached the equal of "Fortune Teller."

That is one example. From the precious platters pressed during the first years of the 45 revolution, by tiny independent labels with zero distribution and marketing, through another half century of withdrawn, deleted, ignored, or simply lost 45s, there is no end to the list of singles that today make hen's teeth look populous by comparison.

And on the other end of the scale, there are the untold millions of 45s that we collect simply for the love of it. "I look back on my old 45s," Elton John told *Uncut* magazine in 2001, "and I remember when they gave me a bit of happiness. Which is more than human beings have ever given me." In the same issue of the magazine, the Human League's Phil Oakey agreed wholeheartedly. "Maybe records meant so much to us because it was all we had. That seven-inch bit of plastic was our lives. And it cost you a load of money."

An entire generation separates the two men—Elton was a child of the 1940s, digging his wax in the first light of Elvis. Oakey struck gold in the 1980s, with Bolan and Bowie to float his boat. Yet both men are correct. The pop record, specifically the three-minute pop 45, is arguably the most intense and important development in the history of human artifice.

It is certainly the most direct. Movies? Yeah, they're great, but once you know the butler did it, who wants to spend another two hours watching while he does it again? Sculpture? Very pretty, lovely lines, and it's your turn to dust its crevices next week. Stamps? Super until your eyesight starts failing, or the hired help needs to mail out the bills. Coins? Bus fare.

But a pile of old 45s? Now you're talking. And now you're dancing.

The first 45 by Sparks, reissued in the UK in 1974, following the band's Island Records breakthrough.

4-TRACK CARTRIDGES: NICE IDEA, BUT NOT ENOUGH CLUNKS

The 4-track tape was, for a short time, the future of rock 'n' roll. Though 4-tracks are barely remembered today and, on the rare occasions when they are encountered, they are usually viewed as a bizarre (or even faulty—what is that big hole in the top where the roller should go?) variation on the 8-track, the 4-track not only preceded its better-known cousin, it actually inspired the creation of that format.

However, whereas 8-track aficionados can look back at their hero's demise at the hands of the cassette and say that the smaller tape was victorious merely because it was cheaper for the record companies to produce, the war with the 4-track was won fair and square.

The 8-track really was superior—at least for the purpose for which it was designed. The fact that 4-tracks offered marginally better sound quality, were less prone to breakage—and due to the (quite deliberate) absence of an internal roller, were easier to maintain—does not even enter into the equation. After all, 8-tracks offered more music, and that's what it's all about.

One Earl Muntz developed the 4-track tape, specifically for use in automobiles. Utilizing the endless loop technology that was exercising so many other designers at the time (see the section about 8-tracks for further details), Muntz created a method by which two "tracks" of stereo sound could be laid side by side, lengthwise, on a piece of tape, to be played on tape decks that read each one in turn.

Although the 4-track technology was originally developed as early as 1956, it was 1963 before Muntz began marketing it, initially in California. Buoyed by the support of several major record companies, the so-called Muntz Stereo-Pak received immense publicity when players were installed in vehicles owned by such stars as Frank Sinatra, Peter Lawford, James Garner, Lawrence Welk, and Red Skelton—and even more when an order was placed to install them in the newly developed Lear Jet.

However, upon delivery, the jet's designer, William Powell Lear, became convinced that he could make a far superior portable tape cartridge. Within a year, he had developed the 8-track, and was moving into many of the same markets that Muntz had hitherto dominated.

Nevertheless the 4- and 8-tracks existed side by side for some time, with canny hardware manufacturers even marketing players capable of dealing with both formats. Retailers, too, saw little difference

Nancy Sinatra and Lee Hazlewood on 4-track.

between the two formats and frequently stocked them in the same racks, while many record companies were happy to see their latest releases issued in both formats as the world watched to see which would ultimately win. Of course it was the 8-track, though it would be as late as 1970 before the victory was finally complete.

As in virtually every other area of record collecting, the most popular act on 4-track today is the Beatles (Elvis did not appear in the format). Capitol was one of the first major labels to strike a licensing deal with Muntz, in 1964, and the company issued its first Beatles 4-tracks that same year. Thereafter, every Beatles album up to their farewell *Let It Be* would appear in the format, together with such early Apple releases as the Lennons' *Two Virgins,* Mary Hopkin's *Postcard,* and George Harrison's *Wonderwall Music.* Paul McCartney's soundtrack to the movie *The Family Way* also made an appearance. The last Beatles-related 4-tracks to appear were the debut solo albums by all four members, in 1970.

Outside of Beatledom, few 4-tracks have any collector value, although fans of individual artists will often find themselves tempted by the occasional find. From the last years of the format's life span, such releases as Cream's *Disraeli Gears,* Jimi Hendrix's *Electric Ladyland* (released across two tapes), the Moody Blues' *Days of Future Passed,* and the Bee Gees' debut album are all of interest, while the 4-track's earlier start also allowed it to make contemporary, as opposed to retrospective, releases for many classic British Invasion albums. This is of especial note to stereo collectors—the most common LPs from this period are, of course, the mono issues. However, 4-tracks were released only in stereo.

A great deal more research can be done about 4-tracks than about 8-tracks, presumably because there are even fewer working 4-track players in existence today than there are 4-track collectors.

Beyond the Beatles, there is very little discographical information available; nor has there yet been published any kind of guide to the occasional musical variations that excite 8-track collectors. That is not, however, to say that they do not exist, with the stereo side of things seeming an especially fruitful domain.

For example, were there any stereo releases that appeared only in the 4-track format? Nobody is going to get rich by answering that question (or any other one related to this format). But the thrill of discovery can be reward in itself.

One final note: When searching for 4-tracks on the Internet, remember that reel-to-reel tapes employed that same terminology. Many more apparent hits will, in fact, be referring to these items, than to their cartridge-clad brethren.

INTERVIEW DISCS: TOO MUCH CHATTER

Since the late '70s, interview discs have proven one of the most popular means by which an unknown label can boast a superstar artist in its catalog. Because spoken word is not covered under any copyright law, any interview material is fair game, and thousands upon thousands of discs—45s, LPs, and CDs—have appeared, bearing the private and public thoughts of rock's greatest names. Few are issued by the artist's home label.

A variety of gimmicks—including colored vinyl, picture discs, and intriguing shapes—have been employed to make these more attractive, but specialist collectors notwithstanding, there is little interest in these releases. However, a handful have become legends of sorts, most notably the *Wibbling Rivalry* Oasis interview, which became the first such release ever to make the UK chart in 1995.

If commercially available interview discs have little after-market value, promo releases fare quite the opposite. Radio transcription discs have a reasonable audience among collectors; issues made to accompany new-release CDs, too, are popular—REM's *Talk About the Weather* and Neil Young's *Silver and Gold* discs are among those in high demand.

There is also an array of radio-interview 45s issued during the early-to-mid-'60s, featuring "open-ended" interviews, in which a script (read aloud by the DJ, of course) provided the questions, while the artist answered back on the disc. Many such discs exist, though they are in short supply—issues by Julie London and Brenda Lee were among those pictured in a special feature in the March 1998 issue of *DISCoveries* magazine.

JUKEBOX ALBUMS: MORE BANG FOR YOUR BUCK

For around fifteen years, roughly between 1960 and 1974, many record companies issued Jukebox Albums, or Little LPs, for use in jukeboxes capable of playing 331/3 rpm 7-inch releases. Often considered a variation on the popular EP format, Jukebox Albums are also frequently found cataloged as promotional issues, in that they were not generally available to the record-buying public.

Jukebox Albums featured between four and (less frequently) six songs from a current LP, usually packaged in two-color picture sleeves depicting the album cover, with an attached title strip for placement in the jukebox's selection index.

Predictably, the most collectible items are by the most collectible bands, including Jukebox Album versions of the Beatles' *Second Album*, Bob Dylan's *Bringing It All Back Home*, and Elvis Presley's 1973 *Aloha from Hawaii*. Some seven different Rolling Stones albums (including the super-rare *Their Satanic Majesties' Request* and *Exile on Main Street*) and Led Zeppelin's *IV* and *Houses of the Holy* are also highly prized.

The Beach Boys, too, boast some very scarce Little LPs in their

Tollie

"All My Loving," The Dowlands (TOLLIE 9002, 7-INCH, 1964)

"Golden Lights," Twinkle (TOLLIE 9047, 7-INCH, 1965)

"I Better Run," Barrett Strong (TOLLIE 9023, 7-INCH, 1964)

"I Want My Baby Back," Jimmy Cross (TOLLIE 9039, 7-INCH, 1965)

"Love Me Do," The Beatles (TOLLIE 9008, 7-INCH, 1964)

"Secret Weapon," The BRATTS (TOLLIE 9024, 7-INCH, 1965)

"Terry," Twinkle (TOLLIE 9040, 7-INCH, 1965)

Their Biggest Hits, The Beatles (TOLLIE TEP 1-8901, COUNTERFEIT EP, 1975)

"Twist and Shout,", The Beatles (TOLLIE 9001, 7-INCH, 1964)

"Winken Blinken and Nod," The Big Three (TOLLIE 9006, 7-INCH, 1964)

discography, including *Surfer Girl*, *Shutdown Volume Two* (but not, apparently, volume one), and *Today*. However, with patience there are many more major acts of the era who can be located on Jukebox Albums, ranging as far afield as Jethro Tull and Marvin Gaye, the Grateful Dead and Eydie Gorme.

Be warned, however: Jukebox Albums basically exist in just two grades—unplayed and still sealed, or played to death and virtually worthless. The latter, of course, are by far the most common.

LABELOLOGY: THE TRAIN NOW STANDING . . .

One of the most frequent questions received at any collecting magazine or website is the one that begins, "I have a copy of such-and-such record, and the label is A) for a different record; B) on the wrong side; or C) upside down [although how that determination is reached, one cannot imagine]—should I quit work now, or hold on a little longer while the price goes up even higher?"

It's not an altogether stupid question. Errors in coins, stamps, and sports cards can often be highly prized, and highly valued, too. Surely it makes sense that what claims to be a copy of Elvis Presley's "In The Ghetto," that instead plays "Any Day Now" (and, when you flip the record over, *vice versa*) should be similar super-scarce?

Well, yes and no. It is an error and there probably aren't many of them around. But, and it's a big but, in these cases you simply have . . . an error, the vinyl equivalent of buying a pair of pants and discovering they're not the size it says on the label. Or ordering a Coke and being handed a Pepsi.

Occasionally a collector might want to pick up such a record for its novelty value. But that, sadly, is all it is—a novelty that is worth no more than a regular pressing, a reminder of a bad split-second at the pressing plant where a record was inadvertently flipped when the labels were being applied.

It also has nothing to do with labelology. This just seemed a good place to mention it.

Labelology is a term that was coined by Japanese record collectors, and it means, quite simply, the study of individual record-label designs. Everything from isolating varieties within the most minute details, and establishing both rarity and, where possible, population reports (the number of known examples) for each of them. It is an exacting pursuit that owes more to such hobbies as bibliophily (book collecting) and, again, philately (collecting stamps) than to music. Much of those pursuits' appeal, after all, is founded upon a collectors'

ability to seek out and identify the tiny variations that denote individual printings and redesigns, with literal fortunes depending upon a correct identification.

So it is with labelology. Exacting students have isolated at least sixteen different printings of the Tollie label pressing of the Beatles' "Twist and Shout" (Tollie 9001), fifteen versions of "Please Please Me," and a dozen of "She Loves You." And that's just for starters.

With the possible exception of Elvis Presley, no other artist has been subject to such microscopic scrutiny as the Beatles; others have been studied, of course, but labelology as a whole is largely restricted to those (and maybe a handful of other) artists and record labels.

Part of the reason for this is the absence of a standard, specialized catalog that is able to elevate the science to the same levels of research and knowledge that do now attend those other hobbies.

In philately, such catalogs as *Scott* and *Stanley Gibbons,* in the US and UK, respectively, document at least the major varieties found in every postage stamp in the world—a multivolume task, admittedly, but one that clearly has a sufficient market to ensure the publication and worldwide distribution of new editions every year.

In record collecting, similar data for no more than a comparative handful of individual records has thus far been published, with the accepted standard catalogs lagging decades behind in making the information available to the public at large.

Thus constricted, labelology can be described as a hobby in search of hobbyists. For those few hundred hardy souls whose time and knowledge is devoted to its furtherance, however, labelology is not simply a vital part of record collecting, it is perhaps *the* most vital.

After all, if you are bidding hard cash for an original first pressing of the Kinks' "You Really Got Me," what do you expect to receive? A record that came off the presses on the first day of manufacture? Or a worthless re-pressing from weeks, months, even years later?

Gong's Radio Gnome Invisible— *unhinged '70s prog rides a flying teapot to the Planet Gong.*

LPS: TWELVE INCHES OF PLEASURE

Let's clear something up right at the start. LPs are pressed on vinyl. Records are pressed on vinyl. Albums are pressed on vinyl. But they are *not* themselves called "vinyl." Or "vinyl*s*," despite both terms having crept into the common vernacular in recent years.

Yes, you can collect vinyl. You can say music sounds better on vinyl. You can even have a vinyl revival. But, in every instance, you are talking about the material that the music is pressed on, The actual thing you are buying is an LP, a record, an album. And having got that out of the way, we continue.

As with 45s and CDs, it is impossible to quantify how to collect LPs—or even what to collect. The three formats so thoroughly dominate our conception of what record collecting is all about that on every page in this book, there will be mention of something that a specialist format collector could (and doubtless does) collect.

Individual artists, labels, genres. Mono variations, stereo specialties. Gatefold sleeves or generic inner sleeves, box sets or Dynoflex (okay, maybe not Dynoflex—an ill-starred super flexible format introduced by RCA during the early '70s, that the company stubbornly persisted with, despite an immediate barrage of complaints regarding quality and fidelity). Even if one were to list every single collectible theme that the LP format has embraced, there would be a deluge of mail the next morning, pointing out all those that were omitted.

The supergroup that never was—Kevin Ayers, John Cale, Nico, and Eno joined forces to headline London's Rainbow Theatre on June 1, 1974.

Historically, the LP is the oldest, and longest surviving, of all recorded formats in use today. Early, unsuccessful experiments in the 1930s notwithstanding, the format was invented by Columbia Records staffer Bill Wallerstein, the 33⅓ long-playing microgroove record made its debut in June 1948, unveiled by Columbia as the disc of the future.

The company had a point. Hitherto, a record album had been precisely what it says—a collection of two-sided records (78 rpm), packaged together into a book-like album. To listen to an entire performance of an opera, for instance, or a symphony, the record owner (or, in better-off homes, one of the record owner's employees) would need to leave his or her seat to change the disc after every song—of course there were no such things as automatic record changers in those days of so-fragile shellac!

Revolving at a significantly slower speed, Columbia's microgroove system allowed the equivalent of six—or more!—individual 78s to be gathered together on each side of a record, affording the unheard-of luxury of up to twenty minutes of uninterrupted listening at a time. It was, in both senses of the word, a revolutionary development, one that would completely change the face of the recording industry.

Indeed, so confident was Columbia in the format's potential to succeed, and so certain of the benefits it would confer on the music industry as a whole (this part may be difficult for modern readers to comprehend), that the company did not even patent the technology employed in the LP's design, development, and manufacture. (Only the term "LP" was trademarked,

10cc's second album, Sheet Music.

and even that trademark was allowed to lapse once it became part of the language.) Rather, the company extended an invitation to RCA Victor, at that time, its greatest rival in the marketplace, to participate in the format's launch.

Of course, history records that RCA Victor flew off in a fit of pique, to develop its own rival format, the 45. Columbia launched the LP alone, then, but it need not have worried over the format's reception; the LP was in every way superior to the 78, and, as RCA discovered to its chagrin, to the 45 as well. Within a year or two, 78 albums were virtually a thing of the past; within five years, it was as though they had never even existed.

The first LPs were issued in a 10-inch format, as were the 78s they were supplanting; there was no technical reason for this, beyond not disturbing the consumer's equilibrium more than was necessary. By

Welsh power trio Budgie was blessed with some of the most spectacular sleeves (and music) of the early to mid-1970s. This, their fifth album, was released in 1975.

the late '50s, however, more and more labels were upgrading to the 12-inch format, in which form LPs would remain.

Significant upgrades to what was so simple and basic a design were few and far between thereafter. The changeover from mono to stereo sound was phased in over almost a decade before the labels finally abandoned mono in 1968, by which time all but the most stubborn consumers had come to terms with the new innovation, from both a sonic and a technical point of view.

Stereo was accepted because it did not require any upgrade of equipment whatsoever, hence the "mono-compatible stereo"

notations applied to many mid-to-late-'60s releases. The 1970s move to quadraphonic sound, on the other hand, foundered on the absence of compatibility, not only with existing equipment, but also between quadraphonic formats themselves.

These periods are, not surprisingly, among the most popular areas for specialist LP collectors who eschew such traditional themes as artists or labels. Quadraphonic is a market unto itself, but both earlier formats have much to offer. Many early stereo albums were produced in painfully minute quantities, to match the market they were intended to meet; they also cost a dollar more than mono, at a time when a dollar actually represented a sizeable chunk out of a young person's allowance.

This differentiation also explains why many late-mono releases have come down to modern collectors in somewhat lamentable condition. Kids bought mono albums because they were cheaper than stereo—and kids are not necessarily the most careful record owners.

Among adults, meanwhile, there was also the matter of perceived value. While today many collectors regard mono recordings as being both sonically and artistically superior to stereo, contemporary consumers regarded stereo as offering bonus extras that were not available on old-fashioned mono—different guitar solos, fabulous effects, speaker-to-speaker panning, and more.

The late-'70s rush into picture discs, too, spun off a wealth of now highly sought-after (if, in many cases, totally unplayable) items. The LP format has also been borrowed for a number of items that, while not technically records at all, also attract collectors—LP-shaped clocks and posters both enjoyed their day in the sun, and online craftsmen still peddle bowls and dishes made from well-warped old records.

The 45 collector's love of foreign picture sleeves is another field that attracts album collectors, as they pursue European and other variants on common American LPs. However, sleeves aren't the only things that change from country to country. The very nature of the records shifts as well. It is well known, for example, that the contents of the Beatles' and Rolling Stones' early (pre-1967) American albums bore little relation to their UK counterparts, even on those occasions when the two releases had a common title. So it was with many other releases of the period, with similar variants then spreading across the globe.

Sharp-eared listeners will instantly detect differences in stereo mixes prepared during this same period for American and British listeners. Capitol, the Beatles' US label, was only one of many labels whose own engineers remixed releases before they were issued, creating a field rich in both incredible variety and eye-popping research possibilities.

To reiterate the point made at the beginning of this article, then, the limits to LP collecting possibilities are defined only by the collector's own imagination. With that in mind . . . you're off.

MIGHTY TINY TOY RECORD PLAYER: BATTERIES NOT INCLUDED

At least one person reading this surely got his or her start in collecting with this.

Ohio Arts's *Mighty Tiny—The World's Smallest Record Player* was marketed during the 1950s. It had a fascinating (if somewhat unreliable) miniature turntable, with a built-in speaker, designed to play correspondingly minute (2-inch) records. Such artists as the Musical Squares, the Harmonettes, and Amy Wilson and Her Guitar headed the popular line of recordings; there were also series of world music and children's songs, all sold in packets of four.

MINIDISCS: TINY TOYS REVISITED

The latest in a long line of post-CD digital formats, the MiniDisc was launched by Sony in September 1992, with the first discs and players hitting the market in time for Christmas that same year.

It was not well received, with critics noting both the high price of players and a signal lack of sales (just 50,000 players were sold during its first year of production). The format was also hamstrung by the fact that it was incompatible with any of the existing digital file formats (wav, mp3, flac, and so on), insisting instead on Sony's own ATRAC encoding. Add the near-simultaneous launch of Philips' DCC—which itself would suffer the same fate of almost immediate obsolescence brought on by the arrival first of recordable CDs, and then the mp3 player—and clearly, the format was doomed.

But it was stubborn, too. MiniDiscs remained in production until 2013, while the format also saw a number of albums released (the majority of them from Sony's own catalog). There is little appetite for them among collectors, but noteworthy releases include David

Bowie's *Hours . . .* , Michael Jackson's *Blood on the Dancefloor*, Pink Floyd's *A Momentary Lapse of Reason*, and Nick Cave's *Murder Ballads*.

MINI-8S: SMALL, BUT SMART

A little-known variant on the 8-track, the Mini-8 was introduced in 1969 by Lear Jet and manufactured by Ampex, as competition to the newly emergent cassette tape, whose runaway popularity was making serious inroads into the traditional 8-track market.

Compatible with existing 8-track players, the tapes' selling point was that they could be folded in half, to more or less the size of a cassette tape—whose own advantage over the 8-track was that it required so much less storage room. The working mechanisms and the tape itself were housed in the front half of the cartridge; the other half folded over to create its own protective box.

The disadvantage was the bugbear of length. Mini-8s could hold no more than thirty minutes of music, rendering them ideal for duplicating singles or EPs, but posing no threat to any longer-playing format. Interestingly, rather than step into the breach left by the recent demise of the PlayTape, and create single-artist tapes built around hits or the most popular cuts from given LPs, the Mini-8 concentrated on various-artists compilations.

It is uncertain how many of these collections were manufactured during the Mini-8's brief life span. The 1970 Ampex catalog lists 150 separate titles, but there were certainly others released before the format was finally abandoned later in the year. However, the nature of the tapes' content has seriously retarded collector interest, condemning Mini-8s to a sparsely populated backwater, where only serious tape enthusiasts dare to venture.

MINI PAC: GONE AND FORGOTTEN

The Mini Pac was an early predecessor of the PlayTape, and was designed by Earl Muntz (inventor of the 4-track cartridge), as an alternative to singles and EPs. Mini Pacs held up to four songs and were compatible with all existing 4-track players. However, the format seems to have existed for a matter of months only, and tapes today are exceedingly rare.

MP3S:
THE INVISIBLE MENACE

In terms of its historical impact, it is all but impossible to divorce the mp3 from its leading role in what we might call the financial decline of the modern music industry, and the conjoined scourges of internet piracy and illegal downloading.

However, the proliferation of legal download sites, ranging from such major players as Apple, Amazon, and eMusic through to such strictly independent concerns as Bandcamp, have seen a wealth of music become available that might never have been heard had a physical delivery format been required.

Furthermore, to cater for those purists who complain that the sound quality here is scarcely anything to write home about, there also exists a growing number of sites that offer (at a price, of course) high definition downloads in various superior, uncompressed, formats. The wav and flac formats are favorites here, later to be joined by the Neil Young–championed Pono, named from the Hawaiian word for "proper," and (according to its backers), offering up songs "as they first sound during studio recording sessions."

All were quick to accrue their followers; all exist (or existed, in the latter instance) within a high-end audiophile niche. But none have come even close to challenging the domination of the mp3.

Archive release projects that might otherwise have been impractical have been made possible by mp3—Third Man's recreation of the near-complete Paramount Records output, for example; Sony's release of Bob Dylan's 1965 live catalog; and Apple's unveiling of great swathes of Beatles archive are all dramatic cases in point. And since the decision was taken to include download sales in the computing of various national Top Forty lists, mp3 singles have become as much a part of the modern landscape as their 7-inch counterparts were to past generations.

There are even labels that focus exclusively upon making the music of the past available on mp3, in the knowledge that there will always be some kind of demand for it, even if it's maybe not enough to justify a physical release.

Anthology Recordings was the pioneer here; the world's first reissues-only download label launched in October 2006 with the stated goal of "keeping it as eclectic as possible," as founder Keith Abrahamsson put it.

An A&R executive with New York City-based indie label Kemado Records, Abrahamsson explained, "I came up with the idea for Anthology about [in 2004] and started putting the idea into motion in December 2005. The idea came from what I thought was missing on the Web. Besides a few blogs, there really was no online resource for rare and out-of-print stuff where someone could get extensive reading material, photos, and artwork and also download the records. It was something I wished existed."

The subject of blogs was very dear to Abrahamsson's heart. "I think blogs are great. Without them, tons of great obscure stuff would go unheard. But what I am doing is creating an outlet that maybe will draw an even larger and broader fan base to some great esoteric music and, in the process, will also give back to the artist."

The logistics behind establishing such an exercise were daunting: not only establishing a secure and reliable website, but also making certain every aspect of the site meets with the actual musicians' approval. Unlike the bulk of the blogging community, Anthology was one hundred percent legal; product was licensed through the official channels, artist royalties were paid in full, and downloads were taken from the highest-possible quality source, usually master tapes that themselves had often been buried away for years.

But Abrahamsson was adamant that "Anthology Recordings is not intended to be an absolute alternative to crate digging. It's a resource for music fanatics who would otherwise not hear these rare titles." With collector prices for this sort of material soaring as fast as any Wall Street investment portfolio, and only a frighteningly finite quantity of actual vinyl copies knocking around out there, "making the music available digitally is an affordable option for both the label and the consumer. "

The label's first wave of reissues was certainly impressive. African Head Charge's 1986 album *Off the Beaten Track* served up a primal slab of Adrian Sherwood–produced dub. Sainte Anthony's Fyre were a late 1960s/early 1970s New Jersey power trio, whose self-titled debut album came in a limited edition of 1,000 and made Blue Cheer sound slick and clean. My Solid Ground were a German trio whose sole album, an eponymous set cut for Bacillus in 1971, is best remembered for its outrageous cover art (naked piggies!), but has also been described as quite possibly the heaviest Krautrock album ever.

Mid-1970s rock 'n' roll revivalists Suicide Commandos were recalled with *The Commandos Commit Suicide Dance Concert*, a live album recorded at the band's final concerts in late 1978 (and given a posthumous release the following year by Twin/Tone).

Early 1980s New York No Wavers China Shop were memorialized by the anthology *21 Puffs on the Cassette*, which rounded up 1983's *Atomic Notions* EP, together with a slew of unreleased cuts, while a self-titled collection by hardcore merchants Moondog delivers up the previously unreleased demos for a 1989 project convened by guitarist Walter Schreifels during the hiatus between the better known Gorilla Biscuits and Quicksand. And, finally, a self-titled 2CD package from Parson Sound covers the Swedish psych-experimentalists' 1967–'68 output, recorded both live and in the studio.

Gary Numan/Tubeway Army

"Are 'Friends' Electric?" (UK BEGGARS BEG 18P, 7-INCH PICTURE DISC, 1979)

BBC Rock Hour (LONDON WAVELENGTH, TRANSCRIPTION DISC, 1980)

"Cars" (UK BEGGARS BEG 23, 7-INCH, DARK-RED VINYL, 1980)

"Down in the Park" (UK BEGGARS BEG 17T, 12-INCH, PICTURE SLEEVE, 1979)

The Fury (UK NUMA CDNUMA 1003, CD WITH ORIGINAL MIXES, 1986)

Images Volumes 1–8 (UK NUMA, GNFCDA 104, FOUR 2-LP SETS, 1986–87)

Telekon (UK BEGGARS BEGA 19, LP, DARK-RED VINYL, 1980)

"This Is My Life" (UK BEGGARS TUB 1, WHITE-LABEL 7-INCH PROMO, 1984)

Tubeway Army (UK BEGGARS BEG BEGA 4, BLUE-VINYL LP, 1978)

Tubeway Army 1978–79 (UK BEGGARS BEGC 7879, CASSETTE, 1985)

Plus, every album came with full artwork and liners, while some albums include even rarer bonus material—a clutch of rehearsal takes on the My Solid Ground album, a video on the Suicide Commandos.

That was the first wave. Many more followed over the next four years, and the label thrived until 2010. It disappeared then for a few years, but relaunched in 2014, by which time, of course, the twinned worlds of unofficial (blog-hosted) and official download releases had exploded out of all proportion.

Physical reservations notwithstanding ("but what exactly am I collecting?"), mp3s were not slow in establishing themselves in the collectible marketplace.

Club DJs had long-since specialized in creating exclusive, personal remixes of existing material to use during their own sets at clubs—Fatboy Slim's UK-chart-topping remix of Cornershop's "Brimful of Asha" started life in this fashion. But when the early 2000s brought a simultaneous explosion of remix software, it fostered a new generation of unofficial (or bootleg) remixers and, with it, a new collecting niche that relied almost exclusively on free Internet MP3 downloads for distribution.

For many people, the appeal of these remixes—christened "Bastard Pop" by some UK commentators—lay in their novelty. Taking one song and blending its key elements with another (or several others), some remarkable soundscapes were produced.

DJ Girls on Top (aka Rich X) scored a major underground hit in 2001 with "I Wanna Dance with Numbers," which married the vocals from Whitney Houston's "I Wanna Dance with You" to the instrumental track of Kraftwerk's "Numbers." Lockarm's "Bring the Music" clashed Public Enemy's "Bring the Noise" with M's "Pop Muzik," while Philly Da Kid's "Eminem vs the Smiths" blended the rapper's "Without Me" with the indie band's "This Charming Man." Bastard Pop indeed.

That these remixes were usually made without the permission of either artist or copyright holder was of little consequence to either collector or creator. The ingenuity and creativity of the mix was the only thing that mattered. The illicit nature of Bastard Pop remixes, of course, ensured that they could not be distributed via any traditional medium: vinyl, cassette, CD, and so on. But they weren't supposed to be.

Bastard Pop was the first musical form to wholly embrace not only the Internet, but also the principle of unlimited, free distribution; and the first to be embraced in kind. It was not unusual for a remix to see more than 50,000 downloads, while there was at least one Internet radio station devoted exclusively to the genre. June 2002 even saw *Newsweek* magazine profile the phenomenon, just one month after Britain's *Record Collector* and *Mojo* magazines offered their own reports.

Of course, such activity and popularity would not go unnoticed in either the pop mainstream or the world of traditional bootlegging. Early 2002 brought a UK No. 1 hit for the Sugababes' "Freaks Like Me," a straightforward cover of another Girls on Top remix, "We Don't Give a Damn About Our Friends," which combined the original talents of Adina Howard and Tubeway Army.

Meanwhile, collectors without the means (or the patience) to gather their mixes from the net were increasingly being tempted by similarly unauthorized bootleg CD collections of the most popular and notorious remixes.

As with so many musical fashions, overexposure and a growing influx of, frankly, grossly inferior product quickly spelled an end to the boom; ally that with the Internet's own grasshopper tendency to spend as little time as possible on any one consuming passion before loping off in search of the next one, and Bastard Pop probably ranks among the shortest-lived musical crazes of all time.

That, however, is unimportant. What it did achieve was to acquaint the public with the notion that Internet-only releases *could* be collected in their own right, not as a substitute (legal or otherwise) for "the real thing," but as a means of expanding physical collections with material that was not available in any other form.

The Bandcamp site is perhaps the leading example of this, with several thousand unsigned artists from around the world now releasing new music solely in mp3 form, or at least primarily; some do also produce limited edition CD, vinyl, and cassette versions.

Again, there is little hope of the purchaser ever recouping even a fraction of the purchase price with a subsequent resale, but outside of the big-ticket box set touts, how many true fans and collectors ever buy a new release with the express purpose of some day reselling it? One is purchasing the immediate pleasure of hearing the music, in the same way as one might rent a movie from an online streaming service—with the major difference being, you can listen to it more than once.

Another area in which mp3 offers a major advantage over absolutely every physical format is in the ease with which music can be arranged on your hard drive.

No matter how you collect, whether by artist or by label (or anything else), being able to string together the catalog in order of release, or recording date, or any other criteria is a boon that can actually become very addictive.

Album tracks can be rearranged, singles dropped into sequence; demos, outtakes, and live recordings likewise. Even if you never get around to playing them in that order, still there is a visual reference that can be most pleasing to behold.

Likewise, mp3s offer a versatility that no other format can match; in fact, their only true drawback, as Neil Young sings on "Driftin' Back," a track from his monumental *Psychedelic Pill* album, is the loss of so much of the music that originally constituted the performance: "When you hear my song now / you only get five percent / you used to get it all."

He exaggerates, but only a little. The process by which mp3s are created employs what is known as "lossy compression," which reduces those aspects of a sound that a system called "perceptual

Lee Hazlewood

"Charlie Bill Nelson" (REPRISE 0667, 7-INCH, 1967)

The Cowboy and the Lady (with Ann-Margret) (LH1 12007, LP, 1971)

Did You Ever (RCA 4645, LP, 1971)

Friday's Child (REPRISE 6163, MONO LP, 1966)

"The Girls in Paris" (MGM K13716, 7-INCH, 1966)

A House Safe for Tigers (CBS 80383, LP, 1975)

It's Cause and Cure (MGM SE 4403, STEREO LP, 1966)

Love and Other Crimes (REPRISE 6297, LP, 1968)

NSVIP, **The NSVIP's** (REPRISE 6133, LP, 1965)

"A Taste of You" (MCA 0613, 7-INCH, 1979)

coding" regards as lying outside of most people's hearing range. Which does not sound like too big an issue until you consider how much of a piece of music is made up of such sounds, and how—even inaudibly—they are a part of what you hear and feel when you play back a piece of music. (And that is without even considering what is meant by "most people.")

Even more alarmingly, according to a 2016 study by the *Journal of the Audio Engineering Society* (*The Effects of MP3 Compression*

on Perceived Emotional Characteristics in Musical Instruments, by Ronald Mo, Ga Lam Choi, Chung Lee, and Andrew Horner), the compression strengthens what researchers described as any "neutral and negative emotional" tones in the music, while weakening the "positive" ones.

If you ask around, you will find plenty of anecdotal evidence of people claiming that listening to music on vinyl makes them feel happy, or at least good; and plenty of others who insist that mp3s give them a headache. We may now have a scientific explanation for why this should be.

Other sonic elements, too, are either discarded or lost; so many, in fact, that the average mp3 might contain as little as one-tenth of the data that constitutes the same song on CD. A point you will swiftly appreciate when you do first hear a piece of music on mp3, after years of listening to it on vinyl or CD (or vice versa).

Of course, mp3's advantages, to many people, far outweigh its disadvantages. The biggest audio library in the world can be stored in the minutest fraction of the room that its physical equivalent would devour. A single terabyte of storage space can hold around 200,000 songs; a ten-terabyte hard drive could thus store two million, which adds up to around twelve years' worth of continuous listening.

Which raises another point that is also pertinent to mp3 collecting. What effect does it actually have upon your listening habits when, for example, you can visit The Grateful Dead Internet Archive Project (GDIAP) and legally access over ten thousand live shows—which, even if you listened to three a day, every day, would take close to ten years to get through? Then multiply that by the number of other artists you collect, or whose works you have downloaded because you were curious.

Once upon a time, the sheer physicality of a music collection ensured that most everything we owned would receive at least one spin, and took any number of years to build up. Thanks to the Internet, the modern collector (who might, under these circumstances, better be termed a hoarder) can effectively download a lifetime's worth of collecting in one evening. In fact, one such collector, author Stephen Witt, admits as much in his book-length study of the impact of the mp3, *How Music Got Free:*

"When I arrived at college in 1997, I had never heard of an mp3. By graduation, I had six twenty-gigabyte drives, all full. By 2005 . . . I had collected 1,500 gigabytes of music, nearly 15,000 albums' worth. It took an hour just to queue up my library." And, had he chosen to listen to it, it would have taken eighteen months to get from Abba to ZZ Top.

Except he never did. "Most of this music I never listened to. I actually hated Abba, and although I owned four ZZ Top albums, I couldn't tell you the name of one." He collected because he could, because "it was effortless: the music was simply there. The only hard part was figuring out what to listen to."

If anything.

So yes, mp3s are here to stay. So is streaming, so is downloading, and so is the accumulation of tens of thousands of songs by tens of thousands of bands.

But is it a collection in the same way as tens of thousands of singles, LPs, cassettes and CDs is a collection? That is for you, the reader, to decide. Just be very, very careful with the "delete" button.

MQS SD: THE LATEST (AS OF EARLY 2018) PHYSICAL MUSIC FORMAT

Pledging, once again, the best possible sonic reproduction, MQS (Master Quality Sound) is a flash drive loaded with flac files, and claiming to deliver up to 6.5 times more data than a CD. Or as one forum poster put it, "perfect sound forever, that I can misplace immediately."

Launched in Asia during 2015, the format arrived in America in December 2016 with the Beatles *1* album as its flagship release.

NIPPER: THE STORY OF HIS MASTER'S VOICE

Possibly the best-known company trademark in the modern music industry is "His Master's Voice," Francis Barraud's much-beloved portrait of his fox terrier, Nipper, listening to a phonograph, or cylinder machine.

Nipper himself was a stray adopted by Barraud's brother, Mark, in 1884. Mark passed away in 1887 and Nipper moved in with Francis, a talented artist. It is uncertain exactly when Barraud painted the picture that would assure Nipper's immortality; however, in 1899 he copyrighted it under the title *Dog Looking at and Listening to a Phonograph*, though he preferred to refer to it by the less formal *His Master's Voice*.

It was, Barraud later said, "the happiest thought I ever had," although his early attempts to sell the painting as

a piece of commercial art met with no success. Finally, sometime toward the end of the year, a friend suggested Barraud rework the picture slightly, replacing the black phonograph horn of the original with a more striking gold one, similar to the ones that had recently been introduced by Emile Berliner's Gramophone Company.

Barraud agreed and, armed with a photograph of his painting, he visited the company's London offices to request the loan of a trumpet. Instead he walked away with a sale. William Barry Owen, the American-born head of the Company's British operation, was so smitten with the image that he immediately commissioned a copy, this time with the entire phonograph replaced by one of his firm's own gramophones.

Barraud received two payments of fifty pounds for his work, one payment for conceding all copyright claims on the picture, the other for granting the Gramophone Company sole reproduction rights. With Nipper at the pictorial helm, the world-famous His Master's Voice (HMV) record label was born soon after.

Back in the US, Emile Berliner was as delighted with the purchase as Owen was, copyrighting the image for the American market in 1900. The following year, Berliner launched his Victor Talking Machine Company, and "His Master's Voice" became that company's trademark as well. A century on, the descendants of those two pioneers, EMI and BMG, continued to utilize the image.

Barraud himself never repeated the success of this one painting. Indeed, by 1913 he was suffering serious financial hardship, with nothing whatsoever to show for his greatest triumph.

Resplendent beneath the faithful hound. 1955's "Dreamboat" was Cogan's first UK chart-topper.

Somehow, word of his plight reached Alfred Clark, the then-chairman of the Gramophone Company. Generously, he commissioned Barraud to paint a third copy of *His Master's Voice* for presentation to the Victor company; over the next eleven years, until his death in 1924, Barraud completed twenty-one further copies for the two companies, while receiving a pension from both of them.

As the single most recognizable logo in music-industry history, Nipper has similarly long been established as a popular collectible in his own right. The most common images, naturally, are those appearing on Victor/RCA/BMG and HMV/EMI's own records. The most faithful of these, perhaps not surprisingly, are the earliest, with HMV's earliest label a deep red with gold lettering that provided an excellent background for the image, which was presented within a semicircular frame on a brown background.

Victor, meanwhile, preferred to place Nipper and the gramophone on a black background that consumed the entire label—an image that remained more or less untouched for the next seventy years, long after HMV's label design moved to a more stylized image. (It should be remembered, incidentally, that RCA's copyright extended only to the Americas and the Far East. Releases elsewhere in the world, including the UK, appeared without the image. Of course, the opposite is true regarding HMV/EMI.)

A vast number of other items bearing the image have appeared over the past one hundred years. Official Victor and HMV record catalogs are, as with similar items issued by every record company, very popular among ephemera enthusiasts; these catalogs frequently appear on the market.

In addition, the HMV chain of record stores in the UK has featured *His Master's Voice* in silhouette on everything from plastic sleeves and shopping bags to security tape. Elsewhere, marketing and promotional items include marbles, plush toys, drinks trays, cast figurines, money boxes, and nearly life-size models of Nipper and his gramophone. All were once a common sight in any store where his owners plied their trade, and all are now a familiar sight in antique marts and mud sales. The modern interest in nostalgia-themed reproductions, meanwhile, has also seen a number of *His Master's Voice* images emerge—one should be careful not to mistake these for original items.

The Beatles' Yellow Submarine Playtape.

PLAYTAPES: THEY WERE TAPES. YOU PLAYED THEM.

The PlayTape was the creation of one Frank Stanton, and was launched at an MGM Records distributors meeting in New York in 1966. Self-winding tapes of anything up to twenty-four minutes in length, selling for between $1 and $3 (battery-operated players cost between $20 and $30), these tapes were touted as the ultimate in portable music, a market that radio had hitherto had to itself.

With backing from a number of record companies, PlayTapes were launched in September 1967 in five formats, each distinguished by the color of the cartridge. PlayTapes in red packaging featured two songs, the equivalent of a 7-inch single. Black cartridges featured four songs; white cartridges featured eight. Full LP releases would thus be spread across two tapes; the Beatles' *The White Album* consumed five.

In addition, there were also collections of children's songs (blue cartridges) and educational/spoken-word issues (gray cartridges). The tapes were packaged in bubble packs, which could be hung on special racks in retail outlets. All releases by individual artists were originally packaged with the same artwork.

There was no shortage of PlayTape releases. MGM artists dominated the field, with PlayTapes by the Animals, Herman's Hermits, the Righteous Brothers, and Steve and Eydie swiftly making themselves known. But other labels also signed on early, including Warner Bros. (Petula Clark, Connie Stevens, Grateful Dead, and Mason Williams); Capitol (the Beach Boys, Nat King Cole, the

Beatles, and the Hollyridge Strings); ABC (the Lovin' Spoonful, the Mamas and the Papas, and the Impressions); Reprise (Frank Sinatra, Nancy Sinatra, Dean Martin, and Jimi Hendrix); A&M (Herb Alpert and Sergio Mendes); and Motown (the Temptations, the Four Tops, Smokey Robinson, and Stevie Wonder).

All releases were in mono; plans to launch stereo PlayTapes never came to fruition, but that didn't seem to matter. By early 1968, the PlayTape catalog featured over 3,000 artists. A marketing tie-in with Pepsi-Cola broadened PlayTape's scope even further, while the electronics firm Discarton, Ltd., launched a fabulous combination portable record (45s only)/PlayTape player that stands as a direct forebear of the music centers of the 1970s.

However, despite having the portable market to itself for much of 1967–'68, PlayTapes' days were numbered. The nature of the system, while similar to 4- and 8-track technology, allowed for only 2-track tapes; it was that which limited the tape's length, and that which gave the rival formats an edge. By late 1968, the first 4- and 8-track portable players were hitting the market, and while PlayTapes did continue (for reasons unknown) to flourish in Germany, by 1969 their American life span was over.

The biggest market for PlayTapes today is limited to enthusiasts of individual artists, fans who are broadening collections that have already swept the vinyl, 8-track, and other common formats. The Beatles, of course, are the most popular act in this respect—most of their LP catalog appears to have been issued on PlayTape, though some releases have eluded discovery thus far. In addition, several Apple releases, including George Harrison's *Wonderwall Music* and Mary Hopkin's *Postcard*, also appeared on PlayTape.

POCKET DISCS: MUSIC FROM THE HIP

The Pocket Disc arrived on the scene in 1966, courtesy of Americom, Ltd. The idea was simple, if perhaps a little ambitious. Pocket Discs were, quite literally, discs you could carry around in your pocket; medium-thickness flexidiscs, admittedly, but discs all the same. (The Enterprise label had made a similar effort during the late '50s and early '60s, for inclusion with boxes of Carnation dried milk.)

Mitch Ryder and the Detroit Wheels

Break Out (NEW VOICE 2002, MONO LP WITH "GOOD GOLLY MISS MOLLY"/"DEVIL WITH A BLUE DRESS ON," 1966)
"I Need Help" (NEW VOICE 801, 7-INCH, 1965)
"Jenny Take a Ride!" (PHILCO HP 4, HIP-POCKET DISC, 1967)
"Jenny Takes a Ride!" (NEW VOICE 806, 7-INCH, MISSPELLED TITLE WITH "TAKES" INSTEAD OF "TAKE," 1965)
"Little Latin Lupe Lu" (NEW VOICE 808, 7-INCH, 1966)
Sock It To Me (NEW VOICE S2003, STEREO LP, 1967)
"Sock It To Me Baby" (NEW VOICE 820, 7-INCH, MUMBLED "PUNCH" IN LYRIC, 1965)
Take a Ride (NEW VOICE S2000, STEREO LP, 1966)
"Too Many Fish in the Sea" (NEW VOICE 822, 7-INCH, PICTURE SLEEVE, 1967)
What Now My Love? Mitch Ryder (DYNOVOICE 1901, MONO LP, 1967)

Just four inches across, Pocket Discs were issued in generic blue or red sleeves, and retailed through Americom's own vending machines. The difference was, whereas many flexis were the fruit of one-off deals that found them glued to magazine covers or arriving unsolicited in the mail, Pocket Discs went straight to the top, striking licensing deals with many top record labels, including, in 1969, Apple. In fact, Apple releases, while extremely scarce, are the best-known and certainly the best-documented of all Pocket Disc releases.

A series of Hip Pocket Discs, marketed by Philco, appeared a short time after the Americom issues. A number of popular issues were made, including a very rare Doors single ("Light My Fire"/"Break On Through"), but the series did not survive long.

POCKET ROCKERS: FOR THE TINIEST TOTS OF THE LOT

Pocket Rockers are one of the most infectious of modern-day tape collectibles, 2-track loop tapes manufactured by Fisher-Price Toys and launched via the larger retail chains in 1988.

Featuring two songs, the tapes were playable only on special Pocket Rockers tape machines, and were packaged complete with miniature album sleeves and a free pocket pop quiz.

Unlike the earlier PlayTapes, which they closely resemble, the target audience was young, those traditionally regarded as not yet ready to get into records, tapes, and hi-fis on their own. However, a surprisingly broad range of artists was incorporated into the series, including Bon Jovi ("Wanted Dead or Alive" and "Livin' on a Prayer"), Huey Lewis ("Hip to Be Square"), and the Fat Boys ("Wipe Out").

Other issues included the Bangles, Belinda Carlisle, Cutting Crew, Debbie Gibson, Exposé; Jan Hammer; Kim Wilde; LeVert; Lisa Lisa and Cult Jam; Los Lobos; Madonna; Mike and the Mechanics; Phil Collins; Pretty Poison; Ray Parker, Jr.; Taylor Dane; Tears for Fears; the Jets; Tiffany; Tom Petty; T'Pau; Whisper; and Whitney Houston. And for more traditional listeners, there were also titles by Bill Haley and the Comets, Chuck Berry, Boston, Danny and the Juniors, and Kenny Loggins.

There appear to have been around forty Pocket Rocker releases altogether, before the format faded from view during the early '90s; some branches of Toys "R" Us were carrying them at heavily discounted prices in 1992.

As collectibles, Pocket Rockers tend to hang out around the novelty end of the market, rubbing shoulders with PlayTapes and Mini-8s. As with those formats, however, the releases are certainly legitimate entries into the relevant acts' discographies—regardless of whether or not one has anything to play them on.

POLISH POSTCARDS: WARSAW PACKED

Although the so-called Polish Postcard singles are widely considered an aspect of flexidisc collecting, the sheer range and novelty of available issues has made them a well-established, if difficult to find, collectible in their own right.

Little firm data has been published surrounding these exotic issues' origins and development. The majority were produced by the Polpress label and are sometimes unsympathetically described as pirate productions, in that the music was not *always* licensed from the Western copyright holders. However, as one of the few rock music media readily available to Polish youth during the Communist era, their status as items of social history necessarily outweighs any legal issues.

Polish Postcard records seem to date back to the 1960s, when Mary Hopkin's "Bylie Taki Dni" ("Those Were the Days") was paired with the Ohio Express's untranslatable "Yummy Yummy Yummy" for an issue much sought after by Apple label collectors. Other known issues from this early period include Procol Harum, the Doors, and Pink Floyd.

Many of the discs (which are shaped and manufactured to the specifications of a regular picture postcard, then embossed with two musical tracks) bear images completely unrelated to their subject—cartoons, street scenes, greetings, and so forth. It also appears that new postcards were not always produced; many postcard singles exist pressed onto cards that clearly predate the song's recording—a 1920s view of Warsaw, for example, playing a 1970s Deep Purple song.

Neither was Poland the only Communist bloc nation issuing music in this form. The Soviet Union itself saw a number of postcard singles issued by the Moscow Photo/Cinema Organization during the late '60s, measuring some 9½" across and playing at 78 rpm. These cards, too, tend to offer totally unrelated images on the postcard side.

Another characteristic of these issues is their extremely limited availability. Some press runs were as tiny as fifty copies. One should also be aware that automatic record players—that is, those whose mechanism automatically returns the playing arm to its rest upon reaching the end of the record—are unable to play them, as the postcard record begins where a conventional 45's label would lie.

Entire LPs were produced in the postcard medium, two songs per card. For obvious reasons, complete sets are extremely rare and highly valued today, particularly those still contained within their own original packaging. Many cards, individual and otherwise, were issued in "picture sleeve" envelopes or wrappers, bearing the artist and song title. Several Pink Floyd titles are known in this format, including the albums *Dark Side of the Moon* and *Meddle,* and a unique compilation, *Super Floyd.* (Pink Floyd itself utilized the wrapper format as packaging for the set of nonmusical postcards included within its *Shine On* box set.)

Polish postcard releases, while actively traded, are nevertheless extremely difficult to find, as is the equipment with which they were made (see "Flexidiscs" for further details). Collectors might spend their entire lives without ever finding one through their traditional record-hunting channels. However, shift one's focus away from record collecting and into the realms of cartophily (postcard collecting), and some finds can be made. Many card dealers have sections of novelty and musical postcards, and while these tend to be dominated by mass-produced American issues, playing state anthems and songs for tourists and the like, more esoteric items abound.

PROMOS: THE CRITICS' CHOICE

"Promo" (or "demo," for "demonstration disc," in the UK) is one of the most commonly used and frequently misunderstood terms in record collecting. In the broadest sense, it refers to absolutely any recording that was not intended for public consumption *in this particular form;* more accurately, however, it describes only records, tapes, and CDs made available to radio stations, journalists, and other members of the media, as a preview of a forthcoming release. Other releases frequently listed as "promos," including discs relating to radio syndication shows (transcription discs), Jukebox Albums, and fan-club items, should in fact be noted under those categorizations.

A number of conditions qualify a record as a promo, but the most pertinent is, it is not intended to be bought and sold. Indeed, the majority of promo releases will carry a notice to this effect somewhere within the package.

This can range from the phrase "DEMONSTRATION: NOT FOR SALE" (or something similar) found on many LP jackets and 45 labels, to wordier warnings declaring the record to be the property of the issuing record company and liable for return upon demand. Other indications that a record or CD is a promo include a punch-hole, the obliteration of the bar code, or some similar defacement. LPs issued to radio stations, in addition, will bear a "timing strip"—a band of paper across the lower half of the front cover, giving song titles and their running times.

The label used for promos, too, is often different from that found on "stock" (or generally available) releases. In the past, many record labels used a predominantly white variation of its regular label (hence the alternate term "white label"), again marked with such terms as "demonstration," "promotion," or "audition copy." (British Invasion–era Imperial label 45s are among the best-loved singles to bear this quaint expression.) Catalog numbers, too, frequently differ from those on the regularly released versions.

Such warnings and admonitions, of course, have no effect on collectors. Promos are eminently collectible, and have been since the first ones appeared, back in the heyday of the 78. Issued in such small numbers that the very existence of many releases (including several Elvis Presley discs) is no more than rumor or supposition, this can prove a very specialized and expensive area to enter. The early years of the 45, however, are little better.

The first promo 45 was, in fact, the first 45 ever issued, a demonstration disc produced for RCA's newly launched automatic record changer and the 45 rpm platters that were developed to accompany it. The *Whirl-Away Demonstration Record* featured excerpts from several of the first releases in this exciting new series, including Eddy Arnold's "Bouquet of Roses" (in terms of actual catalog number, the first commercially available 45), plus a spoken description of the product.

Just one copy is confirmed to exist today, although many were produced, to accompany in-

store demonstration models of the record player. Once the promotion ended, RCA sales representatives descended en masse to retrieve the entire displays. They were then, presumably, recycled or destroyed.

Collecting 45s is the most popular activity for promo collectors, and it's the easiest field to break into. Often readily identifiable by the appearance of a mono mix on one side, stereo on the other (a recording practice that continued into the 1980s), promo 45s can be picked up in almost any used-record store, often at very cheap prices.

Indeed, when contemplating any purchase (or sale) of promo 45s—whether they are mono-stereo couplings or simply promotional label versions of a regular release—one should always remember that virtually *every* 45 of the age was issued in this form, and often in sizable quantities. Indeed, not only are the majority of promos not at all rare, there are many releases (45s, LPs, and CDs alike) that are far more common as promos than as stock copies.

Specialist and completist collectors may show an interest, but in general, a common record is a common record, regardless of its designation. Locate Tori Amos's *Y Kant Tori Read* LP without a promo cutout notch, however, and you have a genuinely sought-after, name-your-own-price item. Find stock copies of Crowded House's "I Feel Possessed" or Jon Anderson's "Surrender" and you might not get the price of a latte for any of them, but at least you have a genuine rarity.

Where promos become especially interesting is in their propensity to offer material in a form that is not otherwise available.

The promo for Long John Baldry's "Cuckoo." The "PLUG SIDE" legend denotes the song that DJs were expected to play.

A 78 rpm promo for Eartha Kitt's so-sultry rendition of the showtune "Let's Do It."

Robyn Hitchcock and the Soft Boys

A Can of Bees (2 CRABS CLAW 1001, 1979)
"Anglepoise Lamp" (RADAR ADA 8, 1978)
Give It to the Soft Boys EP (RAW 5, 1977)
"He's a Reptile" (MIDNIGHT DING 4, 1983)
"I Wanna Destroy You" (ARMAGEDDON AS 005, 1980)
"Love Poisoning" (BOB BOB 1, 1982)
Near the Soft Boys EP (ARMAGEDDON AEP 002, 1980)
"Only the Stones Remain" (ARMAGEDDON AS 029, 1981)
Two Halves for the Price of One (ARMAGEDDON BYE 1, 1982)
Underwater Moonlight (ARMAGEDDON ARM 1, 1980)

Sometimes, this means simply an unusual pairing on a single or EP. Many record labels, when attempting to "break" a new artist to radio and the other media, will produce limited-edition promos featuring key tracks that might interest DJs but that would never be issued as conventional 45s or LPs.

One example, popular among David Bowie collectors, pairs two tracks apiece by Mick Ronson (Bowie's former guitarist) and Dana Gillespie on one EP; another, even scarcer, marries Bowie and Gillespie onto an album, one side each, that was then used to solicit record deals for them both in 1971. (The Bowie side alone was reissued in a replica sleeve for Record Store Day in 2017.)

Others still will highlight potential hits from a new album and serve them up on an EP. The Kinks' *Give the People What They Want* LP, in 1981, was previewed with a very collectible four-track 12-inch. Other EPs cherry-pick entire series of albums—the first twenty-three volumes released in Pearl Jam's 2001 *Bootleg Series* were highlighted on a fifteen-track CD sampler (Epic).

Another popular theme for collectors revolves around the mono promo albums issued in America during the late '60s and well into the 1970s. While 1967–'68 saw record companies across America abandon mono for stereo, radio was somewhat slower to adapt. Many popular albums of the age—what the general public knew as stereo-only releases by Cream, Janis Joplin, the Grateful Dead, and so many more—were mixed into straightforward mono for radio play, a practice that has provided for some truly stellar rarities.

Most 1960s-era mono promos are relatively common. They do fetch a premium, but it should never be high. However, move into the 1970s, and releases by artists who are already considered collectible, and you are looking at a whole different scenario.

Both the Rolling Stones' *Sticky Fingers* and Paul McCartney's *Ram*, released in 1971, were issued in mono mixes (the latter was reissued in 2012); from even later in the day, Led Zeppelin's 1973 album *Houses of the Holy* was also issued as a mono promo. None of these mono albums offered any new musical variation on the stereo experience; their collectibility centers upon their very existence. Remember, however, to ensure that the record's actual label includes the magic word "mono"; remember also that only radio promos were treated thus. Promos issued to other members of the media remained in stereo.

Other promos deviate from released issues in equally spectacular ways. Promos of Art Garfunkel's 1978 LP *Watermark*, featuring the song "Fingerpaint" on side two, became prized above many other Garfunkel issues after the album's running order was changed for full release.

The earliest promos of Michael Jackson's "Ben" 45 featured authentic rat noises behind the music—these were not only removed for public consumption, they were also deleted from all subsequent promo issues as well. Even more disconcerting, however, are promo copies of Wild Cherry's "Play That Funky Music," which were sent to radio with the crucial hook-line "white boy" deleted. Political correctness is not a new development.

Of course, alterations take place with regularly issued LPs as well. There are, for example, two different versions of the mega-selling soundtrack *Saturday Night Fever*, the first featuring a studio recording of the Bee Gees' landmark "Jive Talkin'," the other substituting a live recording. Madonna's first album, 1983's *Madonna*, substituted a guitar-heavy remix of "Burning Up" for the original version immediately after the initial pressing run. Roxy Music's *Manifesto* saw several original mixes replaced by hit remixes during its shelf life.

Generally, these issues are little more than completist curios. Unless there are specific (usually controversial) reasons cited for such changes, stock-copy variations tend to attract only scant attention. Promo variations, on the other hand, are always considered worthwhile.

Promo-only compilations of an artist's greatest hits, designed to arouse interest in his or her new material, are a time-honored device. Another Kinks' issue, *Then, Now and in Between*; *Everything You Wanted to Hear by Jeff Beck but Were Afraid to Ask*; Kiss's *Special Album for Their Summer Tour*; Bruce Springsteen's *As Requested around the World*; Peter Gabriel's *Before Us*; and the Cracker–Camper Van Beethoven *Virgin Years* are just a random fraction of the myriad killer compilations available only on promo LP or CD.

A number of promotional releases sampling forthcoming releases (most notably box sets) have also taken on legendary status. When the Beach Boys' *Pet Sounds 30th Anniversary Box Set* CD was withdrawn from the schedules shortly following dispatch of the promotional samplers, demand skyrocketed, with the promos reaching $100-plus before the box set was finally rescheduled.

Excitement also attended the release of another Capitol sampler, this time previewing 1999's *John Lennon Anthology* box set. Included among the tracks on *howitis* was a version of the John Lennon–Cheap Trick collaboration "I'm Losing You," clocking in at a full minute longer than the released version, and featuring not only a unique count-in, but also an additional bridge section. Such bonuses are not a common feature of samplers, but they do ensure careful listening from collectors!

Fans of tribute albums, meanwhile, should be aware that several have been issued as promotional double CDs, featuring the tributes on one disc and the originals on the other—Black Sabbath's *The Bible According To . . .* is a popular example. And while custom promos rarely cater to audiophiles, the early '80s saw a number of issues apparently aimed at that very market.

Members of the Warner Bros. group of labels issued a number of promos on the high-quality "Quiex II" vinyl, denoted by a sticker on the front cover (the actual records and labels are indistinguishable from regular vinyl issues). Sought-after releases in this series include *The John Lennon Collection* and Fleetwood Mac's *Mirage*.

New releases are not the only newsworthy events to demand noteworthy promos. Following Pink Floyd founder Roger Waters' successful 1990 performance of *The Wall* in Berlin, Columbia issued *The Wall Berlin,* a promo-only CD gathering of Floyd cuts.

But the most popular promos, the bedrock upon which the entire promo-collecting hobby is built, lies in the availability of material that simply hasn't been issued to the general public in any form.

These can take many forms. The simplest are such offerings as the 12-inch Bee Gees mega-mix issued by their UK label at the height of the early-'80s *Stars on 45* medley mania. Or one might find isolated tracks included on collections of otherwise familiar material—Smashing Pumpkins' *1991–1998* included among its eighteen tracks an exclusive acoustic version of "Mayonaise."

Others, however, serve up entire albums' worth of unissued music. In 1996, Robyn Hitchcock marked the thirtieth anniversary of Bob Dylan's legendary Royal Albert Hall Concert (the one that *isn't* featured on Dylan's own *Live 1966* album!) by recreating Dylan's live set for one of his own shows—the *Royal Queen Albert and Beautiful Homer* promo captured the occasion.

The "official bootleg" boom of the mid-'70s saw excellent and long-in-demand live albums by Tom Petty, Nils Lofgren, and Graham Parker; twenty years later, Matthew Sweet's *Goodfriend: Another Take on Girlfriend* delivered demo and live versions of tracks from his critically acclaimed third album. Once again, the album has been reissued for the general public, for Record Store Day in 2016.

Many record companies abandoned the issue of special promo 45s and LPs during the mid-'80s, as their attention turned toward popularizing the CD. Dire Straits' *Brothers in Arms* (Warner Bros. 25264) was the first album to be issued as a promo CD to both US and British radio in May 1985. It seems curious today, but Britain's BBC Radio 1 devoted an entire program to playing the vinyl and CD versions side by side, so listeners could decide for themselves about the sound quality. In the early years of the new format, and indeed, into the early '90s, the majority of media promos were dispatched on cassette tape. It was only as the decade progressed that promo CDs became ubiquitous, and by the end of that span, their day had already passed.

By the early 2000s, many promo albums were being burned onto CD-R; or, to combat piracy, issued with unique identifying watermarks, or with the recipient's name printed on the label. Today, although CD promos are still produced, many more labels prefer simply to service the media with mp3s. Although, in an amusing turn-around of the norm, the British Fruits de Mer label produces CD promos of releases that will be available only on vinyl. In the main, CD promos of full albums can only be valued on a case-by-case basis, though it is true to say that the vast majority are of little value, particularly when they are issued without artwork, or with only limited sleeve information.

Unlike promotional LPs, which possess an inherent collectible value, the deliberately unattractive promo CD (or, worse still, CD-R) is regarded with little more respect than the cassette that preceded it.

Promo collectors should also be on the lookout for what were briefly, if not very catchily, termed "Compact Disc Jockeys" (CDJs)—promotional CD singles, tending to feature just one song. They have a market all of their own, although the sheer number of issues also reduces the field in general to something of a crapshoot, with many used-CD dealers happily selling them off in bulk, so many for a buck or two. It's all a far cry from when they first arrived on the scene, in 1986.

Back then, CDJs (were a prized beast indeed, all the more so since regular CD singles were still struggling to make an impression on either marketplace or marketing departments. At least until 1993, virtually every current hit record one heard on the radio was taken from a CDJ—but few of them were actually available in the stores, and even fewer were on CD. The cassette single still dominated, and collectors were willing to pay $20 or more for CDJs.

Since that time, the market for CDJs has settled down considerably, and even name-artist releases are scarcely noticed any longer. But, of course, exceptions abound. One of the rarest CDs of all time is a CDJ of Nirvana's "Pennyroyal Tea (Scott Litt Mix)," scheduled for release as a UK single in May 1993 to coincide with the band's European tour, then canceled following vocalist Kurt Cobain's death.

While an estimated ten vinyl test pressings were destroyed, an unknown number of CDs, plus printed artwork for the German release, survived. One copy sold for $1,000 on eBay during April 1999; the same month, coincidentally, that a copy of Prince's legendary "Pussy Power" in-house Paisley Park promo, sold for over $600 in the same forum.

QUADRAPHONIC LPS: EXTRA EARS OPTIONAL

Quadraphonic sound has gone down in musical history as one of the greatest and most expensive failures of the vinyl age. Touted, in the aftermath of stereo's so-successful introduction during the 1960s, as the next level in audio entertainment, "surround sound" was originally introduced in 1970 on 8-track, with the first vinyl issues following a year later.

Initially, the majority of releases were targeted toward the audiophile market, with classical and jazz albums high on the schedules. Gradually, the format broadened its scope toward rock and pop performers, with Columbia, RCA, EMI, and two labels under the Warner Bros. umbrella, Elektra and Asylum, among the most prolific issuers, releasing a stream of potentially big-selling albums in the new format.

Unfortunately, that was where quad's downfall lay. It was not bad enough that quad required a special decoder before it could be enjoyed to its full potential—necessitating the purchase of an entirely new sound system. Even worse was the fact that the industry itself had yet to standardize which of several competing quad formats was to be employed, so that anybody wishing to pick up releases from more than one group of labels would need more than one player.

Three major systems were developed: Sansui's QS (quadraphonic-stereo), Sony's SQ (stereo-quadraphonic), and JVC's CD-4 (compatible discrete four channel). A fourth system, Nippon Columbia's UD-4 (universal discrete four channel), perhaps mercifully failed to make it off the ground.

Several labels issued albums in two of the three formats—Virgin in the UK actually issued Mike Oldfield's *Tubular Bells* in all three. But these were the exception. In essence, if you bought one system, you were stuck with one group of labels—Columbia, A&M, and Vanguard, for example, if you chose SQ; Warner Bros. (Elektra and Asylum), RCA, and Phonogram if you opted for CD-4; Command, Impulse, and Ovation with QS.

Had these conflicts been resolved, or had the competing formats at least become compatible with one another, quad might have succeeded. Instead, by decade's end, it was a dead issue.

Billion Dollar Babies *in quad . . . twice as good as the stereo.*

Mike Oldfield's Tubular Bells— *"for people with four ears," insisted a sticker on the front cover.*

Despite the varying formats, quad records have long been popular with collectors, many of whom might never have even seen a quad sound system. Even on a regular stereo, quad remixes can sound spectacularly different, with certain collectors willing to go to considerable financial lengths to acquire recordings that are unique to the format.

Included in this category are releases by such acts as the Doors, John Lennon, Pink Floyd, Bob Dylan, Black Sabbath, Alice Cooper, and Deep Purple—in other words, artists who are collectible in every other format as well. (There were no Beatles albums issued in quad.)

However, the vast majority of quad records are worth little more than their stereo counterparts. Albums by the likes of the Carpenters, Harry Nilsson, Eric Clapton, Carole King, Earth Wind and Fire, Carly Simon, Bill Wyman, Chicago (whose entire quad catalog formed a handsome CD box set in 2016), and Santana seem to clog up every "quad" bin at record fairs, and certainly dominate Internet auction listings.

The depressing absence of any substantial bidding is eloquent enough testimony to the general lack of interest in any sonic delights that these gems may hold. For they do, as a rule, offer the listener a brand new perspective on a recording, even if, as is so often the case, one gets the distinct impression that the remix is designed more to show off the format's capabilities than to enhance the recording itself.

In terms of new releases (both current catalog and remixed older issues), quad was at its peak during 1975–'76. Thereafter it swiftly became apparent that the format was not going to take off, and issues declined alarmingly. By 1978, the whole thing was forgotten.

And thirty years later it was back, in the form of surround sound.

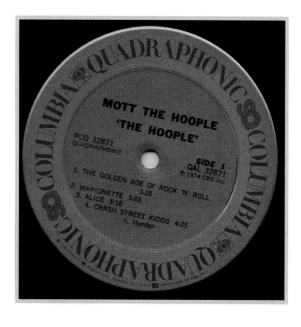

The quad Mott the Hoople's The Hoople is so radically remixed that it sometimes feels like a demonstration disc.

Crucial Quad Varieties

ALICE COOPER, *BILLION DOLLAR BABIES*
(WB BS4 2685)

The entire LP has been completely remixed, but several tracks are of especial note—a guitar-heavy "I Love the Dead" and a powerfully horn-driven "Elected" among them. Elsewhere, "Unfinished Suite" boasts improved and extra-terrifying dentist sound effects, while "Generation Landslide" features an alternate ending, before segueing into a ferocious, colossally superior take of "Sick Things." The art of the quad mix has seldom been put to better use!

BOB DYLAN, *DESIRE*
(COLUMBIA PCQ 33893)

The exclusive availability of a noticeably alternate mix of "Romance in Durango" is responsible for raising this album high in collecting circles; it is not, however, the only reason for listening. The entire LP is vastly superior in every department. The already somber "Joey" is raised to fresh heights of majesty by the newly emphasized violin, while "Black Diamond Bay" benefits immeasurably from its pronounced percussion.

DAVID ESSEX, *ROCK ON*
(COLUMBIA CQ 32560)

If you know the title track—all echo, percussion and echoing percussion—and know how good it sounds in stereo, you can only imagine what it's like in quad. The rest of the album pales by comparison, with a lot of the quad effects sounding almost forced. But for "Rock On" alone, it's a worthwhile investment.

ART GARFUNKEL, *BREAKAWAY*
(COLUMBIA PCQ 33700)

Richard Perry's original production was so extravagant that the quad remix can do little but accent the textures. While the overall sound is superior to the stereo edition, the most marked variations are in the harmonies, and a handful of inconsequential instrumental flourishes, including a slightly drawn-out (and seriously panned) fade to "Waters of March" and more pronounced guitar and percussion during the Paul Simon reunion "My Little Town."

MOTT THE HOOPLE, *THE HOOPLE*
(COLUMBIA PCQ 32871)

One of the most radical, but oddly redundant, of all quad rock releases appears to have been constructed with nothing more in mind than thrilling the listener's ears. Abundant use of echo brings some almost disconcerting effects into play—gently through "Golden Age of Rock 'n' Roll," obtrusively during "Alice," most portentously in "Through the Looking Glass." Sharp ears will discover more conversation beneath the intro to "Pearl and Roy," and more na-na-na ribaldry in the backing chorus, but the highlights here are a fine guitar workover during "Crash Street Kids," the most aggressive cut on the original LP, and an almost Spectorish thunder to "Roll Away the Stone," the most gorgeously, stupidly romantic number in the band's entire repertoire.

MIKE OLDFIELD, *BOXED*
(VIRGIN VBOX 1)

This four-LP box set comprises quad remixes of Oldfield's first three LPs—*Tubular Bells, Hergest Ridge,* and *Ommadawn*—plus an exclusive fourth set, *Collaborations,* featuring material cut with orchestral leader David Bedford, among others.

The remixes add little to Oldfield's already sumptuous recordings, with the most telling departure being an alternate version of "The Sailor's Hornpipe" at the conclusion of *Bells,* featuring a spoken-word passage from master of ceremonies Viv Stanshall. Also worthy of investigation, however, is the remixed conclusion to side one of *Ommadawn,* where the crescendo of guitars builds to levels of palpable intensity. One of the most powerful passages of music in the modern rock idiom just grew even stronger.

PINK FLOYD, *DARK SIDE OF THE MOON*
(HARVEST Q4SHVL 804)

Even in stereo, this was one of the equipment demonstration albums of the age. The quad mix raises many elements to prominence, beginning with the hitherto mumbled spoken passages at the opening of side one and culminating, from a sonic point of view, with a newly deafening alarm clock sequence. The majority of quad enhancements are confined to the spoken and FX portions of the LP, but "Any Colour You Like" is a revelation on headphones.

SIMON AND GARFUNKEL, *BRIDGE OVER TROUBLED WATERS*
(COLUMBIA CQ 30995)

Even if you've never owned another quadraphonic recording in your life, you probably have this one. Yet, what was once a mainstay of every thrift store in the land (and is probably still widely available for a matter of cents) is also one of the most beautiful sounding of all quad releases. For once, the remixers concentrated on what was already on the record, rather than seeking out new and interesting elements to raise into the mix. That said, "Cecilia" is certainly more percussive than its stereo counterpart, with new wind elements as well, while "Baby Driver" may or may not be improved by the raucous saxophones.

QUAD-8S: EIGHT TRACKS, FOUR CHANNELS

Up there with 8-tracks (and as we have just seen), quadraphonic sound is widely regarded as one of the biggest jokes in music-industry history. Put the two together, then, and you will certainly be requiring a new set of ribs.

Yet quadraphonic 8-tracks ("Quad-8s," as they are called) also represent one of the most volatile growth areas in modern record collecting, offering sometimes stunning mixes that simply were never made available in any other format, and though it might seem difficult for non-enthusiasts to believe, frequently boasting sound quality that mere vinyl could never eclipse.

Of especial fascination is the realization that, despite looking identical to stereo cartridges, Quad-8 does not behave at all like a conventional 8-track. While stereo tapes change programs three times as they play through an entire tape (at the conclusion of programs one, two, and three), Quad-8 changes just once, much as the old 4-track tapes did. This was because the four channels of sound that define quad each occupied four bands on the tape, thus creating just two programs. The downside of this was that twice as much tape needed to be crammed into the cartridge, thus rendering Quad-8 tapes even more susceptible to damage and breakage than their stereo cousins.

The technology also necessitated acquiring an entirely new sound system upon which to play the tapes, with specially designed playing heads capable of recognizing the expanded input. This requirement was an expensive drawback at the time, and is an even greater difficulty today. Quad-8 players can play stereo tapes, but conventional stereo players do not satisfactorily play Quad-8.

These waters are muddied further by the number of pseudo-Quad-8 players that appeared on the market as the tapes' own popularity increased, and which seem to predominate today. Bearing such names as 4D, Quad Matrix, Quatravox, and Quadradial, these decks were, simply, stereo systems with two sets of speakers. The inner workings of the quad player, as manufactured by the likes of Akai, Panasonic, Pioneer, and Sanyo (and clearly notated QUAD-8, Q-8, or DISCRETE QUADRAPHONIC 8-track) were far beyond their capabilities.

It is for these reasons that Quad-8 cartridges, even more so than their regular counterparts, constitute a tiny, and extraordinarily specialized, end of the modern market. However, it is a market that is more than happy to pay considerable sums for the tapes it requires.

The first Quad-8 tapes were introduced in fall of 1970, shortly after the unveiling of the quadraphonic reel-to-reel format, but around a year before the first quadraphonic vinyl LP records.

Initially, these constituted simple remixes of strong catalog material—the soundtrack to *The Sound of Music* (RCA OQ8 1001) was the first-ever release. By 1971, however, custom quad mixdowns were being undertaken, often adding new sound effects to the original tape in order to make them more attractive to listeners and (presumably) to justify the extra cost; like quad LPs, the tapes retailed at around $1 more than stereo.

Although Quad-8 releases were widespread, only a handful of record companies seriously got behind the format. Columbia and RCA led the way; A&M, ABC, and Warner Bros. followed. Capitol/EMI released only a handful of tapes, however; the Phonogram and London/Decca groups likewise, and rock releases from these latter companies account for the majority of the format's most spectacular rarities.

These include (but are not limited to) Pink Floyd's *Dark Side of the Moon* and *Wish You Were Here*, Kraftwerk's *Autobahn*, and five titles from ex-Beatles: John Lennon's *Imagine* (Lennon himself supervised the quad remixing of the title track) and *Walls and Bridges*; Paul McCartney's *Band on the Run* and *Venus and Mars*, plus the *Live and Let Die* movie soundtrack; and Ringo Starr's *Goodnight Vienna*. The excitement surrounding these latter releases increases when one realizes that *Imagine* alone was also granted a quad release on vinyl, and that was in Europe only.

Other titles to appear exclusively in Quad-8 (and, very rarely, quad reel-to-reel) include some quite unexpected titles—quadraphonic mixes of albums by Babe Ruth, Bachman-Turner Overdrive, Chuck Berry (the less-than-essential *London Sessions*), and many more were delivered in cartridge form, without ever seeing the business end of a vinyl stamper.

In the classical arena, the few Deutsche Grammophon Quad-8s to have seen release never have difficulty finding homes, while Isao Tomita's synthesized rendition of Gustav Holst's *The Planets,* from 1978, is considered collectible, not only in its own right, but also because it represents the very last Quad-8 release of them all.

Moody Blues

Days of Future Passed (DERAM DE 16012, MONO LP, 1968)

"From the Bottom of My Heart" (LONDON 9764, 7-INCH, 1965)

"Go Now" (LONDON 9726, 7-INCH, BLUE/PURPLE/WHITE LABEL, 1965)

Go Now, The Moody Blues 1 (LONDON LL 3428, MONO LP, 1965)

The Moody Blues (UK DECCA DFE 8622, EP, 1965)

"Nights in White Satin" (DERAM 85023, 7-INCH, CREDITS WRITER AS REDWAVE, 1967)

On the Threshold of a Dream (NAUTILUS NR21, AUDIOPHILE-PRESSING LP, 1981)

Special Interview Kit (THRESHOLD THX 100, PROMO LP, 1971)

"Steal Your Heart Away", Moodyblues (UK DECCA F11971, 7-INCH, 1964)

"This Is My House" (LONDON 1005, 7-INCH, 1967)

REEL-TO-REEL TAPES: HIGH-END AND HOT

The most popular tape format among collectors today is the reel-to-reel, the single-spool packages that were also the first magnetic tapes to be made available to consumers, during the mid-'50s.

At seven inches in diameter (the same size as a 45), reel-to-reels were attractively packaged in cardboard boxes bearing full-color artwork. They were also very exclusive. Reels were marketed toward the audiophile end of their contemporary market—indeed, in general, the tapes were not even available in regular record stores, the majority being stocked instead by high-end equipment and electronics outlets. It is a further indication of the esteem in which reels were held that the first-ever commercially available stereo recordings appeared in the tape format, some time before the first stereo LPs were marketed.

Tapes were issued at three speeds: the professionals-only 15 ips (inches per second), 7 1/2 ips, and 3 3/4, the standard to which both the later 4-track and 8-track cartridges adhered. Available in both mono and stereo, reels were designated "two track," which played in one direction only; "four track" required you to turn over the tape to continue listening at the end of the program.

For much of the format's early life, releases were aimed at what might now be termed a determinedly highbrow audience, with the emphasis on classical, jazz, opera, and theatrical issues. Not until the mid-'60s brought the rising star of the 8-track into view did the reel-to-reel first acknowledge rock music, and even then, it was extremely choosy about who was allowed into the club.

The decision of what to release was taken not by record companies, but by the manufacturing company, Stereotape, which leased the music from the labels, then distributed the tapes through its own network. This arrangement meant that there was often a considerable lag between a new LP release appearing on disc and its arrival on reel—or on any other tape format, for that matter. It would be early 1968 before firm efforts were taken on an industry-wide level to ensure vinyl and tape issues became simultaneous.

Immediately, sales of all the then-current tape formats began to rise, with reel-to-reels showing an especial gain. Emboldened, Bell and Howell (as Stereotape was now known—it would later become Magtec) began issuing more rock music in the format; this period also saw Ampex, hitherto known primarily as makers of 8-track cartridges, move into the field.

The vast majority of readily available rock reel-to-reels date from this period. Although the format remained in use until the early '80s (by which time record clubs had become its principal outlet), the early '70s produced a boom in new releases.

The most collectible artists in the format are, of course, the usual suspects—from the 1960s, Elvis Presley, the Beatles, the Rolling Stones, Jimi Hendrix, Bob Dylan, and Simon and Garfunkel; from the new decade, Pink Floyd, Led Zeppelin, Black Sabbath, and David Bowie, among others. A handful of quad reels issued during the early '70s are also much sought after—the Allman Brothers' *At the Fillmore East,* Bachman-Turner Overdrive's *Not Fragile,* and Caravan's *For Girls Who Grow Plump in the Night* are among the most popular titles.

Since only a select group of artists are featured in the format, most rock reel-to-reels are considered of value today. This is true even when the corresponding vinyl is of little worth—certain Presley and Moody Blues releases fall into this category. However, condition is paramount, as the format was wide open—literally—to abuse and damage.

Finding something to play them on can also be problematic. Although *broken* reel-to-reel machines do seem to turn up a lot, working models are not only expensive, they can also be finicky. In particular, it is crucial to note whether or not the deck is even capable of playing stereo (four-track) tapes correctly. A mono (two-

The reel-to-reel for Simon and Garfunkel's 1979 swansong.

track) player will read both strips of information as one and play them simultaneously, with one in reverse. Stereo players, of course, can handle both formats without difficulty.

That said, new machines are still in production, including several that the audiophile community swears will outperform even the most expensive turntable. A handful of tapes, primarily classical and jazz titles, are also available.

SHEET MUSIC:
PLAY IT YOURSELF

With a history that predates even cylinders by a considerable margin, and with sales that far eclipsed many of the hit records that it featured, sheet music might not be most obvious adjunct to a record collection, but it is certainly one of the most logical.

It is exactly what it says on the tin: a few pages, sometimes as few as one or two, printed in playable form—the lyrics and music of the latest popular tunes, be they the minstrel hits of nineteenth century music hall, or the latest chart smashes of today.

The UK sheet music for Slade's 1974 hit "Everyday."

Its history is immense—what we would now know as sheet music has been excavated, in the form of inscribed tablets, from ancient Sumeria, and dated to 2,000 BC. The ancient Greeks and Romans wrote down music; the medieval monks transcribed it onto manuscript; and the oldest known book to include music, *The Mainz Psalter,* was published in 1457.

What we would today recognize as "sheet music" first appeared during the nineteenth century, as the American music industry consolidated itself around Tin Pan Alley in New York City. There was scant regard for copyright in those days; music publishers (and enterprising private individuals) would simply take the most popular songs of the day, transcribe them onto cheap paper, and sell them without any regard for any composer's (or rival publisher's) rights. This situation changed as the century wore on, of course, but the popularity of the format never wavered.

In an age without radio, and with cylinders and (later) gramophones still prohibitively expensive, for many people, sheet music was often their sole opportunity to hear a song—provided they, or someone they knew, was capable of playing it!

The golden age of sheet music, both for the publishers and for collectors, was the last decade of the nineteenth century through the first of the twentieth. There is no authoritative catalog to refer to, but it has been estimated that some 25,000 new songs were published in sheet music form every year during that period, and sales boomed.

Some songs, "Let Me Call You Sweetheart" and "Down by the Old Mill Stream," for example, are claimed to have sold up to six million pieces of sheet music apiece; others ("A Bird in a Gilded Cage" is one) sold an only marginally less-respectable two or three million..

Yet the music was not the sole attraction for would-be purchasers. Just as modern record collectors are tempted by eye-candy album sleeves, so our century-past predecessors were wooed with likewise cover art. Sometimes it was relevant to the song itself; sometimes it wasn't (nothing has changed). Sometimes it deployed the vision of a leading artist (the great Vargas undertook several commissions illustrating sheet music related to Florenz Ziegfeld's *Ziegfeld Follies*; Louis Gaudin is remembered for his depictions of Josephine Baker); sometimes the artist labored in absolute obscurity.

No matter. Without an iota of musical ability, it is very easy to become utterly entranced by sheet music, simply for the quality of the art; and, when collectors gather, they are as likely to include collectors of, for example, militaria; sport; stars of stage and screen; and planes and boats and trains, and so forth, as fans of jazz, ragtime, dance numbers, Broadway hits, or popular composers. Basically, if songs were written about a topic, then the chances are that sheet music was published of the song, usually with a cover to match. And there will be collectors pursuing it.

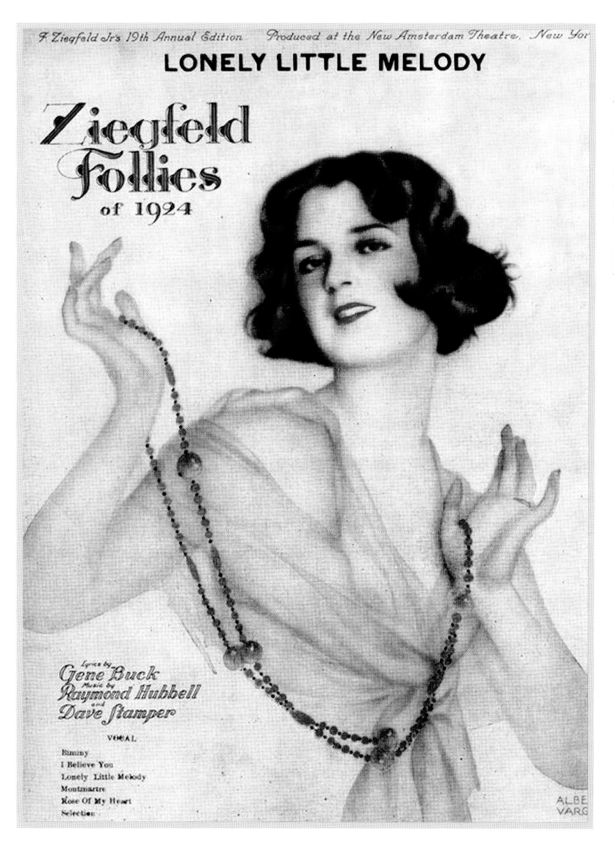

Albert Vargas undertook several sheet music commissions—this, for the 1924 Ziegfeld Follies, is perhaps the greatest of all. The cover model, incidentally, is believed to have been actress Olive Thomas, whom Vargas first painted in 1920, shortly before her death.

Neither does one need to nurse a fascination with the good old days to delve into the hobby. Sheet music continues to be published today, allowing collectors to effectively trace the story of the last hundred and thirty years of recorded sound *without having to play, or listen to, a single recording.*

As with records, of course, there are certain . . . not rules, but guidelines . . . that one should be aware of. For starters, condition is paramount. Just as records were meant to be played, and it would be a very tiresome person who simply filed them away unopened in a vault, so sheet music was meant to be opened and spread across a music stand, and enjoyed.

Consequently, a lot of it has come down to us in decidedly ragged condition. The paper used for sheet music was rarely of the highest quality, particularly during the war years, 1917–'18 and 1941–'45 (1914–'18, 1939–'45 in Europe). Just as it will always be easier to find a 45 in a tattered jacket, so sheet music, too, is most commonly spotted with tears, creases, stains, and more. Paper ages, too; it becomes brittle and flaky. And in exactly the same way as a rare record becomes increasingly less desirable the further down the grading scale it plunges, so the value of a piece of sheet music, too, depreciates quickly if it hasn't been looked after.

Is it complete? Many pieces of sheet music contained a single loose page within a fold-out cover, and obviously, these loose pages were very easily separated from their parent.

Has it been trimmed? The earliest twentieth century sheet music was published in an impressively large format, around 10.5 inches by 13.25. This was then reduced, during World War One, to 9 x 12, and this is the format that has remained in use ever since. Consequently, many of the storage boxes, albums, and so forth that have been produced throughout the last century have themselves adhered to 9 x 12, leaving owners of the larger sheets to either find someplace else to keep them, *or*, to fold or even trim the larger sheets to fit. (Sheet music that has been framed also frequently suffers from such attentions.) Suffice to say, this too will seriously reduce the worth of a piece.

Enough of the pitfalls and problems, though. At least until you have filled your first album or two with the cheaper, more common, material, sheet music is generally affordable (eBay usually boasts a few hundred bulk lots to choose from) and, provided your specialty isn't too specialized, reasonably common.

"Personality" pieces can become harder to find. Composers like Jerome Kern, Irving Berlin, Scott Joplin, and George Gershwin are vastly popular; and while their bigger hits are commonplace, there are rarities here just as there are in every other musical field.

Early movie stars, many of whom featured on sheet music regardless of whether they had any connection to the song, are also widely sought after; and then there are those icons whose very name

Johnny and the Hurricanes

"Beatnik Fly" (WARWICK 520, 7-INCH, PICTURE SLEEVE, 1960)
The Big Sound Of (BIG TOP ST 13-1302, STEREO LP, 1960)
"Crossfire" (WARWICK 502, 7-INCH, 1959)
"Down Yonder" (BIG TOP 3036, 7-INCH, PICTURE SLEEVE, 1960)
Johnny and the Hurricanes (WARWICK W2007S, STEREO LP, 1959)
Live at the Star Club (ATILLA 1030, LP, 1964)
"Red River Rock" (WARWICK 509ST, STEREO 7-INCH, 1959)
"Reveille Rock" (WARWICK 513ST, STEREO 7-INCH, 1959)
"Rocking Goose" (BIG TOP 3051, 7-INCH, PICTURE SLEEVE, 1960)
Stormsville (WARWICK W2010ST, STEREO LP, 1960)

is sufficient to persuade the casual dealer to add a zero or two to the price–Judy Garland, Marilyn Monroe, Jayne Mansfield, Laurel and Hardy. And sometimes, they are justified to do so; sheet music for the first Beatles' single, "Love Me Do," has sold for over $250.

Black Americana is another popular and possibly pricey field. In 2016, a copy of Mose Gumble's "The Hoogie Boogie Dance," published in 1901, sold for $1,400 on eBay. The cover artists can affect a piece's value; and the art, too, can make a difference. In the early 1900s, sheet music produced by the A. Hoen Company featured some fabulous lithographs; one such (illustrating a song by composer ET Pauli) sold for over $1,000 on eBay in 2008.

SUPER AUDIO COMPACT DISCS: THEY'RE COMPACT DISCS, AND THEY'RE SUPER. APPARENTLY.

Launched in 2002 as a rival to the emergent DVD-A, there was very little difference in terms of sound quality between the two formats; where the SACD fell down was initially (and, in fact, for a long time thereafter), at the need for a standalone player that was incompatible with the opposing format.

That said, the SACD quickly accrued (and has retained) its devotees, with well over 500 different labels eventually coming on board, and several artists launching their own specialist SACD labels—including the Chicago and London Symphony Orchestras.

As with what we might describe as other recent niche formats (MiniDisc, DCC, etc.), SACD collecting is a small, if devoted, pursuit, with the greatest rarities including a box set of sixteen Rolling Stones SACDs, remastered and reissued in 2003; Creedence Clearwater Revival's *Absolute Originals* box; the Doors' *Infinite* box; David Bowie's *Scary Monsters;* and Kraftwerk's *Minimum-Maximum* live album. Any number of box sets released by classical specialists Esoteric are also in great demand.

78S: FRAGILITY AS A WAY OF LIFE

If one thinks about it on a purely instinctual level, the idea of rock 'n' roll playing on 78 is absurd. Rock 'n' roll, after all, was the sound of a new generation; a new world, even—vital, thrusting, and coruscating with excitement, and so far removed from the loves and lives of previous generations that it simply could not exist on anything so crusty and square as a 78.

The sounds of "Johnny B. Goode" and "Heartbreak Hotel" are the sounds of the 45, discs as unbreakable as the spirit now coursing through the veins of America's with-it youth, as fresh and filled with fidelity as the new dawn that was breaking across the postwar world. Rock 'n' roll was the sound of teenagers in ascension; 78s were the old world they were crushing beneath their feet.

Johnny Nash

"As Time Goes By" (ABC PARAMOUNT 9996, 7-INCH, PICTURE SLEEVE, 1959)
Composer's Choice (ARGO LPS 4038S, STEREO LP, 1964)
"Deep in the Heart of Harlem" (GROOVE 58-0021, 7-INCH, 1964)
Hold Me Tight (JAD JS 1207, LP, 1968)
I Can See Clearly Now (EPIC KE 13607, YELLOW-LABEL LP, 1972)
Johnny Nash (ABC PARAMOUNT S244, STEREO LP, 1959)
"Out of Town" (ABC PARAMOUNT 9743, 7-INCH, 1956)
"Stir It Up" (EPIC 10873, 7-INCH, 1972)
"Talk to Me" (ARGO 5471, 7-INCH, 1964)
"Teardrops in the City" (CADET 5528, 7-INCH, 1966)

Yet, between whichever date you choose to mark the dawn of rock 'n' roll, and the very end of the 1950s, the 78 wasn't simply the dominant force in the music industry, it was also the most popular. In the US, the 45 did not finally overtake the 78 in terms of units sold until 1957, and remained in production until at least the end of 1959, and maybe even early 1960. Among the very last 78s released are found such gems as "I Only Have Eyes For You" by the Flamingos, "I Got Stung" by Elvis Presley, "Instant Love" by Doris Day, and "Fannie Mae" by Buster Brown. In Britain, the old format was still holding its own in the marketplace until 1961.

Today, it is said, rock 'n' roll 78s are one of the hottest commodities in the record-collecting world, with any survey of America's (or the UK's) most valuable records of the era literally bursting with high-ticket 78s. The market for them might be smaller than for 45s, and the values in the price guides might sometimes seem a little lower. But ask any dealer what he would rather be offering—a set of mint Elvis Sun singles on 45, or a set on 78? There is no competition.

The reason for this, first and foremost, is that 78s simply were not built to last. They were manufactured from shellac, a compound derived from a natural resin secreted by the lac beetle of Southeast Asia. This material is extremely durable, and was ideal for the 78's primary purpose—being rotated at high speeds while a thick steel needle passed over it in a clockwise direction.

Unfortunately, it is also extremely fragile and frighteningly brittle. Even with the most stringent precautions, mailing a 78 means taking its life in your hands, while simply transporting a 78 from one room to another can seem like juggling fine crystal. The 78s that today sell for high prices on the collectors market are not necessarily rare because very

David Bowie released but a handful of SACDs, but all took maximum advantage of the format.

few were made, as is the case with many of the most valuable 45s of the same period. They are rare because not many have survived unbroken.

Emile Berliner, a German citizen who emigrated to the US in 1870 when he was nineteen, was responsible for the birth of the 78. A pioneering student of sound technology, he developed the flat-disc technique not simply to replace the bulky cylinders then in use, but to obviate their most common fault—every time you listened to one, the actual content of the cylinder, the music or whatever it was, would be physically scraped away. And one day, there would be nothing left.

Through the 1880s, Berliner worked to perfect a means of preserving sound permanently and, by 1888, he had come close enough that he was able to unveil his prototype at the Franklin Institute. His first discs were etched in zinc using chromic acid; from there he moved to celluloid and rubber, before hitting upon shellac in 1891. It is a testament to his farsightedness that shellac would remain the industry standard for the next fifty-plus years. (Vinyl began creeping into fashion during the mid-'50s, but never became a standard.)

Of course, 78s were the first records ever to be collected, at least if one discounts those souls who hoarded the earlier cylinders. In the years prior to World War II, the majority of serious collectors sought classical and opera music, allowing pop, "race music" (as the blues was then known), and other genres to pass by unnoticed.

The post-war era, however, saw rising interest in the blues, and the plethora of often-tiny labels that had spent the 1920s and 1930s documenting the phenomenon, a fascination which gave rise, in

turn, to one of the most intriguing, and romantic, phases in record collecting history.

Although most of the old labels—specialist concerns such as Paramount and Genet, as well as the more established Columbia, OKeh, and Victor—fastidiously issued catalogs of their releases, few operated any kind of archive. Or, if they did, not many of these had survived. Famously, when Paramount closed its doors for the last time, furious workers spent the rest of the day throwing everything—records and masters alike—into the nearby river.

Neither were there compilation albums that gathered up the best of a label's output, or reissue labels pumping out past classics. If you wanted to hear the records, you had to get off your ass and search for them, first through the handful of record stores that cared to carry old 78s (there was a small, but thriving network of used dealers, many of whom also advertised in various publications), and then among the very people who had purchased those records in the first place.

Which, in the realm of race records, meant jumping in the car, driving south, and then going door to door, asking whether the residents had any old records they wanted to sell. Accounts of such expeditions, as related by such youthful explorers as John Fahey, Joe Bussard, and Al Wilson (later of Canned Heat) are among the most enjoyable accounts you will ever read in any collecting history. Friendships were cultivated, contacts were made, and records by the score were rescued from the realms of obscurity, to be shared among the finder's closest circle.

Recordings were made onto reel-to-reel tape and passed around; for the majority of these collectors, simply owning what might be the only copy of a certain record was not (as it so often seems to be today) the object of the exercise. The

Rare Blues from the Shellac Age

Long "Cleve" Reed & Harvey Hull: "Original Stack O' Lee Blues"/
"Mama You Don't Know How" (BLACK PATTI 8030, 1927)

Tommy Johnson, "Alcohol and Jake Blues"/"Ridin' Horse" (PARAMOUNT 12950, 1930)

Robert Johnson, "Me and the Devil Blues"/"Little Queen of Spades" (VOCALION 04108, 1938)

Charley Patton, "Poor Me"/"34 Blues" (VOCALION 02651, 1934)

Mississippi John Hurt, "Frankie"/"Nobody's Dirty Business" (OKEH 8560, 1928)

Louie Lasky, "How You Want Your Rollin' Done"/"Teasin' Brown Blues" (VOCALION 02995, 1935)

Tommy Johnson, "Canned Heat Blues"/"Big Fat Mamma Blues" (VICTOR V-38535, 1929)

Cannon's Jug Stompers, "Pretty Mama Blues"/"Going to Germany" (VICTOR V-38535, 1930)

Cannon's Jug Stompers, "Walk Right In"/"Whoa Mule! Get Up in the Alley" (VICTOR V-38611, 1930)

Robert Johnson, "Hell Hound on My Trail"/"From Four Until Late" (VOCALION 03623, 1937)

Buddy Holly and the Crickets

Blue Days, Black Nights (DECCA 29854, 7-INCH, BARS BY LOGO ON LABEL, 1956)

The Chirpin' Crickets (BRUNSWICK BL 54038, LP, TEXTURED SLEEVE, 1957)

Listen to Me (CORAL EC 81169, EP, PICTURE SLEEVE, 1958)

"Love Me" (DECCA 30543, GREEN-LABEL 7-INCH PROMO, 1958)

"Modern Don Juan" (DECCA 30166, 7-INCH, BARS BY LOGO ON LABEL, 1956)

"Stay Close to Me," Lou Giordano (HOLLY ON GUITAR, BRUNSWICK 55115, 7-INCH, 1959)

Terry Noland, Terry Noland (HOLLY ON GUITAR, BRUNSWICK BL 54041, LP, 1958)

That'll Be the Day (DECCA DL 8707, LP, BLACK LABEL WITH SILVER PRINT, 1958)

That'll Be the Day (DECCA ED 2575, EP, PICTURE SLEEVE WITH LINER NOTES, 1958)

"Words of Love" (CORAL 61852, 7-INCH OR 78, 1957)

goal was to bring the music back to life, and allow everyone to hear it.

So many of the rarest 78s of all were discovered in this fashion, discs that even today are known to exist in quantities of just a handful or less (a number are still considered unique, including Charley Patton's "Devil Sent the Rain"—Paramount 13040, in case you have a copy).

But many more escaped discovery of altogether—two of the three records that Willie Brown cut for Paramount; a couple more by St. Louis guitarist Jaydee Short; and a solitary Roebuck Ray 78 that is so obscure that even the title of its B-side has yet to be identified. And that's just from the Paramount catalog!

Those days of discovery are long gone. A few misty-eyed collectors do wax lyrical about the first years of eBay, and the treasures (and trash!) that could be picked up relatively inexpensively in that brief window before every seller became a self-styled expert and every collector scoured the listings. But even then, truly untouched old collections were the exception, not the rule, and genuine bargains were even scarcer. There would always be a few other people bidding for the same items.

Besides, as any specialist 78 collector will tell you, one man's vintage blues (or jazz, or country, or whatever) is another's heap of unresaleable rubbish. And the fact is, the vast majority of 78s released throughout the first half of the last century are—like the vast majority of 45s and LPs released throughout the second half—little more than cultural landfill.

That determination, however, has no bearing whatsoever on the actual quality of the recorded performances. Even today many traditional used record stores still have no idea of how to display or even categorize their 78s.

Rather, collectors flick through the pile looking for the odd name they may recognize, then leave the rest in the least-visited corner, with no thought for even rudimentary preservation. One can always tell, when a store rearranges its stock, where the 78s used to be kept. There will be flakes of broken shellac all over the floor. Which is great, because that means there's a few less to carry out to the skip, the next time they clean up the store.

Rock 'n' roll, like jazz and the blues, is one area in which there are few throwaways., although—with the exception of the best-known artists—collecting its 78 rpm heritage did not really get underway until the mid-late 1970s.

Much of the demand, initially, came from Europe; the UK, where the fifties cult of Teddy Boys was still a powerful cult among the country's youth (and the not so young), and where the old American rock 'n' rollers were still guaranteed vast, sell-out audiences; and

Everly Brothers

"Cathy's Clown" (UK WARNER BROTHERS WB 1, 78, 1960)
Fabulous Style of the Everly Brothers (CADENCE CLP 25040, MAROON-LABEL LP, 1960)
It's Everly Time! (WB PRO 134, PROMO LP, 1960)
"Keep a-Lovin' Me" (COLUMBIA 21496, 7-INCH, 1956)
"Let It Be Me" (CADENCE 1376, 7-INCH, PICTURE SLEEVE, 1959)
"Lucille" (UK WARNER BROS WB 19, 78, 1960)
"So Sad" (WB 5163, GOLD-VINYL 7-INCH PROMO, 1960)
The Everly Brothers (CADENCE CLP 3003, MAROON-LABEL LP, 1958)
"Wake Up Little Susie" (CADENCE 1337, 7-INCH, PICTURE SLEEVE, 1957)
"When Will I Be Loved" (UK LONDON HLA 9157, 78, 1960)

Germany, where 1940s-style "bubble tube" Wurlitzer 78 jukeboxes were enjoying a small but significant boom in popularity.

A familiar sight in the American and British army-run youth clubs of the immediate postwar period, these beautiful slices of nostalgia were off-loaded from storage during the late '70s, and their new owners were now looking to stock them with the music they remembered from their youth.

As the Deutschemarks flew in one direction, and the records sailed off in another, domestic collectors began to reflect upon the format. The boom began, hampered only by the fact that few dealers were even vaguely capable of specializing in the field. No less then than today, to many of them, 78s were the fat, black, breakable things that sat patiently gathering the dust which would then rise up in vast, choking clouds on the rare occasions when somebody—usually an older person, with very specific requirements—chose to leaf through them.

A few of them, however, took the time to learn. Specialist publications sprang up, specialized collecting clubs were launched. The last, traumatic, years of the 78 finally came out of the shadows. With astonishing rapidity, 45s moved into the 78 marketplace. Introduced in 1949 by RCA Victor, by 1952 even tiny independent record labels were producing them, side by side with 78s, but in increasing quantities every year. Had the new format not demanded a new type of record player, it might have taken off even faster; as it was, many consumers preferred to wait until the first players were marketed that could handle all three speeds now on the market—78, 45, and the similarly new 33⅓.

Unquestionably, teenagers were the driving force behind the revolution—45s blended in perfectly with a lifestyle that prided itself on excitement, speed, and devil-may-care bravado. They could be stacked on a turntable for nonstop dancing parties, they could be passed around without fear of breakage, they could be dropped on the floor and propped against the wall, and they might never seem too worse for the wear. On the other hand, 78s . . . you only had to look at them wrong (or, at least, lay them in a box with less than infinite care), and they shattered into irreparable shards.

So the statistics are probably deceptive. While 78s did outsell 45s for much of the 1950s, that's because they sold to fans of jazz, swing, dance band, classical, blues, and opera; 45s were a rock and pop phenomenon.

Nevertheless, vast quantities of every hit issue were produced, with the biggest names in the infant rock world—including Elvis, Chuck Berry, Buddy Holly, Little Richard, and Jerry Lee Lewis—as familiar spinning on a 10-inch shellac platter as on a 7-inch vinyl one.

If one does not care so much for condition (or playability) as for simply owning a handsome artifact, it is not at all difficult, or especially expensive, to build a remarkable collection of early rock 'n' roll on 78. It's only when you attempt to upgrade that you will start running into serious difficulties.

In general, the rarest rock 78s are the most obscure issues on the best-loved labels—early Sun, Chess, and Vee-Jay releases, for example. The most expensive, on the other hand, tend to be those by the best-known artists. It does not take a rocket scientist to realize that a clean 78 pressing of Gene Vincent's "Be-Bop-A-Lula" or Chuck Berry's "Roll Over Beethoven" will attract more attention than "Tennessee" Ernie Ford's "You Don't Have to Be a Baby to Cry" or the Lane Brothers' "Marianne." Which is not to say those latter aren't just as appealing to a specialist, simply that most buyers and sellers' knowledge simply is not that in-depth.

Because Britain continued producing 78s for some years after the US quit, many of the rarest issues do hail from the UK. A number of labels were still issuing 78s at least into summer and fall of 1960, with a number of new releases still reaching stores in time for Christmas—Ray Charles' "Georgia on My Mind" was issued in Britain on 78 as late as November 1960.

Warner Bros., whose British operation was not even opened until April 1960, released several extremely rare 78s by the Everly Brothers, featuring titles that never saw shellac in the US ("Cathy's Clown," "Lucille"); while 78s of Eddie Cochran's "Three Steps to Heaven," Brian Hyland's "Itsy Bitsy Teenie Weenie Yellow Polka Dot Bikini," and Elvis Presley's "Stuck on You," "A Mess of Blues," and "It's Now or Never" will all appear impossibly time warped to the American collector.

Perhaps the most startling 78 discoveries of all, however, are those issued by EMI's India operation. The popular modern image of the subcontinent's music industry is of a land dominated by colorfully packaged cassette tapes. Prior to that medium's invention, however, India devoured shellac and vinyl releases as voraciously as any other land, with the 78 ruling absolutely supreme in areas where the lack of electricity meant that most record buyers were still employing hand-cranked wind-up gramophones.

A full catalog of releases to this market would probably boggle the most even-keeled mind. But let us reel off just four of the 78 rpm discs that haunt the imagination of every completist Beatles enthusiast: "If I Fell," "Tell Me Why," "I'll Follow the Sun," and "Michelle," the latter dating from as late as summer 1965. How about Cliff Richard? "Summer Holiday," "On the Beach," "Don't Talk To Him," "Spanish Harlem." There's even a couple of Elvis 78s dating from 1966! And some people think the Sex Pistols' 8-track is an anachronism!

Pretty Things

"All Light Up" (NORTON PT 109, RED-VINYL 7-INCH, 1999)

Get the Picture (UK FONTANA TL 5280, LP, 1965)

"Honey I Need" (FONTANA 1508, 7-INCH, 1965)

On Film (UK FONTANA TE 17472, EP, 1966)

Pretty Things (FONTANA MGF 27544, LP, 1965)

"Private Sorrow" (RARE EARTH 5005, 7-INCH, 1969)

Rage Before Beauty (SNAPPER, NO CATALOG NUMBER, CD, ROUGH-MIX SAMPLER, 1999)

Rainin' in My Heart (UK FONTANA TE 17442, EP, 1965)

SF Sorrow (RARE EARTH RS 506, LP WITH ROUND COVER, 1969)

"Talkin' About the Good Times" (LAURIE 3458, 7-INCH, 1968)

---

16 RPM: A MERRY-GO-ROUND FOR YOUR TORTOISE

If you've never wondered what the 16 rpm setting on your old-time record player is for, you either don't have an enquiring mind . . . or you already know.

The sound quality was not great, but you could certainly fit a lot onto one side of a disc—16s were thus ideal for spoken-word recordings, and the Argo subsidiary of Decca (*not* the Chess imprint), specialists in that genre, produced a number of releases. They are extremely rare, although there is little general market for examples.

TEST PRESSINGS: JUST TO MAKE SURE IT WORKS

Test pressings (often called "factory samples" in the UK) are, as the name implies, produced at the beginning of a record's final manufacturing process, to ensure that no defects or errors are present in either the recording or the mastering. Test pressings were produced, therefore, for virtually every record ever made, in quantities ranging from one or two to several hundred.

Aside from the absence of a conventional printed label, most are no different from the finished product, beyond being prepared over two one-sided discs, in some cases, rather than on one two-sided platter. Some will be marked "test pressing" (or something similar), others may have hand-written notations; others still will be completely blank. Very few test pressings carry anything more than a nominal premium over a conventional pressing of the same disc—those acts whose test pressings do command high sums tend to be those whose entire catalog, in all its permutations, is considered especially collectible.

Which is not to say there's not a number of extremely scarce test pressings, then, primarily those that reflect either last-minute changes in an album's makeup (the removal or switching of songs, for example), or which represent variations that did not ever appear in any other form.

A 78 rpm test pressing for UK family entertainer Max Bygraves.

Into the CD age, test pressings continued to be produced for disc jockeys.

Test pressings of T. Rex's 1970 hit "Ride a White Swan," with the notation OCTO 1 scratched into the run-off groove, are currently ranked among Britain's rarest singles—the catalog number dates from the brief period during which the newly formed Fly record label was still considering calling itself Octopus.

Those of Neil Young's *Comes a Time* album still bear its original title, *Ode to the Wind*; similarly, tests of his three LP *Decade* compilation feature a lengthier version of the song "Campaigner" than appeared on the released version. Both are hotly pursued.

Test pressings of Bob Dylan's *Blood on the Tracks* LP feature several performances that were deleted prior to the album's release, and replaced with new recordings; the original test-pressing version of Paul McCartney's *McCartney II* solo album is effectively an entire album's worth of material that was eventually scrapped.

Collectors should be aware, however, that it is often difficult to differentiate between a white-label test pressing and a similarly packaged bootleg, particularly on those occasions when a bootleg purposefully echoes the contents of the unissued LP (*Blood on the Tracks* and *McCartney II* are key examples). One should always ascertain whether the correct identification marks (usually matrix and other numbers in the run-off groove) are present before making a major purchase.

The final area of test pressings to be aware of are those issued to clubs and DJs, in the form of prerelease, white-label versions of 12-inch singles. The concept originated in Jamaica, where hot new songs would be rushed from the pressing plant to the sound systems the moment they were off the presses, in the form of what the locals called "dub plates"; in the US and Europe through the mid-'70s, similar issues became the lifeblood of the disco scene—a role that they retain today.

Likewise, it is only in recent years that record companies have stopped pumping out 12-inch singles specifically for the club circuit, with the vast majority of dance tracks made available to the public on CD debuted in the clubs on test-pressing issues. Looking back over the past decade or so, name artists and DJs such as Moby, St. Etienne, Danny Howells, the Orb, Orbital, and DJ Shadow are all avidly collected, not on luxuriously packaged CD, but on next-to-anonymous vinyl.

Finally, mention should be made of the occasional vinyl packages wherein a new release is itself disguised as a test pressing, among them the late 2016 10-inch release of the Doors' *London Fog 1966* live album.

China Street's 1978 "Rock Against Racism" on test pressing.

TRANSCRIPTION DISCS: ON YOUR RADIO

Transcription discs are the recordings that were supplied to radio stations that subscribe to any of the popular syndicated shows broadcast throughout the country every week.

These include such institutions as *America's Top 40, Rock over London, Rick Dees' Weekly Top 40,* and *The National Music Survey,* and music-interview magazine digests like *Off the Record, Robert W. Morgan Special of the Week,* and the BBC's *Top of the Pops* radio program.

There are also transcription discs of one-off specials and series profiling individual artists (*The Lost Lennon Tapes, The Beatle Years,* etc.) and of the live concerts brought into your living room by the *King Biscuit Flower Hour, Superstar Concert, In Concert,* and Cleveland's legendary *Agora Live* series.

Originally issued to broadcasters as either reel tapes or multidisc vinyl packages, radio shows more recently appeared exclusively on CD. Collectors generally eschew only the (easily duplicated) reels, and naturally, prefer packages that include the original cue sheets, two- or three-page documents detailing contents and commercials, with very specific timing information.

Those discs which offer complete (or nearly complete) concerts are the most collectible, and although value is highly dependent upon the featured act, specialist collectors of any artist will at least be sorely tempted by a high-quality, limited-edition, and otherwise unavailable live recording.

Bootlegs, of course, have picked up many of the best-known broadcasts for their own ends, while the BBC and King Biscuit have both made selected performances available to the general public. (Emerson Lake and Palmer's 1974 triple live album *Welcome Back, My Friends, to the Show That Never Ends—Ladies and Gentlemen Emerson Lake and Palmer* was itself originally heard as a KBFH special.) But even the most lovingly presented alternative cannot compete with a genuine, official radio disc, in terms of collectibility.

Detailed discographies for most major (and many minor) acts will feature at least one live broadcast; detailed listings for any of the major concert broadcasters will likewise reveal some incredibly in-demand transcription discs. A complete listing for the *Agora Live* series, for example, numbers over 350 separate concerts recorded between February 1972 (a performance by Tiny Alice) and July 1982 (Robert Pezinski), and includes shows by such giants as Spooky Tooth (8/20/73), Ted Nugent (1/28/74), the Pretty Things (3/18/75), Spirit (6/30/75), Thin Lizzy (4/11/76), Boston (9/27/76), Elvis Costello (12/5/77), Todd Rundgren (11/5/78), and U2 (12/2/81). Only a handful of these performances have seen official release, among them Iggy Pop's 3/21/77 show and one track ("My Generation") from Patti Smith's 1/26/76 performance.

Although the majority of collectors will, naturally, hope to acquire all of a given artist's radio discs, the highest priority tends to attach itself to broadcasts from periods in a band's career when interest among subscribing radio stations was low.

A BBC transcription disc of a Police show from 1978, for example, will fetch several times more than an *Omni College Rock Concert* disc from 1983; U2's first American broadcast, from 1981 *(Warner Bros. Music Show)* is considerably rarer than a concert from the *Popmart* tour in 1997.

Among non-concert discs, documentaries featuring rare and unissued material are the most collectible, with Bob Dylan's 2006–2009 *Theme Time Radio Show* (101 episodes), the *Lost Lennon Tapes* (221 shows), and Paul McCartney's *Oobu Joobu* (seventeen shows) far and away the best known. Dylan's was effectively a crash course in the history of music, punctuated by his own thoughts and comments; the other pair were dominated by music that had never previously been aired and which, for the most part, remains in the vault. And, naturally, bootlegs and downloads have sprung up as affordable alternatives to the "real thing."

A number of syndication companies have also operated in this particular field, producing some very high-quality and well-researched discs—the Santa Monica–based On the Radio's collection of Jimi Hendrix rarities is one such. Probably the most respected individual provider of this type of show, however, is the BBC, whose *At the BBC* series of documentaries resurrected radio sessions that, in some cases, had not been heard since their original broadcast.

Such CD series as the *Peel Sessions* EPs and albums have made a lot of this material readily available. However, the documentaries often feature additional material ignored on official releases—the broadcast *David Bowie at the BBC,* for example, included a 1967 performance of "Love You Till Tuesday," which Bowie's own *Bowie at the Beeb* two-CD set completely overlooked.

News and magazine-style shows, wherein the "exclusive" content is largely confined to interview material and maybe an impromptu live-in-the-studio performance, also have their supporters, though prices and demand tend to be low.

At the very bottom end of the scale, at least in terms of collector demand and interest, are simple Top 40 countdown or personality DJ

Spirit

Clear Spirit (ODE Z12 44016, LP, 1969)
"Dark Eyed Woman" (ODE 122, 7-INCH, 1969)
The Family that Plays Together (ODE Z12 44014, LP, 1968)
"Fresh Garbage" (UK MERCURY MER 1626, 6-INCH, 1984)
"I Got a Line on You" (ODE 115, 7-INCH, 1968)
"Mechanical World" (ODE 108, 7-INCH, 1967)
"Midnight Train" (UK SOUND FOR INDUSTRY/DARK STAR SFI 326, FLEXIDISC, 1978)
"1984" (ODE 128, 7-INCH, 1969)
Spirit (ODE Z12 44004, LP, 1968)
Twelve Dreams of Dr. Sardonicus (EPIC E30267, YELLOW-LABEL LP, 1970)

shows (from Wolfman Jack to Lawrence Welk!), where the content is, at least in collecting terms, as anodyne as radio can be. These are the discs one most frequently finds being sold either in bulk lots or via bargain bins after radio-station clear-outs. And in these circumstances, one can safely say, you get what you pay for.

If purchased carefully, transcription discs make a fabulous addition to any collection. There are a handful of caveats, however. Beware of repeat broadcasts of shows, some of which do not state their origins in their packaging; beware, of course, of bootlegs; and beware of being taken for a ride by sellers who insist they have an all-but-unique item. There are a lot of radio stations in America, and a lot of them subscribe to these shows. There are at least that many other copies floating around out there somewhere.

Two songs made it onto the b-side of the UK 12-inch for the Tubes' "White Punks on Dope."

12-INCH SINGLES: THEY'RE LIKE 45S. ONLY BIGGER.

One of the most exciting, and certainly the most successful, musical innovations of the 1970s was the 12-inch single—literally, a conventional 7-inch (45 rpm) single pressed onto LP-sized vinyl and marketed as a limited edition.

The advantages of the format were manifold. Whether spinning at 33 1/3 (the United States' favored format) or 45 (the UK's speed of preference), the 12-inch single allowed for far more music to be pressed into the grooves, and facilitated a better sound quality as well.

Almost from the outset, then, the primary markets were the dance floors; indeed, the first 12-inch singles issued anywhere in the world were the white-label (test pressing) "prerelease" discs made available

The Lords of the New Church's glorious reconstruction of Madonna's "Like a Virgin."

exclusively to disc jockeys and sound-system owners in Jamaica during the early '70s.

The format reached the US and European disco scene around 1975, with several now-collectible promo issues, including the Rolling Stones' "Hot Stuff." It was fall 1976, however, before the first commercially available 12-inch singles made their debut, with a reissue of the Who's decade-old "Substitute."

Two B-sides, the similarly classic oldies "I'm a Boy" and "Pictures of Lily," took full advantage of the added playing time, and a British Top Ten hit, the Who's first in five years, secured the future of the format, despite costing close to twice the price of a conventional 7-inch single.

Few of the earliest British 12-inch singles were issued in picture sleeves; the unusual format itself was generally considered novelty enough. Generic card sleeves, thicker than traditional singles sleeves, were considered sufficient to house the new format, with only Island displaying any further marketing awareness, by packaging Steve Winwood's "Time Is Running Out" in a sleeve clearly marked "prerelease"—thus trading on both the format and the label's own Jamaican origins.

The first custom 12-inch sleeves began arriving during the late summer of 1977, largely drawn from the ranks of the New York new wave scene. Richard Hell ("Blank Generation"), Blondie ("Rip Her to Shreds"), and the Talking Heads ("Psycho

Killer") were among the earliest, while the Ramones' "Sheena Is a Punk Rocker" 12-inch invited purchasers to send along a proof of purchase and receive, in return, a limited-edition T-shirt.

Several of these releases are now sought after. Television's debut UK single "Marquee Moon" was presented in its full nine-minute glory, as opposed to being broken into two parts, as was the 7-inch version, and furthermore boasted a unique mono mix of the A-side's stereo. The same band's next 12-inch, "Prove It," was issued on green vinyl.

In 1978, the notion of either remixed or extended 12-inch versions passed into common currency. The impetus to extend beyond the traditional barriers of the three-minute single came, again, from the dance floor. Several unabashed disco hits appeared in elongated form in 1977, but it was also an age in which some of rock's heaviest hitters acknowledged the importance of the dance floors.

Among the pioneers of the remix, the Rolling Stones expanded a straightforward, four-minute version of their new single, "Miss You," to an astonishing eight and a half minutes—and then plastered it onto lascivious pink vinyl, as if to ensure that nobody could possibly ignore it.

It was a dramatic gesture, negating all accusations that the band had indeed "gone disco," with one of the most powerful performances of the Stones' recent history. Even more important, it opened the door for a clutch of other acts that might otherwise have thought twice about commissioning what was already being termed as a "dance mix."

Few lived up to the standards set by the Stones. Indeed, the Stones themselves have never equaled, let alone eclipsed, "Miss You" in terms either of dynamics or invention. Too many remixes, it seemed, entailed simply raising the sound of the bass in the mix, and maybe incorporating a few extended passages of percussive repetition; Roxy Music's "Dance Away" raised eyebrows by simply repeating a cymbal

Depeche Mode

BBC Transcription Disc 1985 (BBC TRANSCRIPTION, TRANSCRIPTION DISC, 1985)

"Behind the Wheel" (SIRE PROA 2952, 12-INCH PROMO, 1987)

"Blasphemous Rumours" (SIRE PROA 2271, 12-INCH PROMO, 1985)

B-Sides (UK MUTE, NO CATALOG NUMBER, 4-LP TEST PRESSINGS, 1989)

"Everything Counts" (UK MUTE 10BONG 16; 10-INCH WITH POSTCARDS, STICKER, ETC.; 1989)

"Get the Balance Right" (UK MUTE L12BONG 2, 12-INCH, 1983)

"It's No Good (Club 69 Future Mix)" (UK MUTE BONG 26, 12-INCH, 1997)

"Master and Servant (On-U Sound Science Fiction . . .)" (UK MUTE L12BONG 6, 12-INCH, 1984)

Selections from the Commercially Available Box Sets (SIRE PROA 5192/5242, PROMO LPS, 1991)

"Sometimes I Wish I Was Dead" (UK LYNTONE LYN 1029, FLEXIDISC, 1981)

rhythm for what seemed like hours. Other acts seemed unwilling to go even that far.

The collectibility of 12-inch singles has never been in doubt. Although the early assurance that they were limited editions swiftly evaporated, still very few 12-inchers continued in regular production once a single's chart life was over, regardless of whether or not the 7-inch remained in stock.

The 12-inch reigned supreme throughout the first half of the 1980s, with the most significant releases, appropriately, being delivered by those acts whose careers not only came of age following the birth of the 12-inch, but who could even be said to have prospered because of it.

Sticking with the UK, the early '80s "new romantic" movement might be recalled (at least by its detractors) as a primarily visual medium, but on the club floors it was driven wholly by the 12-inch single, with its leading practitioners—Duran Duran, Spandau Ballet, Soft Cell, and Depeche Mode—responsible for some of the most vibrantly inventive extended mixes yet conceived.

The 1976 UK reissue of the Who's "Substitute" is generally regarded as the first ever commercial 12-inch single.

Longstanding pop barriers were ruthlessly demolished—both Duran Duran's "Planet Earth (Night Version)" and Soft Cell's "Say Hello Goodbye" eschewed the traditional concept of the snappy intro, by running through extended instrumental versions before the singers (Simon Le Bon and Marc Almond, respectively) even opened their mouths. Soft Cell's effort went even further by designating a clarinet the lead instrument.

New Order's own position in the mythology of 12-inch collecting was assured when the group's "Blue Monday" single was issued on 12-inch only. Sensing a major hit, the band's label and its distributors all pressured New Order to release a 7-inch edit; the group refused, sensing that to do so would utterly dilute the performance; the band was rewarded with a No. 9 UK hit.

Other significant issues from this period include a handful of 12-inch box-set releases. Public Image Ltd.'s second album, *Metal Box*, was indeed packaged in a circular tin, akin to a film reel, replicating the album over three 12-inch singles. Spandau Ballet, too, transformed a regular LP to the 12-inch format, with 1982's *Diamond* also sporting

several otherwise unavailable extended mixes of its contents. A six-disc collection of Soft Cell 12-inch issues, *The 12-Inch Singles,* is also worth looking out for if your tastes lean toward the new-romantic electro age.

Mute label stars Depeche Mode, meanwhile, adopted the 12-inch not only as a vehicle for extended mixes, but also as a platform for some quite un-pop-like activities, including a series of very limited editions, and a series of live releases in deluxe sleeves, aimed wholly at collectors. This entire catalog would later be collected into a series of CD box sets.

Frankie Goes to Hollywood employed the medium in a similarly visionary, not to mention vigorous, manner, and today, multiple 12-inch pressings of their first four singles ("Relax," "Two Tribes," "The Power of Love," and "Welcome to the Pleasure Dome") remain hot collectibles. A clutch of late-'80s Kate Bush 12-inchers—preeminently "Cloudbursting (The Organon Mix)"—are similarly prized as much for their musical content as for the format's scarcity.

Outside of the disco market, the 12-inch single was much slower to take control in the US. It was 1978 before Chrysalis's *Disco 33 1/3* and the Warner Bros. series *33⅓ Disco Stereo* marked the first regular 12-inch issues, with Blondie's "Heart of Glass" and Rod Stewart's "Do Ya Think I'm Sexy" among the earliest commercially released 12-inch singles to make an impact on American consumers.

Even in the face of these successes, the bulk of US 12-inch singles, until well inside the new decade, remained promotional only—surprisingly, not only because the format was directly responsible for a massive flowering of artistic breakthroughs, but also because a massive market in UK imports quickly sprang up to fill the void left by domestic labels' reticence.

Billy Idol, for one, credits the 12-inch format with engineering his US breakthrough, after an extended version of "Dancin' with Myself" cut with his earlier band Generation X became a major American club hit in 1980.

Much of U2's transition from cult live attraction to a group of stadium-filling superstars in 1982 can be credited to the tremendous

promo 12-inch remixes of "New Year's Day" and "Two Hearts Beat as One" commissioned from dance producer Francois Kervorkian.

These releases, incidentally, also ignited the still-enduring consumer and collector interest in "name" remixers. Kervorkian was joined in the early '80s vanguard by New York hip-hop producer Arthur Baker, whose work with New Order remains among the mightiest demonstrations of the remixer's art ever.

Such specialist subscription services as Disconet, whose 12-inch remixes offer some of the most collectible variations in any artist's catalog, sprang from this same cult, to dominate the dance floor of the late '80s and the 1990s.

The artists who most surely epitomizes the importance of the American 12-inch, however, are Prince and, even more seismically, Madonna. Her first hits were issued only on now-in-demand promotional 12-inches. But, beginning with 1984's "Borderline," the Material Girl's entire singles output was made available on both

The only place to find the extended mix of Wings' "Goodnight Tonight" was on 12-inch.

7-inch and 12-inch, with Madonna also among the first international artists to realize the benefits of including two or more mixes of the A-side on the commercial issue, thus keeping fans apace with the DJs' own growing demand for alternate versions.

Madonna's 1989 "Like a Prayer" featured five mixes; 1990's "Keep It Together" boasted six, though even those could not compete with a pair of promos issued in 1992—eleven mixes of "Erotica" and *twelve* of "Deeper and Deeper," both released over two 12-inch discs.

The 12-inch boom reached its apogee in the mid-1990s, at least in the UK. Radiohead, [London] Suede, and Oasis can probably point to the most valuable 12-inch releases; in fact the latter issued several extraordinarily limited one-sided 12-inchers during 1994–95, such quantities as 300 ("Cigarettes and Alcohol"); 560 ("Whatever"), and 1,203 ("Cum On Feel the Noize"), clearly issued in full awareness that demand was going to far outstrip supply.

Increasingly, however, record companies were looking to the CD single as a far more economical and convenient format, and by the late 1990s, the 12-inch had more or less returned to its origins, limited edition pressings served up for club DJs alone.

The 12-inch has undergone something of a renaissance in recent years, with the so-called vinyl boom playing a major part in that. But the bulk of new releases today are either straightforward reissues or Record Store Day exclusives. The day of the 12-inch, sadly, seems to be over.

UHQCD (ULTRA-HIGH QUALITY CD): THE ULTIMATE SOUND EXPERIENCE . . . AGAIN

UHQCD is yet another high-end audio format, introduced in Japan in 2016 with releases by King Crimson, Kitaro, Rodney Whittaker and more. To which the cynic, looking back across the thirty-plus years since we were first told CDs deliver perfect sound, can only sigh, "Wouldn't it have been nice if they'd got it right to begin with?"

3 | THE EYE OF THE BEHOLDER— CASE STUDIES FROM THE FRINGES OF OBSESSION

INTRODUCTION

We collect what we want to. We collect *how* we want to. There is no right way to do it, and there is no wrong way. Occasionally, however, we need a nudge, and that is what the following chapters are about. Giving a nudge, pointing out directions that may or may not appeal, but which open up all manner of possibilities regardless.

They are not to be taken literally. For *Dark Side of the Moon*, substitute another album that is more to your liking. For the BBC sessions, seize upon a different broadcast outlet. For 1968, pick a different year. For Elvis Presley, choose another legend. And so on. The point is, a collection can be as vague or as specific as you like, and it can lead you off down all the associated alleyways as you want. You will not, for example, be the only person whose love of David Bowie's Berlin era sent them instead into the realms of Neue Deutsche Welle (the contemporary German answer to electronic punk rock); or the first whose Beatlemania was supplanted by a lifelong pursuit of the rest of the British Invasion; or even the sole soul who read Gemma Files's supremely creepy novel *Experimental Film*, and found themselves collecting Dvorak's tone poems in response. (Or maybe you will. Read the book and see what happens.)

Think of the following, then, as individual case studies, with the individuals themselves excised from the equation. It's a mixed bag, designed to highlight some of the most popular themes in modern collecting, as seen through some not necessarily over-subscribed topics. And while we discuss the "whats" and "wherefores" of each collection, we purposefully omit the "whys."

Because those are for you to decide upon.

THE ALBUM: HOW MANY COPIES OF THAT RECORD DO YOU NEED? THE MYRIAD DARK SIDES OF THE MOON

How many times you have replaced a particular record in your collection. Once? Twice? Five times?

Any other collector, an arctophile, for example, or an entomologist, might go a lifetime without ever again touching a particular favorite in their hoard . . . maybe upgrading if a better conditioned example comes along, but otherwise content in the knowledge that the space

The SACD version of Dark Side of the Moon.

is filled, the gap is plugged, and it doesn't matter how many brightly colored replicas come along, their original acquisition remains inviolate.

Record collectors, on the other hand . . . . You buy an album in 1973. A couple of years later, you upgrade your sound system to quadraphonic, in the days when that was considered the wave of the future. So you buy the album again. Quad withers and dies, and your old stereo copy is looking a little worn. You pick up a new copy and, somewhere around the early 1980s, you maybe grab the picture disc as well, just because it looks so nifty.

The mid-1980s arrive, bearing with them, CD. Out with the old, in with the new. Except the CD doesn't sound half as good, so you pick up the most recent vinyl repressing, then upgrade the CD when the remaster arrives.

Another copy arrives as part of a box set, another turns up in SACD. An anniversary edition promises the best sound quality ever, and a DVD-Audio projects pretty images across your widescreen TV . . . a picture disc with a superiority complex!

And so on and so forth until the fateful day when you're browsing along your Pink Floyd shelf and you realize, to your horror, that you have now purchased no less than a dozen different versions of *The Dark Side of the Moon*, and not one of them sounds as vital as the first one you ever purchased, all those decades before. But, whereas a teddy bear or bug collector would still have his copy filed neatly away, yours went to the used store long ago.

Forty-five years is a long time in the life of a gramophone record, which is one reason why the above analogy doesn't work. Most collectors dread the day when they find they have to physically touch their collectibles, and would never dream of actually using them for the purpose for which they were intended.

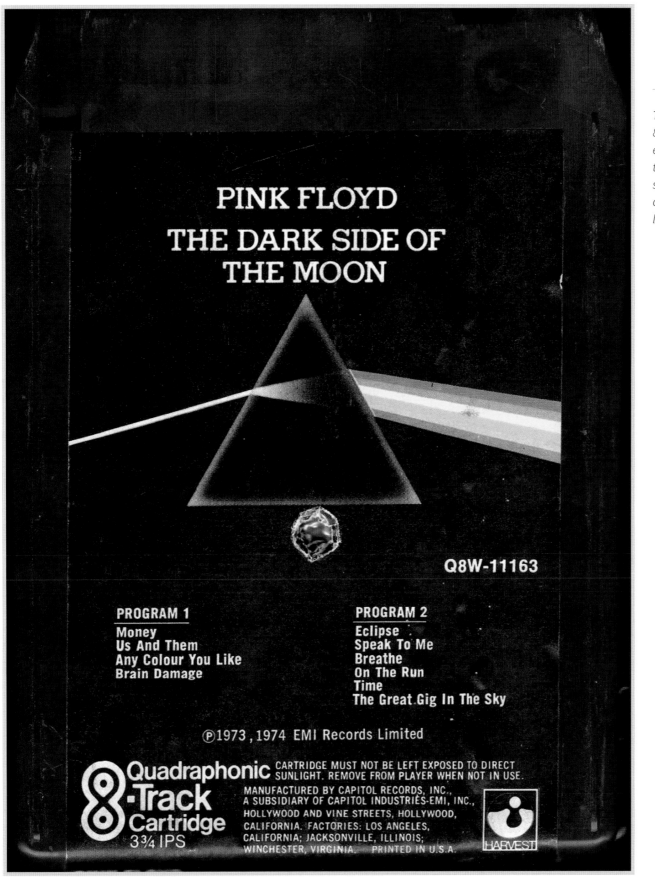

The Dark Side *8-track made no effort whatsoever to maintain the seamless continuity of the album's track listing.*

Record collectors, on the other hand, cannot help but play with their purchases, because what would be the point of owning them in the first place? And some records are simply born to be played and played and played again, until the stylus carves great chasms through the grooves, and the clicks and scratches are as loud as the music, the sleeve becomes tattered and the inserts get lost. . . . Of *course* you have to buy it again, and there's something else you've probably never thought about. Science has spent lifetimes trying to create a perpetual motion machine, without ever realizing that the music industry got there years ago. It's called . . . us.

Then again, *The Dark Side of the Moon* is one of those albums that does inspire undying loyalty. From the moment it was released, on March 17, 1973 (March 24 in the UK and Europe), Pink Floyd's sixth studio album (eighth if you count soundtracks) was regarded as a cut above anything the band had ever released in the past, and a monumental achievement by anybody's standards.

Stereo salesmen, in particular, adored it, and it's still difficult, all these years later, to pass a hi-fi showroom without hearing an excerpt from *The Dark Side of the Moon* wafting out of the door. And if it was good enough for them, then it was good enough for everyone. You would search long and hard to find anybody who was content to keep their copy of the album once it developed a scratch or two, because what is the point of pristine reproduction if it's scarred with extraneous surface noise?

And so the cycle begins.

Including foreign pressings and reissues, multitudinous formats and even alternate sleeves, but ignoring covers, tributes, and non-Floydian remakes, there are probably over a hundred different versions of *The Dark Side of the Moon* out there to be collected—"different," of course, referring to the nature of the packaging it arrives in, as opposed to the music. That, with the necessary exceptions of quadraphonic vinyl and remastered CD, has remained inviolate, and that is exactly how it should be.

No retrospective remixes for this baby, and no modern rerecordings, either, although we could consider Floyd's own live recreations. The earliest dates from January 1972, over a year before the album was released, and the most recent was enacted by former frontman Roger Waters almost forty years later.

Collect every concert rendition that has ever been taped, whether for official release or bootleg, and you could spend the rest of your days listening to nothing else. And, likely, wind up as deranged as the poor lunatic whose plight is documented on the album itself.

We can, however, hoard the highlights of this remarkable disc's timeless journey, beginning with one of its earliest ever complete live performances, at the Rainbow Theatre in London on February 17, 1972.

The first bootleg from the Dark Side *tour.*

In Celebration of the Comet
(THE AMAZING KORNYFONE LABEL, TAKRL 1903)

Pink Floyd had been working on what would become their next album since the end of November 1971, sequestered away at their rehearsal rooms in Broadhurst Gardens, West Hampstead, writing, jamming and resurrecting some discarded old shreds of song.

Equally important, however, was Roger Waters' intention that the entire album should be conceived as one single thematic piece of work, each song flowing into the next, breaking Floyd away from the increasingly interminable side-long epics that had begun to dominate their horizons.

He was, he insisted, "bored with most of the stuff we play," and his bandmates quickly agreed. Shorter songs were the order of the day; how appropriate, then, that they should then present themselves with the shortest of deadlines. The new album was to be written and ready to perform in time for the first concert of the new year.

A concept presented itself; "the pressures of modern life—travel, money, and so on," explained Nick Mason, which only gradually developed into "a meditation on insanity" as well, as Waters grabbed the reins and ran with them. By December 13, the band was ready to begin recording; by January 20, they were ready to unveil the fruits of their labors-so-far.

In the event, Brighton did not receive the expected premier; a tape fault brought "Money" to an unscheduled close and the sound crew was unable to remedy it. The band moved on to a performance of "Atom Heart Mother," and *The Dark Side of the Moon* was forced to wait another twenty-four hours, until the band set up at the Portsmouth Guildhall, to be heard in all its glory.

Tapes exist of almost every night on this British tour (excerpts from the Brighton performance have been officially released within Floyd's own archive projects). As the outing moves on, you can hear the band tinkering with their performance, minor rearrangements that push the songs closer towards what would be their ultimate destiny. "Time" speeds up, "On the Run" seeks its final melody, harmonies twist.

By the time the tour reached the London Rainbow, for four nights in mid-February, the piece even had a title, *The Dark Side of the Moon—A Piece or Assorted Lunatics*. Mere weeks later, British bootleg purchasers were being tempted with *In Celebration of the Comet*, a disc of such high quality that it went on to sell an estimated 120,000 copies and remains one of the finest Floyd boots of all.

Pink Floyd Live at Pompeii
(THEATRICAL RELEASE, 1974; "DIRECTORS CUT" DVD, 2003)

For an album as cohesive as the finished LP would become, *The Dark Side of the Moon* was recorded in remarkably piecemeal fashion. March 1972, for example, saw Floyd in Paris recording an entirely different record, the soundtrack to Barbet Schroeder's movie *La Valee (Obscured by Clouds)*.

They were touring, too, crossing Japan that same month, the US through April and early May, and Germany and Holland later in May. It was June 1 before they returned to the studio, booking in to Abbey Road and, over the next twenty-four days, laying down the basic tracks to "Us and Them," "Money," "Time," and "The Great Gig in the Sky."

A new song, "Eclipse," was added to the brew during this same period and, when Floyd returned to Brighton in mid-month to play an apologetic replacement for the gremlin scarred January gig, this latest piece was firmly in place, rounding out *The Dark Side of the Moon* with fitting finality.

The band was back on the road in the US in September, for a tour that peaked at the Hollywood Bowl, while other distractions include discussions with ballet choreographer Roland Petit for a Floydian soundtrack his production of Proust's *A La Recherche Du Temps Perdu*.

There was also a clutch more live shows, recommended to anybody who can hunt down the tapes for the chance to enjoy *The Dark Side of the Moon* during the days before it became the Biggest Selling Etc. Etc., not only because audiences are, for the most part, sitting quietly (or, at least, not going "whoooo!" over every intro), but also because the songs themselves were still not set in stone.

And they found time for a little more recording. Saxophonist Dick Parry, an old friend of Gilmour's, was recruited during sessions in October to add the now trademark honking to the album; vocalist Claire Torry was introduced during the same sessions by engineer Alan Parsons. Both would go onto create some of the album's most remarkable moments; Torry is, in fact, now credited as a co-composer (with Wright) of "The Great Gig In The Sky," having successfully sued for recognition in 2004.

Returning to Abbey Road on January 18, and working through the month, Pink Floyd finally declared *Dark Side of the Moon* complete on February 1, 1973. The entire process, spread over the past fourteen months, had devoured just thirty-eight days of studio time, but was wrapped up in time for director Adrian Maben to join the band in the studio where they were mixing the finished item, but happily pretended to be recording it for the benefit of his cameras.

Maben had already recorded the band in concert, amidst the stately ruins of Pompeii. The studio footage, though absent from the original 1972 version of *Live at Pompeii*, was added in time for its 1974 reissue, with "On the Run," "Us and Them," and "Brain Damage" among the extra-curricular highlights of what remains one of the all-time great rock concert movies.

The Dark Side of the Moon
(ORIGINAL VINYL RELEASE, HARVEST SHVL 804)

The album suffered an inauspicious birth. Engineer Parsons had created a quadraphonic mix of the album, even though the marketplace required only stereo at that time, and this was to be previewed to the world media at the album's press launch in early March.

Unfortunately, as the day grew closer, it became obvious that EMI was failing in its pledge to wire the London Planetarium for the correct sound system and, though the listening journalists were universally impressed by the album itself, only Rick Wright was present to witness their delight. The remainder of the band stayed home in protest.

There were no complaints, however, regarding the album's performance. By the end of March, *The Dark Side of the Moon* was top of the Billboard charts (it would halt at No. 2 in the UK). The first American single from the album, "Money" (Harvest 3609), was Top Twenty–bound, and the band's latest American tour was the hottest ticket in the land.

And no wonder. From beginning to end, from "Breathe" to "Eclipse," *The Dark Side of the Moon* was spectacular, perhaps the greatest Pink Floyd had mustered so far. But the sleeve, too, was to become iconic, a gatefold designed by Storm Thorgerson of the Hipgnosis design team, and George Hardie of Nicholas Thirkell Associates. It was Hardy, by the way, who contributed the refracting prism that today speaks as loudly for Pink Floyd as any single piece of music.

The surprises did not end with the stark beauty of the sleeve. Within, for purchasers of the original pressing, were two posters, one depicting the band in concert, the other a psychedelic depiction of the Great Pyramid, shot using infrared film. Pyramids also appeared on the sheet of stickers which likewise awaited early bird buyers.

The Dark Side of the Moon
(VINYL QUADRAPHONIC MIX, HARVEST Q4SHVL 804)

The quadraphonic mix over which engineer Parsons labored so long did not go to waste. Ranked among the very first truly successful surround sound mixes ever created, the mix was, in fact, never completed to the engineer's satisfaction. Nevertheless, when Harvest turned to *The Dark Side of the Moon* as one of the jewels in its intended quadraphonic crown, it was to Parsons' mix that they looked.

Released on both vinyl and 8-track, the quad mix is not, in all honesty, too great a departure from its stereo counterpart. A handful of elements, notably guitar lines and spoken vocal passages, are drawn up higher, but it is in the ambience of the music, the sense that you are indeed surrounded by sound, that the mix excels; the

The Yugoslavian quadraphonic version of Dark Side.

instrumental passages that swirl and rush around your ears, those that echo in stereo and now ricochet in quad.

The cataclysmic crashing that rumbles through the speakers in the lead-up to "Time"; the antique clock chimes; and, for the intro to "Money," the clanging of the cash registers—all can bedevil the unsuspecting ears, while both "The Great Gig in the Sky" and a suddenly funky "Any Color You Like" are nothing short of sonic revelations, probably worth the cost of the album in their own right.

All in all, then, it is a remarkable piece of work, yet Parsons' dissatisfaction was, apparently, contagious. When the quad boom passed away, so did the availability of the quad mix and, when Pink Floyd did settle down to consider a surround sound CD of their masterpiece (see below), Parsons' work was only briefly considered before being placed back on the shelf.

A DVD-Audio bootleg did surface, to be passed around sundry Internet sites, but the true vinyl experience—presented, incidentally, with the same ephemeral bells and whistles as the original stereo pressings—was to remain in the hands of collectors alone, at least for a couple of decades.

Fast forward. It is now 1988. Roger Waters has left Pink Floyd, quadraphonic sound has left the lexicon, and vinyl has left the building. What better time, then, to rerelease the quad mix of *The Dark Side of the Moon*, and on pink vinyl yet?

A limited edition confined to Australia alone (Harvest Q4 SHVLA 804), this is one of the more bizarre *Dark Side* spin-offs that the truly enterprising collector can seek out . . . up there with the 1978 Japanese record club edition (EMI/Toshiba HW 5149) that replaced the prism sleeve with a live shot from the *Animals* tour (and was then withdrawn because nobody had thought to secure permission to use the photo), the five-"disc" Polish postcard version (Polpress 003), and the album's first ever appearance in the Soviet Union, as a three-song flexidisc (excerpts from "Time," "On the Run," and "Money") gifted with the magazine *Krugozor*. The full album would not see a Russian release until 1992.

The Dark Side of Radio City
(PIGS ON THE WING 2CD)

Back on the road, this time with *The Dark Side of the Moon* finally available for home stereo comparison, Pink Floyd were astonished to discover their traditionally intent audience had been replaced by an army of youths demanding, all show long, to hear "Money."

It was five years since Pink Floyd had last gone out on tour with a hit single to dictate the makeup of their audience, and they had forgotten just how strange that could be. But that did not dissuade them from releasing a follow-up, "Us and Them."

Andy Warhol was among the guests at the Radio City Music Hall tour highlight in New York on March 17, 1973, while this excellent audience recording captures the entire show as he would have heard it, from the opening reflection on *Obscured By Clouds,* a magnificent "Set the Controls for the Heart of the Sun," replete with a rarely-heard Minimoog, and on to extended trips through "Careful With that Axe, Eugene" and a truly memorable "Echoes" before sliding into *The Dark Side of the Moon.*

It's the kind of set list, and performance, that should peg this among the best of all Floyd boots, and it would, but for one thing. Disc Two (that is, the whole of *Dark Side,* plus "One of These Days" and "Saucerful of Secrets") seems to play just a shade too fast. It's still eminently listenable, of course, but it is a little disappointing.

Eighteen months later, and Pink Floyd were still touring the album, even as their own thoughts turned towards its successor—initially intended to be recorded exclusively on an array of household and kitchen implements, but swiftly scaled down to amore conventional musical presentation. Any number of live shows made it onto bootleg during this period, but perhaps the finest—indeed, the crucial—recounting of *The Dark Side of the Moon* was that broadcast by BBC radio from the band's November 6, 1974, performance at London's Wembley.

This was later remastered as the bootleg *Time in London: 30th Anniversary Edition,* and anybody who heard the broadcast for the first time rattling out of a transistor radio in 1974 could thrill again to what seemed, at the time, to be one of the BBC's greatest-ever offerings.

In terms of sound quality, the CD pressing is all a very long way from the crackle and hiss of old; cleaned up and equalized, it has a stereo impact that almost rivals the studio vinyl (almost: we are speaking in relative terms here), and there are moments of such sublime beauty—the guitar solo through "Time," "The Great Gig In The Sky," "Any Colour You Like"—that Floyd's long-time refusal to release a complete and unabridged document of their '70s live peak becomes ever more baffling.

In terms of past airings, the bonus here is the encore of "Echoes," omitted from the original broadcast and absent from many of the subsequent bootlegs as well. One of the most entrancing versions to be found on any Floyd live recording, it is well worth half an hour of your time, regardless of how many times you've heard the rest of the disc in the past.

Dark Side of the Moon picture disc
(UK DEPICTING PYRAMID, HARVEST SHVLP 804; US DEPICTING PRISM, CAPITOL SEAX 11902)

Was there ever a sillier collecting rage than picture discs? Okay, you don't have to answer that, but really . . . you couldn't play them, because the sound quality was usually rubbish; you couldn't really leave them lying around the house, in case visitors mistook them for placemats; and, if you framed them, then you'd just spent the price of an LP on something that really didn't look any different to the record's original sleeve, or at least an element thereof. So why did people buy them?

Dunno. But almost four decades after this most peculiar of late 1970s/early 1980s fashions fell out of favor, people still seek out the things; indeed, in 2013, a French pressing sold on eBay for almost $350, and there have been others since then that have come close to equaling that.

The Dark Side of the Moon CD
(HARVEST CDP 7 46001 2)

The Pink Floyd catalog was, understandably, one of the earliest mainstream rock concerns to be transferred over to CD, following the upstart format's arrival in the marketplace in 1983. And *The Dark Side of the Moon* was, equally understandably, among the first of their albums to be converted, alongside *Meddle, Wish You Were Here,* and *The Wall.*

That was the good news. The bad news was that they really didn't sound too hot. Nothing you can really put your finger on . . . but you know how it was, the first few goes around, as the promise of CDs restoring original master tapes to the market was hamstrung by the sonic limits of the technology available. Which, of course, opened the door for the next two decades' worth of remastered improvements, as the original discs were enhanced, again and again and again, by successive advances in mastering technology.

At least thirteen different variations of *The Dark Side of the Moon* were produced on CD in the years before the entire catalog was remastered and repackaged during 1994–1995 (see below), and that is without counting those that were purposefully manufactured and marketed as special anniversary editions.

Each of these "regular" editions was manufactured by a different plant. The earliest, manufactured in Japan by Toshiba-EMI, circulated throughout 1983–1984 and do indeed bear a "made in Japan" notice on both sleeve and label. Production then (in 1984) shifted to the Sony plant in Terre Haute, Indiana, before moving on to the Philips DuPont Optical plant in Kings Mountain, North Carolina in late 1986 and, finally, to EMI's own facility in Jacksonville, Illinois, in 1987.

Does anybody care? Yes. But only if the CD comes with its original long-box packaging!

The Dark Side of the Moon
(MOBILE FIDELITY SOUND LAB UDCD 517)

In 1987, in the midst of all the activity surrounding the regular CD pressing of *The Dark Side of the Moon*, this little jewel dropped out of the sky, remastering the album onto the then hi-fi-standard gold disc. Who ever could have guessed that, within less than a decade, the perceived value of gold-colored discs would be so utterly debased by the arrival of CD-Rs?

Audio freaks continue to swear by the sound quality of Mobile Fidelity's output, and certainly *The Dark Side of the Moon* sold well enough for this edition to go into at least two further pressings.

A vinyl pressing, meanwhile, catered towards the still stubborn core of resistance that insisted that compact discs could never replace a good solid 12-inch slice of plastic. And listening to the two alongside one another might well convince you that they were correct.

Shine On
(EIGHT-CD BOX SET, COLUMBIA CXK 53180-S1)

There are box sets and there are doorstops. *Shine On* is definitely one of the latter, and most of Pink Floyd's subsequent boxes have followed suit. Retailing upon release in November 1992 in the region of $100, *Shine On* contained—in no particular order— seven albums and an otherwise unavailable early-years collection, the former repackaged in individual black opaque jewel cases, each enlivened by a small central sticker of the original album art, and bearing an element of the *Dark Side* prism on the spine (file them upright in the correct order and the full effect would be revealed); a fold-out card slipcase in which to keep them; eight postcards; a cover sticker; and a 112-page hardback book of lyrics, photos, and other such ramblings.

It is a gorgeous package. True, you can complain that, with eight CDs at their disposal, the band could surely have accomplished something a little more adventurous than straightforward repressings of *A Saucerful of Secrets*, *Meddle*, *The Dark Side of the Moon*, *Wish You Were Here*, *Animals*, *The Wall* and *A Momentary Lapse of Reason*. You could moan, too, that if they were committed to mere reissues, *The Piper at the Gates of Dawn* and *Atom Heart Mother* should certainly have gone along for the ride.

But they didn't, and *Shine On* is what it is, an expensive but extraordinarily lavish way in which to pick up the Floyd CDs you'd been meaning to buy over the past decade, but hadn't quite got

Pink Floyd's first box set—the impressively packaged Shine On— *kept the extras to a minimum, but if you lined the CD spines up correctly, you were rewarded with the* Dark Side *logo.*

round to. And don't worry if you missed it, the first time around. Subsequent box sets have dragged the same albums out again and again, usually with a lot more CDs as well, but rarely with such tremendous packaging.

The Dark Side of the Moon
(30TH ANNIVERSARY SACD, CAPITOL CDP 7243 5 82136 2 1-US)

In 1993, with the album's twentieth anniversary upon us, EMI packaged up a newly commissioned 1992 remastering of the LP (by Doug Sax) inside a limited edition 5" x 5" collectors edition box, with a twenty-eight page booklet and five Pink Floyd cards. This same remastering was then reissued without the bells and whistles when the entire Pink Floyd back catalog was repackaged during 1994–1995 (Capitol CDP 0777 7 46001 2 5).

Shunting those earlier, nasty-sounding aluminum-colored coasters back into the garbage can, this latest series replaced them all with nicely re-jacketed editions that restored a lot of the little extras that vinyl buffs grew up with, but which earlier CDs had considered strangely unnecessary.

But could the album now be left alone? Of course not, not with *The Dark Side of the Moon*'s thirtieth anniversary now bearing down upon us. Remastered in 2003 from the original master tape, and with the familiar old artwork similarly revised, a "surround sound" Super Audio Compact Disc edition was released with a twenty-page booklet featuring full lyrics, additional photos, and a bonus remastering of the original stereo version, too, for those of us deprived of the fancy new hardware required to play the SACD.

This is the edition, of course, that Pink Floyd themselves preferred to the original vinyl-era quad mix and, in technological terms, they were probably correct to do so. It is a far warmer mix, and enfolds the listener to a far greater extent than Alan Parsons' original vision. At the end of the day, though, we still have just the two ears, and the need for more just muddles our minds. One wonders if anybody ever made a mono mix of *The Dark Side of the Moon.*

Pulse
(2 CDS, LIMITED EDITION LED SLIPCASE EDITION, COLUMBIA C2K 67065)

Recorded live in 1994, as the Waters-less Floyd toured their *Division Bell* album, *Pulse* was marketed largely on the strength of the inclusion, for the first time ever on an official release, of an entire concert presentation of *The Dark Side of the Moon.*

Released in 1995, the performance adds little to the studio version, beyond the gasps of amazement that come out of the audience as sundry visual effects are unleashed. That these are even more impressive on the accompanying concert DVD goes without saying; however, the original CD release of *Pulse* did not come without some visual trickery of its own, namely a solid card slipcase into which was inserted a flashing red light.

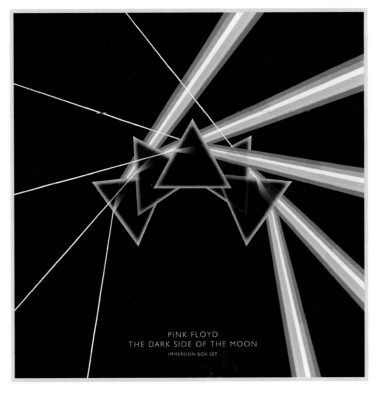

The Immersion boxed version of Dark Side *came complete with marbles and a silk scarf.*

Intended to remain alive for around a year, but actually proving considerably more resilient than that (some copies didn't give up the ghost for five), the LED slipcase was a relatively limited edition of "just" two or three million copies.

The Dark Side of the Moon
(IMMERSION BOX SET, EMI 5 0999 029431 2 1)

By this point, it probably feels like overkill. Nevertheless, among the most fascinating releases of recent years have been the series of three (so far) box sets that Pink Floyd have dedicated to three of their most best loved albums, *Dark Side of the Moon, Wish You Here,* and *The Wall.*

Titled, for reasons that quickly become self-evident, "Immersion" editions, all three are weighted down with more or less every last version of the parent album that you could require.

The Dark Side of the Moon spreads over six discs, opening with the original album (remastered in 2011); then moving on through the 1973 quad mix and the 2003 surround sound mix, both in your choice of bitrate; a live version from the band's 1974 appearance at Wembley in London; a handful of tracks from the Brighton gig; original demos for "Us and Them" and "Money"; the onstage films that the band utilized during their 1974 and 1975 tours; the "Travel Sequence" studio outtake; and even one track from the aborted *Household Objects* follow-up album.

Plus, a couple of books, some so-called collectors cards, replica gig ticket and back stage pass, a scarf (!), nine coasters (!!) and three black marbles (!!!). As bonus trinkets go, they certainly raise the eyebrows. And all packaged in a ten-inch box emblazoned, oddly, with the warning "this is not a toy."

No, it probably isn't.

Next?

What's next, at the time of writing, can only be speculation. It is unlikely that the album's forty-fifth anniversary (2018) will pass unrecognized; and impossible for the fiftieth (2023) to do so. Rumor also insists that the band will be following 2016's *The Early Years 1966–1972* boxed behemoth with a similar package for the half-decade that followed, so we have that to look forward to, as well.

Time to build another shelf?

THE YEAR: IT WAS FIFTY YEARS AGO TODAY (GIVE OR TAKE . . .)— COLLECTING 1968

One of the most popular avenues of collecting is to focus on the releases of a single year—a pursuit, interestingly, which often comes together almost by accident, as you set about cataloging your music for the first time and realize how many of your acquisitions do indeed date from a single year, or at least brief period in time.

Very often, this ties in with the year in which you first became interested enough in music that you started buying records; or to a particular genre that has caught your ear. From there, however, it is but a small step to start looking for other releases from the same period, to build up a sense of how the entire year sounded, and not just a single facet of it.

In this field, the most popular years are those in which, to put it bluntly, "something happened"—1955, with rock 'n' roll first breaking out everywhere; 1964 and the arrival in America of the Beatles; 1967 and the Summer of Love; 1977 and the great punk rock explosion; 1992 and the dawn of grunge.

Or 1968, the year in which the double album came of age, and politics carved its presence into the grooves; the year when the first supergroups arose from the egalitarianism of the past, and profits first became a paramount concern. The year when mono died and bubblegum was born.

But most of all, the year in which rock realized that everything it had accomplished in the past was simply a rehearsal, and that 1968 was the year in which things turned serious.

The previous year had seen record sales in America reach an all-time high. With over a billion dollars' worth of music shifted in just twelve months, record industry profits had more than doubled in a decade.

For the first time, too, LP sales were outstripping singles, and that too made an impact. It would be misleading to say that it was high finance alone that pushed so many bands into new realms of musical seriousness—the ambitious pastures opened up by the Beatles' *Sergeant Pepper* accomplished that, and the artists who followed its lead did so for artistic reasons.

But record companies were another matter entirely. They scented big bucks and they wanted them, and the notion that the youth of America suddenly had previously untold sums of disposable cash to flash and splash on their hairy rock idols was not something that could be easily ignored.

The electrifying debut album from the Crazy World of Arthur Brown—"Fire" was, perhaps significantly, one of the biggest hits of the year.

Bands, too, understood that their audience wanted something more than the lightweight two- or three-minute ditties that had sustained their careers until now. In 1967, many—too many, in fact—had looked towards literature and fantasy for inspiration, and turned out some remarkable music in the process.

But the real world was not like that. It was not peopled with hobbits and goblins and rainbow-riding unicorns. It was a place where bloodshed was commonplace and death was too easy, and rioting was the only means by which a raised voice could be guaranteed to be heard.

This new year was set to offer it another outlet.

In terms of marketing and, therefore, collecting, the year's biggest headline was the wholesale changeover from monophonic sound to stereo—itself a prime mover in the record-breaking album sales of the era, as the first wave of enthusiasts rushed out to replace their scratchy olds with pristine news.

The Who

Excerpts from Tommy (DECCA 734610-3, 4X7-INCH, BOX SET, 1970)
Magic Bus, The Who on Tour (DECCA DL 5064, MONO PROMO LP, 1968)
"My Generation" (UK DECCA AD 1, 7-INCH, EXPORT, PICTURE SLEEVE, 1968)
Ready Steady Who (REACTION 592 001, EP, 1966)
The Who Sell Out (DECCA DL 4950, MONO LP, 1967)
Sing My Generation (DECCA DL 4664, LP, 1966)
"Squeeze Box" (MCA 40475, 7-INCH, PICTURE SLEEVE, 1975)
"Substitute" (ATCO 6409, 7-INCH, 1966)
"Under My Thumb" (UK TRACK 604 006, 7-INCH, 1967)
"Young Man (Blues)" (DECCA 32737, 7-INCH, PICTURE SLEEVE, 1970)

In both the US and the UK, mono would finally be phased out during 1968—indeed, the process was already underway in America, with Simon and Garfunkel's *Bookends* the only truly significant rock album of the year to be released in the now-redundant format.

Mono lingered on in the UK, however, and a number of fascinating curios emerged, with a unique and spectacular mono mix of the Beatles' self-titled double album, also known as "The White Album," and a skull-pummelling mono recreation of the Jeff Beck Group's *Truth* among the most in-demand of all releases from this period.

Elsewhere around the world, the format survived a little longer; mono pressings of the Beatles' *Abbey Road* and the Rolling Stones' *Let It Bleed* were issued in several South American countries in 1969. By 1970, however, mono existed only in radio land, where major label promos mixed the stereo masters down to accommodate AM radio's demands.

As a result, some of the most collectible albums of the 1960s are mono pressings dating from 1967–1968, a roll call that not at all coincidentally includes what are regarded among the greatest albums of all time—*Sgt. Pepper*, the Rolling Stones' *Their Satanic Majesties Request*, Pink Floyd's *The Piper at the Gates of Dawn* and *A Saucerful of Secrets*, the first Grateful Dead and the Doors LPs, Jefferson Airplane's masterpiece *After Bathing at Baxter's*, the Monkees' *The Birds the Bees and the Monkees*, and the Who's astonishing *The Who Sell Out*.

Look out, too, for the mono version of the Crazy World of Arthur Brown's eponymous debut, because for anybody raised on the stereo pressing of this 1968 masterpiece, the mono edition is akin to hearing an entirely different record. Side one is especially notable, with the opening three tracks (including the hit "Fire") present in noticeably longer versions.

The mono "Fire" is much more spare and lacks the friendly trumpets that haunt the stereo version. The epic suite of "Come and Buy"/"Time"/"Confusion," meanwhile, might be almost one minute shorter in mono, but offers up a completely different take, with a new construction.

Unfortunately, very few people bought it. They were more interested in the stereo version—which, for reasons that aren't too difficult to imagine, retailed at a somewhat higher price than mono. Well, you didn't think they were going to give you a whole new speaker's worth of music for free, did you?

The record companies were coining it in, then. But while the music was making money, the sentiments behind the music were somewhat bleaker. The façade of love and peace that sustained youth fashion through 1967 had finally been punctured. The three-year-old Vietnam War was turning ever uglier every day, and the previous year's death toll—9,353 Americans were killed there during 1967—was more than double that of the first two years combined. The launch of the Tet Offensive at the end of January 1968 suggested that, this year, the numbers were set to climb even further.

The anti-war movement was gaining momentum; the Civil Rights movement was gathering arms. Again the previous year, race riots had become commonplace throughout the inner cities, but now the rioters were lethally organized, as Dr. Martin Luther King's dream of peaceful Black Equality was translated into the gun-toting Black Panthers' cry of Black Power. In February 1968, eighth grade students in Brooklyn's Bedford-Stuyvesant all but rioted in protest at the quality of school dinners; in March, Columbia University was stricken by a daylong boycott of classes, organized by anti-war protesters.

The turmoil was not confined to the United States alone. In France, students were agitating loudly against the DeGaulle government's ambition of exemplifying law and order in an increasingly lawless world. In Czechoslovakia, Alexander Dubček took over the leadership of the local Communist Party, and ushered in a Prague Spring of

Wheels of Fire—a four-sided half studio/half live leviathan from the Cream supergroup.

Julie Driscoll, Brian Auger, and the Trinity's revolutionary interpretation of Dylan's greatest basement tape, "This Wheel's On Fire."

enlightenment and—dare the people even breathe the word?—freedom.

In Spain, the Fascist government was experiencing, for the first time, the lashings of a pro-democracy movement, rising in furious disbelief at General Franco's decision to stage a mass for Adolf Hitler on the dead dictator's birthday. In Germany, the younger generation was finally demanding to know what their own elders did during World War Two.

The establishment responded in kind.

In August 1968, Soviet tanks and troops rolled into Prague to crush the incipient democracy. In Los Angeles, the Sheriff's Office was contemplating the purchase of a fleet of armored cars; in Detroit, the local authorities acquired an army-surplus half-track; and, from the depths of the bunkers where the nuclear arsenals grow, *The Bulletin of Atomic Scientists* prepared for Armageddon by pushing forward one hand on the Doomsday Clock, their own iconic contribution to the shaky state of the world. For more than four years, since the days that drove Dylan to warn of "Hard Rain," the hands were frozen at twelve minutes to midnight. Now they hung at seven. (On January 26, 2017, following the inauguration of President Trump, they moved to two-and-one-half minutes to midnight.)

A country that was founded on the principles of freedom was suddenly being ruled by fear, at least if you were young and longhaired. "Hippy" was a dirty word; "student," "pacifist," and "protestor" likewise.

Visiting California the previous year, the English band Cream had expressed their own astonishment at the freedom that seemed to permeate the very streets. True, not every passing cop was willing to look the other way when he stumbled on a gang of kids taking a crafty toke, but he wasn't about to start cracking skulls with his nightstick, either. Overnight, all that had changed, and rock 'n' roll would soundtrack it all.

Cream

BBC Classic Tracks (WESTWOOD ONE, TRANSCRIPTION DISC, 1994)

Classic Cuts (RSO 0152, PROMO LP, 1978)

Cream on Top (UK POLYDOR 2855 002, MAIL-ORDER LP, 1971)

Disraeli Gears (ATCO 33-232, MONO LP, 1967)

Fresh Cream (ATCO 33-206, MONO LP, 1967)

Goodbye (ATCO 141, SAMPLER LP WITH VANILLA FUDGE, 1969)

"Strange Brew" (UK POLYDOR 56315, UNISSUED 7-INCH, 1969)

Wheels of Fire (ATCO 2-700, 2-LP MONO PROMO, 1968)

Wheels of Fire (ATCO 4525, PROMO EP, 1968)

"Wrapping Paper" (UK REACTION 591 007, 7-INCH, 1967)

From the Rolling Stones' "Street Fighting Man" to the Beatles' "Revolution," from Eric Burdon's "Sky Pilot" to the Lettermen's "All the Gray Haired Men," voices were raised in opposition to all that the authorities were bringing to bear.

Jimi Hendrix grasped Bob Dylan's "All Along the Watchtower" before most people had even heard the album from which it came (*John Wesley Harding*) and electrified sentiments that might have seemed mere allegory in Dylan's hands, but became a mantra among American troops fighting in Vietnam. "There must be some way out of here!"

The Stones, in particular, came out fighting. Scrambling to make up the ground (both musical and critical) that they lost with the psychedelic stew of *Their Satanic Majesties Request* the previous year, the Stones hooked up with producer Jimmy Miller to craft an album that would both reconfirm the band's blues traditions and dismiss their (and everybody else's) psychedelic meanderings as simply a passing aberration. And they succeeded with an album that not only restated the Stones' roots, it reinvented them.

The ten songs that made up *Beggars Banquet* fit the band like a glove. Nobody ever believed the group had traveled 2000 light years from home, or spent a night in another land. But the brutal sexuality of "Stray Cat Blues" and the badlands hoedown of "Prodigal Son" merged so perfectly with the Stones' public persona that their imagery became utterly inseparable from the performers—a process that reached its terrifying apogee with "Sympathy for the Devil," a lyric that Jagger wrote after reading banned Soviet author Mikhail Bulgakov's *The Master and Margarita*, but which was far easier to view as unadorned autobiography. Even today, as many legends and myths adhere to "Sympathy for the Devil" as the rest of the band's output put together.

"Sympathy for the Devil" dominates *Beggars Banquet*, but by no means does it outclass it. The scratchy lilt of "No Expectations," the country pastiche "Dear Doctor," the chugging blues of "Parachute Woman" . . . with every passing number, the aura of menace builds and builds, until the valedictory "Salt of the Earth" croaks it to a close that is all the more haunting for its lack of the expected climax. *Beggars Banquet* sounds like it wanted to end with an apocalypse. Instead, it leaves you hanging on the brink, wondering what could ever, possibly, follow it up.

The Stones manufactured their menace. Other songs took on their own foreboding meaning, whether they were intended to or not. Who, among those who were alive and thinking in 1968, can listen to Mary Hopkins' "Those Were the Days," one of the biggest hits of the entire year, without translating the song's eerie edge of sad nostalgia into a lament for the life we led before all Hell broke loose at home and abroad?

Elsewhere, the emergence of the first proto-metal bands, the Jeff Beck Group and Blue Cheer among them, might not have posited a

Eddie Cochran

C'mon Everybody (UK LONDON HA-U 2093, EP, 1959)

"Hallelujah, I Love Her So" (UK LONDON HLW 9022, 78, 1960)

"Mean When I'm Mad" (LIBERTY 55070, 7-INCH, PICTURE SLEEVE, 1957)

Never to Be Forgotten (LIBERTY LRP 3220, LP, 1962)

"Rough Stuff" (CAPEHART 5003, 7-INCH, PICTURE SLEEVE, 1960)

Singin' to My Baby (LIBERTY LRP 3061, GREEN-LABEL LP, 1957)

"Skinny Jim" (CREST 1026, 7-INCH, 1956)

"Three Steps to Heaven" (UK LONDON HLG 9115, 78, 1960)

Twelve of His Biggest Hits (LIBERTY LRP 3172, LP, 1960)

"Twenty Flight Rock" (UK LONDON HLU 8386, 7-INCH,
    BLACK LABEL WITH TRIANGULAR CENTER, 1957)

formal protest against the political machine that was crushing hope and extinguishing promise, but it was a protest nonetheless, the realization that if you turned the volume up loud enough, you might just be able to drown out the screams.

It was no coincidence that, even as the Who worked up what would become *Tommy* (the archetypal story of the blind leading the bland), they were also rehearsing a live set that kicked back into rock's more innocent past, resurrecting Eddie Cochran's "Summertime Blues" and Mose Allison's "Young Man Blues," and reinventing them as virtual talismans, reminders again of happier days twisted through the prism of irony. With the military draft growing louder every day, how wonderful it must have been when your biggest worry was whether or not you'd be able to borrow the car for the evening.

"1968 was a funny old year," the Hendrix Experience's Noel Redding once recalled. "From the point of view of the band—well, there stopped being one. But when we were out on the road, you could see that people were scared, they were looking out at the world and everything they'd been brought up to believe, and everything they thought they were creating in 1967, was falling apart around their ears. "We were insulated from a lot of it; we'd play a town, then move on, but you'd talk to kids and a few months later, reading the paper and looking at the casualty figures, you'd wonder, how many of them had you talked to somewhere a few months earlier? And now they were dead or injured, fighting a war that very few of them seemed to believe in, or even understand."

You could almost hear Arlo Guthrie strike up the opening patterns of "Alice's Restaurant" as he spoke.

But the war was only one part of an equation that appeared to be painting the collapse of civilization in sky-high neon lettering. The assassination of Martin Luther King on April 4 (followed two months later by the death of Democratic frontrunner Bobby Kennedy) carved its own bloodied initials into society's flesh, an outrage that essentially pulled the rug out from beneath anybody who felt America (and, therefore, much of the world) still had a hope of surviving the decade.

Dion's "Abraham, Martin and John," aligning King with fellow martyrs Abraham Lincoln and John F. Kennedy, so captured the mood of the country that it not only gave the singer his first gold disc since "Runaround Sue," but also kickstarted a chart career that had lain dormant since 1964.

The immediate response to the killing, however, was considerably less calm and respectful, as rioting broke out across America—the country's most serious outbreak of civil unrest since the Detroit riots of the previous year.

It might have been worse, too, had it not been for James Brown. Amid the turmoil that exploded in the wake of the first reports of MLK's slaying, Brown broadcast appeals for calm on the radio stations WJBE and WEBB, before hurriedly arranging a live TV broadcast of his scheduled show at the Boston Garden the following evening.

Unquestionably, the gesture quelled at least a little of the violence; Boston, having expected absolute chaos, was almost peaceful that night, and the *Boston Phoenix* subsequently ranked the show among the most important live performances the city had ever seen.

"The show was an absolute tour de force. Brown soothed his mourning audience by dedicating the concert to Dr. King and delivering a million-watt performance packed with greats: 'It's a Man's Man's Man's World,' 'Cold Sweat,' 'That's Life,' 'Try Me,' 'Please, Please, Please,' and more.

"He invited [Boston Mayor Kevin] White to speak to the crowd and the cameras. And when police reacted to fans who rushed the stage at one point, Brown assured them he could handle things himself, pleading, successfully, for everyone to return to their seats. On this night, music literally helped determine the course of Boston's history." The concert broadcast on local PBS station WGBH, together with a wealth of supplemental footage, is now available on DVD.

It would be so misleading, however, to recall 1968 as a year dominated by protest and riot. True, the all-pervading image of the MC5, kicking out the jams at the head of the Detroit underground, is a difficult one to shake free of, and it certainly cannot be divorced from any discussion of the year.

But the MC5 were little more than a local cult at that time, destined for infamy more through their associations with radical kingpin John Sinclair and their unequivocal refusal to tone down the language on their *Kick Out the Jams* debut album. To America and the rock world at large, 1968 was the year of a series of triumphs that could scarcely have been further removed from the political tumult if they'd tried.

Cream, after all, was one of the most apolitical bands you could hope to find, at least in a major rock arena, yet they were also one of the biggest in the land; and their contribution to the unfolding year,

Wheels of Fire, was gargantuan as well. A double set, half of this eye-catching new package drew from the studio recordings Cream had spent the last year working on. The remainder was boiled down from live shows recorded earlier in the year, because it was onstage that Cream's brilliance was at its most vivacious.

A brilliant album, a stunning achievement, a Herculean melding of craft and creativity, the centerpiece of *Wheels On Fire* was the dichotomy that dogged Cream throughout their career: the uneasy marriage of, on the studio disc, a succession of sharp, tight rock songs and, on the other, four sprawling jams.

To modern ears, accustomed as they are to the "legend" of Cream, the two faces are not so extreme. Journeying through the strangely Yardbirds-y "Passing Time," the haunted neo-orchestrations of "As You Said," the lumbering "Politician," and the eerie "Deserted Cities of the Heart," we can slip from the whimsy of the studio record's "Pressed Rat and Warthog" to the thunder of the in-concert "Toad" and easily understand how the same man (drummer Ginger Baker) wrote them both.

At the time, however, they were as divisive as any other facet of the group. Reiterating the complaints it had slung at Cream's last album, *Disraeli Gears, Rolling Stone* opened its review of the album with the admonishment, "Cream is good at a number of things; unfortunately songwriting and recording are not among them. [Their last album,] *Disraeli Gears* was far better."

The live record, on the other hand, was the food of the gods. Preaching at a time when the vast majority of live albums were little more than contractual obligations, poorly recorded and even harder to listen to, the review insisted, "this is the kind of thing that people who have seen Cream perform walk away raving about, and it's good to, at last, have it on a record." Such enthusiasm still holds true. In 2003, *Classic Rock* magazine published its critics' choices of the Top 50 live albums ever released. *Wheels of Fire* came in at number fifty.

But still the divide between the two discs was disconcerting. The band's UK label, Polydor, was so nervous about the LP's schizophrenia that the scheduled double album was also released as two individual discs (the snappy *In the Studio* in August, and the lumbering *Live at the Fillmore* in December), so that fans of one would not perforcedly be saddled with an unwanted other.

Neither was it a wasted gesture. While the full-weight *Wheels of Fire* marched to No. 3 on the UK chart, the slimmed-down *In the Studio* soared almost as high, to No. 7. *Live at the Fillmore*, on the other hand, did not even make the listings.

The record was even bigger in America. The most eagerly awaited new release of a summer that was already girding for fresh albums from the Dead, the Airplane, and Vanilla Fudge, *Wheels of Fire* was released in America in July, and marched straight to the top of the chart, bumping brassman Herb Alpert out of the way in the process.

It remained there for a month, until the latest by the Doors came to push it off its perch, but it was still in the album chart close to one year later.

From the commercially sublime to the disastrously ridiculous: The Kinks' *Village Green Preservation Society* album scarcely sold a bean upon release, although it has long since ascended to that rarified strata of albums that (say it softly) are now widely proclaimed to be "better than *Pepper*." That's a yardstick that may only be worth the weight of whichever critic says it, but still it has ensured the immortality of a record that even Ray Davies describes as "the most successful failure of all time"—successful in that the album said everything he wanted it to; "failure" in that . . . well, in that it barely sold a bean on release.

The people who always loved the album, of course, will always love it and for good reason. From the hymnal title track through to the heart-tearing nostalgia of "Village Green" itself; from the scatty whimsy of "Phenomenal Cat" to the fiendish fairy-tailoring of "Wicked Annabella," *Village Green Preservation Society* is the childhood memory you recall but cannot quite grasp, the favorite TV episode that never turns up in the reruns, the old lover whose photo was eaten by the cat. It is certainly the Kinks' greatest album, and one of the decade's finest as well. 1968 would have been a lot poorer without it.

Valuable, too, is Pink Floyd's *A Saucerful of Secrets*, an album of cosmic rumination and painstaking improvisation that sought only to prove that its makers could survive life without frontman and songwriter Syd Barrett, but wound up creating far more than that. The title track alone remains one of the most pivotal numbers in the Pink Floyd catalog, *not* for what it is, but for what it represented. As guitarist David Gilmour later pointed out, it set the stage for so much of what Floyd would accomplish in the years to come, while bandmate Roger Waters confirmed that "it was the first thing we'd done without Syd that we thought was any good." Their adhesion to those principles over the next five years would ultimately birth *The Dark Side of the Moon*.

Some of the most important records of the age were released in 1968. The Jeff Beck Group uncorked *Truth* and singlehandedly served up the blueprint that would create Led Zeppelin. Jeff Beck remembers the day he sat listening to a white label of Zeppelin's year-end debut album with Jimmy Page. Page was proud of that record, and Beck agreed that he ought to be, at least until the needle hit the third track on side one, and "You Shook Me" shook out of the speakers. The same "You Shook Me" that Beck had included on *Truth*; the same "You Shook Me" that a passing John Paul Jones had gifted with an immortal organ line.

"I looked at him and said 'Jim . . . what?' and the tears were coming out with anger. I thought, 'This is a piss take, it's got to be.' I mean, there was *Truth* still spinning on everybody's turntable . . . .

Then I realized it was serious." It is probably no more accurate to say that without *Truth*, there would have been no *Led Zeppelin I* than it is to argue that without the Velvet Underground (whose *White Light White Heat* sank without trace this same year), there would have been no David Bowie.

But without the Beck Group to pave the way, Zeppelin would certainly have found their own elevation a little harder to pull off, not only because Beck and his own savage brand of *Truth* opened the country up to a whole new style of blistered blues, but also because the man who managed Zeppelin, Peter Grant, was the same man who road-managed the Beck Group, and knew, therefore, precisely which markets would be the most receptive to the new group's dynamic.

Truth hit hard, after all. With radio already primed by advance copies of the record, and a spellbinding reconstruction of "Ol' Man River" receiving so much attention that it was briefly scheduled for release as a single, *Truth* entered the *Billboard* chart buoyed by a crop of genuinely enthusiastic reviews. *Truth*, declared Robert Christgau, was "the best thing from England this year, with the exception of Traffic. Deluged by British blues bands, they said it with a rock 'n' roll difference, a good record characterized by new sounds and a respectable tour." Other reviews were equally complimentary. It was a dynamite album.

What is interesting, however, as we filter through what are today adjudged some of the year's most significant releases, is that few of them were especially huge hits.

Truth reached the giddy heights of No. 15, only five places below Zeppelin's maiden flight. But the Zombies' purposefully misspelt *Odessey and Oracle* barely scratched the Top 100, and who among us paid any attention to such delights as the pioneering fusion of

Otis Redding

The Great Otis Redding Sings Soul Ballads (VOLT S411, STEREO LP, 1968)
The Immortal Otis Redding (ATCO 33-252, MONO PROMO LP, 1968)
Otis Blue (VOLT S412, STEREO LP, 1965)
Pain in My Heart (ATCO 33-161, STEREO LP, 1964)
"Pain in My Heart" (VOLT 112, 7-INCH, 1963)
"She's Alright" (FINER ARTS 2016, 7-INCH, 1961)
"Shout Bamalama" (ORBIT 135, 7-INCH, 1961)
"(Sittin' On) The Dock of the Bay" (VOLT 157, 7-INCH, BLACK-AND-RED LABEL, 1967)
"That's What My Heart Needs" (VOLT 109, 7-INCH, 1963)
"These Arms of Mine" (VOLT 103, 7-INCH, 1962)

Brian Auger-Julie Driscoll Trinity's *Open*? The eponymous debut by the Crazy World Of Arthur Brown made No. 7 on the strength of the all-consuming "Fire," but the Small Faces' *Ogden's Nut Gone Flake* climbed no higher than No. 159 in America, even as it topped the UK chart.

The reformed Byrds had already run out of feathers, as *The Notorious Byrd Brothers* flapped around the lower reaches of the Top Fifty; Moby Grape and the Vanilla Fudge were already in decline; and, though the Mothers of Invention certainly scored their biggest hit yet with *We're Only In It for the Money*, a week at No. 30 was scarcely going to dent the big boys . . . especially when Frank Zappa's second album of the year, the delightful *Lumpy Gravy*, foundered a full 129 places lower down. (Catch the full story behind both albums on Zappa's *Lumpy Money* CD anthology.)

And so on. Of course, one can never judge an act's importance by its popularity, as a swift glance at a list of the year's No. 1 albums will prove. In the United Kingdom, balladeers Andy Williams and Val Doonican and the perennial soundtrack to *The Sound of Music* did battle with the Beatles, Scott Walker, the Hollies, and Tom Jones and, reflecting the UK's long-standing love affair with soul music, hit collections by the Supremes, the Four Tops, and the recently deceased Otis Redding.

In the United States, the picture was no less distorted. The Beatles bookended the year's chart toppers with *Magical Mystery Tour* and the double "White Album," while new offerings by Simon and Garfunkel, the Rascals, Janis Joplin and Big Brother, and the Doors, plus another double album delight from Hendrix, *Electric Ladyland*, pointed to the strength of the relatively recently launched FM radio boom.

Julie Driscoll, Brian Auger and the Trinity, European 45s

"I Don't Know Where You Are" (Brian Auger & the Trinity) (UK MARMALADE 598 006, 1968)
"Lonesome Hobo" (FRANCE MARMALADE 421 180, 1968)
"Red Beans and Rice" (Brian Auger and the Trinity) (UK MARMALADE 598 003, 1967)
"Road to Cairo" (UK MARMALADE 598 011, 1968)
"Save Me" (UK MARMALADE 598 004, 1967)
"Season of the Witch" (FRANCE MARMALADE 421 194, 1968)
"Take Me to the Water" (UK MARMALADE 598 018, 1969)
"This Wheel's On Fire" (UK MARMALADE 598 006, 1968)
"Tramp" (FRANCE MARMALADE 421 168, 1968)
"What You Gonna Do?" (Brian Auger & the Trinity) (UK MARMALADE 598 015, 1968)

But such a triumph for sensible listening is balanced by the three months at the top that were divided between Paul Mauriat and his Orchestra (purveyors of the lush instrumental hit "Love Is Blue"—subsequently covered for a UK hit by Jeff Beck, of all people), country singer Glen Campbell, and the jumping rhythms of Herb Alpert and the Tijuana Brass.

The singles chart offers an even more bizarre barometer. American chart-toppers in 1968 included John Fred and the Playboy Band's stupendously original "Judy in Disguise (with Glasses)," Jeannie C. Riley's "Harper Valley PTA," and Bobby Goldboro's snuff-rock epic "Honey." And bubbling behind them, taking the charts by storm almost every time they released another 45, the arch bubblegum factory of Kasenetz Katz was peaking so high in 1968 that it seemed unlikely they would ever come down again.

How do we explain that?

We do so by remembering the sheer schizophrenia of the American record-buying public of that time, one that not only flourished on either side of the AM/FM divide, but also across the chasm that yawned between the parallel universes of rock and pop. And, in doing so, we can paint some very peculiar lines across the popular face of the underground.

Restricting our generalizations to the best selling artists alone, artists like the Jefferson Airplane (whose 1968 opus *Crown of Creation* really doesn't receive the respect today that it deserves), the Grateful Dead, Hendrix, the Who, the Doors, Cream, and Big Brother (plus comparative veterans like the Beatles, Stones, and Dylan) were popularly believed to represent the conscience of the age. Outside of their domain, everything else was inconsequential pap, marketed and manufactured for an audience whose collective IQ barely reached room temperature.

The divide between pop and rock, between what was "acceptable" and what was not, had grown immense over the last couple of years.

Pop was no longer an abbreviation of "popular"; now it suggested something so wholesome that it was unwholesome, something that crept into your house whilst you slept, cleansed your spirit, corrupted your sister, and left a sticky trail of slime everywhere it went.

It appealed to the idiot masses and led them, sheep-like, into the corporate embrace of The Man, dulling what little spark of intellect the listener might once have possessed with its hypnotic repetition of the message that everything was *fine*.

Rock confronted the burning issues of the day, and through the weight of public opinion, it extinguished them. It was held in the blood-free hands of the Revolution. The pop groups, on the other hand, were the establishment's way of making people forget what was going on in the real world, and bubblegum remains all-pervading image of 1968.

Long after we have tired of alphabetizing all the icons of rock that were released that year; long after we have replaced our original vinyl with a reissue with a CD with a DVD-A with whatever is next; a chorus or two of the Lemon Pipers' "Green Tambourine," of Status Quo's "Pictures of Matchstick Men," of the Ohio Express' "Chewy Chewy," and the 1910 Fruitgum Company's "Goody Goody Gumdrops" is always going to set the old memory banks salivating faster and more furiously than any psychedelic chestbeater or heavy rock anthem.

Add the Beatles' "Lady Madonna" to the mix, and the coloring book craziness of the *Yellow Submarine* movie . . . remember that the Doors' "Hello I Love You" was scarcely less maddeningly memorable than Tommy James' "Mony Mony" . . . and that "Hey Jude" might well have been the longest No. 1 hit of all time, but that most of its lyrics were "na na na na" . . . and it doesn't matter what the rock history books tell us about 1968.

Yes, it was the year that America burned and her children scowled. But it was also the year that we sang "Yummy yummy yummy, I've got love in my tummy" and, arguably, we were all a lot happier because of it. Whether we'd be willing to admit it or not.

Status Quo

"Black Veils of Melancholy" (CADET CONCEPT 7015, 7-INCH, 1969)

Dog of Two Heads (PYE 3301, LP, 1971)

"In My Chair" (UK PYE 7N 17998, 7-INCH, PICTURE SLEEVE, 1970)

"Jealousy" (IRELAND VERTIGO QUO 9, 7-INCH PROMO, 1982)

Ma Kelly's Greasy Spoon (JANUS JLS 3018, LP, 1970)

Messages from the Status Quo (UK PYE NPL 18220, MONO LP, 1968)

"Pictures of Matchstick Men" (CADET CONCEPT 7001, 7-INCH, 1968)

"Roadhouse Blues" (UK PHONOGRAM DJ 005, 7-INCH PROMO, 1972)

Spare Parts (UK PYE NPL 18301, MONO LP, 1969)

"Technicolor Dreams" (UK PYE 7N 17650, WITHDRAWN 7-INCH, 1969)

THE BROADCAST: LIVE AT THE BBC

They lurk in the catalogs of more or less every significant British and American band of the '60s, '70s, '80s, and '90s. They pop up as bonus tracks on more "deluxe" and "expanded" CD rereleases every year. They have been released as stand-alone 12-inch singles and multi-disc box sets. They have been mislabeled as outtakes and bootlegged to eternity.

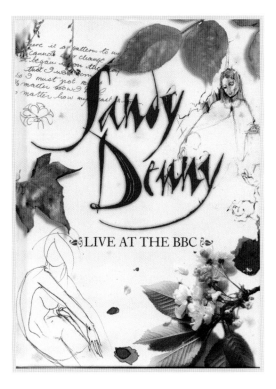

The exquisitely designed boxed collection of all Sandy Denny's BBC recordings.

They are the Peel Sessions, although that itself is a misleading catch-all, because they are also the Bob Harris Sessions, the Anne Nightingale Sessions, the Andy Crowley Sessions . . . and Almost-Every-Other-British-Radio-Disc-Jockey-You-Could-Mention Sessions. The late John Peel just happens to be the one whose name most people seem to recognize.

Back in the early 1990s, when author Ken Farner compiled his epochal *In Session Tonight: Complete Radio One Recordings* book, it was estimated that since the station opened in September 1967, the BBC Radio One archive had grown to contain over 8,000 largely unreleased performances, by some 1,500 different acts.

In the years since then, several thousand further performers have filed into the BBC studios in London to record a clutch of songs for broadcast on one or other of the myriad radio programs which have catered for such recordings.

And this only takes into account the last fifty years. For more than forty years before that, the BBC had been broadcasting exclusive "in session" performances by everyone from vaudeville stars and music hall singers, through light orchestras and jazz bands, skiffle acts and bluesmen, and onto every shade of rock, pop, R&B, and reggae you could ask for.

Not all of them are still with us. Indeed, some were not even taped; they were simply broadcast live on the night, and if they do exist today, it is only because somebody, somewhere, was crouched by their radio, tape recorder in hand. The concept of exclusive radio sessions is a relic of British radio's earliest years. Forever looking to preserve the integrity of its members, most of whom were concert rather than studio musicians, the all-powerful Musicians' Union viewed radio as a serious threat to its well-being. If people could listen to music on the radio, after all, why would they bother going out to shows?

The answer to that question was supplied by "needletime," a draconian piece of legislation that regulated the amount of time that could be devoted to broadcasting gramophone records. And the BBC, a state-run organization that held the monopoly on British broadcasting until the early 1970s, had no alternative but to comply.

Even as its most lenient, needletime was harsh. Little more than twelve hours of prerecorded music was allowed per week, throughout the BBC's entire operation (domestic and abroad), with even top music shows restricted to just half an hour of disc spinning per three- or four-hour broadcast. The rest of the program would thus be devoted to live performances.

By the early 1960s, and the dawn of Britain's rock 'n' roll era, the Union had relaxed its regulations a little, but still, the demands were harsh. The legendary *Saturday Club*, the source for many of the now famous (and oft-bootlegged) early Beatles, Rolling Stones, and Yardbirds performances, was allocated just forty-five minutes of needletime per two-hour show.

Things weren't much better in 1967, when the BBC launched its pop music station, Radio One, to replace the recently outlawed pirate stations that had fermented the British pop boom of the sixties. Overnight, stations like Radio Caroline, Radio London, and many more were obliterated; but overnight, too, the best of their disc jockeys found a new berth in London, on the BBC's brand new venture. John Peel, the man whose name today is synonymous with BBC radio sessions, was among them. And he quickly proved the most resourceful of them all.

The Move

"Cherry Blossom Clinic" (UK REGAL ZONOPHONE, NO CATALOG NUMBER, 7-INCH TEST PRESSING, 1968)

"Chinatown" (MGM 14332, 7-INCH, 1971)

"Ella James" (UK HARVEST HAR 5036, UNISSUED 7-INCH, 1971)

"Fore Brigade" (UK FLY ECHO 104, EP, PICTURE SLEEVE, 1972)

Looking On (UK FLY HIFLY 1, LP, 1970)

The Move (UK REGAL ZONOPHONE LRZ 1002, MONO LP, 1968)

"Night of Fear" (DERAM 7504, 7-INCH, 1967)

Shazam (A&M SP 4259, LP, 1969)

Something Else from the Move (UK REGAL ZONOPHONE TRZ 2001, EP, 1968)

"Tonight" (CAPITOL 3126, 7-INCH, 1971)

Other DJs booked whoever was being offered by record labels and pluggers. Peel, for the most part, booked the artists he liked, and it didn't even matter to him whether or not they had a hit, or even a record label, behind them. If they met his personal musical standards, then they were right for his (late night) show.

And so, new sessions would be taped, old ones would be repeated; and, by the time needletime was abolished at the end of the 1980s, the session had become so entrenched within the Peel Show's makeup that nobody even dreamed of abandoning it.

Through the early fall of 1967, therefore, the BBC studio complexes in London played host to one of the greatest ensembles of rock 'n' roll talent ever assembled under their respective roofs. The Jimi Hendrix Experience, Procol Harum, Denny Laine, Pink Floyd, the Idle Race, the Move, the Crazy World Of Arthur Brown, Traffic, the Nice, Tomorrow, Tim Rose, the Bee Gees, the Incredible String Band: It was a roll call which read like the greatest festival ever, as though every underground happening that had stirred London's psychedelic imaginings that year was being recreated once again, but this wasn't a concert, and it wasn't a dream. It was simply the lineup for the first three installments of Peel's weekly BBC radio show, *Top Gear*.

Perhaps the most difficult thing to understand about the whole business is that it was never intended to create a unique archive of sound. Live sessions were regarded as a necessary evil, a way of airing the top hits of the day whilst staying within the MU's guidelines.

If a band was available to play, they would be invited in to the studio, freeing up two or three valuable minutes for a record whose makers were not around. The tapes would be preserved for subsequent repeats; again, there was no sense of cataloging history. As far as the BBC was concerned, needletime was simply an irritant. It created an institution despite itself.

Most BBC sessions are recorded in one day, and from the modern listener's point of view, that in itself is fascinating. The Cure's Robert Smith once spoke of recording one of his group's later album, "and taking three weeks to get the snare sound right." At the BBC, he would have had three minutes. It is a fast-paced and furious atmosphere, and the results—generally broadcast within a week of the recording—can be fascinating, performances caught almost midway between the live environment and the studio.

Working with tough, no-nonsense BBC producers who know exactly what needs to be done, and how long it takes, even the greatest perfectionist musician has to simply buckle down and get the job done!

Former Nice guitarist Davey O' List, a member of Roxy Music when they recorded their first John Peel session in 1971, remembers, "We just went and did it. We'd start out playing the song through live, taping everything, and then there'd be a little time left over for overdubbing and mixing. But what you hear is pretty much what we did first time."

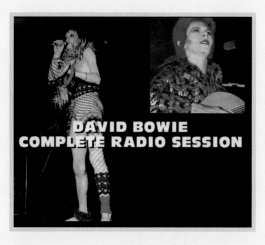

An official box of Bowie's Beeb tracks would eventually appear, but prior to that, CD bootlegs also rounded up this astonishing canon.

A pair of the best-known BBC session CDs highlight this. Neither Yes nor Led Zeppelin, after all, are known as "bang it down and get it out" merchants—indeed, not until the days of punk rock and the new wave did bands start priding themselves on how quickly they could record. But Yes' *Something's Coming* BBC album and Zeppelin's *BBC Sessions* have both been unanimously ranked amongst the most exciting, not to mention spontaneous, recordings in either band's catalog, and they are not alone in that.

Well-known from bootlegs and box sets alike, early sessions by such progressive rock idealists as Genesis, Pink Floyd, and Gentle Giant have an excitement and energy which was rarely recaptured on their regular albums.

That said, not every session by every band is available for release. For starters, every musician involved in the session has to give their approval beforehand, a process which is snarled both by interband politics (attempts to chronicle David Bowie's BBC sessions constantly foundered on this rock before they were finally compiled in the early 2000s), and the players' own memories of the sessions.

"I remember the session being very hurried, and musically we would have preferred to have spent more time getting it right," Genesis keyboard player Tony Banks once reflected. "We weren't that happy with the end result, but we look back with affection." Brett Anderson, vocalist with London Suede, too, acknowledges that when his band is asked to clear sessions for release, "It's very much a case by case basis. Some performances were better than others." Those groups who do simply give the BBC *carte blanche* to release entire blocks of sessions are indeed in a minority—even the Led Zeppelin album would not include everything the group taped for the network until 2016 finally brought an expanded edition of the anthology.

Other artists, however, believe they reached a peak of sorts at the BBC. Eccentric British singer Robyn Hitchcock describes the last session that his band, the Egyptians, recorded as "the best stuff we ever did. It was live, it was mixed by our soundman who's Finnish,

Jimi Hendrix Experience

Are You Experienced (REPRISE R6261, MONO LP, 1967)

Axis: Bold As Love (REPRISE R6281, MONO LP, 1967)

Cry of Love (REPRISE MS 2034, LP WITH W7 LOGO, 1971)

Electric Hendrix (UK TRACK 2856 002, LP, 1971)

Electric Ladyland (REPRISE 2R 6307, MONO PROMO LP, 1968)

"Gypsy Eyes" (UK TRACK 2094 010, 7-INCH, 1971)

Hendrix in the West (UK POLYDOR 831 312-2, CD, 1989)

"Hey Joe" (REPRISE 0572, 7-INCH, PICTURE SLEEVE, 1967)

"Little Drummer Boy"/"Silent Night" (REPRISE PRO 595, 7-INCH PROMO, PICTURE SLEEVE, 1974)

"Stepping Stone" (REPRISE 0905, 7-INCH, 1970)

and there were about twenty people in the other room drinking wine and coffee, and they'd just hold their glasses still for three minutes while we did a take, then we'd do another one. That last session, I think, is the real heart of the Egyptians."

Other acts, too, believe the BBC brought out the best in them. In 1968, the young Dave Edmunds-led Love Sculpture, for example, were so blown away by their six-minute single take version of the classical piece "Sabre Dance" that even after it was rerecorded for the first hit, the BBC version remained their favorite.

And from a year before that, the memory of Pink Floyd's earliest BBC appearances remains so powerful that almost every time British record collectors are asked which sessions they would most like to see released, the Floyd come out well on top—and that despite their very first broadcasts having been wiped many years before. Those that survive finally made it onto the band's 2016 *Early Years* box set.

Of all the sessions taped during the late 1960s, perhaps the most legendary are those laid down by the Jimi Hendrix Experience, as recaptured on his own BBC CD. Between February 13, 1967, and December 15 that same year, Hendrix and the Experience recorded sufficient exclusive BBC material to stuff a double album to bursting point. Twenty-four tracks were taped and completed, some reprising the band's own recent releases; others documenting moments that might never recur again; others still hammering back at songs which the group weren't completely happy with. What is amazing about all this is that it took them just five days of work to do it.

The sessions in question were the Experience's five BBC Radio broadcasts, a series of sense-shattering recordings that catch the band at both its most relaxed, and its very best. These recordings, after all, would be heard the length and breadth of the entire nation, bringing the sound of the Experience into homes that might never have dreamed such a band existed.

But they would also be aired just once or twice, and then filed away and forgotten. So, as another producer told another band, when they were faced with a similar quest: "Make it good . . . but don't make it difficult."

The Experience's first BBC session came on February 13, five days ahead of its scheduled broadcast. Recording in Studio Two, at the BBC's London headquarters, the band would record four songs for broadcast on *Saturday Club*: "Stone Free," "Hey Joe," "Foxy Lady," and "Love or Confusion," plus first-take versions of "Hey Joe" and "Foxy Lady."

The session was unorthodox, to say the least. Producer Bill Bebb recalled the sound mixer Peter Harwood complaining about the feedback he was hearing, "so I opened up the talkback and started saying, 'Er, Jimi, we're getting rather a lot . . . ' when Chas . . . leans over and says, 'Shut up man, that's his sound!'" He may have been shut up, but he still remembered that even with the monitors switched off, "we could still hear Jimi through the soundproof glass, and we could see the glass moving." There were also noise complaints from the Radio 3 Concert Hall, two floors above!

Despite such problems, the band, Bebb, and Harwood (plus engineer Tony Wilson) were back at Studio Two on March 28, for a second *Saturday Club* recording. This time, all three tracks were first takes: "Killin' Floor," "Fire," and "Purple Haze."

In September, 1967, following the arrival of Radio One, the Experience—by now one of the biggest bands in Britain—were amongst the earliest guests invited to appear on *Top Gear* show. Recorded at the Playhouse Theatre in London, with Bev Phillips and Pete Ritzema, it was to prove an epochal recording.

The band recorded five songs for broadcast (on October 15): "Little Miss Lover," "Driving South" (a second take was attempted, but didn't quite make the grade), "Burning of the Midnight Lamp,"

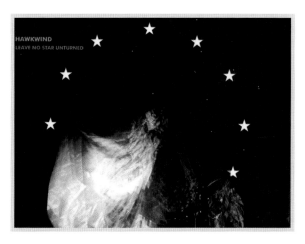

Hawkwind's 1972 appearance on the BBC's In Concert *was finally released on CD as 2011's* Leave No Star Unturned.

"Hound Dog," and "Experiencing the Blues" (mistitled "Catfish Blues" on the 1989 *Radio One Sessions* album). But it was a cut they left in the can that intrigues.

Stevie Wonder was also at the studio, being interviewed by Brian Matthews, and when Mitch Mitchell disappeared to the bathroom, Wonder took over his drumstool, for ninety seconds of his own "I Was Made to Love Her," followed by seven minutes more of what engineer Ritzema calls "mucking around," but was actually a very loose version of "Ain't Too Proud to Beg."

"Hendrix I remember as being very giggly and camp," Ritzema reflected. "He was very self-conscious about doing his vocals. He insisted on having screens put up round his mike when he was overdubbing his vocals, because otherwise . . . Noel and Mitch would make him laugh."

On October 17, the Experience were at Studio Two of the BBC's Aeolian Hall complex, recording a session for the BBC World Service's *R&B* show, hosted by Alexis Korner. Produced by Jeff Griffin and Joe Young, the performance opened with Korner himself joining the band for a driving version of "Hoochie Coochie Man," plus a performance of Dylan's "Can You Please Crawl out of Your Window," and a suddenly aborted version of "Driving South." As the song drew close to its conclusion, Jimi broke a string, and Mitch finished off the performance with a drum solo.

The Experience's final BBC session was another marathon. Recorded on December 15 at the Playhouse, with Phillips and Ritzema again in attendance, the songs are familiar, even if the *Sessions* album does again get several details wrong. The session opened with Jimi messing around with a Radio One jingle, before matters got underway with Noel's fabulous lead vocal on "Day Tripper" (credited, for reasons unknown, to John Lennon alone on the *Sessions* album). "Spanish Castle Magic," "Getting My Heart Back Together Again" (*Sessions* retitles this "Hear My Train A-Coming"), and "Wait Until Tomorrow" followed. An earlier take of "Getting My Heart" also exists, the atmosphere building as Hendrix encouraged onlookers— mainly people from his office—to join in on the jam.

Hendrix would not return to the BBC studios—a sad departure, but an understandable one. He would, after all, be spending so much more time in the US, while his own rising fame suddenly deemed these one-off promotional sessions an irrelevance. What he left behind, however, remains as timeless as anything else he recorded, and that remains true regardless of whether or not he intended it for release.

If Hendrix rationed his BBC appearances, Fleetwood Mac took full advantage of the corporation's requirements. Between November, 1967 and January, 1971, no single rock band made more live recordings for the BBC than they. Twenty sessions, close to ninety songs— Fleetwood Mac might as well have taken up residence at the

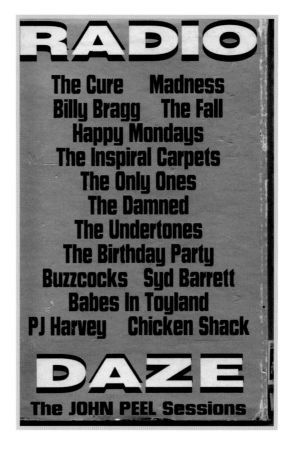

Another visit to the BBC vaults, courtesy of an early 1990s UK magazine cover-mounted freebie.

BBC, and the moment the band's own *Live at the BBC* sessions CD was announced in 1995, so Mac fans began drawing up wish lists.

Thirty-five songs, little more than one-third of the archive, ultimately appeared on the two-disc set, with twenty-one of them dating from the latter part of the era. Mick Fleetwood himself coordinated the project, and maybe he had his own reasons for not wanting us to hear Mac's "Psychedelic Send-Up Number," or the immortally titled "Bee-I-Bicky-Bop Blue Jean Joney Babe Meets High School Hound Dog Hot Rod Man."

Not that really mattered. What he did unleash was sufficient enough to remind us that right there, right then, Fleetwood Mac was the most important blues band to come out of Britain. Ever.

Purists will smirk at that, and it's true, that whole premise is strangely oxymoronic: blues from the Surrey delta. But what made Fleetwood Mac special was not the ease with which they could recreate the past masters, but the way they could make that past become the present. For most exponents of British blues, the source material was a museum piece; for Fleetwood Mac it was a living entity. And that by cross-referencing that entity with other rock influences, they themselves became part of its lifeforce. No one hearing Peter Green's own "Rattlesnake Shake," which kicks off disc one, could doubt that.

In his contribution to the accompanying booklet, Mick Fleetwood remarked that one of the things he hoped this set would do was show "a very different side to the band that many of you may not have known even existed." He probably meant those who came to the collection expecting *Rumours*, Stevie, and Lindsay, but for the rest of us too, there was a lot to be learned.

Each of the three guitarists, Green, Jeremy Spencer, and Danny Kirwan, could have led the group; the fact that they shared that duty was as integral to this lineup's eventual, piecemeal, disintegration as any other factor. But it was also integral to its brilliance, and while it lasted, all three took their turn at the helm, whether for the soulful blues that Green favored ("Long Grey Mare" from Mac's first ever session opens disc two in fiery fashion), for Kirwan's more meditative pop, or for the gratuitous rock 'n' roll of the band's revivalist alter-ego, Earl Vince and the Valiants.

Jeremy Spencer was the ringleader there. Indeed, if he hadn't been playing the blues, he could have out-rocked Sha Na Na. And while "Someone's Gonna Get Their Head Kicked in Tonight," the Spencer-penned B-side to "Man of the World," is the Valiants' only vinyl manifestation, live, Spencer indulged his fascination to the limit. *Live at the BBC* was dominated by Spencer's predilections.

"You Never Know What You're Missing," from March, 1969, introduces his spot-on Elvis persona, while an entire session from the following August is given over to renditions of "When Will I Be Loved," "Heavenly," "Buddy's Song," and "Honey Hush." Further into the collection, a romping "Tallahassee Lassie" rounds out the sequence. For anybody whose only experience of vintage Mac is "Albatross" (included here in very a slapdash rendition), these tracks are a revelation.

Spencer also provides a majestic version of Tim Hardin's "Hang Onto a Dream," pre-empting, if not predating, the Nice's more bloated rendition. And though elsewhere, *Live at the BBC* remains locked firmly within traditional Mac territory, still the overall impression is of a band which truly knew no limits, a belief that the nature of the BBC sessions only encouraged.

The set closes with "Man of the World," the haunting masterpiece which would, within a year, become Green's self-composed epitaph. Before dismissing that prescience as simple coincidence, however, think on this.

When Peter Green formed the band in 1967, the multitude of lineup shifts for which Fleetwood Mac would become so famous for were still far off in the future. Why, then, did he name the group, *his* group, for its rhythm section? Was it really just luck? Or did he somehow know that they would not only outlast him, they'll probably outlive the rest of us, too?

Historically, the BBC sessions that exist today can be divided into four "golden" eras, each corresponding with a similarly golden era in the history of rock. The first dates back to before the creation of Radio One, to a time when television barely acknowledged the existence of pop music.

Back then, shows like *Easy Beat*, an earlier show called *Top Gear* (neither of which, incidentally, are related to the boys-with-toys automobile program of more recent televisual vintage) and, most important of all, *Saturday Club,* as hosted by the effervescent quickfire conversationalist Brian Matthews, were many peoples' sole contact with "live" pop music. And if these programs by necessity reflected the popularity of some bands, they also played a major part in introducing others.

The Zombies, Episode Six (whose lineup included two future members of Deep Purple) and so many others can all point to their radio work for whatever early success they had, while even the Beatles might have moved much slower were it not for the support of the BBC. *Saturday Club*, after all, was the source for many of the cuts included on the two volumes of *Beatles at the Beeb* released so far.

Similarly, the Yardbirds and the Who's official BBC anthologies, not to mention countless Rolling Stones bootlegs, pay further testament to this show's massive influence.

The second great era was the 1967–68 period, following the creation of Radio One, and a time when the BBC was actively campaigning for high profile acts to appear, to help establish the station as Britain's Number One. The third, in terms of the sheer number of legends who continued pouring into the BBC studios, ran through the early 1970s, when you could turn on the radio any time of the evening and catch groups like Stackridge, the Sensational Alex Harvey Band, the Heavy Metal Kids, and Dr. Feelgood in session—alongside a plethora of acts who never stood a chance of cracking the daytime radio shows.

Peter Green's Fleetwood Mac

"Black Magic Woman" (EPIC 10351, 7-INCH, 1968)

English Rose (EPIC LN 24446, WHITE-LABEL MONO PROMO, 1969)

Fleetwood Mac (EPIC LN 24402, WHITE-LABEL MONO PROMO, 1968)

"Green Manalishi" (UK REPRISE RS 27007, 7-INCH, PICTURE SLEEVE, 1970)

"Hungry Country Woman" (with Otis Spann) (BLUE HORIZON 304, 1970, 7-INCH, 1970)

"I Believe My Time Ain't Long" (UK BLUE HORIZON 3051, 7-INCH, 1967)

In Chicago (BLUE HORIZON 3801, 2-LP, 1970)

"Oh Well" (REPRISE 0883, 7-INCH, 1970)

"Rattlesnake Shake" (REPRISE 0860, 7-INCH, 1969)

"Stop Messin' Around" (EPIC 10368, 7-INCH, 1968)

Of them all, Queen's BBC sessions are among the most fondly remembered, not only by listeners but by the band members, too. Two collections of this material have now been released, the original 1990s' *Queen at the Beeb* and, in 2016, the six-CD *Queen on Air* box set (sadly bloated beyond reason by the inclusion of no less than three discs' worth of interviews).

The band's first BBC session took place on February 5, 1973 (for broadcast ten days later), two months before the group signed with EMI, and featured four tracks later to surface on their debut album—two of which, "Liar" and "Keep Yourself Alive," would be reprised five months later on July 25, for a Bob Harris session. "Liar," "Son and Daughter," and, perhaps surprisingly, the then-unreleased slow blues "See What a Fool I've Been" were broadcast on August 13; "Keep Yourself Alive" was held over until September 24.

Over the next eighteen months, Queen recorded three further sessions (one for Peel, two for Harris), the first two highlighting the *Queen II* sophomore album and the third, naturally, previewing material from *Sheer Heart Attack*. It was the second of these sessions, together with the 1973 debut recording, that was selected for inclusion on *Queen at the Beeb*—a total of just eight tracks out of a possible twenty-four.

Queen remained occasional visitors to the BBC over the next three years, appearing on television's *Top of the Pops* in January, 1975 (performing "Now I'm Here") and again during summer, 1977 ("Good Old Fashioned Lover Boy"). BBC TV and radio also offered a simulcast (simultaneous broadcast) of the group's 1975 Christmas Eve concert at London's Hammersmith Odeon, and filmed the following year's Hyde Park free concert. It was fall, 1977, however, before the group again recorded exclusive material for radio broadcast, with a return to the John Peel show.

It was, at the time, a surprising choice—for the previous year, the bulk of Peel sessions had concentrated on either prog-tinged cult heroes (the reformed Van Der Graaf Generator and the newly-formed National Health and 801 also broadcast sessions around the same time), or the newly emergent punk scene, which barely and rarely had any time whatsoever for old-time hard rockers like Queen.

At the same time, however, Queen do have a significant role in punk history—it was their last-minute withdrawal from an early evening television spot on December 1, 1976, that prompted EMI to offer the show's producers another of the label's roster, a little-known combo called the Sex Pistols. Utterly unaware of what the band represented, the show agreed—and that evening, viewers across London and the southeast sat transfixed as the Pistols assaulted host Bill Grundy with a stream of foul-mouthed obscenities. In the emergence of punk as a mainstream musical style, the *Today* show remains one of the crucial watershed moments. And it was all down to Queen.

Punk and the Pistols, of course, had no part to play in Queen's Peel session, as they got down to the serious business of recreating four tracks from the then-newly released *News of the World* album, and more than a few regular Peel listeners were somewhat mortified to hear the likes of "We Will Rock You" and the minor epic "Spread Your Wings" coming over airwaves more traditionally associated with the Lurkers, the Adverts, and the Subway Sect.

Peel sessions were recorded on just eight tracks at Studio 4 in Maida Vale, with bands allocated little more than half a day in which to get their performance recorded, mixed, and delivered to the show's producer, John Walters. It is intriguing, then, to consider how a band like Queen, relentless perfectionists as they were, contrived to knock out four remarkably accurate facsimiles of their original records in the same amount of time, and on the same equipment, as it took the most basic punk band to get down four of theirs.

"It's a strange thing," guitarist Brian May reflects. "You work for hours and hours in the studio for days and weeks, to put down the structure of a song, but once you have it it's not too difficult to recreate it. It's doing it the first time which is the hard thing. So generally we recreated things quite quickly for a couple of tracks, because time was so short, then we'd sort of stretch out a bit on the others."

Almost gleefully, he reiterates, "You certainly couldn't spend all day in the Beeb because there just wasn't the time." He will not be drawn on the relative merits of the performances, however. "I think they were fun at the time and it's nice to look at them again. They do have a roughness and a freshness which is enjoyable."

The aforementioned punk rock era, of course, sums up the fourth of our putative golden ages, a musical movement that John Peel—almost alone of the BBC staff—did much to popularize. Many bands landed record deals only after appearing on his show, while Siouxsie and the Banshees almost joined the BBC's own record label, so fervent was Peel's belief in them.

Later still, the Smiths numbered their first Peel session amongst the biggest breaks they ever got, while New Order recorded some of their most haunting music ever for the show. But perhaps the most legendary of all the eighties sessions was the BBC debut by Nirvana, a Seattle band that was still three long years away from superstardom.

Nirvana were undertaking their first European tour at the time, a grueling thirty-six shows in forty-two days beginning in October 1989. They stopped off at the BBC's Maida Vale Studio 4 on October 26, less than a week after touchdown, to record a session for the John Peel show.

With ex-Mott The Hoople drummer Dale Griffin in the producer's chair, and Kurt Cobain in particularly fine form, the trio hammered down a blistering four track session, comprising versions of their debut single, "Love Buzz"; "Spank Thru'," from the *Sub Pop 200* compilation; "Polly," a new song they had recently attempted for the *Blew* EP; and "About a Girl," from the band's recently released debut album, *Bleach*.

The session went unaired for close to a month, finally going out on November 22, two weeks before the band went home. A year later, back in London, the band was back at the BBC. Drummer Chad Channing had left by now, to be replaced by Dave Grohl—he had been a band member for mere weeks before he was scooped up and taken to Europe for the band's second continental tour, opening for L7.

A new single, coupling "Sliver" and "Dive," was imminent, but the tour was also timed to keep the band occupied while their own future fell into place: the management company Gold Mountain and a clutch of major record labels were all in hot pursuit of the group, with Geffen and Charisma rapidly emerging as the favorites.

All that, of course, was a long way away as the band returned to Maida Vale (Studio 3 this time) on October 21, 1990, with Dale Griffin once again in the producer's chair. Three of the four songs that Nirvana recorded that afternoon have since been given an official release: "Son of a Gun," "Molly's Lips," and a thunderously crooked version of Devo's "Turnaround" all featured on the *Incesticide* odds and sods compilation, leaving only the cover of the Wipers' "D7" out in the cold—it would, however, be featured on the Australian *Hormoanin'* compilation, before resurfacing on the B-side of the "Lithium" CD single and, later, the *Nevermind* deluxe edition.

Again, almost exactly twelve months elapsed before Nirvana were back in town, with Nirvana's third BBC session being recorded a full two months before broadcast, on September 3, 1991 . . . one of their last acts before *Nevermind* blew the band's lives out of the water. Now occupying Maida Vale Studio 5, but still enjoying the now familiar embrace of Dale Griffin, Nirvana previewed the forthcoming album with "Drain You" (again available on the *Nevermind* deluxe edition) and "Endless Nameless," the latter a freeform jam that wasn't even credited on the record and appears on the BBC's own records under the name "No Title As Yet." The other cut, the older "Dumb," was more conventional. Find the latter pair aboard the band's *With the Lights Out* box set.

Just two months later Nirvana were back in the UK, arriving on November 3, the same day as the John Peel session was finally broadcast. Aside from a string of long sold-out shows, the band was also booked for a wealth of television appearances that included, amongst others, an anarchic rendering of "Smells Like Teen Spirit" on *Top of the Pops*, and a frighteningly raw performance on the *Jonathan Ross Show*. (Both feature on Nirvana's official live video, *Live! Tonight! Sold Out!*)

They also found time, on November 9, to record a session for the Mark Goodier Show. Working with producers Miti Adhikari and John Taylor in Studio 4, they turned in the very accomplished, but slightly tour-fatigued versions of "Been a Son" and "Aneurysm," which would subsequently appear on *Incesticide*, and a punked-up rendering of "Polly," which that same collection would subtitle "[New Wave]." The best of the batch, however, would be the moody, atmospheric take on "Something in the Way" that finally saw release on the *Nevermind* deluxe edition.

Although it is relatively small, and contrarily omits many of the band's better known hits, Nirvana's BBC legacy is one of the most important elements in the band's catalog. Certainly it is of greater musical value than the live and outtake material that generally preoccupies bootleggers and official guardians of Nirvana's repertoire, filling a gap, in fact, between those two extremes, and bringing another dimension both to this remarkable band's canon, and to the BBC's own operations during the first half of the 1990s.

The BBC's support certainly played a major role in the explosion of new British talent that was grouped together as Britpop, with London Suede, Oasis, Sleeper, and Blur only the best-known of the bands whose careers were inestimably assisted by their sessions for the Beeb. Twenty years on, the mid-1990s can be regarded as another golden age for BBC rock 'n' roll.

Despite having so much history at its fingertips, the BBC was slow in comprehending just what a vast resource it had at its disposal. Through the early 1980s, the corporation had been periodically producing one-off radio specials highlighting some band's BBC recordings, knowing that such exercises in unabashed nostalgia attracted huge audiences. The Beatles and the Stones, David Bowie, and T. Rex were amongst early broadcasts, but it was only when these shows started reappearing on bootleg that the commercial—and historical—possibilities of the vault become apparent.

Few bootleggers, for example, appeared to know exactly what they had, which is why radio sessions are frequently described as either studio outtakes, or live recordings when, as we have already seen, they are neither. (For some reason, the Rolling Stones and London Suede bootleg catalogs are particularly encumbered by this.)

Finally, then, a record label, Strange Fruit, was set up to begin marketing the sessions. Although the emphasis was on punk and early '80s era material, Strange Fruit's series of *Peel Sessions* EPs was a success from the start, so much so that a second label, catering to live recordings from the *In Concert* and *Old Grey Whistle Test* television series, was inaugurated, followed by a third, covering world music recordings.

The response remained staggering. Soon, artists and fans alike were deluging the offices with offers and suggestions. Performances that were officially presumed lost began turning up as fans volunteered recordings they had made at home years before (several BBC cuts on the King Crimson collection *Epitaph* were restored from such sources). A vintage 1964 Rolling Stones recording reappeared years after it was said to have been wiped, apparently when a recording engineer announced he'd hung onto it for technical reference purposes.

Other bands approved the release of old sessions because they highlighted a side to the group that might otherwise have been lost forever, as they experimented with their own songs, or tried out other people's. Jimmy Page's willingness to release Led Zeppelin's sessions stemmed from this belief, while Fairport Convention used their BBC sessions to play material they would never include on their own albums. Great swathes of this catalog have since been released, first on the self-released 1987 *Heyday* collection; and, thirty years later, the four-CD *At the BBC* box set.

Yes might never have released their epochal sixteen-minute version of Paul Simon's "America" if they hadn't first tried it out on John Peel. And Billy Bragg fans still rave about the rendition of "Route 66" he performed for Peel in 1983, replacing the traditional words with a roadmap between two eastern English towns.

The major appeal of the BBC sessions remains their exclusivity. More than anything else, a session preserves a moment in time in a band's history with a quality and a veracity that nothing else, neither live recordings nor studio outtakes, can emulate.

Sessions show a band simultaneously on its best behavior, and at its most crazily vulnerable, working simply for that moment, with nothing else on its mind. And that honesty remains the sessions' greatest asset . . . that, and the almost illicit thrill of knowing that the music you are listening to was never recorded with posterity in mind.

Yet you do not need to halt your hunting with the sessions alone. The internet plays host to a vast army of enthusiasts who collect recordings of entire shows, and post them to be shared with fellow collectors. Sites such as the John Peel-centric peel.wikia.com and offshoreradio.com, with its emphasis on the pirate stations that once ruled British airwaves, are the portal into literally days', if not months', worth of vintage recordings, many of which were taped off the air by listeners in the day, and offer up portraits not only of the hits and heroes of the time, but also the also-rans and no-hopers, interspersed with the disc jockey's chatter, the news of the day, and more.

Not every hour of every station was recorded; the most prolific survivors tend to be those that have always had the greatest audience among enthusiasts—Peel, of course, and Radio Caroline. But others are out there: Radio Essex, Radio Sutch, Radio Invicta, and more from the pirate era; Tony Blackburn, Alan Freeman, and Kenny Everett from among Peel's workmates; and other stations, too.

London's local Capital Radio and Manchester's Piccadilly were among the first legal stations to challenge the BBC's monopoly on pop radio broadcasting, after independent stations were legalized in 1973, and there was a brave new wave of pirates, too: Radio Jackie, Radio Geronimo, Radio North Sea International, and, of course, Radio Caroline—the only original pirate that did not close down

when the law changed in 1967, and the last one standing again in 1980, when nature finally did what the British government had never been able to do, and crashed the station's ship against a sandbank *while the station continued broadcasting.*

Listening to these tapes today is very little different to listening to them at the time—the same vagaries of atmospherics and drifting signals; the same attempts by the British government to jam the signal; and the same absolute disregard for the playlisted niceties of the BBC and Capital.

Names like Crispian St. John, Andy Archer, and Samantha Dubois—one of the first women DJs in British broadcasting history, and one of the most beloved, too—live on through the hours of mp3s that can be downloaded today, and which form the heart of a collection that reminds you, maybe, why you fell in love with music in the first place.

It was radio that did it.

THE SINGLE: THE BEST OF PUNK ROCK— THE FIFTY MOST NECESSARY

Punk rock was all about singles. Of course the bulk of the bands made albums as well, and jolly fine some of them were. Later, the albums spawned compilations and the compilations have grown into box sets and anthologies.

But if you want to know—and, more importantly, comprehend—what punk rock was really all about, what do you reach for? A dog-eared copy of "One Chord Wonders," or the multi-CD Ramones box set? A crackly, worn pressing of "Piss Factory," or six sides of the Clash's *Sandanista*? Do you go foaming with the Germs? Or into the Valley of the Dolls with Generation X?

Every time, it's the 45—or, at least, it should be. Even at their most punky-powered frenzied, albums (and box sets) are for relaxation and, later, dotage, when you're too tired or decrepit to get up and change the record.

Singles, on the other hand, were frantic, fast and furious, slapped down and lapped up in less time than it takes to tune a guitar—a couple of minutes of glorious noise, and then onto the next one with a flick of the stylus.

Today, the abuse to which those old 45s were subjected is apparent every time you look at another old-timer's record collection. So is the sheer volume of releases that were slammed out to conform with the demands of the punk-era audience.

From the grandest major label to the tiniest back alley bed room, singles simply hurtled out in search of their post-Warholian fifteen seconds' worth of fame (for who had fifteen *minutes* to waste on such nonsense?), ricocheted around the consciousness for as long as it took to play them, then were slipped back into their picture sleeves, to sleep their way back to obscurity.

Some of them were lucky—they were great records. A few were luckier—they became hits. And a handful were even luckier still—they kickstarted careers that are still going today.

But most were simply one-offs and one-shots, released because they could be, not because they needed to be. There was a lot of great music released in the name of punk rock. But there was even more rubbish and, for that reason, the fact that there was so many swine rubbing noses with the pearls, it is very difficult to quantify just what constitutes a "rare" punk single.

Is it rare because there were only a hundred copies pressed, and the songs were so horrible that all went unsold? Is it rare because on the eve of release, a jealous rival snuck into the pressing plant and stuck poisoned safety pins into the only master tape? Or, is it rare because, though there's a few thousand copies knocking around, there's even more thousands of collectors searching for them? That, for the most part, is what this guide constitutes, a rough survey of the fifty singles that the majority of collectors will have heard of, a lot of them are searching for, and a few of them will one day wind up owning.

Even the rarest of them all, the legendary A&M pressing of the Sex Pistols' "God Save the Queen," has been known to surface on eBay, while most of the other 45s documented here spent at least a few weeks in a high street retailer's new releases bin—as opposed to a few days in the small ads of a local fanzine, because that was the best distribution that the truly specialized rarities could manage.

As for what these records are actually selling for these days, nothing on the list should set you back more than a few thousand bucks (the Pistols again, with XTC close behind), the majority should come in at well under $50, and a few will barely scrape into double figures. But, as any seasoned collector will tell you, that's only what they're selling for. You have to find a copy that's for sale first.

Adam and the Ants, "Young Parisians"
(DECCA F13803, PAPER LABEL, PICTURE SLEEVE) 1978

The Ants' brief period with Decca produced a flurry of demos, but only one actual release, a 1978 45 that disappeared almost as quickly as the band's tenure with the label. Following Adam and his insects' ascension to international pop stardom in the early 1980s, however, Decca returned to those old, long-forgotten recordings, reissued "Young Parisians," and saw Antmania send it soaring to No. 9 in January 1981. The reissue features a die-stamped label; original pressings carry a paper one.

The Adverts, "Cast of Thousands"
(RCA PB 5191, PICTURE SLEEVE) 1979

The Adverts had already shattered when RCA pretended to issue this, their seventh and final single. Edited down from the full-length title track to the band's second album (and backed by the equally atypical, but supremely creepy "I Will Walk You Home"), "Cast of Thousands" was a far cry from the Adverts of "One Chord Wonders"/"Gary Gilmore's Eyes" fame and acclaim.

Driven by choir and keyboards, and drenched by a wide-screen Tom Newman production, it was probably doomed to failure whatever happened. The absence of the band from the promotional circuit simply confirmed that fate, and it is uncertain whether copies of the single were actually even delivered to the stores. It has never been reissued.

ATV, "Love Lies Limp"
(SNIFFING GLUE SG 75 RPS, FLEXIDISC) 1977

Editor of the seminal punk fanzine *Sniffin' Glue*, Mark Perry began entertaining notions of forming his own band around the same time as he tired of his print escapades. Alternative TV was his solution, a ragged outfit whose original lineup was most notable for the presence of former Generation X drummer John Towe, and who debuted on this loose-limbed epic of sexual dysfunction, issued as a flexidisc with the final issue of *Sniffin' Glue* (No. 15). The song would be reissued a little over a year later, on the flip of ATV's "Life" single, but the original flexidisc is the one to look out for.

The Bizarros, "Lady Doubonette"
(GORILLA RECORDS GNR 7639, PICTURE SLEEVE) 1976

Better known for its appearance on the Clone label in 1978, this was the Akron-based Bizarros' vinyl debut, one of four tracks on the self-released *Lady Doubonette* EP sold out of the Hodeo's Discodrome record store in Cleveland. (Frontman Nick Nicholis was also responsible for establishing Clone.)

The Buzzcocks, *Spiral Scratch*
(NEW HORMONES ORG 1, PICTURE SLEEVE) 1977

The first Buzzcocks EP was also one of the first self-releases to emerge from the punk ferment. Recorded, pressed, bagged, and distributed under the band's own aegis, the four songs that make up the *Spiral Scratch* EP—"Boredom," "Time's Up," "Friends of Mine," and "Breakdown"—would each become near-anthems of the age, with the swift deletion of the release adding an all-but-legendary cachet to them.

Finally, responding to both public demand and spiraling collector prices, *Spiral Scratch* was reissued in August 1979, the reproduced picture sleeve now crediting it to "Buzzcocks with Howard Devoto"—the band's founding vocalist quit the band shortly after the original January 1977 release to form his own Magazine. The reissue breached the UK Top Forty; the original just kept on going up in price.

Unsurprisingly, a fortieth anniversary reissue also arrived in early 2017, packaged alongside an album's worth of other Devoto-era recordings, the *Time's Up* collection.

John Cooper Clark, "Splat/Twat"
(EPIC 7982, PICTURE SLEEVE) 1979

Acerbic Manchester poet John Cooper Clark had already issued a handful of singles, plus a couple of albums, by the time "Splat" came out in October 1979—of these, 1977's *Innocents* EP and 1979's strangely shaped orange vinyl "Gimmix" are frequently regarded as the hardest to find, when it is "Splat/Twat" that causes collectors the most problems.

Released, like "Gimmix," at the height of the UK record industry's obsession with ever new and noteworthy ways of drawing attention to its latest releases, "Splat/Twat" arrived in a picture sleeve emblazoned with the legend "a twin grooved single recorded live at the Marquee and messed about with at Molinaire"—and indeed it was.

Utilizing a technology best known from a mid-'70s Monty Python album, whereby two sets of grooves wind side by side across the face of the record, "Splat/Twat" featured two versions of the same poem, with no way of determining which one the needle was going to find. "Twat" is an unexpurgated rapid-fire tirade of insults that never ceases to amuse; "Splat" is the same rant with sound effects added to enhance the experience (and obscure a few obscenities).

Clone Records

Bizarros/Rubber City Rebels, *From Akron* (CLONE CL-001, 1977)
Bizarros, *Lady Doubonette* EP (CLONE CL 000, 1977)
Bizarros, "Laser Boys" (CLONE CL 003, 1978)
Harvey Gold, "Experiments" (CLONE CL 005, 1978)
Tin Huey, "Breakfast with the Hueys" (CL 004, 1978)
Tin Huey, *Tin Huey* EP (CLONE CL 002, 1977)
Human Switchboard, "I Gotta Know" (CLONE CL 007, 1978)
John Rader, "One Step at a Time" (CLONE CL 009, 1979)
Teacher's Pet, "Hooked On You" (CLONE CL008, 1978)
The Waitresses, "In 'Short Stack'" (CLONE CL 006, 1978)

Ork Records 45s

Alex Chilton, "Singer Not the Song" (ORK 81978, 1977)
Mick Farren and the New Wave, "Play with Fire" (ORK 81980, 1977)
Richard Hell and the Voidoids, *Another World* EP (ORK 81976, 1976)
The Idols, "You" (ORK NYC 2, 1979)
The Marbles, "Red Lights" (ORK 81977, 1976)
Prix, "Girl" (ORK 81979, 1977)
The Revelons, "The Way (You Touch My Hand)" (ORK NYC 3, 1979)
Chris Stamey, "The Summer Sun" (ORK 81982, 1977)
Television, "Little Johnny Jewel Parts 1 and 2" (12-INCH, ORK NYC 1, 1979)
Television, "Little Johnny Jewel," (ORK 81975, 1975)

Unfortunately, the thinness of the grooves that was a prerequisite of the format ensures that most surviving copies end up playing a medley of the two, as the needle skips and scratches around. The record itself isn't too hard to find. A clean copy is.

The Clash, "Capital Radio"
(CBS CL 1, PICTURE SLEEVE) 1977

A promotional offering hatched between CBS and the *New Musical Express* saw the first 40,000 copies of the Clash's eponymous UK debut album arrive with a red circular sticker affixed to the inner bag. Detached and mailed in to the newspaper's office, this treasure entitled the bearer to a copy of what remains the rarest of all Clash 45s and one of the first punk-era artifacts ever to be bootlegged.

Three tracks were included on the EP, the now classic "Capital Radio" (rerecorded by the band in 1979, for the *Cost of Living* EP), the instrumental "Listen," and an only occasionally audible interview with *NME* staffer Tony Parsons, apparently recorded on a speeding tube train.

Of wryly incidental interest: copies of the original green-labeled bootleg now seem even scarcer than copies of the original item.

Controllers, "(The Original) Neutron Bomb"
(WHAT RECORDS? WHAT 03) 1978

One of the first bands ever to play Los Angeles's legendary Masque club linked with the Eyes ("Don't Talk to Me") and the Skulls ("Victim") for their first release, one of the most incendiary singles ever to emerge from California.

Elvis Costello, "Neat Neat Neat

(RADAR SAM 83) 1978

The Clash were not the only new wave acts to offer early purchasers of their latest albums a free gift. The first 50,000 copies of Elvis Costello and the Attractions' sophomore set, *This Year's Model*, were similarly enhanced, although it certainly seems hard to believe that there really was that many. (Compare finding a copy of this with a search for the next album's *Live at Hollywood High* giveaway.)

Featuring otherwise unavailable versions of the soon-to-be-classic country air "Stranger in the House," and a radical reinterpretation of the Damned's "Neat Neat Neat," SAM 83 remains one of the most musically intriguing of all Elvis Costello singles, as the man who was otherwise still laboring beneath the media tag of "the new Bob Dylan" proved himself to have George Jones and Brian James just as much in mind.

Crash Course in Science, "Cakes in the Home"

(GO GO RECORDS 004, PICTURE SLEEVE) 1979

Synth-driven post punk from Philadelphia, all homemade electronics and analog drum machines, "Cakes in the Home" was released on local DJ Lee Paris's label, and helps predict a lot of what would be coming from the club scene a year or two later.

The Damned, "Stretcher Case Baby"

(STIFF DAMNED 1, PICTURE SLEEVE) 1977

Another *New Musical Express* promotion, a limited edition 45 comprising two stunning new James compositions, "Stretcher Case Baby"/"Sick of Being Sick," was available through both an *NME*-sponsored competition in the early summer of 1977, and at the door for the Damned's first anniversary party/gig at London's Marquee Club in August. Distinctively picture sleeved, ownership bragging rights have been only mildly reduced by the two songs' subsequent reappearance on a myriad Damned compilation albums.

The Desperate Bicycles, "Smokescreen"

(REFILL RR 1, PICTURE SLEEVE) 1977

Pipped to the post only by the Buzzcocks, the south London–based Desperate Bicycles were one of the earliest bands to truly epitomize the DIY ethic of punk, launching their own Refill label and self-financing the release not only of "Smokescreen," but also three further singles, an EP, and an album. This, the debut, is the most sought after, a desperately limited edition cut at a time when the band truly had no idea whether or not anybody would pay any attention. Later releases came once they knew that they would.

Doctors of Madness, "Bulletin"

(POLYDOR 2058 921, PICTURE SLEEVE) 1977

A shade too early to take advantage of punk, but thematically and stylistically allied to many of the same impulses and desires, the Doctors of Madness were well on their way to completing their third (and final) album when Polydor finally got around to releasing their first single in mid-1977.

An alternate version of a song that would feature on that third LP, "Bulletin" was the Doctors' lament for the already-incipient decline of the punk movement, with the media soundly singled out to take responsibility for that fact. The "Dadomo" character name checked in the first verse, incidentally, is Giovanni Dadomo, a writer for the music weekly *Sounds* and, later in the year, guiding light behind the Snivelling Shits. (See below.)

The Doctors of Madness were three albums old before they released their debut single.

Ian Dury,
"Sex and Drugs and Rock and Roll"
(STIFF FREEBIE 1, PICTURE SLEEVE) 1977

Originally issued as Stiff BUY 17, the ultra-anthemic "Sex and Drugs and Rock and Roll" was deleted from the label catalog at a time when many observers felt it was odds on for a UK chart placing—it did, in fact, succeed elsewhere in Europe, climbing as high as No. 12 in Sweden, and there was a hectic trade in import pressings once the original vanished from the shops.

Forever aware of the importance of this collectors market, Stiff Records lost little time in reissuing the track—but added a little twist by ensuring it was even harder to find this time around than it had been before.

Coupling the song with an otherwise completely unavailable rendering of "England's Glory," a song Dury wrote for comedian Max Wall, "Sex and Drugs and Rock and Roll" was available in just two ways—by winning a competition in the *New Musical Express*, or by gaining admission to the paper's Christmas party.

The Electric Eels, "Agitated"
(ROUGH TRADE RT 008) 1978

Recorded in rehearsal in 1975, three years before it was released as their debut single, "Agitated" is the sound of pre-punk Cleveland already knowing exactly what the future demands of it. The Eels themselves had been around since 1972, self-described "art terrorists" whose musical arsenal included lawnmowers, anvils, sledgehammers, and a confrontational attitude towards bandmates and audience alike.

Mick Farren and the New Wave,
"Lost Johnny"
(ORK RECORDS 81980) 1977

British journalist and ex-Deviants frontman Farren was based in New York when he cut this, a speedball demolition of a song he originally composed with Lemmy for the latter's then-band Hawkwind. Screaming guitars and lethal vocals are the order of the day, with Farren almost visibly living the lyric. It's punk rock, but it makes most of the others sound like the Eagles.

Journalist and musician Mick Farren's incendiary version of Hawkwind's "Lost Johnny" made even Motörhead's take on the song sound anemic by comparison.

Fear, "I Love Living in the City"
(CRIMINAL RECORDS, NO CAT #, PICTURE SLEEVE)

Fear were always the L.A. band that the outside world considered The Most Likely To. For a short time in 1978, you could barely switch on the radio without their "I Love Living in the City" single assaulting your ears and, three years later, still serving up the same discordant menu as they always had, Fear became the first L.A. punk band to play *Saturday Night Live*.

It was a remarkable accomplishment. For all the show's New York–centricity, the Ramones never made *SNL*, Television never got there, and even Blondie only did it once they'd gone all squeaky-clean and disco. But Fear did it, and when they got home, they immortalized the experience in a new song, "New York's Alright If You Like Saxophones."

Mick Farren/Deviants

All Screwed Up (UK STIFF LAST 4, EP, 1978)

The Deviants, The Deviants (UK TRANSATLANTIC TRA 204, LP, 1969)

Disposable, The Deviants (UK STABLE SLP 7001, LP, GATEFOLD SLEEVE, 1968)

"Half Price Drinks" (UK LOGO GO 321, 7-INCH, 1979)

Human Garbage (Live . . . 1984), The Deviants (UK PSYCHO 25, LP, 1984)

"Lost Johnny" (ORK 1980, 7 INCH, 1976)

Mona (The Carnivorous Circus) (TRANSATLANTIC TRA 212, LP, 1970)

Partial Recall, The Deviants (UK DROP OUT DOCD 1989, CD, 1992)

Ptooff!, The Deviants (UK UNDERGROUND IMPRESARIOS IMP 1, LP, 1967)

"You Got to Hold On," The Deviants (UK STABLE STA 5601, 7-INCH, 1968)

Generation X, *Day By Day*
(GENERATION X GX 1, WHITE LABEL) 1977

Although Generation X were, by spring 1977, widely regarded among the most promising of the up and coming punk bands, they remained unsigned until comparatively late in the day. Anxious to get some kind of product into their fans' hands, however, the band themselves privately pressed up a four-track white label EP for sale at gigs.

Marketed as an official bootleg, the EP reprised the group's well-received April 1977 John Peel session, comprising the future classics "Day By Day," "Your Generation," "Youth Youth Youth," and "Listen," all of which would be rerecorded later in the year for the Chrysalis label.

The Germs, "Foaming"
(WHAT? RECORDS 001, PICTURE SLEEVE)

Multiple repressings of the L.A. legends' debut 45 render this a rat trap for anyone hunting down the earliest pressing. Look for white labels with black print affixed to the wrong sides of the record, with "true mono" printed to the left of the center hole, and a picture sleeve offering a special $1 offer.

The Heartbreakers, "Chinese Rocks" (12-inch single, picture sleeve)
(TRACK RECORDS 2094-135) 1977

Having dispensed with original bassist Richard Hell shortly after the band's formation, New York Dolls Johnny Thunders and Jerry Nolan relocated to London in late 1976, and swiftly built a reputation for uncompromising time . . . and time-keeping. Few Heartbreakers gigs ever started on schedule, but they were always worth waiting for, even when the night was clearly not panning out as planned. Which also happened a lot.

Jilted John's eponymous tale of lost love and childish spite remains one of punk's most enduring novelties.

Their debut album emerged a divisive mess of sonic misrepresentation that nevertheless has an inestimable charm, and their debut single (cowritten by Thunders and Dee Dee Ramone) remains one of the key heroin songs of the twentieth century.

Richard Hell and the Voidoids, "Blank Generation"
(SIRE 6078-608, 12-INCH SINGLE, PICTURE SLEEVE) 1977

Rerecorded from an earlier single released by Ork (Stiff in the UK), "Blank Generation" became the ralying cry title track of Hell's major label debut album, a scything guitar-led anthem over which Hell's glorious whining vocal imbibes every last lyric with maximum impact. The 12-inch adds nothing to the 7-inch in terms of the performance's length, but it *sounds* fabulous.

The Jam, "Going Underground"
(POLYDOR POSPJ 113/2816 024, PICTURE SLEEVE, DOUBLE-PACK) 1980

By early 1980, the Jam were arguably the biggest band in Britain, effortlessly firing singles to the top of the chart and, if the truth be known, no more in need of gimmicks and limited editions than a crab needs lessons in scuttling sideways.

No matter—with their last single, "Eton Rifles," having peaked at No. 3, all concerned were adamant that "Going Underground" was to go all the way, hence the not-too-limited-edition addition of a three-song live EP, attractively packaged in a gatefold 7-inch picture sleeve, with initial pressings of the single.

"Down in the Tube Station at Midnight," "The Modern World," and "Away from the Numbers" offered in-concert reprises of three of the band's best-loved oldies, and the offering did the trick. "Going Underground" not only reached No. 1, it actually entered the chart at that position, the first single to do so since the halcyon days of the glam rocking Slade, seven years before.

Jilted John, "Jilted John"
(RABID TOSH 105, PICTURE SLEEVE) 1978

Comedian Graham Fellow's plaintive lament was one of the surprise hits of 1978, whining its way to No. 4 on the back of a chorus that packed more juvenile slang and insults into a couple of chords than the rest of the punk pack had managed in two years, a savage dismissal of a girlfriend who had thrown him over for a friend. "She's a slag and he's a creep, she's a tart, he's very cheap . . . ." Ah, teenaged poetry at its finest.

The hit version, released on EMI's EMI International imprint, is easy enough to find—far trickier is the original pressing on the Manchester-based Rabid label (home, among others, to early releases by John Cooper Clarke and Slaughter and the Dogs). It was the regional success of this release that prompted EMI to move in for Mr. Jilted, repressing the single on their own imprint (but retaining the original's picture sleeve), and subsequently unleashing the lad across an entire LP, *True Love Stories*. But that's another beast-to-find altogether.

Johnny Thunders

"Chinese Rocks," The Heartbreakers (UK Track 2094 135, 12-inch, 1977)
"Crawfish" (with Patti Paladin) (UK Jungle JUNG 23, 7-inch, picture disc, 1985)
"Get Off the Phone" (UK Beggars Banquet BEG 21, 7-inch, 1979)
"Hurt Me" (France New Rose 27, 7-inch, 1984)
"In Cold Blood" (France New Rose 14, 7-inch, 1982)
"It's Not Enough," The Heartbreakers (UK Track 2094 142, withdrawn 7-inch, 1978)
"Que Será Será" (UK JUNGLE JUNG 33, 12-INCH, 1987)
Too Much Junkie Business (ROIR 118, CASSETTE, 1984)
What Goes Around (BOMP 4039, LP, 1992)
"You Can't Put Your Arms Around a Memory" (UK REAL ARE 3, 12-INCH, BLUE- AND PINK-VINYL, 1978)

Klark Kent, "Don't Care"
(KRYPTONE KK 1, PICTURE SLEEVE, BLACK VINYL) 1978

Who is Klark Kent? That, if the media hype was to be believed, was the question on everybody's lips during the summer of 1978—or, at least, it would have been if television's *Old Grey Whistle Test* hostess Anne Nightingale hadn't let the cat out of the bag when the Police appeared on the show one night.

Drummer Stewart Copeland probably wasn't too bothered at this unexpected denouement, however—a combination of fetching Kryptonite green vinyl and a jolly catchy, punky snarl had already sent "Don't Care" speeding bullet-like into the Top 40, at a time when the Police themselves had still to even sniff such success.

Indeed, more than nine months would elapse before bandmate Sting was able to unveil any song (a reissue of "Roxanne") that could out-perform "Don't Care," although once he'd started, he didn't stop. Klark Kent, on the other hand, released just one more single and was then retired. For collectors, incidentally, it's the black vinyl pressing of "Don't Care" that raises the pulse rate. The green one is as common as any forty-year-old Top 40 hit should be.

LaPeste, "Better Off Dead"
(BLACK RECORDS CB 711, PICTURE SLEEVE) 1978

LaPeste (French for the plague) may have been Boston's finest. Ultra-cool, urban and urbane, they were also responsible for what *Subway News* fanzine proclaimed "rock's most terrifying moment." Far more unsettling than Gene Simmons' flames, or Alice Cooper's guillotine, you didn't know what fear was until you caught a Boston audience singing along to the refrain of "Kill Me Now." "Alice and Kiss . . . are comic fantasy. LaPeste incite a threatening vision."

"Better Off Dead" is not "Kill Me Now." If anything, it's even better.

The Lewd, "Kill Yourself"
(SCRATCHED RECORDS ME 101, PICTURE SLEEVE) 1979

Formed in Seattle in 1977, then relocating to San Francisco in 1979, the Lewd opened for the Ramones a couple of times in their home city, and recorded their self-released debut in their own home studio in early 1978. An earlier incarnation of the band, by the way, was called Sixteen Year Old Virgins, which has to be one of the all-time great band names.

The Lurkers, "Shadow"
(BEGGARS BANQUET BEG 1, PICTURE SLEEVE, BLACK VINYL) 1977

The maiden release on the now internationally established Beggars Banquet label, "Shadow" is not the greatest Lurkers release by a long chalk, but it is, in its original form, the hardest to find. Why? Because nobody cared at the time. Thus, while subsequent Lurkers

The Psychedelic Furs' debut single was originally to be released on the Epic label before they were switched to CBS. A handful of early promos predate the change.

singles arrived to thrill the fan club with a panoply of accompanying gewgaws, ranging from free gold flexidiscs to picture discs and double packs, poor old "Shadow" simply sat, indeed, in the shadows and nobody paid it a blind bit of attention.

As the Lurkers' renown increased, of course, so did demand for this debut disc, at which point Beggars kindly reissued it, with copies spread evenly across fetching red, white, and blue colored vinyl. Boring black wax didn't get a look in, though, which means completist collectors in search of such a treasure still need hunt down an original pressing. Bon chance.

The Members, "Solitary Confinement"
(STIFF ONE OFF OFF 3, PICTURE SLEEVE) 1978

Another independent release that, once in the clutches of the majors, took on a fresh life of its own, "Solitary Confinement" was originally released via the Stiff label's short-lived One Off subsidiary, a fascinating concern that essentially allowed bands to release and promote their own record, without incurring all of the expenses of actually doing it themselves.

The success of the venture can be gauged from the fact that the series stretched to four very collectible singles, but the Members were the only act to actually break out of the shop window, hence the increased demand for OFF 3.

Signing to Virgin in 1979 and scoring an instant hit with "Sound of the Suburbs," the Members rerecorded what remains one of the ultimate anthems of suburban angst for inclusion on their debut album, *At the Chelsea Nightclub*. (The rerecording also made it onto the B-side of the minor hit "Off-Shore Banking Business." In a perfect world, it would have again been an A-side in its own right.)

The Neighborhoods, "Prettiest Girl"
(ACE OF HEARTS AHS 102, PICTURE SLEEVE) 1979

The Neighborhoods managed just three singles, but not only did they win the 1979 battle of Boston's bands, The Rumble, they also looked dead set to follow the Cars straight out of town. Instead, they just went round the ring road.

That said, the 'Hoods' vision of DMZ meeting Generation X "got real big, real fast," says guitarist Dave Minehan. "We just thought, 'We're going straight to the top.'" They had faith, they had commitment, but they also had "total delusions of grandeur." The major labels they'd been expecting to call never came, and when the decade imploded, so did the Neighborhoods.

The "hip pocket" version of Radio Stars' "From a Rabbit" was just six inches across.

The Only Ones, "Lovers of Today"
(VENGEANCE VEN 001, PICTURE SLEEVE) 1977

Peter Perrett's Only Ones are described, even by those who loved them, as one of the great lost opportunities of late 1970s British rock, punk or otherwise. They had everything—great songs, talented musicians, and a former member of Spooky Tooth, but a combination of drugs, disinterest, and record company politics ultimately doomed the group to near-obscurity, and a legacy of three magnificent albums that are still only just being rediscovered.

Released on their own Vengeance label in June 1977, some months ahead of the band's eventual recruitment to CBS, "Lovers of Today" is a faintly glammy, plaintively whiny little number that has little in common with the punk pack that the Only Ones were roped into, an impression that the flirtatious schoolgirl-draped picture sleeve only amplifies. It is the original, self-distributed pressings of the single that is hardest to find—just 500 copies of both the 7-inch and 12-inch were manufactured in the first run; the more common subsequent pressings were handled by the national Bizarre Distribution.

Pere Ubu, "30 Seconds over Tokyo"
(HEARTHAN RECORDS HR 101) 1976

Destined to become one of America's leading post-punk leviathans—a genre they were pioneering pre-punk as well—Cleveland's Pere Ubu debuted with this remarkable slab of experimental rock, and all of their future ingredients were already plain to see.

Psychedelic Furs, "Sister Europe"
(EPIC EPC 8179) 1980

One of the last truly memorable bands to emerge from the London Roxy Club, in December 1977, the Furs signed with Epic in mid-

1979, releasing their debut 45, "We Love You," that fall. The follow-up, the epic "Sister Europe" (backed by the outtake "Fuck, " now politely retitled "****"), was scheduled for issue the following February 14, and the first copies had already come off the presses when the group switched from Epic to the parent CBS label.

The Epic issue was scrapped and destroyed long before any saw the inside of a shop, but around twenty-five promotional copies, featuring "Sister Europe" on both the A- and B-sides, did escape to bedevil Furs completists forever more.

Public Image Ltd., "Death Disco"
(VIRGIN VS 274-12, 12" SINGLE, PICTURE SLEEVE) 1979

The Artist Formerly Known as Johnny Rotten not only tore up his former image when he formed Public Image Ltd., he also threw away the mold that he'd manufactured with the Sex Pistols. PiL was a dense roar within which swirled a dark cocktail of funk, dub, and non-electronic electronics. While their first album and eponymous debut single at least offered listeners some form of musical escapism, by the time the band reached its sophomore LP, mercy was the last thing on their minds.

The entire *Metal Box* album, originally released as a clutch of 12-inch singles packaged within a circular tin, remains an endurance test for anybody who claims they like their entertainment raw, but it is the 12-inch version of "Death Disco," the band's second single and a reworking of the album's "Swan Lake," which remains the peak of their achievement—and that despite it becoming an absolutely astounding Top Twenty hit. More or less readily available in unadorned form, "Death Disco" is eminently collectible in picture sleeve, of which just 5,000 copies were produced.

Chiswick

"Anti-Social," Skrewdriver (CHISWICK NS 18, 7-INCH, 1977)

"Brand New Cadillac," Vince Taylor (CHISWICK S2, 7-INCH, 1976)

"From a Rabbit," Radio Stars (CHISWICK NS 36, HIP-POCKET DISC, 1978)

I Wanna Be a Cosmonaut, Riff Raff (CHISWICK SW 34, EP, 1978)

The Jook, The Jook (CHISWICK NS 30, EP, 1978)

"Keys to Your Heart," The 101ers (CHISWICK S3, 7-INCH, 1976)

"Motörhead," Motörhead (CHISWICK S13, 12-INCH, 1977)

"Saints and Sinners," Johnny and the Self Abusers (CHISWICK NS 22, 7-INCH, 1977)

"Sex Cells," The Table (CHISWICK NS 31, 7-INCH, 1978)

"Television Screen," Radiators from Space (CHISWICK S10, 7-INCH, 1977)

Radio Stars "From a Rabbit"
(CHISWICK NS 36, 6" HIP POCKET EDITION, PICTURE SLEEVE) 1978

With the advent of the 12-inch single, the humble 45 had grown as big as it was ever likely to. The Chiswick independent, then, began to consider other ways of making their product stand out, eventually settling upon the opposite extreme. Although a six-inch diameter single is, of course, just one inch smaller than a conventional 45, still the so-called Hip Pocket Edition of the Radio Stars' ode to body-building, "From a Rabbit," is an odd-looking creation.

There was nothing especially new about the format—in fact, an even smaller four-inch vinyl disc had been marketed under much the same name ("Pocket Discs") in the United States by Philco as far back as 1966. Those, however, were nothing more than medium-thickness flexidiscs. "From a Rabbit" was real, honest-to-goodness vinyl, but it

Public Image Ltd.'s "Death Disco"—the 12-inch is the essential version, but the 7-inch still moved mountains.

John Cooper Clark's acerbic "Twat" was also recorded in a cleaned-up version. However, double-groove technology ensured you never knew which one you were going to hear.

swiftly became apparent why the concept had never caught on in the past. The reduced size so compacted the grooves that the lightest scratch became a sonic graveyard, while the growing fashion for automatic turntables ensured the six-inch disc did more favors to the stylus-making industry than it did Radio Stars or Chiswick.

"From a Rabbit" was also pressed on regular 7-inch vinyl and isn't too hard to find. A pristine copy of the Hip Pocket Edition, however, is another matter entirely.

The Sire label's reissue of Patti Smith's debut single from 1974.

The Ramones, "Sheena Is a Punk Rocker" UK numbered 12-inch single)
(SIRE RAM 001) 1977

There were no extended versions for the Ramones' debut 12-inch single, no dance floor remixes or any other musical gimmick. But you were buying into a limited edition, and if you followed the instructions on the sleeve, you could grab yourself an exclusive Ramones T-shirt.

Rich Kids, "Rich Kids"
(EMI 2738, BLACK VINYL, PICTURE SLEEVE) 1978

Sacked Sex Pistol Glen Matlock wasted no time in putting his past behind him. Within months of departing that band, he was helming another, and rubbing salt into his old mates' chagrin by promptly signing with EMI, the label that had itself sacked the Pistols after just one single. "Rich Kids," his new band's eponymously titled debut, was released in January 1978, with initial pressings aping the Pistols' "Anarchy in the UK" debut by arriving in an unlabelled picture sleeve that was the exact same color as the vinyl within—in this case, red.

A Top Thirty hit, "Rich Kids" was also released in regular black vinyl (still with the red picture bag) but, of course, nobody paid that any attention. Now everybody's after it. Funny how that happens, isn't it?

Rikki and the Last Days of Earth, *Oundle 29/5/77* EP
(WHITE LABEL, ONE SIDED) 1977

Widely touted as the most hated band of the entire punk movement, Rikki and the Last Days were a highlight of the Roxy club calendar during the summer of 1977 and, the following spring, released what remains one of the most misunderstood albums (with two accompanying singles) of the entire age.

Recorded in concert in, not surprisingly, Oundle around a month before the group made its Roxy debut, this one-sided EP served as both the band's first demo and a neat piece of merchandise to sell at early gigs. Nobody seems to remember precisely how many were produced, but their scarcity today would suggest there were very few.

The Saints, "(I'm) Stranded"
(FATAL RECORDS, NO CAT #)

Their timing was exquisite. One minute, the Saints were another ragged Australian garage band, vaguely following in the beery, blues-drenched footsteps of a rougher AC/DC; the next, they were opening for the Ramones at the Roundhouse, "I'm Stranded" was an all-time punk anthem, and they never even had to get their hair cut!

Unrepentantly hirsute, irredeemably pub rock, the Saints' debut album (titled, of course, for the anthem) remains a burning slice of misbegotten R&B; timelessly troubled in a way that had worked for every bar band since the Stones. They wrote songs like the Stones as well, though, which is what raised the Saints above the rest of the punk pack jetsam they sailed with; wrote them, and kept on writing them.

Sex Pistols, "God Save the Queen"
(A&M 7284) 1977

Signed and sacked in the space of one week, the Sex Pistols' A&M sojourn is the stuff from which punk rock legends were made—all the more so since production of their "God Save the Queen"/"No Feelings" 45 was already in full flow.

With rumors swirling that outraged A&M superstars had deluged the office with complaints and disgust, unable to believe such a nice, sedate label had inked a pact with Satan's foulest demons, the label commenced destroying every manufactured copy of the record the moment the Pistols were fired. And, when "God Save the Queen" did finally appear two months later, it was on a different label (Virgin), with a different B-side ("Did You No Wrong"—the A&M version of "No Feelings" finally resurfaced on this year's Pistols box set).

The A&M single lived on, however. Anything up to 300 copies are now believed to have escaped the cull (earlier estimates were considerably more conservative), with the band members apparently owning several apiece. Another dozen were distributed among redundant A&M executives following the UK label's closure in 1999.

Siouxsie and the Banshees, "Mittageisen"
(POLYDOR 2059 151, PICTURE SLEEVE) 1979

From the very outset of their career, Siouxsie and the Banshees courted controversy, although few of their gestures so inflamed the self-righteous as their taunting flaunting of the swastika—which, of course, is why they did it. Like their detractors, the group itself had no support for fascism in any shape or form. Unlike their detractors, they were smart enough to realize that the ruthless suppression of any idea, no matter how wrong that idea may be, is in itself a form of fascism, all the more so when it is compounded by ignorance.

This point was hammered home by the release first of "Metal Postcard" (on the band's *The Scream* debut album), then with the appearance of this German language version, as a single in late 1979. Once it became known that the song's lyric was lifted directly one of Herman Goering's speeches, you could cut the condemnation with a ceremonial SS dagger—not, however, because the words themselves were any more inflammatory than anything else the head of Hitler's air force ever said, but because everybody knew who (and what) Goering was, and simply knee-jerked their way to the obvious conclusion.

The song's real inspiration, John Hartfield, was as obscure in the complainants' minds as any 1930s-era anti-Nazi propagandist-in-exile could be, and how the Banshees chortled as the Anti-Nazi League leaped at their throats, accusing them of promoting Hitler and co.

Backed by a rendering of the live favorite "Love in a Void," but rendered unsuitable for radio play by virtue of its foreign language lyric, "Mittageisen" crept to No. 47 on the UK chart and then disappeared. It remains the least known and, consequently, the most sought-after of all regular Banshees' 45s.

Patti Smith, "Hey Joe (Version)"
(MER 601) 1974

Patti Smith was a poetess with a severe Keith Richard fixation, and was already into her late 20s by the time she started performing regularly. She'd done pretty much everything else, though, so why not?

She'd published her first book, a slim poetry volume called *Seventh Heaven*. She was writing regularly for *Creem*, *Crawdaddy*, and *Rock Scene*, was a improv stage veteran, and had made her acting debut, in roommate Robert Mapplethorpe's *Robert Having His Nipple Pierced*. But most crucial of all, she was already hanging with Lenny Kaye, a guitarist and rock archivist who worked at Village Oldies record store. Together, the pair played poetry readings at the Mercer Arts Center and St. Mark's, and by 1974, they'd been joined by keyboard player Richard Sohl.

It was this trio that recorded the now-legendary "Hey Joe"/"Piss Factory" single, financed by Mapplethorpe and released on their own Mer label in January, 1975, the old '60s murder ballad rewired as a lament for Patty Hearst, the newspaper heiress whose kidnap and apparent conversion by the guerilla Symbionese Liberation Army dominated the headlines of the day. It's a remarkable performance, all the more so when you play it to a Jimi Hendrix fan—as British TV's *Old Grey Whistle Test* proved two years later, when Smith's live performance of the track was segued almost immediately into vintage footage of Jimi's rendering. Patti's single was reissued (with picture sleeve) by Sire in 1978.

The Snivelling Shits, "Terminal Stupid"
(GHETTO ROCKERS PRE 2, PICTURE SLEEVE) 1977

Journalist Giovanni Dadomo created the Snivelling Shits as the ultimate punk band—virtual non-musicians playing virtual non-

---

Patti Smith

"Ask the Angels" (FRANCE ARISTA 2C00698529, 7-INCH, PICTURE SLEEVE, 1976)

Big Ego (GIORNO POETRY SYSTEM 012-13, LP, 1978)

"Brian Jones" (FIERCE FRIGHT 017, 7-INCH, 1988)

"Hey Joe" (MER 601, 7-INCH, 1974)

King Biscuit Flower Hour 2/76 (KBFH, TRANSCRIPTION DISC, 1976)

Nova Convention (GIORNO POETRY SYSTEM 014-15, LP, 1978)

"Privilege" (UK ARISTA 12197, 12-INCH, PICTURE SLEEVE, 1978)

Sugar Alcohol and Meat (GIORNO POETRY SYSTEM 016-17, LP, 1978)

Wave (GREECE ARISTA 06262516, BLUE-VINYL LP)

"White Christmas," Link Cromwell (JASON J60568, 7-INCH, 1977)

songs, while offending as many people as possible with their sentiments. "Terminal Stupid" has become an anthem of sorts, but the real gem was the B-side, the sexual dismay of "I Can't Come," which develops, as a taut guitar riff and a frankly strangled vocal continue, into an A-Z of famous people who can. It is, of course, hysterically funny, possibly the only record on earth to mention both Hayley Mills and the Birdman of Alcatraz, whilst managing to drop in more references to masturbation than most people even knew existed.

Since reissued and repackaged on several occasions, the original single release is also the only one guaranteed to feature the original, vastly superior, version of the song. Most subsequent issues pack a decidedly weaker take.

Soft Boys, *Give It to the Soft Boys* EP
(RAW RAW 5) 1977

Robyn Hitchcock and the Soft Boys' monumental debut opens with what remains one of their best-loved tracks, "Wading Through a Ventilator." Originally recorded as a demo for the Raw label (in which form it was subsequently released in 1984), then rerecorded for the group's debut EP, either version stands as essentially a rough draft of everything the Soft Boys would go on to achieve.

It's essential stuff. But when *Give It to the Soft Boys* appeared in the spring of 1977, barely a soul paid it any attention. Alongside "Ventilator," "Hear My Brane" and the monumental "Face of Death" are especially notable for their sheer exuberance, and Hitchcock himself admits, "the Raw thing was beginners' luck, it was a really good session. The first Soft Boys recordings were among the best things I've ever been involved in, I think."

Give It to the Soft Boys in its entirety was an early highlight of Rykodisc's acclaimed 1976–'81 Soft Boys CD retrospective, taking the edge off a fanatical collectors market. The Raw original, however, is worth crawling on your knees across a field of upturned parrot beaks for.

The Stranglers, "Peasant in the Big Shitty"
(UA FREE 3, RED PICTURE SLEEVE, "WHAT DO YOU EXPECT . . . " IN RUN-OFF GROOVE) 1977

Another in the litany of singles delivered free with the purchase of an album, the immortally titled "Peasant in the Big Shitty" (b/w "Choosy Susie") fell out of the first 10,000 copies of the Stranglers' debut album, *Rattus Norvegicus IV*, and was immediately acclaimed among the principle rarities of the early punk era.

Featuring live versions of songs that the Stranglers had been performing since infancy, but that would not be addressed in the studio until their second album, the single has been repressed on at least two occasions, first by the band's SIS fan club, and then by United Artists' Liberty successor. Of the two, the first-named most closely resembles the original, although there are no excuses whatsoever for being misled. Not only is the picture sleeve black, rather than the first issue's red, the inscription in the run-off groove has been changed to "'Ello 'Elen."

Television, "Little Johnny Jewel"
(ORK RECORDS 81975) 1975

Formed by school friends Tom Verlaine and Richard Hell, Television grew up quickly. Hell was into short, sharp shocks, "Blank Generation" and "You Gotta Lose"; Verlaine favored ten-minute soundscapes that reveled in improvisation: "Jewel," "Kingdom Come," "Elevation," and "Marquee Moon."

A parting was inevitable, but while Hell fled for the sonic immediacy of the Heartbreakers, and later his own Voidoids, Television just kept on extending, and with ex-Blondie bassist Fred Smith in Hell's place, they cut their debut single, "Little Johnny Jewel," for Terry Ork's eponymous label.

Recorded in mono, with its full length split across both sides of the record, "Little Johnny Jewel" introduced Television to the world at a time when their reputation had scarcely spread outside of the Bowery. There are no musical surprises awaiting anyone drawn to the band by the later *Marquee Moon* debut album, but still the sheer rawness of the band, with guitar solos etched in ice and embedded in glass, marks them out as something special.

The Urinals, "Black Hole"
(HAPPY SQUID HS 002, PICTURE SLEEVE) 1979

The opening cut on the L.A. band's sophomore release, *Another EP* and, at a minute twelve in length, the longest song in sight, "Black Hole" catches the Urinals in full minimalist mode, the most angular of all their hometown's punk progenitors.

The Vibrators, "Bad Times"
(RAK 253) 1977

The first of the punk bands to land a major record deal, with Mickey Most's RAK concern, the Vibrators had already issued two singles by the time the rest of the pack began catching up with them—"We Vibrate," under their own name, and "Pogo Dancing," co-credited to guitarist Chris Spedding.

Both are well worth seeking out, for both their musical and their scarcity value, but the real jewel is the group's third single, "Bad Times"/"No Heart," scheduled for release in early 1977 but abandoned when the Vibrators broke away to sign with Epic. Promo copies of the release have, apparently, been sighted over the years, although no firm evidence that either they, or any stock copies, truly exist.

Unnatural Axe, "They Saved Hitler's Brain"
(VARULVEN 87-66, PICTURE SLEEVE) 1978

Boston's Unnatural Axe managed just one 45, but it was a beauty, an adrenalined roar of B-movie sound effects (tribute to the song title's source) and absurdly brilliant lyrical couplets. Where else are you going to hear "staff car" rhymed with "glass jar"?

X—X, "Your Full of Shit"
(DROME RECORDS DR-2, PICTURE SLEEVE) 1979

Former Electric Eel John Morton led X—X ("X Blank X," as they were also known) across a couple of singles and a live album; this was the B-side of the first, and reprised an old Electric Eels track to the *n*th degree.

XTC, "Science Friction"
(VIRGIN VS 1988, PICTURE SLEEVE) 1977

Intended as the Swindon art attack's debut single, "Science Friction"/"She's So Square" had already been pressed when the powers that be opted to abandon the 7-inch version of the release, and market only the three-song 12-inch 3D EP (VS 188-12—"Dance Band" completed this package). The majority of known copies of the scrapped 7-inch appear in plain Virgin company bags, and are valued in the three-figure range. Picture sleeved copies go for around ten times as much.

Jerry and Jeff were, in fact, Kasenetz and Katz.

THE GENRE: WE ALL GOT HIGH ON BUBBLEGUM

History, sadly, has not recorded who first applied the term "bubblegum" to pop music. The substance itself had been around since the early 1900s, when one Frank H. Fleer marketed a gooey substance called "Blibber Blubber," although certain teething problems, such as the difficulty one encountered when trying to blow a bubble which didn't automatically stick to your face, took twenty years to iron out. When Dubble Bubble gum was finally introduced around 1928, however, it was an immediate success.

In wartime Europe, gum was up there with dairy chocolate and silk stockings in every sexually active GI's basic survival kit. In Borneo, headhunters kidnapped a diplomat and demanded Dubble Bubble as ransom. And in 1950s America, a mouthful of gum was as vital to the teenage revolution as any leather jacket, Elvis quaff, or James Dean sneer.

In 1955 the Scholastic label, a subsidiary of Folkways, released *33 Skip Rope Games*, an LP recorded on the streets of Chicago by folkie Pete Seeger, and consisting of the rhymes children chanted as they skipped. One such rhyme was "Bubblegum," and a decade on, the progenitors of the later musical genre might well have had a copy of the chant alongside the piano when they first began piecing together the ingredients they required.

Ingredients which included: a hint of "The Nitty Gritty," a dash of "Loop De Loop," a sprinkling of "Yellow Submarine," and a hefty dose of Richard Berry's "Louie Louie" riff, arguably the most

The Singing Orchestral Circus in all its sprawling glory.

important noise to emerge from post-Beatle-whipped America, and the inspiration behind a pioneering boom in garage bands, so named because they tended to form, and sometimes even live, in garages. And, from there, find their own way into the percolating bubblegum stew, as the Shadows of Knight were destined to discover.

The other key player in this story is Neil Bogart, a record company bigwig whose only other claim to fame at the time was a smattering of long-forgotten Midwest pop stardom in the guise of Neil Scott, teen idol. Mark Stein, who later found fame as a member of mogodon pomp quartet Vanilla Fudge, later recalled, "When I was eleven . . . my dad got me into a rock and roll show, emceed by Neil, who had a song ('Bobby') in the charts. He became my manager. I was eleven and Neil was sixteen."

Now Bogart was vice president of Cameo Records, one half of Cameo Parkway, and the poorer half at that. While Parkway had launched Chubby Checker and the Twist, Cameo struggled on with a sporadic series of turntable favorites and the odd regional breaker, and when Bogart picked up on another local hit, "96 Tears" by the mysterious ? and the Mysterions, few folks expected his luck to change.

Instead the song gave Cameo their first ever No. 1, and while neither Cameo, Bogart, nor the Mysterions were ever to repeat that one great success, Bogart was suddenly established as a man with a finger on the pulse. He picked up the fledgling Bob Seger, grooming him for his later success, and had Iggy Pop not split for Chicago and left his teenaged band the Prime Movers for dead, he too, is said to have been high on Bogart's totem.

Bubblegum from the Fruitgums.

And so it was, during the summer of 1967, that Bogart signed two studio whiz kids, Jerry Kasenetz and Jeff Katz, to Cameo. Natives of Long Island, the pair had been working together for a little under eighteen months, primarily with low-key proto-punk outfits whose efforts were for the most part not even to leave the studio. Because when they did, they sank.

Rare Breed, who debuted the duo's production talents in the marketplace, chalked up two resounding zeros in a row, first with "Beg, Borrow and Steal," a frantic adaptation of the basic "Louie Louie" riff, spiced up with a few nice hook-lines, then with "Come On Down to My Boat (Baby)."

Shortly after that, The Music Explosion's "Little Black Egg" failed to hatch. But within a year, Kasenetz-Katz were riding high in the chart, both in their own right (The Music Explosion's "Little Bit O' Soul") and by proxy, when Every Mother's Son took their own version of "Come On Down to My Boat" into the Top Ten.

"Little Bit O' Soul" was the crystallization, in embryonic form at least, of everything Kasenetz-Katz had been working towards. Their earlier efforts revolved primarily around the dexterous reproduction of innumerable proto-punk archetypes, crammed together in an uneasy alliance of sloppiness and pomp; this time, however, the duo loosened up a little, allowing vocalist Jimmy Lyons more room in

Crazy Elephant's greatest hit was, in fact, recorded by the future 10cc.

which to maneuver, and providing the rhythm section—Butch Stahl and Bob Avery—with a beat even Moulty, the Barbarians' hook-handed drummer, could have tapped out in his sleep.

Although Kasenetz-Katz's career was still very much in its infancy, Neil Bogart was swift to win an introduction to them. He sensed an immediate chemistry; when Kasenetz-Katz spoke of their ambitions, he saw his own being spelt out before him. They wanted to create a sound as individual as Phil Spector's, as dynamic as Andrew Oldham's, as instantly recognizable as Leiber-Stoller's, and somehow Bogart knew that if anybody was entitled to such lofty aims, it was these earnest, likable young New Yorkers. Watching them work in the studio for the first time only confirmed his first impressions.

For Kasenetz-Katz, Bogart was the only man they'd met who offered them exactly the terms they wanted—the promise of being able to work in any way they wished, with the minimum of bureaucratic interference. They had a dream, but it was an exclusive one. They wanted to build an empire in which the sound, the groups, the music, and the marketing were as one. All they needed was the money to pay for it, and a backer with the belief to stand by them even if success was not immediately apparent.

In the event, their first effort for Cameo was a hit. Confident that the failure of Rare Breed's "Beg, Borrow and Steal" had been due almost entirely to their having tried introducing their techniques to the marketplace a little at a time, rather than in one all-embracing, devastating single blow, they virtually rebuilt "Little Bit O' Soul" around the Ohio Express' interpretation of the older song. By the end of November, they had another smash on their hands.

The Ohio Express, like the Music Explosion, were primarily a studio-based outfit, comprising Dale Powers (vocals), Doug Grassel (guitar), Dean Kastran (bass), Jim Pfayler (keyboards), and Tim Corwin (drums). They operated out of Mansfield, Ohio, and legend had it that they rehearsed in a deserted railroad station.

One night a huge crowd gathered around them, but not—as the band thought—to listen to them. Rather, the Ohio Express, a super-fast freight train, was due through, and everybody wanted to get a look at it. The band immediately renamed themselves after the train in the hope that people would find them as exciting as the puff puff evidently was.

In truth, the name—like the band itself—was simply one of Kasenetz-Katz's inventions. A ready-made band would have been of little use to them; they required intransigence, the knowledge that absolutely *anybody* they chose could play for the Express. Their vision of artistic control could not be fulfilled if they had to deal with an actual band, with all the ego trips and demands that that would involve. Session men, on the other hand, might not enjoy playing what they were given, but at least they would play it, and play it well.

The success of "Beg, Borrow and Steal" was followed by a surprising flop, "Try It." But when Neil Bogart left Cameo for his own (misspelled) Buddah label, he was not slow to offer Kasenetz-Katz similar freedoms within the new company as they had enjoyed at the old—something Cameo's next president, Allen Klein, is unlikely to have agreed to.

Buddah was established primarily as a light- (as opposed to easy) listening label, a principle borne out by the company's first chart success, the Lemon Piper's "Green Tambourine." Of course Bogart could not expect to have the entire bubblegum market to himself; what was to set Buddah apart was the guile with which that market would be courted. With the exception only of a handful of licensed British acts, nothing even remotely threatening was to sully Buddah's name. Even Crazy Elephant, Kasenetz-Katz's brilliant concession to the growing "heavy" market, were farmed out to the Bell label.

Carole King

"**Baby Sittin'**" (ABC PARAMOUNT 9986, 7-INCH, 1958)

"**Goin' Wild**" (ABC PARAMOUNT 9921, 7-INCH, 1958)

"**He's a Bad Boy**" (DIMENSION 1009, 7-INCH, 1963)

"**It Might As Well Rain Until September**" (COMPANION 2000, 7-INCH, 1962)

"**Main Street Saturday Night**" (CAPITOL SPRO 8863, 12-INCH PROMO, 1978)

Now That Everything's Been Said (ODE Z12 44012, LP, FULL-COLOR COVER, 1968)

"**Oh Neil**" (ALPINE 57, 7-INCH, 1959)

"**A Road to Tomorrow**" (TOMORROW 7502, 7-INCH, 1966)

"**Short Mort**" (RCA VICTOR 47-7560, 7-INCH, 1959)

Tapestry (ODE HE 44946, HALF-SPEED MASTER LP, 1980)

Bogart was confident that the aims with which he founded Buddah would be successful. American pop was still struggling to reestablish itself after the British Invasion, and with Herman's Hermits' peculiar hybrid of English music hall standards and equally innocent sub-beat boppers still holding the preteens in their sweatless grasp, American business was still vitally concerned with manufacturing a homegrown response.

Kasenetz-Katz knew what it should be: a return to the musical values that had dominated pop before the invaders arrived. A return to the so-called hit factories, wherein the era's most gifted writers would effectively clock in and every day and work nine-to-five writing songs. Or, as English songwriter Graham Gouldman (who would later join Kasenetz-Katz's own setup) put it, "We were employed to write songs. Every morning we would clock in, go up to our offices, sit down at the piano, and write. It was like any factory, only instead of little bits of cars you'd make little bits of music."

The criteria that bound the factory workers' efforts were equally simple. Was a song easy to learn, easy to sing? Was it a hit? That was all that mattered. And so the likes of Carole King, Gerry Goffin, Bobby Darin, Barry Mann and Cynthia Weill, Neil Diamond, Gary Sherman, Neil Sedaka, and Howie Greenfield churned out the classics, and that was the mentality that Kasenetz-Katz intended to recreate.

They did not only want hit songs, though. They also demanded a hit *sound,* a unique sonic imprimatur that would become as reliable a brand as any before them. And they nailed it with their first production for Buddah Records, the 1910 Fruitgum Company's "Simon Says."

"Simon Says" was brilliant. It operated on a nursery-rhyme level; indeed, Simon Says itself is a long-established playroom game in which the participants are given a variety of commands, and eliminated if they follow any not prefaced by the words "Simon says." The song followed those rules to the letter, and over five million copies were shifted, sold to parents wanting to give Junior a game to play, to teachers hoping to introduce first graders to drama through a medium with which they were already familiar, and to preteens simply because they
liked it.

The Fruitgums—whose name allegedly came from a gum wrapper discovered in the pocket of some antique clothes they were looking through—followed "Simon Says" with "1-2-3 Red Light," in August, 1967. In the interim, the Ohio Express clocked up their second hit with "Yummy Yummy Yummy" and together, they launched the western world into the age of bubblegum.

Kasenetz-Katz were in full stride. By the end of 1968, with seven Top Forty hits under their belts, and a production team that included Art Resnick, Joey Levine, and Ritchie Cordell, their sound—The Sound of Super K—was, exactly as they had predicted it would be, no less recognizable than Spector's, and at this point in time, no less salable.

When they put together the Kasenetz-Katz Singing Orchestral Circus, they claimed to have sold out Carnegie Hall on the strength of their reputation alone. In fact, they didn't; the entire story was simply the backdrop to the release of their Singing Orchestral Circus's eponymous debut album, a cornucopia of bubblegum that included such (equally fictional) superstars as Lt. Garcia's Magic Music Box

(how the Deadheads must have appreciated that one), the Teri Nelson Group, the 1989 Musical Marching Zoo, JCW Rat Finks, and the St. Louis Invisible Marching Band, alongside the more established hitmakers.

The Circus LP was and remains regarded as Super K's masterstroke, the ultimate culmination of their chosen art form; a reminder that Kasenetz-Katz was now a brand name at least as well-known as the bands themselves. Like Wile E. Coyote and his eternal patronage of ACME Products, you didn't ask for the new Fruitgums single, you asked for the new Kasenetz-Katz.

Yet it was also, perhaps, a request for a little respect. Kasenetz-Katz had made their way to the peak of their profession, but who cared? Kids bought their records, bought them in prodigious quantities. But kids didn't talk in hushed, reverent tones of the stunning production techniques, and the revolutionary use of echo. They simply knew the Sound of Super-K in the way their mothers knew which brand of washing powder to use.

Kasenetz-Katz wanted a little credibility, and the only way they could get it was by letting everybody else in on the joke.

Thus Jerry and Jeff, Super K themselves, whose solitary single featured a pre-Dawn Tony Orlando on vocals. Thus the Circus, the Marching Band, and the Magic Music Box. Thus Captain Groovy and His Bubblegum Army (the single of the same name), and the Rock 'n' Roll Dubble Bubble Trading Card Company of Philadelphia, 1941.

And thus, the record that in overall sonic terms, surely represents the culmination of all that Kasenetz-Katz had achieved: "Oo Poo Pah Susie," by Professor Morrison's Lollipop, a record so far-sighted that, almost half a century later, it was as thrilling to rediscover within the *Pink Boots and Lollipop* glam and bubblegum series of compilations as it was on an original scratchy White Whale label single.

The songs weren't hits, but they weren't expected to be. They were statements of intent, woven in and around the records that Super K knew would maintain their chart profile. "Quick Joey Small," released under the name of the Circus, was a brilliantly constructed jailbreak song, one of the best of all time. The Shadows of Knight's "Shake" was equally well-made, and prompted considerable comment from without, if only from people trying to work out what a mean-lookin' bunch of garage critters like the Shads were doing making records with Kasenetz-Katz.

If they reread the sleeve notes to the band's first album, they would have understood: "If you invited them over for dinner your parents would, at first, have you examined, or call the police, or run screaming to the neighbors. If your parents stayed around, they would find the Shadows are polite, quiet, considerate, and that they might even grow to like them."

No brooding carbon-monoxided punk image here; the Shadows of Knight were good boys who only sounded like they'd strangle your granny as soon as look at her. In reality, they'd probably want to help you feed her.

Yet despite so much brilliance, 1969 saw the Super K bubble come perilously close to bursting. With the exception of Crazy Elephant, a band the duo maintained were discovered in a Welsh coal mine, they were to launch no new successes all year. Their own Super K label was visibly foundering—launched a year previous, it had still to rack up a single hit, and that despite employing the services not only of the proven Buddah stable, but also Buckwheat (not the Our Gang member, but a dubious sextet of the same name), The Shadows of Knight, and Jerry and Jeff . . . yes, that Jerry and Jeff.

The Hollies

"(Ain't That) Just Like Me" (UK PARLOPHONE R5030, 7-INCH 1963)

"The Baby" (EPIC 10842, 7-INCH, PICTURE SLEEVE, 1972)

"Carrie Ann" (EPIC 10180, 7-INCH, PICTURE SLEEVE, 1967)

Hear! Here! (IMPERIAL LP 9299, LP, 1965)

The Hollies (IMPERIAL LP 9265, LP, BLACK LABEL WITH STARS, 1964)

I Can't Let Go (UK PARLOPHONE GEP 8951, EP, 1966)

"If I Needed Someone" (IMPERIAL 66271, 7-INCH, 1968)

"Just One Look" (IMPERIAL 66026, 7-INCH, 1964)

"Stay" (LIBERTY 55674, 7-INCH, 1964)

"Yes I Will" (IMPERIAL 66099, 7-INCH, 1965)

Even worse, both the Fruitgums and the Express were showing unmistakable signs of debilitation, a process that quite audibly reached its nadir when the Fruitgums were exposed to the full Phil Spector treatment on "When We Get Married," a wall of unremitting bubblesound that could have impressed none other than Spector himself. If nothing else, the master must have thought it proved that these Super K upstarts weren't quite as hot as they thought. Nobody that hot would even dream of tarting their baby up in somebody else's hand-me-downs.

It was also telling that Super K's sole success of the year was one they had delegated down to their most faithful lieutenants, Ritchie Cordell and Joey Levine. The Elephant's "Gimme Gimme Good Loving" had very little in common with Kasenetz-Katz, but an awful lot to do with the heavy rock boom now beginning to glower over the horizon.

Above a pounding rhythm, a piping organ, and scything guitars, the Crazy Elephant—featuring Bob Avery from the Music Explosion and Fruitgum Ralph Cohen's brother Kenny—chanted their way into every hit parade in the west. It was quintessential super pop, but it pinpointed not the direction in which Kasenetz-Katz were intending to move, but that in which the rest of the world was directing its thoughts.

An attempt to broaden the team's horizons even further faltered, even after English songwriter Gouldman was brought into the factory, and then sent back home again when he revealed that he had a fully equipped studio of his own to work in back home, and a willing team of co-conspirators, too: Eric Stewart, Lol Crème, and Kevin Godley—who, together with Gouldman would soon be leading 10cc to glory.

A proven hit writer in his own right, with smashes for the Hollies, the Yardbirds, Herman's Hermits, and more already behind him, Gouldman recalled, "Kasenetz-Katz decided they wanted to get legit, so they wanted someone a little more valid in their factory. Artistically, it was not a good move on my part, but there's always good comes out of things like that, and actually they did contribute to 10cc coming together, because I was working in New York, and I said, 'Look, I'm fed up here. I've got involved in this studio back in Manchester, Strawberry, I want to take all the stuff we're recording here, and do it with my own guys back in England.' So Strawberry got a tremendous amount of business, and those records, the early ones, were Kevin, Lol, and myself, and Eric was engineering them."

In fact, the first Kasenetz-Katz sessions took place in London, while Strawberry Studios were being properly equipped; together, however, the Gouldman-Stewart-Godley-Creme team wrote and played on a host of Super K Productions records, released under varying names around the world.

Kevin Godley remembers, "We briefly and uncomfortably became Crazy Elephant, Ohio Express, Silver Fleet, Fighter Squadron, Festival, and fuck knows who else under the production tutelage of the late Richie Cordell, brought in from New York to keep the crazy Brits in check. Crazy Brits? This was a guy who ate pickled onions straight from the jar and nothing else. I think Richie introduced spliff into our lives. Thank you Ritchie."

The hits kept coming, though. Gouldman's "Have You Ever Been to Georgia" was a smash for many artists, including Tony Christie, another Kennedy Street act. He was also responsible for two Ohio Express hits, "Sausalito" and "Tampa Florida," while a latter-day version of the old Merseybeat novelty act Freddie and the Dreamers sold a million copies of "Susan's Tuba" in France, with Gouldman writing and singing.

But bubblegum was losing its flavor, in Europe as well as the United States, and here's why: if there was any flaw in the Super K gameplan, it was that while they had sewn up the singalong, dancealong market, they had made no provision whatsoever for their audience's other prime fixation—love.

Sure they sang about it, but they did so in a most impersonal way. You could like the 1910 Fruitgum Company, you could even look at their pictures on the record sleeve and think they were cute. But unless you could get to know them intimately, you could never fall in love with them.

In 1970, around the same time as the last truly great Kasenetz-Katz records emerged, US prime time television began airing a new musical sitcom, *The Partridge Family.* Pop was still its raison d'être. But so was the young David Cassidy. The age of the teenybop idol had arrived.

THE EVENT: RECORD STORE DAY

It's one of the modern world's most predictable cycles. No sooner have the doors closed on another Record Store Day, and sometimes even before that, than the day's biggest sellers will start turning up on eBay, often at prices far in excess of whatever they sold for in the first place. Which, considering that Record Store Day prices do sometimes seem to incorporate some kind of early bird premium, makes for a fair whack of change.

Nobody is surprised. Nothing seems to say "limited edition" faster than an object's swift appearance in online auctions, usually at a considerable premium, and often in such quantities that one wonders whether any genuine purchasers even had a chance to get a copy. And every year since Record Store Day first entered the calendar, there's been a handful of releases that seemingly everyone wants,

and a strictly limited edition to make sure they don't get it. Because someone who *doesn't* want it got their first, and is now sitting back to watch the bids pile in.

The rights and wrongs of that should be left to the various internet forums whose members discuss such things. Besides. For everyone who picked up an extra copy of the pink vinyl pressing of Pink Floyd's "See Emily Play," for example, there's plenty more lumbered with multiples of yet another Flaming Lips offering, desultorily following up their initial Record Store Day release, *Heady Nuggs,* which is tooth-achingly pricey today.

Indeed, no matter how limited an edition may be, participating retailers always seem to be stuck with a handful of several long after the event. Meaning, even a deliberately designed "collectors item" is only really worth creating if the collectors are out there. Which in many cases, they are not.

This isn't a dilemma unique to record collecting, of course. Back in the '80s and '90s, the world's postage stamp and coin collecting hobbies were awash with limited edition items from all around the world, all being touted as future rarities—and many of them are now in the equivalent of the dollar bin.

And why? Because collectors, despite what manufacturers think, are not stupid and do not all fall into Pavlovian paroxysms of mouth-foaming ecstasy the moment they see the words "rare" or "limited edition" attached to something that just came out of the factory.

Maybe in the wider world of late night TV infomercials, there will be sufficient bored insomniacs who truly believe "a genuine replica gold vinyl repro of the Beatles' first album with certificate of authenticity signed by someone you've never heard of" is an heirloom for the ages (don't bother looking for it; I just made it up). But Beatles fans themselves would just sniff and file under "novelty item," preferring to save the cash for something with more of a cachet.

Bobby Fuller Four

The Bobby Fuller Four (MUSTANG MS 901, STEREO LP, 1966)

"**Fool of Love**" (EXETER 126, 7-INCH, 1964)

"**I Fought the Law**" (EXETER 124, 7-INCH, 1964)

"**King of the Beach**" (EXETER 122, 7-INCH, 1964)

KRLA, King of the Wheels (MUSTANG MS 900, STEREO LP, 1965)

"**Never to Be Forgotten**" (MUSTANG 3011, 7-INCH, 1965)

"**Not Fade Away**" (EASTWOOD 345, 7-INCH, 1962)

"**Saturday Night**" (TODD 1090, 7-INCH, 1963)

"**Those Memories of You,**" as Bobby Fuller and The Fabtastics (DONNA 1403, 7-INCH, 1965)

"**You're in Love**" (YUCCA 140, 7-INCH, SLOW VERSION/FAST VERSION, 1961

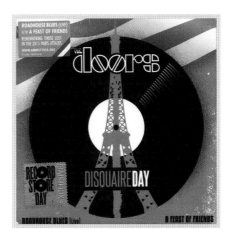

An exclusive Doors single for RSD 2016.

And so it is at Record Store Day. The event was launched on April 19, 2008, as a means of celebrating the survival of what was then, contrarily, a rapidly diminishing number of "mom-and-pop" record stores around the United States and United Kingdom—around 300 participated in this first year.

The idea was, by persuading labels and artists to create limited edition releases that would only be available on the day, it would also persuade fans and collectors to arrive early and spend big. And so it proved. With members of Metallica being designated unofficial ambassadors, and inaugurating the event at Rasputin Music in Mountain View, California (Billy Bragg took the same role in the UK), ten Record Store Day exclusives were produced, including releases by Death Cab For Cutie, R.E.M., Stephen Malkmus, Vampire Weekend, the Teenagers, Black Kids, and Jason Mraz.

The following year saw eighty-five new releases rolled out, 500 stateside stores involved (plus another thousand across Canada and western Europe), and New York Mayor Mike Bloomberg announcing that his city officially recognized Record Store Day. It just kept on growing from there, soon proving so successful that a second date was introduced, a special Black Friday showing that, while considerably lower key in terms of both releases and turnout, nevertheless offered indie store owners a welcome start to the Christmas shopping season.

Indeed, while many purists complain that Record Store Day has effectively degenerated into a major-label feeding frenzy, utterly sidelining the indie labels that pioneered the concept, the fact is, the event brings vast quantities of customers (and therefore money) into bricks-and-mortar record stores on two guaranteed days a year.

From the store owner's point of view (and that of the store's continued survival), does it even matter whether those customers are buying a colored vinyl single by a band no one else has heard of, or a lavishly packaged Grateful Dead live box set?

It's not all weighted in the dealer's favor, of course. For starters, Record Store Day exclusives cannot be returned if they don't sell. Neither can stores pick and choose between the offered releases; they receive what they are sent, which is why a lot of people spend almost as long on eBay that evening as they did on line outside the store that morning, looking for the records that didn't arrive. (Or were sent in such minute quantities that they'd already been snapped up.)

But the positives do outweigh the negatives. Otherwise, nobody would bother.

Hardly surprisingly, it's the major label releases that have seen the most appreciation in value—again, because more people are interested in owning them. At the same time, however, what might now seem like no-brainer investment items were not necessarily conceived as such, by either manufacturers or purchasers.

New releases within the (at the time of writing) ongoing series of David Bowie picture disc 45s, for example, are now a guaranteed sellout, because the earliest discs in the series are selling in the range of three figures apiece. Yet history itself was against the series, because Parlophone's modern series is by no means the first go-round for such an extravagance.

As far back as 1982, ten of Bowie's past 45s were repressed as picture discs in the *Fashions* box; the following year, twenty were reissued in custom picture sleeves in the *Lifetimes* series. A lot of people passed them by at the time, because . . . well, they'd already got the original pressings, and these looked more like a tacky cash-in.

Soft Cell's "Say Hello Wave Goodbye" remixed for a RSD 2018 12-inch exclusive.

A Bob Dylan singles box set for RSD's 2011 Black Friday event.

Record Store Day 2018 inside Rainbow Records of Newark, Delaware. (Photo by Amy Hanson)

Even today, individual releases within the two series are readily available at reasonable prices, which only really add up if you collect the entire set. Who could possibly have predicted that the twenty-first century series would fare any better? But it did, and the run already boasts a couple of entries that are worth more as stand-alone singles than the entire *Fashions* series combined.

Previously unissued David Bowie live LPs. Vinyl-only "alternate" versions of sundry Fleetwood Mac LPs. One-off reissues for classic albums of the early 1990s. Established cult collectibles rendered even more desirable by colored vinyl and picture discs. They all have one thing in common: People want them. Or, if they didn't before, they will now.

More than any of the so-called classic artists, however, what is especially gratifying is the sight of what older generations might consider "new talent"—that is, anyone who arrived on the scene post 1980-something—laying the groundwork for future generations of collectors.

Names like Nirvana, Soungarden, Mad Season, and Pearl Jam from the mid-1990s grunge scene all have Record Store Day releases that now push the three-figure mark; the White Stripes, the Black Keys, and Radiohead too. And one of the most valuable Record Store Day releases of them all arrives courtesy of the electro mavens Daft Punk, with copies of the *Tron* triple 10-inch package nudging the $1,000 mark less than a year after release.

Ten classic Stiff Records 45s repressed for your RSD pleasure.

Other prized items include U2's *Songs of Innocence*, released in 2015 in a worldwide edition of 5,000 copies; one of the 1,000 green vinyl box sets of Type O Negative's *None More Negative* (released 2011); the Cure's "Friday I'm in Love," an implausibly scarce (100 copies) 45 from 2012; the eye-catchingly liquid-filled 12" single of Jack White's *Sixteen Saltines* (2012); Haim's 2013 offering "Better Off" (another edition of 100); Elvis Presley's 2014 live album *Showroom*

The 2014 RSD saw a "mystery disc" pair Love's "7 & 7 Is" with Rush's cover. You only discovered that, though, once you played it.

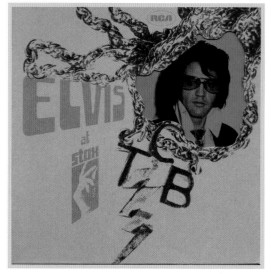

Not officially a RSD release, but this limited edition on split translucent black and gold vinyl was released in time for the Black Friday event in 2015.

Internationale; punk rocker Ed Banger's *The Bee Sides* box of five 7" singles (2011); and the twelve-inch remix of Paul McCartney's "Nineteen Hundred and Eighty Five" (2016).

And there are plenty more where they came from.

THE ARCHIVE: JIMI HENDRIX— THE EARLY YEARS

Rolling Stone put it best. Reviewing the then-newly (2010) released Jimi Hendrix anthology, *West Coast Seattle Boy*, Will Hermes' review announced, "For Jimi Hendrix fanatics, the selling point of this four-disc set is a full CD of songs on which the guitarist doesn't sing lead and barely solos.

"Instead, he plays sideman to Little Richard, Don Covay, and others on fifteen R&B smokers. The tracks offer glimpses of a prodigy straining at the bit: The hot-shit solo on the Isley Brothers' 1964 'Testify,' all of ten seconds long, is like an early Marlon Brando screen test, coiled drama springing to life; the reverb-soaked, Curtis Mayfield-style licks on the Icemen's sublime 1966 '(My Girl) She's a Fox' offer a taste of the exploded-soul magic Hendrix cooked up later on 'Castles Made of Sand.'"

The collection, for the first time ever, attempted to place Hendrix's entire career in perspective, not via simply running through the greatest hits and wildest solos, but by chasing Jimi back to the very dawn of his career, working as a sideman on what was unflatteringly known as the Chitlin Circuit of early 1960s America,

Hidden away among soul man Covay's Goodtimers: the young Jimmy Hendrix.

It was a courageous undertaking—not because so much of the music barely featured a solitary iota of the qualities for which Hendrix is today revered, but because documentation of precisely what he did and didn't play on is generally contradictory at best, and often altogether nonexistent.

The collection's own provenance cannot be debated. Since 1997, the Hendrix family's own Experience Hendrix foundation has been diligently working to cut through the confusion (not to mention bulk) wrought by the activities of the estate's earlier administrations, reissuing and remastering each of his core albums, while supplementing the catalog with a host of live and unreleased recordings.

Their initial efforts concentrated exclusively upon the four years 1966–'70, during which Hendrix was at his creative and commercial height, completely overlooking all that occurred at the opposite end of the chronological scale. And wisely so. But sooner or later, they knew, they needed address the nest of snakes so venomous that no single record label had ever attempted to delve definitively into it.

Indeed, even *West Coast Seattle Boy* only scratched the surface of what may or may not be out there, a point proven in 2015 with the release of *You Can't Use My Name: The RSVP/PPX Sessions*, which focused in on the best-known (and, on this occasion, -documented) phase of Hendrix's pre-fame career, working alongside singer Curtis Knight.

And yet, Hendrix's pre-fame career, the three-year span 1963–'66, during which he worked as a backing musician for whomsoever would employ him, itself abounds with LP releases, often bearing more familiar imagery, most times arriving with minimal track information and occasionally proving utterly preposterous.

Unlike many musicians, Hendrix rarely talked in any depth about his apprenticeship. Out of that vagueness, however, have been conjured at least a couple of hundred LPs and CDs, released all around the world, which claim to feature Hendrix playing alongside one name or another, with the most ubiquitous offender being his time alongside bluesman Lonnie Youngblood.

Youngblood himself has testified that barely a handful of titles actually live up to that billing, and the fact that the fraudulent issues include some of the best-known of all "early" Hendrix titles only amplifies the sheer audacity of these claims.

For the record, such "early Hendrix" classics as "Spiked with Heady Dreams," "She Went to Bed with My Guitar," and "Strokin' a Lady On Each Hip," first issued on a series of LPs by the Pan/Saga labels in the early 1970s, are nothing of the kind. Neither are such enticing titles as "Funky," "Feel That Soul," "Gangster of Love," "Hey Leroy," and "Young Generation."

Nevertheless, Youngblood was the first artist to record the young Jimmy (as he was then) Hendrix in Philadelphia during 1963, and the pair appear together on two Youngblood 45s issued at the time by the Fairmount label, "Go Go Shoes" and "Soul Food." Other songs recorded at this time, but unreleased until after Hendrix's death, include "Sweet Thang," "Groovemaker," "(She's a) Fox," and multiple versions of "Wipe the Sweat" and "Under the Table. " All were mono recordings—however, stereo mixes of the latter two tracks, with new overdubs, were prepared in 1971 prior to their release on the Maple label album *Two Great Experiences Together*, a set that actually reached No. 127 on the US chart.

The albums *Rare Hendrix, The Genius of Jimi Hendrix,* and *For Real!* round up the remainder of authentic Hendrix/Youngblood material in the most concise manner; other titles, while possibly featuring one or two of the Hendrix performances, overwhelm it with other Youngblood material—which is no bad thing if you're a Youngblood completist, but is disappointing for Hendrix fans. Do not, however, overlook all of Hendrix's recordings with Youngblood. A post-fame reunion of the two is among the undisputed highlights of Jimi's 2018 *Both Sides of the Sky* compilation.

By 1964, Hendrix had moved onto the Isley Brothers' band, again remaining on board for two singles, "Testify" (the first ever release on the brothers' own T-Neck label) and "The Last Girl" for Atlantic. He quit the band that fall, but rejoined them in the studio a year later to guest on a third 45, "Move Over and Let Me Dance."

The Isleys themselves would reissue these tracks on their own *In the Beginning* album, although all were either remixed, or offered alternate takes to the originally issued sides. (The original 45 version of "Testify" would remain unavailable until its inclusion on the Isleys' *It's Your Thing* box set in 1999.)

A 45 released in 1972, just one of the multitude of posthumous cash-ins that percolate through Hendrix's catalog.

The following year, 1965, also saw Hendrix playing in Little Richard's band and again there's a wealth of releases whose titles are somewhat deceptive (*Friends from the Beginning* and *Together* rank among the most common). However, Little Richard's 1965 single, the two-part "I Don't Know What You've Got But It's Got Me," represented Hendrix's first ever taste of chart success, when it reached No. 12 on the US R&B chart (No. 92 on the pop listings). Another song from the same session, "Dancin' All Around the World," was unearthed for the 1971 Little Richard compilation *Mr. Big*, together with a composite version of the single.

West Coast Seattle Boy documents Hendrix's studio stints alongside Don Covay and the Goodtimers ("Mercy Mercy," "Can't Stay Away"), the aforementioned Icemen, Jimmy Noman ("That Little Old Groovemaker") and Billy Lamont ("Sweet Thang"); included, too, are singles recorded with Ray Sharpe ("Help Me (Get the Feeling)"), King Curtis ("Instant Groove"), and Rosa Lee Brooks ("My Diary") during 1965–'66.

Hendrix also worked with actress Jayne Mansfield in late 1965, although his labors were not issued until summer, 1967—"Suey" was the B-side to Mansfield's "As the Clouds Drift By." The session was significant, however, in that it was arranged by Ed Chapin, manager of Curtis Knight and the Squires, with whom Hendrix would spend some time between 1965–'67.

This is the best-documented phase of Hendrix's pre-London career, a prolific period that saw him featured on some sixty-five studio recordings, together with over two hours' worth of live material, apparently recorded at two separate shows in late 1965. This material appeared across a colossal number of releases over the years, prior to

Another 1972 production.

The first official release for Hendrix's oft-circulated Curtis Knight catalog.

the release of *You Can't Use My Name*, beginning with two singles released during 1966, "How Would You Feel" and "Hornet's Nest."

Following Hendrix's breakthrough in 1967, this material began appearing with considerably more regularity. A reissue of "How Would You Feel," with new B-side "You Don't Want Me," was scheduled for release on the UK Decca label in August 1967 before an injunction threatened by Track, Hendrix's current label, saw the release switched to that imprint before any Decca pressings were issued.

Further legal investigation then restored the rights to this material to Decca (Capitol in the US); it also ignited the breach of contract disagreement that would finally be resolved by Hendrix delivering a full album of new material to Capitol, the *Band of Gypsies* live album.

Capitol themselves issued two albums of Hendrix/Knight recordings during 1967–'68, *Get that Feeling* and *Flashing: Jimi Hendrix Plays, Curtis Knight Sings*; the London label, in the meantime, issued a single of "Hush Now" in October, 1967, following through with a British release of *Get that Feeling*; a second collection, *Strange Things;* and a double album apparently issued in the Netherlands only, *The Great Jimi Hendrix in New York.*

All included material recorded both during Knight and Hendrix's original partnership, and in 1967, when the pair reunited for a jam during Hendrix's first "post-stardom" visit to New York. Interest in these releases was low at the time; none offered more than the most rudimentary information and, while Hendrix was indeed present on almost every track released in his name, neither the sound quality nor the performances themselves exactly lived up to the standards the world had come to expect from the guitarist.

By late 1968, both London and Capitol had given up on this archive. Perhaps inevitably, however, London returned to it following Hendrix's death, rushing out the somewhat sensationally titled "The Ballad of Jimi" 45, but defraying the inevitable accusations of opportunistic sensationalism by including (with the German release) a purported copy of the original studio sheet giving the recording date as September 18, 1965.

Knight himself later claimed this possibly premonitory song was composed after Hendrix himself predicted his death earlier that year, although several observers have questioned how Hendrix could have been playing a very audible wah-wah some two years before the effect unit itself was actually available. Another single rushed into production in late 1970 was the now very scarce "No Such Animal," deceptively credited to Hendrix alone, but in reality dating again from the Knight sessions.

Beginning 1970, a number of labels then licensed Knight's Hendrix archive for a succession of releases, many of which continued to draw new and unheard performances from the vault without ever coming close to offering a complete survey of the duo's entire recorded repertoire. Significant among these are the early 1970s UK LPs *What'd I Say/Early Jimi Hendrix* and *Birth of Success*, budget-price releases that introduced the first live recordings to the catalog.

They were followed into this same poorly recorded, but generally entertaining territory by the Ember label's *Early Jimi Hendrix*, *In the Beginning* (complete with added false applause), and *Looking Back with Jimi Hendrix*. These, and several other similar albums were all issued between 1971–'75, and were generally regarded as worth picking up, at least at the time. The bewildering plethora of such albums issued since then, however, has seriously impacted the material's collectibility.

Particularly over the last decade, it has become almost second nature among Hendrix fans to disregard any attempt to repackage the guitarist's pre-fame material, for reasons ranging from the aforementioned lack of concrete information (not to mention Hendrix), to wariness of investing in another fly-by-night budget label's wares, and on to a general weariness with the subject in general.

Hendrix's longtime studio associate Eddie Kramer might have been overly harsh when he described Hendrix's early canon as "crap" in a mid-1990s interview, but he was not too far off the mark either. Though the Hendrix heard on these early recordings, the Isleys material in particular, was already unquestionably a magnificent guitarist, the innovation and inventiveness that became his trademarks are scarcely even hinted at.

Fascinating glimpses into his future are present—from the Knight days, the Beatles' "Day Tripper," the Albert Collins–inspired "Drivin' South," and Howlin' Wolf's "Killin' Floor" would all reappear in the Jimi Hendrix Experience's live repertoire. However, it is also plain that much of the material was either simply a job to be done or, again among the Knight material, a bit of fun laid down while the tape was still rolling.

For the historical record alone, there is a need for this entire period to be compiled together into one cohesive and, most essentially, well-annotated package. Until that time, however, if you're looking for a collecting challenge, and the chance to do some detective work too, welcome to the world of Jimmy Hendrix.

THE BAND(S): TWO SUPERGROUPS TOGETHER— THE STONES AND BEATLES COLLABORATIONS

It's a sign of the sophistication of twenty-first century record collectors and students that one of the greatest scams of the '70s-and-beyond bootleg world really does seem to have disappeared from view today. There was a time when it was the easiest thing in the world to walk into your friendly neighborhood underground LPs emporium, cross the salesman's hand with silver, and shortly thereafter emerge the proud owner of Rock's Most Fabled Beast—an honest-to-goodness, true-as-I'm-standing-here, real life, authenticated Beatles-Stones outtake.

Neither band was any stranger to this particular phenomenon. Indeed, many can claim at some point to have fallen prey to what are generally known as "out-fakes"—that is, recordings that have been credited to them without a shred of evidence that there is any relationship whatsoever. It just happened to the Beatles and the Stones more than most.

Back in 1968, Martin Lewis was a young journalist penning a piece on unreleased Beatles songs for Britain's weekly *Disc and Music Echo* newspaper; and, in those days of minimal research facilities, rapidly running out of song titles to include. So he invented some, and then watched with disbelief as his fiction became accepted as fact across wide swathes of emergent Beatle fandom.

He explained, "At that time, Apple and EMI were denying the existence of any song the Beatles hadn't already released, even things we knew were out there, like 'What's Your New Mary Jane.' So I thought, 'Sod it, they're only going to deny everything anyway, so why don't I just . . . ?'"

The four spurious titles he added to his article were poems he himself had written as a schoolboy. "Atrocious things," he shuddered, but that did not deter him. "Pink Litmus Paper Shirt" he recredited to George Harrison; "Deckchair" to a dream Harrison/Steve Winwood collaboration; "Left Is Right (And Right Is Wrong)" and "Colliding Circles" he gave to John. And for some three decades thereafter, at least two of those titles had become an integral part of Fab Four folklore.

Lewis himself is regarded as one of Beatledom's premier scholars, hosting regular conventions, running several excellent websites, and coordinating marketing for the band's own *Anthology* series in the mid-1990s. Immersed in the world of real Beatle rarities, then, "I really hadn't given the made-up songs a second thought. Then one day I picked up a Beatles discography book, and saw them listed there."

That book was Neil Stannard's *Long and Winding Road*, and the plot only thickened from there. Walter Podrazik's *All Together Now: The First Complete Beatles Discography* was also out there, with the author singling out "Colliding Circles" and "Pink Litmus" for especial veneration; while there was also a 1982 feature in Britain's *Record Collector* magazine that echoed Stannard's description of the same two songs, with profound authority, as *Revolver*-era outtakes.

That same year, "Colliding Circles" itself took on a new life of its own, when it transpired that George (and not John) really had written and demoed a song called "Circles," available in its original form on the Yellow Dog bootleg label's *Unsurpassed Demos*, and then rerecorded by Harrison for 1982's *Gone Troppo* album. Lewis, incidentally, was not aware of Harrison's song when he wrote his original story—"it was pure coincidence."

The bandwagon rumbled on. Serial Beatles author Geoffrey Giuliano utilized three of the titles as chapter headings in one of his books on band rarities; and even today, "Colliding Circles" and "Litmus" can still be found on sundry Beatles websites, where their existence is not only taken for granted, it is actually discussed. (Curiously, says Lewis, those two songs are the ones which seem to have stuck the fastest, leaving the true completists alone to search out "Deckchair," and the supremely Bolshy Lennony–titled "Left Is Right.")

But how long could the joke survive? "When Mark Lewisohn's book [*The Beatles Recording Sessions*] came out," Lewis admitted, "I knew I was finished. 'Oh damn, anybody who believed it before is never going to now.'"

Facts, however, rarely get in the way of a good piece of fiction. Lewisohn, after all, listed only the songs that the Beatles took into Abbey Road studios. Countless more exist as simple home-recorded fragments, as scraps of paper in Paul McCartney's bottom drawer, or as song titles alone, copyrighted by the band in the early-mid 1960s, and maybe never taken anywhere after that.

Lewis continues, "When I was researching the discography for Hunter Davies' book [1968's authorized *The Beatles*], I was given carte blanche to go through the files at Dick James Music, this huge card system, where every title the Beatles registered was listed. "The cards themselves probably don't even exist any more, but I got all the lists of all the song titles, and we know a lot of them were never recorded, or were very early working titles for other songs, and so on. Obviously, a lot of these never got into the studio, so Mark Lewisohn

Mick Jagger's CD best-of included the first official release of his Lennon collaboration "Too Many Cooks."

wouldn't have included them. But they did exist in some form or another . . . " and enough of them are known to the public today, that what did a couple more matter in the greater scheme of things?

They mattered a lot, Lewis learned. "I've already had one person ask, 'Who is Martin Lewis, and what does he know about it anyway?' and others who've been very defensive about these songs, who tell me they actually know people who've heard the songs themselves. Which is weird, because I wrote them, and I still don't know what they sound like."

This story is instructive in many ways. Forget Martin Lewis's status as a Beatles expert. Paul McCartney, too, has described, incredulously, encounters during which his own personal memories of events are flatly contradicted by fans who either read, or concocted, an alternate scenario, and refuse to accept his version, even though he's the one the story is about. Authors, too, and biographers in particular, can likewise tell tales of being taken to task for getting things wrong, after publishing firsthand accounts of the events being written about. Their critics, it seems, would rather believe that the speaker—a person that they might have spent their entire lifetime obsessing over—is either extremely forgetful, or an outright liar, than countenance the possibility of their own beliefs being contradicted.

On this particular occasion, we were assured, there was no question about what we were hearing. Erase the hiss of the tenth-generation tape, strain your ears round the clicks, pops, and crackles, and there they were—John, Bill, George, Mick, Charlie, Keith, Brian, Ringo, Paul, and Stu wrapping dulcet tones and unmistakable chops around a crop of songs that really were as good as they ought to have been.

Even the song titles were unmatchable gems—"Shades of Orange," "Loving, Sacred Loving," "Too Many Cooks"—and you'd sit there with your copy of *When Two Legends Collide*, the Tuna label's bootleg bonanza of precisely what its title claimed, utterly oblivious to the fact that, a few years down the road, you'd be buying at least two of the same songs once again, in the belief that someone had finally dug out some long-lost Brian Jones compositions . . . and again, a few years later, when they turned out to be by The End, a Bill Wyman production from the late 1960s that was finally reissued in the late 1980s.

Both "Shades of Orange" and "Loving, Sacred Loving" have been classified as out-fakes (see previous chapter) ever since, and don't you feel silly for falling for that? "Too Many Cooks" has a slightly more authentic pedigree, in that it at least features Messrs Lennon and Jagger. But it dates from just before Christmas 1973, when Jagger dropped by a Harry Nilsson session that Lennon was producing at the Record Plant West, and it really isn't that hot. Indeed, when an unauthenticated acetate of the performance (on which Jagger alone is audible; Lennon merely produced) turned up at a London auction in February, bidding stalled at just 1,400—a far cry from the 10,000 estimate that the auction house itself placed upon it. And when the track finally turned up as an authorized release, on 2007's *Very Best of Mick Jagger*, it scarcely merited a second glance.

And that's because collectors had long since moved on, to dream now about the couple of other songs that the pair recorded that merry evening—a version of "Hey Paula," with Lennon and Jagger trading off the lyrics, and substituting one another's names for the song's originals, and a version of Sam Cooke's "Bring It On Home to Me."

Because with those, the subject of further undiscovered Beatles/Stones collaborations is officially closed. Instead, the world has finally come to believe what the Stones and the Beatles themselves said all along. They did very little recording together, and what there was has all been released. And you probably already own it all.

The relationship between the Beatles and the Stones dates back to the earliest days of the latter's lifetime—Beatle George was among their earliest admirers, catching the band for the first time at the Crawdaddy on April 14, 1963, and later recalling, "it was a real rave.

The Beatles' "Baby You're a Rich Man" with added sax from Stone Brian Jones.

The audience shouted and screamed and danced on the tables. The beat the Stones laid down was so solid it shook off the walls and seemed to move right inside your head. A great sound!"

Days later, acting on a tip from a journalist friend, the Fabs' London press agent Andrew Loog Oldham caught the Stones for himself at the Station Hotel and was similarly impressed—more so, in fact. By the end of the following week, Oldham was installed as the nascent band's manager, a role he would ultimately retain for the next four years. Still it was pure serendipity that placed John Lennon and Paul McCartney in a London cab inching down Tottenham Court Road just as Oldham walked out of the Stones' latest rehearsal session, frustrated at the group's inability to come up with a song suitable to become their all-important second single.

Gazing out of the taxi's window, the pair spotted him—and spotted his dark mood as well. Oldham recalls, "I explained that I had nothing to record for the Stones' next single. They smiled at me and each other, told me not to worry . . . " and, within minutes, "the boys got to work teaching the Stones 'I Wanna Be Your Man'."

Period Stones associate James Phelge continues, "the band was in between numbers . . . when in walked Andrew. At first glance it looked as if he had two well-heeled businessmen in dark coats and suits following behind. The pair was, in fact, John Lennon and Paul McCartney.

"The few privileged onlookers watched with surprise as the two Beatles and the Stones greeted each other like old friends. With Paul looking on, John explained that they had a song they'd written for themselves, but not yet recorded. They would be happy to let the Stones record it instead as a single, if they were interested."

Of course they were. Phelge reckons it took no more than twenty minutes for the band to nail the song, twisting the Beatles' dynamics

Sam Cooke

Encore Volumes 1–3 (KEEN 2006-08, EPS, PICTURE SLEEVES, 1958)

"Forever," Dale Cooke (SPECIALTY 596, 7-INCH, 1957)

"I'll Come Running Back to You" (SPECIALTY 619, 7-INCH, 1957)

I Thank God (KEEN 86103, LP, 1960)

Sam Cooke (KEEN A2001, LP, 1958)

Songs by Sam Cooke Volumes 1–3 (KEEN 2001-03, EPS, PICTURE SLEEVES, 1958)

"Stealing Kisses" (KEEN 2005, 7-INCH, 78, 1958)

"Teenage Sonata" (RCA VICTOR 47-7701, 7-INCH, 1960)

Tribute to the Lady Volumes 1–3 (KEEN 2012-14, EPS, PICTURE SLEEVES, 1959)

The Wonderful World Of (KEEN 86106, LP, 1960)

to their own ends while the writers looked on, smiling as Brian Jones added a wild slide guitar to the brew, and leaving Oldham content in the knowledge that this next record was going to make the Stones' debut, "Come On," "sound limp by comparison. The force of the title and the writers would demand attention, and the power of the collaboration and execution of the same would guarantee the hit."

Lennon, in later years, was somewhat less magnanimous about the entire affair. He told *Playboy*, "'I Wanna Be Your Man' was a kind of lick Paul had . . . it was a throwaway. The only two versions of the song were Ringo [who performed it on the Beatles' next album, the UK *With the Beatles*] and the Rolling Stones. That shows how much importance we put on it. We weren't gonna give them anything *great*, right?"

National Lampoon excerpted further Lennon-ian musings on the subject for the classic "Magical Misery Tour," the remarkable parody featured on the comedy troupe's *Radio Dinner* album. "Where does [Mick Jagger] come off saying all those tarty things about the Beatles when every fokkin' thing we ever did he tried to copy . . . you know we even wrote his second fokkin' record for him . . . ." Wonderful stuff!

Lennon's retrospective misgivings notwithstanding, "I Wanna Be Your Man" reached No. 12 on the UK chart in November 1963, confirming the ascendancy of the Stones, even if the band themselves weren't yet ready to take the Beatles on at their own game. That would come the following year, once Mick Jagger and Keith Richard inaugurated the songwriting partnership that would swiftly prove just as prolific as (and ultimately far longer-lived than) Lennon/McCartney's. They would not be needing Beatles castoffs ever again.

But the two bands remained close regardless, in the eyes of the media that loved nothing so much as a good, old-fashioned feud between the clean-cut Fabs and the scruffy, long-haired Yobs; and in their own private circles as well. Members of the two bands frequently socialized around London—the Ad Lib in Leicester Square was one favorite hangout; later, as the city settled deeper into its role as the swinging-est metropolis on the planet, the party shifted to the Bag O' Nails and the Scotch of St. James, exclusive niteries that, some nights, boasted so many pop celebrities, it was as though the room was physically wallpapered with them.

The confines of the recording studio, however, remained sacrosanct so far as Beatles and Stones alike were concerned. Under the watchful gaze of, respectively, producers George Martin and Andrew Oldham, even family and friends had a hard time just "hanging out" while the groups were working. Rival pop stars were right out. It would be four more years, then, before the two groups again witnessed one another in the act of actual creation, although once the ice had been broken, it seemed as though it might never be repaired.

On February 10, 1967, Mick Jagger, Keith Richards, and Brian Jones joined sundry other Beatle-people at Abbey Road's Studio One, to watch George Martin and Paul McCartney put the finishing touches to "A Day in the Life"—by conducting a symphony orchestra through one of the most unusual pieces they had ever been commissioned to play, a twenty-four bar free-form chord that began at the lowest possible note of every instrument, and rose to the highest.

As an example of the sheer ingenuity that was now the Beatles' to command, merely watching the session was an inspirational experience—one that would, of course, soon be resonating within the Stones' own work. Few observers (or even participants) deny that the band's next album, *Their Satanic Majesties Request*, was written and recorded almost wholly in the shadow of the Liverpudlians' *Sgt. Pepper*. Before those sessions even began, however, the two bands would interact on at least three further occasions.

On May 11, the Beatles abandoned their customary haunt at Abbey Road Studios and shifted instead to Olympic—the Stones' own most-favored base—to record "Baby, You're a Rich Man." Hardly surprisingly, the Stones were also around, and twenty-one years later, during his marathon exhumation of the Beatles' recorded archive, researcher Mark Lewisohn discovered a brief notation on one of the two tape boxes that documented the evening's recording and mixing: "The Beatles + Mick Jagger?"

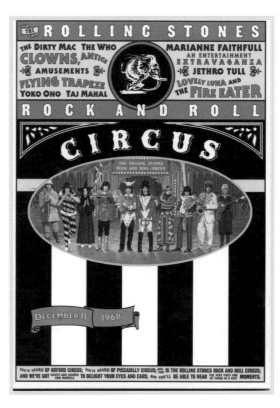

The Stones' Rock and Roll Circus *extravaganza comes to DVD.*

One of the myriad bootlegs offering up something that really didn't exist.

"Jagger did attend the session," Lewisohn confirms. "It is feasible that he sang backing vocals in the free-for-all choruses near the end of the song."

Considerably better documented are the events of June 8, and the next union of the two supergroups. Back at Abbey Road, that night saw the Beatles' latest session joined by Brian Jones. Paul McCartney had invited him along, but remembers being very surprised to discover that Jones had not arrived unarmed. "He brought along a sax. I remember him turning up in this big Afghan coat at Abbey Road and he opened up a sax case."

Never wanting to be caught by surprise on their own turf, the Beatles swiftly put their guest to good use. "We said, 'We've got a little track here . . . '." Over the past couple of nights, the Beatles had been working on what even they regarded as a "crazy" number, a somewhat disjointed and certainly discordant Lennon composition/comedy routine called "You Know My Name (Look Up the Number)." The Beatles had already added flute, organ, and tambourine to the piece; that night's schedule included overdubbing vibraphone, bongos,

harmonica, and bird whistles. Why not an alto sax as well? "It's a funny sax solo," McCartney continued. "It isn't amazingly well-played, but it happened to be exactly what we wanted, a ropey sax, kind of shaky. Brian was very good like that."

Sadly, Jones would not live to see the fruits of his work released—"You Know My Name" would remain on the shelf for another three years, before finally appearing as the B-side to what proved to be the Beatles' final single, "Let It Be." Alongside Jagger and Richard, however, Jones would take his place within the iconography that surrounds the Beatles' very next 45, lining up among the myriad guests invited to participate in the group's *Our World* telecast, singing along to the world premier of "All You Need Is Love." The trio are, of course, indistinguishable from any of the other voices on the recording, but all three were visible in the telecast—a presence, incredibly, that we are fortunate to be able to view at all.

The Stones were now laboring within the painfully protracted aftermath of Jagger and Richard's so-highly publicized Redlands drug bust back in February. The trial itself was still some three weeks away, but the British media seemed already to have delivered its verdict on the duo, with the BBC—as broadcasters of the telecast—grimly debating whether such notorious fiends should even be glimpsed by the cameras.

Less censorious heads ultimately prevailed, and the broadcast went ahead with the pair in full view. But, as the Stones set to work on their own next single the following week, it was in the knowledge that not only might it be their last, it would also need to run the gamut of BBC approval to have even a hope of radio airplay.

They'd better make it a good one, then, and the plain truth is, they did. Indeed, "We Love You" can be considered the very last of the Stones' truly *great* singles, a *tour de force* of studio trickery, psychedelic effects and electrifying harmonics that sums up all the hopes and fears of that tempestuous summer without ever making reference to one of them.

Yet the Stones knew that the scales of justice were heavily weighted against them and, just two weeks after the basics of "We Love You" were recorded, the court handed down sentences that only lent conclusive credence to the duo's convictions. For drug offenses that would normally have merited little more than a judicial slap on the wrist, Richard was given twelve months, Jagger three.

Released on bail pending the inevitable (and ultimately successful) appeals, the band quickly returned to Olympic to complete "We Love You," with both Lennon and McCartney dropping by to add backing vocals to the proceedings. Andrew Oldham, himself undertaking his final Stones production, recalled, "You have to know this about the twin Moptops. They never let love and peace bring or slow them down."

While other bands—his own charges among them—let the psychedelic mood of the day clog the creative process to Quaalude slow-mo, Lennon and McCartney remained a hive of intuitive energy and instinct. "[They] didn't listen to the 'We Love You' track for much longer than they'd spent running down 'I Wanna Be Your Man.' They picked up the cans and sniffed each other out like two dogs in heat for the right part. Harmonic results from the Stones were, for the most part, either 'interesting' or the result of hard work. John and Paul just glided in and changed a runway into an aeroplane with wings. I'd just seen and heard a fuckin' miracle."

He had also overseen the last occasion upon which the Beatles and the Stones would unite on record. Although rumor insists that the pair also lent some tonsil to "Sing this Altogether," a track destined for the forthcoming *Satanic Majesties* album, nobody has ever seen fit to corroborate the suggestion—and why should they? It probably didn't happen.

The two bands' paths would continue to cross, of course. Brian Jones' saxophone reappeared briefly during the McCartney-produced sessions for Mike McGear and Roger McGough's 1968 album, while Lennon and Richards would share a stage at the Stones' Rock and Roll Circus, members of the crowd-thrilling supergroup that turned in an all-time definitive version of the White Album's brittle "Yer Blues."

But hopes for any further interaction between the two greatest bands of the British Sixties were destined to remain in fluffy cloud cuckoo-land, a wondrous place where the most whimsical whisper can be distorted as fact, and wishful thinking butters parsnips for all. Such as the report, in the British *People* newspaper, on October 15, 1967, which announced that the Beatles and the Rolling Stones were intending to go into business together. Already, the story said, they were "looking for new studios in London, probably to record unknown pop groups. And they may make films together." But there was, the story reassuringly concluded, "no question of the two pop groups merging."

Well, at least they got that bit right.

THE THEME: EVERY DAY IS HALLOWEEN

For whatever reason, few holidays offer up anywhere near as many musical possibilities as a Christmas collection (see "The Guilty Pleasure," below)—you could maybe fill a blank CD with the songs that celebrate New Year, Easter, Hanukah, Kwanza, Guy Fawkes Night, and Independence Day. And, on first inspection, Halloween doesn't seem to offer that many more possibilities: "Monster Mash," "Spooky," Marilyn Manson's "This Is Halloween," Dead or Alive's "Something In My House"—there are others, but every time All Saints Eve rolls around, and one dives onto the internet in search of the season's most suitable songs, you wind up with a bunch that have nothing more in common with creepiness than their titles.

LA witch Louise Huebner's Seduction Through Witchcraft *blends spellbinding philosophy with dramatic electronics.*

Norman Greenbaum's "Spirit in the Sky" is *not* a song about ghosts. The Cranberries' "Zombie" is *not* about the living dead. And the *Rocky Horror Picture Show*'s "Time Warp" only makes sense in this context if you've seen the movie, and even then it's debatable. Do the people who make these lists even *listen* to the songs?

Cross everything you first thought of off the wants list and begin again.

Because Halloween does serve up a wealth of collecting (and collectible) possibilities, even if one utterly boycotts those songs that simply happen to mention ghosts, ghouls, and unnamable somethings—or even namable ones: cue a chorus of "Flying Purple People Eater" here, followed by Marc Almond's "This House Is Haunted," and Godley-Creme's "Under Your Thumb."

In fact, a number of records, both singles and albums, have been released that take a somewhat more sober look at the holiday's occult inspirations; records that range from live recordings of Wiccan initiations, through to full-blown Satanic masses. Many of these are excruciatingly difficult to find today, with one of the most challenging dating from as recently as 2011, albeit in a limited edition of around 200 vinyl copies (some sources say 205).

The various artists collection *Do What Thou Wilt: The Satanic Rites of British Rock 1970–1974* was itself the first ever modern repository for a host of private pressings and acetates recorded during that timespan by such utterly unknown hard rock and heavy metal acts as Tonge, Shado, Grind, Wooden Lion, Pony, Heatwave, Yellow, and Unicorn; plus one at least relatively well known mega-rarity in the form of Lucifer's "Fuck You" single.

Released in a hand painted sleeve with a xeroxed booklet, *Do What Thou Wilt* was titled from what is probably Aleister Crowley's best known quote—Crowley himself being the self-styled "wickedest man in Britain," a constant delight for sensationalist journalism and

Barbara the Gray Witch's so-scarce collection of music and magic.

(barely remembered among all the other legends), author of some of the most significant occult writings of the last century-plus. He also penned an often-hilarious column for early issues of *Vanity Fair* magazine.

But he is also the quavering, and distinctly *un*wicked-sounding voice that can be heard behind the crackling on a series of LPs and CDs released under a variety of titles over the past thirty years (*The Great Beast Speaks*, *Live Rituals and Chants,* and, again, *Do What Thou Wilt* among them). Originally recorded on a series of wax cylinders between 1910–1914, and then transferred to 78 rpm acetates, the sound quality is dire; so much so that Crowley's exact words can often be difficult to make out. The recordings are not especially rare, with new CD versions appearing on a fairly regular basis. However, the original cylinders are probably unique; while even the earliest British vinyl pressings, dating from the mid-1980s, can prove expensive—the unlabeled *Aleister Crowley* and the Goetia label's *The Hastings Archive* (catalog number 666, in case you wondered).

Many listeners will admit that a few minutes of Crowley's voice are all they can reasonably take, in which case a CD compilation dating from 2015, the Cleopatra label's *The Occult Box*, should satisfy most—alongside five CDs' worth of atmosphere, mood, and magic from the likes of Joy Division, Rozz Williams, Switchblade Symphony, and more, the package also includes a bonus Aleister Crowley 45.

The "golden age" of what we might call occult vinyl was the late 1960s and early 1970s, when

Joy Division

"Atmosphere" (SORDIDE SENTIMENTALE 33002, 7-INCH, 1980)

Closer (FACTORY FACT 25, LP WITH TEXTURED SLEEVE, 1980)

A Factory Sample, Various artists (FACTORY FAC 2, DOUBLE 7-INCH PACK EP WITH FIVE STICKERS, 1979)

The Ideal Beginning (ENIGMA PSS 138, 12-INCH EP, 1981)

"An Ideal for Living" (ANONYMOUS ANON 1, 12-INCH REISSUE, 1978)

"An Ideal for Living" (ENIGMA PSS 139, EP WITH FOLD-OUT PICTURE SLEEVE, 1978)

"Komakino" (FACTORY FAC 28, FLEXIDISC, 1980)

Short Circuit, Live at the Electric Circus, Various artists
(VIRGIN VCL 5003, 10-INCH EP; ORANGE, YELLOW, OR BLUE VINYL, 1978)

Still (FACTORY FACT 40, 2-LP WITH HESSIAN SLEEVE, RIBBON, 1981)

Unknown Pleasures (FACTORY FACT 10, LP WITH TEXTURED SLEEVE, 1979)

it emerged from the psychedelic underground as a corollary (logical or otherwise) to the ongoing drive into transcendental meditation. Viewed in both political and cultural terms, it was a timely intervention—the world *was* becoming darker and, for many people, the Rolling Stones exemplified the mood with the one-two punch of 1968's "Sympathy for the Devil" and "Jumping Jack Flash."

But there was more. In 1968, William Burroughs recorded a seventy-minute narrative track for a reissue of the 1922 Scandinavian silent movie *Haxan: Witchcraft Through the Ages.* (It is now available on CD.) Aleister Crowley peers out from among the faces on the Beatles' *Sergeant Pepper's Lonely Hearts Club Band.* The Crazy World of Arthur Brown earned a No. 1 hit with an invocation of the God of Hellfire; British blues legend Graham Bond revealed himself as a loudly practicing occultist who revealed all on his 1970 album *Holy Magick.* Led Zeppelin's Jimmy Page not only lived in Crowley's old house, he also soundtracked director Kenneth Anger's *Lucifer Rising* movie. Barbara, The Gray Witch released a fabulous double album, featuring twenty fabulously atmospheric chants and songs. A Detroit practitioner, Gundella, conjured *The Hour of the Witch*—an album's worth of spells and charms derived, she said, from the green witches of Scotland, from whom she was descended. And actor Vincent Price narrated a double album's worth of occult history across *Witchcraft - Magic: An Adventure in Demonology.* All attracting high prices on the collectors' market.

Across the western world, interest in the occult was soaring; in the movies, in publishing, in art, and in music. Black Sabbath—for many, the very epitome of "occult rock"—admitted they took a great

The tale of the 1612 Pendle witch trials, exquisitely performed by ERC and actress Maxine Peake.

swathe of their inspiration from watching the crowds pour into the cinema to watch a newly released horror movie. If people were willing to pay good money to be scared by a film, what would they pay to be scared by a record?

Sabbath frontman Ozzy Osbourne later insisted that the closest his bandmates ever came to the Dark Arts was a box of chocolates (Black Magic was a popular British confectionary), but neither band nor, as a solo performer through the 1980s and beyond, Osbourne himself ever truly distanced themselves from the howling winds, tolling bells, and doomwatch guitar chords that marked out their entry into the music scene in 1970.

And where Sabbath led, others quickly followed. Indeed, even more dramatic than the Sabs were Coven, an American outfit whose 1969 LP *Witchcraft Destroys Minds and Reaps Souls* featured a sidelong Satanic mass, and was withdrawn from sale in the US after an *Esquire* magazine article on Satanism highlighted the album's existence (it has since been reissued), although that, too, is growing increasingly hard to find).

Enthralling, too, were Black Widow, a band whose theatrical dreams soared so high that they even approached the self-styled King and Queen of British witches, Alex and Maxine Sanders, to help them choreograph a projected Satanic opera, a musical spectacular titled *Sacrifice.* Staged in its entirety on only a handful of occasions, but recorded for release as 1970's *Sacrifice* LP, the project remains one of the crucial albums of its age, not only as a musical accomplishment, but also for its cultural resonance.

Witchcraft itself had only been legal in the UK for a matter of fifteen or so years; in the eyes of the tabloid press, it was still the domain of the twisted, sick, and perverted. The idea that any band could even compose, let alone release such a record on a major label (CBS in the

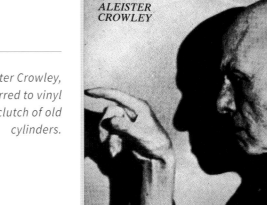

Aleister Crowley, transferred to vinyl from a clutch of old cylinders.

UK, United Artists in America), was almost inconceivable—as were the predictions in sundry reviews that the spin-off 45, "Come to the Sabbat," was a surefire tip for the top of the UK charts.

Slapped with an outright ban by the broadcast monopoly of the BBC, both album and single ultimately foundered. But the forces that Black Widow marshaled, and that Black Sabbath (in the face of equally fierce opposition, but considerably less censorship) exemplified, would only grow more powerful, and fascinating.

Alex Sanders followed up his dalliance with Black Widow by releasing a record of his own. *A Witch Is Born* appeared in 1970, a vérité recording of an actual Wiccan rite, frank and unforgettable (although the random slabs of classical music that were dubbed behind the rites are unnecessary), with Maxine's rendering of "The Charge of the Goddess" (here retitled "the *Legend* . . . ") a truly dramatic performance. Furthermore, readers of the Sanders' best-known student, author Janet Bord, can hear her receiving her initiation into the faith across one whole side of the album.

There was further instruction to be gleaned from *Seduction Through Witchcraft,* a 1969 spoken-word album that pairs electro whizz Bebe Barron and Los Angeles occultist Louise Huebner across an album that is as discomforting as it's delicious. But you'll only know that if you own a copy, and that's a lot harder to accomplish without resorting to the modern reissue market.

Beyond its original target audience, most people encountered *Seduction Through Witchcraft* for the first time courtesy of David Bowie's *His Master's Voice* bootleg, where excerpts from a couple of tracks were spliced into an off-air recording of ABC TV's broadcast of Ziggy's 1973 farewell concert. Why was it there? Who knows. For atmosphere, maybe. No matter; super-spacey synthy mystery music, and a dark, seductive voice intoning the correct conditions under which to stage an orgy seemed to blend perfectly with Bowie's Ziggy-era message. *Seduction Through Witchcraft* was an electronic psychedelic guide to getting it on with magic, and it's exquisite in every way, from the cover shot of Huebner smoldering out from that arterial blood-red background, onto a musical soundscape that could almost double as an electric storm in Hell.

Which just happens to be the title of the final track on another of 1969's most disquieting releases, *An Electric Storm* by White Noise (Island Records)—an experimental electronics outfit formed by a couple of members of the BBC Radiophonic Workshop, Delia Derbyshire and Brian Hodgson, and American classical musician David Vorhaus.

It is Derbyshire's involvement that establishes this album's status among the era's most wanted—best known, perhaps, for creating the distinctive theme to television's *Doctor Who* (itself an incredibly

innovative work in its original form), she also rates among the most visionary electronic musicians of the age. And the most disconcerting; White Noise revel in the connotations of their name, soundtracking nightmares that have yet to be dreamed. And its closing "Black Mass: An Electric Storm in Hell" is only the most overtly named.

From sonic madness to an oasis of calm: Rosemary Brown was a London housewife and medium who, according to her own testimony, was awoken one night by the ghost of Franz Liszt and, beginning in 1964, became the conduit for both his "latest" compositions, and those of a slew of other deceased classical legends. Debussy, Brahms, Bach, Rachmaninoff, Schubert, Chopin, Grieg, Beethoven, Mozart, and Liszt all flocked to Brown's unassuming London home to dictate music, which Brown—by her own confession, a very unaccomplished pianist—would painstakingly take down.

Her claims, perhaps unsurprisingly, found few supporters within the world of classical experts. But 1970 saw Philips, one of Europe's leading classical labels, release a full album of "her" music, as played by both Brown and pianist Peter Katin, and titled *A Musical Seance*. An enclosed booklet gives the album's background, and the first track on side two has Brown detailing her encounters in her own words. It's a remarkable story . . . and the music's not bad, either.

Brown (together with Huebner, Crowley, and Black Widow) is also a featured performer on what we can only describe as the ultimate spooky sampler album, author and researcher Nat Freedland's 1973 collection *The Occult Explosion*.

A companion to the book of the same name, also featuring excerpts from recordings by Anton LaVey, the founder of the Church of Satan; UFOlogist Stanton T. Friedman; and yoga instructor Indra Devi, it's a lavishly presented double album, loaded with reading

Question Mark and the Mysterians

Action (CAMEO C2006, MONO LP, 1967)

"Can't Get Enough of You Baby" (CAMEO 467, 7-INCH, 1967)

"Funky Lady" (LUV 159, 7-INCH, 1975)

"Girl" (CAMEO 479, 7-INCH, 1967)

"Hang In" (SUPER K 102, 7-INCH, 1969)

"I Need Somebody" (CAMEO 441, 7-INCH, 1966)

"Make You Mine" (CAPITOL 2162, 7-INCH, 1970)

96 Tears (CAMEO C2004, MONO LP, 1966)

"96 Tears" (PA-GO-GO 102, 7-INCH, 1965)

"Talk Is Cheap" (CHICORY 410, 7-INCH, 1968)

material, and a magnificent summary of the field, one-stop shopping for the butterfly Fortean.

But, of course, it merely scraped the tip of the iceberg.

An entire genre of occult folk grew (and continues to grow) as the decade moved on, much of it inspired by what was ranked among the most in-demand movie soundtracks of all time, Paul Giovanni's soundtrack to the legendary horror epic *The Wicker Man.*

Unreleased in its own right until 2002, both the songs and the spirit of the movie nevertheless became a veritable touchstone for successive generations of performers, with the Swedish duo Us and Them delivering perhaps the most glorious tribute in the shape of 2011's *Summerisle* EP, and its chilling recreations of four of the soundtrack's best-loved songs.

Another movie to take a remarkable hold upon the musical imagination was *Quatermass and the Pit*, a late '60s Hammer Studios remake of a decade-old BBC production in which evidence of mankind's earliest beliefs are uncovered during building work at a London underground railroad station. This itself was a chilling visualization of a prophesy delivered in 1860 by "the Reverend Doctor John Cumming: "The forthcoming end of the world will be hastened by the construction of underground railways burrowing into infernal regions and thereby disturbing the Devil.""

Scottish-based psychogeographer Drew Mulholland, under his Mount Vernon Arts Lab pseudonym, revisited these fears in 2001 to record *The Seance at Hob's End*, an album of stark sound and fission whose rapid disappearance at the time was remedied by a reissue on the Ghost Box label in 2015. Indeed, Ghost Box itself can be considered something of a trailblazer within these realms.

Asked to sum up Ghost Box's overall output, cofounder Jim Jupp explains, "The music is largely, although not entirely, electronic, and mainly instrumental (though increasingly less so). Its artists share influences in library music, TV soundtracks, vintage electronics, folk music, weird fiction, and forgotten films and TV shows. We think of it as a kind of world where pop culture from the mid-'60s up to the early eighties is happening all at once, in a kind of parallel world. Not historically accurate, but naggingly familiar."

Those musical moments from horror movies that ensure you jump in the right place; the background music to old public information films; children's TV themes and old radio sound effects—back in 2004, when Jupp (who records as Belbury Poly) and partner Julian House (aka the Focus Group) launched the label, this was largely untapped territory.

The likes of Current 93 and Broadcast were moving in that direction, and probably remain the grandparents of it all. But "Hauntology," as the labelers labeled the emergent sound, had still a long way to go before even tapping its full potential, and Ghost Box has remained at the forefront, both in the UK (where its primary sources and influences certainly lie) and elsewhere.

"I guess this strange old British stuff comes over as more exotic or just plain weird," says Jupp. "But it seems to strike a chord anyway—particularly in America where we have our biggest audience outside of the UK (even more than any other European country)."

The discography is deliciously streamlined: the Other Voices and Study Series of 45s, and a succession of albums that are as varied as the sources that can be said to have inspired them. For even a blanket summary of Hauntology's contents can only go so far.

A pinch of Delia Derbyshire and the aforementioned White Noise LP is a touchstone that many commentators eventually arrive at, but don't stop there because the most haunting Hauntology draws its imagery from everywhere—imagine a movie that has never been made, but is built around every scene you've ever seen that made you laugh, cry, scream, or hide. Then conjure the sounds that every still image feels like and, across releases by Belbury and the Focus Group, Eric Zan and the Advisory Circle, Roj (ex-Broadcast) and Pye Corner Audio, Hintermass, Jonny Trunk, former Ultravox mainstay John Foxx, and Broadcast, the label has cornered what Jupp laughingly describes as "ahem . . . mature record collecting types into soundtracks, vintage electronics and obscure psych or prog and weird old TV programs.

"They're also a fairly literate and academic bunch, judging by the number of interview requests we get from research students writing about Hauntology or Retromania." It was a slow process. Early releases were CD-R only, with manufactured discs following once an audience started not only to swell, but also to prove loyal—a process aided immeasurably by the label's own sense of identity. "We've always put a lot of time and effort into our artwork and concepts. The visual identity of the label wears its references on its sleeve (even if they are a little obscure sometimes) so I guess that helps drag in the right audience."

For the most part, the recordings are Ghost Box's sole interaction with audiences, and that too plays a part in the overall mythos. "Our artists don't do much live performance, and are happy to remain fairly anonymous. So the label acts as a kind of identity for everyone—getting equal billing to the performer name.

"Effectively, we're a small collective of very like minded artists that work on solo projects and often collaborate [although] we also have occasional guests like the Soundcarriers and the Pattern Forms who are more like regular bands. The main thing is, though, that everyone understands and fits into the Ghost Box aesthetic."

Equally enterprising in these waters are the likes of the Mortlake Book Club, Soul Party, and absolutely anything touched by A Year in the Country, the label and website whose series of *Audiological Transmission* CDs, downloads, and most recently, a book have been transfixing listeners since 2014.

Neither is A Year in the Country averse to venturing deeper into the realms of more traditional Halloween. From a 2015 single by London singer-songwriter She Rocola, "Molly Leigh of the Mother Town" is the kind of nursery rhyme you never learned at your mother's knee, but which buried itself in your memory regardless, to peer out of the soil while you're hopscotching past, and wrap bony fingers round your ankle. The other, "Burn the Witch," is freakish fiddles (by Andrea Fiorito) that scratch behind She's icy vocal and spectral harmonies, a Hammer film condensed to two minutes of sound and effects.

And if all of that's not enough, the memorials staged around the 2012 anniversary of Britain's Pendle Witch Trials (1612) produced a veritable concept album by the Eccentronic Research Council, *1612 Underture*. A twelve-chapter sound poem, fantastically voiced by actress Maxine Peake, it describes itself as "One part political commentary and feminist manifesto and two parts theatrical fakeloric sound poem," which may or may not lure in the unsuspecting listener. But from its Kraftwerkian opening, through to the almost childlike chorus of "Another Witch is Dead" at the end, *1612 Underture* is utterly riveting. Your Halloweens, not to mention your record collection, will never sound the same again.

THE FIFTIES: IT WASN'T ALL ROCK 'N' ROLL

Looking back on his childhood, Rolling Stones bassist Bill Wyman shudders at what passed for light entertainment. "I was nine when [World War Two] ended, I was thirteen in 1949, I was fifteen in 1951, and rock 'n' roll just wasn't around. When I was in my teens, my early teens, there weren't bands. Rock 'n' roll hadn't been invented, skiffle wasn't even around. It was dance bands, dance music by Benny Goodman, Glen Miller and all that lot.

"There wasn't pop music; pop music was sung by very ordinary, horrible people in evening clothes, that copied American hits . . . and it was bloody awful."

Britain, in the years before rock 'n' roll came along, is often regarded as a wasteland today, and anyone who lived through it seems more

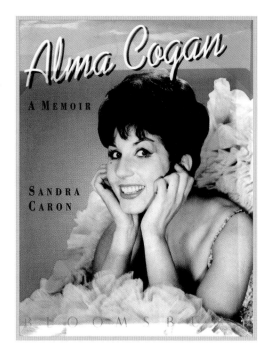

Alma Cogan's life story, as told by her sister.

than happy to perpetuate that belief. The first record Wyman ever bought was a 78 of Les Paul and Mary Ford's "The World Is Waiting for the Sunrise," and he still remembers rushing home to play it on the family's wind-up record player. "Johnny Ray was the first singer I saw who had a bit of balls. I saw him at the London Palladium on my grandmother's television; the kids tore his trousers off, and that was the first time I ever saw fans attack someone on stage.

"But all the rest of it was dance bands, from my first memories of music, what I heard on my aunt's radio, or my gran's radio. There was no scene." What there was, was a sense of futility. For Wyman, and for the generation born immediately after him, the one that was conceived while German bombs rained down on British cities, and young marrieds snatched just a few days together before the men folk went back to the battle, life was simply something that was laid out before you, cold, gray, and immutable.

Ramsey Lewis

Down to Earth (MERCURY SR 60536, STEREO LP, 1965)

Gentlemen of Jazz (ARGO 627S, STEREO LP, 1959)

Gentlemen of Swing (ARGO 611S, STEREO LP, 1959)

Hang on Ramsey! (CADET LPS 761, STEREO LP, 1966)

"Hi Heel Sneakers" (CADET 5531, 7-INCH, 1966)

"Just Can't Give You Up" (COLUMBIA 10937, 12-INCH SINGLE, 1979)

"Santa Claus is Coming to Town" (CADET 5377, 7-INCH, 1966)

Sound of Christmas (ARGO EP 1084, EP, 1961)

The "In" Crowd (CADET LPS 757 WITH ARGO LABEL, LP, 1965)

Upendo Ni Pamoja (COLUMBIA CQ 31096, QUAD LP, 1972)

You accepted what you were offered because there was no alternative. Adolescence stretched out like a looming no-man's land, the final rite of passage before you stepped into your father's shoes and followed him to the office . . . to the shop . . . but first, two years serving in the armed forces.

National Service, the compulsory induction of every able-bodied school-leaver into one of Her Majesty's Armed Forces, was introduced in 1948, in part to halt a massive upsurge in juvenile crime in the immediate postwar period and in part to ensure that Britain, so unprepared for Hitler in 1939, would never be caught napping again. When the United Nations waded into Korea in 1951, National Servicemen supplied nearly sixty percent of Britain's infantry force; when Britain marched into Egypt in 1956, the conscripts were in the frontline again. Everywhere that Britannia was perceived to be under threat, a fresh crop of eighteen-year-old boys was draped in green and dispatched to duty to serve their nation—with their blood if they had to. And, like the rest of their impending adult existence, there was very little they could do to prevent, or even postpone, it.

From 1956, Cogan's version of movie hit "The Birds and the Bees."

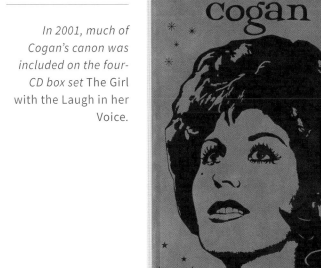

In 2001, much of Cogan's canon was included on the four-CD box set The Girl with the Laugh in her Voice.

Maybe that's why rock 'n' roll would become so important. Fourteen, fifteen years into a life that had been mapped out before it had even begun, rock 'n' roll had an unpredictability that wasn't simply exciting, it was liberating.

No one had ever heard anything like it, no one had ever sung anything like it; and how satisfying it was, after a hard day's obeisance to a crinkled adult world, to simply let rip with the feelings that you really felt meant something: "Yes sir, no sir, three bags full sir, and awop-bop-a-loo-bop to the whole damned lot of you." But, until that happened, it was a matter of just gritting your teeth and waiting.

The British *New Music Express* published its first pop chart on November 15, 1952—No. 1 was Al Martino's "Here in My Heart." Jo Stafford, Kay Starr, Eddie Fisher, Perry Como, Guy Mitchell, the Stargazers . . . over the next six months, as it was for the next three years, the best-selling 78s (there were very few 45s being released in Britain at that time) were showtunes, ballads, movie themes, and novelty numbers.

Occasionally, a local star rose to joust with the Americans, and at least insert a hint of unpredictability into the brew. But they were the exceptions. Wyman again: "You had David Whitfield and Lita Roza and Dickie Valentine, doing all these songs like 'Green Door,' 'How Much Is that Doggy in the Window,' all the Doris Day songs, all the Connie Francis songs, they were all covered by these quite ordinary, middle-aged people."

But just because it looks like a wasteland, and sounds like a wasteland, that doesn't necessarily mean it was a wasteland. The state-owned BBC held the monopoly on broadcasting in Britain. But though the family wireless was perpetually tuned to the Beeb's brand of entertainment—light orchestral music and live dancing contests, prewar comedians and mind-broadening lectures—there were alternatives.

Radio Luxembourg, beaming out of the European principality of the same name, was powerful enough to be picked up across much of Britain and, though the reception was invariably lousy, the R&B and blues records that filtered through the crackling ether at least hinted at a life beyond Sam Costa and Dorothy Carless.

Specialist record shops in the bigger city centers, too, splashed the edges of Gray Britain with a dash of welcome color—namely the blues that crept in on fragile imported 78s, to be treasured by the youths who would one day become the Blues Incorporated, the Cyril Davis All Stars, and, indeed, the Rolling Stones.

And, if you waited a few decades, one day you'd realize that the BBC itself wasn't so bad, as Deep Purple's Roger Glover explains. "Growing up in the '50s in England, the BBC . . . played every kind of music there was. And, though we complained about it, in retrospect that was a great education.

"Without the BBC we'd not have heard gospel music and classical music, folk, blues, and jazz. They'd dip into everything and it wasn't done with any style or anything. But in retrospect it wasn't so bad, because you look at kids growing up now, they get force-fed a particular sub-genre of music, and that's it. They don't have the wide overview. They're very channeled. We heard everything, and we could take what we wanted."

And it wouldn't be long before they started giving back. Rock 'n' roll was just around the corner, and the Beatles and the Beat Boom were on their way as well. Yet the stars of the '50s were not to fade so swiftly as the history books insist.

Hitmaking careers that predated rock 'n' roll continued on long after it had established itself, with many of the earlier era's biggest stars now ascending to the ranks of something approaching showbiz royalty. And of them all, none was so regal as Alma Cogan, one of the aforementioned local stars who arose in the years before Elvis and co., and who so effortlessly shrugged off the drab austerity of the day that, at first glance you'd swear she was another Hollywood starlet.

But her accent was pure London and her homegrown style so captivated the country that, a decade later, Paul McCartney was writing songs for her; Andrew Loog Oldham was producing a single for her; and, at least according to the tabloids, Brian Epstein was planning to marry her. The pair had, after all, been seen "stepping out" together, and if you didn't know the Beatles' dapper young manager as well as his friends did, what more natural arrangement could there be?

Epstein's little moptops, after all, were the biggest pop sensation of the time; had been ever since they yeah-yeah-yeahed their way into the nation's heart almost exactly one year before. But Cogan was just as big, and at thirty-one (two years Epstein's senior), she had almost sixteen summers of totally self-managed success behind her. Pair her

experience with Epstein's enthusiasm, and however they pooled their talents, the results could only be spectacular.

Of course it was not to be. On February 7, 1964, the *New Musical Express* stated categorically that fans could "discount rumors linking Alma Cogan's name romantically with Brian Epstein," as Cogan insisted that she simply wasn't interested in finding "Mr. Right." Her career was far more important. "Sometimes I feel that I only come to life when I walk on to the stage. The people out there in the darkness, or sitting in front of their TV seats. I feel I really do belong to them."

She was certainly a key figure in the Beatles' circle of friends. Paul McCartney guested as drummer on her 1964 recording "I Knew Right Away," pushing the original single into the three-figure range when copies come up for sale; McCartney and John Lennon gleefully teased her with their childhood memories of her earliest hits whenever they met. Lennon was just thirteen, and McCartney eleven, when Cogan scored her first hit single, "Bell Bottom Blues," in 1954, and such was her omnipresence that they could not avoid growing up listening to the singer whom the media dubbed "the girl with the laugh in her voice." Years later, on the twentieth anniversary of her death, McCartney would contribute liner notes to a new compilation of her best work.

Born in Golders Green, north London, in 1932, Cogan was fifteen when she played her first professional engagement, at the Grand Theatre in Brighton. Two years later, she was a chorus girl (alongside Audrey Hepburn) in the postwar smash "High Button Shoes," and in 1950, aged seventeen, she signed to the HMV label.

Over the next decade, she would run up twenty hit singles for the company, the UK home of Francis Barraud's portrait of Nipper the Dog: "I Went to Your Wedding," "Bell Bottom Blues," "Canoodlin' Rag," "Skokiaan," "Skinnie Minnie," "I Can't Tell a Waltz from a Tango" . . . .

Cogan was a revelation. Her voice alone belied her youth; strident, but never over-bearing—when casting opened for Lionel Bat's musical version of Charles Dickens's *Oliver* in 1960, her ebullience made her a natural Nancy, as the ensuing cast album proves. But she was also capable of slipping into almost childlike innocence—"Never Tango With an Eskimo," one of eight hits she scored in 1954, remains an evergreen throughout western Europe, including Iceland, where she toured in 1962, and delivered a word-perfect rendition in her audience's native tongue.

She possessed a natural flamboyance that dazzled a British nation still recovering from the austerity of the war years. As a child, Cogan dreamed of becoming a dress designer; now, she put those dreams into practice, creating the outlandish flounce and frill bedecked bouffant skirts that became as much a trademark as her voice.

When she performed "Twenty Tiny Fingers," a song about the birth of twins, her dress had twin dolls sewn into one pocket. By the time she scored her first number one, 1955's "Dreamboat," she was arguably the best-loved British entertainer of the decade, and nothing—not the onset of rock 'n' roll, nor her late 1950s interest in jazz—could dislodge her. Nor could the transition from 78s to 45s; indeed, she consistently sold better on 7-inch vinyl and, in 1958, "There's Never Been a Night" became her final release in the old format.

Between 1958 and 1962, Cogan visited New York, most of Europe, Africa, Australia, Israel, and even Japan, where her 1962 single "He Just Couldn't Resist Her with Her Pocket Transistor" proved one of the biggest hits of her career. Proof of her massive popularity lies in the (relative) ease with which her records can be found, and their (relative) inexpensiveness, too. As with so many other names from this period in music history (an observation that can then be spread throughout the so-called "easy listening" genre), Cogan is not a major figure in modern collecting, nor an especially challenging one.

There are rarities, of course. A demonstration (promo) copy of the album *I Love to Sing* sold for over $230 on eBay in 2013; a red vinyl Japanese pressing of "Tell Him" hit $160 in that same year. And, of course, the Beatles connection guarantees a flurry of excitement around several of her titles, despite it being the sudden revolution prompted by that band that brought Cogan back to earth, in the UK at least.

Though her sales were dipping, however, her celebrity never lapsed. Her friendship with the Beatles kept her on the front pages, and the rumored relationship with Epstein was a godsend to hungry columnists. She was a regular sight around Swinging London's most prestigious niteries, and when she did eventually fall in love, it was with Brian Morris, owner of the Ad Lib club. The parties she threw at the house she shared with her mother in Kensington, too, were legendary: the guest list for her thirty-second birthday on May 19, 1964, included all four Beatles, Epstein, producer George Martin, American legends Chuck Berry and Carl Perkins, comedian Noel Coward, and the head of EMI Records, Sir Joseph Lockwood.

It was after one such bash that McCartney knocked out the melody that eventually became "Yesterday," tapping out the notes on Cogan's own piano, and Cogan repaid the honor a year later, when she recorded her own, extravagantly orchestrated version of the same song. In fact, her final album, *Alma*, featured several Lennon-McCartney songs, the singer working with arranger Stan Foster to completely redefine them, including a swing version of "I Feel Fine," and a strings and horn–led "Eight Days a Week." Lennon and McCartney attended the October 9, 1965, session and were said to have been completely blown away by it.

It was during 1965 that Cogan fell ill. Rushed to hospital, she was informed that she was suffering from appendicitis; in fact, she had inoperable stomach cancer, a fact which was kept hidden from her, presumably to save her further distress. Unperturbed, then,

Cogan completed work on the *Alma* album, and in September 1966, set out on a Swedish tour. Coming offstage following the final show, she collapsed and was rushed home. She died shortly after, on October 26.

Since that time, Cogan's reputation has ensured she is seldom far from the new releases rack, at least in terms of compilations. Of these, 2001's 4-CD box *The Girl with a Laugh in Her Voice* is a spectacular tribute, running through all her hits, select LP cuts, and a clutch of previously unreleased numbers, including three tacks recorded towards a projected single produced by Andrew Loog Oldham: "Now That I've Found You," "I Know," and "Love Is a Word." A true labor of love, the box remains precisely the monument that Cogan's memory deserves.

THE SOUNDTRACK: QUADROPHENIA ON DISC, ON STAGE, ON FILM "THE STORY IS SET . . . ON A ROCK . . . IN THE MIDDLE OF A STORMY SEA."

Quadrophenia was Pete Townshend's masterpiece. Other Who albums, of course, have their fans; others, perhaps, feature better songs, stronger performances, more dynamic music. But if Townshend's oeuvre, as everything he worked towards from the *A Quick One* mini-opera onwards insists, was to create a seamless blending of story and song, with an underlying philosophy and an overwhelming intensity, *Quadrophenia*—as befits its title—would become a four-way showcase for all that made the Who truly special, the last of their albums to even make that attempt, and the first to actually succeed.

And yet of all the Who's albums, at least those which any right-minded fan would consider their best, *Quadrophenia* remains the most misunderstood and, in a way, the most misrepresented. Even at the time of its release, in late 1973, no album in the band's repertoire thus far had proven so divisive as *Quadrophenia*, Pete Townshend's manifesto for the disaffected youth of a decade past (and a half-decade to come: the movie version of *Quadrophenia* was single-handedly responsible for the Mod revival of the late 1970s).

Who biographer Dave Marsh hated it, for instance, and never missed the opportunity to tell us why, while Townshend himself came close to clipping five minutes off the original double album to fit the whole thing when it came time for its 1996 CD remastering.

Common sense ultimately prevailed, and the new-look *Quadrophenia* reached the shops that June, spread across two slabs of silver, with the vinyl version's original booklet reproduced in its entirety, and the whole thing boasting a remastering job that not only wiped the floor with any past version, but also kicked the hindquarters off every other album in the band's latest reissue series. It still does, too. In 2011, *Quadrophenia* reappeared as a deluxe box set, including another remaster and two discs of demos (previously spotlighted over a pair of recent Record Store Day 10-inch releases); and in 2014 it turned up again in surround sound on Blu-ray, and it truly had never sounded better.

Which, again, isn't bad for an album that a lot of people chose to all but write off when it first came out. The story begins on a rock, and ends up in the sea. One Mod's struggle to find some meaning to his life probably isn't the most appetizing synopsis of a rock 'n' roll album (although its scarcely any less absurd than a disjointed fable about a pinball-playing messiah).

But, in running the gamut of musical moods for which the Who justly became famous, from pounding semi-metal ("The Punk and the Godfather") to impassioned balladeering (the closing "Love Reign O'er Me"), '50s-style rock 'n' roll ("5.15") to almost folky jig-a-jigging ("The Rock"), *Quadrophenia* was not only the last significant album of The Who's own career, it was conceivably also the first significant album of the late 1970s—and that despite being released a full three years before even the Sex Pistols had heard of punk rock.

The success of the 1979 movie notwithstanding, *Quadrophenia* tapped into the hearts of a youth movement that was, almost

2094 115

The French picture sleeve release of "5.15."

literally, still wearing short trousers when it was originally issued. But the quest for individuality running in tandem with the need for acceptance was one of the underlying elements not only of punk, but also of the disparate youth movements that splintered out of punk, culminating in the Mod revival of 1979, which coincided so crucially with the movie. For a few months that summer, culture turned back the clock fifteen years. For a few months, *Quadrophenia* was reality.

"Being Mod meant a lot more in Britain than it ever did America," Roger Daltrey—who Townshend credits with having the idea for *Quadrophenia* in the first place—told audiences on the Who's winter 1973 American tour. "I think you think of it as maybe being in Carnaby Street and things . . . but it was far more than that."

Indeed it was. Less a cult than a way of life, less a rebellion than a complete reassessment of the meaning of Youth, Mod was about living fast, staying high, and holding down a job while you did it. For

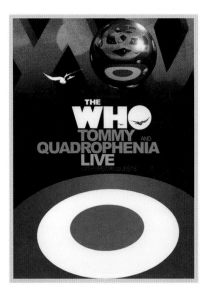

Live on DVD, the Who recount their greatest concept (plus Tommy) *in the late 1990s.*

Glam Rock

"Bed in the Corner," Cockney Rebel (UK EMI 2233, WITHDRAWN 7-INCH, 1974)

"Do the Strand," Roxy Music (ISLAND WIP 6306, UNISSUED LIVE 7-INCH, 1976)

"Hear Me Calling," Slade (UK POLYDOR 2814 008, 7-INCH PROMO, 1971)

"Moonage Daydream," Arnold Corns (UK B&C CB 149, 7-INCH, 1971)

"Rebel Rebel," David Bowie (RCA 0287, 7-INCH, DIFFERENT MIX, 1974)

"Ride a White Swan," T. Rex (UK OCTOPUS OCTO 1, TEST PRESSING, 1970)

"Slaughter on 10th Avenue," Mick Ronson (UK RCA 11474XST, FLEXIDISC, 1974)

"Take Me I'm Yours," Jobriath (UK ELEKTRA K12129, 7-INCH, 1974)

"Teenage Revolution," Hello (UK BELL 1479, 7-INCH PROMO, 1976)

"Va Va Va Voom," Brett Smiley (UK ANCHOR 1004, 7-INCH, 1974)

the first time in history, British youth had money, influence, power. In a few years' time, youth might even have the vote. Mod celebrated the future, and the boundless possibilities it embodied. And it was drove the adults crazy, as Pete Townshend later recalled.

"It was fashionable, it was clean, it was groovy. You could be a bank clerk, it was acceptable. You got them on your ground. They thought, 'Well there's a smart young lad.'" But it was a double-edged sword. "We made the establishment uptight, we made our parents uptight, and our employers uptight, because although they didn't like the way we dressed, they couldn't accuse us of not being smart. We had short hair and were clean and tidy."

Mod was the audience with which the Who first identified, even as they struggled to find their own identity. Original manager Pete Meadon was a Mod, and so were the audiences that hung around the local west London venues where the Who most regularly played. "We weren't Mods," Townshend admitted, "but we became Mods. We looked at it and said, 'That's incredible, let's be involved in it.' We had to learn all that stuff. I was at Art College, had long hair, was smoking pot and going with girls with long red hair, and all that. Painting farty pictures and carrying my portfolio around. And I had to learn how to be a Mod."

Quadrophenia, taken at face value, was Townshend passing those lessons on to anyone who now cared to listen. But as Daltrey would tell audiences in 1973, "it's not just a looking back, it's a kind of bring up to date. *Quadrophenia* is about where we're all at today—and maybe you too."

In Britain, 1973 was the year of glam rock, a year in which the headlines were dominated by David Bowie, and the charts by Slade and Gary Glitter. To an audience weaned on the glittering savagery of glam, the Who were a relic of a past that few folk remembered, an age of tassled jackets and flashing peace signs, wooly-hatted Woodstock casualties, an age where dinosaurs roamed the earth and listened to concept albums on their headphones.

The 1979 soundtrack to the Quadrophenia *movie.*

The fact that two years had elapsed since the Who's last all-new album, the chart-topping *Who's Next*, only exacerbated the group's redundancy. So did the knowledge that despite the success of *Tommy*, and the failure of *Lifehouse*, its projected follow-up, Townshend still hadn't got the concept bug out of his system. Nor his own sense of the band's importance.

Latter-day Who biographer and long time Townshend ally Richard Barnes wrote: "[Townshend] explained to me one day at his house that he was going to write an all-embracing story of the group that would, at the same time as reviewing their Mod past, free them from it completely. He felt they were too involved in their own legend, and he wanted to cut this connection so they could search for new directions."

There was never any doubt, then, that *Quadrophenia* was to be Townshend's baby, more so than any other album in the band's catalog. Past Who albums, even *Tommy*, had at least acknowledged some written contribution from bassist John Entwistle. *Quadrophenia*, however, would be composed by Townshend alone.

And while the songs he was writing and demoing at his home studio might have reflected the band's background, they were his experiences alone, their exclusivity only exaggerated by Townshend's insistence that his own eight-track demos become the blueprints for every song on the album. According to Ron Nevison, an engineer at the Who's still only partially completed Ramport Studios in Battersea, "Pete's demos had him playing pianos, synthesizers, all guitars and drums, plus some sound effects. It was silly to try and redo it, so the demos were used to work to, and as they overdubbed parts, they wiped Pete's originals. They added John's bass and Keith's drums, and wiped off Pete's demo bass and drum tracks."

A mid-1990s bootleg rounding up an assortment of demos for both Quadrophenia *and the earlier abandoned* Lifehouse.

This is noticeable throughout the raft of *Quadrophenia*-era demos that leaked out first on bootlegs through the '80s and '90s, then via Townshend's own official *Scoop* anthologies, and finally in the box set. There were, however, some revealing variations, most notably Townshend's original take on "The Real Me," which has a lot more in common with the later disco throb of "Who Are You" than it does with the familiar track. Inversely, one is also struck by the similarities between "I've Had Enough" and the earlier "Pinball Wizard," something else the band treatment would successfully camouflage.

And in the liners to the first *Scoop* collection in 1983, Townshend himself remarked of the "Love, Reign O'er Me" demo, "the piano part from [the] demo was used as the basic track for the Who version . . . . I still glory in the fact that the piano reveals new things to me every time I sit down to play. I am still a poor player, but in a sense, as a writer, that helps. This is composed almost entirely on the black notes."

Several of the demos also feature alternate lyrics in their demo form, heightening their allure for the album's acquisitive admirers, while *Scoop*—until the box set, the primary source for *Quadrophenia* outtakes, also included a sequence of sparse instrumentals that Townshend quaintly dubbed "Unused Piano," "Recorders," and "Brrr."

They amount to less than ten minutes of the music known to have been sliced from the original *Quadrophenia* project; more was confirmed by Townshend in a 1996 interview with *Mojo* magazine. "There is quite a lot of material which didn't get on the original album, there are two or three tracks. There's one called 'Joker James' [the story's hero is named Jimmy], another called 'Four Faces' [a reference both to Jimmy's quadrophenia] . . . which we included on the film soundtrack just to confuse everybody."

Other titles were confirmed by John Astley, overseeing the 1996 remastering of *Quadrophenia*, in a March, 1996, interview with *ICE* magazine. "I've found some outtakes but I haven't listened to them yet, so I don't know if they're up to it yet. There's a song called 'Wizardry,' one called 'Bank Holiday,' and a couple more. If they're any good, I'll put them on the record." Apparently they weren't . . . so he didn't.

Then again, the sessions at which *Quadrophenia* was completed were so chaotic that it is a wonder anything wound up "good enough" to be put on a record.Politically, the Who were as close to disaster during this period as they had ever come in the past, as first Daltrey, then Townshend, fell out with the band's long-established management team of Kit Lambert and Chris Stamp, albeit for very different reasons.

Gary Glitter

"Alone in the Night," as Paul Raven (UK DECCA F11202, 7-INCH, 1960)
"Another Rock 'n' Roll Christmas" (UK ARISTA ARISD 592, SHAPED PICTURE DISC, 1984)
"Dance Me Up" (UK ARISTA ARISD 570, 7-INCH PICTURE DISC, 1984)
"Do You Wanna Touch Me" (UK BELL 1280, 7-INCH, PICTURE SLEEVE, 1973)
Gary Glitter (UK BELL REBEL 1, EP, PICTURE SLEEVE, 1976)
"Musical Man," as Paul Monday (UK MCA MU 1024, 7-INCH, 1968)
"Shout Shout Shout" (UK ARISTA ARICV 586, 7-INCH MIRROR DISC, 1984)
"Tower of Strength," as Paul Raven (UK PARLOPHONE R4842, 7-INCH, 1961)
"Wait for Me," as Paul Raven (DECCA 32714, 7-INCH, 1970)
"We're All Livin' in One Place," as Rubber Bucket (UK MCA MK 5006, 7-INCH, 1969)

While Daltrey seethed over what he believed were the unaccounted-for millions the Who had surely earned, Townshend was raging over the more prosaic problem of Lambert's time-keeping. He didn't have any. Despite the presence of Glyn Johns in the studio, Lambert was nominally the band's producer. But according to Richard Barnes, it was Townshend who was "left holding the baby for the production, which was bloody difficult."

Having started work at Keith Richards' home studio, the band then moved on to the Who's own studio, Ramport, in south London. Unfortunately, the Who's dream of creating a studio no less ambitious and complex than the album that would launch it was doomed to failure. They envisaged equipping it with quadrophonic sound, then widely regarded as the wave of the future (and certainly an influence on the new album's title), but even as recording commenced, the studio was still incomplete.

The Who were not prepared to wait. While engineer Nevison and his partner, Chris Fawcus, raced to complete the planned sixteen-track control room, the Who made do with Ronnie Lane's eight-track mobile, which was parked outside. The air conditioning and acoustic ceiling tiles were literally installed in between takes, but the most ironic incident took place while the band, augmented by pianist Chris Stainton, were recording "Drowned." A flash summer storm erupted outside, flooding the streets and of course, the studio. According to Richard Barnes, "the piano booth filled up . . . [but] everyone was so into the track that they just continued recording."

Neither did the band forget their grand tradition of auto-destruction. Daltrey, for instance, sang so loudly on two (unnamed) tracks that he blew up the microphone, while Keith Moon succeeded in destroying every percussion instrument in the studio in the course of just one take . . . one note.

Ron Nevison recalled, "There was this big note at the end [of 'Love Reign O'er Me'], and we got all these percussive things out for Keith, loads of them and there was only one take. He didn't know what to hit, and Pete was going, 'just hit everything,' so he did. He got the tubular bells and dumped them over into everything else. There was this incredible crash . . . ."

The recording finally, and laboriously, completed (even the sound effects proved troublesome: Townshend demanded stereo and quadrophonic sounds, but the FX libraries only carried mono), Townshend retired to his cottage in Goring On Thames to mix the album, again applying all that technology had to offer. He used a synthesizer to process the voice of top BBC newsreader John Curle, reading a 1964-style report on Mod violence, for example, while there were also some unexpected expenses to deal with as well. Desperate for the sound of a train whistle at the beginning of "5.15," he had to bribe a train driver to sound his horn within range of a waiting microphone.

At the same time as completing the album, Townshend was also supervising American photographer Ethan Russell's work on an album package that would prove as lavish as the music within: Townshend required a forty-four page booklet, featuring scenes from what was then still his personal mind movie, providing a visual framework to the progression of the story. Although the actual cover art was shot by Daltrey's cousin Graham Hughes, it is Russell's work that remains the firmest image of *Quadrophenia*, from the row of terraced houses on the front of the booklet to those frozen frames that would, six years later, provide an equally firm framework around which director Franc Roddam would create the movie.

It was the booklet that caused many of the manufacturing delays that slowed down the album's eventual release. While the two-LP *Quadrophenia* appeared in the US on October 19, 1973, the British release continued to run into problems, and when the band took the stage for the first live performance of this new magnum opus, at Stoke's Trentham Gardens, *Quadrophenia* was still pending. Bootlegs preserve Townshend's apology. "Now we'd like to do something from the forthcoming album. We're still finding our way with it. We were expecting the album to be out and in your possession by now, but of course it isn't."

Quadrophenia finally hit the stores in mid-November, with a single, an edited version of side three's opener, "5.15" (backed by the two-year-old "Water" outtake) paving the way. It was an inspired choice, and that despite the lyric's unabashed attempt at some form of glam rock modernity—"he man drag in a glittering ballroom," sang Daltrey, and seemingly mindless of the incongruity of the image; "gaily outrageous in my high-heeled shoes."

Unfortunately, "5.15" climbed no higher than No. 20 in the UK, and Track's American office came to choose a 45, they went for the epic "Love Reign O'er Me," which ran out of steam at No. 76! (An edit of "The Real Me," in February, 1974, performed even more poorly, barely even making the Top 100.)

Quadrophenia itself mustered a more accurate reflection on the Who's standing. It reached No. 2 on both sides of the Atlantic, selling over a million in under three weeks even as it was held from the British top by the ever-extraordinary charms of David Bowie's *Pin Ups*—itself a musical tribute to the very era the Who were trying to exorcise. It was blocked in America by an equally poignant (and pricey) double album competitor, Elton John's *Goodbye Yellow Brick Road*.

The Who continued touring, and *Quadrophenia* continued to prove an awkward beast to live with. Despite the unfamiliarity of the material, and the vast amount of prerecorded tapes required to recreate it, the band allowed themselves just two days in which to rehearse their live set, of which one was completely washed out after Daltrey and Townshend began brawling—a confrontation that ended when Daltrey knocked the guitarist unconscious with a blow to the chin. Townshend came round in the hospital, suffering from temporary amnesia, which probably didn't help *Quadrophenia*'s cause much either.

The few rehearsal tapes that have leaked out, most notably two tracks on the Whoopy Cat label bootleg *The Punk Meets the Godfather,* indicate just how woefully unprepared the band was to attempt anything like a representative version of *Quadrophenia* in concert. "Drowned" and "I'm One" pack plenty of raw rock 'n' roll punch, but the sheer majesty of their studio counterparts is nowhere to be found. Just days into the tour, the Who came to realize that just maybe it was too much to expect that it could have been.

Quadrophenia was inserted into the middle section of the Who's live set, but was dogged with difficulties from the outset. The band's naturally ramshackle live set was thrown completely out by the need to play along with the tapes' preset tempos, while audiences seemed completely unmoved by the experience. By the fourth night of the British tour, at Manchester's Belle Vue on November 2, the band had dropped five new songs from their set. They were contemplating cutting even more when finally, disaster of a different nature struck.

On November 5, the British holiday so appropriately known as "Fireworks Night" to millions of schoolchildren, soundman Bobby Pridden jumped the gun with one of the cues and set one of the tapes rolling too early. In front of a packed Newcastle Odeon, Townshend exploded. Dragging Pridden away from the sound desk, sending an amplifier sprawling in the process, he proceeded to attack the tape machines, wrecking weeks of work in a matter of seconds. Pridden quit on the spot (he was persuaded to return later that night), and after a thirty-minute cooling off period, the Who ended their set with a solid greatest hits routine, culminating with Townshend smashing his guitar to smithereens. Fireworks Night indeed!

Neither did matters improve when the band reached the United States, as Daltrey admitted as the band took the stage at San Francisco's Cow Palace on November 19. "We'd like to carry on our present act with the new album, or parts of it. We've had a few problems and we've cut a few songs out. We'll do what we're comfortable with." This, of course, was the night that has since passed into legend as the evening Keith Moon passed out on stage and, while Daltrey threatened him with a punch in the stomach and a custard enema, a member of the audience, Scott Halpin, took over for the last three songs of the set—"Smokestack Lightning," "Spoonful," and "Naked Eye."

Moon was back in form for the next show, at the L.A. Forum, and bootlegs emanating from this show remind us that when the show was good, it was excellent, with ripping versions of "The Real Me," "The Punk and the Godfather," "I Am One," "Helpless Dancer," "5.15," "Sea and Sand," and "Drowned."

Even more impressive, however, is the FM broadcast made from the Capitol Center, Largo, in early December. The bootleg *Decidedly Belated Response* (aka *American Tour* and *American Tour 1973*) not only includes the full show, but also Daltrey's attempts to maintain the storyline with his spoken intros to each song.

These introductions, some of which threatened to run even longer than the actual songs, were not popular with audience and critics alike, and Daltrey acknowledged, "in a couple of months, when everyone knows the album, we won't have to explain." Indeed, by the time the tour returned to Britain, for the Who's four-night Christmas performance at north London's Edmonton Sundown, Townshend's attempts to explain what was going on were tersely interrupted by a loud voice from the stalls . . . "We know!"

The Sundown shows have also been preserved on bootleg, with the *Quadrophenia* portion of the set featured on *Merry Xmas Mr Who Volume 2,* living proof that the prolonged problems with executing the album on stage had seen the set drastically pruned until it really was, at Daltrey put it, representative purely of "what's good to play on stage. We started off playing it all, and it was bloody awful."

It would be another twenty-two years before he and Townshend felt confident enough to return *Quadrophenia* in its entirety to the stage; in the meantime, when the Who went back on the road in February 1974, *Quadrophenia* received little more attention than any earlier album in the band's canon, highlighting not only the band's unhappiness with their attempts to present it, but also their audience's.

The album's sales were healthy, and critics and public alike were generally approving (if a little uncertain): indeed, *Quadrophenia* was voted second best album of the year in the 1973 *New Musical Express* magazine poll. But still, *Quadrophenia* can only be regarded as a failure, at least under the terms the Who had made their own.

Both of the new album's predecessors, *Tommy* and *Who's Next*, had matched their commercial success with immediate cultural success, only piling on fresh accolades as time passed. By those criteria, *Quadrophenia* was still at the starting post, overtaken even by the comparative insignificance of *A Quick One*.

Richard Barnes was among those close associates of Townshend who realized just how hard the composer was hit by *Quadrophenia*'s failure to make it three social phenomenons on the trot. "[The Who's] inability to put across *Quadrophenia* at the time had a profound effect on Pete. Its failure to take off as a major album shook him. He had put a lot into the album, and staked the Who's future on its being able to allow them to stop having to play *Tommy* and the '60s stuff on stage."

Instead, the *Quadrophenia* tour had barely ground to a halt than *Tommy* was rubbing their face in its failure, as Australian entrepreneur Robert Stigwood announced his plans to make a movie of the tale. And as if that wasn't enough, on December 13, Lou Reizner presented the second of his live *Tommy* extravaganzas at the London Rainbow, following the massively successful 1973 effort with a somewhat lower key, but musically far superior show starring the likes of Roy Wood, David Essex, Viv Stanshall, and Marsha Hunt. (A bootleg of this performance was culled from a December 26 London radio broadcast.)

Even more alarmingly, *Quadrophenia*'s so-called failure apparently left a severe dent in Townshend's own belief in the Who. *The Who By Numbers* and *Who Are You*, the two albums which followed (and the last of the original lineup's career) both offered more than a suggestion that Townshend's commitment to the group was in marked decline.

The past, on the other hand, never went away. A two-album compilation of the band's hits, *The Story of the Who* (accompanied by the first commercially available 12-inch single in British rock history, coupling "Substitute," "I'm a Boy," and "Pictures of Lily"), reached No. 2 in the fall of 1976, a year after *By Numbers* faltered at No. 7, while 1979's *The Kids Are Alright* documentary movie would rank amongst the most eagerly awaited cinematic events of the year.

Add to that the groundswell of both sympathy and interest aroused by Keith Moon's death on September 7, 1978, and add to *that* the vintage Who's rehabilitation into the halls of British pop legend, courtesy of new wavers the Jam's constant praise . . . by the time the British press became aware of the so-called Mod Revival, we were already halfway through what the media would subsequently dub "1979: The Year of the Who." And Townshend was certainly realistic enough to know that catchy expression told only part of the story. 1979 was really the year of the Who's back catalog.

Director Franc Roddam's movie version of *Quadrophenia* was originally conceived in 1977–'78, when the band's new manager, Bill Curbishley, entered into negotiations over financing with Polytel, the film wing of the band's UK label, Polygram. Roddam, the band's unanimous choice for director, had never made a feature film before, but his BBC television play, *Dummy*—the story of a deaf teenaged prostitute—had made a major impression on the Who, not least for its mischievous play on the title of their own sensorily impaired little hero.

Unlike Ken Russell's overloaded cinematic take on *Tommy*, *Quadrophenia* was never conceived as a vehicle for the Who themselves, as the principle roles in the movie were spread amongst a largely untried cast. Initial attempts to recruit Sex Pistol Johnny Rotten having fallen through, Phil Daniels, a cocky young cockney actor, portrayed Jimmy, the mixed up Mod whose tale *Quadrophenia* is; actress Lesley Ash plays his (sometime) girlfriend; the only vaguely musical star in sight was Sting, leader of the then still largely unknown Police, who took the role of the Ace Face.

Quadrophenia continued to occupy the band's thoughts, however. In January, 1979, Keith Moon's successor was announced, in the form of the Small Faces' Kenney Jones, and the Who's 1994 *Thirty Years of Maximum R&B* box set preserves his audition, a version of "The Real Me" taped at Ramport, in January, 1979. Jones would make his live debut with the band on May 2, at the London Rainbow.

In the meantime, too, the Who worked on the movie's soundtrack, rerecording and/or remixing three songs originally written for the album ("Get Out and Stay Out," "Four Faces," and "Joker James") plus looking again at another ten tracks from the original *Quadrophenia* project ("I Am The Sea," "The Real Me," "I'm One," "5.15," "Love Reign O'er Me," "Bell Boy," "I've Had Enough," "Helpless Dancer," "Dr. Jimmy," and "The Punk and the Godfather"). The embellishments were seldom more than cursory, but still the result was a fabulous soundtrack to a marvelous movie, both as true to the album that spawned it as to the era which inspired it: Dave Marsh, that most maddening opponent of *Quadrophenia* in all its guises, would subsequently complain that Roddam "got much of the period detail wrong," but even he had to concede that *Quadrophenia* "was exciting in just the way *Tommy* hadn't been—the script even made sense of the plot."

Newsweek called it "a damn good movie," even as American audiences left the theaters baffled by the fast-paced cockney accents and fast-moving portrayal of a lifestyle that had no equivalent in American culture; Richard Barnes describes it as "one of the most realistic and entertaining films about adolescence ever to come from the British film industry."

It was also one of the most successful. Playing to packed theaters from the moment it premiered on August 16, 1979, *Quadrophenia* became one of the year's biggest-grossing British films, while the soundtrack album would rise to No. 23 in Britain, and No. 46 in America—no mean feat, considering the album's primary audience, Who fans, had already forked out for one double album of old material that year (*The Kids Are Alright* soundtrack) and were now being asked to do the same again. An America-only single of "5.15" also charted, at No. 45.

The movie and soundtrack versions of *Quadrophenia* seldom appear as much more than a footnote in biographies of the Who, an oversight that not only overlooks, but actually negates, the vast impact it was to have on the band's subsequent standing. Since 1971, and the spectacular success of *Who's Next*, the band had arguably spent close to a decade alternating between creative and critical freefall. *Quadrophenia* had been a tremendous album, but it failed, a victim of Townshend's refusal to accept that in 1973, the kids wanted fun and frivolity, not introspection and soul-searching; *Who Are You*, contrarily, would be few people's idea of a classic, and yet in the prevalent mood of the time, with Moon so recently dead and the Jam so violently alive, it became both their biggest- and fastest-selling record yet.

The movie, in so firmly linking past with present, then, is nothing less than the Philosopher's Stone for which Townshend had been searching for over a decade, the event that made sense of his restless search for meaning within his own career. Understandably uncomfortable with the popular notion that his last record was always better than his next (a common failing in both the public and media's perception of the Who) but equally, painfully, aware that he had spent the mid-late 1960s singlehandedly breeding the flock of pop albatrosses that now hung around his neck, Townshend finally realized, with the movie *Quadrophenia*, that rock history is relative.

If a mood he captured in 1974 could still be current five years later, then it only followed that a record he made twenty years before would still be brand new to somebody hearing it for the first time today. And with that knowledge, Townshend was finally free from *Tommy*, from "My Generation," from the Who itself. Though the band would soldier on for another couple of albums, and another couple of years, still it can be said that the band itself ended with *Quadrophenia*. It broke up when Jimmy's motorbike plunged off a cliff into the English Channel in the final moments of the movie.

That is why, discussing the *Quadrophenia* performance that was to be the highlight of a June, 1996, spectacular in London's Hyde Park, Townshend acknowledged that though the show reunited him with erstwhile bandmates Daltrey and John Entwistle, it was not a Who concert. Rather, with a wealth of guest performers and musicians, it was simply a spectacular event he had been scheming for years. "It'll be like the Spiders from Mars meets *The Wall*." From London, the show moved to New York, opening a week of performances at Madison Square Garden on July 16, 1996, before heading out on tours captured on DVD in the 2005 package *Tommy and Quadrophenia Live*.

It surfaced again in 2010 at a charity gig at the Royal Albert Hall; and then went back out on tour in 2012–'13, this time as the Who . . . now reduced to Townshend and Daltrey alone, with the late Entwistle and Moon appearing in video footage. The final night of that outing, at London's Wembley Arena, became the *Quadrophenia Live in London* DVD. The box set and the Blu-ray of the original album followed; Townshend's demos were collated for the first time, complete within the box set and highlighted across a pair of 10-inch EPs. And even they are merely components within a Who reissue program that has also seen their entire 45 rpm catalog (including "5.15") reissued on vinyl. Finally, after forty years, with the vinyl, the tour, and the movie far behind it, Pete Townshend's most dramatic vision had finally reached the end of its journey.

It's time you cleared off a shelf for it.

THE GUILTY PLEASURE: ALL I WANT FOR CHRISTMAS IS . . . SOMETHING DIFFERENT TO COLLECT

It is a historical fact that more records are sold in the weeks leading up to Christmas than at any other time of year. It is a fact, too, that more "unusual" (read "novelty") songs are released with a shout of success, with seasonal offerings not only paramount on the release sheets, but also on record buyers' minds.

Christmas would not be Christmas without Slade's 1973 seasonal floor-shaker.

The upshot of all this activity is a collecting field that, while scorned by many enthusiasts, nevertheless attracts some of the most dedicated specialists in the hobby, with prices for the most in-demand pieces at least pursuing the best-known rock 'n' roll rarities into the stratosphere.

In 1998, Tim Neely, one of America's foremost collectors and experts in the field, isolated a lengthy catalog of Christmas releases with current values in excess of $500, including festive offerings by such comparative unknowns as the Moonglows ("Just a Lonely Christmas," Chance 1150, red vinyl), the Orioles ("What Are You Doing New Year's Eve," Jubilee 5017), the Five Keys ("It's Christmas Time," Aladdin 3113) and Georgia Harris ("Let's Exchange Hearts for Christmas," Hy-Tone 117), alongside such hobby staples as odd variations on Elvis Presley's Christmas album, the Beatles' annual Christmas flexidiscs (since reissued on solid vinyl as a 2017 box set), and original (1966) pressings of Booker T. and the MGs' *In the Christmas Spirit*.

Voicing the wishes of many a teenybopper, comedienne Dora Bryant admits "All I Want for Christmas Is a Beatle."

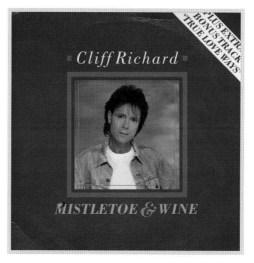

Band Aid's "Do They Know It's Christmas," raising funds for the Ethiopian famine appeal in 1983.

Cliff Richard has been scoring UK hits since 1958. "Mistletoe and Wine" was his Christmas 1988 offering; his ninety-ninth single, it became his twelfth UK number one and the biggest selling 45 of the year.

However, it is also safe to say that even among the most unremarkable Christmas releases, there lurk rarities and obscurities that evade the most completist collector's grasp, even when—as in many instances—the record in question was a sizable hit. Kate Bush's "December Will Be Magic Again," Queen's "Thank God It's Christmas," and David Bowie's "Peace on Earth"/"Little Drummer Boy" duet with Bing Crosby are classic examples of original 45s that, unreleased in the US and generally available only for the seasonal period elsewhere, disappeared much faster than their Top Thirty chart positions might suggest.

Crosby, of course, is probably the artist most responsible for the enduring popularity of Christmas records. His "White Christmas" is reckoned among the best-selling records in world history, having been re-pressed and reissued on countless occasions. Several of these pressings are now as rare as the song itself is popular; for example, finding original 78 and 45 issues from both the US and UK is a challenging proposition for any collector. The sheer popularity of that song, incidentally, is challenged only by "Little Drummer Boy"—a US Top 30 hit for five years running (1958–'62) for the Harry Simeone Chorale, and a staple release for myriad acts every year since then.

The history of Christmas records is almost as old as records themselves, and rounds up legends as disparate as bluesmen Blind Lemon Jefferson and Leadbelly, the Alabama Sacred Harp Convention and the Reverend J.M. Gates. However, the rock 'n' roll Christmas record was launched by Elvis Presley. Accompanied by the EP *Elvis Sings Christmas Songs*, *Elvis's Christmas Album* was originally issued in 1957, in a deluxe gatefold sleeve with a booklet of photographs. Although the LP itself has remained a catalog staple, that grand, early packaging was already a thing of the past for the 1958 season, rendering the original pressing a highly sought-after item.

In Elvis's wake, a host of artists cut their own Christmas albums—as, indeed, they still do. From Frankie Avalon to the Partridge Family, from the Brady Bunch to the Backstreet Boys, no teen idol's year seems complete without a festive disc, though it is, perhaps, a sorry indictment of the overall quality of these releases (combined with the enormous quantities that are so optimistically manufactured) that precious few have taken on any serious value among collectors.

There are, however, exceptions, artists intent on proving that Christmas not purely the province of the kitschy and sentimental. Phil Spector weighed in with some of the most sensational Christmas records of all time, collected together on the legendary and oft-reissued *A Christmas Gift to You*. It is hard to believe, therefore, that the original album release, in 1963, was an absolute flop, largely because its release coincided with the assassination of President John F. Kennedy, an event that essentially canceled Christmas across the US.

It would be 1972 before a reissue on the Beatles' Apple label (SW 3400) brought the record the critical and commercial favor it

Taking a break from album-length opuses, Mike Oldfield recounts the medieval carol "In Dulce Jubilo."

merited. In the meantime, however (and, of course, across the years since then), singles pulled from the LP have become avidly collectible. Look for Darlene Love's "Christmas," "Xmas Blues," and "Winter Wonderland" (125X); the Ronettes' "I Saw Mommy Kissing Santa Claus" backed by the Crystals' "Rudolph the Red Nosed Reindeer"; and the promo "Phil Spector's Christmas Medley," issued (like the Ronettes 45) to coincide with a 1981 rerelease of the LP. None will disappoint.

Those other giants of American pop record production, Brian Wilson and Bob Crewe, also masterminded Christmas records. Crewe led the Four Seasons through *The 4 Seasons Greetings* in 1962, spinning off the singles "Santa Claus Is Coming to Town" and "I Saw Mommy Kissing Santa Claus"; Wilson's *The Beach Boys' Christmas Album* followed in 1964, again trailing some remarkable 45s, "Little Saint Nick" (Capitol 5096) and "The Man with All the Toys" (Capitol 5312). The latter title, incidentally, is also the source for one of the scarcest of all British Christmas singles, a cover version by the Variations (UK Immediate IM 019); the Beach Boys' own efforts, meanwhile, were subsequently paired with an abandoned second Christmas album, dating from 1977, as 1998's *Ultimate Christmas* CD.

If Christmas albums can sometimes prove a little too much of a good thing, Christmas singles exert a fascination that even avowed anti-Christmas listeners find difficult to avoid, and festive shoppers seem unable to resist. Billboard even published a special Christmas chart between 1963–'72, and again from 1983–'85, since so many Santa songs were invading the regular Top 100.

Even today, it is hard to turn one's back on such seasonal delights as Charlie Ace's "Jingle Bells Cha Cha," Santo and Johnny's "Twistin' Bells" (one of an entire subgenre of Christmas records dedicated to the twist dance sensation), the surfing silliness of the Surfaris' "Santa's Speed Shop," or the Paris Sisters' "Man with the Mistletoe Mustache."

Motown was another reliable source of Christmas material during the 1960s, with suitable (if not necessarily excellent) offerings across the stable. The Temptations' "Rudolph the Red Nosed Reindeer," Stevie Wonder's "Some Day at Christmas," the Supremes' "Children's Christmas Song," and, as late as 1972, Marvin Gaye's "Christmas in the City" are among this avenue's brightest highlights.

Perhaps the most collectible individual field within the Christmas hobby, predictably, relates to the Beatles. Their own festive flexis notwithstanding, the group's enormous success launched a string of 45s seemingly guaranteed to appeal to lovelorn Beatles fans everywhere, as they waited to see what Santa would bring them. The craze was launched in 1963 by English comedy actress Dora

Bryan, who announced "All I Want for Christmas Is a Beatle." It was perpetuated the following year by TV puppet stars Tich and Quackers, who demanded "Santa Bring Me Ringo," a ditty so contagious that it even provoked a cover version by America's Christine Hunter.

That same year, 1964, had already seen the Beatles' sudden fame provoke such tributes as Donna Lynn's "My Boyfriend Got a Beatle Haircut," the Four Preps' "A Letter to the Beatles," and Annie and the Orphans' "My Girl's Been Bitten by the Beatle Bug." But as Christmas loomed, the floodgates truly opened. Becky Lee Beck, Jackie and Jill, and the Fans all strived for success with the plaintive "I Want a Beatle for Christmas." Cindy Rella begged "Bring Me a Beatle for Christmas," while the Beatles' drummer was also the subject of Garry Ferrier's Canadian 45 "Ringo-Deer." The Beatles' own response to all this action, incidentally, does not appear to have been recorded.

The Beatles' own contributions to the festivities, meanwhile, remained locked on those aforementioned flexidiscs, until after the band's dissolution. In 1971, however, John Lennon's "Happy Christmas (War Is Over)" was issued (it became a hit the following year), with George Harrison's "Ding Dong" following in 1974; Paul McCartney weighed in with "Wonderful Christmas Time" (although if you listen to it a few times in succession, you might find yourself questioning its sentiment) in 1979; and Ringo Starr unleashed his *I Want to Be Santa Claus* album in 1999.

Included among that latter set's highlights, incidentally, was a cover of one of the Beatles' own Christmas flexi performances, "Christmas Time Is Here Again." None of these solo efforts are especially rare, incidentally, but there are some neat variations: green-vinyl pressings of the Lennon 45, blue-and-white custom labels for the Harrison issue, and a red-vinyl reissue of McCartney's song.

Even more recent is McCartney's teasing description of how, in the early 1970s when his children were young, "I went into my studio and made loads of tracks. I have a little CD actually, called *Christmas Songs*, and it's just all stuff I've made up. I multitracked them all in the studio and they're kind of nice! So rather than sitting around a piano, normally we would play that CD while everyone's cooking. It's a nice little CD actually . . . ."

It has never been released, and very well might never be. But if there is such a thing as a Christmas holy grail for collectors to lie awake dreaming of, this is it.

If the majority of Christmas action took place in the US during the 1960s, the scene shifted to the UK throughout the early 1970s. Chart regulars Mud, Showaddywaddy, Slade, Wizzard, the Wombles, and Gilbert O'Sullivan all scored with seasonal smashes between 1973–'75. The festive fancy also struck as far afield as singer-songwriter

Chris de Burgh ("A Spaceman Came Traveling"), progressive rocker Greg Lake ("I Believe in Father Christmas"), folkies Steeleye Span ("Gaudete"), and multi-instrumentalist Mike Oldfield ("In Dulce Jubilo").

Elton John scored a minor British hit with the now remarkably hard to find "Step into Christmas," though in terms of fabled rarities, none can touch Marc Bolan and T. Rex. A super-limited fanclub flexidisc, *Christmas in a T. Rex World* (Lyntone), in 1972, was followed by "Christmas Bop," scheduled for release for Christmas 1975, but pulled before the pressing plant even began production. All that exists today of this release are a couple of sets of paper labels for the A- and B-sides, although the song itself is now readily available on sundry compilations.

The late seventies and thereafter saw no letup in the weight of Christmas records released, though chart placings became considerably scarcer. Although the UK charts continued to turn up at least one monster smash every Christmas, in America the highest-placing festive single of the entire decade was the Eagles' "Please Come Home for Christmas"—which peaked just inside the top twenty. Oddly, this is also the only Eagles single ever issued with a custom picture sleeve.

In the 1980s, glam veteran Gary Glitter, teen idols Wham! (featuring George Michael), and the Kinks all cut very credible Xmas offerings for the UK market, while an American radio promo *Christmas Rarities on CD* compilation, issued in the late '80s, rounded up a number of the most collectible recent issues, including the aforementioned Queen and Kate Bush titles, oddities by REM (including "Ghost Reindeers in the Sky"), and songs by Elvis, the Beach Boys, and many more.

The highest-selling Christmas record of all time, even eclipsing any individual issue of "White Christmas," also dates from the 1980s. Band Aid's "Do They Know It's Christmas?" was issued in 1984 to raise relief funds for victims of the Ethiopian famine. It drew in guest performances from across the contemporary British pop and rock spectrum: U2, David Bowie, Paul Weller, Duran Duran, Culture Club, Bananarama, Spandau Ballet, Paul McCartney, and Status Quo are just some of the acts who are featured on the recording.

It is not rare in any format, though a handful of variations might at least be of interest. A 12-inch remix contributed by Frankie Goes to Hollywood mastermind Trevor Horn features an otherwise unheard lead vocal from Sting; while a 1989 Band Aid II remake, produced by Stock-Aitken-Waterman, involves Cliff Richard,

Kevin Godley, Wet Wet Wet, and the returning Bananarama, backed by a somewhat less-than-stellar gathering of the producers' own stable of stars.

Further rerecordings in 2004 (Band Aid 20) and 2014 (Band Aid 30) brought in their own selection of current superstars—Daniel Bedingfield, Keane's Tom Chaplin, Dido, and the returning Bono and Paul McCartney were among the biggest names in 2004; Angélique Kidjo, Coldplay frontman Chris Martin,, Sinéad O'Connor, Olly Murs, and teen sensations One Direction (plus Bono again!) in 2014.

With and without his contributions to Band Aid II, Cliff Richard is also very high among the biggest-selling artists of the Christmas genre. Richard, a consistent hitmaker since 1958, had his first-ever religiously themed Top 20 hit with 1982's "Little Town (of Bethlehem)." Since that time, "Another Christmas Day," "Mistletoe and Wine," "Saviour's Day," "We Should Be Together," and "The Millennium Prayer" not only helped maintain Richard's record of scoring at least one chart-topper in every decade since his career commenced, but have also outperformed the expectations of both his fans and his detractors.

"The Millennium Prayer," recorded for Christmas 1999, was rejected by EMI, Richard's record label for the previous forty-one years. Richard responded by quitting the company for his manager's own Papillion label, and "The Millennium Prayer" topped the UK chart for three weeks.

These vast successes have not obscured some extremely collectible items within this canon. Despite being a comparative unknown in the US, Richard is avidly collected in the UK and elsewhere, and each of his festive offerings has arrived with its own unique limited

Marc Bolan

"Chariot Choogle," T. Rex (EMI SPRS 346, 7-INCH PROMO, 1972)

"Christmas Bop," T. Rex (EMI MARC 13, LABELS ONLY, 1976)

Electric Warrior Preview Single, T. Rex (FLY GRUB 1, 7-INCH, PINK-ENVELOPE SLEEVE, 1971)

Hard on Love (TRACK 2406 101, LP TEST PRESSING, 1972)

"Hippy Gumbo" (PARLOPHONE R5539, 7-INCH, 1966)

"Midsummer Night's Scene," John's Children (TRACK 604 005, 7-INCH, 1967)

"Ride a White Swan," T. Rex (OCTOPUS OCTO 1, 7-INCH TEST PRESSING, 1970)

"The Third Degree" (DECCA F12413, 7-INCH, 1966)

"The Wizard" (DECCA F12288, 7-INCH, 1965)

Zinc Alloy and the Hidden Riders of Tomorrow, T. Rex
(EMI BNLA 7751, PROMO LP WITH THREE-WAY FOLD-OUT SLEEVE, NUMBERED, 1974)

edition—a picture disc of "Little Town," an Advent calendar insert with the 12-inch "Mistletoe and Wine," and a 7-inch double-pack of "We Should Be Together," for example.

Christmas-themed novelties, long a popular field, have also flourished over the years, with punk-speed carols a period one particular specialty. From the Yobs (aka punk band The Boys), who kicked the field off with 1977's "Run Rudolph Run," to X and Bad Religion (who contributed a mach ten "Silent Night" to an Atlantic label promo), and on to indie favorites Silkworm, Dandy Warhols, the Flaming Lips, and Metal Mike, the alternative rock era has seen a plethora of amusing, wry, or just plain breakneck holiday fare.

Reggae is another genre that has a long and often hilarious history of revising our expectations of another traditional Christmas singalong. Eek A Mouse ("The Night Before Christmas") and Jacob Miller ("Deck the Halls with Lots of Colly") are among the staples of countless Christmas collections but, as with so many other Jamaican records, can be tricky to hunt down in their original homeland pressings.

Be prepared to search long and hard for most of them, though. Many were issued as limited-edition 45s, others appeared only on now-rare promo collections, and others still were intended merely as Christmas gifts to a band's fan club or friends. Pearl Jam's annual offerings are insanely collectible, though one of the rarest (and greatest) such issues was British rockabilly hero Howlin' Wilf's "Bugger My Buttocks for Christmas." As its title suggests, it is an indelible slab of ribaldry, guaranteed to enliven any festive gathering.

The bootleg boom of the 1980s and 1990s also unearthed a number of quite unexpected Christmas-themed outtakes from some of the giants of '60s rock. A Rolling Stones' *Satanic Majesties*-era outtake, "Cosmic Christmas," relayed "We Wish You a Merry Christmas" via freaky electronics. Pink Floyd were caught in a riotous mood with the 1969 release "The Merry Xmas Song."

U2 frontman Bono was captured on bootleg reciting the poem "Driving to Midnight Mass on Christmas Eve" by Irish poet John F. Dean over his band's "New Year's Day" on an Irish radio broadcast, while Brit-pop heroes Elastica cut a driving version of "Gloria in Excelsis" for the BBC's John Peel show. Neither have either the quantity nor the occasional brilliance of the Christmas record faded, with LeAnn Rimes' 2014 cracker "I Want a Hippopotamus for Christmas" just one

recent example of an utterly irresistible performance dropping down the chimney.

Even its adherents admit that collecting Christmas records is neither the most culturally hip, nor the most musically fulfilling, field in which to specialize. Nevertheless, the genre continues to blossom in collectibility, as surely as every Christmas brings another cartload of records to be collected.

78S: A SHELLAC SUPERSTAR

By March, 1941, Britain had been embroiled in the Second World War for exactly eighteen months, and enduring sustained enemy bombing for six. It was a time of tremendous personal courage and sacrifice, and an era, too, in which the islanders' world-renowned "Bulldog Spirit" flowed with even greater potency than ever before.

Nightly, German bombers filled the skies, raining destruction down upon the country's cities, and after a while, it became routine. Home from work, time for tea, then down to the shelter to wait out Mr. Hitler's latest tantrum.

Some people even stopped going to the shelters. If the Germans wanted to kill them, a popular saying went, they'd have to find them first, and so the nightclubs and theaters started reopening evenings,

Al Bowlly fronts the Waikiki Serenaders on this foxtrot.

White Town's UK chart-topping "Your Woman" sampled Bowlly's "My Woman."

Al Bowlly's "Lady of Spain," a hit in 1931.

pubs and cafes stopped closing when the air raid sirens sounded, and all over London, the hottest topic of conversation was the upcoming reopening of the Royal Albert Hall for a series of promenade concerts in June.

Although the bombers did still come over, their numbers had dropped and continued dropping, and the massive raids of just a few months earlier were suddenly little more than inconveniences—lethal ones, admittedly, but nothing compared to the carnage they had once represented.

Two events within a few weeks of one another, however, not only shocked the people out of their burgeoning complacency, they also robbed the British music scene of two of its most vital talents. "Snake Hips" Johnson, the band leader at the Cafe De Paris and one of the first black superstars on the London scene, was killed in March when a pair of German bombs hit the Cafe itself. Singer Al Bowlly died in a raid the following month. But while "Snake Hips" is almost completely unknown today, Bowlly continued to exert his influence decades later.

Guitarist Richard Thompson says, "my parents saw Al Bowlly sing at Hammersmith Palais during the war. I quite like him . . . I don't think he was Bing Crosby or anything, [but] he was the Great British Hope." Thompson subsequently introduced the singer to a brand new generation with a track on 1986's *Daring Adventures* album, "Al Bowlly's in Heaven."

Nine years before that, Bowlly's music was one of the star turns of a new BBC TV wartime drama, *Pennies from Heaven*, and amongst the millions of rapt viewers was a young Jyoti Mishra, the boy who would grow up to become 1996's "Your Woman" hitmaker White Town.

"I remember there was a piece of music in there by Al Bowlly, called 'My Woman,' which I just loved and remembered for years. Then, when I was writing 'Your Woman,' that was the kind of feel I wanted, so I went back to the Al Bowlly song." And so it came to

pass, in January, 1997, that two years shy of the centenary of his birth, Albert Alick Bowlly found himself at the top of the British chart, hypnotically sampled into one of the most memorable singles of the entire decade. Let's see Bing Crosby top that.

Neither was that Bowlly's first encounter with modern popular culture. In 1980, his recording (with bandleader Ray Noble) of "Midnight, the Stars and You" was included in the soundtrack to Stanley Kubrick's movie *The Shining*, and in 2016, an eBay user paid $1,500 for a copy of the original US Victor 78. It is, by far, his most in-demand recoding . . . even more so than "My Woman."

Although Thompson is right to call him the Great British hope of his era, Al Bowlly was actually born to a Greek father and Lebanese mother in Maputo (Lourenco Marques) in the Portuguese colony of Mozambique, in 1899. The family moved to Johannesburg, South Africa, while Al was still a child, and by the early 1920s, Bowlly was working at his uncle's barbers shop, supplementing his income singing and playing guitar, banjo, and ukulele in various local dance halls.

It was there that he was discovered by jazz pianist Edgar Adeler, and recruited into his band the Syncopaters in time for a tour of Asia. The group would travel throughout the Indian subcontinent, and were just about to head for Singapore when Bowlly and Adeler had a major falling out. Bowlly was fired on the spot, and left stranded in Calcutta, to make his own way home.

In 1926, Bowlly made his recorded debut with Calcutta's own Lequime's Grand Hotel Orchestra, playing banjo (but not singing) on their HMV release "Soho Blues"/"The House Where the Shutters are Green." Shortly after, however, he met American band leader Jimmy Lequime at the Grand Hotel, and joined his group just as they themselves were departing for Singapore.

By 1927, Bowlly was in Berlin, recording with both German and visiting American groups—two months apart that summer, he recorded versions of "Ain't She Sweet" with Arthur Brigg's Savoy Synchopators Orchestra (for Deutsche Grammophon) and the Salon Symphonic Jazz Band (for the Czechoslovakian Homochord label), while also cutting records with the Rene Dumont Jazz Band, John Abriani's Six, Billy Bartholomew's Delphians, and soloist Fred Bird. All told, Bowlly cut more than fifty sides alongside these acts between 1927–'28, while he also renewed his friendship with Edgar Adeler. They, too, were busy in the studio—titles such as "All Day Long," "I'm Alone in Athlone," "I'm Looking for a Bluebird," and "Blue Skies" were all cut in Berlin (for Homochord), and it was one of these recordings that brought Bowlly to London in the summer of 1928.

The controversial jazzman Fred Elizalde had just been appointed leader of the resident band at the Savoy Hotel—more out of respect for his public popularity than for the traditionally highbrow Savoy's love of Elizalde's saucy "hot" jazz style—and was playing through his record collection in search of suitable musicians. Bowlly's smooth, seductive vocal style fit Elizalde's bill perfectly, and within days, the singer was on his way to England.

In July, Bowlly cut his first record with Fred Elizalde & his Music, "Just Imagine [Good News]"/"Wherever You Are." Further studio sessions later in the year brought "If I Had You," "I'm Sorry Sally," and "Misery Farm," all released in the UK by Brunswick.

Unfortunately, the Savoy was not the only establishment that found Elizalde too hot to handle. The BBC, too, was unimpressed,

"Judaline," recorded by Bowlly with the Ray Noble Orchestra.

and when the corporation announced it intended to cease its regular live broadcasts from the Savoy, for fear of Elizalde's style offending listeners, the hotel management had no choice. The band was sacked and broke up soon after, and Bowlly found himself out of work and penniless.

He remained in dire straits for most of 1929, simply singing and playing wherever he could find work. In April/May, he cut sides with Percival Mackey & his Concert Orchestra, and joined band leader Len Fillis for some sessions with Linn Milford & his Hawaiian Players & Singers. Later in the year, he worked with another of Fillis' Hawaiian-themed acts, the Honolulu Serenaders, cutting a terrific "Pagan Love Call," and was on call again when Fillis and pianist Sid Bright required a guitarist for "Anita."

December then brought a studio reunion with Fred Elizalde and his latest band, the Rhythmicians, for the Metropole release "After the Sun Kissed the World Goodbye," and now Bowlly was back on his feet, singing at the newly opened and fashionably prestigious Monseigneur Restaurant with the Ray Fox Band. He would later join a splinter danceband formed by Fox sideman Lew Stone, but by far the more important engagement came when Bowlly was invited to join Ray Noble's famed New Mayfair Orchestra, in November, 1930.

Noble was director of light and dance music at the HMV Gramophone Company, and had been turning out a succession of smooth hit records for the

More than a quarter of a century after his death, Bowlly is commemorated on this 1966 album.

label for over a year now. Most featured some kind of vocal refrain, but usually an understated performance by anonymous performer. For his latest disc, however, Noble required something a little more special—"How Could I Be Lonely" was a beautiful song, but one which required someone who could do more than simply sing. They also needed to be versed in what journalist Brian Rust later called "the modern rhythmic idiom," and Bowlly—obscure though he might have been—was the best in town. "Without any shadow of a doubt," *Melody Maker*'s review of the record announced, Bowlly was "the leading style singer in the country. His phrasing, diction, and intonation are superb, whilst the individualism he manages to get into his renderings is really amazing."

Neither was it a one-off. By the end of 1930, Bowlly and Noble had recorded three more songs, including the monster-selling waltz "Underneath the Spanish Stars," the vigorous "Sunny Days," and the rousing "Make Yourself a Happiness Pie."

But it was the Orchestra's next session, in February, 1931, that would truly establish Bowlly as Britain's number one. "Goodnight, Sweetheart" would become *the* closing number at dance clubs all over the country, not just at the time, but for decades after; a true standard that has since been reinterpreted by any number of singers, but never with the sheer panache Bowlly brought to its bittersweet lyric. "When he sang a love lyric, it really got him," Ray Noble reflected. "The sincerity came through. I have seen him sing at the mike in front of the band, and there have been tears in his eyes as he turned away after finishing."

Buoyed by such success, Bowlly and Noble suddenly seemed unstoppable. Bowlly himself became the first singer ever to be granted a solo spot on BBC radio, and recorded over 250 songs during 1931 alone. (A number of these tracks have been anthologized within Vocalion's *HMV Sessions 1930–34* series of CDs.)

David Bowie, 12-inch Singles

"Absolute Beginners" (EMI AMERICA V-19205, 1985)

"Beauty and the Beast" (RCA PC-11,204-PROMO, 1978)

"Cat People (Putting Out Fire)" (BACKSTREET L33-1759 PROMO, 1981)

"Hallo Spaceboy" (12-inch Remix) (VIRGIN SPRO-11513 PROMO, 1996)

"Heroes" (RCA JD-11151 PROMO, 1977)

"John I'm Only Dancing (Again)" (1975) (UK RCA BOW12 4, 1979)

"Pallas Athena" (live) (as Tao Jones Index) (ARISTA/BMG 512541, 1997)

"Star" (live) (RCA DJL1-3255 PROMO WHITE VINYL, 1978)

"Up the Hill Backwards" (RCA PD-12249, 1981)

The Continuing Story of Major Tom (RCA DJL1-3,795 PROMO, 1980)

Most were hits: indeed, both "Time On My Hands" and "Lady of Spain" kept the cash registers screaming for years, while "Pages of Radioland" offered dancers a swinging medley of nine of the day's biggest hits (spread over two sides of a disc), and "Lights Of Paris" tied their feet in knots with one of the trickiest time signatures ever devised, a nine-eight-one step. Perhaps inevitably, this became one of the Noble/Bowlly team's biggest flops, and its composer, Tolchard Evans (author, too, of "Lady of Spain") vowed never to try such an experiment again.

All told, Bowlly recorded some 700 sides between 1930–'34, not only with Noble and his various musical permutations (the New Mayfair Dance Orchestra, the New Mayfair Novelty Orchestra, the New Mayfair Orchestra, the Night Club Kings, and the Novelty Orchestra) but also alongside Lew Stone (with and without his Monseigneur Band), Jack Leon, his old friend Len Fillis, and more.

In 1934, Noble and Bowlly decided to take their talents to New York, and after some initial union-led teething problems, America, too, took the singer's cool, good looks and rich, dark voice to its heart. He performed at the Rainbow Room; recorded some ninety sides for the Victor, Bluebird, and Decca labels; and was even involved in a few unseemly incidents where excited female fans attempted to remove his clothing and hair for souvenirs.

Such sights were never seen in staid old Britain (there, fans merely fainted at the sight of him, hence Bowlly's reputation as "The Swoon of the Thirties") and Bowlly—happily married to his second wife, Marjie—had to be rescued by the police, and promise never again to leave his hotel room unaccompanied.

Bowlly's American sojourn ended when Ray Noble was offered a regular spot alongside comedians George Burns and Gracie Allen on radio's *Burns and Allen Show*, which launched in September 1936. Already homesick, Bowlly decided against seeking new opportunities in the US, and returned to London in January, 1937.

He arrived home to discover that times had changed dramatically during his absence. A handful of solo sides recorded during the year (including "Blue Hawaii," "Hometown," and "On a Little Dream Ranch") fared poorly, and while a return to New York at the end of the year would see him cut the much-loved "Every Day's a Holiday" and "Half Moon on the Hudson," it was clear that new singers and new styles had moved up to displace him.

Bowlly would enjoy some success working with the famed trumpeter Nat Gonella, and continued to record some quite masterful records, often alongside Lew Stone. But then a throat operation pushed him even further away from the limelight. It would be late

1938 before Bowlly was back to his performing best, by which time he was regarded as even more old-fashioned.

His marriage crumbled along with his career, and when war broke out in September, 1939, Bowlly seized the only opportunity for regular work that was available, entertaining the troops with a new stage routine built solely upon his nostalgia value—a surefire hit, it transpired, in a world which was getting darker by the day. By early 1941, Bowlly's career was again in the ascendent.

On April 2, taking a break from his concert schedule, Bowlly went into the studio with guitarist Jimmy Mesene and pianist Pat Dodd, in the guise of Radio Stars with Two Guitars, to cut two new songs, "Nicky the Greek (Has Gone)" and "When that Man Is Dead and Gone." It was, he would say, a rare night off indeed when he could simply return to his London flat, curl up in bed with a cowboy novel, and read himself to sleep.

Wednesday, April 16 was one of those rare nights. Unfortunately, it was also one of the now-equally infrequent occasions when the German Luftwaffe decided to put on a major show of force in the London skies. According to one eyewitness, writer Charles Graves, the Stuka dive bombers came in so low "that I mistook [them] for taxi cabs," and the following morning, the city left the shelters to find over a thousand people dead, some 80,000 houses damaged, Chelsea's beautiful Old Church demolished, the Admiralty headquarters wrecked, and one magical voice stilled forever.

A bomb had exploded in the street immediately outside the bedroom of Bowlly's apartment, blowing in one entire side of the building, and killing the singer instantly. "Goodnight, Sweetheart" would never be sung quite so sweetly again.

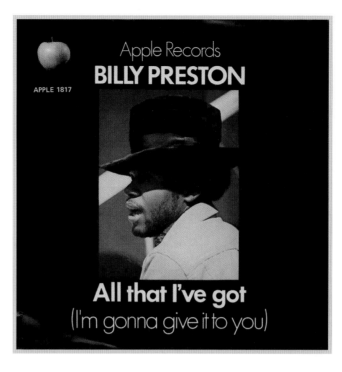

Billy Preston was one of the Beatles' most trusted sidemen, and an Apple label star as well.

The Bowlly catalog abounds with what are now considered rarities—even the big hits, after eighty-plus years, survive in ever-decreasing quantities, while his first releases from Germany and Czechoslovakia are extraordinarily elusive, even in their countries of origin.

His contributions to the Durium label's shortlived series of flexible 78s are in demand, even if they are not especially expensive, and when you step off the beaten track and move into the world of test pressings, some true marvels emerge—none more than the contents of a 2012 eBay auction, offering up 110 tests that had been sent to bandleader Howard Godfrey, from which he would select which "take" of a song should be released. Many of the titles ran to four or five different versions; all but one was destined to remain unreleased; and no less than fifteen of the recordings featured Bowlly. The entire lot sold for over $5,000.

Pre-10cc

"I'm Beside Myself," Frabjoy and the Runcible Spoon (UK MARMALADE 598 019, 1969)

"Impossible Years," Graham Gouldman (RCA VICTOR 47-9453, 7-INCH, 1968)

"Joker," Garden Odyssey (UK RCA 2159, 7-INCH, 1972)

"Sad and Lonely," Garden Odyssey Enterprise (UK DERAM DM 267, 7-INCH, 1969)

"Stop Stop Stop," Graham Gouldman (UK DECCA F12334, 7-INCH, 1966)

"That's How," The Mockingbirds (ABC PARAMOUNT 10653, 7-INCH, 1965)

"Umbopo," Dr. Father (UK PYE 7N 17977, 7-INCH, 1970)

"Upstairs Downstairs," Graham Gouldman (UK RCA 1667, 7-INCH, 1968)

"Windmills of Your Mind," Graham Gouldman Orchestra (UK SPARK SRL 1026, 7-INCH, 1969)

"You Stole My Love," The Mockingbirds (UK IMMEDIATE IM 015, 7-INCH, 1965)

THE LABEL: MICK JAGGER IS THE A&R MAN

Although it feels like a modern innovation, ripe with the promise of the internet and the pleasures of "cutting out the middle man," the concept of an artist-owned record label was already an old one even when the Beatles launched the best known of the lot, Apple in 1968.

Both Frank Sinatra (Reprise) and Herb Alpert (A&M) had entered these waters before the Fab Four, while sundry producers and managers, too, had long since established their own concerns. However, it was with the launch of Apple that the idea of the artist at least appearing to be in control of their own destiny, and that of the artists they favored, took hold with a fascination that remains ripe even today.

Such concerns as dBpm Records (owned by Wilco), Richter Scale (. . . And You Will Know Us By the Trail of Dead), Third Man (Jack White), and G.O.O.D. Records (Kanye West) have all flourished in recent years; and, looking back, NPG (Prince), Rocket (Elton John), Hot Wax (Marc Bolan), Purple Records (Deep Purple), and Threshold (the Moody Blues) can all point to some remarkable successes.

In collecting terms, such labels are both a blessing and a curse—the former, because they place great swathes of an artist's catalog "under one roof"; the latter because the artist often tended to be the only significant performer on the label, which leaves the collector scrambling for some decidedly obscure one-off 45s and albums. Many of which, in truth, they would not even consider allowing into the house if it were not for the sake of the collection.

As aforementioned, Apple is the "big daddy" of the artist-owned labels, launched with much fanfare in August, 1968, with the release of three 45s—the Beatles' own "Hey Jude" joining Mary Hopkin's "Those Were the Days" and Jackie Lomax's "Sour Milk Sea." A fourth issue, released in the UK only, was the Black Dyke Mills

George Harrison

"All Those Years Ago" (DARK HORSE PRO A949, 12-INCH PROMO, 1981)

The Best of George Harrison (CAPITOL ST 11578, ORANGE-LABEL LP, 1976)

"Dark Horse" (APPLE 1877, 7-INCH, PICTURE SLEEVE, 1974)

Dark Horse Radio Special (DARK HORSE, NO CATALOG NUMBER, PROMO LP, 1974)

"Devil's Radio" (DARK HORSE PRO A2889, 12-INCH PROMO, 1987)

"Ding Dong" (APPLE 1879, 7-INCH, BLUE/WHITE PHOTO LABEL, 1974)

"Give Me Love" (APPLE P1862, 7-INCH PROMO, 1972)

"Love Comes to Everyone" (DARK HORSE 8844, 7-INCH, PICTURE SLEEVE, 1979)

"My Sweet Lord" (APPLE 2995, 7-INCH, BLACK STAR ON LABEL, 1970)

"What Is Life" (APPLE 1828, 7-INCH, PICTURE SLEEVE, 1971)

Band's "Thingumybob." Uniquely for a new label (but, perhaps, not surprisingly for a Beatles-related concern), both "Hey Jude" and "Those Were the Days" topped the UK chart.

Apple was conceived amid a flurry of other ambitious projects (movie, electronics, publishing, tailoring, and merchandising divisions were also founded). Emphasizing artists whom the Beatles themselves personally wished to nurture, the label's early signings also included the Iveys (soon to become Badfinger), Billy Preston, Doris Troy, Ronnie Spector, David Peel, James Taylor, and Hot Chocolate—notably only the latter two truly met with lasting success, both after they departed Apple.

The bulk of these non-Beatle recordings were made during the label's first three years of operation; by late 1972, the label's output was almost exclusively confined to John and Yoko Lennon, Paul McCartney and Wings, George Harrison, and Ringo Starr. Of Apple's other recruits, only Elephant's Memory, Badfinger, and the utterly obscure Lon and Dereck Van Eaton would release further music (one 45 and LP apiece) on the label. Paul McCartney departed in 1975; Apple ceased operations, as far as new releases were concerned, in 1976.

With fewer than seventy LPs and one hundred 45s released in either the UK or US (including several that appeared only in one or the other market), the Apple catalog is small, but surprisingly difficult to amass in its original form.

A promotional box set comprising the first four UK singles and an EP available only through the British Walls Ice Cream company are very rarely sighted; also of immense value is the banned UK APPLE 8, "The King of Fuh," by New York singer Brute Force. Outraged by lyrics that included the immortal "Oh hell! The Fuh King," distributors Parlophone refused to press the single. Apple therefore manufactured it privately, but it failed to sell and copies swiftly disappeared.

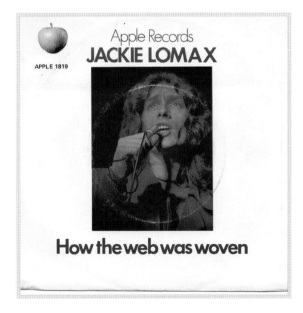

George Harrison was responsible for signing Lomax to the label.

The first and only releases on the extraordinarily short-lived experimental subsidiary Zapple, in May 1969 (John and Yoko's *Unfinished Music 2: Life with the Lions* and George's *Electronic Sounds*) are highly prized, as are the eight mono LPs that Apple released in the UK during late 1968 and early 1969. This includes the Beatles' own *The Beatles* and the *Yellow Submarine* movie soundtrack, together with further LPs by Harrison, the Lennons, James Taylor, Mary Hopkin, Jackie Lomax, and the Modern Jazz Quartet.

Apple also produced a handful of special-edition LPs, featuring ephemeral extras that are now very difficult to come by. The Lennons' *Wedding Album* featured several items of a celebratory nature; *Live Peace at Toronto* included a free calendar. The Beatles' final album, *Let It Be*, was issued in a box set with an accompanying booklet; so were George Harrison's *All Things Must Pass* and *The Concert for Bangladesh*. The greatest rarity of all, however, is a Christmas 1970 Beatles LP issued only for fan-club members. *From Then to Us* compiled all of the group's annual Christmas flexidiscs and has since been extensively bootlegged.

Other high-ticket items include a Mary Hopkin hits collection, *Those Were the Days,* and Indian sitarist Ravi Shankar's *In Concert 1972*, a two-LP live set that sold extremely poorly at the time, but that has since become a grail of sorts. Pressings of a Delaney and Bonnie album scheduled for release, but ultimately canceled, exist, but they surface very rarely.

Apple's US office was also responsible for a handful of 4-inch Pocket Disc releases, manufactured in 1969 in conjunction with the company Americom, for sale via vending machines. These account for many of the label's greatest rarities: the Beatles issues comprise "Get Back," "The Ballad of John and Yoko," "Yellow Submarine," and a unique 3:25 edit of "Hey Jude." Mary Hopkin's "Those Were the Days" and "Goodbye," the Iveys' "Maybe Tomorrow," the Plastic Ono Band's "Give Peace a Chance," and Billy Preston's "That's the Way God Planned It" also appeared in this unusual format.

In addition to UK and US releases, international Apple releases also offer a considerable challenge. Many were issued with otherwise unavailable picture sleeves, and occasionally, incomprehensible titles—Mary Hopkin's "Bylie Taki Dni" ("Those Were the Days") was a major hit in Poland; Hopkin also rerecorded several of her singles in foreign languages, including French, German, Spanish, Italian, and Japanese.

Apple specialists might also care to pursue acetates recorded at the Apple studios, distinguishable (of course) by the blank Apple label affixed to many. Among the rarest of these can be counted the first-ever recording by British band 10cc, "Waterfall."

Apple's full catalog has yet to see any kind of orderly CD reissue program, with only sporadic releases for certain titles appearing until 2010 brought a seventeen-disc box set featuring albums by Badfinger, Mary Hopkin, Billy Preston, Jackie Lomax, the Modern Jazz Quartet,

An Apple release raising funds and awareness for the legally beleaguered UK magazine Oz.

James Taylor, Doris Troy, the Radha Krishna Temple, and John Tavener, plus two discs of rarities. More recently, 2017 saw the much-anticipated arrival of New York band Mortimer's second album (following a debut for Philips), recorded in London but left unreleased.

There have also been several reissues for Yoko Ono's catalog (the most recent launched in late 2016 featured both CD and vinyl releases) including the three experimental albums cocredited with Lennon. Impressively, almost half a century on from their original release, all three are still capable of infuriating the inhabitants of those online forums where music lovers go to discuss things. There are not many albums you can say that about.

Although Apple is often described as a failed experiment, at least inasmuch as many of its extracurricular enterprises all failed quite spectacularly, two ex-Beatles would go on to launch their own labels later in their careers; Ringo Starr's Ring O, and George Harrison's Dark Horse.

Harrison was still under contract to EMI/Apple when he launched Dark Horse in May 1974, initially as an outlet for new talent, but also, from 1976, for his own releases. The label's original distributor was A&M; a fractious relationship ended after just eight LPs, in November 1976. Harrison then switched distribution to Warner Bros.

Dark Horse got off to a good start with the UK success of Splinter, a band featuring members of the Apple-signing Elastic Oz Band. Splinter's "Costa Finetown" 45 and *The Place I Love* debut album were immediate hits, but the band's subsequent releases were less successful, setting the stage for two years of underachievement.

Dark Horse's next release was Ravi Shankar's *Family and Friends*; in common with other Harrison-related Shankar LPs, the value of this release is constantly rising. A Shankar and Friends single, "I Am Missing You," is a seldom-seen score.

Lesser known, but similarly scarce, is a self-titled set by Jiva, while a solo album by Henry McCullough, *Mind Your Own Business*, proudly boasts two Beatle links—McCullough was previously guitarist with Paul McCartney's Wings. Other Dark Horse artists during the A&M period included the Stairsteps and Attitudes, an ad-hoc band featuring session musicians David Foster, Danny Kortchmar, and Jim Keltner.

Harrison's *Thirty Three and ⅓* was the first release under the Warner Bros. deal in late 1976, but a promising start for the new arrangement—with four albums issued in under twelve months (further sets by Attitude and Splinter, and a debut by Keni Burke)— swiftly petered out. There would be no further Dark Horse activity until 1979 brought Harrison's eponymous set, since which time the Dark Horse logo has been invoked for his releases alone.

Naturally, the late Harrison was the label's most consistently collectible artist, with his British 45s catalog featuring several scarce items. These include a picture-disc edition of 1979's "Faster" and limited boxed editions of 1987's "When We Was Fab" and "Got My Mind Set on You." Reissues of his albums, meanwhile, have seen box set editions on both CD and vinyl.

The Rolling Stones were the first major act to follow the Beatles into the realms of boutique labels; after eight years with Decca (UK) and London (US), the Rolling Stones launched their own self-titled label in 1971. Having entertained bids from virtually every major label in the business, they linked with Atlantic Records for distribution, while appointing Marshall Chess (son of Chess label founder Leonard) as label manager.

The intention was for the new label to handle both the Stones' own output (and planned solo releases) and to showcase new talent discovered by the band members. In fact, only a handful of non-Stones records were ever issued during the label's time with Atlantic: two underachieving solo sets by bassist Bill Wyman (*Monkey Grip* and *Stone*

The Iveys, James Taylor, Jackie Lomax and Mary Hopkin were all featured on this promotional EP available via mail order from Walls Ice Cream in 1969.

Alone); a collection of Moroccan pipe music recorded by the late Brian Jones; the *Jammin' with Edward* collection of loose jams and grooves, featuring sundry Stones members and associates; a Keith Richards solo single; and just one unrelated LP (and 45), by Kracker. Interestingly, the extracurricular careers embarked upon by Messrs. Wyman, Watts, Richard, and Wood during the 1980s and 1990s all took place far from the auspices of their own label—only Mick Jagger deployed the familiar logo on his mid-'80s albums *She's the Boss* and *Primitive Cool*.

The European end of the Atlantic distribution deal expired in 1976 and Rolling Stones Records moved to EMI. A new numbering series was instituted; the Atlantic COC prefix was replaced by CUN, continuing a delightfully schoolboyish ribaldry. However, again, extracurricular albums were at a premium, with reggae star Peter Tosh

Led Zeppelin

"Communication Breakdown" (UK ATLANTIC 584 269, 7-INCH PROMO, 1969)

"Dazed and Confused" (ATLANTIC EP 1019, 7-INCH PROMO, 1969)

"D'yer Maker" (UK ATLANTIC K10296, 7-INCH PROMO, 1973)

Houses of the Holy (ATLANTIC SD 7255, MONO PROMO LP, 1973)

Led Zeppelin III (ATLANTIC SD 7201, MONO PROMO LP, 1971)

Led Zeppelin IV (ATLANTIC SD 77208, JUKEBOX ALBUM, 1972)

"Stairway to Heaven" (ATLANTIC STPR 269, 7-INCH PROMO PICTURE DISC, 1979)

"Trampled Under Foot" (UK SWAN SONG DC 1, 7-INCH PROMO, 1975)

"Wearing and Tearing" (UK SWAN SONG SSK 19421, WITHDRAWN 7-INCH, 1979)

"Whole Lotta Love" (UK ATLANTIC 584 309, WITHDRAWN 7-INCH, 1969)

the sole new arrival. He would bring the label its only significant non-Stones chart success, when a cover of the Temptations' "Don't Look Back" made No. 81 in 1978. Rolling Stones Records has since been handled by CBS (beginning in 1986), Virgin/EMI (1994), and Universal (2008), all of whom have reissued the band's own catalog and brought together their own compilations of material. However, no further outside talent has been recruited to the label.

The vast majority of collectibles on the label are, then, the Stones' own, and include a slew of CD singles in the 1990s and, more recently, a very impressive forty five–CD box set of every own-label Stones single, released in 2011. True, multiple remixes of their latter-day releases are not always the first thing you'll throw on the player every day, but the initial run of releases from "Brown Sugar" (1971) to "Mixed Emotions" (1989) represents some of the most superlative music they ever made.

Beyond the Stones' catalog, the Kracker, Brian Jones, and *Jammin'* albums are sought after, while quadraphonic mixes of Wyman's two solo LPs are extremely hard to find. These are the only quad releases on the label. Another popular item is a red-vinyl 12-inch of the infamous "Cocksucker Blues," which purportedly appeared as an official Rolling Stones Records promo release in the late '80s. In fact, this release was a bootleg—the only official release of "Cocksucker Blues" remains its appearance on a limited-edition, one-sided 7-inch offered with the German four-LP box set, *The Rest of the Best of the Rolling Stones*, in the mid-'80s.

The early 1970s were a heyday of sorts for the artist-owned label; few, however, were built for the long haul and most, sadly, spared barely a glance for outside talent. One that did branch out in quite spectacular style was Manticore, the property of the progressive-rock band Emerson Lake and Palmer.

The label took its name from one of the mythological creatures depicted on the sleeve of the group's sophomore LP, *Tarkus.* The label was distributed through Cotillion in the US and Atlantic in the UK.

The label debuted in 1973 with a solo album by King Crimson songwriter Pete Sinfield, *Still*—ELP's 1971 live album *Pictures at an Exhibition* would subsequently be reissued on Manticore in the US. *Photos of Ghosts,* by Italian band PFM (Premiata Forneria Marconi), followed, together with ELP's own new album, *Brain Salad Surgery.* Albums by Hanson, Stray Dog, Junior Hanson, and a second PFM set followed during 1973–'74, while ELP released a second live set, the ambitious triple LP *Welcome Back My Friends*, that same year.

In 1975, Manticore's US distribution moved to Motown, for a series of LPs that includes further sets by Stray Dog and PFM, plus debut offerings by Keith Christmas (first released in the UK the previous year) and another Italian band, Banco, and two sets by the putative supergroup Thee Image (ex–Iron Butterfly, Cactus). A fourth PFM

LP, *Chocolate Kings* (K53508), and Keith Christmas's second, *Stories from the Human Zoo* (K53509), appeared in the UK alone in 1976, but there was no new material from ELP. The band was in the midst of what would become a three-year break, and upon their return to action in 1977, Manticore was nowhere to be seen.

In collecting terms, the label is nevertheless dominated by ELP. The aforementioned LPs are joined by two singles: 1973's "Jerusalem" and "Still . . . You Turn Me On." Both were distinguished by otherwise unavailable B-sides; Manticore also released a promotional flexidisc through the UK newspaper *New Musical Express,* excerpting the *Brain Salad Surgery* album and offering the cuts in a gatefold sleeve similar to that of the parent LP. Also of interest are the UK label releases of Greg Lake's solo 45 "I Believe in Father Christmas" and Keith Emerson's "Honky Tonk Train Blues."

Generally overlooked, however, is the fact that Manticore also released 45s by its other signings. In the US, this includes Hanson's "Love Knows Everything" and "Boy Meets Girl" and PFM's "Celebration" and "Mr. Nine to Five." These releases can prove extremely challenging to find.

Equally impressive, in terms of both success and scope (and lastly in this brief roundup), was Led Zeppelin's Swan Song. Titled for an unreleased Jimmy Page solo recording, Swan Song launched in 1974 with the US release of the British band Bad Company's eponymous debut LP (the UK version was released by Island Records) and 45 "Can't Get Enough." In Britain, the debut release arrived some six months later, with a garish party at Chislehurst Caves launching the Pretty Things' *Silk Torpedo* album.

Zeppelin did not appear on the label until 1975 brought the *Physical Graffiti* double album. Distribution was handled through Atlantic, to whom the band had been signed since its inception in 1969.

Over the next six years, four further Led Zeppelin albums were issued by Swan Song—the double live *The Song Remains the Same, Presence, In Through the Out Door*, and, issued following the group's disbandment, *Coda.* Of these, *In Through the Out Door* is notable for being released with six different sleeves, labeled A to F and individually paper-bagged so that purchasers would not know which sleeve they were receiving. Complete sets of all six, with the bags intact, are relatively easy to assemble but fetch a considerable premium on the collectors market. Also of note are white-label test pressings of *Physical Graffiti,* issued within a mock-up of the album's eventual sleeve.

Led Zeppelin understandably dominates the label from a collector's point of view, with several of the group's most sought-after rarities emanating from the Swan Song catalog. Paramount among these is a withdrawn UK single coupling "Wearing and Tearing"/"Darlene," scheduled for release to commemorate the band's Knebworth Park concerts in July 1979. Better known, and considerably more common, is a similar issue for the 1975 Earl's Court concerts, coupling "Trampled Under Foot"/"Black Country Woman"—this same coupling, of course, appeared as a regular 45 in the US, one of three Led Zeppelin singles issued by Swan Song. "Candy Store Rock" and "Fool in the Rain" complete the sequence. No Led Zeppelin singles were ever issued in the UK.

Swan Song's next non-Zeppelin releases were both US-only issues, Maggie Bell's *Suicide Sal* and Bad Company's *Straight Shooter*. Bad Company remained with the label until the band's breakup in 1982, releasing four further albums and nine singles. Zeppelin aside, it was the label's most successful act, although Dave Edmunds ran it a close second. Joining Swan Song in 1976, the Welshman cut four albums and a total of fourteen singles (some UK or US only).

A second Pretty Things album, *Savage Eye*, appeared in 1975—as with its predecessor, attendant singles are common; the following year brought the arrival of the underrated but not especially sought-after Detective, featuring ex-Yes keyboard player Tony Kaye, Steppenwolf guitarist Michael Monarch, and former Silverhead vocalist Michael Des Barres. *Detective* was followed by *It Takes One to Know One*.

Led Zeppelin disbanded following the death of drummer John Bonham in September 1980; Swan Song began to wind down at the same time. The last new signings were Midnight Flyer, who cut two Swan Song LPs featuring the returning Maggie Bell, and the Manchester band Sad Café, whose one album was produced by 10cc's Eric Stewart—US promo copies of the attendant "La-Di-Da" 45 are common enough to have earned the title of the biggest non-collectible in the entire Swan Song catalog.

The label closed down with the first solo recordings by Jimmy Page (the *Death Wish II* soundtrack) and Robert Plant (*Pictures at 11*). A UK 12-inch single from the latter, "Burning Down One Side" (SSK 19429T), fittingly closed the catalog with another rarity.

AND FINALLY: THE REBIRTH OF VINYL— FORGIVE ME IF YOU'VE HEARD THIS ONE BEFORE

It's one of *the* musical headlines of the mid-2010s . . . vinyl is *back*. And not just back on the racks, it's back in people's hearts as well, up there alongside internet streaming and highly-priced box sets as *the* principle musical delivery format of the age.

The statistics are certainly impressive. In April 2016, the fortune.com website reported, "Revenues from vinyl sales last year were higher than those of on-demand ad supported streaming services, such as YouTube, Vevo, and Spotify's free service, which only accounted for $385 million, according to the RIAA."

In December, digitalmusicnews.com proclaimed, "sales of LPs and 45s are outstripping digital sales in the UK, according to the Entertainment Retail Association (ERA)." Over a seven-day period at the dawn of the holiday shopping season, "sales of vinyl reached £2.4 million ($3.03 million) . . . while digital purchases only reached £2.1 million ($2.64 million)."

The numbers are impressive, all the more so since they account only for new vinyl sales. Factor in the used market, both on and offline, and the figures are certainly far higher. Yet the mid 2010s do not mark the first time a vinyl resurgence has been celebrated. Two decades earlier, in the mid-1990s (that is, less than five years after LPs were effectively phased out of mainstream production), all the signs and celebrations were that wax had simply been on hiatus, and was now preparing to launch the comeback of the century.

The signs were indeed convincing. In November 1994, Pearl Jam's *Vitalogy* album was released on vinyl two weeks before its CD counterpart emerged, and promptly entered the chart at No. 55. The point being *not* that the most eagerly awaited new album of the season could only debut at No. 55. It is that it did so on the strength of a limited edition of 35,000 copies of a format that was supposedly dead and buried.

And that was in the United States—which, according to figures published the following year, was the last of the world's major markets not to be experiencing a serious resurgence of vinyl consumption. The Japanese had never really stopped stocking vinyl, while 1994 also saw Tower Records in London's Piccadilly devote an entire floor to the resurgent wax.

Nor, contrary to continued propaganda, was it indie 45s alone that took up so much space. More UK new releases were appearing on vinyl than at any time all decade, while the Top Thirty singles chart remained as readily available on plastic as it ever was. The only difference was, there were fewer high-street retailers stocking the things. Both WH Smith's and Boots, two of the largest general merchandisers to carry music products, had renounced vinyl a couple of years earlier.

In terms of overall sales, compact disc did still rule the roost, particularly in the realm of archive-scouring bonus tracks and anthologies—the last serious stab at rivaling its supremacy was Rykodisc's early 1990s series of David Bowie reissues, (almost) every one appended with bonus tracks spread across a second piece of vinyl. But the series was curtailed long before it was complete, and a lesson appears to have been learned.

The death, in 2011, of singer Trish Keenan brought to an end the remarkable career of Broadcast, one of the most extraordinary experimental acts of the century so far.

The singles market was a very different beast, with the revived fortune of the 7-inch joined by a simultaneous revival of its 12-inch sibling. Indeed, it was even suggested that the only thing keeping CDs ahead in sales terms was the then-current policy of releasing the discs in two, or even more, versions, each bearing a crop of different B-sides; and that advantage was looking shaky.

Both CD editions of [London] Suede's "The Wild Ones" single appeared on 12-inch, while Morrissey—a record collector himself—went one better by restricting his *Boxers* EP to just one CD and an identical 12-inch. The situation in the US was not so clear-cut. Major league country singles were still appearing on 7-inch vinyl, catering primarily for the lucrative jukebox market, while the club scene's dependence on 12-inch white labels had yet to be seriously challenged.

But there was action in the rock market, too. Capitol Records accrued considerable collector mileage from a red vinyl Beatles collection, while Warner Brothers were not averse to the occasional promo 45.

Albums, however, remained a prickly prospect. Import sales of UK LPs were strong, particularly those that either predated, or differed significantly from the US CDs (releases by Shane MacGowan and St. Etienne were cases in point). And while this was more suggestive of collector activity than a mass-market move back to wax, collectors were scarcely a new innovation. If they now formed a large enough chunk of the market to send Pearl Jam into the Top Sixty on the strength of vinyl sales alone, then surely they were worthy of consideration elsewhere?

The indie labels had already sensed this, and the majors were watching them closely. All along, however, one significant issue hung unanswered. Should they have decided to act, and sponsor a wholesale return to vinyl, how could they best address the issue?

It was, after all, a public relations disaster in the making. Having finally persuaded most everyone that CDs were the wave of the foreseeable future, and having successfully survived both the great Self-Destructing Lacquer scare and the surprisingly prevalent belief that digital sound causes brain cancer (actually, it just gives you a headache), the music industry could scarcely turn around and say, "Oops, sorry; we goofed."

The audiophiliac Mobile Fidelity was the first to take such a step, pledging its support to the vinyl renaissance through their licensing of various comparatively low-profile alternative releases—Matthew Sweet's *Girlfriend* and *Altered Beast* albums both landed on the schedule, despite the former having sold less than 500,000 copies, and the latter, around half of that. Other, similarly cult releases would follow.

Neither was Sony's vinyl Pearl Jam effort unique. A&M had done something very similar with Soundgarden's *Superunknown*, while Atlantic (Page and Plant's *No Quarter*) and Geffen (Nirvana and Siouxsie & the Banshees) had likewise catered for vinyl lovers. Furthermore, the latter pair also adopted the collector-oriented Bomp indie's long-established love for 10-inch vinyl mini-albums with releases by, respectively, Bettie Serveert and Elastica.

And it all amounted to . . . nothing. The Britpop explosion that fed Britain's vinyl revival faded; the Pearl Jam and Soundgarden experiments were never seriously repeated. Vinyl returned to the history books, at least so far as the majority was concerned, and while there would remain a steady trickle of indie releases and reissues, by the end of the first decade of the twenty-first century, new vinyl accounted for precisely 2,800,000 unit sales. That in turn was divided almost exactly between new releases and catalog sales, with the latter then skewed further by the long-awaited release of the Beatles' *Abbey Road*, destined to remain the best selling vinyl record in America for the next four years.

But there *was* something going on. A million more records were sold in 2011 than in 2010. By 2013, vinyl had more than doubled its total of three years before. When 2014 brought a total figure in excess of nine million, a 260% increase in just five years, clearly something was afoot.

How significant was it? According to the IFPI trade body, vinyl sales still accounted for just two percent of total music sales, at a time when the total trade revenue generated by the music industry worldwide had fallen by 0.4 percent to $14.97 billion.

Or, as *Billboard* put it in April 2014, "Vinyl remains a niche part of the market, and no one is saying the old-school format is the saviour of the industry, artists, and for entertainment retailers. Consider it a feel-good story in a time when technology and digital streaming models dominate talk on the future of music distribution."

Hard numbers are one thing, however. Anecdote and experience are something else entirely. Keith Jones, whose specialist Fruits de Mer label is one of the collecting sensations of the era (and is stubbornly devoted

> ## Dawn 7-Inchers
>
> *Barrelhouse Player*, Bronx Cheer (DAWN DNX 2512, EP, 1971)
> **"Crippled with Nerves,"** Kilburn and the High Roads (DAWN DNS 1102, 7-INCH, 1975)
> *Diana*, Comus (DAWN DNX 2506, EP, 1970)
> *I Can't Lie to You*, Atlantic Bridge (DAWN DNX 2507, EP, 1971)
> *Reason for Asking*, Paul Brett (DAWN DNX 2508, EP, 1971)
> *I Put a Spell on You*, Demon Fuzz (DAWN DNX 2504, EP, 1970)
> **"Love Is Walking,"** Quiet World (DAWN DNS 1005, 7-INCH, 1970)
> **"Ricki Ticki Tavi,"** Donovan (DAWN DNS 1006, 7-INCH, 1970)
> **"Stand by Me,"** Atomic Rooster (DAWN DNS 1027, 7-INCH, 1972)
> **"Whoa Buck,"** Paul King (DAWN DNS 1023, 7-INCH, 1972)

From Finland, the Octopus Syng are one of the key acts on the Mega Dodo label.

to vinyl-only releases) explains, "As a vinyl fan, it's got to be good news—amongst all the dull reissues, there are some real gems being released that would otherwise never have seen the light of day. Running a small vinyl label, it's tough. The major labels that turned their backs on vinyl are back with a vengeance and they're doing their best to push the small guys to the back of manufacturing and distribution queues that simply didn't exist when we started back in 2008.

"It's not had a noticeable effect either way on Fruits de Mer sales, as far as I can see. I'm sure some of the new recruits to collecting vinyl will stay around, getting seriously hooked on the music (and not just the format) and enjoy their obsession with music, bands, and labels—an obsession that those of us who grew up in the '60s and '70s lived for and still revel in.

"But much of it's a fad. It's inevitable that the novelty will wear off, interest in reissues will fall, 'limited editions' (of 5,000 and more!) will remain unsold." Unapologetically, he predicts a day when the current boom becomes a bust, and vinyl—at least as a must-have, must-buy accoutrement to everyday living—falls out of the media spotlight and becomes, again, the province of hardcore collectors, fans, and obsessives. Just like it did in the '90s, just like it did in the '80s.

Which isn't such a bad thing. A lot of modern reissues do seem unnecessary, particularly in those instances where an album that is already as common as muck on the used circuit, and can be picked up for a buck or two there, is repurposed as a "modern collectible," maybe bound up into a box set with a clutch of the artist's other releases, and retailed for sums in the low three figures.

But we take the bad with the good—other rereleases look into the very depths of the archive, to restore to vinyl albums that have been out-of-print for decades, and have a strong following of would-be owners pursuing them. Whoever would have believed, at any point

The first-ever release on the eminently collectible Fruits de Mer label, Schizo Fun Addict's irresistible retreads of George Martin's "Theme One" and the Small Faces' "Ogden's Nut Gone Fluke." Both were originally instrumentals. Schizo added vocals.

Current 93's The Inmost Light collects 1996's All the Pretty Horses album, plus two associated 12-inch EPs.

Ten Top Finds from the Last Days of Vinyl

Achtung Baby, U2 (ISLAND 510347-1, 1991)

Check Your Head, The Beastie Boys (CAPITOL C1-98938, 1992)

Cocteau Twins, Cocteau Twins (CAPITOL SPRO79066/7, 1991)

Erotica, Madonna (MAVERICK PRO-A-5904, 1992)

First Kiss, Last Licks, Kiss (MERCURY 792-1, 1990)

Metallica, Metallica (ELEKTRA 61113, 1991)

No Fences, Garth Brooks (CAPITOL NASHVILLE R173266, 1990)

Tripping the Live Fantastic, Paul McCartney (CAPITOL C1-94778, 1990)

U2, Negativland (SST 272, 1990)

We Die Young, Alice in Chains (COLUMBIA CAS2192, 1990)

since 1968, that it would one day be possible to buy brand-new, and newly pressed mono editions of the entire Kinks, Beatles, and Rolling Stones catalogs? Entire artistic oeuvres, from Marvin Gaye to Bruce Springsteen, from Barry White to the Monkees, have been restored to the racks in monstrous LP box sets? Nineties-and-later albums that never even saw vinyl in the US now take their waxen bow.

That LPs that sold just a handful in their day, and have scarcely been seen outside of museums since then, would now be just a mouse click away, in pristine, factory-fresh condition? That not only would select new releases be appearing on CD, download, and vinyl as well, but that some—and Fruits de Mer are simply the leaders of this parade—would forego digital and disc altogether, and *only* appear on record?

With all that in mind, it wouldn't matter if the vinyl bubble was to burst again tomorrow. The past five years have already gifted record collectors with a whole new world full of records to collect. And they aren't going any place.

What do you mean, vinyl is back? It never really went away.

4 | THIRTY COLLECTIBLE RECORD LABELS

INTRODUCTION

Without record labels, we would have no records. That is, perhaps, a simplistic statement that is open to pedantic debate on a thousand levels, particularly since the internet proved that self-released albums, whether physical or downloaded, are just as effective a means of getting the music out there as any hitherto inviolable business plan.

It is, however, also true. The very act of manufacturing a record and providing would-be purchasers with a contact address necessitates the creation of some kind of corporate identity, and the more records that are produced, the firmer that identity becomes.

It is that strength of identity that convinces many collectors to eschew the so-called obvious route of collecting records by individual bands and artists, and to concentrate instead on the releases of entire labels, and any affiliated companies (commonly called subsidiaries and/or imprints).

The advantages of such an approach are manifold. While there are several labels that are avidly pursued by collectors of all persuasions, the vast majority represent comparatively untapped territory, allowing the diligent enthusiast to build a substantial collection at relatively little cost. For every high-ticket item in a label's catalog, there will be many more releases that are regarded as little more than filler, regardless of their scarcity, even by the authors of the price guides.

Collectors who prize the music more than its theoretical "value" are even better served. What better way to expose oneself to a wide variety of new sounds than to play through a few years' worth of releases from any given label?

That said, some labels' catalogs are simply too vast to ever approach from a heroic "all or nothing" point of view. Staff changes, rosters revolve, musical fads and fashions pass—a label's very nature might undergo any number of complete changes during the course of its existence. Some of the best-loved companies in the world were in operation for thirty, forty, fifty years. How could they have done anything but adapt?

With this in mind, many collectors choose to specialize in certain areas only—a favored label design, perhaps; the reign of a chosen artist or a certain producer or A&R man; a time during which the label's output was considered to be at a peak; and so on. Several of these designations, it must be confessed, have been reflected in the entries that follow, with the CD age given deliberately short shrift when compared to the earlier years.

While there are doubtless still label enthusiasts out there for whom a recent promo CD single is as thrilling a discovery as an old DJ 45 was for their forebears, experience and observation insists that they are firmly in a minority. Few labels of the last few decades have even

halfheartedly courted enthusiasts of their own, with the exceptions being those that tend toward self-defined genres. The ska-oriented Moon Records, the punk Epitaph/Hellcat/Nitro family, Seattle's Sub Pop and C/Z, and such modern prodigy as Fruits de Mer and Mega Dodo are all well appreciated among specialists.

So are the reissue labels that have sprung up in such vast numbers, ranging from comparative veterans Rhino, Edsel and Bam Caruso, Italy's Akarma, Germany's Repertoire, and the UK's Ace through to more recent concerns like Dust-To-Digital, Light in the Attic, Sundazed, and Norton.

Few of these are included here. Rather, it is the vinyl specialists of earlier times that dominate this survey. Many of the labels listed here are what we would today consider "majors"—that is, imprints wholly owned or at least distributed by the giant companies of their respective ages. However, a number of smaller independent concerns are also covered, together with a handful of operations so tiny that the vast majority of readers might never even have heard of them.

Throughout, the implication is not that these labels are somehow better, brighter, or more collectible than the thousands that are not included. They can, however, be considered representative of the spirit of those that are absent.

For this is not a complete list of record labels. Even today, as the world wrings its hands at the thought of the entire European and American music industry being in the thrall of a mere handful of multinational megaconglomerates, there are several thousand labels/imprints still turning out music. Over the last fifty years, that total multiplies so many times over that it is probably impossible to calculate exactly how many different record labels have existed in the US and UK alone.

Captain Beefheart

Bat Chain Puller (WARNER BROS., NO CATALOG NUMBER, TEST PRESSING WITH DIFFERENT TRACKS, 1978)

"Click Clack" (REPRISE 1068, 7-INCH, 1972)

"Diddy Wah Diddy" (A&M 794, 7-INCH, 1966)

"Moonchild" (A&M 818, 7-INCH, 1966)

"Plastic Factory" (BUDDAH 108, 7-INCH, 1969)

Safe As Milk (BUDDAH BDM 1001, MONO LP, 1967)

Strictly Personal (BLUE THUMB BTS 1, BLACK-LABEL LP, 1968)

"Too Much Time" (REPRISE 1133, 7-INCH, 1972)

Trout Mask Replica (STRAIGHT 2-STS 2027, 2-LP, 1970)

"Yellow Brick Road" (BUDDAH 9, 7-INCH, 1967)

However many it is, the labels profiled in the following pages represent a mere drop in the ocean—albeit an extraordinarily significant one. All have been selected for their value to collectors today; some as entities in their own right (Sun, Immediate, Stiff, and Sub Pop spring to mind), and others because their catalogs bristle with names and records of import. And some are profiled because they had the fortune to release one record, or sign one band, that just happened to change the world.

Each label biography provides the most basic information collectors will require to begin their own investigation of its output: when the label was launched and when it folded. First and final releases are given wherever possible. Numerals appearing in parentheses refer to original catalog numbers.

Each entry also notes the most significant artists to record for the label, with especial attention paid to rarities, novelties, and other unusual or noteworthy releases. Obviously, this information can only be considered a general guide and introduction to the subject—specialist collections demand specialist knowledge.

A&M

Los Angeles–based A&M Records was the brainchild of Jerry Moss and songwriter-trumpeter Herb Alpert, who joined forces in 1962 to head a self-avowedly middle-of-the-road (MOR) label. According to legend, their combined resources amounted to just a few hundred dollars. When they sold the label to the PolyGram group twenty-seven years later, it was worth around half a billion dollars.

Alpert had previously been in a partnership, as an independent producer, with Lou Adler (among their clients were the then-little-known Jan and Dean, at Dore Records). However, he had all but abandoned hopes of making a successful career in music when he met Jerry Moss, at that time a freelance promotions man who also dabbled in record production.

Their first collaboration came when Alpert played trumpet on a session organized by Moss in 1961. By early 1962, they had launched their own label, Carnival, debuting with a 45 credited to Dore Alpert, "Tell It to the Birds" (Carnival 701). Almost immediately, the Dot label purchased the release for $750, which Herb and Jerry plowed into setting up their own recording studio in Alpert's garage.

Their first recording here was "Lonely Bull," a uniquely mariachi-flavored instrumental credited to Herb Alpert and the Tijuana Brass. It was originally scheduled for release on Carnival; however, learning of another label with the same name, Alpert and Moss renamed their concern A&M (from their last initials).

Released in October 1962 as A&M 703, "Lonely Bull" was a massive hit, prompting an immediate LP of the same name and igniting a period of massive chart success for Alpert and his band—at one point in 1966, Alpert had five albums in the US Top 20 simultaneously, while 1968 brought a worldwide No. 1 with "This Guy's in Love with You" (A&M 929).

A&M moved from Alpert's garage to new offices on Sunset Boulevard in early 1963, before taking over the Charlie Chaplin movie studio on Sunset and La Brea in late 1966. The label's roster expanded to match its growth. Adhering to Alpert's own stranglehold on adult listening tastes, early recruits included the Baja Marimba Band (formed by Julius Wechter, a former member of Martin Denny's band), Sergio Mendes, Chris Montez, Claudine Longet, the Sandpipers, We Five, and Evie Sands, a New York singer whose "Any Way That You Want Me" (1090) was one of those big-hits-that-wasn't in 1969. The checkered career of the superlatively talented Sands has continued sporadically since then, peaking with 1999's much-acclaimed CD *Women in Prison* (Train Wreck TW 009).

In 1967, Moss opened A&M's doors to the rock market, and two years later, released one of the label's most prized rarities, a eponymous LP by Spirits and Worm (4229). Though the Italian label Akarma later reissued the set, original pressings, of which very few were manufactured, are extremely scarce.

Moss also concluded licensing deals with the British labels Regal Zonophone and Island. Over the next three years, A&M would become the US home for such British stars as Procol Harum, the Move, Spooky Tooth, Fairport Convention, Free, Jimmy Cliff, Cat Stevens, the Strawbs, and Humble Pie, while domestic recruits included Phil Ochs, organ virtuoso Lee Michaels, and country-

The Carpenters

Battle of the Bands at the Hollywood Bowl (CUSTOM FIDELITY PRIVATE PRESSING, 1966)

California State University, Long Beach Celebrates 25 Years Of A Cappella/University Choir 1959–1984 (CSU, 1984)

Carpenters (A&M SP 3502, WHITE LABEL PROMO, 1971)

Carpenters Anthology (A&M AMP 98001, JAPANESE VINYL BOX SET, 1985)

Horizon (A&M QU 54530, QUADRAPHONIC, 1975)

Now then and Always: A Carpenters Special (WESTWOOD ONE, 1989)

Offering (A&M 4205, 1969)

Navy Presents the Carpenters (US NAVY PUBLIC SERVICE RADIO GXTV 8185/86, 1970)

The Singles 1969–1973 jukebox single (A&M LLP 3601, 1973)

Star magazine interview disc (A&M, 1973)

rockers Dillard and Clark and the Flying Burrito Brothers. A&M was also behind one of the most unconventional live successes of the age, Joe Cocker's legendary Mad Dogs and Englishmen outing.

The concert album that documented that tour went on to sell over a million copies, becoming the most successful double live album ever released up to that point—a title that was not surrendered until another A&M act, Peter Frampton, issued 1975's *Frampton Comes Alive*, and wound up with one of the biggest-selling records of all time.

Maintaining a reputation for signing classy acts, A&M continued to grow throughout the 1970s. Styx, Rick Wakeman, the Tubes, and Supertramp, among many others, expanded the label's rock output, while the earlier MOR sensibilities were more than adequately served by the presence of the multimillion-selling Carpenters, the Captain and Tennille, Irish singer-songwriter Chris de Burgh, and Joan Armatrading.

From a collector's point of view, then, it is ironic that the rarest record in the entire A&M catalog was the result of what Derek Green, head of the company's UK operation, ultimately conceded to be a serious error in judgment—signing, and a week later, sacking punk rock icons the Sex Pistols in March 1977. Manufacture of their proposed label debut, the single "God Save the Queen" (AMS 7284), had already commenced when the band was dumped. The records were scrapped, with an estimated 300 survivors now regarded among A&M's (and punk's) most fabled rarities.

Punk did surface on A&M, however. A licensing deal with the I.R.S. label brought both the Police and Squeeze to the label in 1978, while the 1980s saw further diversification via Amy Grant, Captain Beefheart, Joe Jackson, Suzanne Vega, Bryan Adams, John Hiatt, and the Neville Brothers.

Following the label's sale to PolyGram in June 1989, Alpert and Moss continued on in management roles until 1993. Six years later, PolyGram merged into the Universal Music group, at which point A&M all but ceased operations as a functioning record label, and became simply a reissue imprint.

Linda Ronstadt's 1976 Asylum debut followed a string of LPs for Capitol.

The Sex Pistols notwithstanding, A&M catalog rarities are determined more by the collectibility of the artists than by the actual releases. The Carpenters are especially popular, with several now-scarce picture-sleeve 45 releases and a hard-to-find debut album (Offering—SP 4205).

The British label also produced a number of limited-edition, colored-vinyl releases during the late '70s: the Police's "Can't Stand Losing You" (blue wax), Klark Kent's (actually Police drummer Stewart Copeland's) "Don't Care" (green), and Squeeze's "Up the Junction" (lilac) remain popular, even if black vinyl pressings seem oddly harder to find. Other Police-related scarcities include the British Police *Six Pack* wallet of six blue-vinyl singles (with wallet, inserts and discs all present) and a 10-inch pressing of their debut album. With all pre-1973 releases, the most desirable editions of individual LPs tend to be those bearing the original all-brown label; later pressings feature a new silver-gray label design with the letters A&M in brown.

ASYLUM

To the fan and collector of early '70s folk-rock, Asylum Records represents the mother lode. From Jackson Browne and Linda Ronstadt to the Eagles and Andrew Gold, Asylum dominated the genre, and though few of the label's releases are especially rare, quantity (mercifully allied to quality) alone ensures a constantly challenging pursuit.

Asylum Records was created by a former agent at the William Morris talent agency, David Geffen. He had originally hoped to work with movie stars, but having been assured that his youth was against him, he turned instead to rock management. Quitting the agency, his first client was singer-songwriter Laura Nyro, followed by Crosby, Stills and Nash, before Geffen decided he didn't enjoy management after all, and having sold his interests to Elliot Roberts, he returned to agency work.

In 1972, Geffen and Roberts formed their own management company to represent singer-songwriter Jackson Browne. They were unable to find a record deal for the artist; finally, Ahmet Ertegun at Atlantic suggested they launch their own company, with Atlantic handling distribution.

Browne was the first artist signed to Asylum; he was followed by John David (J.D.) Souther, Judy Sill (her debut LP was Asylum's first release—SD 5050), David Blue, and the Eagles, a band formed at Geffen's own suggestion. JoJo Gunne, featuring ex-Spirit member Jay Ferguson, brought Asylum its first major hit 45 in the summer of 1972, when "Run Run Run" (11003) reached No. 27. Before the end of the year, Jackson Browne's "Doctor My Eyes" (11004) and "Rock Me on the Water," (11006) as well as the Eagles' "Take It Easy" (11005) and "Witchy Woman" (11008) had all marched into the Top 20. The label was printing LPs the way other institutions print banknotes.

Linda Ronstadt

"Alison" (UK ASYLUM K13149, 7-INCH PICTURE DISC, 1979)
"Blue Bayou" (ASYLUM AS 11431, BLUE-VINYL 12-INCH, 1978)
DIR Special (DIR, NO CATALOG NUMBER, TRANSCRIPTION DISC, 1982)
"Dolphins" (CAPITOL 2438, 7-INCH, 1969)
"Lago Azul" (ASYLUM 45464, PROMO 7-INCH, 1978)
Living in the USA (UK ASYLUM K53085, RED-VINYL LP, 1978)
Simple Dreams (NAUTILUS NR 26, AUDIOPHILE-PRESSING LP, 1982)
"So Fine," The Stone Poneys (SIDEWALK 937, 7-INCH, 1968)
"Somewhere Out There" (UK MCA MCAP 1172, 7-INCH PICTURE DISC, 1987)
"Up to My Neck in High Muddy Water," The Stone Poneys (CAPITOL 2110, 7-INCH, PICTURE SLEEVE, 1968)

The SD 5000 series, representing Asylum's first year in action, is the most collectible. Many of the LPs here have been re-pressed and reissued on numerous occasions; first printings, most bearing either an all white or cloudy blue (with circled logo) label and Atlantic Records information, are obviously the desirable ones, and include label debuts by Sill, Browne (5051), Blue (5052), Gunne (5053), the Eagles (5054), Souther (5055), the Byrds (5058), Tom Waits (5061), and Rod Taylor (5062).

The arrival of Linda Ronstadt (from Capitol) and Joni Mitchell (from Reprise) added further weight to Asylum. Mitchell's *For the Roses* (5057) and Ronstadt's *Don't Cry Now* (5064) are common, but worthwhile, acquisitions; contrarily, albums by Batdorf and Rodney (5056) and Mick Jagger's brother Chris (5069) are seldom seen.

In late 1973, with Asylum's success still speeding ahead, Geffen sold Asylum to Warner Bros., though he would remain head of the company. At the same time, Elektra Records head Jac Holzman was keen to step down from the day-to-day running of the company—whose own distribution was through Warner Bros. In a surprising, but nevertheless logical, move (stylistically there were numerous similarities between the two catalogs), the labels were merged under Geffen's control, consolidating their catalogs within the same numbering system: the 7E-1000 series for LPs, the 452 series for singles.

Immediately, the union made headlines with the arrival of Bob Dylan from Columbia. Unhappy with the label he'd spent the past decade with, and infuriated by its clumsy efforts to blackmail him into renewing his contract (including raiding the outtakes bin for the *Dylan* album), Dylan joined Asylum in 1973, linking with the Band to cut 1974's *Planet Waves* (E 1003) and the live album *Before the Flood* (AB 2001). Point made, he then returned to Columbia in 1975.

Asylum and Elektra retained their label identities (and, therefore, their own artists and A&R departments), with the merger. Asylum releases continued from both established and new artists—aside from Dylan, these latter included Tim Moore (7E 1019); Traffic (7E 1020); Essra Mohawk (7E 1023); Orleans (7E 1029); Albert Brooks (7E 1035); John Fogerty (7E 1046); and Jack the Lad, a spin-off from the successful British act Lindisfarne (7E 1014)—Lindisfarne itself was signed to Elektra.

The lesser-known artists tend to be the most challenging for the collector; both on 45 and LP, Asylum's hit acts tended to sell in such vast quantities that condition alone affects value and collectibility. One should, however, also note the introduction of a new 6E numerical sequence in 1977—several 7E series LPs were reissued within this new series. (Singles moved to the 455 series at the same time.) The 5E series launched in 1978.

The ensuing commonsense caveats aside, a number of albums are considered rare, drawn from the label's small but so select band of quadraphonic releases. This catalog features Joni Mitchell's *Court and Spark* (EQ 1001) and *Hissing of Summer Lawns* (EQ 1051), Dylan's *Planet Waves* (EQ 1003), the Eagles' *On the Border* (EQ 1004) and *One of These Nights* (EQ 1039), Jackson Browne's *Late for the Sky* (EQ 1017), and the Souther-Hillman Furay Band's *Trouble in Paradise* (EQ 1036).

Another popular variant is the pursuit of UK releases. Although Asylum's chart profile was considerably smaller, the release schedule was just as hectic. Prior to 1976, LPs bear an SYL prefix (sometimes with a fourth letter), and thereafter, the letter K5; singles were originally AYM, changing to K1. British quad releases also exist.

As the late '70s progressed, Asylum releases became scarcer within the catalog, all the more so following David Geffen's departure in 1980 to launch his own Geffen label. Of almost 300 LPs released between 1977–'81, fewer than sixty bore the Asylum identity. The label is still issuing today, but remains a mere shadow of its former self. Most serious collectors therefore concentrate only on the 45s and LPs of the David Geffen period.

ATLANTIC

One of the crucial players in the American music industry, Atlantic Records is also among the most avidly collected, with particular attention being directed toward the run of essential soul-R&B releases of the 1960s, and the label's near-monopoly on the rock explosion of the early '70s. On either side of these key sequences, Atlantic's 1940s–1950s jazz catalog is second to none, while the 1980s and 1990s have each produced their fair share of eminently collectible acts. In addition, the Atco and Cotillion subsidiaries (the latter originally a publishing wing, formed in 1964) also merit serious consideration.

New York–based Atlantic was formed in 1947 by Ahmet Ertegun, the son of Turkey's US ambassador, along with a Brooklyn-born jazz promoter, Herb Abramson, a part-time record producer with National Records. In 1946, Abramson and Jewish comedy producer Jerry Blaine launched Jubilee Records; Abramson left in September 1947 to concentrate on jazz and blues recordings, linking with Ertegun to form Atlantic the following month. Abramson was president, Ertegun and Abramson's wife, Miriam, were VPs. The trio was joined in 1953 by *Billboard* journalist Jerry Wexler (the man who created the term "rhythm and blues," to replace the earlier "race records" on the magazine's chart). Wexler became a VP and in-house R&B producer. Ertegun became Atlantic's president in 1958, three years after Abramson moved to Atco.

Swiftly establishing a reputation for fair dealings, Atlantic prospered, both artistically and commercially. Early signings included vocal groups Delta Rhythm Boys, the Clovers, and the Cardinals; bluesmen Leadbelly and Sonny Terry; and jazz musicians, ranging from Art Pepper and Erroll Garner to Dizzy Gillespie and Sarah

Atlantic Records

"A Beggar for Your Kisses," The Diamonds (ATLANTIC 980, 7-INCH, 1952)

Blues Ballads, LaVern Baker (ATLANTIC 8030, LP, 1959)

"Devil or Angel," The Clovers (ATLANTIC 1083, RED-VINYL 7-INCH, 1956)

"Don't You Know I Love You," The Clovers (ATLANTIC 934, 7-INCH, 1951)

"I'm Gonna Dry Ev'ry Tear," Bill Haley and the Comets (ATLANTIC 727, 78 RPM, 1947)

Love Ballads, Clyde McPhatter (ATLANTIC 8024, LP, 1958)

"Love Love Love," Oscar Black (ATLANTIC 956, 7-INCH, 1952)

"Sweet Talk," Faye Adams (ATLANTIC 1007, 7-INCH, 1956)

"Teardrops from My Eyes," Ruth Brown (ATLANTIC 919, 7-INCH, 1950)

What Am I Living For? Chuck Willis (ATLANTIC 612, EP, 1958)

Vaughan. Within five years, Atlantic could boast hits by Ruth Brown, Stick McGhee, Joe Turner, Professor Longhair, Laurie Tate, and Joe Morris, while Ertegun was also proving a successful composer—the Clovers' chart-topping "Don't You Know I Love You" became the label's second R&B No. 1.

As early as March 1949, Atlantic issued its first 33⅓ rpm long-playing (10-inch) record, poet Walter Benton's *This Is My Beloved* (Atlantic 110), narrated by John Dall over musical accompaniment by Vernon Duke. The same material was perforcedly spread over three 12-inch 78s, effortlessly proving the efficiency of the new format. Atlantic's first 33⅓ 12-inch LP followed in early 1951, scenes from Shakespeare's Romeo and Juliet, by Eva Le Gallienne and Richard Waring (ALS-401).

Following the arrival of Ertegun's brother Nesuhi as head of the LP division in 1955, Atlantic would become renowned for some of the best-quality, best-value LPs on the market, factors which still influence collectors today. All are characterized by high-quality sleeves, more tracks than other labels' offerings, and of course, a plum selection of artists. Atlantic was also a pioneer of stereo technology, cutting its first recordings in 1958.

While Nesuhi's beloved jazz formed the backbone of the LP catalog, with the Modern Jazz Quartet its crown jewel, the arrival of the Drifters in 1953, brought Atlantic its first long-term success. The group would remain with the label for the next fourteen years, scoring close to forty R&B chart hits, beginning with their debut. "Money Honey" (45-1006) topped the chart that winter.

Clyde McPhatter, LaVern Baker, and Ray Charles also became chart regulars, while Joe Turner's "Shake, Rattle and Roll" (1026) not only topped the R&B chart in 1954, it also provided the springboard for country band Bill Haley and the Comets' leap to stardom via a new musical genre that the group, and their not-so-different adaptation of Turner's hit, was now creating: rock 'n' roll.

Instrumental in Atlantic's early domination of this field was the arrival of songwriters Mike Stoller and Jerry Leiber, co-owners (with Lester Sill) of the Los Angeles–based Spark label. With them came two members of Spark's biggest band, the Robins, which was promptly renamed the Coasters, and under Leiber and Stoller's guidance, ran up a string of hit 45s for Atco. Other Leiber-Stoller hits, of course, were spread throughout the Atlantic roster, including the Drifters' "There Goes My Baby," the label's biggest crossover pop hit to date.

The Spark connection also drew producer Phil Spector to Atlantic in 1960. His greatest successes there were, ironically, as a musician—he played guitar on hits by the Drifters, the Coasters, and Ben E. King. Productions, including tracks by the Top Notes, Ruth Brown, Jean DuShon, Billy Storm, and LaVern Baker fared poorly, but Atlantic was merely a stopgap for Spector. By 1961 he and Lester Sill had departed to form Philles.

In 1960, Atlantic was introduced to the Memphis independent Satellite, picking up national rights to the regional hit "Cause I Love You," by Carla and Rufus Thomas, for release on Atco. It was the dawn of a relationship that, based on a handshake deal between Wexler and Satellite head Jim Stewart, would see Atlantic become proud distributors, manufacturers, and (apparently unbeknownst to Stewart) owners of the Stax Records catalog.

Yet Stax was only one string of the label's R&B bow. With Solomon Burke, Sam and Dave, Aretha Franklin, Wilson Pickett, and many more also on board, Atlantic was poised to dominate the field as comprehensively as Motown—and, arguably, with much more consistency. Indeed, for many collectors, Atlantic's R&B output constitutes a category in its own right.

But R&B was not the label's only forte. Indeed, by the mid-'70s, such concerns had all but petered out, with Scottish funk band the Average White Band alone representing new talent. Elsewhere, the label was forging ahead with inspired magnificence. The [Young] Rascals headed a pop boom that began as early as 1965; and while the bulk of Atlantic's rock output was placed with Atco, the late '60s and the 1970s saw the parent label retain Stephen Stills (and, eventually, the Crosby, Stills, Nash and, sometimes, Young supergroup); Led Zeppelin; Yes; Mott the Hoople, for the group's first four albums; the J. Geils Band; King Crimson; the early Hall and Oates; Bryan Ferry; and ELP (following the dissolution of the group's Manticore subsidiary), among many others.

In 1967, Atlantic was purchased by the Warner Seven Arts Corporation, which in turn was purchased by the Kinney Corporation in 1969. Atlantic continued to operate as a separate entity, however, with a culture and catalog that remained irresistible to many artists.

The Rolling Stones' decision to link their newly formed, eponymous label to the company in 1971 was almost wholly based on the members' love of all that the label stood for—other companies had offered far more money than Atlantic had. At the same time, the Kinney Corporation's decision to establish a unified record division that incorporated Atlantic, Warner Bros., and the newly purchased Elektra into one major company, WEA, created a power bloc that even the established major labels were hard-pressed to compete with.

In commercial terms, Led Zeppelin dominated Atlantic's output through the first half of the 1970s, just as they dominate its collectibility today. Some of the most valuable Atlantic releases (or, at least, promos and the like) of the entire decade are Zeppelin-related, with the band's own label Swan Song itself distributed by Atlantic, continuing the relationship through the remainder of the decade.

However, the English hard rockers were by no means the label's sole success. The Swedish pop group ABBA joined Atlantic in 1974, following victory in Europe's annual Eurovision Song Contest; its rarities, too, exert considerable influence on the modern market.

In common with so many classic major labels, Atlantic's subsequent collectibility is driven by individual artists rather than by the label itself, a situation exacerbated, of course, by the uncertainty engendered by a decade's worth of mergers and similar corporate shenanigans. The Warner Bros. group itself is now a part of the multimedia AOL Time Warner group.

Further reading: *The Last Sultan: The Life and Times of Ahmet Ertegun*, by Robert Greenfield (Simon & Schuster, 2012)

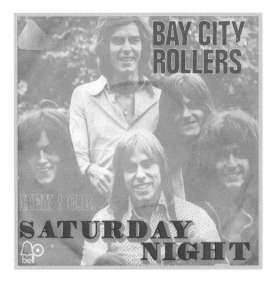

The original "Saturday Night" 45, before the Rollers rerecorded it for a worldwide smash.

BELL

The Bell label was launched in New York City in 1954, with its emphasis firmly on pop and comedy recordings—few of which today are regarded as anything more than curios. The label's forte was for orchestral cover versions of the day's most popular hits, collected onto LPs with such titles as *Songs That Sold a Million* (multiple volumes), *Moods from the Movies* (BLP 15), and *Best of Broadway* (BLP 33). By 1961, Bell had been all but superseded by its subsidiaries Amy and Mala, finally coming back to life in 1964 under the ownership of Larry Uttal. A handful of 45s during 1964–'65 was followed in 1966 by the launch of the 6000 series of LPs, itself opened by Georgia Gibbs' *Call Me* (6000).

The label's first major hit was Syndicate of Sound's "Little Girl," reissued from an earlier 45 on Hush (228). It reached No. 8, the first of three hits the San Jose garage band would enjoy, and was celebrated immediately with an album, also titled *Little Girl* (6001).

Over the next three years, Bell went from strength to strength, not only scoring memorable 45s, but also unleashing a stream of remarkably intelligent LPs. Singles by Alex Chilton and the Box Tops, including the smash hits "The Letter" and "Cry Like a Baby," were released on the Mala label, but Bell handled the group's LP output. (A similar situation existed with the Van Dykes.) Gladys Knight and the Pips, who released half a dozen singles on the Fury subsidiary between 1961–'63 (that is, prior to their successful Motown reign), were celebrated with the *Tastiest Hits* compilation (6013).

A run of classic soul singles by the O'Jays were complemented by the 1968 album *Back on Top* (6014); similarly, a pair of excellent albums by James and Bobby Purify join the duo's ten Bell singles, a run that includes the immortal "I'm Your Puppet." Other much-sought-after Bell LPs from this period include releases by Dale Hawkins (6036) and Pacific Northwest favorites the Wailers (6016).

In 1968, Bell released English folk-rock duo Nirvana's *The Story of Simon Sociopath* (6015), licensed from Britain's Island Records. Overlooked for many years, Nirvana was catapulted to prominence in the early '90s following the emergence of a Seattle band with the same name. The "original" Nirvana launched a highly publicized legal action against its modern namesake; in the resultant flurry of attention, the group's entire back catalog was reissued, while values for original pressings skyrocketed.

The situation has calmed considerably in recent years, but *Sociopath* and its 1969 successor, *All of Us* (6024), still command prices far in excess of their pre-Cobain peaks. Three Bell singles, "We Can Help You" (715), "You Are Just the One" (730), and "Trapeze" (739), are likewise highly prized. (Anybody doubting whether the similarity of the two bands' names did cause any confusion, incidentally, need

Alex Chilton

"Hey Little Child" (UK AURA AUS 117, 7-INCH, 1980)

"Hold On Girl," The Box Tops (HI 2242, 7-INCH, 1973)

"The Letter," The Box Tops (PHILCO HP 27, HIP-POCKET RECORD, 1968)

The Letter/Neon Rainbow, The Box Tops (BELL 6011, MONO LP, 1968)

"No Sex" (FRANCE NEW ROSE 69, DOUBLE 7-INCH PACK, 1986)

"O My Soul," Big Star (ARDENT 2909, 7-INCH, 1974)

"September Gurls," Big Star (ARDENT 2912, 7-INCH, 1974)

The Singer, Not the Song (ORK 1978, EP, 1976)

"Watch the Sunrise," Big Star (ARDENT 2904, 7-INCH, 1972)

"When My Baby's Beside Me," Big Star (ARDENT 2902, 7-INCH, 1972)

only have attended the Seattle Public Library sale in spring 2001. Multiple unplayed copies of several Nirvana UK CDs were available there for just $1 apiece.)

Other collectible British bands joining Bell in the late '60s included another Island UK band, Spooky Tooth (another act whose US singles were handled by Mala) and the Scaffold, featuring Paul McCartney's brother, who called himself Mike McGear. Five Bell 45s, including the UK chart-topper "Lily the Pink" (747), are among the prime ephemerals pursued by arch Beatles collectors.

Merrilee Rush's "Angel of the Morning" (705) and Crazy Elephant's "Gimme Gimme Good Lovin'" (763) rank among the label's biggest singles of the late '60s (both artists also produced collectible Bell LPs); the latter named are also hotly pursued by fans of the British band 10cc. "There Ain't No Umbopo" (875) was a rerecording of a song cut for Pye (UK) by the four future band members, under the name Dr. Father; bassist Graham Gouldman was also a contract songwriter for Crazy Elephant producers Kasenetz-Katz.

Among other much-sought-after albums from the turn of the decade are a set celebrating the Apollo 11 moon shot (1100); the movie soundtrack *Nicholas and Alexandra* (1103)—other movie titles were placed in the 1200 series and are uniformly sought after—and the fourth LP (but first for Bell) by Orpheus (6061), a painstakingly ambitious folk-rock band from Worcester, Massachusetts. Together with three LPs cut for MGM, Orpheus was reissued in an extravagant two-CD package by the Italian Akarma label in 2001.

Bell's biggest acquisition of the early '70s was the Partridge Family. Columbia Screen Gems purchased co-ownership of the label (alongside Uttal) in the late '60s. The hook-up brought Bell the rights to the Monkees' back catalog (evidenced by the Refocus compilation,

6081), and spawned a now-popular solo album by singer Davy Jones (6067); it also ensured that the label would become the home for soundtrack recordings emanating from this new television series. Nobody could have foreseen the sheer commercial enormity of the venture, with both the Partridge Family and frontman David "Keith Partridge" Cassidy emerging as stars of the first magnitude.

Their modern collectibility is scarcely less prodigious today, and that despite contemporary sales in the multimillions. Of particular note today are copies of the 1971 *Christmas Card* album (6066), with an attached Christmas card, and 1972's *Shopping Bag* (6072), with of course, a free shopping bag. Several of the group's later singles, too, are extremely difficult to find. Cassidy releases, while equally sought after, are more common.

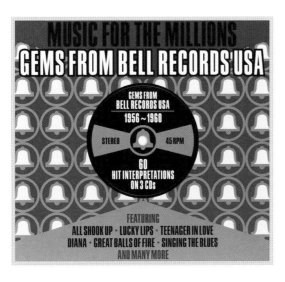

A CD collection of hits from the early years of Bell.

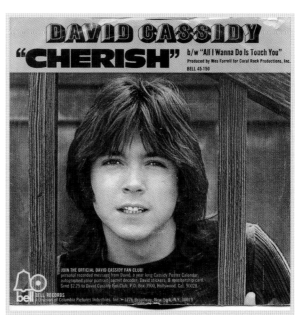

And here he is, with the international chart topper "Cherish."

Genuinely scarce, however, are Bell singles by fellow Family regular Shirley Jones; she cut three during 1971–'72: "I've Still Got My Heart, Joe" (119), "Ain't Love Easy" (253), and "Walk in Silence" (350). The show also made a passing fancy out of juvenile Ricky Segall—his *Ricky Segall and the Segulls* LP (1138) offers a taste of the precocious child star squawking at its most post–Jimmy Osmond appalling; the single, "Sooner or Later," (429) at least minimizes the torment. Mercifully hard to find.

Other high-selling (if somewhat less collectible) Bell artists of the early '70s include the Fifth Dimension, Tony Orlando and Dawn, Terry Jacks, and Melissa Manchester. With artists and successes like these, Bell's American profile was distinctly middle-of-the-road. Not so in the UK. There, Bell—under the expert guidance of former Philips A&R man Dick Leahy—was at the forefront of the glam-rock movement, its output headlined not only by Cassidy, but also by homegrown sensations Gary Glitter and the Glitter Band, Hello, and Showaddywaddy. At one point during 1972–'73, the label was operating on a hit ratio of almost one in four, a spectacular achievement in one of the most competitive climates in pop history.

Bell's UK label launched in 1968 with the Box Tops's "Cry Like a Baby" (1001), the most successful of the group's eight British 45s over the next two years. The Delfonics (consigned to the Philly Groove subsidiary in America) were an early cult success, scoring on the Northern Soul club circuit with "La La Means I Love You" (1006), "Ready or Not" (1042), and a trilogy of excellent LPs.

Tony Orlando and Dawn were a predictable success in the very early '70s, topping the UK chart in 1971 with "Knock Three Times" (1146), while UK pop maverick Jonathan King brought a handful of hits to the label, including the Piglets's "Johnny Reggae" (featuring *EastEnders* TV star Wendy Richards) (1180), and "Keep On Dancing" (1164), the first-ever release by an unknown Scottish band called the Bay City Rollers. A major rarity from this period is "Oh Baby" (1121) by Dib Cochran and the Earwigs—a pseudonym disguising Marc Bolan, Rick Wakeman, Tony Visconti, and Mick

The UK maxi-single for the Partridge Family's 1972 hit "Breaking Up Is Hard to Do." Two previous hits appeared on the b-side.

Ronson. (Rumors that David Bowie also appears on the track can be discounted upon the insistence of all participants.)

Domestic talent remained an inconsistent proposition until mid-1972 brought the launch of Gary Glitter. "Rock and Roll" (1216) hit No. 2 that summer, igniting a peerless run of success and a string of eleven successive Top Ten hits that extended into 1975. The Glitter Band (as their name suggests, the band was made up of Gary's backing musicians) scored seven hits of their own between 1974–'76 and behind them, the glam floodgates simply exploded.

Jonathan King

"Everyone's Gone to the Moon" (PARROT 9774, 7-INCH, 1965)

"It's Good News Week," Hedgehoppers Anonymous (DECCA F12241, 7-INCH, 1965)

"It's the Same Old Song," The Weathermen (UK B&C CB 139, 7-INCH, 1971)

"Johnny Reggae," The Piglets (UK BELL 1180, 7-INCH, 1972)

"Just Like a Woman" (PARROT 3005, 7-INCH, 1966)

"Leap Up and Down (Wave Your Knickers in the Air)" St. Cecilia (UK POLYDOR 2058 104, 7-INCH, 1971)

"Lick a Smurp for Christmas," Father Abraphart and the Smurps (UK PETROL GAS 1, FLEXIDISC, 1978)

"Loop Di Love," Shag (UK 45-49007, 7-INCH, 1972)

Or Then Again . . . (PARROT PAS 71013, STEREO LP, 1967)

"Sugar Sugar," Sakharin (UK RCA 2064, 7-INCH, 1971)

Bell made several attempts to launch glam into the US mainstream. From the Nicky Chinn–Michael Chapman songwriting stable, the Sweet (an RCA act in Britain) scored US hits with "Co-Co" (45-126), "Little Willy" (45-251), and "Blockbuster" (45-361), all gathered on an eponymous LP (1124) before the band was allowed to slip away to Capitol.

Another Chinn-Chapman act, Mud, saw two singles issued, "Crazy" (415) and "Tiger Feet" (602), while a third from the same stable, Detroit-born Suzi Quatro, released two Bell LPs and five 45s, including 1973's minor hit "All Shook Up" (45-477). Quatro passed by unnoticed, however, until she was transferred to Big Tree, where "Can the Can" at least made the Top 60. (Quatro's biggest US hits ultimately came with RSO.) Both Mud and Quatro were signed to Mickie Most's RAK label in the UK; Bell also briefly carried another RAK act, Hot Chocolate, releasing its "Rumours" (45-390) and "Emma" (45-466) singles, before they too moved to Big Tree . . . where a reissue of that second single promptly became a Top Ten hit.

Yet another RAK act, meanwhile, offers Bell collectors one of the US label's greatest 1970s-era rarities. Former Herman's Hermits vocalist Peter Noone scored a major UK hit with his version of the then-unknown David Bowie's "Oh! You Pretty Things," featuring Bowie himself on piano. Promo copies of Bell's US release are relatively common; stock copies (45-131), however, are all but unknown.

Bell had no more luck with Gary Glitter, despite scoring a major smash with "Rock and Roll" (45-237) and following through with a minor hit, "I Didn't Know I Loved You" (45-276). Glam was never to become more than a marginal interest in the US, and subsequent Glitter releases (singles and LPs) fell on deaf ears, only to be picked up for major hits by acts ranging from Brownsville Station to Joan Jett. The Glitter Band's only sniff of American success, meanwhile, was with a funk-rock instrumental, "Makes You Blind," discarded as

Hello were one of the UK label's highest hopes for 1974–75, but are ultimately best remembered for recording the original version of Ace Frehley's solo hit.

a B-side in their home country and released on Arista following its absorption of Bell.

Barry Blue scored four big hits in the UK; just one of them, "Dancing on a Saturday Night" (45-391/UK 1295), even saw an American release, at which point it was covered by Flash Cadillac and the Continental Kids (Epic 511102). Hello fared even more poorly. In the UK, its reputation is based on a pair of solid hit 45s, a fine album, and one of the great Bell UK rarities, the withdrawn 45 "Keep Us off the Streets" (1479). In the US, the group is known only for cutting the original version (1438) of Kiss guitarist Ace Frehley's

Brownsville Station

Air Special (EPIC JE 35606, ORANGE-VINYL PROMO LP, 1978)

Brownsville Station (PALLADIUM P-1004, LP, 1970)

"Let Your Yeah Be Yeah" (BIG TOP 161, 7-INCH, 1973)

"Love Stealer," as Brownsville (EPIC 50695, 7-INCH, 1979)

Motor City Connection (BIG TOP BTS 89510, LP, 1975)

A Night on the Town (BIG TOP BTS 2010, LP, 1972)

No BS (WARNER BROS. WS 1888, LP, 1970)

"The Red Back Spider" (BIG TOP 156, 7-INCH, 1972)

"Rock and Roll Holiday" (HIDEOUT 1957, 7-INCH, 1969)

"Rock with the Music" (BIG TOP 144, 7-INCH, 1972)

Amy Records

Authentic Ska, Various artists (LP AMY 8002, 1964)

"Cards of Love," Tico and the Triumphs (AMY 876, 1963)

"Cry, Li'l Boy," Tico and the Triumphs (AMY 860, 1962)

"I Can't Believe My Ears," Del Shannon (AMY 947, 1966)

"The Lone Teen Ranger," Jerry Landis (AMY 875, 1964)

"Mary Jane," Del Shannon (AMY 897, 1961)

"Motorcycle," Tico and the Triumphs (AMY 835/MADISON 169, 1965)

Ride Your Pony, Lee Dorsey (AMY S-8010, STEREO LP, 1962)

"War Cry," the Ramrods (AMY 846, 1962)

"Wildflower," Tico and the Triumphs (AMY 845, 1962)

"New York Groove" anthem. Even less recognition awaited other Bell UK successes Harley Quinne, rock 'n' roll revivalists Showaddywaddy, and the girl duo the Pearls.

Another Bell act that seemed destined to remain as obscure in the US as they were enormous in Britain was the Bay City Rollers. Since "Keep On Dancing," the band had completely vanished from the commercial radar, issuing a string of now-super-rare flop 45s and getting nowhere fast. They re-emerged in 1973 with a new tartan-drenched image, a new songwriting team (veterans Bill Martin and Phil Coulter), and an effervescent sound previewed on the 45 "Remember" (1338). (Two versions of this exist: an original take with vocalist Nobby Clarke, swiftly replaced by a new recording with Clarke's replacement, Les McKeown.)

"Shang-a-Lang" (1355) followed, and for two years, the Rollers ruled the UK chart, scoring five Top Ten hits and two No. 1s during 1974–'75 alone. America didn't even look twice at any of them. It was not until Arista came into being that the band's US fortunes changed, and today, the group's Bell catalog is in great demand—and scarce supply.

The last years of Bell also saw the emergence of Barry Manilow. During 1973–'74 he released four singles on the label, including the hits "Could It Be Magic" (45-422) and "Mandy" (45-613), plus a pair of LPs (1129, 1314). Again, however, it was with the advent of Arista that his career truly took off.

Arista was the brainchild of Clive Davis, former head of Columbia Records, who became president of Bell following the departure of Uttal to his own Private Stock label (home of the early Blondie, Arrows, and Starsky & Hutch TV star David Soul). The Arista identity was initially ushered in amid the small print of the latter-day Bell releases ("Bell Records, Distributed by Arista Records . . . "); by the end of 1974, however, it was a done deal. The existing Bell catalog was absorbed into the new company, while many artists were either dropped or departed of their own accord—David Cassidy fled for RCA, Tony Orlando and Dawn signed with Elektra, and the Fifth Dimension moved to ABC.

In Britain, the Bell identity persisted until early 1976. Its final major hit was scored by Slik, a Glaswegian band fronted by the then-unknown Midge Ure. "Forever and Ever" (1464) topped the UK chart and might have succeeded in the US as well. Unfortunately, injuries sustained in a road accident sidelined Ure just as Arista released the group's debut LP, and by the time the band returned to action, its carefully nurtured teenybop audience had moved on.

For many years, the Bell label was overlooked by collectors—even as subsidiaries Amy, Philly Groove, Fury, and so on became major sellers. But for the generation whose formative musical tastes developed during the half decade spanned by Bell's greatest successes, 1971–'76, the familiar silver label has a magic all its own, one that traditional collecting outlets utterly overlooked until internet auctions rudely informed them that records they'd been pumping out at a buck or two a throw were actually in extraordinary demand.

BESERKLEY

One of the great pioneering indie labels of the new wave movement, Beserkley predated that vehicle by over a year, launching in 1975 after founder Matthew King Kaufman found himself unable to land a record deal for Earth Quake, a band he'd been managing since the early '70s (they had already released two LPs on A&M). Other early signings included Greg Kihn, the Rubinoos, and most significantly, Jonathan Richman.

Beserkley's first release was a 45 coupling Earth Quake's version of the Easybeats's "Friday on My Mind" with Richman's anthemic "Roadrunner"; Earth Quake also backed Richman on his recording. Both tracks reappeared on the *Beserkley Chartbusters* LP (BZ 0044), which introduced the label as the "Home of the Hits"—a short-lived Beserkley subsidiary of this same name was responsible for the first issue of the Modern Lovers' self-titled debut in 1975 (a collection of demos and unreleased tracks recorded for Warner Bros. two years earlier). The album reappeared on Beserkley the following year.

Another well-received issue from this period was the Beserkley Six Pack, which contained 45 rpm versions of several of the LP's cuts, plus a controversial blank 45 by the Sons of Pete—it was titled "Silent Night." Albums by Earthquake, Greg Kihn, Richman, and

Jonathan Richman/Modern Lovers

"Buzz Buzz Buzz" (UK BESERKLEY BZZ 25, 7-INCH, PICTURE SLEEVE, 1978)

Jonathan Richman and the Modern Lovers (BESERKLEY BZ 0048, LP, 1976)

The Modern Lovers (HOME OF THE HITS HH 1910, LP, 1975)

"The Morning of Our Lives" (UK BESERKLEY BZZ 7, 7-INCH, 1978)

"New England" (BESERKLEY 5743, 7-INCH, PICTURE SLEEVE, 1976)

The Original Modern Lovers (BOMP 4021, LP, 1981)

Penthouse/Omni College Rock Concert (LONDON WAVELENGTH, TRANSCRIPTION DISC, 1983)

"Roadrunner" (BESERKLEY 5701, 7-INCH, PICTURE SLEEVE, 1975)

"Roadrunner" (UK UNITED ARTISTS UP 36006, 7-INCH, 1975)

"That Summer Feeling" (UK ROUGH TRADE C52, 12-INCH, 1985)

the Rubinoos followed between 1975–'77, the period of Beserkley's greatest collectibility and success.

Although Richman never scored a US hit, "Roadrunner" was picked up for UK release by UA in 1975. It did not chart but was greeted with excellent reviews and a reissue two years later on Beserkley's newly opened UK subsidiary (BZZ 1) made the UK Top 20. It was followed into the chart by "Egyptian Reggae" (BZZ 2) and "The Morning of Our Lives" (BZZ 7), while the album *Rock 'n' Roll with the Modern Lovers* (BSERK 9) was a Top 50 hit. No other Beserkley act did as well in Britain, but the label's UK catalog is well worth pursuing.

Beserkley's early US releases were distributed by Playboy; Janus/GRT took over between 1977–'79 and Elektra/Asylum handled the label from 1979 until its dissolution in 1984. These changes all had an impact on the catalog—*Beserkley Chartbusters*' original US catalog number, BZ 0044, became JBZ 0044 under Janus, and so on. The Elektra deal then saw a new numbering sequence, the BZ 10000 series, launched with further reissues.

New signings under the Janus deal included the Tyla Gang, a band formed from the ashes of British pub-rockers Ducks Deluxe, and the frantic instrumentalist Spitballs. No new acts joined the label thereafter; indeed, Beserkley's last years saw it dedicated almost exclusively to reissues and new Greg Kihn recordings.

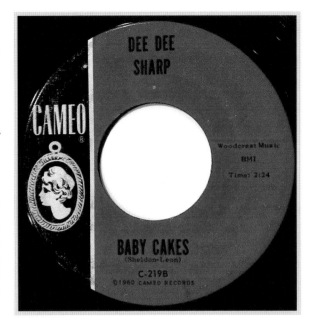

The incomparable Dee Clark.

CAMEO-PARKWAY

The Philadelphia-based Cameo and Parkway labels were among the staples of the late-'50s and early '60s American pop scene, home to the clean-cut likes of the Rays (whose "Silhouettes"—Cameo 117—was the label's first major hit in 1957), Bobby Rydell, Dee Dee Sharp, and the Orlons, and the source of a magnificent stream of 45s, almost all of which are in heavy demand by modern collectors.

The label's LP output, too, is legendary, opening in 1958 with *An Adventure in Hi-Fi Music*, by *Today* TV host Dave Garroway (1001)—a decade later, Ed McMahon would also release an album on the label (2009). Sets by Denise Darcel, the Imaginary Five, Dave Appell, Bernie Leighton, and Jack Wiegand followed in the years before Rydell burst onto the scene; among the titles thereafter, a sequence of 1961–'62 LPs immortalizing the great dances of the day is especially noteworthy.

Meyer Davis Plays the Twist (1014), the Carroll Brothers' *College Twist Party* (1015), and the various-artists set *12 Top Teen Dances 1961–1962* (1016) are all collector favorites today, with the latter an

especially desirable piece. Comprising such Cameo-Parkway gems as the Dovells, the Apple Jacks, the Dreamlovers, and of course, Chubby Checker—the man who set the country twisting in the first place—the album is both a fascinating period piece and a crash course into the brilliance of the Cameo family.

Dee Dee Sharp arrived at Cameo in early 1962, fresh from duetting on Chubby Checker's "Slow Twist" 45 for Parkway, and armed with a dance craze of her own, the "Mashed Potato" (212). "Gravy (For My Mashed Potatoes)" followed, and Sharp's debut album promised, quite logically, *It's Mashed Potato Time* (1018). Later in her career, Sharp would incite America to "Do the Bird" (244); however, she also cut a number of non-locomotive 45s, and continued scoring hits into 1965.

The Orlons also proved to have considerably more staying power than the dance that brought them, too, to prominence, summer 1962's "The Wah Watusi" (218). The Cameo-Parkway set-up's earlier preeminence was, however, slipping, and attempts to leap aboard other passing bandwagons met with little success. The interestingly named Three Young Men from Montana made a gallant stab at catching the folk train with, indeed, *Folk Song Favorites* (1025); Eddie Greensleeves followed suit with *Humorous Folk Songs* (1031), and Sunny Schwartz went so far as to raid the same traditional repertoire as Joan Baez and the grittier protest singers for *Sunny's Gallery of Folk Ballads* (1030).

By late 1963, the label's most consistent releases were hits collections for Rydell, Sharp, and the Orlons, interspersed with collections of

Hawaiian, organ, camping, cowboy, and orchestral pop music, and annual "biggest hit of the year" releases from, again, Rydell. Among these, "Magic Star," from *All the Hits Volume Two* (1040) is avidly sought by fans of English producer Joe Meek, being a lyrical version of the Telstars' instrumental "Telstar," otherwise available only on one of Meek's own scarcer productions, by Kenny Hollywood.

There were some inspired releases, of course. The demise of the Dovells in 1963 deprived Parkway of one of its most consistent hitmakers, but when vocalist Len Barry launched a solo career at Decca, Cameo was on the ball immediately, releasing the *Len Barry Sings with the Dovells* collection (1082).

Another fascinating release is 1964's *You Be a Disc Jockey* album (1075), a so-called instructional record that offered, on side one, an entertaining recreation of a radio broadcast, complete with jingles, weather reports, time checks, commercials, and interviews (with Rydell and Sharp), all conducted by a real live DJ. Flip the disc, and the exact same recording is repeated, this time without the DJ. A script booklet allows the listener to fill in the gaps. Needless to say, the disc's collectibility is most dependent on the presence of that booklet, but even without it the album offers an entertaining glimpse into the world of radio in the last days before the British invaded.

For perhaps the first time in its history, Cameo was surprisingly slow to recognize the impact of the new musical climate. Only one Invasion-era band had an impact on the label, the minor-league Ivy League, whose "Tossing and Turning" (377) limped to No. 83 in late 1965, despite its being bolstered by an LP of the same name (2000). Indeed, with so little action on the hit singles front, Cameo and Parkway alike were slowly sinking into a quagmire from which neither new owner Allen Klein, nor a freak No. 1 by Michigan garage punks ? and the Mysterians, "96 Tears" (428), could extract them.

Collectors, on the other hand, salivate over the two albums that the band issued on the now-conjoined Cameo-Parkway label in 1966 and 1967, *96 Tears* (C2004) and *Action* (C2007), while the absorption of the Lucky Eleven label brought another future garage rarity to the party, *Reflections* by Terry Knight and the Pack (2007, also Lucky Eleven SLE 8000). Label VP Neil Bogart was largely responsible for these final oases of brilliance in the catalog.

Following a rare hit with Ohio Express's "Beg Borrow and Steal" (483), Cameo-Parkway moved to MGM for distribution in 1967. A second Ohio Express single, "Try It" (2001), debuted the deal, but the new arrangement was very much a last hurrah. Two final albums appeared in 1967, by Ohio Express (20,000) and the Village Stompers (20,001); the label then lay fallow for several years, before being reborn as Klein's ABKCO (Allen B. Klein Company).

CAPRICORN

The Capricorn label was one of the enduring successes of the so-called Southern-rock movement of the early '70s, not only pioneering the boom in the first place, but outliving it by several years. Though only the label's first years truly excite collector interest today, the entire catalog pursues the multitudinous strands of the genre to the very end of the 1970s, with a host of genuinely intelligent CD releases now appearing to both upgrade and enlarge many of Capricorn's original releases.

Allman Brothers

"Ain't Wastin' Time No More" (CAPRICORN 0003, 7-INCH, 1972)

The Allman Brothers at Fillmore East (NAUTILUS NR 3, AUDIOPHILE 2-LP, 1982)

Beginnings (ATCO SD 2-805, 2-LP, 1973)

Early Allman, The Allman Joys (DIAL 6005, LP, 1973)

Eat a Peach (MOBILE FIDELITY 1-157, AUDIOPHILE LP, 1984)

"Heartbeat," The Hour Glass (LIBERTY 56002, 7-INCH, 1967)

The Hour Glass, The Hour Glass (LIBERTY LST 7536, STEREO LP, 1967)

"Morning Dew," Duane and Gregg Allman (BOLD 200, 7-INCH, 1973)

"Ramblin' Man" (ROLLING STONE/CAPRICORN, FLEXIDISC, 1975)

"Spoonful," The Allman Joys (DIAL 4046, 7-INCH, 1966)

The label was the brainchild of Phil Walden, manager of R&B singers Otis Redding, Percy Sledge, and Sam and Dave. In 1967, Walden approached Atlantic Records to help finance a recording studio in his Macon, Georgia, hometown. The label suggested he form a record label instead, and in 1969, Capricorn was launched with two signings, Johnny Jenkins and a band formed by Muscle Shoals studio guitarist Duane Allman and his brother Gregg, the Allman Brothers.

Under the terms of the Atlantic deal, the first Capricorn LPs were released through Atco, bearing that label's catalog numbers and label, with mention of Capricorn confined to the LP jacket alone. The first three Allman Brothers albums, including the breakthrough *At Fillmore East* (SD 2-802) double live album, were issued in this fashion, together with sets by Jenkins (33-331), Livingston Taylor (33-334), and Cowboy (33-351). In addition, a back-to-back reissue of the first two Allman albums appeared on Atco (with no reference to Capricorn whatsoever), as 1973's *Beginnings* (SD 2-805).

In 1971, Atco gave Capricorn its own numbering system and label, an arrangement debuted by Alex Taylor's *With Friends and Neighbors* (860). Wet Willie, Jonathan Edwards, and further sets by Livingston Taylor and Cowboy followed, before the new year saw Capricorn shift from Atco to Warner Bros. for distribution.

The first major hit under the new regime was the Allmans' *Eat a Peach* (CP 0102); other popular releases followed from Captain Beyond, White Witch, Wet Willie, Maxayn, and the Marshall Tucker Band, but even this early, it was clear that nothing was going to challenge the Allmans' supremacy, as 1973's *Brothers and Sisters* (CP 0111) LP topped the US chart, and the group co-headlined the massive Watkins Glen festival in front of an crowd estimated to number half a million.

Such vast success notwithstanding, one of the few true rarities in the Capricorn catalog dates from this period, a flexidisc presented with *Rolling Stone* magazine featuring tracks from the then-forthcoming *Brothers and Sisters* and the first album by the Marshall Tucker Band (CP 0112).

With the Allmans embarking on what amounted to a two-year sabbatical, punctuated by solo activity, Capricorn moved into a period of uncertainty and confusion. Gregg Allman's *Laid Back* (CP 0116) solo set was a Top 20 hit in late 1973, but it would be close to a year before Capricorn returned to the chart, this time with fellow Allman Dickey Betts's *Highway Call* (CP 0123).

Another year, and thirty-one LP releases, would elapse before the Allmans' *Win Lose or Draw* album broke another hitless sequence—before the band itself shattered.

This lack of mainstream chart success is no reflection, of course, on the quality of Capricorn releases throughout this period—career-best sets from Marshall Tucker, Martin Mull, and White Witch were joined by spellbinding label debuts by Hydra, Elvin Bishop, and Grinderswitch, while 1974 saw soul veteran Percy Sledge arrive at Capricorn with the LP *I'll Be Your Everything* (CP 1047). Of course it doesn't measure up to his classic '60s material, but it was a great listen regardless. Other new arrivals during this period included Bonnie Bramlett, Dobie Gray, and John Hammond.

Following the Allman Brothers' split, Capricorn released two archive projects, the "best of" set *The Road Goes on Forever* (2CP 0164), a double album reissued in admirably expanded (two-CD) form in 2002, and the live *Check the Windows* collection. Sales were disappointing, however, and a change in distribution, to Phonogram, did not reignite Capricorn's fortunes. Neither did the label's latest signings achieve much, and that despite including the likes of Dixie Dregs, Billy Joe Shaver, Sea Level (featuring several former Allman musicians), Billy

Thorpe, Priscilla Coolidge-Jones (sister of Rita and wife of Booker T.), and the now-veteran (but still vital) Black Oak Arkansas.

The Allmans' 1979 reunion did bring back at least a taste of the good times, but the following year saw Capricorn declare bankruptcy. The label's last taste of chart action came with Delbert McClinton's *Keeper of the Flame* LP (CPN 0223); the last release, oddly appropriately, was Sea Level's *Long Walk on a Short Pier* (CPN 0227).

It would be a decade before Walden resurrected the label, distributed again by Warner Bros., but based in Nashville. Athens jam band Widespread Panic launched the rebirth in 1991 with a self-titled debut album (9 10001-2); subsequent releases included Col. Bruce Hampton and the Aquarium Rescue Unit, the Zoo, Billy Burnette, 311, and the revitalized Lynyrd Skynyrd. Capricorn has also hosted a number of excellent archive exhumations of vintage labels Scepter, Fire/Fury, Cobra, Jewel/Paula, and Swingtime, while also undertaking a massive re-evaluation of its own archive, courtesy of its current co-owners and distributors, Universal.

Further reading: *Capricorn Rising: Conversations in Southern Rock*, by Michael Buffalo Smith (Mercer University Press, 2016)

CHESS

One of the most legendary, and certainly among the most evocative, of all American record labels, Chess is also, arguably, the most avidly collected label of the 1950s and 1960s. Its roster is a veritable who's who of the blues, and rather than document the artists whose material is regarded as collectible, it would probably be easier to note those who aren't. It would be a ridiculously short list.

Checker

"Broken Heart," Memphis Minnie (CHECKER 771, 7-INCH, 1953)

"Country Boogie," Elmore James (CHECKER 777, 7-INCH, 1953)

"Darling I Know," The El Rays (CHECKER 794, 7-INCH, 1954)

"It Must Have Been the Devil," Otis Spann (CHECKER 807, 7-INCH, 1954)

"I Was a Fool to Love You," The Teasers (CHECKER 800, RED-VINYL 7-INCH, 1954)

"Juke," Little Walter (CHECKER 758, RED-VINYL 7-INCH, 1952)

"Off the Wall," Little Walter (CHECKER 770, RED-VINYL 7-INCH, 1953)

"Tired of Crying over You," Morris Pejoe (CHECKER 766, RED-VINYL 7-INCH, 1953)

"When I Look at You," The Encores (CHECKER 760, 7-INCH, 1953)

"White Cliffs of Dover," The Blue Jays (CHECKER 782, 7-INCH, 1953)

The British Invasion was largely fueled by the importance of Chess—according to legend, future Rolling Stones Keith Richards and Brian Jones were introduced by a copy of Muddy Waters' *Best Of* LP (LP 1427)—Richard had a copy, and Jones wanted to know where he got it. They formed the band soon after, and named it for another Waters song, the B-side of his first-ever Chess 78. Elsewhere around the UK, so many other bands cut their teeth on the Chess catalog that you could create the most star-studded tribute imaginable to the label without ever leaving the British-beat boom.

Chess grew out of brothers Leonard and Philip Chess' involvement with the Aristocrat label, formed by Charles and Evelyn Aron, in Chicago, in 1947. Prior to this, the brothers (Polish immigrants who arrived in the city in 1928) had operated the Macomba nightclub, specializing of course in blues. It was their dissatisfaction with the recordings then being made of these performers that first prompted them to make records themselves.

Aristocrat released a number of seminal records, including issues by bandleader Sherman Hayes, the singularly named Wyoma, Billy Orr and Andrew Tibbs and Jump Jackson, plus several hits by Muddy Waters. When the brothers bought out their partners' interest in Aristocrat and relaunched the label as Chess in 1950, Waters automatically became the new label's first superstar—but not its first release. That honor was reserved for saxophonist Gene Ammons' "My Foolish Heart" (1425), with Waters' "Walkin' Blues"/"Rollin' Stone" (1426) following soon after.

Others, however, soon followed—Howlin' Wolf was licensed from Memphis record producer Sam Phillips (later to launch his own Sun label) and Little Walter was drawn from Muddy Waters' band. Sonny Boy Williamson, Lowell Fulson, Memphis Slim, Jimmy Rogers, and John Lee Hooker all followed, while the arrival of Chuck Berry in 1955 brought Chess its first consistent hitmaker. Beginning with "Maybellene" (1604) and "Roll Over Beethoven" (1626), credited to Chuck Berry and His Combo, the young St. Louis native would notch up twenty-five Top 100 hits over the next decade.

More importantly, however, he did so with songs that would help define rock 'n' roll—"School Day" (1653), "Sweet Little Sixteen" (1683), "Johnny B. Goode" (1691), "Carol" (1700), and so many more. Berry even delivered Chess's final chart-topper, when the ribald "My Ding-a-Ling" (2131) went to No. 1 on both sides of the Atlantic, in late 1972. The majority of Berry's releases are not especially rare, even in 78 form. But they are extraordinarily desirable.

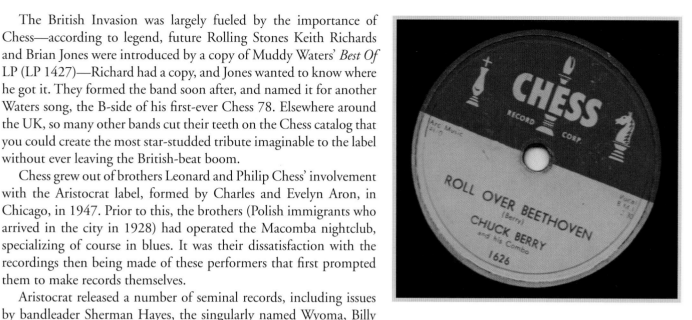

Chuck Berry's "Roll Over Beethoven" on a 1956 Chess 78.

In 1956, Chess released its first long-playing records, initially on the Argo subsidiary. The debut Chess release was the teen-sploitation movie soundtrack *Rock, Rock, Rock* (1425), widely regarded as the first-ever release in that field. Chuck Berry's *After School Session* (1426) and the aforementioned Muddy Waters compilation followed, though just nine Chess LPs were issued before the end of the decade (six further LPs within the same 1400 numbering system were issued by Checker).

Among these, the most sought after are the Moonglows' *Look* (1430), Berry's *One Dozen Berrys* (1432) and *On Top* (1435), Howlin' Wolf's *Moanin' in the Moonlight* (1434), and a pair of compilations, *Oldies in Hi Fi* (1439) and *A Bunch of Goodies* (1441). The rare promotional copies of this latter brace, incidentally, were issued on multicolored vinyl.

Surfing Singles

"Barbie," Kenny and the Cadets (RANDY 422, COLORED-VINYL, PINK-LABEL 7-INCH, 1962)

"King of the Beach," Bobby Fuller (EXETER 122, 7-INCH, 1964)

"Miserilou," Dick Dale and the Deltones (*BILLBOARD* MAGAZINE, FLEXIDISC, 1963)

"One Pine Box," The Royal Flairs (MARINA 503, 7-INCH, 1965)

"Shoot the Curl," The Honeys (CAPITOL 4952, 7-INCH, PICTURE SLEEVE, 1963)

"The Surfer Moon," Bob & Sheri (SAFARI 101, 7-INCH, 1962)

"Surfin'," The Beach Boys (X 301, 7-INCH, 1961)

"Three Surfer Boys," Gary Usher and the Usherettes (DOT 16158, 7-INCH, 1963)

"Volcanic Action," The Belairs (ARVEE 5054, 7-INCH, 1963)

"Wipe Out," The Surfaris (DFS 11/12, 7-INCH, 1963)

Chess's impact was not limited to the Chicago-Mississippi blues scene. A number of artists were recruited from the fertile melting pot of New Orleans, including Clarence "Frogman" Henry. Argo proved as influential in jazz circles as Chess and the Checker imprints were in the blues. The vocal groups the Flamingos and the Moonglows both brought further renown to the Chess family, even though it took white-cover versions to popularize their biggest hits—the Moonglows' "Sincerely" (1581) and the Flamingos' "I'll Be Home" (Checker 830). An extensive line of religious and gospel releases also has a fervent following among modern collectors.

The arrival, from the King label, of A&R director Ralph Bass enabled the Chess group to add R&B and soul to its repertoire, via Etta James (at Argo, and later both Cadet and Chess), the Dells (Cadet), Billy Stewart (a former member of Bo Diddley's band, who cut singles for Argo and Chess in 1956, then returned to Chess in 1962 for a run of solid soul hits), Fontella Bass (Checker), and others.

Chess remained a major force in American music through the late '60s, with the roster constantly reflecting the changing local scene. Among the most in-demand later releases is an album by Canadian psychedelic band the Baroques (1516). As the decade ended, however, a succession of key personnel changes saw the label's once intuitive understanding of the music decay. The death of Leonard Chess in October 1969, shortly after he and Phil sold the label to General Recorded Tape, was another major blow, and by mid-1972, the label barely functioned anymore. Even the massive success of "My Ding-a-Ling" sounded a hollow ring; even among die-hard Berry aficionados, few would claim the song to be one of Chess's finest releases. Chess finally closed its doors in August 1975, with the rights to the catalog sold to All Platinum. It is now held by Universal.

Further reading: *Spinning Blues into Gold: The Chess Brothers and the Legendary Chess Records*, by Nadine Cohodas (Iconoclassic Books, 2012)

DEL-FI

The Del-Fi story is, essentially, that of Bob Keane, a clarinetist and former bandleader (both in his own right and for Artie Shaw), who recorded for the GNP and Whippet labels before joining the Siamas brothers' Keen label in 1957. From there he launched Del-Fi, specializing in recording Los Angeles–based Mexican musicians. Ritchie Valens was his first star, hitting in 1958 with "C'Mon Let's

Shirelles

Baby It's You (SCEPTER SPS 504, STEREO LP, 1965)
"Dedicated to the One I Love" (SCEPTER 1203, WHITE-LABEL 7-INCH, 1958)
"Hurry Home to Me (Soldier Boy)," Valli (SCEPTER 1233, 7-INCH, 1962)
"I Met Him on a Sunday" (as the Honeytones) (TIARA 6112, 7-INCH, 1958)
"My Love Is a Charm" (DECCA 30669, 7-INCH, 1958)
Sings to Trumpets and Strings (SCEPTER SPM 502, LP, LABEL WITH LOGO IN SCROLL, 1962)
"Stop Me" (DECCA 30761, 7-INCH, 1958)
"A Teardrop and a Lollipop" (SCEPTER 1205, WHITE-LABEL 7-INCH, 1959)
Tonight's the Night (SCEPTER SPM 501, LP, LABEL WITH LOGO IN SCROLL, 1961)
A Twist Party (SCEPTER SPS 505, STEREO LP, 1965)

Go" (4106) and "Donna" (4110), before his death alongside Buddy Holly and the Big Bopper in February 1959. "La Bamba," since established as Valens' personal anthem, was originally issued on the flip side of "Donna"; of course, it has since far eclipsed its running mate in popularity, although when Del-Fi launched a subsidiary label, it was named for "Donna."

Valens remains Del-Fi's best-known and most-collected artist. Other releases include "Fast Freight" (4111), released under the name Arvee Allens, and "That's My Little Susie" (4114), "Little Girl" (4117), "Stay Beside Me" (4128), and "The Paddiwack Song" (4133). Two eponymous EPs (DFEP 101, 111) are extremely rare; LPs include 1959's *Ritchie Valens* (DFLP 1201—first pressings include diamonds in the black border around the sleeve; later issues eschew the decoration); *Ritchie* (1206); the seldom-seen *In Concert at Pacoima Jr. High* (1214); *His Greatest Hits* (1225—the white-jacket variety is relatively common, but the black-jacket issue is very scarce); and *His Greatest Hits Volume Two* (1247).

Valens also dominates the label's rarest LP release, a green-vinyl promo titled *The Del-Fi Album Sampler*, issued in 1959 and also including cuts from LPs by the Balladeers (DFLP 1204), Voices of Africa (DFLP 1203), Tony Martinez (DFLP 1205), and Keane's own (and confusingly misspelled) Bob Keene Quintet (DFLP 1202)—Keane was also a member of the Voices of Africa. Individual releases by these acts are seen very infrequently.

A pair of Mother's Day and Father's Day releases by the sweet little Nilsson Twins, along with releases by Bill Tracy, Little Caesar and the Romans, the Rookies, the Addrisi Brothers, Prentice Moreland, Buddy Landon, the Nitehawks, and Chan Romero were Del-Fi successes during the late '50s and early '60s, while the label also enjoyed massive local (southern California) impact with a long series of guitar-based surf and hot-rod albums, featuring the Lively Ones, the Surf Stompers, Dave Myers and the Surftones, the Sentinels, the Surf Mariachis, the Impacts, and more. The final Del-Fi release was within this sequence: *Big Surf Hits* (DFST 1249) in 1964.

Among the rarest of these are future Beach Boy Bruce Johnston's Surfing Band's *Surfer's Pajama Party* (1228)—which was almost immediately reissued with the same catalog number and sleeve, but credited to the Centurions. This version features different songs and carries no reference to Johnston. However, Johnston would reappear across the *Battle of the Surfing Bands* LP (1235), itself issued in three collectible varieties, named for the radio stations KFWB, KYA, and KPOI (different DJs appear on the sleeves).

Other peculiar issues, as sought after for their off-the-wall nature as for their links with Del-Fi, include Sheldon Allman's *Sing Along with Drac* (1213) collection of dreadful puns and horror spoofs; and the same artist's *Drunks* (1217), which collected the recorded statements of various anonymous drunks, encountered by Allman around Los Angeles's bars.

Del-Fi closed in 1965, when Keane launched his Mustang label. However, a new series of Del-Fi releases and reissues appeared on CD beginning in 1994. Among these, Frank Zappa's pre–Mothers of Invention *Rare Meat* EP (70010) has already become a solid collectible.

ELEKTRA

Founded in 1950 as an outlet for folk, jazz, gospel, and ethnic music, Elektra Records would develop into one of the most visionary labels of the mid-to-late '60s with a string of inspired signings, including the MC5, the Stooges, David Peel, and of course, the Doors, the four acts around whom much of the label's modern collectibility revolves.

Later, following a merger with Asylum, Elektra became party to the explosion of West Coast soft-rock talents that dominated the American 1970s; later still, the company helped popularize the so-

Jobriath was not one of Elektra's most successful signings, but this 1974 promo single proves the label tried.

called new wave in the US, via the recruitment of the Cars. Today, with the imprint now over fifty years old, Elektra remains a vibrant concern, home to talents as divergent as Icelandic maverick Björk and jam leviathan Phish. Small wonder, then, that Elektra boasts one of the most devoted collector followings of all American labels, with each decade bringing an entirely new generation of enthusiasts into the fold.

Elektra is also widely regarded as the first "modern" label to issue a budget-priced label sampler designed to draw new listeners into the fold—a promo collection (SMP 1) appeared in 1954 to encourage airplay; two years later, SMP 2 was marketed to the public as well, not only igniting interest in Elektra, but firing an entirely new field of record promotion.

Label founder Jac Holzman was inspired to form a label after attending a performance by soprano Georgianna Bannister at St. John's College in Annapolis, Maryland, where he was a student. In late 1950, he recorded a fresh version of the same recital, issuing it as the LP *New Songs by John Gruen* (the composer) in March 1951 (EKLP 1). Just 500 copies were pressed and few were sold, establishing this first release among Elektra's greatest rarities.

From college, Holzman opened a record store, The Record Loft, in Greenwich Village—it was there he met Elektra's next signing, folk singer Jean Ritchie. In stark contrast to its predecessor, the ensuing *Jean Ritchie Singing the Traditional Songs of Her Kentucky Mountain Family* (EKLP 2) quickly sold out of its entire pressing.

Elektra developed slowly but surely. Between 1952–'54, Elektra issued twenty-four albums, including sets by folk singers Frank Warner, Shep Ginandes, Cynthia Gooding, Hally Wood, and Tom Paley, as well as two titles by bluesmen Sonny Terry and Brownie McGhee, along with field recordings from as far afield as Haiti and Nova Scotia. Actor

Lovin' Spoonful

Alive and Well in Argentina, Zalman Yanovsky (BUDDAH BDS 5019, LP, 1968)

The Best Of (KAMA SUTRA KLP 8056, 2-LP WITH FOUR COLOR PHOTOS, 1967)

Daydream (KAMA SUTRA KLPS 8051, STEREO LP, 1966)

"Daydream" (KAMA SUTRA 208, YELLOW-LABEL 7-INCH, PICTURE SLEEVE, 1966)

"Did You Ever Have to Make Up Your Mind?" (KAMA SUTRA 209, 7-INCH, PICTURE SLEEVE, 1966)

Do You Believe in Magic? (CAPITOL RECORD CLUB ST 90597, LP, 1965)

"Do You Believe in Magic?" (KAMA SUTRA 201, 7-INCH, RED-ORANGE LABEL, 1965)

"She's a Lady," John Sebastian (KAMA SUTRA 254, 7-INCH, PICTURE SLEEVE, 1968)

"You Didn't Have to Be So Nice" (KAMA SUTRA 205, 7-INCH, RED-ORANGE LABEL, 1965)

You're a Big Boy Now (KAMA SUTRA KLP 8058, LP, 1967)

Jeff Barry

"All You Need Is a Quarter" (RCA VICTOR 47-7821, 7-INCH, 1960)

"The Face from Outer Space" (RCA VICTOR 47-7797, 7-INCH, 1960)

"I'll Still Love You" (RED BIRD 10-026, 7-INCH, 1965)

"It's Called Rock 'n' Roll" (RCA VICTOR 47-7477, 7-INCH, 1959)

"Lenore" (DECCA 31089, 7-INCH, 1960)

"Much Too Young" (UA 40429, 7-INCH, 1969)

"Never Never" (DECCA 31037, 7-INCH, 1959)

"Sweet Saviour" (BELL 45 140, 7-INCH, 1971)

"Walkin' in the Sun" (A&M 1422, 7-INCH, 1973)

"We Got Love Money Can't Buy" (UA 440, 7-INCH, 1962)

Theodore Bikel cut a collection of Israeli folk songs for Elektra in 1955 (EKL 32) and remained with the label until 1961.

Another early coup was the arrival of folk singer Josh White. Hitherto contracted to Decca, he joined Elektra after being blacklisted for alleged communist sympathies during the McCarthy era. His first release, *The Story of John Henry and Ballads, Blues and Other Songs* (EKL 701), was the label's first double album (two 10-inch discs); it was also the first Elektra release to appear on both 10-inch, and later 12-inch, vinyl (EKL 123).

Elektra's development through the late '50s and early '60s was dictated by the mood of the folk community, itself undergoing a massive revival. Glenn Yarbrough, Peggy Seeger, Oscar Brand, Shel Silverstein, Bob Gibson, and Paul Clayton recorded now-scarce albums for the label. Elektra also dipped into the fertile Caribbean scene, with in-demand releases by the Original Trinidad Steel Band (EKL 139) and Lord Foodoos and His Calypso Band (EKL 127). Further indication of Holzman's willingness to experiment is seen in the 1960 release of English comedienne Joyce Grenfell's *Presenting* (EKL 184), a collection of extraordinary monologues about the life of a school teacher. All but unknown in the US, this album is much in-demand among British comedy collectors. Other fascinating specialist items appear within the Nonesuch classical and Nonesuch Traveler series of LPs, the latter developing what future generations would term world music.

Elektra's biggest star of the early '60s was Judy Collins, signed in 1961 in response to the Vanguard label's Joan Baez, but rapidly emerging as a diamond talent in her own right, both via such early LPs as *Maid of Constant Sorrow* (EKL 209) and *Golden Apples of the Sun* (EKL 222), but also via a clutch of excellent singles—"Turn, Turn, Turn" (45008), her first, was an early success in Elektra's newly inaugurated series of 7-inch releases.

Tom Paxton, Phil Ochs, and the Ian Campbell Folk Group joined in 1964, while Elektra also handled two of the seminal folk compilations of the age, the three-LP box set of Woody Guthrie's *Library of Congress Recordings* (EKL 271), and the British Topic label's The Iron Muse (EKL 279) compilation of folk songs from the Industrial Revolution.

Other significant signings from this period included the Dillards and the Even Dozen Jug Band, a sprawling twelve-piece whose membership included John Sebastian, Maria Muldaur, Stefan Grossman, and Steve Katz—the group's eponymous debut album (EKL 246) appeared in 1964 and is much sought after today. Producer Paul Rothchild, very much Holzman's right-hand man, meanwhile, was responsible for moving the label into the electric-blues arena with the inspired signing of the Paul Butterfield Blues Band in 1965. Famously, Rothchild recorded the group's self-titled first album (EKL 294) three times before he was satisfied with the results; the first two sets of sessions were issued thirty years later as *The Original Lost Elektra Sessions* (Rhino R2 73505).

The success of the Butterfield album saw Elektra begin moving closer to the pop mainstream it had hitherto kept at a deliberate arm's length. The label came close to signing the Lovin' Spoonful, actually exchanging contracts before it was discovered that the group's publishing deal already bound them to the Kama Sutra label. Elektra was more fortunate with Los Angeles band Love, scoring its first hit single with spring 1966's "My Little Red Book" (45603). Love's debut album (EKS 74001) followed, and despite the general unpredictability of the band's music (sometimes brilliant, sometimes . . . not so brilliant), it remains one of the best-loved acts of the age—with its only serious competition coming from Elektra's next venture into rock, the Doors.

The success, popularity, and legends surrounding these two acts has conspired to ensure a thriving collectors market exists around both. In the Love camp, mono and promo pressings of its first three albums—*Da Capo* (4005) and the much-lauded *Forever Changes* (4013) followed their debut—are much sought after despite the latter's offering nothing more than a simple mono reduction of the stereo mix; these releases are joined as grade-A collectibles by the single "Que Vida"/"Hey Joe" (45613).

The Doors are more challenging by virtue of the almost preposterous recycling and reissue programs that have clouded a relatively straightforward discography over the past forty-plus years—vocalist Jim Morrison's death in July 1971 marked the end of the band but the birth of an industry. Mono pressings of the first three albums exist, with the *Doors* (EKL 4007) debut characterized by a radically different mix than its stereo counterpart. *Strange Days* (4017) and *Waiting for the Sun* (4027) again offer mere fold-ins.

Scarce 45s include picture-sleeved original yellow-and-black-label copies of the band's "Break On Through" debut (45611) and an initial run of "Hello I Love You" (45635), retitling the song "Hello I Love You, Won't You Tell Me Your Name?" Audiophile and quadraphonic pressings of the 1970s *Best of the Doors* compilations, too, enjoy some popularity, though there appears to be no shortage of the latter format.

The Doors' "Light My Fire" (45615) gave Elektra its first chart-topping single; fresh signings, including Tim Buckley, Ars Nova, David Ackles, and Eclection, seemed set to further that success, while the sale of the label to Warner Bros. in 1967 (with Holzman remaining on board, of course) only amplified Elektra's visibility. At the same time, however, the label's traditional penchant for the extraordinary and the eccentric continued to bear strange fruit—Britain's Incredible String Band, former Velvet Underground chanteuse Nico, the Holy Modal Rounders, and New York street performer David Peel were as bizarre as any Elektra watcher could hope for, while the arrival of Detroit hard rock bands the MC5 and the Stooges saw Elektra pursue its vision to the extremes of rock iconography.

With the exception of the Incredible String Band, none of these acts released more than a handful of records for the label, although again, reissues and archive discoveries have complicated matters considerably. Nico's catalog was confined to just one album, 1968's cult classic *Marble Index* (74029), as was the MC5's—the definitive *Kick Out the Jams* (74042) and a single of the title track (45648). Look for first pressings of the album, with a gatefold sleeve and John Sinclair's original liner notes, matching the band blow-by-blow for incendiary impact—they were removed for later pressings and would not be seen again for almost three decades, before finally reappearing on the *Ice Pick Slim* EP (Total Energy/Alive 8).

The Stooges' catalog stretched a little further, embracing two albums: *The Stooges* (74051), produced, like *Marble Index*, by former Velvet Underground bassist John Cale, and *Fun House* (74101). Look also for two super-scarce 45s, "I Wanna Be Your Dog" (45664) and "Down on the Street" (45695). Time, however, has allowed a wealth of associated documents to emerge, most notably an eight-CD box set of the sessions that made up the second Stooges album. A limited edition within the Rhino Handmade series, *The Complete Fun House* (RHM 2-7707) is arguably the ultimate test of the liberated mind. If you can sit through twenty-eight successive takes on "Loose," spread across two discs, you can sit through anything.

David Peel, too, released two albums, themselves since reissued across one disc in the Rhino Handmade series (RHM 2-7713); *Have a Marijuana* (74032) and *The American Revolution* (74069) are both relatively common, but are favored by Apple label completists—1971 saw the performer fall into John Lennon's orbit, at the outset of the ex-Beatle's New York sojourn, cutting the album *The Pope Smokes Dope* (Apple SW 3391).

If Elektra ended the 1960s as a haven for some of the most unique freak shows in the American mainstream, it entered the 1970s as a repository for another musical force entirely. The mature ruminations of David Gates's Bread debuted on the label in 1969, with the single "Any Way You Want Me" (45666) and a self-titled album (EKS 74044). By 1971, when singer-songwriters Harry Chapin and Carly Simon were added to the roster, Bread ranked among Elektra's biggest-selling acts ever. Simon would swiftly join the group at the top, and by the time Holzman retired in 1973, and the label merged with Asylum, Elektra was poised to dominate the middle of the soft-rock road.

Of course, the label's historical love for the oddball continued to shine through, and it is in this area that the greatest collectibles exist. Queen, the British hard rock band whose appeal embraces everyone from dyed-in-the-wool headbangers to students of absurdly tongue-in-cheek satire, are rightly ranked among the most collected bands in the world. Elektra signed the band in 1975, and over the next six years, Queen unleashed the greatest music of its long career, ranging from the mock-operatic "Bohemian Rhapsody" (45297) to the shuddering funk of "Another One Bites the Dust" (47031); from the two-sided sporting anthem "We Are the Champions"/"We Will Rock You" (45441), to the two-headed collaboration with David Bowie, "Under Pressure" (47235).

Also in heavy demand today are releases by an artist who, ironically, Elektra could barely give away at the time. Glam-rocker Jobriath was brought to the label by Jerry Brandt, Carly Simon's manager, and afforded one of the most lavish, not to mention expensive, launches in rock history. Unfortunately, all the money in the world could not persuade the public to buy his records, and for many years, the albums

Link Wray

"Ace of Spades" (SWAN 4261, 7-INCH, 1967)

"Batman Theme" (SWAN 4244, 7-INCH, 1966)

"Good Rockin' Tonight" (SWAN 4201, 7-INCH, 1965)

Great Guitar Hits (VERMILLION 1924, LP, 1966)

"I Sez Baby" (KAY 3690, 7-INCH, 1958)

"Jack the Ripper" (RUMBLE 1000, 7-INCH, 1961)

Link Wray and the Waymen (EPIC LN 3661, LP, 1960)

"Rumble" (CADENCE 1347, 7-INCH, 1958)

"Rumble Mambo" (OKEH 7166, 7-INCH, 1963)

Yesterday and Today (RECORD FACTORY 1929, LP, 1963)

Sparks

"Beat the Clock" (ELEKTRA 11412, 12-INCH PROMO, 1979)

"Cool Places" (ATLANTIC 89866, 7-INCH, PICTURE SLEEVE, 1983)

Excerpts from Gratuitous Sax and Senseless Violins
(UK LOGIC 74321 24302, PROMO CD, GATEFOLD SLEEVE, 1994)

"Forever Young" (COLUMBIA 10579, 7-INCH, 1977)

Halfnelson, Halfnelson (BEARSVILLE BV 2048, LP, 1971)

"I Predict" (ATLANTIC 325, 12-INCH PROMO, 1982)

"I Want to Hold Your Hand" (UK ISLAND WIP 6282, 7-INCH, 1976)

"Looks Looks Looks" (ISLAND 043, 7-INCH, 1975)

"Tips for Teens" (RCA PD 12252, 7-INCH TEST PRESSING, 1981)

"Wonder Girl" (BEARSVILLE 0006, 7-INCH, 1971)

Jobriath (75070) and *Creatures of the Street* (7E 1010) could be found propping up bargain bins across the country. Two UK singles, "Take Me I'm Yours" (K12129) and "Street Corner Love" (K12146), were also released to deafening apathy.

The early '90s, however, saw such stars as Morrissey and the Pet Shop Boys begin to voice their admiration for the star-that-never-was, and slowly, eyes and ears opened. A decade later, albums and associated singles alike are snapped up the moment they appear, while one of the most exciting items ever to emerge on eBay in 2001 was a reel of unreleased material recorded by Jobriath with producer Eddie Kramer, shortly before he signed to Elektra. Together with the two released albums and excerpts from an uncompleted third, this material forms the basis for yet another Rhino Handmade CD collection.

Sparks, a band whose career probably touches more record labels than Link Wray's, issued one album through Elektra, 1979's massively influential *No. 1 In Heaven* (6E 186). Boston new wave band the Cars opened their Elektra career in 1978 with the quirky "Just What I Needed" (45491), and closed it a decade later as one of the entire genre's most reliable hit machines—at least in America.

In the UK, where the group was launched with the single "My Best Friend's Girl" (UK Elektra K12301), they remain best recalled as the vehicle for a spot of marketing shenanigans that came close to crippling the entire concept of "limited" special editions of new releases, with a "rare" picture disc that rapidly transpired to be anything but. The Cars' British collectibility never really recovered.

British Elektra also produced apparently copious "limited" versions of another American new wave act's records—Television's "Marquee Moon" (K12252) is, again, far more common as a 12-inch single than an edited 7-inch, while red-vinyl pressings of the group's sophomore album, *Adventure* (K52072), also appear more common than perhaps they should.

In 1982, Elektra founded its own jazz-rock oriented subsidiary, Elektra Musician, while maintaining its presence in the rock mainstream as skillfully as ever. Rabidly collectible artists recruited during the 1980s include the Cure and Depeche Mode (via licensing deals with the British Fiction and Mute labels, respectively), the Sugarcubes (and following their demise, Björk), Metallica, Third Eye Blind, and rap star Ol' Dirty Bastard. Indeed, in an age when the spirit of many of rock's traditionally collected labels has been utterly subverted by the advent of the CD, Elektra has managed to retain and even strengthen its ties with the community, simply via the artists it signs. Not all are great, not all are collected by even the label's most staunch fans. But those that are more than make up for the shortfall.

Further reading: *Becoming Elektra: The True Story of Jac Holzman's Visionary Record Label*, by Mick Houghton and Jac Holzman (Jawbone Press, 2017)

FACTORY

Chiswick and Stiff may have set the pace for British independent labels, but into the early '80s, even they were no competition for Factory, the Manchester-based concern established by local scene-maker, BBC producer and TV host Tony Wilson.

From the outset, the label's musical policy was beyond reproach. Concentrating almost exclusively on Manchester and its environs, Factory's first signings represented a virtual *Who's Who* of local luminaries, including Joy Division, Cabaret Voltaire, John Dowie, and Durutti Column. Taking a leaf out of Stiff's book, Factory brought on board a house producer of soon-to-be-proven renown, Martin Hannett; taking another, Wilson also identified the collectors' need to be constantly challenged and entertained by a hobby.

Particularly through its first five years of activity, the Factory catalog would intersperse records with a plethora of other oddities, issued in strict numerical order, regardless of format or nature. These range from label stationery and posters (the label's very first release, FAC 1, was one such) to real estate: FAC 51 was the Hacienda nightclub, built and operated by Factory from May 1982, and soon to become the focal point for Manchester nightlife. FAC 98 was the hairdressing salon opened in the Hacienda's basement in October 1983. As for the oddities, FAC 99 was New Order manager Rob Gretton's

Björk

"Birthday + 3," The Sugarcubes (UK ONE LITTLE INDIAN 7TP7CD, CD, 1987)

Bitid fast i vitid, Tappi Tikarris (ICELAND SPOR SPOR 4, LP, 1981)

Björk (ICELAND FALKINN FA 006, LP, 1977)

Celebrating Wood and Metal (UK ONE LITTLE INDIAN BJORK FC1, CD, 1996)

Debut (UK ONE LITTLE INDIAN TPLP 31, LP WITH LYRIC BOOK, 1993)

"Enjoy" (UK ONE LITTLE INDIAN 193TP12DM, 12-INCH, 1996)

Gling glo, Trio Gudmundar Ingolfssonar (ICELAND SMEKKLEYSA SM 27, CD, 1990)

"Joga + 12-inch (UK ONE LITTLE INDIAN TPLP 81, 3X12-INCH SINGLES, 1997)

"Possibly Maybe" (UK ONE LITTLE INDIAN 193TP12TD, 12-INCH, 1996)

"Songull", Kukl (ICELAND GRAMM GRAMM 17, 7-INCH, 1983)

dentistry bill, paid for by Factory after he was beaten up by associates of A Certain Ratio.

Few of these, of course, were obtainable by the average fan. Even among the label's more conventional releases, however, the chances of completeness were slim. Factory's first vinyl release was the EP *A Factory Sample* (FAC 2), a limited edition that swiftly went out of print. Early singles by A Certain Ratio and the fledgling Orchestral Maneuvers in the Dark ("Electricity," FAC 6) vanished swiftly, and who has ever seen a Factory egg-timer (FAC 8)?

Even Joy Division and New Order, the label's brightest stars, have a catalog replete with scarcities and seeming impossibilities, and while Factory LPs tended to remain on the catalog long enough for all interested parties to pick them up, the original packaging was not always so reliable. *Unknown Pleasures* (FACT 10), Joy Division's debut, initially appeared with a textured sleeve; *Still* (FACT 40), the

The Cure on Fiction

"Catch" (UK FICTION FICSP 26, CLEAR-VINYL, CLEAR-LABEL 7-INCH, 1987)

"The Caterpillar" (UK FICTION FICSP 20, 7-INCH PICTURE DISC, 1984)

Disintegration (UK FICTION FIXHP 14, LP PICTURE DISC, 1990)

Entreat (UK FICTION FIXCD 17, LIMITED-EDITION LP WITH YELLOW SLEEVE, 1990)

Faith/Carnage Visors (UK FICTION FIXC 6, CASSETTE WITH B&W SLEEVE, 1981)

"I'm a Cult Hero," The Cult Heroes (UK FICTION FICS 006, 7-INCH, PICTURE SLEEVE, 1979)

Kiss Me Kiss Me Kiss Me (UK FICTION FIXHA 13, 2-LP SHRINK-WRAPPED WITH BONUS ORANGE-VINYL 12-INCH, 1987)

"Never Enough" (UK FICTION FICDP 35, PICTURE-CD SINGLE, 1990)

"The Walk" (UK FICTION FICSP 18, 7-INCH PICTURE DISC, 1983)

Wish (UK FICTION CUREPK 1; PROMO BOX SET WITH DIGIPACK CD, VIDEO, EPK; 1992)

group's posthumous third, was issued in a Hessian sleeve with card inners and white ribbon.

New Order's *Brotherhood* (FACT 150) LP first arrived in a metallic sleeve (its CD counterpart boasted a metallic booklet) and Durutti Column's *Return Of* (FACT 14) made its debut with a sandpaper sleeve—a gimmick that was swiftly quashed by the retail sector. Any other album that came into contact with it was promptly shredded!

The list goes on—at least one Factory collector believes that it is possible to find at least one collectible variant with every release in the catalog, and while this may be an exaggeration, it probably isn't much of one. Further confusion can be enjoyed if one also includes the Factory Benelux subsidiary in one's calculations— operating for some sixty releases (numbered FBN 1-55, and apparently randomly thereafter), between 1980–'87, the label offered both alternatives to and expansions of a number of the parent label's releases, aside from taunting completists with a number of unreleased (but nevertheless extant) issues.

Factory folded in 1992 with two final albums, Steve Martland's *Wolfgang* (FAC 406) and the Happy Mondays' . . . *Yes Please!* (FAC 420).

Further reading: *Factory Records: The Complete Graphic Album* by Matthew Robinson (Thames & Hudson, 2007)

Former Pink Floyd frontman Syd Barrett's debut album, 1969's The Madcap Laughs.

HARVEST

Best known as home to some of the undisputed giants of the 1970s British rock scene—Pink Floyd and Deep Purple paramount among them—EMI's Harvest subsidiary was established in 1968 by Malcolm Jones to provide a fertile environment for "progressive" bands hitherto spread across the EMI catalog.

That brief was fulfilled, with room to spare. The label's first UK releases, in June 1969, comprised 45s by free-festival regulars the Edgar Broughton Band ("Evil," HAR 5001), singer-songwriter Michael Chapman, the classically inclined Barclay James Harvest, and light-rockers Bakerloo. The following months brought LPs by Deep Purple (*Book of Taliesyn*, SHVL 751), poet Pete Brown, folk singers Shirley and Dolly Collins, and Chapman, all of which were previewed on the impossibly rare (100 copies) *Harvest Sampler* (SPSLP 118).

This mixed bag set the standards by which Harvest would operate for at least the next five years. Purple and Floyd (the latter of which arrived via ex-frontman Syd Barrett's two solo albums, before

unleashing its own *Ummagumma* (SHDW 1/2, 1969)) may dominate the label in terms of its best-known collectibles, but to dwell on either is to overlook the almost obsessive zeal with which Harvest hunters pursue now-scarce albums by the Third Ear Band, the Panama Limited Jug Band, Forest, Tea and Symphony, Quatermass, Chris Spedding, Spontaneous Combustion, Babe Ruth, and so many more. As with other UK prog-inclined labels of the day, the one- or two-album act was the rule, and the Harvest label overflows with them.

Singles by these bands are colossally hard to collect. Purple and Floyd (the latter, again, via Syd Barrett—the band itself released no UK Harvest singles whatsoever until 1979) are the ones everybody seems to be searching for, with values for Barrett's "Octopus" (5009) outpacing virtually everything else on the label.

Practically every other Harvest 45 issued prior to 1972 is scarce, however, and that includes releases by such putative stars as the Broughtons ("Out Demons Out," 5015; and "Apache Drop-Out," 5032, actually made the UK Top 40), Roy Harper, Kevin Ayers (whose Harvest output is possibly the highlight of the entire catalog), and the last days of '60s hit-makers the Move, as members Roy Wood and Jeff Lynne moved toward their respective destinies in Wizzard and the Electric Light Orchestra.

Those bands would bring Harvest its first reliable hit-single acts, with Wizzard scoring two successive No. 1s in 1973. Of course, 1973 also brought the Floyd's monstrous *Dark Side of the Moon* (SHVL

804), still one of the biggest-selling albums in history, and it is at this point that many Harvest collectors lose interest, since the label stopped operating as a welcoming home for rock's dottiest denizens and began functioning like just another conventional record label.

Certainly this impression is borne out by the official label history, published in the Harvest Festival box set. Again and again, interviewees wax rhapsodic about the label's early days, but few have more than a few facts and figures to relate about the post–*Dark Side* era. Nevertheless, some intriguing prospects are realized by a careful trawl through this period, including further gems from Ayers and Harper, interesting sets by Strapps, Gryphon, the last days of Focus, and the Soft Machine.

Releases by Japanese rockers Sadistic Mika Band and Bill Nelson's Be Bop Deluxe are extremely collectible, while the late '70s saw Harvest plunge headfirst into the punk scene with the release of *The Roxy, London WC2*, a lo-fi live document of the seminal punk venue, which gave vinyl debuts to future superstars the Wire (who remained Harvest artists), Buzzcocks, the Adverts, and X-Ray Spex. Australia's Saints, New York's Shirts, and power-pop hopefuls the Banned are also worthy of investigation.

Harvest dipped into roots reggae with very collectible albums by Britain's Matumbi and Jamaica's Israel Vibration; the steel band Trinidad Oil Company scored an unexpected hit with "The Calendar Song" (5122); there was even a dose of disco from La Belle Epoque. European metal band Scorpions and former Jam bassist Bruce Foxton also made collectible excursions—indeed, Foxton's "Playing this Game to Win" 45 (5239) was the final Harvest release, in July 1985.

HOMESTEAD

One of the most important of all US independent labels of the alternative age, Homestead was launched by Gerard Cosloy in 1984 with the eponymous debut LP by Boston's Blackjacks (HMS 001). Following through with sets by Salem 66, the Dogmatics, and Great Plains, Homestead received its first national notice after linking with maverick producer Steve Albini's controversial Big Black.

One of Harvest's biggest hits in 1971, Deep Purple's Fireball.

The group's "Racer X" 12-inch, in April 1985, was one of several characteristically confrontational releases by the band, all of which are now sought after by hardcore punk aficionados.

Another key Homestead release was the compilation *Speed Trials* (HMS 011), featuring rare material from across the extreme rock spectrum of the day—the Fall, the Beastie Boys (the hyper-rare "Egg Raid on Mojo"), Lydia Lunch, Sonic Youth, and the Swans all contributed, with the latter also issuing the "Raping a Slave" 12-inch (HMS 017). Among other crucial Homestead releases from this early period are Australia's Died Pretty's 12-inch *Out of the Unknown* (HMS 014) and several early releases by the then-unknown Dinosaur Jr. (the earliest pressings were originally, and collectibly, released credited to "Dinosaur").

Seattle's Green River, precursors of the later Mudhoney–Pearl Jam axis; New York noise terrorists Sonic Youth; Death of Samantha; and Live Skull also made several now-valued releases. Boston-based Live Skull's origins were also recalled with a 12-inch by the earlier Uzi, *Sleep Asylum* (HMS 055).

Hitherto, Homestead's appeal had remained strictly cult American; 1986, however, saw the arrival of Scraping Foetus off the Wheel, Australians Nick Cave and the Bad Seeds, and Einstürzende Neubauten, from the UK label Mute. Cave's 12-inch Homestead singles are extraordinarily difficult to find today, particularly when compared with their UK counterparts.

Breaking Circus, the Membranes, Big Dipper, Phantom Tollbooth, and the Volcano Suns arrived during 1986–'87, alongside New Zealanders the Verlaines, the Chills, the Clean, and the Tall Dwarfs, all of whom helped introduce America to that country's Flying Nun label, one of the most important (and itself collectible) of all Antipodean labels. Controversial punk G.G. Allin also made a number of Homestead releases—interestingly, his brother was once a member of the Boston band Thrills, alongside Blackjacks frontman Johnny Angel.

Growing awareness of the scene unfolding in the Pacific Northwest brought a now-much-in-demand split 45 featuring two of that area's most vital acts, Beat Happening and Screaming Trees (HMS 110); late-'80s and early '90s releases by the Pastels, Sebadoh, Giant Sand, and two astonishingly prolific acts, Daniel Johnston and the Happy Flowers, are also worth looking for.

Homestead offered up several classic archive releases, including a mass of material by Cleveland punk pioneers the Styrenes (*It's Artastic*, HMS 173) and the Electric Eels (*God Says Fuck You*, HMS 174). However, the sheer weight of major-label interest in the now-burgeoning alternative scene was taking its toll on Homestead's

ability to attract and retain the talent that had once established its reputation.

The changing marketplace, too, affected the label's willingness to issue either 7-inch or 12-inch releases; it preferred to concentrate on full-length CD albums. This certainly affected the collecting market, although the occasional break in this rule—Soul-Junk's "1945" 7-inch (HMS 225), for example—remains in high demand.

Homestead wound down in the mid-'90s, following releases by William Parker, Hoosegow, and the Joe Morris Ensemble (HMS 233).

IMMEDIATE

Immediate was the brainchild of businessman Tony Calder and Andrew Loog Oldham, manager and producer of the Rolling Stones and the first of the new wave of entrepreneurs to shake the cobwebbed halls of traditional British pop during the so-called Swinging Sixties.

More importantly, however, Immediate was also the role model for almost every independent UK label of the next decade and beyond (both Chiswick and Stiff, pioneers of the punk-era DIY label boom, were fiercely indebted to Immediate's example), while the company's pop-art imagery and eye for catchy slogans still dominates rock iconography. The fact that the label's actual output almost universally lives up to these same high standards is simply the icing on a fabulous cake.

Immediate debuted in August 1965, with the first fruits of a licensing deal with the US Bang label, the McCoys' "Hang On Sloopy" (001). The group would ultimately see six 45s issued on the label, and it is perhaps surprising to learn that of the twenty-two singles released by Immediate during its first six months, the only other chart entry was the McCoys' own follow-up, "Fever" (21).

Ignored by the record-buying public in the interim were releases by future Velvet Underground vocalist Nico ("I'm Not Saying," 003—one of several Immediate releases produced by Jimmy Page); Gregory Phillips ("Down by the

The Edgar Broughton Band's 1970 "Out Demons Out" 45 was edited down from a ten-minute live recording that would remain in the vaults for the next twenty-four years.

Flying Nun

"Ambivalence," Pin Group (NZ, FLYING NUN 001, 7-INCH, 1981)

Boodle Boodle Boodle, The Clean (NZ FLYING NUN 003, EP, 1982)

"By Night," The Bats (NZ FLYING NUN 024, 7-INCH, 1983)

"Death and the Maidens," The Verlaines (NZ FLYING NUN 014, 7-INCH, 1983)

Eric Glandy Memorial Band, Eric Glandy Memorial Band (FLYING NUN 049, EP, 1986)

"Schwimmin in der See," The Builders (NZ FLYING NUN 006, 7-INCH, 1982)

"Show Me to the Bellrope," This Sporting Life (NZ FLYING NUN 011, 7-INCH, 1983)

"Tally Ho!" The Clean (NZ FLYING NUN 002, 7-INCH, 1981)

"Tired Sun," The Able Tasmans (NZ FLYING NUN 043, 7-INCH, 1985)

"Uptown Sheep," Crystal Zoom (NZ FLYING NUN 030, 7-INCH, 1984)

Boondocks," 004—later covered by Depeche Mode's Martin Gore); another US license, the Strangeloves ("Cara-Lin," 007); John Mayall and the Bluesbreakers (the classic "I'm Your Witch Doctor," 012—featuring Eric Clapton); comedian Jimmy Tarbuck (a Rolling Stones cover, "Wastin' Time," 018); and the Mockingbirds ("You Stole My Love," 015—performed by Graham Gouldman, with Julie Driscoll on backing vocals; the song was later covered by the Jimmy Page–era Yardbirds).

Debuts by such proto-psychedelic legends as the Golden Apples of the Sun, the Factotums, and Les Fleur de Lys, and a solo single by Glyn Johns, now far better known as one of Britain's top producers, also passed by.

Immediate's first homegrown hit was Chris Farlowe's version of another Stones song, "Think" (023), and over the next year, Jagger-Richard compositions remained Immediate's only other chart entries: "Sitting on a Fence" (recorded by Twice as Much, 033) and "Out of Time" and "Ride On Baby" (Farlowe again, 035, 038—"Out of Time" brought the label its first chart-topper).

The Rolling Stones' dominance of the Immediate catalog was finally broken by Steve Marriott and Ronnie Lane of the Small Faces. They joined the label in late 1966, immediately handing Chris Farlowe another hit, "My Way of Giving" (041), before displacing him as Immediate's biggest-selling act. The band's own string of classic 45s was joined by two LPs, including the legendary *Ogden's Nut Gone Flake* (IMLP/IMSP 012), and sufficient unreleased demos, outtakes, and sessions to ensure that "new" Small Faces material has been appearing ever since. The Charly label's four-CD *The Immediate Years* (CD IMM BOX 1) box set is probably the most complete summary of this material, though there are omissions even there. (Other Immediate acts similarly summarized by Charly include the Nice and Humble Pie.)

P.P. Arnold, Fleetwood Mac, and Amen Corner also rank among Immediate hitmakers; Duncan Browne, Mike D'Abo, and the young Rod Stewart rate among the most promising hopefuls. Neither commercial nor critical support could prevent Immediate from collapsing in financial disarray in 1970, however—the final single, perhaps appropriately, was the Amen Corner's coupling of "Get Back"/"Farewell to the Real Magnificent Seven" (084). The last album was a label sampler, *Happy to Be Part of the Industry of Human Happiness*—with the extremely odd catalog number IMLYIN 2 (say it fast).

The collectibility of the Immediate label (and its short-lived Instant subsidiary) has never been in doubt; original releases are scarce across the entire eighty five–single and thirty six–LP catalog, with a handful of albums fetching genuinely serious money, including the supposedly Keith Richards–led Aranbee Pop Symphony Orchestra's *Today's Pop Symphony* (IMLP/SP 003), original editions of the Small Faces' *Ogden's*, and rare British pressings of the German *In Memoriam* (IMLP 022) collection, along with barely released albums by Billy Nicholls (*Would You Believe?*, IMCP 009), Duncan Browne (*Give Me Take You*, IMSP 018), and Michael D'Abo (*Gulliver's Travels*, Instant INLP 003).

Another Instant release manages to combine the obsessiveness of record collectors with the fanaticism of soccer fans—*Recorded Highlights: European Cup Final 1968* (INLP 001) offers commentary from Manchester United's 4-1 win over Benfica, and is Britain's rarest sports record by far.

Of the singles, all are worth seeking out, but special mention must be made of the Apostolic Intervention's version of the Small Faces' "(Tell Me) Have You Ever Seen Me" (043), the Australian Playboys' "Black Sheep" (054), picture-sleeved editions of the Small Faces' "Tin Soldier" (062), and promo pressings of the same combo's "Afterglow

Small Faces

"Almost Grown" (PRESS 5007, 7-INCH, 1969)

"My Mind's Eye" (RCA VICTOR 47-9055, 7-INCH, 1966)

Ogden's Nut Gone Flake (IMMEDIATE Z12 52009, LP WITH ROUND COVER, 1968)

"Sha La La La Lee" (PRESS 9826, 7-INCH, 1966)

Small Faces (UK DECCA LK 4790, RED-LABEL LP, 1966)

Small Faces (UK IMMEDIATE AS 1, ONE-SIDED 7-INCH PROMO, 1967)

There Are but 4 Small Faces (IMMEDIATE Z12 5002, LP WITH COLOR COVER, 1967)

"Tin Soldier" (IMMEDIATE 5003, 7-INCH, PICTURE SLEEVE, 1968)

"Understanding" (RCA VICTOR 47-8949, 7-INCH, 1966)

"What'cha Gonna Do About It?" (PRESS 9794, 7-INCH, 1965)

of Your Love" (077), inadvertently pressed with an alternate version of the B-side, "Wham Bam Thank You Ma'am."

Releases on Immediate's American wing, too, are much sought after. Included among these are an otherwise unavailable version of the Small Faces' "Mad John" (5012) and one 1969 single that has no UK equivalent, "Sylvie," performed by Chris Farlowe's backing band the Hill (5016).

Given the rarity and desirability of so many Immediate originals, it might appear queer that many of these apparent obscurities now seem as familiar as the greatest hits in history—and most of them probably are. Almost from the moment Immediate closed its doors in 1970, the catalog has been recycled, reissued, and revived on so many occasions that only the classic Sun label can reasonably claim to have received more cavalier treatment.

From odd issues on the Springboard (US) and NEMS (UK) labels during the 1970s, to a string of compilations and reissues masterminded by Sony in the early '90s, and on to the seriously collector-oriented issues from Charly and the Castle/Sanctuary Group of decade's end, there is scarcely a single Immediate recording left that has not now been reissued, with the arrival in 2000 of Castle's six-CD recounting of the entire Immediate singles catalog, plus releases for even the Billy Nicholls and Duncan Browne albums the crowning glory. Only the European Cup album remains totally unavailable in some form or other.

Further reading: *The Immediate Records Story: One of the Greatest Accounts of Sixties Rock 'n' Roll Life*, by Simon Spence (St. Albans Press, 2016)

ISLAND

Chris Blackwell's Island records was launched in Jamaica in 1958, transferring to the UK in 1962 and concentrating its output on its erstwhile homeland: over the next five years, the quality and quantity of Island's ska-rocksteady catalog was rivaled only by the Melodisc/Blue Beat and Dr. Bird labels, and when, in 1967, founder Blackwell decided to shift Island's focus toward Britain's own rock scene, he did so only after transferring Island's multitudinous Jamaican contacts and catalog to a new, co-owned venture, Trojan Records.

For Island records collectors, the so-called Jamaican era is a law unto itself. Some 400 45s and thirty LPs were released between 1962–'67, many of them now-avowed classics of the genre. In addition, the subsidiaries Brit, Black Swan, and Aladdin pumped out almost one hundred more, also primarily Jamaican, or at least Caribbean. The Sue imprint, headed by maverick producer Guy Stevens, was responsible for an equally collectible hoard of classic R&B releases.

Through this period, Island catalog numbers were prefixed with the letters WI. When 1967 brought the move into rock, a new series was launched—WIP (the P stood for "pop")—and the label made almost immediate inroads into that market. The second-ever release, Traffic's "Paper Sun" (6002), made the UK Top Five, establishing that band among the best-loved groups of the age (two further singles made the Top Ten that year), and confirming Island's arrival on the scene.

From the outset, Island regarded singles as little more than trailers for

The final Immediate release, the Hill's "Sylvie" did not even get beyond the promo stage.

The Anglo-American five-piece Sparks broke through in the UK with 1974's Kimono My House LP.

albums, a mindset that communicated itself to both purchasers, and subsequently, to collectors. Although many Island singles are considered choice rarities, far more enthusiasts pursue the label's LPs, in particular the pink-label issues that appeared between 1967–'70. This incorporates key releases by Mott the Hoople, King Crimson, Free, Jethro Tull, Fairport Convention, Traffic, and Nick Drake, all of which are extremely collectible today, plus lesser-known (but equally desirable) sets by John Martyn, Clouds, Blodwyn Pig, Tramline, the Bama Winds, Quintessence, Dr. Strangely Strange, and more.

Many collectors believe that the Island rock LP series was launched with the introduction of the ILPS numbering series (that is, John Martyn's 1969 LP *The Tumbler*, 9091). In fact, the first releases—Traffic's *Mr. Fantasy* (ILP 9061), Art's *Supernatural Fairytales* (ILP 967), and Spooky Tooth's *It's All About* (ILP 9080)—appeared within the label's already existing numerical sequence, sandwiched, as the gaps between numbers indicates, between the traditional reggae and the R&B fare. The "S" designation, perceptive readers may already have realized, was introduced when the label commenced issuing stereo recordings only.

The pink Island label went through three phases, all of which are crucial to identifying original pressings: between 1967–'69, it featured an eye motif, and "island" in large lowercase letters at the foot of the label. A transitional design used for a handful of issues in late 1969 had the word "ISLAND" within a black box that extended up to a swirl design around the spindle hole; the final type, into 1970, simply bore a large, lower-case "i" at the bottom of the label. This was abandoned in late 1970, when a new palm tree logo was introduced. Cat Stevens' *Tea for the Tillerman* (9135) was the last album to be issued with a pink label of any kind.

Widely regarded as the next era in Island's development, the early '70s saw the label move away from its unabashedly underground origins and begin actively pursuing hit singles, an approach that reached fruition following the appointment of producer Muff Winwood to the A&R department. Although both Free and Cat Stevens enjoyed hits during the early '70s, both were still considered primarily album artists. The arrival of Roxy Music in 1972, and Sparks two years later, reversed that equation—though both did make phenomenal LPs, their singles were better still (and usually featured non-album B-sides, adding to their appeal). By the time of the next label-design change, to a deeply stylized tropical sunset scene, the original collecting cognoscenti had long since moved away.

The change was not as radical as some people would have you believe. Bands like Sharks (featuring guitarist Chris Spedding), the Sutherland Brothers, and Quiver and Jade Warrior maintained at least a light grip on the underground values of old; the soap operatic saga of Fairport Convention continued in full force; Bad Company married the best of old Free and Mott the Hoople into one seamless unit; and Bob Marley, signed to the label in 1971, began his march toward world superstardom and headlined a still vibrant crop of reggae releases in the Island catalog.

Indeed, even under the new regime, Island remained a provocative concern. The popularity of Roxy Music spun off Bryan Ferry's massively successful solo career, but it also brought solo ventures from bandmates Andy Mackay and Phil Manzanera, neither of which sold especially well. Both are now heavily collected, although CD reissues on Manzanera's Expression label have taken some of the sting out of prices.

Also desirable are releases by the group's original electronics player, Brian Eno—he quit Roxy in 1973 to launch an utterly idiosyncratic solo career, highlighted in the rarity stakes by the singles "Seven

The peak of British punk's fascination with roots reggae, the all-girl Slits' debut album Cut.

Roxy Music's self-titled debut album, from 1972.

Island Anthology two-CD set). Another Cale rarity involves the *Helen of Troy* LP (9350), originally issued with the controversial "Leaving It All up to You" included. Early into the manufacturing run, the decision was made to replace the song with "Coral Moon"—only for the decision to be reversed immediately thereafter. Only a handful of amended versions appear to have been made; in terms of scarcity, they rank alongside any of the Velvet Underground's so widely feted rarities.

There are several similar issues in the Island catalog, including copies of the first Mott the Hoople album (9108) with the song "Road to Birmingham" inadvertently included. Corrected pressings followed very swiftly; "Birmingham" itself was the also B-side of the group's debut single, "Rock 'n' Roll Queen" (6072).

Another extremely popular, if intensely controversial, release was Derek and Clive Live, a private recording of comedians Peter Cook and Dudley Moore at their most foul-mouthedly funny, which gathered cult pace so quickly that when Island finally released it in 1976 (9434), some two years after its conception, it made the UK Top 20 on word of mouth alone (radio certainly couldn't touch it). More than a quarter of a century of ever-plummeting societal standards later, it remains the most abusively and gratuitously obscene record ever to become a major hit.

Into the late '70s, Island remained ambitious. In 1977, a band called Warsaw Pakt made national headlines by rehearsing, recording, manufacturing, and shipping an album, *Needletime*, in under twenty-four hours (9515); three years later, Toots and the Maytals' *Live in London* album was put together with similar haste.

New signings the B-52's, Grace Jones, and many more established the label at the forefront of the artier new wave scene. Although the label's inherent collectibility declined utterly during the 1980s and 1990s, individual artists remained frequently fascinating. It should also be remembered that two of the most deliberately collector-

Deadly Finns" (6178), and unlikely as it sounds, "The Lion Sleeps Tonight" (6233). The Roxy family catalog left Island in 1977 at the expiration of the label's contract with the EG Management company (King Crimson also departed); rereleases followed on the Polydor and Virgin labels.

Eno was also involved in a venture that, had certain of its participants had their way, might well have developed into a full-time supergroup, as he joined recent Island recruits Kevin Ayers, John Cale, and Nico (the latter two ex–Velvet Underground members) for a joint concert at the London Rainbow. June 1, 1974 (9291). A live album commemorating the show is all that became of the union, but the promise of the union remains palpable.

Cale and Ayers both released now-rare Island singles around this time—Cale's "The Man Who Couldn't Afford To" (6202) is especially sought after for its non-LP B-side, "Sylvia Said" (since included in the

Kevin Ayers' 1974 The Confessions of Dr Dream and Other Stories was his first for Island, after five years at Harvest.

The promo for New York glam band Milk'n'Cookies' UK debut single.

oriented labels of the age, Stiff and ZTT, were both distributed by Island at the height of their zaniness.

Island's biggest act of the age—indeed, of the last twenty years—was U2, regarded among the most collectible bands to have emerged since the halcyon days of the 1950s and 1960s. The group joined the label in 1980, debuting with the UK single "11 O'Clock Tick Tock" (WIP 6601), since which time they have, of course, gone from strength to strength.

There is little value attached to any of the band's conventional releases—singles and albums alike have sold in such vast quantities that even novice collectors need to dig some way below the surface in search of truly unusual items. A wealth of international picture sleeves offer one popular route; in-concert and other radio broadcasts from King Biscuit, Westwood One, the Album Network, and many more also have a devoted following; while a number of fascinating limited-edition items have cropped up over the years, ensuring that U2's collectible status spans its entire career, as opposed to a handful of rare releases at the outset.

Among the most popular items are *The Joshua Tree Collection* (Island 6:1-6:5), a box set replicating the blockbuster *The Joshua Tree* LP across five singles; and a second set, *The Joshua Tree Singles* (Island U2PK 1), which merely rounded up the four officially released 45s from the set in a custom PVC wallet. Singles from both 1983's *War* and 1984's *The Unforgettable Fire* albums were issued as double singles in gatefold sleeves; "The Unforgettable Fire" itself appeared briefly as a shaped picture disc (Island ISP 220).

Several of the band's early to mid '80s UK 12-inch singles are becoming increasingly difficult to find; so, at the opposite end of the scale, are such latter-day issues as 1992's "Even Better than the Real Thing" (Island REAL U2) and 1997's "Mofo" (12IS 684), which was issued in an impossibly limited run of just 2,000 copies. The majority of U2 CD singles, too, are becoming scarcer.

Nevertheless the key to a comprehensive U2 collection does lie within its earliest releases; the irony for any collector who regards U2 and Island Records as one of the era's most reliable double acts is that all appear on the Irish wing of CBS Records, to whom the group was contracted since 1979. Reissues have rendered 12-inch pressings of the group's debut single, the *U2:3* EP (CBS 12-7951) relatively common—certainly they are more visible than the 1979 7-inch, or the four colored-vinyl reissues that followed in 1980. However, further singles are extremely difficult to locate, including "Another Day" (CBS 8306), "11 O'clock Tick Tock" (8687), "A Day Without Me" (8905), "I Will Follow" (9065), "Fire" (1376), "Gloria" (1718), and "A Celebration" (2214). Even more troublesome to locate are three 7-inch anthologies, issued between 1982–'84, and each

comprising four singles in a plastic wallet. *4 U2 Play* (PAC 1), *PAC 2* (PAC 2), and *PAC 3* (PAC 3) are essential but challenging digests for the collector, with the first-named also presenting a bewildering variety of colored-vinyl variations.

Chris Blackwell sold Island to Polygram during the 1990s; the label continued on for a while, but as its roster was shifted elsewhere into the empire, Island gradually became regarded primarily as a reissues imprint and is today part of the massive Universal group. Under this administration, many classic recordings of the 1960s and early '70s have finally resurfaced, to inform a new generation of the original label's audacity and ingenuity.

Further reading: *The Story of Island Records: Keep On Running*, by Suzette Newman and Chris Salewicz (Universe, 2010)

KING/FEDERAL

The King label is best known for its nurturing of the Godfather of Soul, James Brown, from the time of his emergence in 1956 until his departure for Polydor at the end of the 1960s. No matter that the label had already been operating for more than a decade when Brown came along (it was founded in 1943); no matter that label head Sydney Nathan's pioneering vision of a label that boldly went where the majors refused to go remained King's modus operandi for much of its life span. Mention King, and the general collector sees a pile of classic James Brown 45s—and the pile of dollars it would cost to purchase them all.

It is odd, then, to discover that King was initially a country-based label, with so-called race records not entering the catalog until around 1945, when Nathan launched the Queen label to cater to that market.

King/Federal

"Eternally," The Swallows (KING 4501, BLUE-VINYL 7-INCH, 1952)

"Every Beat of My Heart," The Royals (FEDERAL 12064AA, BLUE-VINYL 7-INCH, 1952)

"Flame in My Heart," The Checkers (KING 4558, 7-INCH, 1952)

"I Know I Love You So," The Royals (FEDERAL 12077, 7-INCH, 1952)

"I'll Cry When You're Gone," The Platters (FEDERAL 12164, 7-INCH, 1964)

"Moaning Blues," John Lee Hooker (KING 4504, 7-INCH, 1952)

"Moonrise," The Royals (FEDERAL 12088, BLUE-VINYL 7-INCH, 1952)

"Night's Curtains," The Checkers (KING 4581, 7-INCH, 1952)

"Tell Me Why," The Swallows (KING 4515, 7-INCH, 1952)

Wynonie Harris, Wynonie Harris (KING 260, EP, 1954)

Early releases were licensed from elsewhere—Bull Moose Jackson and Slim Gaillard were the first artists recorded by Nathan himself.

Queen folded in 1947 and Nathan launched a new R&B label, King Race. Three years later, Deluxe and Federal came into being, the latter's early catalog immortalized by Billy Ward and the Dominoes. The first R&B group ever to cut an LP, an eponymous 10-inch (Federal 295-94) issued in early 1955, their record has been ranked among the all-time rarest and most valuable releases in the hobby.

Federal's next major star was Hank Ballard and the Midnighters; its third, although Nathan would never have believed it at the time, would be James Brown and the Famous Flames. Nathan had not wanted to sign Brown in the first place—it was A&R man Ralph Bass who made the decision, and who felt the full force of the label head's wrath when, after scoring a shock No. 1 with his debut, "Please Please Please" (12258), Brown's next nine singles all flopped. Nathan was on the verge of dropping Brown from the roster when "Try Me" (12237) finally ended this luckless sequence, to open a period of absolute chart domination for Brown and the Famous Flames. Two years and seven hits later, Nathan finally transferred the singer from Federal to the higher-profile King label.

If Nathan was initially unable to see Brown's potential, it might well have been because the King stable was literally swimming in talent. The country and gospel stables were full; the blues, R&B, and vocal departments were brimming—an accounting of acts on the three labels would include Albert King, Annie Laurie, Big Jay McNeely, Bill Doggett, Champion Jack DuPree, Earl Bostic, Eddie Vinson, Freddie King, Ivory Joe Hunter, Jimmy Witherspoon, John Lee Hooker, Johnny Guitar Watson, Little Willie John, Little Willie Littlefield, Lonnie Johnson, Lucky Millinder, Lula Reed, Memphis Slim, Otis Williams and the Charms, Roy Brown, Sonny Thompson, Tiny Bradshaw, Todd Rhodes, Wynonie Harris, Little Esther (Phillips), the Chanters, the Checkers, the Five Keys, the 5 Royales, the Ink Spots, the Platters, the Royals, and the Swallows. Further bolstering the catalog, the sacred Glory and country-oriented Bethlehem labels were purchased, the budget Audio Lab was inaugurated, and Beltone was distributed.

All are very collectible today; most scored signature hits that enabled the King empire to continue growing, and many released LPs that today fetch sums far in excess of equivalent releases by other labels. One reason for this appears to have been Nathan's natural caution—even with guaranteed bestsellers (the Brown titles, for example), print runs for LPs never exceeded what he knew he could sell straight off the bat; if demand exceeded supply, a fresh run would be produced.

This policy resulted in a rash of minor variations between pressings, with some especially successful albums boasting four, five, or even

six notably different sleeves and/or labels. Many King collectors have become specialists in this field, and accepted prices for the scarcest varieties—a copy of Brown's *Try Me* (635) LP with "King" two inches wide on the label, or *Think* (683) with it expanded to three inches—approach the four-figure mark.

Despite his dominance of this vast empire, Brown was dissatisfied enough with his standing that, even after his move to King and the pleasure of issuing the label's biggest hit LP ever, *Live at the Apollo* (826), he jumped ship at the earliest opportunity, signing to Mercury's Smash Record subsidiary on the premise that his King contract only applied to vocal performances.

Nathan sued, and while a string of Smash instrumentals duly followed, a court eventually ruled in Nathan's favor and Brown returned to King, on hugely improved terms. He would remain with the label for the remainder of the decade, during which King would grow to become the sixth-largest record company in the land.

Nathan's death in March 1968 brought a sudden halt to this miraculous development. Subsequent owners Starday Records and Lin Broadcasting maintained the catalog but did little to improve upon it, and in 1971, Lin sold Brown's contract to Polydor, then sold the remainder of the label—virtual shell though it now was—to Leiber and Stoller's Tennessee Recording and Publishing company. King, and the newly revived DeLuxe and Federal labels, spent much of the remainder of the decade as a reissues label, first under TR&P, and then for the Gusto label.

MOTOWN

Its admirers call it the greatest soul-R&B label in the world and even its detractors admit there has never been anything like it in music history, a phenomenon that rose out of one man's vision and became not simply one of the most successful black-owned businesses in the world, but one of the most successful businesses, full stop.

Berry Gordy, Jr., was already a successful songwriter and producer when he launched Motown—his earliest productions appeared on Mercury, George Goldner's Mark X and End labels, and the lesser-known Kudo and HOB concerns during 1957–'58. These included efforts by the Miracles, Eddie Holland and his brother Brian, Herman Griffin, and Marv Johnson.

In 1958 Gordy, Jr., formed his own publishing company, Jobete, named for his three children, Hazel JOy, BErry IV, and TErry. The following January, he borrowed $800 from his family's loan fund and opened Tamla Records—his original choice of name, Tammy, had already been taken. Marv Johnson's "Come to Me" 45 (101) launched the label and won Johnson a deal with United Artists—his next single, "You Got What It Takes" (UA 0030) became producer Gordy, Jr.'s first pop Top Ten hit.

Gordy, Jr. launched a second label, Motown (a play on hometown Detroit's Motor City nickname), soon after, debuting it with the Miracles' "Bad Girl" (G1/G2, also TLX 2207—either pressing is impossibly rare, valued in excess of $1,000 in all but the vilest condition). This time it was Chess who moved in for a fast-percolating local hit, and while the reissue (1734) did not break the national chart, it established both the group and its producer as names to watch. That observation paid off with Barrett Strong's "Money" (Tamla 54027—his second 45, following "Let's Rock," 54022). Leased to Gordy, Jr.'s sister Anna's label, itself called Anna, whose own distribution deal with Chess placed it in a far stronger position than either of Gordy, Jr.'s labels, "Money" became a pop Top 30 hit. It also signaled the start of the Hitsville Revolution.

Collecting Motown is not a hobby. It is a full-time job (and it requires a full-time job as well, simply to finance the purchase of the earliest releases). Any one of some two dozen Motown acts could claim a place in the Top Ten of the world's most collectible bands and artists—and Smokey Robinson and the Miracles, Diana Ross and the Supremes, the Temptations, Marvin Gaye, and Michael Jackson and the Jackson Five would probably all be correct in their assumption.

For that reason alone, many Motown collectors prefer to concentrate their attentions either on one particular group (or group of groups— particularly during the 1960s, Gordy, Jr., loved teaming his bestsellers together on one-off singles and LPs), or on the work of one writer or producer. Among the most collectible are Holland-Dozier-Holland, who masterminded many of the Four Tops' greatest hits before decamping to launch their own Invictus-Hot Wax concerns. Other collectors concentrate on Gordy, Jr., or on Norman Whitfield, who led first the Temptations, and then Motown itself, into the tempestuous waters of late-'60s psychedelia and protest.

UK Motown releases are a popular field. Early issues were licensed through the London label (a total of eleven singles), Stateside (forty-five), Oriole (nineteen), and Fontana (four), before a joint Tamla-Motown label was launched with the Supremes' "Stop! In the Name of Love" (Tamla Motown TMG 501) in March 1965.

Many of these pre-Motown discs are extremely hard to find; among them, the scarcest are a 78 by Paul Gayton, "The Hunch" (UK London HLM 8998), the Valadiers' "I Found a Girl" (Oriole CBA 1809), and promo or demonstration copies of 1969's withdrawn "Oh How Happy," by Blinky and Edwin Starr (Tamla Motown TMG 720).

Another popular area covers Motown subsidiaries. Having bought up his sister's Anna label, Gordy, Jr., then launched the imprints Soul, VIP, Gordy, Melodyland, Hitsville, Mowest, and Prodigal, together with the more specialized Black Forum (spoken word), Workshop Jazz (jazz), Rare Earth (rock) ,and Weed, a late-'60s concern whose one LP, by Chris Clark, bore the slogan "Your Favorite Artists Are on Weed." One must make of that what one will.

Motown was one of the first record labels to sign up for the PlayTape system, in April 1967, and a number of the label's biggest stars can be collected in this fascinating (if short-lived) format; the deal was significant in that Motown had hitherto resisted overtures to tie itself to nonvinyl formats. Only Ampex's high-end reel-to-reel tapes had persuaded Gordy, Jr., that they offered an alternative to the 45 and the LP, and these, too, offer a challenging topic.

Other enthusiasts will choose one era of the label's history—the first mad flurry of early '60s fame, when every single to leave the studio seemed to have "hit" stamped into the very vinyl; the early '70s, when albums rose to the forefront of the label's consciousness for the first time, and Marvin Gaye, Stevie Wonder, Edwin Starr, and the Undisputed Truth painted their hard-hitting political messages across an unsuspecting Top 40; or the disco years, when Thelma Houston, the Commodores, and Diana Ross led a pulsating revolution of their own.

Over the years, Motown has come to mean so many things to so many people that it is a sour soul indeed who cannot find something of joy within that vast catalog. In 1976, Gordy, Jr., remarked, "I earned 367 million dollars in sixteen years. I must be doing something right!" A quarter of a century later, more than forty years after the label's inception (and almost fifteen years after Gordy, Jr., sold the company to the Universal Music Group), that "something right" is still taking place.

Further reading: *The Motown Encyclopedia* by Graham Betts (Createspace, 2014)

Motown/Soul/Gordy

"Angel," The Satintones (MOTOWN 1006, 7-INCH, 1961)

"Bad Girl," The Miracles (MOTOWN G1/G2, TLX 2207, 7-INCH, 1959)

"Camel Walk," Saundra Mallett and the Vandellas (TAMLA 54067, 7-INCH, 1962)

"Do the Pig," The Merced Blue Notes (SOUL 35007, 7-INCH, 1965)

"If Your Heart Says Yes," The Serenaders (MOTOWN 1046, 7-INCH, 1963)

"In My Diary," The Spinners (MOTOWN 1155, 7-INCH, 1969)

"Let's Rock," Barrett Strong (TAMLA 54022, 7-INCH, 1960)

"Since I Fell for You," The Skyliners (MOTOWN 1046, 7-INCH TEST PRESSING, 1963)

"Sweeter As the Days Go By," Frank Wilson (SOUL 35019, 7-INCH, 1966)

"You're Gonna Love My Baby," Barbara McNair (UK TAMLA MOTOWN TMG 544, 7-INCH, 1966)

PARLOPHONE

The story of Parlophone is, basically, the story of George Martin, the former Navy pilot who joined the label in 1950, as assistant to A&R manager Oscar Preuss. It was a tiny label at the time, dwarfed by its compatriots within the EMI Group: HMV, Columbia, and Regal Zonophone. It was content with an output of orchestral, dance, light jazz, and children's music. Martin recorded all this and more—Eve Boswell and Cleo Laine, Kenneth McKellar and Jimmy Shand, the Luton Girls' Choir, and the Kirkintilloch Junior Choir all passed through his studio.

Preuss retired in 1955 and Martin stepped up to replace him, immediately making changes in the Parlophone policy. The label's bread and butter remained much the same as before (one now-notable recording featured Dick James, later renowned as owner of the DJM label, voicing the TV theme "Robin Hood," MSP 6199), but Martin also began bringing in new talent: singer Edna Savage, the skiffle band the Vipers, and the King Brothers.

In December 1959, Adam Faith brought Parlophone (but not Martin—Faith's producer was John Burgess) its first-ever British No. 1 45, "What Do You Want" (R4591); he followed up with the equally successfully "Poor Me" (R4623). But if Parlophone was renowned for any one thing at this time, it was for Martin's painstaking recruitment of the cream of Britain's radio comedy community. Such records were unheard of in Britain at that time, but under Martin's aegis they became one of the fastest-selling genres of the late '50s.

Spike Milligan, Harry Secombe, Peter Sellers, and Michael Bentine, individually brilliant and collectively The Goons, cut a string of hits with Martin; so did the musical duo Flanders and Swann, as well as actors Bernard Cribbens, Peter Ustinov, and Charlie Drake.

It wasn't all the Beatles and Merseybeat over at Parlophone!

The Temperance Seven event provided Martin with his own first UK chart-topper, when their "You're Driving Me Crazy" (R4757) went to No. 1 in May 1961. Had Martin never made another "musical" record in his life, his modern collectibility would be assured by the barrage of comic brilliance that Parlophone issued between 1955–'62.

In 1962, however, the Beatles joined the label, and Parlophone embarked upon its next phase, as home to the most successful act in recording history. Today, the black Parlophone imprint, dominated by a giant 45 that was introduced in 1962, shortly after the release of the Beatles' "Love Me Do" debut (R4949), is among the best-known identities of all, and one of the most heavily researched.

Whereas labelology—the minute study of record-label design and variations—has long been an accepted part of the record-collecting hobby in the US and Japan, British collectors have seldom shown any interest in pursuing it. It was, therefore, an American collector, Mitch Scharoff, author of the privately published handbook *The Beatles: Collecting the Original UK Pressings 1962–'70*, who first ventured into the field, to be followed by members of the Tokyo Beatles fan club in Japan.

Their research isolated and dated the most minute Parlophone label varieties and even cracked the long-standing mystery of the indented numbers printed on the push-out center of Parlophone 45s, identifying them as coded references to EMI pricing and the government's Purchase Tax (then-equivalent to the American sales tax and the modern European VAT). These letters can now be used to date the period during which a particular record was pressed, an important factor in identifying 45s that remained in print, and largely unchanged, for over a decade.

Liverpudlian comedian Jimmy Tarbuck tries his hand at Lennon/McCartney's "All My Loving."

The Beatles aside, 1963–'65 saw the label issue hit after hit by Cilla Black, Billy J. Kramer and the Dakotas, the Hollies, and so many more. Of course these are highly collectible, but so are many less successful releases for which Martin and Parlophone were responsible, acts like Freakbeat pioneers the Action, the Toggery Five, pop-soul specialists the Marionettes, the Roulettes (Adam Faith's former backing band), and a host of others.

Martin departed the label in 1965 to concentrate on his responsibilities as the Beatles' producer. His years at the label are best chronicled within the box set *Produced by George Martin: 50 Years in Recording* (EMI 07253 532631 2 6).

His replacement was Norman Smith, engineer at the very first Beatles session, and since then, the man responsible for bringing both Pink Floyd and the Pretty Things to EMI. The change did not affect Parlophone's output; neither did the Beatles' own departure to establish their own Apple imprint (distributed, of course, by Parlophone) in 1968. In 1965 the young Marc Bolan joined the label (his "Hippy Gumbo," R5539, is one of the label's highest-priced non-Beatles issues). Art Woods was introduced in 1966, featuring Deep Purple's Jon Lord and Ron Wood's brother Art. The year 1967 introduced Nick Lowe's Kippington Lodge and Simon Dupree and the Big Sound, the pop band that would soon metamorphose into prog heroes Gentle Giant; 1968 saw Parlophone secure Love Sculpture, featuring guitarist Dave Edmunds, and the return of Jon Lord, with Deep Purple.

Nevertheless, the 1970s would see the label enter a period of sharp decline, and in 1973, Parlophone was closed, to be merged (alongside Columbia, HMV, Stateside, and several other EMI subsidiaries) into the new EMI imprint.

Parlophone re-emerged in the late '70s with Beatle Paul back on board, and new wave hopefuls the Flys heading a small but impressive roster of new talent—McCartney's "Goodnight Tonight" 12-inch (12R 6023) is an entertaining rarity from this period. Another quiescent period then ended in 1985, when the label was revitalized with the arrival of Duran Duran and the Pet Shop Boys. By the mid-1990s, Parlophone had utterly re-established itself as a major power on the UK scene, with acts as disparate, but universally acclaimed, as Morrissey, My Life Story, Radiohead, Supergrass, and the Sundays maintaining this new era of prosperity, a period that was capped by the restoration of the classic 1960s Parlophone label design.

Many of these latter-day signings have proven as collectible (almost) as any past Parlophone artist, and the story continues today, with Parlophone now established among the leading reissue labels of the 2010s. However, the label's own inherent collectibility is firmly locked within those first generations of George Martin–inspired talent.

One of Spector's greatest triumphs and Philles' biggest hits.

PHILLES

The Philles label is simply one component in the vast world of collectible Phil Spector releases—albeit, in many ways, the best known. The label was launched in late 1961 by Spector and Lester Sill; the label's name combines the two founders' Christian names, though Spector purchased Sill's interest in September 1962. Philles' first release was the Crystals' "There's No Other (Like My Baby)" (100).

The Crystals then supplied four more of the label's first ten singles, including the immortal "Uptown" (102), "He Hit Me" (105), "He's a Rebel" (106), and "He's Sure the Boy I Love" (109). The first two Philles LPs were also by the Crystals: *Twist Uptown* (PHLP-4000) and *He's a Rebel* (4001). A Crystals hits collection (4003) was called for just two years after their arrival. It should be noted, incidentally, that original pressings of these albums featured a blue-and-white label; the more common red-and-yellow Philles label was introduced in 1965 and appears only on re-pressings of earlier LPs.

Bob B. Soxx and the Blue Jeans, the group that was the architect of the next Philles LP (4002), are best remembered for the hit title track, "Zip-a-Dee-Doo-Dah" (107); two further singles comprised the LP's epic "Why Do Lovers Break Each Others' Hearts?" (110) and "Never Too Young to Get Married" (113).

Darlene Love emerged with "(Today I Met) The Boy I'm Gonna Marry" (111—two pressings offer different B-sides, "Playing for Keeps" and "My Heart Beat a Little Faster"). The Ronettes arrived on the Philles scene with "Be My Baby" (116), which was swiftly followed up the chart over the next year by "Baby I Love You" (118), "(The Best Part Of) Breaking Up" (120), "Do I Love You" (121), and "Walkin' in the Rain" (123). The Ronettes's first LP, *Presenting the Fabulous Ronettes Featuring Veronica* (4006), was released in late 1964.

All four of Philles' maiden chartbusters were gathered together on what is surely one of the greatest collections of all time, 1963's *Today's Hits* (4004). Or perhaps that honor is better bestowed upon the label's next issue, the legendary *A Christmas Gift to You* (4005), widely regarded as the greatest Christmas album ever issued.

The year 1965 opened with the recruitment of the Righteous Brothers, hitherto a none-too-distinguished duo recording for the Moonglow label. "You've Lost That Lovin' Feeling" (124) was their first and biggest hit; Spector produced four further singles with the pair, together with three epic albums.

One of Philles' most unexpected releases followed, an album by comedian Lenny Bruce. *Lenny Bruce Is Out Again* (4010) was a reissue of what was already an extremely rare LP that Bruce issued on his own Lenny Bruce label around 1962. (A second set on that imprint, *Warning: Sale of this Album,* is even more desirable; its contents include routines cited as evidence for the prosecution during Bruce's obscenity trial.)

Even more rare are US pressings of Ike and Tina Turner's *River Deep Mountain High* (4011), manufactured but left unreleased following the chart failure of the title track. Spector, who personally believed "River Deep" represented his greatest achievement yet, was mortified by the single's poor performance. It is widely believed that this single defeat precipitated his virtual retirement the following year; certainly it sounded the death knell on Philles.

ABBA

The ABBA Special (ATLANTIC PR 436, 2-LP PROMO, 1983)

Anniversary Boxed Set (UK EPIC ABBA 26, 26X7-INCH, BLUE-VINYL, 1984)

"Happy New Year" (ATLANTIC PR 380, 7-INCH PROMO, 1980)

"Lay All Your Love on Me" (DISCONET, NO CATALOG NUMBER, 12-INCH PROMO, 1980)

Live (ATLANTIC 81675, LP, 1986)

Nightbird and Company 11/74 (US ARMY RESERVE, 2-LP TRANSCRIPTION DISC, 1974)

"Ring Ring" (UK EPIC EPC 1793, YELLOW-LABEL 7-INCH, 1973)

Robert W. Morgan Special of the Week 6/81 (WATERMARK 812, TRANSCRIPTION DISC, 1981)

"Summer Night City" (UK POLYDOR ABBADJ 1, ONE-SIDED 12-INCH PROMO, 1993)

"Waterloo" (ATLANTIC 3035, 7-INCH, PICTURE SLEEVE, 1974)

A mere handful more singles were released before the end, including a run of three successive Ike and Tina singles that, in many ways, are at least the equal of their illustrious predecessor: "Two to Tango" (134), "I'll Never Need More Love Than This" (135), and "I Idolize You" (136). "I'll Never Need More Love Than This," incidentally, is backed by the infamous "The Cash Box Blues or (Oops, We Printed the Wrong Story Again)."

Philles was reborn briefly in 1972, when a compilation, *The Phil Spector Spectacular* (PHLP 100), was issued to radio stations. The Beatles' Apple label had already engineered a reissue for the *Christmas* album (SW 3400); it is believed that *Spectacular* was intended as a follow-up to that. This series was ultimately canceled; 1975, however, saw the launch in the UK of the Phil Spector International label, which included material from both the Philles era (including several in stereo for the first time), and elsewhere.

Further reading: *Out of His Head: The Sound of Phil Spector*, by Richard Williams (E.P. Dutton, 1972)

Phil Spector

Back to Mono, Various artists (ABKCO 711831, PROMO CD, 1991)

A Christmas Gift for You, Various artists (PHILLES 4005, PROMO LP, 1963)

"I Really Do," The Spectors Three (TREY 3001, 7-INCH, PICTURE SLEEVE, 1959)

Phil Spector's Christmas Medley (PAVILION AE7 1354, 7-INCH PROMO, 1981)

Phil Spector '74–79, Various artists (UK PHIL SPECTOR INT'L 2307 015, LP, 1980)

The Phil Spector Spectacular, Various artists (PHILLES PHLP 100, PROMO LP, 1969)

Rare Masters Volumes 1 and 2, Various artists (UK PHIL SPECTOR INT'L 2307-08, LPS, 1976)

The Teddy Bears Sing! (IMPERIAL LP 12010, STEREO LP, 1959)

Thanks for Giving Me the Right Time
   (PHILLES, NO CATALOG NUMBER, 7-INCH PROMO, SPECTOR LABEL, 1965)

Today's Hits, Various artists (PHILLES 4004, PROMO LP, 1963)

POLAR

Best regarded on the international scene for the development and success of ABBA, the Stockholm, Sweden–based Polar label actually predated the formation of that act by more than a decade.

Polar was launched in 1963 by Swedish music publisher Stig Anderson and his partner, Bengt Berhag. Anderson was a prolific songwriter who had his first composition published in Sweden in 1950, when he was nineteen years old. In 1953, he became Sweden's

Abba—back on the scene in 2018. But will they ever sound this great again?

most successful music publisher, after launching what would become a startlingly successful modus operandi. Picking his material from Radio Luxembourg, the continent's premier popular music station, Anderson would write Swedish-language lyrics to the biggest hits of the day, then recruit local musicians to record them for a never-ending string of hit 45s.

In 1959 "Klas-göranö" went gold throughout Scandinavia and the Netherlands, and by the time he launched Polar, Anderson's Sweden Music was already handling Scandinavian publishing for most of the major Anglo-American houses. Naturally, this supply would dominate Polar's output through the 1960s.

Polar's first successes came with the folky Hootenanny Singers, featuring Björn Ulvaeus, later of ABBA. Their "Jag väntar vid min mila" single and EP were the first-ever releases on the label in 1963,

while another 45, "No Time," was picked up for a full American release by United Artists (UA 991). Over the next two years, the LPs *Hootenanny Singers Basta* (Polar POLL 101), *Sjunger evert taube* (204), and *International* (206) all proved major hits, the first in an impressive stream that continued into the early '70s.

Ulvaeus met fellow songwriter Benny Andersson, at that time a member of the beat group the Hep Stars, in 1965. According to legend, the first song Ulvaeus and Andersson ever wrote together, "Isn't It Easy to Say," was composed the evening they met, to appear on the Hep Stars' self-titled third album (Olga LP 004). That same fall, Andersson guested on the Hootenanny Singers' own next album (their fourth), *Många ansikten (Many Faces)* (209).

Further collaborations were sporadic—it would be two years before Andersson and Ulvaeus launched a full-time musical partnership.

In the meantime, Ulvaeus stepped outside the Hootenanny Singers in 1968 to launch a solo career, debuting in April with a Swedish-language version of Stig Anderson's latest American acquisition, Bobby Goldsboro's "Honey." "Raring" (POS 1056) was a major hit, to be followed by versions of "Harper Valley PTA" (1062) and "Where Do You Go to, My Lovely" (1073), and a new Andersson/Ulvaeus composition, "Partaj-aj-aj" (1088).

The Hep Stars broke up following a summer 1969 tour; immediately, Ulvaeus and fellow bandmates Svenne Hedlung and his wife, Charlotte "Lotta" Walker (a former member of American girl group the Sherrys), combined with Andersson for a floor-show tour. During this same period, Ulvaeus and Andersson also composed and recorded a clutch of songs for the movie soundtrack *Inga II*, including a single issued under the Björn and Benny name in March 1970, "She's My Kind of Girl"/"Inga Theme" (Polar POS 1096). Backing vocals were supplied by the songwriters' girlfriends, Anna-Frida "Frida" Lyngstad and Agnetha Fältskog—both were already established singers, with the Cupol and EMI labels, respectively.

Lyngstad and Fältskog reappeared on Björn and Benny's debut album, *Lycka (Happiness)* (113), in 1970, together with a new single, "Hej gamle man" (1110); further Swedish hits included "Det kan ingen doktor hjälpa" (POS 1130), "Tänk om jorden vore ung" (POS 1140), and "En karusell" (POS 1154).

Following the suicide of Polar co-founder Berhag in 1971, Stig Anderson gave Andersson and Ulvaeus a production partnership within the Polar setup. With the duo at the helm, Polar was responsible for a stream of extremely successful singles during the early '70s.

Most, if not all, of these featured future members of ABBA—in either production, writing, or musician roles—and tend to be priced accordingly. These include Brita Borg's "Ljuva sextital" (POS 1072); Arne Lambert's "O mein Papa" (POS 1094); Borg and Rolf Bengtsson's "Jop jo na na men" (1100); Lena Anderson's "Scarborough Fair" (POS 1129), "Säg det med en sång" (POS 1148), and "Better to Have Loved" (POS 1149); and Jarl Kullo's "Jag ar blott en man" (POS 1162).

The year 1971 also saw work begin on what was intended to become the second Björn and Benny album; by March 1972, the sessions were all but complete, Polar had assigned the opus a catalog number (230), and everything was gearing up for what was certain to be a banner release. The release, in June, of a trailer from the LP, the song "People Need Love" (POS 1156), changed all of that forever. For the first time from the quartet, it was a fully collaborative venture, all four vocalists sharing lead duties.

Polar issued the single under the name "Björn and Benny, Agnetha and Anni-Frid"; a minor hit in Sweden, "People Need Love" was also issued in the US by the tiny Playboy label (P50014). Playboy issued

two more singles during 1972–'73, though promo mono/stereo issues only are known: "Another Town Another Train" (P50018) and "Rock 'n' Roll Band" (P50025).

A tour of the Swedish folkpark circuit followed, spawning one of the rarest of all pre-ABBA releases, a one-sided 45 titled *En halsning till vär parkarrangorer (Greetings to Our Park Arrangers)* (POR 1), featuring the quartet members talking about themselves and their music—there was no actual music on the disc.

The tour's success encouraged the quartet to persevere with the new format, placing the Björn and Benny LP on hold (it would eventually be scrapped) and cutting a new group single, "He Is Your Brother" (1168). By now, Frida, too, was a Polar artist—her EMI contract expired in July 1972, and she had already issued her Polar debut, the single "Man vill ju leva lite dessemellan" (1161).

In late 1972, Björn and Benny were invited to contribute a song for consideration as Sweden's 1973 Eurovision Song Contest entry—"Ring Ring," the ensuing effort, was released in February, uniquely, in two formats: a Swedish-language version (1171), and the following week, an English version (POS 1172). The song was not, ultimately, selected for the competition itself, but it still became a massive hit. While the Swedish version climbed to No. 1 on the Swedish chart, its English doppelgänger rested at No. 2. The song (available now in a German-language version) was also successful across mainland Europe, though a UK release through Epic (EPC 1793) did nothing.

Ring Ring (242), the debut album by the still unwieldy Björn and Benny, Agnetha and Anni-Frid, was issued in Sweden in March 1973; it, too, was a major hit—Sweden's chart, at the time, combined LPs and singles together. Within two weeks, the album was at No. 3, behind the two versions of its title track. A new single, June's "Love Isn't Easy" (1176), was soon racing in its wake, and through the summer, Björn and Benny, Agnetha and Anni-Frid toured Sweden to scenes of wild popularity.

Back at Polar, meanwhile, Stig Anderson was desperately trying to think of an appropriate name for the quartet. His favorite, drawn from the quartet's initials, was ABBA, and when the issue was put to a newspaper vote, the public agreed. So, fortunately, did the management of the ABBA canned-fish company—who might otherwise have rewritten the next decade of pop history with barely a second thought.

That history truly got under way in March 1974. Once again, the group had entered a song for the Swedish heats of the Eurovision Song Contest and this time, it triumphed—not only at the local level, but on the main stage as well. "Waterloo," the winning song, was the first record released under the new ABBA name, and the last to appear in simultaneous Swedish (1186) and English (1187) versions. Henceforth, the group would record one version for all markets.

Success saw ABBA's releases slowly take prominence in both the musicians' schedule and the label's schedule; the quartet's explosion to international fame essentially spelled the end for any outside activities. Following the release of "Waterloo," a mere handful of extracurricular releases appeared on the label, with the majority of them, too, having some kind of connection to ABBA. Look out for former Hep Stars Sven and Lotta's Swedish-language version of ABBA's "Bang a Boomerang" (1204), and one of the most prized of all regular-issue Polar singles, the same duo's "Funky Feet" (1231), the first public appearance of an Andersson-Ulvaeus song written for, but dropped from, ABBA's *Arrival* album.

Another massive rarity is Frida's final solo single, 1975's "Fernando" (1221). Taken from her *Frida ensam* album (265), it offers a Swedish-language version of the later ABBA hit. Fältskog also debuted a future smash that year, with her solo version of "SOS" (Cupol CS 303).

ABBA collectors also prize Kicki Moberg's "Men nattan är vår" (POS 1276), an Agnetha Fältskog composition targeted at the 1980 Eurovision Song Contest, and Fältskog's own first solo single in four years, "It's So Nice to Be Rich" (POS 1347), from the soundtrack to the movie *P and B*.

Notable Polar albums from the late '70s and early '80s include an album of children's music by Fältskog and her daughter Linda, *Nu tandas tosen julejus* (POLS 328), a solo set by ABBA backing vocalist Tomas Ledin, *The Human Touch* (POLS 364), and Frida's collaboration with English songwriter Kirsty MacColl, 1984's *Shine* album. (This set also produced a very collectible white-vinyl 12-inch of the title track—POLM 14.) Also notable is the 1983 various-artists collection *Äntligen sommarlov* (POLS 377), a compilation of songs dedicated to summer. A live version of ABBA's "Summer Night City" makes its only appearance on this disc.

Individually, the members of ABBA offer some interesting highlights of the Polar label catalog; collectively, they utterly dominate it. ABBA maintained its stranglehold on the world charts for the next nine years, releasing a dozen albums and almost two dozen 45s. Rarities abound worldwide, with the Polar catalog responsible for surprisingly few of them, placing less emphasis on limited-edition gimmicks than other markets. However, the rarest release in the entire ABBA catalog is a Polar issue—the "Sang til Gorel" 12-inch recorded (with Stig Anderson) as a thirtieth birthday present for Polar VP Gorel Hanser. Just fifty copies were pressed.

ABBA ceased operations in 1982, at which point Polar's output, too, declined. The label's final internationally noted release, in 1986, was ABBA's *Live* (412), the long-awaited release for concerts recorded back in 1977 and 1979. This is also the rarest regular ABBA album of them all—it spent just two weeks on the Swedish chart, and was barely even released in the US.

The music industry was quick to honor Polar's role in ABBA's career. An honorary member of the Royal Swedish Academy of Music, Anderson also became only the second non-American (after Brian Epstein) to receive *Billboard* magazine's prestigious Trendsetter Award.

Anderson reciprocated such honors in 1989, shortly after selling his companies to the Polygram group (he remained chairman of the board for Sweden Music AB and Polar Music International, posts he retained until his death in 1997). Although it would take another three years before the award was up and running, that year saw the endowment of the Stig Anderson Music Prize Fund of the Royal Swedish Academy of Music, or the Polar Music prize. "The world's biggest music prize" was to be "awarded for significant achievements in music and/or musical activity"; winners to date include Burt Bacharach, Bruce Springsteen, Elton John, Dizzy Gillespie, and Paul McCartney.

RED BIRD

One of the most popular labels of the American mid-'60s, Red Bird's output was short on quantity but incredibly high on quality. Formed by George Goldner and songwriters Jerry Leiber and Mike Stoller, Red Bird was dominated by what are now regarded as the quintessential American girl groups of the era, the Shangri-Las and the Dixie Cups, both of whom are very collectible in their own right. But the remainder of the label's output is also hotly pursued, all the more so since reissues of Red Bird material, on both vinyl and CD, have been uniformly dogged by atrocious sound quality.

The Dixie Cups launched the label with "Chapel of Love" (10-001), which was also the title of their debut LP (RBS 20-100) in 1964. Six further 45s failed to have the resonance of that debut, while

Shangri-Las

"Footsteps on the Roof" (MERCURY 72670, 7-INCH, 1967)

I Can Never Go Home Anymore (RED BIRD 20-104, LP, 1965)

I Can Never Go Home Anymore (UK RED BIRD 40-004, UNRELEASED EP, 1966)

"I Can Never Go Home Anymore"/"Bulldog" (RED BIRD 10-043, 7-INCH, 1965)

"I'll Never Learn" (MERCURY 72645, 7-INCH, 1966)

Leader of the Pack (RED BIRD 20-101, LP, 1965)

"Past, Present and Future" (RED BIRD 10-068, 7-INCH, 1966)

The Shangri-Las (UK RED BIRD 40 002, EP, 1965)

Shangri-Las' Golden Greats (MERCURY SR 61099, STEREO LP, 1966)

Shangri-Las-65 (RED BIRD 20-104, LP, 1965)

among Red Bird's most in-demand releases. Other popular Red Bird releases include two classics by the Jelly Beans ("I Wanna Love Him," 10-003, and "The Kind of Boy You Can't Forget," 10-011) and three by Trade Winds. However, Red Bird released just two further albums, a collection of speeches by politician Adlai Stevenson (20-105) and the debut by singer Steve Rossi (20-106), both of which are extremely obscure.

SKYDOG

Marc Zermati and Pieter Meulenbrocks' Skydog label launched in Paris, France, in 1972, with the first legitimate pressing of the legendary Jimi Hendrix/Jim Morrison/Johnny Winter jam session, *Skyhigh* (SGSH 2017378), and the Flamin' Groovies' *Grease* EP (FGG 001). This early incarnation of what became France's most legendary label ended following the issue of a Velvet Underground bootleg, *Evil Mother* (LP 003).

a major hit with 1965's "Iko Iko" could prompt nothing more than a reissue of *Chapel of Love*, with a new sleeve and title (Iko Iko, of course—10-003).

The Shangri-Las arrived with "Remember (Walking in the Sand)" (10-008), the first in a stream of peerless teen classics whose highlights alone could fill a romance novel: "Leader of the Pack" (10-014), "Give Him a Great Big Kiss" (10-018), "Maybe" (10-019) . . . by the time the Shangri-Las' Red Bird career wound up in 1966, with the stately "Past, Present and Future" (10-068), the group's influence on American teenagers simply could not be overstated.

Two Shangri-Las albums were issued during the group's heyday, *Leader of the Pack* (20-101) and *Shangri-Las-65* (20-104); the latter was reissued later in the year with the same catalog number, but retitled for the girls' latest hit, "I Can Never Go Home Anymore" (10-043); that song was added to the album, in place of "The Dum Dum Ditty" (not in place of "Sophisticated Boom Boom," as reported elsewhere).

Issued in 1965, the collection *Red Bird Goldies* (20-102) sums up Red Bird's major hits and reacquaints us with the most successful act on the short-lived Blue Cat subsidiary, the Ad-Libs. Their "The Boy from New York City" (102) is a masterpiece. Also included, and of great significance among collectors of the girl-group sound, are the Butterflys—in actuality, songwriter Ellie Greenwich. Two singles, "Goodnight Baby" (10-009) and "I Wonder" (10-016), are

Zermati then linked with Larry Debay, of London's Bizarre record store, to launch Bizarre Distribution, the first independent record distribution company in Europe. Releases by Kim Fowley (*Animal God of the Street*, LP SGKF 001), British pub-rock favorites Ducks Deluxe (*Jumpin'*, EP 005) and the Groovies' *Sneakers* 10-inch (MLPFGG 003) followed, with Skydog coming to international attention with the 1976 release of *Metallic KO* (62232), a cinema verité account of Iggy Pop and the Stooges' final live show in Michigan, in 1974.

The Stooges have remained a staple of the Skydog catalog for over a quarter of a century since, with a number of equally collectible titles—the live EP *(I Got) Nothing* (SGIS 12) and the CDs *We Are Not Talking Commercial Shit* and *Wake Up Suckers* included.

With a keen appreciation of rock history, Skydog engineered a 1976 release for two early Lou Reed recordings, "You're Driving Me Insane" and "Cycle Annie," released under the French-language pseudonym Velour Souterain (SP SMAC 001). With a sharp understanding of rock's present, meanwhile, an early link with Britain's Stiff label saw Skydog handle the French issue of debut 45s by the Damned and Motörhead; the Tyla Gang and the Gorillas also issued on Skydog, but a planned release for an early demo version of the Stranglers' "Peaches" never made it.

In 1976, Zermati was involved in the famous Mont de Marsen punk festival, with several of Skydog's French acts appearing alongside

Iggy Pop and the Stooges

"Down on the Street" (ELEKTRA 45695, 7-INCH, 1970)

Fun House (ELEKTRA EKS 74101, RED-LABEL LP, 1970)

"I Got a Right" (SIAMESE 001, 7-INCH, 1977)

"(I Got) Nothing" (FRANCE SKYDOG SGIS 12, 12-INCH, PICTURE SLEEVE, 1978)

"I Wanna Be Your Dog" (ELEKTRA 45664, 7-INCH, 1969)

Jesus Loves the Stooges (BOMP 114, EP, PICTURE SLEEVE, 1977)

Kill City (BOMP 1018, GREEN-VINYL LP, 1977)

Raw Power (COLUMBIA KC 32111, LP, 1973)

"Search and Destroy" (COLUMBIA 45877, 7-INCH, 1973)

The Stooges (ELEKTRA EKS 74051, RED-LABEL LP, 1969)

STAX

With the possible exception of Motown, Stax is the most famous soul/R&B label in the world and home to some of the best-loved artists. Otis Redding, Sam and Dave, Rufus Thomas, the Bar-Kays, Isaac Hayes, Eddie Floyd, and Johnnie Taylor did more than create great records, they laid the foundations for much of what the genre went on to achieve. In terms of quality alone, Stax richly deserves its reputation as the most collectible R&B label of the age. It is simply a bonus (or not, depending upon whether or not you own a copy) that the label is also host to some of the genre's most favored rarities.

Stax formed in September 1961, after owners Jim Stewart and Estelle Axton's original label, Satellite, was prompted to change its name (ST-AX was arrived at by combining the first letters of their surnames). The new label's numbering sequence picked up more or less where Satellite left off. Satellite 107, the Mar-Keys' hit "Last Night," became Stax 107; the label's final issue, 111, was renumbered 113, with 112 being granted to the Mar-Keys' second 45, "Morning After."

Swiftly following the Mar-Keys was Booker T. and the MGs, originally a house band at the subsidiary Volt label, and the instrumental prowess of these groups (the latter in particular) remained Stax's most identifiable feature. But it was with vocal talent that the company made its name. Carla Thomas, William Bell, the Mad Lads, Sam

the British contingent; he also arranged the following year's follow-up event. In 1977 Titus Williams, America's first black punk band, cut their *Message of Love* EP for Skydog. Just 200 copies were pressed before the release was canceled; it is now considered Skydog's rarest item, and was one of the highlights on the stellar CD *Skydog Poubelles: The Singles Story* (Japan P-Vine PVCP 8736).

This same period also brought recordings with Shakin' Street, who recorded for Skydog before becoming the first French band ever signed to the CBS major; the Phantoms; 84 Flesh ("Salted City," SGH 15); and the Rockin' Rebels (SGRB 16).

Two compilations, *Creme de Skydog* (P SGC 0017) and *Skydog Commando* (P SGSC 0018), released in 1978, wrapped up Skydog's early career, followed as they were by the collapse of Bizarre Distribution. The label relaunched in 1983 with archive and new releases by the Flamin' Groovies (SKI 2224); the Flying Padovanis (SKI 2225); the Heartbreakers spin-off Heroes—featuring Walter Lure and Billy Rath (SKI 6101); the London Cowboys (SKI 2102); and with a Blue Öyster Cult live album dating from 1972 (MAXI 62237-1). The late '80s and the 1990s, meanwhile, saw much of Skydog's legacy transferred to CD.

Skydog went on to release a slew of Iggy/Stooges related records. But this, featuring a handful of recordings from their last-ever show, remains the hardest hitting of them all.

and Dave, Johnnie Taylor, Isaac Hayes, and Eddie Floyd joined the roster over the next five years, often performing songs written and/or produced by members of the MGs. That band's output, incidentally, includes such unmistakable signatures as "Green Onions" (127) and "Time Is Tight" (0028), and a string of LPs, beginning with Stax's first-ever full-length, also titled *Green Onions* (701).

Like Motown, which was Stax's only genuine competitor in the R&B field, the label's primary preoccupation was singles. This is reflected in the collectors market by the relative availability and inexpensiveness of all but a handful of releases. The label's 1960s LP output, on the other hand, is less frequently encountered—just twenty-six albums were released during this golden era, with even the seemingly undesirable (and certainly out-of-character) Gus Cannon's *Walk Right In* (702) commanding a good price.

The majority of albums in this series were issued in both mono and stereo; the latter tend to be scarcer. Noteworthy, too, are the two separate covers for Booker T. and the MGs' Christmas album (7013), first released in 1966, then reissued the following year. Clumsy counterfeits of one unissued LP, Carla Thomas's *Live at the Bohemian Cavern* (7024), have also been reported—the catalog number, incidentally, was reused for Booker T.'s *Doin' Our Thing*.

Stax's long-standing relationship with Atlantic Records came to a close in May 1968, and Stewart sold the label to Gulf and Western; two years later he and DJ Al Bell bought it back, as a new generation moved up to take Stax into the 1970s. The 2000 LP series, with close to fifty titles, testifies to the importance of the label during this period.

The undisputed star of the newly formed Enterprise subsidiary, Isaac Hayes emerged from the shadows of songwriting and sessions to become a superstar; the Staple Singers, the Emotions, and the Dramatics followed, while the group the Bar-Kays was reborn first as the new Stax house band, then as a hitmaker in its own right. Wattstax, a 1972 daylong festival showcasing the best of current Stax talent, spun

The 2010s have seen the gradual rejuvenation of much of the classic Stax/Volt catalog—including this gem.

off one of the most successful music movies of the early decade, along with a dynamite soundtrack of the same name (STS 2-3010).

Stax also released successful soundtracks to several so-called blaxploitation movies, including *Sweet Sweetback's Badasssss Song* (STS 3001), and via Enterprise, the granddaddy of them all, Isaac Hayes' *Shaft*. Expanding even further, Stax launched a comedy label, Partee, and scored a major hit with Richard Pryor. Other new subsidiaries included Hip, Gospel Truth, and Respect. The label even moved into rock, with Knowbody Knows (aka Black Oak Arkansas) appearing on both Hip and Enterprise, while UK prog act Skin Alley headed for Stax. Despite the band's American obscurity, copies of its *Two Quid Deal* album (STS 3013) are surprisingly common, certainly when compared to its UK equivalent (on the Transatlantic label).

By the mid-'70s, however, the label's importance and impact alike were fading. The problems dated to 1972, when Columbia Records took over Stax's distribution on the understanding that the parent label would pay Stax for every record, regardless of sales and/or returns. It was an unprecedented deal, and when Columbia head Clive Davis was replaced in 1973, his successors quickly changed the terms of the deal, slashing payments by forty percent. Within two years, Stax was teetering on the brink of bankruptcy.

Of all the desperate measures that the label took during these last years, perhaps the most notorious was the signing of teenaged English singer Lena Zavaroni, an unashamedly MOR performer discovered via a primetime TV talent contest called *Opportunity Knocks*. For anybody encountering her *Ma, He's Making Eyes at Me* LP (STS 5511), Stax could fall no further from grace—and so it proved. On January 12, 1976, the courts ordered the label's closure.

Since that time, successive owners have worked hard to keep the label's name and artists alive. The nearly complete Satellite/ Stax/Volt singles catalog has been presented within four CD box sets; in

Booker T. and the MGs

And Now (STAX STS 711, STEREO LP, 1966)

Booker T. and Priscilla (A&M SP 3504, LP, 1971)

"Chinese Checkers" (STAX 137, 7-INCH, 1963)

"Green Onions" (STAX 127, GRAY-LABEL 7-INCH, 1962)

Green Onions (STAX 701, MONO LP, 1962)

"Green Onions" (VOLT 102, 7-INCH, 1962)

In the Christmas Spirit (STAX STS 713, LP, FINGERS-AND-KEYS SLEEVE, 1966)

"Jellybread" (STAX 131, 7-INCH, 1963)

"Mo' Onions"/"Fanny Mae" (STAX 142, 7-INCH, WITHDRAWN B-SIDE, 1963)

Soul Dressing (STAX 705, MONO LP, 1965)

addition, a wealth of reissues, compilations, and even new collections (a multidisc Otis Redding live set, for example) have ensured that little of the label's crucial output remains unavailable to interested listeners. (The label's fiftieth anniversary has been especially generous to collectors.) These releases have not, of course, had an impact on the values of the original vinyl; indeed, if anything, they have encouraged the collectibility of the original issues, as an entirely new audience discovers the magic of the original Stax sound.

Further reading: *Respect Yourself: Stax Records and the Soul Explosion*, by Robert Gordon (Bloomsbury, 2015)

STIFF

In early spring of 1976, in the "records for sale" section of the UK music press classifieds, a new record company announced its birth. It demanded no fanfare, and made no extravagant promises, but anybody who had followed pub-rock group Brinsley Schwarz through its seven-year career would have paid attention regardless. "So It Goes" (Buy 1) was the debut 45 by Schwarz songwriter Nick Lowe; it was also, though nobody knew it at the time, the maiden release for what would become the most exciting British record label of the late '70s.

Never before had a label garnered its supporters not only through its artists, but also through its own identity. Stiff collectors bought Stiff records regardless of the records' musical merit, and most later

Stiff Records was never a full-bore punk label, but the acts that it did sign were among the movement's most significant. This is the Adverts' "One Chord Wonders" debut.

agreed it would be three years and fifty-plus new releases before the label first let them down. Which wasn't at all bad for a company that was only ever intended to be a showcase for a few passing pub rockers, launched by Dr. Feelgood road manager Jake Riviera with a loan from his employers.

From the start, Stiff set about doing things differently. "Mono, enhanced stereo," insisted the credits to Lowe's debut. "The world's most flexible record label," pledged the company's logo. "Artistic breakthrough: double B-side!" bellowed the first release by the Tyla Gang (BUY 4); and further witticisms quickly followed. When David Bowie released a new album called *Low*, Lowe responded with an EP called *Bowi* (LAST 1). And then there was the infamous promotional button that insisted, "If it ain't Stiff, it ain't worth a fuck," a legend that proved so instantly popular that bootleg versions were appearing on the streets within weeks, and Stiff's reputation was guaranteed. Bootleg buttons, indeed.

"So It Goes" arrived with what remains the most sensible catalog number in recorded history, a plaintive, pleading, BUY ONE. It only followed, therefore, that subsequent releases would exhort even more grandiose purchases: the Pink Fairies' "Between the Lines" begged BUY TWO; Roogalator's "All Aboard"—BUY THREE . . . by the time the label finally closed, in 1987, it was suggesting that fans BUY 259.

Things moved quickly. In October 1976, Stiff signed the Damned and unleashed the first punk single ever, "New Rose" (BUY 6—and a lot of people did), which was the first record by any British punk band, beating the Sex Pistols' "Anarchy in the UK" by three full weeks. Within weeks, Stiff had landed major-label distribution via UA; within months, the label was opening its own retail outlet. By summer 1977, Elvis Costello was preparing to score his first chart hit; by fall, the Live Stiffs tour was the hottest ticket on the concert circuit, and names like the Damned, the Adverts, Ian Dury, and Wreckless Eric were bywords for the wider pastures roamed by the new wave cognoscenti.

Indeed, it took Stiff no time at all to transform itself from a pub-rock nursing home to a punk rock institution, without changing the company's outlook one iota. Stiff released records by other company's artists—the *A Bunch of Stiff Records* sampler included contributions from Graham Parker (Mercury) and Dave Edmunds (Swan Song). Stiff trawled the halls of musical eccentricity in search of the next Max Wall (a vaudevillian comedian), Humphrey Ocean (an established and respected artist), or Jona Lewie (a wacky keyboard player with an outstanding haircut). And Stiff still made "mistakes" that an amateur might have avoided, such as shipping the Damned's debut LP (SEEZ 1) with a photograph of Eddie and the Hot Rods inadvertently placed on the back.

Fully aware of the label's popularity among collectors, Stiff bent over backwards to keep things interesting. Announcing "We're a record company, not a museum," the label delighted in deleting records as soon as they became popular—and sometimes, before they were even issued. Motörhead's "Leaving Here" (BUY 9) vanished from the catalog immediately, before it reached the stores; Ian Dury's "Sex and Drugs and Rock and Roll" (BUY 17) was withdrawn just as it seemed poised to enter the chart.

Early 1978 saw Riviera depart to launch a new label, Radar—he took Costello, Lowe, and the Yachts with him. A new generation of Stiffs sprang up regardless, revolving around Mickey Jupp, Lene Lovich, Jona Lewie, and schoolgirl country singer Rachel Sweet; both Lovich and Lewie scored significant hits over the next two years. In the 1980s, they were joined by Kirsty MacColl, both a performer and a writer (she penned Tracy Ullman's "They Don't Know" smash, BUY 180). Other Stiff acts of the era were Madness, Dave Stewart and Barbara Gaskin, Tenpole Tudor, the Belle-Stars, and the Pogues, acts whose stellar success and future collectibility in many ways camouflages the less interesting releases that were now littering the catalog—Joe "King" Carrasco, Dirty Looks, Any Trouble, and the Equators.

The label's creative decline could be charted across any sampling of its post-1980 releases, but still there were moments of sheer, shining glory, isolated moments of musical majesty from John Otway, a brace of classics by Department S., and unlikely efforts from the Untouchables and the immortally named Pookiesnackenburger. And when it did all wrap up, it

was with breathtakingly circular purity, as the label's first-ever friend became its last-ever signing, and Dr. Feelgood came back to reclaim its loan.

Since then, of course, Stiff has remained on the release sheets, across a string of compilations and reissues spread between a dozen different labels worldwide, each one harking back to the days when Dave Robinson's explanation for Stiff's existence genuinely did ring true. "If major record companies were really good," he once admitted, "then we wouldn't be here."

Further reading: *Be Stiff: The Stiff Records Story*, by Richard Balls (Soundcheck Books, 2015)

SUB POP

Alongside the same city's C/Z, the Seattle-based Sub Pop was the driving force behind the PNW/Seattle Sound grunge movement of the late '80s and early '90s. Formed by Bruce Pavitt and Jonathan Poneman in the early '80s, originally as a fanzine (which accounts for the first nine Sub Pop catalog releases), Sub Pop dedicated itself to developing a label spirit that, in the alternative era, is analogous only to the early years of Stiff—acts seemed to be signed as much for what they could bring to Sub Pop as for what Sub Pop could do for them.

Swift deletion polices; limited-edition, colored-vinyl, and picture-sleeve releases; and the generally small runs that were Sub Pop's

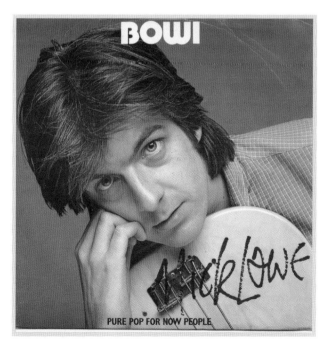

raison d'être have all contributed to the label's high collectibility. As with Stiff, however, to concentrate on the gimmickry is to overlook the label's vital role in documenting (and, indeed, shaping) a significant moment in time.

During the five years of operation that preceded the grunge explosion—indeed, within Sub Pop's first twenty-five releases—almost every one of the acts that would eventually put Seattle on the musical map passed through Sub Pop. The seminal compilation *Sub Pop 100* (10) was followed by individual releases by Green River (the *Dry As a Bone* EP, 11), Soundgarden (*Screaming Life*, 12), Mudhoney ("Touch Me I'm Sick," 17), Tad ("Ritual Device," 19), and Nirvana ("Love Buzz," 23).

Neither did the label confine itself to local environs. Oklahoma City's Flaming Lips (28), San Francisco's Helios Creed (30), Cincinnati's Afghan Whigs (32), Ann Arbor's Big Chief (53), and Chicago's Smashing Pumpkins (90) all released early material through the label. France's Les Thugs (29) and England's Billy Childish (71) came from even further afield. Many of these releases were included within the much-collected Sub Pop Singles Club series.

Launched in November 1988, with the aforementioned first single by the then-unknown Nirvana, the Singles Club, too, brought fresh air to the US market, with limited-edition 45s appearing every two months for the next five years. Other highlights included now extremely rare releases by Sonic Youth (26), Rapeman (40), the Dwarves (50), Fugazi (52), the Rollins Band (72), Elastica (275), and Gene (294), before the series ended with Lou Barlow's "I Am Not Mocking You." (The Club was relaunched in April 1998, since which time Luna, Jesus and Mary Chain, Dot Allison, and Imperial Teen have contributed.)

Amid such activities, Sub Pop first came to major attention in the UK, following well-received tours by Mudhoney, Soundgarden, and Nirvana, among others. Even before Geffen signed Nirvana in 1991, Sub Pop was creeping into the American consciousness. Once *Nevermind* hit, however, Sub Pop became ubiquitous, marketing its own name with merciless precision, particularly following the label's partial acquisition by Time Warner.

The decline of grunge's mainstream popularity naturally led to a downswing in Sub Pop's visibility; however, intelligent signings continued to distinguish Sub Pop through the remainder of the 1990s, with the 1998 capture of St. Etienne a particularly noteworthy accomplishment.

Further reading: *Loser: The Real Seattle Music Story*, by Clark Humphrey and Art Chantry (Misc. Media, 1999)

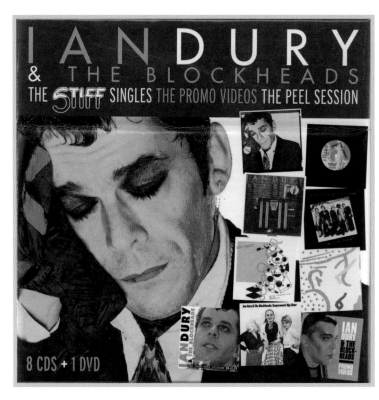

A CD box set rounding up Ian Dury's Stiff singles catalog.

SUN

Disc jockey Sam C. Phillips opened the Memphis Recording Service in 1950, initially recording local musicians (including Phineas Newborn) for the local Modern Records label before he joined forces with another local DJ, Dewey Phillips (no relation) to form their own label, It's the Phillips. The label issued one single, Joe Hill Louis's "Boogie in the Park"/"Gotta Let You Go" (9001/2); Sam Phillips then moved Louis over to Modern and resumed his own work for that company.

Over the next year he worked with B.B. King, Roscoe Gordon, and Walter Horton, but fell out with Modern after leasing sessions with Howlin' Wolf and Jackie Brenston (the immortal "Rocket 88") to Chess. That relationship prospered for a time, but by 1952, Phillips was looking again for a reliable outlet for his production work. When none was forthcoming, he decided to do it himself, launching Sun in February 1952. (His brother Judd was involved for a time, before launching his own Judd Records label. Judd was also Jerry Lee Lewis's manager for many years.)

Phillips intended the first Sun release to be "Blues in My Condition," by Jackie Boy and Little Walter (174); a poor response from radio, however, persuaded him to can it in favor of Johnny London's "Drivin' Slow" (175). The next scheduled release, Walter

Bradford's "Dreary Nights" (176), too, was canceled and it was eight months before Sun stirred again, with releases by Joe Hill Louis, Willie Nix, and Jimmy Walter.

Sun's first hit (and the first release to appear on both 45 and 78) was Rufus Thomas's "Bear Cat" (181), a response to Big Mama Thornton's "Hound Dog." Thomas's "Tiger Man" (188) proved a popular follow-up. Other hits came from Little Junior Parker; Billy "The Kid" Emerson; and Little Milton Campbell and the Prisonaires, a vocal group formed by inmates at the Nashville State Penitentiary. "Just Walkin' in the Rain" (186) was covered for pop success by Johnny Ray in 1956. Subsequent Prisonaires' singles "A Prisoner's Prayer" (191) and "There Is Love in You" (207), appeared in late 1953 and summer 1954, respectively.

Memphis Recording Service's first brush with Elvis Presley came in 1953, when the truck driver dropped by to record a birthday present for his mother, "My Happiness," using the studio's "make your own record" services. Phillips was absent that day; secretary Marion Keisker is thus credited as Elvis's discoverer. It would be another eight months before Phillips finally acceded to her demands that he contact Presley—the rest, of course, is history.

Presley issued five singles on Sun, "That's All Right, Mama" (209), "Good Rockin' Tonight" (210), "Milkcow Blues Boogie" (215), "Baby Let's Play House" (217), and "I Forgot to Remember" (223). Phillips then sold Presley's contract and recordings to RCA Victor for $40,000.

Presley's success put Sun firmly on the map, drawing in a wealth of ambitious talent. June 1955 brought the first Sun release by Johnny Cash ("Cry Cry Cry"—221); Carl Perkins' "Let the Jukebox Keep On Playing" (224) arrived in August; Roy Orbison debuted with "Ooby Dooby" (242) in May 1956; Jerry Lee Lewis extended "Crazy Arms" (259) that December. All of these artists would prove major successes, both at Sun and thereafter; all would cut some of the most important records in early rock 'n' roll history.

The vast majority of Sun releases were singles—78s, then 45s. Only twelve LPs were issued bearing the Sun label, seven of which were by Johnny Cash. The Phillips International subsidiary was responsible for four more. Of these, the scarcest are generally reckoned to be Carl Perkins' *Dance Album* (Sun LP 1225), along with two Phillips International issues, one by Frank Frost (PILP-1975) and the other by Frank Ballard (PILP-1985).

It is, contrarily, surprising to learn that the majority of big-name Sun singles are not especially rare—valuable, yes; exceedingly highly priced, yes. But unless pristine condition is a prerequisite, rare, no—a state of affairs which is a due to a combination, more or less equally, of high sales, vast popularity, and the long-held belief that a Sun record is somehow "special." Today, of course we know it is, but it's interesting to learn that even at the time of the records' original release, many people felt that way. Presumably, the cachet that Sun had for being Elvis's first label impressed everyone.

It was this vast success that ultimately brought Sun down. One by one, as the 1950s faded into the 1960s, Sun's stars departed—Cash was the last to go, moving to Columbia in 1962. This time, however, Phillips was unable to replace his stars. From packing some of the hottest shots in rock in 1959, Sun's 1961 catalog offered nothing more noteworthy than George Klein, Tracy Pendarvis, Wade Cagle, Anita Wood, Harold Dorman, Shirley Sisk, Tony Rossini, Don Hosea, Bobby Wood, and Ray Smith. Once the final offerings from Cash, and a handful of desultory late releases by Jerry Lee Lewis, were out of the way, what was Sun but another regional record label that had once scored a few hits?

Sun would linger on until 1969, but releases were few and far between—just twenty-four singles between January 1963 and the final release, Loads of Mischief's "Back in My Arms Again" (407), in January 1968. Finally, Phillips sold the catalog to Mercury Records producer Shelby S. Singleton, Jr., who commenced reissuing (and leasing for reissue) this newly acquired gold mine. It has been estimated that since then, the Sun catalog has been recycled more than any other label on earth.

Further reading: *Good Rocking Tonight: Sun Records and the Birth of Rock 'n' Roll*, by Colin Escott and Martin Hawkins (St. Martins Griffin, 1992)

VANGUARD

Though it would subsequently become (and is certainly characterized as) the most important folk label in US music history, the Vanguard label was initially launched to pursue founders Maynard and Seymour Solomon's love of jazz. Utilizing a $10,000 advance from their father Benjamin, the Solomon brothers established two labels to cater to their tastes, Vanguard and the Bach Guild, the latter of which was an ambitious project intended to release recordings of all of its classical composer namesake's choral work.

Original Vanguard releases, in keeping with industry standards, were issued on 10-inch LPs. Between 1953–'55, Vanguard released some twenty different jazz albums in this format, including well-received and respected titles by Vic Dickenson, Sir Charles Thompson, Joe Newman, Buck Clayton, Don Elliott, and Ruby Braff—many produced by the legendary John Hammond. However, a glimmer of the label's future came in the form of Brother John Sellers' *Sings Blues and Folk Songs* collection in 1954, and in 1956, Vanguard released its first album by Pete Seeger and the Weavers (9001)—a courageous move at a time when the group's political stance saw them all but boycotted by the rest of the industry. (Paul Robeson, another blacklisted performer, joined the Weavers at the label.)

Releases by Martha Schlamme and Cisco Houston followed, and by the end of the 1950s, Vanguard was the biggest folk game in town. In his *Follow the Sun* autobiography, Jac Holzman, head of the then-fledgling Elektra Records, recalls, "In the early days [Elektra launched itself as a specialist folk label in 1950] my competition had been Moses Asch at Folkways. [But] as Elektra grew . . . we moved beyond Folkways, Tradition, and Riverside. By the late '50s, we were nosing level with Vanguard." Elektra might even have sneaked ahead, but for one crucial difference. Vanguard had Joan Baez.

Now based at Columbia, John Hammond had already rejected Baez (or been rejected by her—the story shifts, depending upon who is telling it) when she first arrived at Vanguard's Greenwich Village offices. It was Hammond's superiors' subsequent dismay that led, in swift succession, to Columbia's recruitment of Carolyn Hester and Bob Dylan; the latter was the only other figure on the local folk scene with any hope of outselling Baez, and the former was one of the few who was even remotely capable of out-singing her.

That Hester's first husband, Richard Fariña, would later marry Baez's sister, Mimi (while Dylan, who guested on Hester's first Columbia album, soon became Baez's consort), is indicative of just how compact the folk scene was at that time. That the Fariñas would then join Baez at Vanguard, on the other hand, proves the wisdom of the Solomons. What nobody could have imagined then was how time would bear out so many other of their signings.

Spread across three albums (including the posthumous *Memories*, 9263), the Fariñas' dulcimer-driven folk-rock and proto-psychedelic imagery were undeniably eccentric by contemporary folk standards. By Vanguard's standards, however, eccentricity was the spice of life. Few of the label's signings ever opted for convention and normalcy; indeed, to describe Vanguard as a folk-oriented concern is to utterly belittle the sheer adventurousness that was the Solomons' true nature.

This adventurousness is reflected in the label's modern collectibility. Many of Vanguard's best-known releases have since been reissued by the label's current owners,

the Welk Music Group, with the British Ace and Italian Comet picking up sundry lesser-known classics.

The value of original LP pressings has only risen since the restoration of such oddities as two LPs worth of electronic tomfoolery by Perrey-Kingsley (and two more by Jean-Jacques Perrey alone). Also valued are a pair of scratchy psychedelic monsters from Circus Maximus (featuring a pre-"Mr. Bojangles" Jerry Jeff Walker) and one-offs by such unknowns as Steve Gillete (9251), Elizabeth (6501), the Far Cry (6501), Listening (6504), and the Serpent Power (9252—the band was led by poet David Meltzer, author of a very rare solo album in his own right, 6519). The 45s by these bands are equally highly prized.

Also worth watching for are three albums by the Frost, a Detroit hard rock band fronted by future Lou Reed/Alice Cooper/Peter Gabriel sideman Dick Ezrin. A fourth LP, *Early Frost*—79392—appeared in 1978, years after the band's demise.

A handful of releases by guitar virtuoso John Fahey have also become increasingly popular since his death in early 2001; the interest has also spilled over to Fahey's own Tahoma label, home to some excellent early recordings by another future Vanguard artist, Robbie Basho.

Elizabeth's fabulously decorated Vanguard debut album.

The Fariñas' collectibility, too, has been enhanced in recent years, via the publication of author David Hajdu's *Positively 4th Street* (FSG, 2001) and Mimi's tragic death just months later. An album recorded in London in 1963, by husband Richard and Erik Von Schmidt (Folklore F-LEUT 7), has long been much in-demand for the presence of a pseudonymous Bob "Blind Boy Grunt" Dylan; it is now equally sought after for its maker's own magic.

Vanguard's biggest names, of course, are Joan Baez, Buffy Sainte-Marie, and Country Joe and the Fish. All three artists' catalogs bristle with rarities, including copies of Country Joe and the Fish's *Feel Like I'm Fixin' to Die* (79266) LP, containing a free Fish Game poster, and Baez's "Pack Up Your Sorrows" single (35040), an excerpt from a rock LP she was recording with Richard Fariña at the time of his death in 1966, and which she abandoned immediately after.

Also of considerable interest are Vanguard's live documents of the Newport Folk Festival, issued in 1959, 1960, 1963, and 1964. The range of artists spread across these discs tells the story not only of the folk boom, but also the blues and bluegrass revivals that grew alongside it. Three volumes (2053–55) cover the 1959 event, and they include Joan Baez's first-ever released recording, a duet with Bob Gibson; two LPs covered the 1960 event (2087–88—a third disc was issued by Elektra, EKL 189). The 1963 festival brought six separate albums (9144–49), two of which feature otherwise unavailable Bob Dylan material, and 1964 delivered up seven LPs (9180–86), highlighted by debut performances from Buffy Sainte-Marie and Judy Roderick.

Roderick's *Woman Blue* LP (9197) is another seldom-seen gem that has since been reissued on CD; unfortunately, there is still no sign of an earlier LP, alluded to in the *Woman Blue* liner notes, and damnably elusive, apparently at any price. Thankfully, those same

liner notes suggest it isn't very good, so even Roderick completists probably aren't missing much. Piling up behind the folkies, however, there awaited a host of freakish beat monsters that make the Fish look positively abstinent. The story that best sums up Circus Maximus is: Nobody yet seems to have told their story. Even Jerry Jeff Walker, rhythm guitarist and vocalist across the Texan band's two albums, devotes just a dozen pages of his autobiography to them, with much of that spent discussing the Carnegie Hall Electric Christmas concert that the band co-headlined in December, 1967, on the whim of an organizer who saw modern psychedelia as the logical sonic successor to certain medieval forms. Which, of course, it was.

Walker does, however, spare one thought for posterity, when he contemplates the irony of his situation. Growing up, he had devoted great swathes of his listening time to the Vanguard label, repository of some of the greatest folk music of the age. Now he was signed to that very label—and was playing psychedelic rock.

Circus Maximus formed as the Lost Sea Dreamers, in which form they were discovered by independent producer Dan Elliot. He introduced the group to Vanguard in mid-1967 and, with staff producer Sam Charters helping oversee the sessions, the Lost Sea Dreamers (LSD—geddit?) began work on their debut album.

The sessions were still underway when the group was offered a residency at a new club opening on St. Mark's Place in New York, the only condition being that the band change its name to match the venue. Circus Maximus was born. It wasn't a bad move, either—certainly the new name gave Vanguard's copywriters plenty to work with as they prepared for the band's launch. "Under a visual big top of flowing, multi-colored light," promises the sleeve to Circus Maximus' eponymous debut album, "Circus Maximus is the biggest circus, the circus of the mind, theatered in a tent on imagination."

The music was pretty far out as well: scratchy guitars and abrasive rhythms, a post-garage freak out built around both Walker and lead guitarist Bob Bruno's songwriting and vocals, with Bruno's scintillating hard psych guitar work savage enough to merit its own channel on the headphones.

It was during the sessions for *Circus Maximus* that Walker composed the song for which he is today best remembered, "Mr. Bojangles." Of course it found no place on the group's debut, nor on their second album the following year—rather, *Neverland Revisited* emerged a rather disappointing effort, slower and calmer than its predecessor, more prone to reflection and all but devoid of the manic guitars which scythed through the best of Circus Maximus.

The heavily harmonic "Negative Dreamer Girl" was a neat choice for a single, though, and the backward tape freak out–led "Neverland" suggested that the band hadn't quite run out of ideas yet. They had, however, run out of steam. *Neverland Revisited* was barely issued when the band broke up, with Walker alone remaining at Vanguard for an acoustic solo album the following year (*Driftin' Way of Life*).

Undeterred by the desultory saga of Circus Maximus, Vanguard was gripped by psychedelic rock—and the more skewed and shaded the better. 1967 saw the arrival of David Meltzer, a San Francisco poet who formed the Serpent Power with his wife, Tina, in 1966. With the lineup also featuring former Grass Roots guitarist Denny Ellis and bassist David Stenson, the Serpent Power made their live debut on November 27, 1966, at a benefit concert for the Telegraph Group Neighborhood Center.

It was, from all accounts, a spectacular performance, with Ed Denton, manager of Country Joe & The Fish, sufficiently enthused to immediately contact Vanguard, suggesting they sign the band. The following year saw the release of *The Serpent Power*, and it is still apparent that Denton's enthusiasm was not misplaced. Mature pop rides some delicious harmonies in a manner not altogether removed from a vision of the early Jefferson Airplane, if they'd continued down the route opened up by their own debut—they didn't, so the Serpent Power made the journey for them.

The closing "Endless Tunnel," in particular, is a revelation; Meltzer's lyrics are, perhaps, a little overwrought, and thirteen minutes of slowly building, darkly undulating, organ-led percussion can seem somewhat indebted to the Doors. But then J.P. Pickens' electrified five-string banjo takes over, and the performance goes somewhere else entirely. Unfortunately, the band broke up once they got there. The Serpent Power disbanded following the album's release, leaving the Meltzers alone to cut a second Vanguard album in 1969, *Poet Song*.

In 1966, with Elektra having picked up the Paul Butterfield Blues Band, Vanguard signed Charley Musselwhite and Harvey Mandel, fresh from Steve Miller's Chicago-based Goldberg-Miller Band. The ensuing album, *Stand Back!*, is widely regarded among the key Chicago blues documents of the age, while the next couple of years saw Vanguard's musical pendulum swing to some staggering extremes.

First, 1968 brought Peter Walker's aforementioned second album, which we repeat remains one of the finest American excursions into Indian territory you're going to find; there was a brace of albums by the ever-exquisite John Fahey; and the same period also delivered the one and only LP by Elizabeth, a Philadelphia band whose lineup once included future Nazz drummer Stewkie Antoni, and whose guitarist, Steve Weingart, is responsible for some of the most concisely uncontrolled guitar playing in the entire label catalog, a little under two minutes into "You Should Be More Careful."

Received wisdom insists *Elizabeth* is a fairly average rock album and, once past one of the most eye-catching covers in the history of the Vanguard art department, that might be true. The problem is not, however, the music itself, but rather the band's reliance on two songwriting guitarists, who might have meshed on an instrumental level, but had little in common in the compositional stakes. Thus, while Bob Patterson unleashes the multitextured rockers, Steve Weingart draws upon more placid folk rockers and never the twain shall meet.

But 1968 also saw Vanguard turn its attentions north of its New York City base, to Boston, to pick up the perpetrators of two of the most disconcerting (but extraordinarily effective) Vanguard releases of them all.

An eponymous set by the Far Cry was essentially the blistered ruminations of a heavy psychedelic blues band, rising into a class of its own first via Jere Whiting's vocals—a standard blues bellow with delusions of Arthur Brown operatic grandeur; then though the insertion of a freeform tenor sax into even the raunchiest rocker. Five years later, the Far Cry could have given King Crimson a run for their money. Sadly, they'd long since disbanded by then.

Listening (pointedly christened without a definitive article), on the other hand, were a superbly melodic, but deceptively madcap outfit whose psych-pop masterpieces in no way disguised the band members' past affection for the Beach Boys and the British Invasion.

Indeed, Walter Powers, (credited on Listening with "bass and feelthy literature") was a former member of just such a band, the Lost, who cut three singles for Capitol during 1966–'67. As an aside, it was there that first Powers ignited his friendship with another Beantown superstar, Willie "Loco" Alexander—who guests on Listening's mock-Latin freak out "Cuando" and would later reunite with Powers in the early '80s band the Confessions.

There was an astonishing album by the Cleanliness and Godliness Skiffle Band, the amusingly titled *Greatest Hits*. Country Joe, maintaining his reputation as a traveling A&R department, was responsible for a couple of bands who appeared on Vanguard at the end of the 1960s, and proceeded to blow away all the label's associations with gentle folk, wacked psychedelia, even King Crimson. Both the Frost and the Third Power hailed from Detroit, as all the era's loudest bands seemed to; Country Joe encountered them on his latest tour, and realized instinctively that there was a sound bleeding out of Motor City that made San Francisco and London sound positively old-fashioned.

Over at Elektra, Jac Holzman had already drawn from this rich new vein (and done immeasurable harm to his own folky tag) by picking up the Stooges and the MC5; Maynard Solomon, chasing the same critically acclaimed golden ring, promptly booked himself and producer Sam Charters on a flight to Detroit, and began scouring the clubs. The two groups they emerged with have not, by any means, attracted the same attention as Elektra's dynamic duo, although both are responsible for alluring early 45s on local labels—the Frost's "Bad Girl" appeared on Date, Third Power's "Snow" on Baron.

They also feed into other sainted corners of the hard rock lexicon—Third Power's guitarist, Drew Abbott, went on to Bob Seger's Silver Bullet Band; the Frost's Dick Wagner became part of a studio team, alongside producer Bob Ezrin and fellow axeman Steve Hunter, whose achievements range from Lou Reed's Rock 'n' Roll Animal tour to Peter Gabriel's debut album, and a string of Alice Cooper records as well.

Their own records, meanwhile, are in a class of their own. A thunderous, but otherwise unadventurous debut album, *Believe*, brought Third Power a modicum of attention (think Blue Cheer without the melodies) but little else, and they drifted away soon after. The Frost, however, were made of sterner stuff.

Having kicked off their Vanguard career with a second 45, "Mystery Man," the band then uncaged *Frost Music*, a Panzer division of sound and energy which steamrollered to No. 168 on *Billboard*, virtually on the strength of local sales alone. Suitably emboldened, the band tapped further into their hometown strengths by recording side two of their *Rock and Roll Music* sophomore set live at Detroit's Grande Ballroom.

Sales boomed—according to Sam Charters, "the Frost sold over 100,000 albums." And while their chart profile barely flickered (the album peaked at No. 148), they did land a prestigious gig at the Fillmore West. Unfortunately, they were opening for B.B. King, whose audience of devout blues aficionados was less than impressed with the Frost's barrage of Midwestern mayhem. "It was," Charters continued, "a long, discouraging weekend for everyone." The band broke up soon after.

Equally spellbinding but located on quite the opposite side of the sonic spectrum was the duo of Baldwin & Leps. A guitar and fiddle–fired unit, they appear to have spent much of their time busking on the streets, performing a Michael Baldwin–composed repertoire of gritty ballads that escaped accusations of mundanity by virtue of Leps' maniacal violin.

It cuts through the vinyl (and, latterly, Comet's CD reissue) like a knife through all the clutter of a well-behaved, and tastefully orchestrated folk rock band—four years later, Dylan would borrow the same fiddle-in-yer-face approach for elements of his *Desire* album (and accompanying tour); in 1971, however, Baldwin & Leps' approach was, perhaps, just a little too unique for mainstream listening tastes.

A similar fate befell the Wildweeds. Best remembered today for supplying NRBQ with guitarist Al Anderson, and for 1967's massively minor (No. 88) hit "No Good to Cry" (on the Cadet label), the Wildweeds were also one of the most inventive bands trawling the clubs of the Northeast, with a well-adjusted ear for the sounds of the Southwest.

Had they hailed from California, had their cheeky absorption of Beethoven into beat ("Someday Morning") received any kind of airplay at all, and had pigs grown wings and flapped them vehemently, the Wildweeds might easily have attained at least the same heights as the Charlatans, or the early Steve Miller Band. Instead, they're an obscure little footnote in the NRBQ story (Anderson didn't join until the Wildweeds split, in 1971), and a one-hit wonder of the most minute caliber, cult heroes in every sense of the phrase.

Ah, but it's a hearty, healthy cult, all the more so since the Wildweeds' demise did not end the members' associations. The rhythm section of Bob Dudek and Al Lepak remained alongside Anderson for several further recordings, including "Come On If You're Coming," a great little number now available as a bonus track on Anderson's self-titled 1972 solo album, itself recorded with Lepak still in attendance.

The early 1970s were, however, a less than fertile time for the label, with the departures of Joan Baez and Buffy Sainte-Marie seriously denting its public profile. Releases became less frequent and, sadly, less intriguing—Vanguard's biggest hit over the next few years was Benny Bell's novelty "Shaving Cream" and for a time Vanguard's new releases followed its humorous lead.

There was a flurry of interest around Camille Yarborough's *The Iron Pot Cooker* in 1975; and a flurry more when it was reissued with liner notes describing it as "a precursor to Lauryn Hill," but other releases were less lovable—and that includes the label's shortlived dalliance with disco. By the late 1970s, it was clear the company's day had passed.

A revived Vanguard emerged in the mid-1980s, following the Solomon's sale of the label to the Welk Music Group, the outfit responsible for the welcome flood of reissues that highlighted the 1990s; it has changed hands several more times since then, but for collectors, these later shenanigans scarcely register. It is those ten-or-so years in the '60s and early '70s that safeguard Vanguard's place in the history of rock (and folk and jazz and blues), and which confirm it, too, among the most collected labels of the era.

VERTIGO

Although the Vertigo imprint has been in use for over thirty years now, an easily identifiable warning of an impending heavy metal onslaught from the former Phonogram group of labels, its collectors concentrate on one era, and one era only—the four-year span during which Vertigo's label design displayed, indeed, a vertiginous swirl of black and white, which consumed one whole side of the label

Vertigo Swirl Albums

Asylum, Cressida (UK VERTIGO 6360 025, LP, 1971)

Ben, Ben (UK VERTIGO 6360 052, LP, 1971)

Changes, Catapilla (UK VERTIGO 6360 074, LP, 1972)

Clear Blue Sky, Clear Blue Sky (UK VERTIGO 6360 013, LP, 1970)

Gracious, Gracious (UK VERTIGO 6360 002, LP, 1970)

Red Boot, Legend (UK VERTIGO 6360 019, LP, 1971)

2nd of May, May Blitz (UK VERTIGO 6360 037, LP, 1971)

Space Hymns, Ramases (UK VERTIGO 6360 046, LP, 1971)

3 Parts to My Soul, Dr. Z. (UK VERTIGO 6360 048, LP, 1971)

Tudor Lodge, Tudor Lodge (UK VERTIGO 6360 043, LP, 1971)

and which, when placed on the turntable, brought an entirely new dimension to watching a record go round.

Vertigo was launched in 1969 within the same flurry of progressive activity that prompted Pye to form the Dawn and Middle Earth imprints, EMI to create Harvest, and Decca to grow Nova. Immediately, however, Vertigo set itself apart—and not only via its choice of label design. The first 45 the label ever released, a frenetic rendering of Bo Diddley's "Who Do You Love?" by Juicy Lucy (V1), made the UK Top 20; the second release, by Black Sabbath, "Paranoid" (6059 010), hit the Top Five.

At a time when the progressive-rock movement was so furiously opposed to everything that the mainstream pop industry stood for—so opposed that some bands really did ask their audiences not to dance during the performance—Vertigo took two of the heaviest records, by the heaviest acts on the entire scene, and got them on *Top of the Pops*.

Of course, it was a fluke, and one that was seldom repeated during the lifespan of the swirl label. A second Juicy Lucy single, "Pretty Woman" (6059 015), reached No. 44, but that was it. Theoretically appealing releases by onetime '60s chart darlings Manfred Mann (in its Chapter Three phase), the follow-up hit-hunting Black Sabbath, the Sensational Alex Harvey Band, and Rod Stewart (yes, even Rod Stewart) made no impression whatsoever.

Move into the lesser-heralded realms of Affinity, Beggars Opera, Warhorse, Assegai, Legend, Graham Bond, and Magick and Ronno (a short-lived combo formed by Mick Ronson around what would become David Bowie's Spiders from Mars), and without exception they disappeared without trace. They rank, today, among the rarest major-label metal 45s of all time.

They are joined in those rarified echelons by their long-playing contemporaries. Vertigo launched in 1969 with the simultaneous issue of albums by Colosseum (*Valentyne Suite*, VO 1), Juicy Lucy (*Juicy Lucy*, VO 2), and Manfred Mann (*Chapter Three: Volume One*, VO 3). Debuts by Stewart (VO 4), Sabbath (VO 5), and the little-known Cressida (VO 7) followed before Vertigo adopted a new LP numbering system, the 6360 series, with Fairfield Parlour's *From Home to Home* (6360 001).

A total of eighty-four Vertigo albums were issued with the swirl label, of which a mere handful can even be loosely described as familiar today. Vertigo releases by Status Quo, Black Sabbath, Rod Stewart, the Sensational Alex Harvey Band, Gentle Giant, and Uriah Heep have each been re-pressed and reissued on numerous occasions, and tend to attract lesser prices than efforts from, for example, Gracious, Magna Carta, May Blitz, Nucleus, Dr. Strangely Strange, and Clear Blue Sky.

However, even among these "superstars," there are items to watch for. Few of these later issues duplicated all the little extras for which original Vertigo releases were also prized—the gatefold and poster sleeves that decorated the first seventy-four releases, for example, or the lavish box and poster packaging that accompanied Sabbath's 1971 masterpiece, *Master of Reality* (6360 050). In addition, of course, the discontinuation of the swirl label in 1973 (it was replaced by a rather exciting spaceship design) removes even more allure.

The rarest Vertigo albums are, of course, those that sold the fewest copies at the time, a competition that was, apparently, won hands-

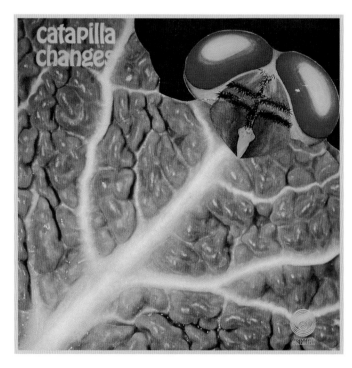

Catapilla's Changes *was released in a fabulous bug-shaped die cut sleeve.*

The Australian collection The Vertigo Trip *offered a double album's worth of swirl-era highlights. Its sleeve design dates from the same Keef photo session as the better-known UK* The Vertigo Annual *compilation.*

down by Dr. Z. Having already released an obscure 45 on Fontana, "Lady Ladybird" (6007 023), Dr. Z. was discovered by Patrick Campbell-Lyons, whose own band, Nirvana, issued its own very collectible LP and single on Vertigo in 1971.

Such patronage did not help, however. Total sales of *3 Parts to My Soul* (6360 048) have been estimated as high as nine or ten copies (and as low as three), firmly placing it at the very peak of Vertigo collectibles. Perhaps mercifully, an accurate vinyl facsimile of the original album, lavish Barney Bubbles artwork included, was among

the handful of Vertigo classics reissued by the Italian Akarma label during the 2000s.

Hotly pursuing Dr. Z. in the rarity stakes are sets by Daddy Longlegs, Ben, Gravy Train, Catapilla, and Hokus Poke. Non-Vertigo specialists, meantime, compete for releases by Freedom (featuring ex–Procol Harum founder Bobby Harrison), Ramases (the self-proclaimed, if misspelled, reincarnation of an Egyptian god, accompanied by 10cc), Greek superstar act Aphrodite's Child (featuring Vangelis and Demis Roussos), and the German electro-mavens in the group Kraftwerk.

Kraftwerk's self-titled debut album (6641 077) was one of three final Vertigo albums to bear the swirl label in 1973—the others were sets by Thomas F. Browne (6343 700) and somewhat at odds with the rest of the catalog, singer-songwriter Jim Croce (6360 701).

The introduction of the aforementioned spaceship label (and, thereafter, a generic molded label pressed into the vinyl itself) did not end Vertigo's career as a collectible label—Alex Harvey, Black Sabbath, Status Quo, Thin Lizzy, and many more maintained the label into the late '70s, alongside a bevy of attractive lesser lights.

As with so many other labels, however, the loss of a favorite label design often spells the end of whatever personal affinity it is that attracts a fan or collector in the first place. Vertigo is a very collectible label. But only the early releases are hypnotically so.

Further reading: *The Vertigo Swirl Label: Worldwide Discography and Price Guide*, by Ulriche Klatte and Marcel Koopman (Edition Books, 2016)

Kraftwerk: The Robots on 45

"Autobahn" (VERTIGO VER 203, 1974)

"Computer Love" (WARNER BROS. 49795, 1981)

***Kraftwerk's Disco-Best* EP** (CAPITOL SPRO-8866 PROMO, 1979)

"Les Mannequins" (CAPITOL 8502, 1977)

"Musique Non Stop" (12-inch) (WARNER BROS. 0-20549, 1986)

"Numbers" (WARNER BROS. 49795, 1981)

"Pocket Calculator" (WARNER BROS. WBS-49723, 1981)

"The Telephone Call" (remix) (WARNER BROS. 0-20627, 1986)

"Tour de France" (French version) (WARNER BROS. 0-20146, 1983)

"Trans Europe Express" (CAPITOL SPRO-8638 PROMO, 1977)

VIRGIN

Virgin Records would establish itself among one of the world's major labels, a monolithic concern whose very name became branded as firmly into the twenty first–century consciousness as McDonald's, Nike, or Microsoft. It is impossible to believe, then, that when the label launched in the UK in 1973, it was as marginal a concern as any other homemade label; that it was essentially formed as a vehicle for one LP, and had that album not taken off the way it did, the entire story might have ended there and then.

That album was Mike Oldfield's *Tubular Bells* (V2001), recorded during downtime at label founder Richard Branson's Manor Studios and released on Virgin only after being rejected by every other label in the land. It went on to become a worldwide hit, establishing Oldfield as an international superstar (albeit, according to contemporary press reports, an extraordinarily reluctant one), and placing Virgin in a limelight that even Branson could never have envisioned.

Oldfield aside, little of Virgin's early output was especially saleable. Although the label did enjoy some chart successes with German electronic band Tangerine Dream, its main impact was critical.

Among the most important, and now collectible, acts from these formative years was Gong, whose legendary Radio Gnome Invisible trilogy was launched with the second Virgin LP, *Flying Teapot* (V2002). (Gong's supremely budget-priced *Camembert Electric*, VC 502, introduced a whole new audience to the antics of the Pothead Pixies.) German experimentalist group Faust (also launched for less than the cost of a 45 with the seminal *Faust Tapes*, VC 501) is also among the most important, as are Kevin Coyne, ex-John Peel's Dandelion label; avant-garde pioneers Henry Cow and Hatfield and the North; modern composer David Bedford; *Tubular Bells* coproducer Tom Newman, whose "Sad Sing" (VS 120) featured Oldfield on a delightfully twiddly guitar solo; and Scottish doggerel poet Ivor Cutler. Also worth watching for are releases on the budget-priced subsidiary Caroline, but be warned. They are not budget-priced today!

Virgin was also heavily involved in the reggae scene, eventually launching the now-legendary Front Line label to deal with the wealth of material being issued. CD reissues of much of this material throughout the 1990s peaked with a post-'90s box set, issued in 2001. *The Front Line Box Set* testifies to the sheer collectibility of this entire catalog.

Most of the early Virgin 45s catalog is now very rare. Although Oldfield scored several hit singles, he also put his name to some remarkable flops—including the first Virgin single, "Mike Oldfield's Single" (VS 101), released with a rare picture sleeve depicting two frogs copulating and an otherwise unavailable B-side, "Froggy Went a-Courting"; and a similarly obscure collaboration with Bedford and former bandmate Kevin Ayers, "Don Alfonso" (117).

The rarest Virgin single from this period, however, is Slapp Happy's "Johnny's Dead" (VS 124), a musical murder that attracted much attention (and fatal censorship) for its employment of an innocently chirpy school choir to sing the chorus. All the above-mentioned releases, incidentally, appeared with the original Virgin label design: two extraordinarily artistically rendered

Dr. Z's one and only album is the highest-valued album in the entire Swirl series.

young ladies who were seated, for no apparent reason, with a dragon. This design was dropped in 1975, in favor of a blue-into-white design, with the Virgin name picked out in electric red. For the vast majority of Virgin collectors, that change marks the end of their interest, though the label continues to turn out some fine music—and some precious collectibles.

Another German act, Can, brought the label an unexpected hit in 1976 with the sibilantly insistent "I Want More" (VS 153); the following year, the arrival of the Sex Pistols thrust Virgin into both the headlines and the charts.

None of the Pistols' conventional Virgin releases are at all uncommon (though most dealers overprice them); however, a handful of rarities are worth noting: a Christmas flexidisc (LYN 3261) issued to journalists in December 1977; a handful of mispressings dating

Smashing Pumpkins

The Aeroplane Flies High (VIRGIN DPRO 11590, 12-TRACK CD SAMPLER, 1996)

"Daughter" (REFLEX, NO CATALOG NUMBER, FLEXIDISC, 1992)

"Drown" (EPIC ESK 4733, CD PROMO SINGLE, 1992)

Live in Chicago 23.10.95 (FRANCE DELABEL DE 3629, PROMO CD, 1995)

Moon (DEMO CASSETTE SOLD AT GIGS, 1989)

1991–1998 (VIRGIN, PROMO CD, 1998)

"1979" (VIRGIN 7243 8 38522, 7-INCH, 1996)

Pisces Iscariot (CAROLINE CAR 1767, GOLD-VINYL LP, HAND-NUMBERED, WITH FREE 7-INCH, 1994)

Siamese Dream (CAROLINE CAROL 1740, MAROON-VINYL 2-LP, 1993)

"Tristessa" (SUB POP SP 90, COLORED-VINYL 7-INCH, 1990)

Kirsty MacColl, 12-inch Singles

"A New England" (UK STIFF BUYIT 216, 1984)

"Angel" (Apollo 440 remix) (UK ZTT ZANG 46T, 1993)

"Berlin" (UK NORTH OF WATFORD NOWX 100, 1983)

"Days" (UK VIRGIN KMAT 2,1989)

"Free World" (UK VIRGIN KMAR 1, 1989)

"He's on the Beach" (UK STIFF BUYIT 225, 1985)

"Innocence" (Guilt Mix) (UK VIRGIN KMAT 3, 1989)

"My Affair" (Ladbroke Groove Mix) (UK VIRGIN VST 1354, 1991)

"Terry" (UK STIFF SBUY 190, 1983)

"Walking Down Madison" (UK VIRGIN VST 1348, 1991)

all maintained their collectibility through this period. Such passing fancies as Lenny Kravitz and the Spice Girls have enjoyed at least moments of intense scrutiny. Branson himself is long gone, having sold the catalog to EMI in order to finance other ventures. He later returned briefly with a new label, V2.

Collectors searching for an easy entry into the Virgin catalog are best directed toward *V* (VD 2502), a two-LP sampler issued in 1975 that wraps up a number of rare and unreleased cuts by many of the original label's greatest attractions. A series of three three-CD box sets released for the label's fortieth anniversary in 2013 are also a source of great delight.

Further reading: *Virgin: A History of Virgin Records*, by Terry Southern (A Publishing Co., 2004)

from the post–Johnny Rotten band's *Great Rock 'n' Roll Swindle* era; and three basic varieties on the original band's one and only album, *Never Mind the Bollocks* (V 2086).

The first pressing was ready to ship when the band announced that it had one more song to add, "Submission." Virgin added this as a free one-sided single (VDJ 24) packaged with the LP; a free poster completed the package. With "Submission" incorporated into the LP, a transitional sleeve was then printed, lacking a track listing on the back cover, before the now-familiar LP appeared. All this happened within a matter of days, ensuring that even informed collectors missed out on the early varieties. There is also a *Bollocks* picture disc, dating from 1978, that appeals.

In the wake of the Pistols' arrival, Virgin picked up a number of other punk/new wave acts, including Penetration, the Motors, and X-Ray Spex. At the end of the decade, Virgin was at the forefront of British pop's next major upheaval, the new romantics.

Both the Human League and Culture Club are heavily collected today, with 12-inch pressings of the latter's first two singles ("White Boy," VS 496-12, and "I'm Afraid of Me," VS 509-12) especially sought after. Most of the group's subsequent releases also appeared as either picture discs or colored-vinyl limited editions—most are relatively common, though gimmick-enhanced singles from the end of the band's career can prove difficult to find. The rarest Human League releases revolve around a plethora of limited-edition gatefold picture sleeves, and the withdrawn 12-inch pressing of the five-track EP *Holiday 80* (SV 105-12).

As is the case with so many labels of the 1980s and beyond, Virgin's collectibility is today centered around individual artists as opposed to any sense of label identity—Simple Minds, Phil Collins, Peter Gabriel, and Genesis (acquired with the Charisma catalog in 1985), as well as Iggy Pop, Massive Attack, and the Smashing Pumpkins have

ZTT (ZANG TUMB TUUM)

Formed by producer Trevor Horn, wife Jill Sinclair, and journalist Paul Morley in 1983, ZTT emerged on the UK scene that August, with the first release by the Art of Noise, a team of studio and session musicians joined for the occasion by Horn and Morley.

The *Into Battle* EP (UK ZTIS 100) was, by the standards that ZTT would soon be setting, a very restrained release, appearing only as a 12-inch single and a cassette single. Readily acknowledging the impact of record collectors on the marketplace, and with marketing executive Morley taking his lead from Italian futurist Russo's use of "zang tumb tuum" to describe the sound of rapid machine-gun fire, ZTT would indeed soon be spitting out a stream of releases, remixing

Anne Pigalle's "Why Does It Have to Be This way" 12-inch single.

and reformatting individual singles to such an extent that even devoted ZTT collectors readily admit they still aren't sure whether every variant has been cataloged.

It was an at-times-unparalleled blitzkrieg, comparable only to Factory Records' penchant for slapping a catalog number on anything it could, from the label's Hacienda nightclub to stationery, unreleased artwork, and advertising campaigns. ZTT did not go that far, but it did venture to extremes.

Art of Noise's third 45, "Close (To the Edit)" (UK ZTPS 01), exists in seven separate versions; Frankie Goes to Hollywood's chart-topping "Relax" debut (UK ZTAS 1) in nine. (These are the primary numbers only. ZTT singles also bore irrelevant "Incidental Series" and "Action Series" numbers, a deliberate ploy to further intrigue collectors. Other numbers in sequence were deliberately omitted for the same reasons—there are no 4, 6, 10, 11, 13, 14, 16–20, 23, or 27 within the ZTAS series, while the ZTIS issues feature 101 and 108 only.)

The success of Frankie Goes to Hollywood, and the sheer weight of product released in that band's name, ensures that ZTT is primarily remembered for that one act alone. However, both Art of Noise and German electronica band Propaganda also enjoyed hitmaking careers strewn with limited-edition releases. Propaganda's Claudia Brucken would also cut several records for the label, under her own name and alongside electronics maven Thomas Leer in a new band, Act. Its "Snobbery and Decay" (28) was the final release in the ZTAS series.

Other early signings, Andrew Poppy and Anne Pigalle, were less fortunate, however, their fates perhaps echoing the reasons behind Art of Noise's eventual departure from the label—too much marketing, not enough promotion.

Originally distributed by Island Records, ZTT didn't become a true independent until 1987, when the label severed its ties with the major. However, post-1987 releases were less collectible than the label's earlier output.

Frankie, ZTT, and Mao.

INDEX